TAKING SECURITY:
LAW AND PRACTICE

TAKING SECURITY: LAW AND PRACTICE

Richard Calnan

JORDANS

Published by
Jordan Publishing Limited
21 St Thomas Street
Bristol BS1 6JS

British Library Cataloguing-in-Publication Data

A catalogue record for this book is available from the British Library.

ISBN 0 85308 995 7

Typeset by Columns Design Ltd, Reading
Printed in Great Britain by Antony Rowe Ltd, Chippenham, Wilts

PREFACE

The purpose of this book is to describe how security is taken in England. It is therefore concerned with one aspect of the law of property – the creation and enforcement of proprietary rights taken to secure the payment of a monetary liability. But security does not exist in a vacuum. It is taken to protect a creditor from the effect of his debtor's insolvency, and this book is inevitably as much concerned with the law of insolvency as it is with property law. It is only in an insolvency that the strength of a proprietary right is really tested.

My primary intention has been to produce a book which can be used by those taking or enforcing security, although I hope it will also be of interest to those on the other side of the transaction – giving or challenging the security. I have attempted to explain the underlying principles of the law of security and how they operate in practice. I have not tried to refer to all the cases which touch upon the law of security. That would have required a very different, and a much longer, book. Instead, I have used the cases to illustrate the principles which underlie the law of security. I have also concentrated on those issues which I believe to be of most importance in practice.

The inspiration for much of this book comes from two, very different, men. The first is James Lingard, a former partner of Norton Rose, with whom I sat as an articled clerk. When I did so, I had every intention of becoming a corporate lawyer but, by the end of my seat, I was determined to join him in the (to my mind, inevitably intertwined) joint disciplines of banking and insolvency law.

If my initial fascination for, and knowledge of, the subject was germinated by James Lingard, both were nurtured as a result of attending Roy Goode's seminars on credit and security at what was then Queen Mary College in the University of London. Roy was the best sort of teacher. His knowledge was immense but, even more importantly, his enthusiasm for the subject was infectious. And he also introduced me to my wife.

Both men have written on the law of security – James Lingard on security documentation and Roy Goode on problems of credit and security – but neither has written a book on the principles of taking security. This book tries to fill that gap. They may disagree with some of the conclusions in this book, but they have both, in their different ways, contributed a great deal to it. And it is fitting that one is a practitioner and the other an academic. I have absolutely no doubt that we need to bridge the gap between practitioners and academics, and no-one has done more than Roy Goode in bringing together academics and practitioners for the better understanding and development of commercial law in this country.

It is customary in a preface to thank those who have contributed to the book in question. In my case, to do so individually to all of those who have helped me would be unduly to increase the length of this book. They know who they are and, I hope, that I am very grateful to them all. But I must mention my friends and colleagues at Norton Rose (both now and in the past) who have contributed to this book in so many ways and, in particular, to my secretary Sandra Pratt, who has, like me, lived and breathed the law of security for what must seem like an excessively long period.

I have done my best to state the law as it was on 1 January 2006.

Richard Calnan

January 2006

CONTENTS

TABLE OF CASES

TABLE OF STATUTES

TABLE OF STATUTORY INSTRUMENTS

TABLE OF EUROPEAN MATERIALS

References are to paragraph number

TABLE OF INTERNATIONAL MATERIALS

Chapter 1

INTRODUCTION

1.1   Over the last few years, there has been an unprecedented level of debate about the rights and wrongs of the law of security in England. The purpose of this book is to explain the conceptual basis of the law of security and to discuss how it works in practice. The purpose of this chapter is to describe the structure of the book and to put the debate about reform into context.

The structure of this book

1.2   A creditor who has taken security over an asset has three principal concerns. He wants to ensure that:

- the security is effective in the insolvency of the debtor;
- the security will take priority over anyone else who obtains a proprietary interest in the asset concerned; and
- the security can be enforced when required, even if the debtor is in insolvency proceedings.

1.3   The creditor may also want to know to what extent security can arise by operation of law, what alternatives he may have to taking security and how his rights are affected in a cross-border transaction.

1.4   This book is accordingly broken down into the following sections:

- Types of security (**CHAPTERS 2–4**): what types of security are available to a creditor, what are the differences between pledges, mortgages and fixed and floating charges, and what are their advantages and disadvantages?
- Creating security (**CHAPTERS 5** and **6**): how is security created in practice and what requirements are there to register the security?
- Priority of security (**CHAPTER 7**): what are the priorities between the creditor and another person who obtains an interest in the secured asset?
- Enforcing security (**CHAPTERS 8** and **9**): how is security enforced, what liabilities can be incurred as a result of enforcing security, and how can the onset of insolvency proceedings against the debtor affect the enforcement of security?
- Security arising by operation of law (**CHAPTER 10**): in what circumstances is security created without the necessity for an agreement between the debtor and the creditor?
- Alternatives to security (**CHAPTERS 11** and **12**): to what extent can a creditor protect himself against the insolvency of the debtor in other ways, for instance, by taking a guarantee from a third party or by relying on a right of set-off?

● International security (**CHAPTERS 13** and **14**): what issues arise where the transaction is of a cross-border nature?

Reform

1.5 Proposals to make substantial changes to the law of security were mooted as long ago as 1971 in the Crowther Report.[1] Those proposals were renewed in 1989, when the Diamond Report was published,[2] but the debate only really took off when the Law Commission published its Consultation Paper on Company Charges in 2002.[3] A further Consultative Report on Company Security Interests was published in 2004;[4] and the Law Commission's final Report on Company Security Interests was published in August 2005.[5]

1.6 The Law Commission's proposals developed during the 3-year period between the publication of the first Consultation Paper and the publication of the final Report. A brief discussion cannot do justice to the range of the issues discussed in the Law Commission's three papers, but three issues stand out as being particularly important.

1.7 The starting point for the Law Commission was the introduction of a new security system based on art 9 of the US Uniform Commercial Code. Their purpose was to treat security in a functional way so that, if a transaction had the economic effect of security, it would be treated in the same way as if a security interest had actually been created. By the time of the final Report, this proposal had largely been abandoned, although some vestiges of it remain.

1.8 A second key feature of the Law Commission's initial proposals was the wish to rewrite the priority rules relating to security interests. Elements of these proposals remain, although it is unlikely that many of them will be implemented for security interests in the absence of a review of the priority of proprietary interests generally.

1.9 The third main proposal by the Law Commission was to alter the way in which charges are registered. The proposal was to replace the current registration procedure with a system of 'notice filing', which would also remove the time limit within which charges have to be registered. This proposal has broadly remained unchanged.

1.10 Over the 3-year period of the gestation of the Law Commission's proposals, there was a vigorous debate of the rights and wrongs of the proposals.[6] Then, in July 2005, the Department of Trade and Industry (DTI)

---

1   Report of the Committee on Consumer Credit, Cmnd 4596 (1971).
2   Diamond *A Review of Security Interests in Property* (1989).
3   *Registration of Security Interests: Company Charges and Property other than Land*, Law Com Consultation Paper No 164 (TSO, 2002).
4   *Company Security Interests: A Consultative Report*, Law Com Consultation Paper No 176 (TSO, 2004).
5   *Company Security Interests*, Law Com No 296 (TSO, 2005).
6   A flavour of the debate concerning the proposals can be gleaned from the three Law

issued a consultation document.[7] It asked for comments on three options – to do nothing, to implement the Law Commission's proposals or to improve the current registration scheme. In November 2005, the government indicated that there was no consensus of support for the Law Commission's proposals, that the Company Law Reform Bill (which is due to be passed in 2006) 'will provide a mechanism for implementing certain changes in respect of company charges, on matters of company law (as against property law) if wished' and that: 'The government will continue to consider and to discuss with interested parties exactly what changes should be implemented.'[8] It therefore seems likely that there will, at some stage, be changes to the registration system in respect of company charges, but that the Law Commission's other proposals are unlikely to be carried forward in their current form.

1.11   The Law Commission's proposals have nevertheless prompted a debate about the utility of the current English law of security; and the main purpose of this chapter is to discuss the extent to which the law does meet its objectives.[9] The starting point is to define those objectives. It is suggested that the main requirement of the law of security is that security should be capable of being created and enforced with the maximum of flexibility and certainty and the minimum of cost, delay and formality consistent with appropriate safeguards for the debtor's unsecured creditors and others dealing with the debtor. The question is the extent to which the English law of security meets these requirements.

1.12   In this chapter, the discussion will be limited to corporate debtors because they are by far the most important in practice and because, although the problems with the bills of sale legislation are manifest, the question of the extent to which individuals (particularly consumers) should be able to create security involves issues which are not central to the issues raised in this chapter.

1.13   When considering the utility of the current law of security, this chapter will adopt the same structure as the rest of the book.

Types of security

1.14   The types of security which are available are discussed in **CHAPTERS 2** to **4**. Pledges are a useful form of security in international trade transactions, but

---

Commission papers and from the following: Calnan 'The Reform of the Law of Security' (2004) 3 JIBFL 88; Beale 'Reform of the Law of Security – Another View' (2004) 4 JIBFL 117; Calnan 'The Reform of Company Security Interests' (2005) 1 JIBFL 25; and the reports of the Financial Law Committee of the City of London Law Society (http://www.citysolicitors.org.uk – go to Financial Law Committee).

7   DTI *Consultation Document on the Registration of Companies' Security Interests (Company Charges)* (July 2005).

8   Ministerial statement of Alun Michael, Minister for Industry and the Regions, on Thursday, 3 November 2005, which is available on the DTI's website (http://www.dti.gov.uk) as part of the material relating to the Company Law Reform Bill, published in 2005.

9   The following discussion is based on a chapter by the author 'What is wrong with the law of security?' in De Lacy (ed) *Personal Property Security Reform in the UK: Comparative Perspectives* (Cavendish Publishing, forthcoming 2006).

the requirement that the debtor obtains, and retains, possession of a tangible moveable asset restricts its usefulness to a relatively small number of cases. In most cases the creditor's choice is between a mortgage and a charge. Legal mortgages are frequently taken over existing land, goods and shares, but are not generally available over other types of asset and, in particular, are not available in relation to future assets. In many cases, therefore, it will be an equitable charge which will be of most value to a creditor – sometimes a fixed charge, in other cases a floating charge.

Creating security

1.15 The way in which security is created is discussed in **CHAPTERS 5** and **6**. The advantage of a charge is that it is simple and easy to create, with a minimum of formality. In essence, there are only two requirements for the creation of a charge by a corporate debtor – first, evidence that the debtor intended the charge to be created over an identifiable asset for the purpose of securing an identifiable liability and, secondly, the effecting of any necessary registration at Companies House. Practically any type of asset is capable of being the subject of a charge, including future assets. The effectiveness of the security in the debtor's insolvency proceedings is not prejudiced by the fact that the creditor does not have legal or beneficial title to the asset concerned. A creditor who has a charge has a sufficient equitable proprietary interest in the charged assets that they can generally be taken outside the insolvency and dealt with by the secured creditor.

1.16 The advantage of this approach is that it gives the parties the ability to create security in a straightforward, simple and flexible manner. There are very few formalities and it is not necessary, as it is in some jurisdictions, to use different procedures depending on the identity of the assets being charged. It is possible for the debtor to create, in just one document, security over all of its present and future assets by means of fixed and floating charges. The advantages for the creditor are obvious, but the benefits for the debtor are equally real. If it is unable to raise finance on an unsecured basis, it will need the ability to create security and, the more straightforward the process, the quicker and cheaper it will be to create security. This is important for the debtor because it will invariably have to pay the costs of its creation.

1.17 The disadvantage of the ease of creation of charges is that it makes it difficult for persons dealing with the company to make themselves aware of the extent to which the debtor has created security over its assets. It is for this reason that most charges created by companies must be registered at Companies House, failing which, for most purposes, they will be void.

1.18 In general terms, therefore, it is suggested that the English law of security does what it ought to do. It provides a relatively simple, straightforward and flexible method for the creation of security over all the present and future assets of the debtor, whilst providing safeguards for third parties by means of a registration system. That is not to say that there are no problems at all. There are two issues, in particular, which are in need of reform. The first concerns the distinction between fixed and floating charges, the second the registration system.

Floating charges

1.19 One of the most intractable problems which has besetted the law for more than 25 years is the distinction between fixed and floating charges. Although it is relatively easy to state the test of whether a charge is fixed or floating, its application to the facts of any particular case involves a great deal of uncertainty. The reason why we need to draw the distinction is almost entirely because of insolvency legislation, which treats floating charges less favourably than fixed charges. One of the major uncertainties of the English law of security would be solved if insolvency legislation were altered by removing the requirement for the distinction to be drawn.[10]

Registration at Companies House

1.20 The other area which could usefully be reformed is the law relating to the registration of company charges, which is discussed in CHAPTER 6. There are three principal problems.

1.21 The first is the undesirability of having a list of those charges which are registrable. The list has grown incrementally over the years in a rather haphazard way, the result of which being that it is often difficult in practice to know whether a charge over a particular type of asset is, or is not, registrable. Subject to the requirements of the Financial Collateral Directive,[11] it would be more consistent with the purpose of the registration system to require the registration of all charges created by companies incorporated in England.

1.22 The second issue concerns the effect of non-registration. A charge which has not been lodged for registration within the required period is void in the liquidation or administration of the debtor or against creditors with security over the same asset. But it is not void against subsequent purchasers of the asset concerned, nor does it prevent a secured creditor from enforcing the security before a liquidation or administration of the debtor and thereby avoiding the problem. This seems unnecessarily complicated. It would be simpler for a charge which has not been registered in time to be void in all respects, but without prejudice to the effectiveness of the underlying secured obligation.

1.23 The third concern is the so-called *Slavenburg* registrations. At present, charges are registrable against oversea companies in certain circumstances even if they have not registered a place of business in England. Since there is no effective means of searching charges created by these companies, the requirement to register serves no useful purpose. It would make more sense if the requirement for registration were restricted to companies which are incorporated in England. If the requirement does have to extend to oversea companies, it should only extend to those which have actually registered a place of business in England at the time the charge is created.

---

10 See Calnan 'Floating Charges: A Proposal for Reform' (2004) 9 JIBFL 341.
11 Directive 2002/47/EC of the European Parliament and of the Council of 6 June 2002 on financial collateral arrangements.

1.24 In summary, it is suggested that there is little which requires changing in relation to the creation of security. On the contrary, it works very well in practice. There are, however, two areas which could usefully be reformed. The first (which is essentially a matter of insolvency law) would be to do away with the necessity to distinguish between fixed and floating charges in insolvency proceedings. The second would be to make certain relatively minor changes to the registration procedure to enable there to be more certainty about which charges are registrable, the effect of non-registration and the extent, if at all, to which oversea companies are affected by the registration requirement.

Priority of security

1.25 Priorities are discussed in CHAPTER 7. Although the law concerning the creation of security generally works well in practice, there can be no doubt that the law concerning the priority of security interests is much more intractable. This should not come as a surprise. English priority rules are detailed and complicated, but then so are priority rules in other jurisdictions.

1.26 Priority issues generally arise when a debtor wrongfully, and in breach of an undertaking to a secured creditor, creates security over, or effects an outright disposal of, the asset charged to that creditor. Such cases normally involve fraudulent action on the part of the debtor and there have, thankfully, been few cases in the last 50 years in which such issues have had to be resolved by the courts in the context of company security interests. That is not to say that we do not need rules concerning priorities, simply that such issues are not the main concern of those taking security.

1.27 It is also extremely difficult in practice to establish the 'right' answer to a priority dispute. Because it will normally involve two innocent parties, each of whom has been duped by the debtor, there is often room for doubt as to which of the parties ought to suffer as a result. It would be naïve of us to assume that we now have all the answers to issues which have perplexed judges in reported cases for more than 300 years.

1.28 The approach of the Law Commission was, essentially, to ditch the existing law, and start again. It is suggested that this may not be the best approach, that there are features of the current priority rules which are useful, and that some relatively minor changes to the existing rules could make them work better, at least until there is a general review of priorities in the context of property law generally.[12]

Enforcing security

1.29 The ability to enforce security simply and cheaply is as important to a secured creditor as its creation and priority. Security is a means to an end, not an end in itself. Its value consists in the ability of the creditor to turn the

---

12 Proposals for the reform of priority law are made in Calnan 'Reforming Priority Law' (2006) 1 JIBFL 4.

security into money in order to repay the secured obligations. The ability to enforce the security is required not only whilst the company is outside insolvency proceedings, but also when it is the subject of them.

1.30 Enforcement of security is considered in **CHAPTER 8**. There is no doubt that the underlying default rules concerning powers of enforcement are out of date and unsatisfactory. In practice, this is of little real concern because security documents invariably contain detailed enforcement powers. It would nevertheless be helpful if the default powers of all secured creditors could be set out clearly in statute. The current default powers are unclear in many respects: they differ depending on the nature of the security interest concerned and the nature of the asset which is the subject of the security, they contain methods of enforcement (such as foreclosure) which are not used in practice, and the restrictions on enforcement contained in the Law of Property Act 1925 do not reflect current practice.

1.31 A simplified set of default rules which would apply to all security interests over all assets and would reflect the practice in security documentation would be useful, not least because it would sweep away the necessity to consider a great deal of arcane case-law which is no longer of any practical relevance. Legislation could, for instance, make it clear that any secured creditor had the power, on default, to appoint a receiver of the assets concerned, enter into possession of them or sell them. The legislation would need to make it clear that these powers could be expressly or impliedly extended or limited in any particular case, thus giving the required degree of flexibility to the parties to shape the enforcement powers to the particular context of their transaction.

1.32 The effect of the debtor's insolvency on the enforcement of security is discussed in **CHAPTER 9**. Until relatively recently, English law did not restrict a secured creditor's powers of enforcement if a debtor was in insolvency proceedings. There is no doubt that recent changes have made the law more complicated and uncertain. Most of the practical problems faced by secured creditors at present do not derive from concerns about the law of security but from developments in insolvency law. The problems include:

- the complexity caused by the proliferation of different insolvency procedures which are intended to achieve the same object (particularly administrative receivership and administration);
- the ability of an administrator to prevent a secured creditor from enforcing his security when he wishes to do so (and the consequent potential for the value of the security to be reduced); and
- the way in which insolvency legislation overrides the rights of floating chargees and thereby creates an unnecessary conflict between the rights of fixed and floating chargees.

1.33 In the short term, there is unlikely to be much change to the way in which insolvency law affects secured creditors. The law was changed substantially in 1986, and again in 2002, and there is little likelihood of any more major changes in the next few years, certainly not changes which would improve the lot of secured creditors.

Security arising by operation of law

1.34   Liens are discussed in **CHAPTER 10**. The circumstances in which a legal lien is created are relatively clear and, because the possession of goods by the creditor is a requirement of all legal liens, they do not create too many problems in practice. The same cannot be said of equitable liens. They arise in a multitude of different situations, and it is well-nigh impossible to establish a conceptual basis for their imposition. There is much to be said for abolishing most (if not all) equitable liens, but this could only sensibly be done in the context of a general reform of non-consensual proprietary rights, including outright interests created under a constructive trust.

Alternatives to security

1.35   One of the most important aspects of English law is that it does not recharacterise a transaction as a secured transaction merely because it has the same economic effect as if security had been created. This issue is considered in part 3 of **CHAPTER 6 (6.32**ff), and it is undoubtedly a strength of English commercial law. Parties favour the use of English law in international financial transactions precisely because they can be assured that the English courts will not generally recharacterise the transaction. This leaves it open to the parties to structure their transaction either as a secured loan or in some other way – for instance, a finance lease, a sale and lease-back or a sale of receivables.

1.36   There are two alternatives to security – guarantees and rights of set-off – which are frequently used in conjunction with a security interest and are therefore discussed in this book.

Guarantees

1.37   Guarantees are discussed in **CHAPTER 11**. The effectiveness of the law of security does not depend solely on the ability of debtors to create security over their assets. As important is the ability of a third party to assume liability for the debtor's obligations, particularly because business enterprises tend to be structured as groups of companies. In broad terms, this requirement is amply met by English law. The creditor can take a guarantee (or an indemnity, or both) and, if required, can take security for the guarantor's obligations. Alternatively, if it does not require a personal undertaking to pay, it can take a third party charge, by which a person other than the debtor creates a security interest over its assets to secure the liability of the debtor.

1.38   The main practical problem with guarantees under English law (and, indeed, in many other jurisdictions) is that the guarantor does not usually obtain any benefit which is commensurate with the liability which it incurs as a result of giving the guarantee. Most problems with guarantees result from the one-sided nature of the contract. Some are inevitable, and will always trouble the creditor in one form or another. The most obvious example is that it will always be easier to have a guarantee set aside than a principal liability. Where the guarantor is a company, the courts can use fiduciary duty concepts to enable a guarantee to be set aside if no reasonable board of directors would have considered the guarantee to be in the company's interests and the creditor knew, or ought to have been aware, of that fact. Where the guarantor is an individual, the application of undue influence principles can also result in the guarantee being set aside. Judges have found it very difficult to settle upon a basis for the doctrine of undue influence with which they can all agree, but there is no doubt that the nature of a guarantee makes it a prime target for an undue influence claim.

1.39 These disadvantages of guarantees are inherent in their nature and, although their precise scope can be a matter for debate, they are necessary protections for those who assume someone else's liability. There are, however, two aspects of the law relating to guarantees which could usefully be reformed. The first concerns the formalities required in order to enter into a guarantee, the second the equitable protections available to guarantors.

1.40 Section 4 of the Statute of Frauds 1677 imposes two requirements for the creation of a guarantee – it must be in writing, or evidenced by a memorandum in writing, and it must be signed by the guarantor or his agent. Whatever the justifications there might have been for such a requirement in the seventeenth century, it cannot be justified in the twenty-first. One of the advantages of the English law of contract is its lack of formality. Formal requirements simply make it more difficult for a court to give effect to the parties' intentions. There is no doubt that the law should protect guarantors in appropriate cases. But this should be achieved by substantive rules which consider whether, in the circumstances of the case, the guarantor deserves protection. A blanket formality rule can work positively against the interests of justice.

1.41 A further consequence of the one-sided nature of a guarantee is the various protections which the courts have developed for guarantors. Their effect is that most arrangements between the creditor and the debtor in relation to the guaranteed debt after the guarantee has been entered into will render the guarantee ineffective unless the guarantor agrees to them. In one sense, these rules are of little importance in practice because they give way to the contrary intention of the parties, and they are invariably contracted out of in practice, at least in guarantees given in relation to financial transactions. It would nevertheless be useful if the underlying rules could be clarified and simplified. The authorities contain an alarming number of different approaches to the circumstances in which the guarantor is released from liability, and the extent of that release. There is much to be said for an attempt to simplify the underlying law in this area, taking into account current practice in contracting out of them. It may not be of much practical significance in relation to financial transactions, but it can be of concern in non-financial commercial transactions, where documentation is often less elaborate.

Set-off

1.42 Rights of set-off are discussed in CHAPTER 12. They are of great importance to secured and unsecured creditors. Unlike some other jurisdictions, English law has always favoured rights of set-off. From the creditor's point of view, it has two particularly important aspects. In the first place, although rights of set-off outside insolvency proceedings are relatively narrow, they can be extended by contract, and this is invariably done in financial transactions. Secondly, English law has always given creditors broad rights of set-off in insolvency. Some problems were caused in the 1970s and the 1980s as a result of doubts about the extent to which liabilities which were contingent at the date of insolvency could be set off and whether a creditor could take a charge over his own deposit. But these doubts were resolved by case-law in the 1990s, and there is now no real concern about the extent of set-off in English law either before or after the debtor goes into insolvency proceedings.

International security

1.43 Cross-border security and insolvency are discussed in **CHAPTERS 13** and **14**. Inevitably, any attempt to reform them needs to have one eye firmly on European and other international developments.

1.44 There is nevertheless much to be said for clarifying those English conflict of laws rules which establish which law determines the proprietary effect of transactions. In **CHAPTER 13**, it is suggested that there are essentially two rules – that the proprietary effect of a transaction in relation to a tangible is decided by the law of its location at the time the transaction is entered into; and that the proprietary effect of a transaction in relation to an intangible is decided by the law which governs the intangible. Although these principles have a broad level of support, the position is not entirely clear, and there are undoubtedly exceptions to both principles. The position could usefully be clarified in the same way that the Rome Convention has clarified a number of contractual conflict of laws issues.

1.45 Cross-border insolvency is considered in **CHAPTER 14**. The main issue is the extent to which insolvency proceedings in one jurisdiction will affect security located in, or governed by the law of, another jurisdiction. There is little case-law and the EC Insolvency Regulation[13] has fragmented English law by distinguishing between those cases where the debtor's centre of main interests is within the European Union, and those cases where it is outside it. There is much to be said for attempting to establish a single set of rules which applies to all debtors.

1.46 A further problem with cross-border insolvencies is that the EC Insolvency Regulation places so much reliance on the concept of the debtor's centre of main interests – the location of which is likely to be uncertain in many cases. It may be crying in the wind to ask for it to be changed, but there can be little doubt that a rule based on the place of incorporation of the debtor, rather than on its centre of main interests, would produce a great deal more certainty in the law.

---

13 Regulation 1346/2000/EC, as amended by Regulation 603/2005/EC of 12 April 2005.

Conclusion

1.47 It was suggested that a successful system of security law enables security to be created and enforced as simply and cheaply as possible, with a minimum of formality and the maximum of flexibility and certainty, whilst at the same time protecting unsecured creditors and others who deal with the debtor. English security law meets these objectives well, and it does so largely because of three things – a law of contract which generally gives parties the freedom to make their own bargains, a law of equity which enables proprietary interests to be created simply and with a minimum of formality, and statutory provisions which require the registration of non-possessory security.

1.48 As a result, the English law of security has the following very material benefits:

- it is easy to create, without many formalities;
- it is a unified system, without the necessity to use different types of procedure for different types of asset;
- it is flexible, and gives creditors the choice of using more formal procedures or relying on the informality of an equitable charge;
- within limits, it allows the parties freedom to vary their rights and duties by contract;
- it is concerned with the substance, rather than the form, of transactions; and
- it provides a registration system for non-possessory security which enables third parties to become aware of security which has been created.

1.49 It is therefore suggested that there is no need for any major structural change to the English law of security, although there are a number of incremental changes to the system which would assist its smooth operation. The real problem is not security law, but insolvency law, not least because of its insistence on drawing an artificial and uncertain distinction between fixed and floating charges.

TYPES OF SECURITY

Chapter 2

PLEDGES

Part 1: INTRODUCTION

2.1   Historically, there were two main ways in which a debtor could give security to a creditor over his assets. The debtor could either transfer the title to the asset to the creditor, or he could deliver possession of it to the creditor; and, once the secured debt had been paid, the creditor would re-transfer title or re-deliver possession of the asset to the creditor. Both types of security interest are still available. The former is a mortgage, the latter a pledge. The purpose of both is to give the creditor a proprietary interest in the asset as security for the discharge of a monetary liability. The importance of them both is that they survive the insolvency of the debtor.

2.2   In essence, a pledge is created when goods are delivered by a debtor to his creditor as security for a monetary obligation.[1] It is, therefore, a form of bailment – an expression which encompasses any type of consensual arrangement by which the possession of goods is separated from their ownership. Indeed, pledge was the fourth type of bailment described by Holt CJ in one of the seminal cases on bailment – *Coggs v Bernard*[2] in 1703.

2.3   The delivery of the possession of an asset to secure repayment of a debt is an obvious, and ancient, form of security. In the past, it has been used extensively, particularly by individuals borrowing small amounts of money on the security of their goods. Such an arrangement was generally known as a 'pawn', and the extent of its use and the prospect of abuse by the creditor resulted in substantial regulation of pawnbrokers in the nineteenth century.

2.4   Such arrangements are still used by individuals today, hence their continued regulation under the Consumer Credit Act 1974. But, as a means of providing security for business credit, the pledge has severe disadvantages when compared with other forms of security such as a mortgage or a charge. A business debtor will normally require the use of its assets for the purpose of running its business, and their delivery to the creditor is not normally a practical proposition. As we shall see, however, there are cases where pledges can be used to create security in a business context, and they do have certain

---

1   *Coggs v Bernard* (1703) 2 Ld Raym 909.
2   (1703) 2 Ld Raym 909.

advantages over mortgages and charges, the most important in practice being that pledges are not registrable under the Companies Act 1985 or the Bills of Sale Acts 1878–1891.

2.5 There are two features of a pledge which it is important to describe at the outset. The first relates to the way in which a pledge is created, the second to the nature of the creditor's interest in the pledged asset.

2.6 The way in which a pledge is created is very different from the way in which a charge is created. A charge is created by an act by the debtor which evidences his intention to create a charge. In many cases, his intention can be manifested orally but, almost invariably, it is in practice effected by the execution of a document by the debtor, in which event it is the document which creates the security. It follows that, once such a document has been executed, it will generally continue to protect the creditor in accordance with its terms until the secured debt is repaid.

2.7 By contrast, a pledge is not created by a document. It is created by the transfer of possession of an asset to the creditor, and its efficacy is generally dependent on the creditor's continued possession of the asset. It is rare, in practice, for a pledge to be created without a document being executed by the debtor, but the document does not create the pledge, it merely evidences it: the pledge is created by the transfer of possession.[3]

2.8 The second important feature of a pledge is that it is a common law concept, and the creditor therefore obtains a legal proprietary interest in the pledged asset, even though he does not obtain title to it. A pledge accordingly has certain advantages over an equitable security interest, such as a charge, particularly in relation to its priority over other proprietary interests. Subject to fairly limited exceptions, a legal proprietary interest is effective against anyone who obtains a subsequent proprietary interest in the asset concerned. If, for instance, the debtor tries to sell the pledged asset to a third party, in principle that third party will not obtain title to the asset, even if he gave value for it and acted in good faith, unless he falls within one of the relatively small number of exceptions to the nemo dat principle (the principle that a buyer gets no better title than his seller).[4] If the same thing were to happen to an asset over which the creditor only had an equitable interest (for instance, by way of charge) the position would be very different. An equitable interest in an asset is ineffective against a person who acquires the legal title to the asset for value and without notice of the equitable interest.

2.9 The rest of this chapter considers how pledges are created, their effect and how they are used in practice. It is divided into the following parts:

- Part 2 (**2.10ff**) – which types of asset can be the subject of a pledge?
- Part 3 (**2.22ff**) – in what ways can possession of the asset be given to the creditor?
- Part 4 (**2.45ff**) – to what extent must the creditor always retain possession of the asset in order to retain an effective pledge?

---

3   *Re Hardwick, ex parte Hubbard* (1886) 17 QBD 690.
4   See the Sale of Goods Act 1979, ss 21–26.

- Part 5 (**2.62ff**) – what formalities are involved in the creation of a pledge?
- Part 6 (**2.73ff**) – what is the effect of a pledge?
- Part 7 (**2.87ff**) – how are pledges used in practice?

Part 2: WHAT ASSETS CAN BE PLEDGED?

Goods

2.10 An asset can only be pledged if it is transferable by delivery of possession. The principal type of asset which can be pledged is therefore goods.[5]

2.11 A question which frequently arises when there is a transfer of the possession of goods is whether or not the transfer also constitutes a transfer of title (for instance, by way of sale). Title to goods can be transferred by a document (sometimes called a bill of sale) or by delivery. If title passes by delivery, no document is required to effect the transfer, although a document will frequently evidence the intention of the parties in relation to the transfer. But a transfer of the possession of goods does not necessarily have the effect of passing title to them. A transfer of possession is also susceptible to another interpretation – that the goods have been bailed (for instance, by way of a lease or a pledge), with the effect that the possession of the goods has been divided from the title to them.

2.12 Whether a transfer of possession also carries with it a transfer of title depends on the intention of the transferor. If the transferor intends to transfer title, then (subject to the terms of any contract) this can be effected by the transfer of possession. If not, then only a possessory interest will pass to the transferee, the nature of which (ie whether it is a lease, a pledge or some other form of bailment) will also depend on the intention of the parties. The important point is that a transfer of possession of goods *need not* also transfer title, though it *can* do so. Goods can be pledged because title to them is *capable* of being transferred by delivery.

2.13 It follows that neither land nor intangibles are capable of being pledged. The title to land can be separated from its possession (for instance, under a lease) but land can only be transferred by deed,[6] subject to the appropriate formalities, not by delivery of possession. Most intangibles are, by their very nature, incapable of being rendered into possession, and therefore cannot be transferred by delivery. A debt, for instance, cannot be possessed and can therefore only be transferred by a legal process such as an assignment.

---

5   *Coggs v Bernard* (1703) 2 Ld Raym 909. In this book, the expression 'goods' will be used, rather than 'chattels'. The expressions are broadly synonymous, and 'goods' is the more modern expression. In this context, 'goods' means any tangible moveable asset.

6   Law of Property Act 1925, s 52.

2.14   Apart from goods, there are two other types of asset which are capable of being transferred by delivery, and which are therefore capable of being pledged. These are documents of title to goods and documents of title to intangibles.

Documents of title to goods

2.15   The most common example of a document of title to goods is a bill of lading. A bill of lading is a document executed on behalf of the owner of a vessel and addressed to the shipper of goods on board the vessel which acknowledges his delivery of those goods to the carrier. In this context, the importance of a bill of lading is that it represents the goods on the vessel. If a bill of lading is endorsed and delivered by the owner to a buyer with the intention of effecting an outright transfer (for instance, under a contract of sale), the buyer obtains title to the underlying goods in exactly the same way as if the goods had themselves been delivered to the buyer. The bill of lading is, therefore, a 'symbol of property'.[7] It is a document of title to the goods it represents because it carries with it the benefit of the carrier's obligations to deliver the goods.

2.16   Whilst the goods are at sea, the title to them can accordingly be transferred by the endorsement and delivery of the bill of lading to successive purchasers. Indeed, the bill of lading continues to be effective in this way even when the goods are on shore until there has been a complete delivery of them by the ship's master.[8]

2.17   Because the bill of lading represents the goods, the endorsement and delivery of the bill of lading can transfer possession not only of the piece of paper itself, but also of the underlying goods. Whether the transfer is a transfer of title or merely a transfer of possession depends on the intention of the parties. In *Sewell v Burdick*,[9] the House of Lords held that the endorsement in blank and the delivery of a bill of lading by way of pledge passed the possession of the underlying goods to the pledgee, but not the title to those goods, because that was the intention of the parties.

2.18   The reason why a bill of lading is a document of title to the underlying goods is because that was how it was treated by merchants, and its effect became incorporated in the common law as a result of the law merchant.[10] It might have been thought that other documents executed by a person in possession of the goods belonging to others (for instance, a warehouseman) would also become documents of title for the same reason, but the common law has not recognised any documents other than bills of lading as constituting documents of title. Certain statutes have accorded the status of documents of title to particular types of instrument, but it is important to ensure that the particular document which is intended to be pledged is actually a document of

---

7   *Meyerstein v Barber* (1866) LR 2 CP 38 at 45, per Erle CJ.
8   *Meyerstein v Barber* (1866) LR 2 CP 38 at 45, per Erle CJ.
9   (1884) 10 App Cas 74.
10   *Official Assignee of Madras v Mercantile Bank of India* [1935] AC 53 at 59, per Lord Wright.

title. If it is not, a pledge of it will only give the creditor rights to the piece of paper itself, and not to the underlying goods.

Documents of title to intangibles

2.19 There is one exception to the principle that intangibles are incapable of being pledged. If they are represented by a document, and title to them can be transferred by delivery (and, if necessary, endorsement) of the document, they are capable of being pledged. Thus, in *Carter v Wake*,[11] Jessel MR decided that a deposit of bearer bonds by way of security created a pledge. The reason why a pledge can be created over documents of title to intangibles, such as bearer securities, is that the document represents the underlying intangible asset in the same way that a bill of lading represents the underlying goods. Delivery (and, if necessary, endorsement) of the document can pass title to the underlying intangible, without the necessity for an assignment.

2.20 It follows that a pledge is not available where the instrument is not a document of title. Most securities of English companies are in registered, rather than bearer, form. Transfer of title to registered shares is effected by the registration of the transferee in the register of members of the company concerned. Accordingly, it is not possible to pledge registered shares, the share certificate being merely evidence of title, and not a document of title.[12]

Summary

2.21 In summary, a pledge can only be created over an asset the title to which is capable of being transferred by the delivery of possession (and, if necessary, endorsement). There are three categories of such assets:

- goods;
- documents of title to goods (such as bills of lading); and
- documents of title to intangibles (such as bearer securities).

Because the pledge requires delivery of possession of the asset concerned, a pledge is only available in respect of existing, identified assets, and cannot extend to future assets.

Part 3: DELIVERY OF POSSESSION TO THE CREDITOR

2.22 It is relatively easy to describe the types of asset which are capable of being pledged, but much more difficult to establish definitively the ways in which possession can be delivered to the creditor for the purpose of establishing an effective pledge. The uncertainty is largely due to the difficulties

---

11 (1877) 4 Ch D 605.
12 *Harrold v Plenty* [1901] 2 Ch 314.

of establishing precisely what is meant by 'possession' in English law. In spite of the extensive analysis by Pollock and Wright in the leading text *Possession in the Common Law*,[13] the precise nature of possession remains elusive.

2.23   The main problem is that a distinction is sometimes drawn between the physical possession of goods and the legal possession of them. Some examples can illustrate the issues which are involved.

2.24   In the first place, the courts draw a distinction between possession and custody, particularly in the context of an employment relationship. If goods are physically held by an employee, he will have custody of them but his employer will have possession of them.

2.25   More importantly in practice in relation to taking security, a distinction is sometimes drawn between the physical possession of goods and their constructive possession. One example of constructive possession has already been discussed – where a person's possession of a document of title to goods also gives him possession of the goods which the document represents. Another type of constructive possession is created where one person, who initially holds goods on behalf of their owner, then undertakes at the owner's request to hold them on behalf of a third party. In such a case (known as an attornment), the third party becomes the person in constructive possession of the goods. Attornment is considered at **2.37ff**.

2.26   Because there is a distinction between the legal concept of possession and its factual incidence, possession is a difficult concept to define, and this makes it hard to describe how possession is transferred. At its most general, possession connotes an intention to exclude others – the ability of a person to be able to control an asset, even though that control can be effected through employees or agents. This part will consider a number of ways in which possession can be delivered by the debtor to the creditor, thereby constituting a pledge over the assets concerned. The list may not be exhaustive, but it comprehends the main types of case which have arisen in practice:

- physical delivery of the asset to the creditor;
- physical delivery to the creditor of something which represents the asset;
- attornment in favour of the creditor by a third party who has physical possession of the asset; and
- retention of the asset by the creditor by way of security in a case where he previously held it in a different capacity.

In the first and last cases, the creditor obtains actual possession of the goods concerned. In the second and third cases, he obtains constructive possession. But in all these cases the creditor obtains possession of the asset concerned because he is able to control it in a way which excludes interference by the debtor; and it is the ability of the creditor to control the asset without the debtor's interference which is the hallmark of possession.

---

13   Clarendon Press, 1888.

Physical delivery of the asset

2.27 The most straightforward example of delivery of possession under a pledge is where the debtor physically delivers the asset to the creditor. It is also the type of case which is most rare in practice, at least in commercial transactions. The reasons are obvious. It is normally impracticable for a business debtor to deliver assets physically to the creditor. There are, nevertheless, cases where it can be done, particularly in relation to objects of high value which are not immediately needed in the debtor's business, for instance, precious metals deposited in a bank's vaults.

Physical delivery of something which represents the asset

2.28 It has been seen that a document of title to goods[14] or intangibles[15] represents the underlying assets, in the sense that the transfer of the document also effects the transfer of the underlying assets. The physical delivery to the creditor of such a document will pledge not only the document, but also the assets which the document represents.

2.29 This principle can also apply where the asset which is delivered to the creditor is not a document of title but is something else which represents the asset. In such a case, in order to obtain possession of the goods concerned, the creditor needs to establish that he controls them and that the debtor has no ability to interfere with that control. Its scope is best considered by looking at three cases, in the first two of which it was held that a pledge had been created, and in the third of which it was not.

2.30 The first case is *Hilton v Tucker*.[16] D had deposited goods in a room owned by a third party. As security for a debt, D wrote to C that the key to the room was with another party and that it was entirely at C's disposal, although it appeared that D also had some access to the room. D became insolvent and the question arose whether the arrangement with C constituted an unregistered bill of sale (in which event it would have been void) or a pledge (in which event it would have been valid). Kekewich J held that a pledge had been created and therefore that the arrangement was effective in D's insolvency.

2.31 A similar conclusion was reached in *Wrightson v McArthur and Hutchisons*.[17] In that case the goods were stored on D's own premises, but D gave the creditor the key to the room and a licence to remove the goods from it. Rowlatt J held that the arrangement created a pledge and was effective even though it had not been registered as a bill of sale.[18] Unlike in *Hilton v Tucker*, the room in which the goods were stored was on the debtor's own premises.

---

14   *Sewell v Burdick* (1884) 10 App Cas 74.
15   *Carter v Wake* (1877) 4 Ch D 605.
16   (1888) 39 Ch D 669.
17   [1921] 2 KB 807.
18   Unlike Kekewich J in *Hilton v Tucker*, Rowlatt J was of the opinion that the mere fact that the arrangement was a pledge did not mean that it could not also constitute a registrable bill of sale. The reason why he held that it was not registrable was because the creditor's rights arose

Rowlatt J nevertheless considered that there was an effective pledge because, in addition to having a key to the room, C had a licence to remove the goods from the room.

2.32 Neither case is straightforward. In principle, in order to obtain possession, the creditor needed to establish that he had control over the assets and that the debtor had no ability to interfere with that control. Whether this was so in these cases is open to some debate. In *Hilton v Tucker*, the room was in a third party's premises but the debtor did have some access to it. *Wrightson v McArthur* was an even weaker case, the room being on the debtor's own premises, albeit that the creditor had a licence to enter them. In both cases, it could be established that the creditor had some degree of control over the assets, but whether that was to the exclusion of the debtor's right to interfere is more debatable.

2.33 Ultimately, these cases are simply examples of the types of case where the court has been prepared to decide that possession of a symbol of assets (such as a key) gives possession of the assets themselves. All such cases are decided on their own facts, and it would be unwise to place too much reliance on these authorities if, in any particular case, the creditor does not, in fact, really control the assets in the sense that the debtor cannot interfere.

2.34 An example of a case in which it was held that the creditor did not have sufficient control is *Dublin City Distillery v Doherty*.[19] C lent money to D on the security of whisky stored in D's warehouse. The whisky could only be removed on the joint instructions of D and an excise officer, and C was given a warrant by D stating that particular whisky was deliverable to C. The security was not registered and D went into liquidation. The question arose whether C had effective security, notwithstanding that it was not registered. The House of Lords held that C did not have a valid pledge. That would have been sufficient to decide the case, but they went on to decide that, even if C did have a pledge, it was nevertheless a registrable bill of sale and, not having been registered, was void. That aspect of the decision will be considered in part 5 of this chapter (**2.62ff**). For present purposes, the relevant issue is why their Lordships considered that C did not have an effective pledge.

2.35 Lord Atkinson pointed out that a contract to create a pledge is not, of itself, an effective pledge. 'Delivery is, in addition, absolutely necessary to complete the pledge; but of course it is enough if the delivery be constructive, or symbolical, as it is called, instead of actual.'[20] But in this case C had not obtained constructive possession of the whisky. The warrants were not documents of title to the whisky, and their delivery to C did not of itself create a pledge. Nor had there been constructive delivery of the whisky itself. It remained in D's warehouse and was not under the control of C.

---

as a result of the delivery of possession, rather than a document. This issue is considered further in part 5 of this chapter (**2.62ff**).

19   [1914] AC 823.
20   [1914] AC 823 at 843.

2.36   In summary, a pledge can be created by the physical delivery to the creditor of something which represents the asset. The delivery of a document of title to goods or intangibles is clearly sufficient to create a pledge. Whether the delivery of anything else is sufficient depends on whether the item which is delivered (such as the key to premises) gives the creditor control over the asset concerned to the exclusion of the debtor.

Attornment by a third party who has physical possession of the asset

2.37   A very clear description of attornment is contained in the speech of Lord Wright in *Official Assignee of Madras v Mercantile Bank of India*:[21]

'At the common law a pledge could not be created except by a delivery of possession of the thing pledged, either actual or constructive. It involved a bailment. If the pledgor had the actual goods in his physical possession, he could effect the pledge by actual delivery; in other cases he could give possession by some symbolic act, such as handing over the key of the store in which they were. If, however, the goods were in the custody of a third person, who held for the bailor so that in law his possession was that of the bailor, the pledge could be effected by a change of the possession of the third party, that is by an order to him from the pledgor to hold for the pledgee, the change being perfected by the third party attorning to the pledgee, that is acknowledging that he thereupon held for him; there was thus a change of possession and a constructive delivery: the goods in the hands of the third party became by this process in the possession constructively of the pledgee.'

2.38   An attornment can therefore be used where the assets concerned are in the physical possession of a third party who holds them to the order of the debtor, the debtor accordingly being the person who has legal possession of them. The attornment is effected by:

● the debtor giving a notice to the third party requesting him to hold the assets on behalf of the creditor; and
● the third party giving a notice to the creditor acknowledging that he holds them on behalf of the creditor.

The result is that the third party, who was originally holding the assets for the debtor, is now holding them for the creditor. As a result of the attornment, the constructive possession of the assets has passed from the debtor to the creditor.

2.39   An example of the use of an attornment to create a pledge is *Re Hall, ex parte Close*.[22] D borrowed money from C, which was to be secured over goods held by T on behalf of D. D gave a delivery order to T, requesting him to hold the goods to the order of C. T then gave an advice note to C confirming that they were held to C's order. D became insolvent and his trustee in bankruptcy contended that the delivery order was a bill of sale which, being unregistered,

---

21   [1935] AC 53 at 58–59.
22   (1884) 14 QBD 386.

was void. Cave J held that the transaction amounted to a pledge and therefore was not registrable under the Bills of Sale Acts 1878–1891. The security was accordingly effective against D's trustee in bankruptcy. The delivery order given by D to T and the advice note given by T to C transferred the possession of the goods from D to C.

Retention of possession by a creditor

2.40 It is not always necessary for there to be a delivery of (actual or constructive) possession by the debtor to the creditor. The creditor normally obtains possession by delivery, but it is possession which is required, not delivery.

2.41 If an owner of goods sells them to a buyer and agrees to store them for the buyer, there is a change in the nature of the seller's possession. Before the sale, he was in possession as owner. After the sale, he is in possession as bailee. The creation of a pledge without delivery is less likely to arise. It is possible for C to sell his goods to D and then to take a pledge over them to secure the purchase price, but this is unlikely to happen in practice because C could simply reserve title until payment. But, if such a case does arise, possession of the assets is not delivered by D to C. C retains possession, but the nature of that possession changes from that as outright owner to that as pledgee.[23]

Cases where the assets remain with the debtor

2.42 In principle, there can be no constructive delivery or attornment in cases where the debtor remains in possession of the assets. In *Dublin City Distillery v Doherty*,[24] it was decided that a warrant stating that particular whisky was deliverable to the creditor did not constitute constructive delivery to the creditor. The whisky remained with the debtor, and the creditor did not have control over it. For the same reason, an attornment is only effective if it is a third party who has custody of the assets concerned.[25] If the debtor has the assets, a purported attornment by him does not transfer possession to the debtor.

2.43 There are, however, some cases which are difficult to reconcile with these principles. In *Martin v Reid*,[26] D agreed that C would have a pledge over certain goods. C left the goods with D on the basis that C could have them when he chose. The Court of Common Pleas held that there had been a constructive delivery to C, even though D remained in actual possession. The reasoning of the court is a little difficult to follow. It clearly wished to give effect to the commercial agreement, but it is difficult to see how C could have obtained possession of the goods in circumstances where they remained under the

---

23 See *Dublin City Distillery v Doherty* [1914] AC 823.
24 [1914] AC 823.
25 *Official Assignee of Madras v Mercantile Bank of India* [1935] AC 53; *Dublin City Distillery v Doherty* [1914] AC 823.
26 (1862) 11 CB NS 730.

control of D. This case seems wrong in principle, and should not be relied on. It is safest to assume that a pledge cannot be created where the debtor remains in custody of the assets.

Summary

2.44 In summary, an effective pledge requires the creditor to obtain possession of the asset concerned. On the assumption that the asset is of a type which is capable of being pledged, the creditor can obtain possession of the asset:

- by receiving physical delivery of it;
- by receiving physical delivery of a document of title to it;
- by receiving physical delivery of a symbol representing it (such as a key to premises where the asset is situated) if it gives control over the asset to the creditor without interference by the debtor;
- where a third party has physical possession of the asset on behalf of the debtor, by the debtor attorning to the creditor in respect of it; or
- where the creditor has possession of an asset in one capacity, by the debtor agreeing that the nature of his possession has changed, and that the creditor now holds the asset as a pledgee.

There is some authority which indicates that the creditor can obtain possession of assets which physically remain with the debtor. That authority is inconsistent with the principles outlined above and with the other authorities, and it would be unwise to rely on it.

Part 4: RETENTION OF POSSESSION BY THE CREDITOR

2.45 It has been seen that the possession of an asset by the creditor is a requirement of an effective pledge. Because the pledge is created by the creditor's possession of the asset concerned, the general rule is that the creditor must remain in possession of the pledged asset, failing which the pledge will be lost. This is one of the weaknesses of a pledge in comparison with a charge. Most charges are created by documents and, once the document has been executed, the charge remains effective until the secured liability is discharged. A pledge, on the other hand, is effective because the creditor has possession of the asset concerned. If he loses possession, he loses the pledge. So if, for instance, the creditor returns the asset to the debtor, his rights under the pledge are lost.[27]

2.46 There are, however, two exceptions to this principle. They apply if:

- the assets concerned are returned to the debtor for a limited purpose as agent or trustee for the creditor; or

---

27 *Babcock v Lawson* (1880) 5 QBD 284.

- the assets concerned are re-pledged by the creditor as security to a third party.

When properly understood, the first of these is only an apparent exception, but the second appears to be a real one.

Re-delivery to the debtor for a limited purpose

2.47 The first exception is illustrated by two cases. In *North Western Bank v John Poynter, Son, & MacDonalds*,[28] D had delivered bills of lading to C by means of a pledge. C handed the bills of lading back to D to hold them on trust for C for the purpose of selling the goods which were the subject of the bills of lading, and then paying the proceeds to C. The House of Lords held that C's pledge continued, notwithstanding the re-delivery of the bills of lading to D. D had acted as agent for C for the purpose of selling and paying the proceeds to C.

2.48 Similarly, in *Re David Allester*,[29] D pledged bills of lading to C to secure an overdraft. When the time came to sell the goods, C re-delivered the bills of lading to D against a letter of trust executed by D which confirmed that D was receiving the bills of lading on trust for C and undertaking to hold the goods and their proceeds on trust for C. D went into liquidation and the liquidator claimed that the letters of trust were bills of sale and therefore void for non-registration. Astbury J held that the letters of trust were not bills of sale and therefore that C's security was effective in D's liquidation. He gave two reasons for this conclusion. The first was that C had preserved its pledge. It could have realised the goods itself, but decided to do so through the agency of D, who was better qualified to do so. The alternative ground for the decision was that, even if D did not have a pledge, the letter of trust was not registrable. One of the exceptions from the requirement to register a document as a bill of sale is where the document is used in the ordinary course of business as proof of possession or control of goods; and it was held that the letter of trust (often called a trust receipt) was such a document.[30]

2.49 On the face of it, the re-delivery of the pledged assets to the debtor ought, in most circumstances, to terminate the pledge. But there are good practical reasons for the decisions in these two cases. A pledge over bills of lading is a short-term security. It is effective whilst the goods concerned are at sea and until they have been delivered by the master of the vessel, but the goods will normally need to be sold in order for the creditor to be repaid. It would be possible for the creditor to effect the sale itself, but it makes more sense for it to be done by the debtor, who is likely to have more experience of such matters than the creditor. The re-delivery of the bills of lading to the debtor, for the limited purpose of selling them and paying the proceeds to the bank, fulfils the purpose of the pledge for the benefit of both debtor and creditor.

---

28   [1895] AC 56.
29   [1922] 2 Ch 211.
30   This provision is discussed in part 6 of **CHAPTER 6 (6.130ff)**.

2.50 This is not really an exception to the principle that re-delivery of possession of the pledged assets to the debtor determines the pledge. The creditor's legal possession continues through the agency of the debtor, the debtor merely obtaining physical possession of the goods, as Lord Wright made clear in *Official Assignee of Madras v Mercantile Bank of India*.[31]

2.51 In these cases, physical possession of the pledged assets was re-delivered to the debtor for a purpose connected with the pledge – the sale of the goods and payment of the creditor. There is one case which it is sometimes suggested goes further than this. In *Reeves v Capper*,[32] in consideration for a loan, D, who was a ship's captain, told C 'I make over to you, as your property, until [the loan] is repaid, my chronometer'. The chronometer was in the possession of its makers. D recovered it from them, gave it to C and then took it back again for the purpose of using it on a voyage. It was then returned to the makers, when D wrongfully pledged it to T. There was then a priority contest between C and T, in which there was a finding of fact by the jury that the chronometer was the property of C.

2.52 T argued that C only had a pledge and that the re-delivery to D had terminated the pledge. C argued that he was the owner of the chronometer under a legal mortgage and, since he had a mortgage rather than a pledge, possession of the chronometer was irrelevant to his security. Tindal CJ held that C had acquired the legal title to the chronometer as security and that all that D had was the reversionary title to it. In other words, C had a legal mortgage over the chronometer, rather than a pledge. That was sufficient to decide the case in favour of C because, if C had a legal mortgage, T's rights would necessarily be subject to it, even if he was not aware of it.

2.53 Unfortunately, Tindal CJ went on to say that C had retained his 'pledge' because the delivery to D was not a parting with C's possession, it being given back to D for the limited purpose of use on the voyage. This dictum is much more difficult to follow than the reasoning in *North Western Bank v Poynter* and in *Re David Allester*. In those cases, the asset concerned was re-delivered to the debtor for the purpose of enabling the pledged asset to be realised and the creditor to be repaid. The arrangement could be seen as being a part of the pledge, to enable the pledged asset to be realised in the most efficient way for the benefit of both parties. In *Reeves v Capper*, on the other hand, the asset was re-delivered to D for his own purposes, which had nothing to do with the pledge, and it is difficult to see how C could properly be seen to have retained possession in such circumstances. Otherwise, all that would be required to create an effective pledge would be a momentary delivery of possession to the creditor followed by re-delivery to the debtor for some purpose which was expressed to be limited.

2.54 The references to the retention of C's pledge are probably not part of the ratio of the case, it having already been decided that C had a legal mortgage over the chronometer. Most decisions in relation to pledges since the mid-nineteenth century have revolved around the question as to whether the

---

31   [1935] AC 53 at 63–64.
32   (1838) 5 Bing (NC) 136.

security concerned was a pledge (in which case it was not registrable) or a mortgage or charge (in which case it was registrable). This was not an issue when *Reeves v Capper* was decided, because the bills of sale legislation had not yet been introduced. There was accordingly no need to distinguish between a mortgage and a pledge for this purpose; and the basis of the decision seems to have been that C had a legal mortgage which took priority over T's pledge.

2.55 In summary, the re-delivery of the asset concerned to the debtor for the limited purpose of selling it and paying the proceeds to the creditor will be effective to preserve the creditor's possession as pledgee, but a re-delivery to the debtor for any other purpose will not do so, and will terminate the pledge.

Re-pledge by the creditor to a third party

2.56 It has been seen that the re-delivery of the pledged goods to the debtor for the limited purpose of selling them is not a real exception to the principle that the creditor must retain possession in order to retain his pledge. In such a case, the creditor does retain constructive possession, the debtor only obtaining physical possession of the goods concerned for a limited purpose and time. Such reasoning is not, however, available where the creditor re-pledges the goods concerned to a third party.

2.57 In *Donald v Suckling*,[33] D deposited debentures with C as security for a debt, and C was given a power of sale over the debentures if D defaulted on payment of the secured debt. Before the secured debt became payable, C deposited the debentures with T as security for a larger debt he owed T. D then attempted to recover the debentures from T on the basis that the actions of C had terminated the pledge and that D was therefore entitled to their immediate possession.

2.58 The Court of Queen's Bench held that, although such a re-pledge was a breach of contract as between D and C, the pledge in favour of C continued and D was therefore only able to recover the debentures from T by tendering the amount of the debt it owed to C.

2.59 D had argued that a pledge requires continued possession of the asset by the pledgee and that, having given up possession to T, the pledge had ceased to exist. Shee J accepted this reasoning, but the majority of the Court of Queen's Bench found in favour of C. They held that the pledge in favour of C continued even though there had been a re-pledge. Their reasoning was that a pledge confers on the creditor a special property in the assets concerned which gives the creditor a proprietary right which is capable of being assigned. Although the sub-pledge was in breach of the original pledge, it was not so inconsistent with it that it amounted to a repudiation of it. Accordingly, although C might be liable to D for breach of contract, the pledge continued.

---

33   (1866) LR 1 QB 585.

2.60 It is not at all easy to follow this line of reasoning. It is clearly correct to say that a pledgee has a proprietary interest in the pledged assets (this is considered in part 6 of this chapter (**2.73ff**)). It is therefore possible for the pledgee to assign the secured debt and the pledge to a third party, who will take possession of the asset on the same terms as the original pledgee. It may also have been the case that the breach of contract by the creditor was insufficient to amount to a repudiation of the contract of pledge. But pledges are not solely matters of contract. They are created by contract but they also have proprietary effects, which is why they are effective in the debtor's insolvency. As a matter of property law, it is fundamental to a pledge that the creditor has possession of the pledged asset. If he loses that possession, it is difficult to see how the pledge can continue. An assignment of the debt and the pledge simply replaces one pledgee with another, but a re-pledge as security for a different debt gives possession to someone other than the creditor, and it is difficult to see how this can be consistent with a continuing pledge in favour of the creditor.

2.61 *Donald v Suckling* is nevertheless authority for the proposition that a re-pledge does not destroy the first pledge. It may simply have to be seen as an anomalous exception to the basic principle that a pledge is only effective if the creditor obtains and retains possession of the pledged asset. In practice, it would nevertheless be preferable for the creditor to ensure that he retains possession of the asset throughout the period of the pledge.

Part 5: REGISTRATION AND OTHER FORMALITIES

2.62 It has been seen that the creation of a pledge requires the creditor to obtain and (generally) retain possession of an asset which is capable of being transferred by delivery. No documentation is required, although there will normally be a document which evidences the terms on which the pledge has been created. This part considers whether there are any registration requirements or other formalities required to create a pledge.

Registration

2.63 A pledge is not registrable either under the Bills of Sale Acts 1878–1891 or under the Companies Act 1985.

2.64 The reason why the bills of sale legislation does not apply is clearly explained by the Court of Appeal in *Re Hardwick, ex parte Hubbard*.[34] D deposited goods with C as security for a loan. At the same time, he entered into an agreement which recited the deposit of the goods, acknowledged receipt of the loan and provided for the sale of the pledged goods on default. The question arose whether the agreement amounted to a bill of sale. The Court of Appeal decided that it did not. It held that the pledge was created by the

---

34   (1886) 17 QBD 690.

delivery of possession of the goods to C. The agreement did not create the pledge, and nor did it give C the right to take possession of the goods. He had already obtained possession under the pledge. All that the document did was to regulate the terms on which C held the goods by way of pledge. A pledge is created by possession of an asset. There will normally be a document involved, but that will only *evidence* the terms of the pledge, it will not *create* the pledge.

2.65　As far as registration under the Companies Act 1985 is concerned, the reason why a pledge created by a company is not registrable is simply because the registration provisions of the Companies Act 1985 only apply to mortgages or charges created by companies. The relevant provisions are not expressed to apply to pledges.[35]

2.66　The reason neither the bills of sale nor the companies legislation require the registration of pledges is because their purpose is to publicise non-possessory security interests, not possessory ones. The statutory requirement for registration stems from a concern that creditors and other persons dealing with a debtor could be unaware that he has created security over his assets. If the security must be registered, a person dealing with the debtor will be able to search the register in order to establish whether any security has been created. But where the debtor is not in possession of the assets concerned because the creditor has possession of them under a pledge, there is no necessity for registration because it will be apparent to those dealing with the debtor that he is not possessed of the asset concerned.

2.67　This rationale is explained in *Re Hall, ex parte Close,*[36] which has already been discussed. The question at issue was whether a pledge created by an attornment was, or was not, registrable as a bill of sale. Cave J held that the attornment created an effective pledge and that pledges were not registrable as bills of sale. He described the mischief at which the bills of sale legislation was directed as being the apparent ownership of assets by a debtor:[37]

> 'The mischief here pointed at is the false appearance of credit arising from the possession, and so apparent ownership, of property which the grantee of a bill of sale is really entitled to, and of which he has the power of taking possession. This is not the mischief which arises from a pledge; for in that case, the possession being transferred to the pledgee, the pledgor cannot get false credit from an apparent possession giving rise to a false notion of ownership.'

2.68　The bills of sale legislation is not aimed at pledges; and the same is true of the companies legislation. Registration is intended to give notice to the world of the existence of security over assets of which the debtor might appear to be the unrestricted owner. Such registration is not required if the assets are in the possession of someone else, because the debtor does not appear to be the owner of them. It has been seen that there are certain limited cases where the assets are capable of being re-delivered to the debtor without the pledge being

---

35　Companies Act 1985, ss 395(1) and 396(4).
36　(1884) 14 QBD 386.
37　(1884) 14 QBD 386 at 391.

destroyed, but these are limited to cases where the pledge is being enforced and the debtor is unlikely to be in possession of the assets concerned for anything more than a limited period.

2.69   There are, nevertheless, statements in some of the cases which suggest that pledges might be registrable in certain circumstances. In *Dublin City Distillery v Doherty*,[38] the House of Lords held that the transaction concerned did not create a valid pledge, and was therefore registrable. There are, however, certain dicta of their Lordships in that case which indicate that, even if there had been a pledge, it would have been a bill of sale and would therefore have been registrable. For instance, Lord Parker stated that the expression 'mortgage or charge' in the Companies Act included a pledge but that, if a pledge was complete without requiring a document, it was not registrable. There are dicta in other cases to a similar effect.[39]

2.70   These statements seem to assume that it is possible to create a pledge otherwise than by transferring possession of the asset concerned to the creditor, and that a debtor can give constructive possession to a creditor by a document, but still remain in actual possession of the assets concerned. It is true that such an arrangement is registrable. But that is not because it creates a registrable pledge, but because it creates a registrable charge. It has been seen that a pledge is created by delivery of possession. If there is no delivery of possession, there can be no pledge, in which event the security concerned must, if it is to be effective, be a mortgage or a charge. It is accordingly suggested that, notwithstanding these dicta, the overwhelming weight of principle and authority establishes that a pledge is not registrable either under the Bills of Sale Acts 1878–1891 or under the Companies Act 1985.

2.71   There is one further point to make in relation to registration. It has been seen that the policy justification behind the principle that pledges are not registrable is that the debtor does not appear to be the owner of assets in the possession of third parties. The one exception to the principle that the pledge terminates if the goods are returned to the debtor is where they are returned for the limited purpose of sale and payment to the creditor. There is, in fact, a further reason why such an arrangement is not registrable, which was the second ground for the decision of Astbury J in *Re David Allester*[40] (which is referred to in part 4 of this chapter at **2.48**). One of the exceptions from the requirement to register documents creating security is where those documents are used in the ordinary course of business as proof of the possession or control of goods; and Astbury J decided that a trust receipt was such a document and was therefore not registrable even if it created a charge, rather than evidenced a pledge.[41]

Consumer Credit Act 1974

2.72   The only other formality required in relation to pledges is where they fall within the scope of the Consumer Creditor Act 1974. It is beyond the scope of

---

38   [1914] AC 823.
39   See, for instance, the judgment of Rowlatt J in *Wrightson v McArthur and Hutchisons* [1921] 2 KB 807.
40   [1922] 2 Ch 211.
41   This is discussed further in part 6 of CHAPTER 6 (**6.130ff**).

this book to consider the detailed provisions of the Consumer Credit Act 1974 and the various regulations made under it. Suffice it to say that, where the Act applies, there are very detailed requirements concerning the form and nature of the documentation required to effect the pledge. The Act does not, however, apply if the debtor is a company; and, even where the debtor is an individual, it does not apply if the amount of the credit is in excess of a particular amount, presently £25,000.[42]

Part 6: THE EFFECT OF A PLEDGE

2.73   It has been seen that the essential nature of a pledge is that the creditor has possession of the asset concerned. The creditor does not obtain legal or beneficial title to the asset, but it does obtain what is often referred to as a 'special property' in the asset to secure repayment of the secured debt.[43] The expression 'special property' is used to distinguish the creditor's rights from those of the ultimate owner, who is said to own the 'general property' (ie the reversionary title) in the asset. This special property is a type of proprietary interest and gives the creditor various rights:

- The creditor's interest is effective against an insolvency officer of the debtor.
- The creditor can sell the pledged asset on default by the debtor.
- The creditor has the right to immediate possession of the asset and therefore the ability to sue the debtor and third parties in conversion if the asset is taken away from him during the continuance of the pledge.
- The creditor has a legal interest in the asset, which gives the pledge certain priority advantages over equitable mortgages and charges.

2.74   The debtor retains title to the asset (the 'general property') and, because the pledge is a form of security interest, has the right to redeem the pledge (ie to recover unencumbered title) on payment of the secured debt.

Priority on insolvency

2.75   The main value of a pledge (as, indeed, of any other form of security interest over the debtor's assets) is that it is enforceable not only whilst the debtor is solvent, but also where he is insolvent. The pledge takes the asset outside the scope of the insolvency proceedings, and the debtor's insolvency officer has, in general, no better rights than the debtor in respect of the pledged assets. The effect of insolvency proceedings on secured creditors' rights is considered in more detail in CHAPTER 9.

---

42   Consumer Credit Act 1974, ss 8(2) and 189(1). There is currently draft legislation which would extend the scope of the consumer credit legislation, in particular by removing the monetary limit on its application.

43   *Coggs v Bernard* (1703) 2 Ld Raym 909.

Power of sale

2.76   Because the creditor only obtains possession of the pledged asset, not title to it, it might have been thought that his powers of sale would be limited. But this is not the case. Because the creditor's rights are held as security for a debt, he is entitled to sell the pledged asset on default by the debtor, and pay himself out of the net proceeds.[44] Unlike a legal mortgagee, a pledgee cannot, however, foreclose (ie apply to the court to become the unencumbered owner of the pledged assets). This is because, unlike a legal mortgagee, a pledgee does not own the pledged asset, he only has possession of it.[45] He has a special property in the asset, but not the general property.

2.77   When the creditor sells, he must act properly.[46] The duty of the creditor when selling is described by Lord Mersey in *The Odessa*:[47]

'If the pledgee sells he does so by virtue and to the extent of the pledgor's ownership, and not with a new title of his own. He must appropriate the proceeds of the sale to the payment of the pledgor's debt, for the money resulting from the sale is the pledgor's money to be so applied. The pledgee must account to the pledgor for any surplus after paying the debt. He must take care that the sale is a provident sale ...'

The duty of the creditor is effectively the same as that of a mortgagee or a receiver – to sell at the best price which can reasonably be obtained at the time he sells. Any surplus, after repaying the secured liability, is held on trust for the debtor.[48]

2.78   Although the creditor has an implied power of sale on default, it is normal for documents evidencing pledges to give creditors wide powers of enforcement. The powers of enforcement of secured creditors are considered in more detail in **CHAPTER 8**.

Rights in conversion

2.79   Whilst the pledge continues, the creditor has the immediate right to possess the pledged asset. If the pledged asset is taken away from him by a third party, the creditor can therefore sue in conversion, and the debtor cannot.[49] Indeed, the creditor can recover the full value of the asset, even if it is in excess of the amount of the secured debt, but is liable to pay the surplus to the debtor.[50]

2.80   During the continuance of the pledge, the debtor has no immediate right to possession, and therefore cannot sue the creditor or third parties in

---

44   *Re Morritt, ex parte Official Receiver* (1886) 18 QBD 222 at 235, per Fry LJ; *Pothonier & Hodgson v Dawson* (1815–1817) Holt 383.
45   *Carter v Wake* (1877) 4 Ch D 605.
46   *Coggs v Bernard* (1703) 2 Ld Raym 909 at 913.
47   [1916] AC 145 at 159.
48   *Mathew v T M Sutton* [1994] 1 WLR 1455.
49   *Owen v Knight* (1837) 4 Bing (NC) 54.
50   *Swire v Leach* (1865) 18 CB NS 479.

conversion. But, once the debtor has paid the secured debt or has tendered the payment of it to the creditor, the creditor's special property in the asset ceases and the debtor has the immediate right to possess it and can therefore sue the creditor in conversion.[51]

A legal interest

2.81 Pledges are recognised at common law, and the creditor's 'special property' in the pledged assets is a legal, rather than an equitable, right. A legal interest in an asset generally gives a creditor greater priority rights than an equitable interest. Once a person obtains a legal interest in an asset, there are only limited circumstances in which that interest can be defeated. Where a creditor has an equitable interest, however, it will be defeated by a bona fide purchaser of the legal interest in the asset concerned for value and without notice of the creditor's equitable interest.

2.82 Pledges also have a practical advantage over other forms of security interest when it comes to defending priority. The fact that the creditor is in possession of the pledged asset means that it is much more difficult for a third party to acquire an interest in the asset without notice of the creditor's security interest.

2.83 There are, however, circumstances where the creditor's rights under a pledge will be subject to those of a subsequent bona fide purchaser of the assets concerned. The creditor's rights are most vulnerable when he has returned the custody of the pledged assets to the debtor (for instance, under a trust receipt) in circumstances where there is an exception to the nemo dat rule. In such a case the creditor has lost both the practical and the legal advantage described above.

2.84 An example of such a case is *Lloyds Bank v Bank of America*.[52] C had a pledge over bills of lading owned by D, and returned them to D under a trust receipt for the purpose of the sale of the underlying goods. D wrongfully pledged them to T, who took his interest in good faith and without notice of C's interest. The Court of Appeal held that T took priority over C. Because the bills of lading had been returned to D, D had been able to persuade T that they were unencumbered. In most cases, this would not have mattered because C's legal interest under his pledge would still have taken priority over T's because of the so-called nemo dat rule, under which a person cannot transfer to another a greater interest than he has himself.[53] However, one of the exceptions to the nemo dat rule is contained in s 2(1) of the Factors Act 1889. That section gives a bona fide purchaser of goods or bills of lading priority over a pledge if the purchaser acquired its interest from a mercantile agent in possession of the bills of lading with the consent of the owner. The Court of Appeal held that D had obtained the bills of lading as agent for C under the trust receipt and was, in the circumstances of that case, a mercantile agent. They also decided that D

51　*Gledstane v Hewitt* (1831) 1 Cr & J 565.
52　[1938] 2 KB 147.
53　*Cole v North Western Bank* (1875) LR 10 CP 354 at 362, per Blackburn J.

was in possession of them with the consent of the owner; the 'owner' meant the person who could authorise the dealing and therefore meant C and D together or, after a default, C.

2.85 The priority of security is considered further in CHAPTER 7.

The debtor's right to redeem

2.86 Because the creditor only has a 'special property' in the goods, rather than absolute legal title, the debtor has a legal right to redeem on payment of the secured debt to the creditor[54] or on tendering the amount of the secured debt to the creditor.[55]

Part 7: PLEDGES IN PRACTICE

2.87 The fact that a pledge requires the creditor to obtain and (generally) to retain possession of the pledged asset means that pledges are not generally used as security devices by companies raising finance.

2.88 Pledges do, however, have certain advantages over other types of security interest. There are two in particular:

- Because pledges are not registrable under the Bills of Sale Acts 1898–1891 or the Companies Act 1985, they are particularly useful in securing short-term financings where registration might be cumbersome.
- Because the creditor's rights under a pledge are legal (as opposed to equitable) and because the creditor normally has physical possession of the asset concerned, a pledge can have priority advantages in a dispute with someone else who has a proprietary interest in the asset concerned.

2.89 There are two particular types of case where pledges are useful in practice. The most important is the financing of international trade. It is commonplace for banks to secure the financing of international trade by taking pledges over bills of lading. The short-term nature of many of these financings means that the absence of a requirement to register is useful, and the trust receipt enables the pledged assets to be realised in the most effective way.

2.90 The other type of case in which pledges can be useful is much less common in practice. Where creditors wish to take a mortgage or charge over goods owned by an individual, they need to comply with the provisions of the Bills of Sale Acts 1878–1891. The requirements of these Acts are discussed in part 6 of CHAPTER 6 (**6.130**ff) but, in essence, they make it impracticable, in most cases, for lenders to take such security over goods owned by individuals. If a pledge can be taken over the assets concerned, the restrictions contained in

---

54 *Coggs v Bernard* (1703) 2 Ld Raym 909.
55 *Ryall v Rolle* (1749) 1 Atk 165.

the Bills of Sale Acts 1878–1891 can be avoided and a relatively simple form of security structure can be effected. The creditor is still required to take possession of the assets concerned, but this can frequently be done by means of an attornment. For example, if the individual debtor is an art dealer, it is possible for works of art owned by him which are in the physical possession of an auction house to be pledged to a creditor by means of an attornment by the auction house.

2.91 Although pledges have, to a very large extent, now been superseded in practice by mortgages and (to an even greater extent) by charges, there are still some circumstances in which they can provide more cost-effective security than other forms of security interest.

Chapter 3

MORTGAGES AND CHARGES

Part 1: INTRODUCTION

3.1 It has been seen in CHAPTER 2 that the requirement of a pledge that the creditor has possession of the pledged asset severely limits its use in commercial transactions. But this limitation is of little practical importance because of the availability of two other forms of security – mortgages and charges. Although they are conceptually different, they will be treated together because, in practice, the distinctions between them are not great. More important are the factors which link mortgages and charges. They are both created by evidence of the intention of the debtor, they are both effective without any necessity for the creditor to obtain possession of the secured asset and they both give the creditor a proprietary interest in the secured asset which (although the nature of the interest varies depending on whether the security is a legal mortgage, an equitable mortgage or a charge) is effective in the debtor's insolvency.

What is a mortgage?

3.2 A mortgage involves the transfer of the title to an asset as security for a liability.

3.3 The nature of a legal mortgage is described by Lindley MR in *Santley v Wilde*:[1]

> 'The principle is this: A mortgage is a conveyance of land or an assignment of chattels as security for the payment of a debt or the discharge of some other obligation for which it is given. This is the idea of a mortgage: and the security is redeemable on the payment or discharge of such debt or obligation ...'

3.4 An equitable mortgage has similar characteristics, the main differences being that it involves the transfer of beneficial (rather than legal) title and that it is available in respect of assets other than land or chattels.

3.5 There are therefore two elements of a mortgage:

---

1   [1899] 2 Ch 474 at 474.

- In the first place, title to an asset must be transferred to the creditor or to someone on his behalf. If it is legal title which is transferred, the mortgage is a legal mortgage. If beneficial title is transferred, it is an equitable mortgage. Either way, the creditor obtains a proprietary interest which remains effective in the insolvency of the debtor. It is not necessary for the creditor to take possession of the asset.
- The second element is that the transfer must be by way of security. The creditor is not intended to have the absolute entitlement to the asset concerned. It has been transferred to secure a liability and, once that liability has been discharged, the debtor is entitled to have the asset re-transferred to him. This right, which is itself a proprietary interest, is generally referred to as an 'equity of redemption'. It is considered further in part 6 of this chapter (**3.295ff**).

What is a charge?

3.6 A charge is less easy to define. In distinction from a mortgage, the creditor does not obtain either legal or beneficial title to the charged asset. But what he does obtain is an equitable proprietary interest in the asset by way of security.

3.7 There have been a number of attempted definitions of a charge in the cases but, in one of the most recent, *Re Bank of Credit and Commerce International (No 8)*,[2] Lord Hoffmann recognised the difficulty of providing an exhaustive definition. He contented himself with describing a charge as being a proprietary interest granted by way of security without a transfer of title or possession. It is also common to describe a charge as the appropriation of an asset in discharge of a liability. An example of such a description is that given by Peter Gibson J in *Carreras Rothmans v Freeman Mathews Treasure*.[3] He said that a charge is created 'by an appropriation of specific property to the discharge of some debt or other obligation without there being any change in ownership either at law or in equity ...'.

3.8 These descriptions show that there are two elements of a charge:

- The creditor obtains an equitable proprietary interest in the secured asset, but does not obtain either legal or beneficial title to it. Nor is it required that the creditor takes possession of it.
- The creditor's interest is given to him by way of security for the discharge of a liability so that, when the liability has been discharged, the charge terminates.

3.9 The second element is common to all types of security, but the first has caused more difficulty. It is easy to state what a charge does not involve: it does not involve the transfer of legal or beneficial title to the asset concerned, nor does it require possession to be transferred. But it is much more difficult to define the precise nature of the interest obtained by the creditor in the asset concerned. Two things are, however, clear:

---

2   [1998] AC 214 at 226.
3   [1985] 1 Ch 207 at 227.

- A charge is an equitable concept, and the creditor's interest is therefore equitable. The creditor does not obtain any common law rights in the asset concerned.
- The creditor's right is proprietary, rather than merely personal, and is therefore effective in an insolvency of the debtor. For the same reason, it will bind the charged asset in the hands of third parties, subject to the rules concerning priorities, which are discussed in CHAPTER 7.

Does the distinction matter?

3.10 It has been seen that the main distinction between a mortgage and a charge is that a mortgagee obtains legal or beneficial title to the asset concerned, whereas a charge does not. Is the distinction important?

3.11 There have been cases where the distinction between a mortgage and a charge has been important. During the First World War, for instance, there was legislation in force which provided for security to have a different effect depending on whether it was a mortgage or a charge. The Court of Appeal had to consider that legislation in *London County & Westminster Bank v Tompkins*,[4] and the requirement to do so led that eminent common lawyer, Scrutton LJ, to say[5] that, although there was a distinction between a mortgage and a charge, 'equity judges appear to use the terms with no such precise distinction'.

3.12 This failure to distinguish between mortgages and charges is understandable. They both give the creditor a proprietary interest in the asset concerned which is effective in the debtor's insolvency. As far as rights against subsequent encumbrancers are concerned, the important distinction is not between mortgages and charges but between legal mortgages, on the one hand, and equitable mortgages and charges, on the other. It is generally easier to enforce legal rights against third parties than equitable rights (not least because of the principle that a person who acquires a legal interest in an asset for value and without notice of an earlier equitable interest will take free of that equitable interest).

3.13 Mortgages and charges are also generally treated in the same way in the relevant legislation. In the Companies Act 1985, which provides for the registration of charges created by companies, the expression 'charge' includes a mortgage.[6] The Law of Property Act 1925, which is the key legislation concerning security over land, conversely (but to the same effect) defines 'mortgage' to include a charge.[7]

3.14 There are two minor differences between mortgages and charges. First, because a chargee does not obtain legal or beneficial title to the asset concerned, his powers of enforcement are more circumscribed than those of a mortgagee. Unlike a mortgagee, a chargee does not have a right of foreclosure

---

4   [1918] 1 KB 515. The legislation is no longer in force.
5   [1918] 1 KB 515 at 528.
6   Companies Act 1985, s 396(4).
7   Law of Property Act 1925, s 205(1)(xvi).

or, in the absence of express provision in the charge document, a right to possession of the charged asset. In practice, however, charges invariably contain extensive powers of enforcement which give the chargee substantially the same powers as those of a mortgagee. These limitations on a chargee's powers of enforcement are therefore of little relevance in practice. The powers of enforcement of secured creditors are considered in more detail in CHAPTER **8**.

3.15 Secondly, it has been seen that a mortgagor's equity of redemption enables the mortgagor to require the re-transfer of the asset to him on payment of the secured debt. This is not necessary where the creditor only has a charge over the asset concerned, because the charge terminates as soon as the secured liability has been paid. In the words of Stuart V-C in *Kennard v Futvoye*:[8]

> 'If there be a simple charge without an equity of redemption, that is, if there be nothing more than a debt charged upon an estate, without any conveyance of the estate to the creditor, or any right or equity of redemption reserved, such a security is not a mortgage … because a charge is at once extinguished by payment of the debt, and from its nature must subsist til the debt is satisfied.'

3.16 Although there is a conceptual distinction between a mortgage and a charge, the practical differences between them are therefore insufficiently important to require them to be considered separately. There is, however, an important distinction between:

- legal mortgages; and
- equitable mortgages and charges.

3.17 One of these distinctions has already been mentioned – the fact that it is generally easier to enforce a legal proprietary interest against third parties than an equitable one. This issue is considered further in CHAPTER **7**. The distinction between legal and equitable interests is also very important when it comes to creating the security. There are more formal requirements for the creation of a legal mortgage than an equitable mortgage or a charge. It is also possible to create security over more types of asset in equity than it is at law. These issues are discussed further in this chapter. For all these reasons, it will be the distinction between legal and equitable security interests, rather than that between mortgages and charges, which will be pursued in this chapter.

Statutory intervention

3.18 Although the basic principles relating to the creation of security have been developed by the common law and equity, there has been a substantial amount of statutory intervention. In the business context, the most important effect of statute on the law of security is the requirement to register most mortgages and charges against the debtor and, in some cases, against the asset over which the security has been taken.

---

8   (1860) 2 Giff 81 at 92–93.

3.19 In practice, the main registration requirement is that contained in the Companies Act 1985, which requires most mortgages and charges created by companies to be registered, failing which they will be void for most purposes. The companies legislation was foreshadowed by the bills of sale legislation, which requires certain types of mortgage and charge created by individuals to be registered, with similar consequences for failure to do so. Registration against the debtor is discussed in CHAPTER 6.

3.20 Other legislation has provided for the registration of mortgages and charges created over particular types of asset, such as land, ships and aircraft and certain types of intellectual property. Failure to register in these asset registries only affects the priority of the mortgage or charge concerned, rather than its effectiveness in an insolvency. These statutory provisions are considered in part 9 of CHAPTER 7 (**7.251**ff).

3.21 Legislation has also affected the way in which some types of mortgage and charge are created. Before the 1925 property legislation, legal mortgages of land were effected by the conveyance of the land to the creditor, on terms that it was to be re-conveyed to the debtor on payment of the secured liability. As a result of the Law of Property Act 1925, legal mortgages of land are now normally created by the execution of a document described as a 'charge by way of legal mortgage', rather than by the transfer of the legal title to the land to the creditor. This has had no practical impact on the effect of a legal mortgage. The creditor continues to have the same powers he would have had if the property had been transferred to him. It is simply the form of the transaction which has changed. This is discussed further in part 2 of this chapter (**3.25**ff).

3.22 Legislation has also had an effect on the creation of security over intangibles. The Judicature Act 1873 provided a statutory means of creating security over intangibles, without having to rely on an equitable mortgage or charge. The relevant legislation is now contained in s 136 of the Law of Property Act 1925. But, again, the practical effect of the legislation is relatively minor. It is considered in part 5 of this chapter (**3.175**ff).

3.23 Unlike the requirement for registration, which permeates the whole of the law of security, these other changes to the way in which security is created have, therefore, been relatively unimportant.

Structure of this chapter

3.24 The rest of this chapter considers the following issues:

- Part 2 (**3.25**ff) – how legal mortgages are created.
- Part 3 (**3.57**ff) – how equitable mortgages and charges are created.
- Part 4 (**3.140**ff) – establishing the scope of the security.
- Part 5 (**3.175**ff) – the particular rules concerning security over intangibles.
- Part 6 (**3.295**ff) – the debtor's rights: the equity of redemption.

Part 2: LEGAL MORTGAGES

3.25 There are three main requirements of a legal mortgage:

- it must be taken over an asset which is recognised as property at common law;
- the legal title to the asset must be transferred to the creditor; and
- the transfer must be made by way of security for the discharge of a monetary liability.

Types of property

3.26 Since a legal mortgage requires the transfer of legal title to the asset concerned, it can only be taken over those assets which the common law regards as property and which are therefore capable of being transferred at common law. Land and goods are regarded as property by the common law, and are therefore transferable, but most types of intangible are not, and nor are future assets.

Land

3.27 In practice, most legal mortgages are taken over land. Since the 1925 property legislation, however, it has no longer been possible to create a legal mortgage over land by transferring title to the creditor. There are now two ways in which a legal mortgage can be created over land. One, which is rarely used (and which is no longer available over registered land),[9] is for the debtor to lease the land to the creditor (or, in the case of a mortgage of leasehold property, to sub-lease it for a shorter term) on the basis that the creditor's interest determines on payment of the secured liabilities. The alternative method of creating a legal mortgage, and by far the most common, is for the debtor to execute what is described in the Law of Property Act 1925 as a 'charge by deed expressed to be by way of legal mortgage'. Such an interest, which is commonly (if misleadingly) called a 'legal charge', does not transfer title to the land to the creditor but does give the creditor what are effectively equivalent rights. Where the land concerned is freehold, the creditor obtains the equivalent of a 3,000-year lease. Where the property is leasehold, the creditor obtains the equivalent of a leasehold interest for a term of one day less than the leasehold term.[10]

3.28 It is been seen that a charge is an equitable concept, not recognised at common law. Although, by statute, it is now possible to create a charge by way of legal mortgage, it is important to appreciate that it creates a legal, rather than an equitable, interest in the land concerned.[11] As a result, although a legal mortgage of land is no longer created by the transfer of legal title to the creditor, both types of mortgage now available give the creditor a legal interest

---

9   Land Registration Act 2002, s 51.
10   Law of Property Act 1925, ss 85–87.
11   Law of Property Act 1925, s 1(2)(c).

in the land and give him effectively the same rights as he would have had if the land had been transferred to him by way of security. The form may have changed, but the substance has not.

3.29 Most land in England is now registered at the Land Registry or requires to be registered as soon as it is next transferred. Registration is required of all material interests in land, whether they are freehold or leasehold.[12] A mortgage of a registered interest in land will only operate as a legal interest once it is registered[13] and, as will be seen in CHAPTER 7, registrable interests rank in order of registration.[14] In practice, therefore, a legal mortgage over land requires to be registered at the Land Registry.

Goods

3.30 The common law recognises two ways in which security can be taken over goods – by a pledge or by a mortgage. Because, in commercial transactions, it is normally impracticable for the debtor to give up possession of its goods, it is much more common for them to be mortgaged. Large items of equipment, such as plant and machinery, are capable of being the subject of legal mortgages; and, although they are frequently charged, rather than mortgaged, there are priority advantages in obtaining the legal title. Priority issues are discussed in CHAPTER 7.

3.31 There are, however, three practical limitations on taking legal mortgages (or, indeed, fixed equitable charges) over goods. The first is that large items of plant and machinery may well become fixtures, attached to the land on which they are placed. If so, the goods will become part of the land and therefore the subject of a mortgage over the land, rather than of a separate mortgage over the goods. This issue is discussed further in part 4 of this chapter (**3.140ff**).

3.32 Secondly, major items of equipment are frequently financed by way of lease, rather than mortgage. Instead of the user acquiring the equipment under a mortgage, the financier will acquire the equipment and lease it to the user, which will pay lease rentals of an amount which represents the acquisition costs plus interest over the period of the lease. The economic effect is broadly the same, whichever method of financing is adopted.

3.33 The other limitation relates to goods which are disposed of in the ordinary course of the debtor's business, such as stock-in-trade. The requirement to release the security each time the goods have to be sold means that it is impracticable for a legal mortgage (or a fixed equitable charge) to be created over stock-in-trade. Security over stock-in-trade is the province of the floating charge, which is considered in CHAPTER 4.

3.34 The availability of a legal mortgage over goods is therefore more circumscribed than might at first glance appear. At one end of the spectrum,

---

12   Leases for 7 years or less are not registrable: Land Registration Act 2002, s 4(1)(c).
13   Land Registration Act 2002, s 27.
14   Land Registration Act 2002, ss 28–30 and 48.

large items of plant and machinery may not be capable of being the subject of a mortgage because they are fixtures or because they are leased to, rather than owned by, the debtor. At the other end of the spectrum, it is impracticable to take a mortgage over stock-in-trade. It is only between these two extremes that goods are capable of becoming the subject of a legal mortgage and, even then, they will often be the subject of an equitable charge rather than a legal mortgage. In practice, it is only very large items of moveable capital equipment (such as ships) which are likely to be of sufficient value to make it worthwhile to take a legal mortgage rather than to rely on an equitable charge.

Intangibles

3.35 Although the common law recognises that tangible assets (ie land and goods) are capable of being transferred, it does not generally recognise the transferability of intangibles (ie assets which cannot be possessed).[15] One of the most important assets available to any business is its intangible assets (such as the debts owing to it by third parties). Generally speaking, the common law does not recognise the transferability of these assets[16] and it is not, therefore, possible to take a legal mortgage over them.

3.36 There are, however, exceptions to the basic common law rule that intangibles are incapable of being transferred, two of which are particularly important in practice.

3.37 It has been seen in CHAPTER 2 that certain types of intangible are recognised as being 'contained' in a document, so that the transfer (and, if necessary, endorsement) of that document will transfer the right to the intangible concerned. It is possible to transfer a bill of exchange or other negotiable instrument at common law simply by delivering the instrument to the transferee and, if necessary, endorsing it. Similarly, bearer securities are transferable by delivery. Whether the delivery of such an instrument to the creditor is by way of mortgage or pledge depends on whether the intention of the parties was to transfer title, or just possession, to the creditor.[17]

3.38 There are also certain types of intangible the transfer of which is recognised at common law, even though the intangibles are not themselves 'contained' in a document. The most important example is shares and debentures of companies. Since the mid-nineteenth century, the companies legislation has recognised that shares and debentures of companies are capable of being transferred even if they are registered, rather than bearer, securities. The transfer is effected by the removal of the name of the transferor, and its replacement by that of the transferee, in a register held by the company for that purpose. Share certificates and debentures in registered form are not documents of title to the shares or debentures concerned. Such securities are not transferable by delivery of the certificates, but only by the entry of the name of

---

15 In this book, the expression 'intangibles' will be used in preference to 'choses in action' because it is the more modern usage, and better describes the nature of the assets concerned.
16 *Master v Miller* (1791) 4 TR 320.
17 *Sewell v Burdick* (1884) 10 App Cas 74.

the transferee in the register concerned. But, because the companies legislation recognised that such transfers could be effected, the common law followed suit. It is, therefore, possible to obtain a legal mortgage over registered shares and debentures by the creditor becoming registered as the owner of them in the relevant register held by the company.[18]

3.39 Since, however, the common law does not recognise the transfer of most other types of intangibles, security over them is generally taken either by means of an equitable mortgage or charge or by means of a statutory form of security under s 136 of the Law of Property Act 1925.

3.40 Security over intangibles is considered in more detail in part 5 of this chapter (**3.175**ff).

Future property

3.41 It has been seen that there are significant restrictions on the types of asset which are capable of being the subject of a legal mortgage. In addition, the common law does not allow a legal mortgage to be taken over future property. It is not possible to create a legal mortgage over an asset unless:

• the asset is in existence at the time the mortgage is created; and
• it is owned by the mortgagor at that time.

3.42 The position was stated clearly by Latham CJ in the High Court of Australia in *Akron Tyre Co Pty Limited v Kitson*:[19]

'A simple assignment of "future property", i.e. of property which does not exist or in which the assignor at the time of the assignment has no proprietary interest, is completely nugatory at law.'

3.43 An example of the common law rule is provided by *Lunn v Thornton*.[20] D had created a security bill of sale in favour of C over all of his present and future goods on a particular property. Goods were brought on to the property after the creation of the bill of sale. C attempted to enforce his bill of sale and seized the after-acquired goods. D sued him in conversion, claiming that C did not have title to them. The Court of Common Pleas gave judgment for D. Title had not passed to C under the bill of sale because, at common law, it is only possible to transfer property which belongs to the transferor at the time of the execution of the document. The transferor cannot give what he has not got.[21]

3.44 At common law, the execution of a mortgage over assets which are not yet owned by the debtor will not give the creditor any proprietary rights in them. The creditor will not become the mortgagee of those assets when they are acquired by the debtor. Title will only pass to the creditor if, once the debtor owns the assets, there is a new act by the debtor which is intended to complete

---

18 *Société Générale de Paris v Walker* (1885) 11 App Cas 20.
19 (1951) 82 CLR 477 at 484.
20 (1845) 1 CB 379.
21 (1845) 1 CB 379 at 386.

the original mortgage. In the words of Tindal CJ,[22] there must be a 'new act done by the grantor, indicating his intention that these goods should pass under the former bill of sale'.

3.45 The position at common law in relation to future property is therefore as follows:

- If the debtor purports to create a legal mortgage over property which he does not then own, the mortgage will not extend to that future property simply because it is acquired by the debtor.
- In order to obtain a legal mortgage, once the debtor has acquired the future property, he must perform some further act in relation to that property sufficient to evidence an intention to transfer title to the creditor. Such a further act could be the execution of a new document or the delivery of possession to the creditor.
- Because the new act creates a new mortgage, any necessary registration requirements need to be effected in relation to the new mortgage, even if the original mortgage had been duly registered.

3.46 It will be seen in part 3 of this chapter (**3.57ff**) that the position of the creditor in relation to future property is much stronger in equity than it is at common law.

Equitable interests

3.47 There is one further limitation on the ability of a debtor to create a legal mortgage over his assets. It is only possible to create a legal mortgage over a legal interest in an asset. This follows from the requirement of a legal mortgage that it is legal title to the asset concerned which is transferred to the creditor. If the debtor only has an equitable interest, he clearly cannot do so. Although, in the commercial context, the inability to create a legal mortgage over trust funds is of little importance, equitable interests can be important in commercial transactions. One example is where the debtor wishes to create a second security interest over an asset which is already the subject of a legal mortgage. If the debtor has created a legal mortgage over the asset, his remaining interest in the asset is an equitable one, and he can therefore only create an equitable security interest over it. Express trusts are also used quite frequently in certain types of financing transaction, with one company holding assets on trust for another. In such cases, the beneficial owner can only create an equitable mortgage or charge over its beneficial interest in the asset concerned.

Transfer of title

3.48 The second requirement of a legal mortgage is that the legal title to the asset concerned is transferred to the creditor. The method of transferring title depends on the nature of the asset concerned. Since it is not generally possible to transfer intangibles at common law, the main categories of commercial asset

---

22   (1845) 1 CB 379 at 388.

which are likely to be the subject of a legal mortgage are land, goods, documents of title to goods and intangibles, and shares and debentures of companies.

Land

3.49 It has been seen that a legal mortgage of land no longer involves the transfer of title to the land, although the mortgagee obtains substantially equivalent rights under a statutory charge by way of legal mortgage. Nevertheless, the necessity for the creditor to obtain a legal interest in the mortgaged land means that certain formalities are required to create it. A transfer of title to land has to be made by deed.[23] More importantly, as has been seen above, a legal mortgage of registered land must be registered at the Land Registry.

Goods

3.50 The only requirement for the transfer of legal title to goods is that the transferor intends to pass title to the transferee. In practice, not least for evidential reasons, there is normally some external manifestation of that intention. In the context of an outright transfer of goods (ie one which is not intended to be made by way of security), that is normally the transfer of possession. Whether or not the transfer of possession is intended to carry with it the transfer of title depends on the intention of the parties. The intention of the parties will determine whether the transfer is:

- an outright transfer of title, for instance, by way of sale or gift;
- a transfer of title by way of security (ie a mortgage); or
- a transfer of possession only (ie by way of pledge or some other form of bailment).

3.51 It has been seen that the advantage of a legal mortgage over a pledge is that the creditor does not require the possession of the asset concerned. A legal mortgage is, therefore, normally created by an act other than the transferring of possession. The act must provide sufficient evidence of the intention of the debtor to transfer title to the creditor by way of security. In theory, it is possible to create a legal mortgage over goods orally although, in practice, the security is invariably created by a document, which is generally described as a bill of sale or a mortgage.

3.52 There are generally no formal requirements for the creation of a legal mortgage of goods. It does not have to be in writing,[24] although it normally is; and there is no requirement for a deed. There are, however, particular requirements for certain types of goods, such as ships. A legal mortgage of a ship must be in a particular form if it is to be registered at the British Ship Registry.[25] Since, as will be seen in **CHAPTER 7**, registration gives priority

---

23 Law of Property Act 1925, s 52(1).
24 *Newlove v Shrewsbury* (1888) 21 QBD 41.
25 Merchant Shipping Act 1995, Sch1, para 7.

advantages, this is normally done. Because the required form is very brief, it is common for the further provisions which are required by the mortgagee to be set out in a separate document, usually known as a deed of covenants.

Documents of title to goods and intangibles

3.53 The requirements of a transfer of title to goods are equally applicable to documents of title to goods (such as bills of lading) and documents of title to intangibles (such as negotiable instruments and bearer bonds). In the case of such instruments, title may be transferred by delivery and, if necessary, endorsement of the instrument concerned. Alternatively, it may be transferred by evidence of the debtor's intention to do so, normally by the debtor executing a mortgage document.

Shares and debentures

3.54 The position is different with respect to shares in, and debentures of, companies. Unless they are bearer securities (which are rare in England), the legal title to shares and debentures passes by the insertion of the name of the transferee in the appropriate register held by the company. The owner of the instrument will normally have a document, such as a share certificate or loan note, which evidences his entitlement to the shares or debentures concerned, but it is not a document of title. Legal title passes to the transferee when he becomes the registered holder of the shares or debentures, rather than by the transfer of the document.

Intention to create security

3.55 The third requirement of a legal mortgage is that the transfer to the creditor is made by way of security for a monetary liability. The document creating or evidencing the legal mortgage will normally make it clear that title is being transferred to the creditor as security for the discharge of a particular liability. If this is the case, it is implicit (and is often made explicit) that the asset will be re-transferred to the debtor once the secured liabilities have been paid in full.

3.56 A transfer is, however, sometimes expressed in absolute terms when it was actually intended to be by way of security. In such a case, the court is not restricted to looking at the document itself. As a result of normal principles of construction of documents, it will construe them in the light of the surrounding circumstances. If it was the intention of the parties that the transfer was to be by way of security, the court will give effect to that intention. This issue is discussed further in part 4 of this chapter (**3.140ff**).

Part 3: EQUITABLE MORTGAGES AND CHARGES

3.57 Equitable mortgages and charges will be considered together. Although they are conceptually distinct, there is no practical difference between them and it is often difficult to distinguish between them in the cases.

3.58 An equitable mortgage involves:

- the transfer of beneficial title in an asset to the creditor,
- by way of security for the discharge of a monetary liability.

3.59 A charge involves:

- the creation, in favour of the creditor, of an equitable proprietary interest in an asset,
- by way of security for the discharge of a monetary liability.

3.60 There is no practical distinction between an equitable mortgage and a charge. They both give the creditor a proprietary interest in the asset concerned. They are both given by way of security, and therefore both terminate on the discharge of the secured liability. (A charge is released automatically; in the case of a mortgage, the mortgagee may have to re-transfer beneficial title to the mortgagor, but it can be compelled to do so.) They are both effective in the insolvency of the debtor and they are both effective against third parties who claim an interest in the asset concerned, subject to the priority rules (which are the same for equitable mortgages as for charges).

3.61 The fact that one involves the transfer of beneficial title and the other does not is of no consequence in practice. The remedies of a chargee are less extensive than those of an equitable mortgagee but, in practice, this distinction is of little importance because of the wide powers invariably given to chargees and mortgagees in the security document itself. It should, therefore, come as no surprise that the distinction between the two is very rarely drawn in the cases.[26]

3.62 The discussion of equitable mortgages and charges in this part is broken down into the following sections:

- how and why equitable proprietary interests are created;
- the requirements for the creation of an equitable mortgage;
- the requirements for the creation of a charge;
- the types of asset which can be the subject of an equitable mortgage or charge;
- taking security over future assets;
- the two main requirements for the creation of an equitable mortgage or charge:
  - intention to create security;
  - identification of the secured asset;

---

26 See, for instance, the opinion of Lord Templeman in *Downsview Nominees v First City Corporation* [1993] AC 295 at 311.

- when consideration is required to create an equitable mortgage or charge; and
- what formalities are required to create an equitable mortgage or charge.

Equitable proprietary interests

3.63 Before considering equitable mortgages and charges in detail, it is necessary to explain, in general terms, how equitable proprietary interests are created. Many features of equitable security interests are common to all types of equitable proprietary interest, and an appreciation of the reasons why equitable proprietary interests are created is necessary for an understanding of how equitable mortgages and charges actually work.

3.64 At common law, it is generally not possible to transfer title to assets simply by agreeing to do so. Some other formality often needs to be complied with. With some assets, such as registered land and ships, the transferee's interest needs to be registered in a central registry. With other assets, such as shares and debentures of a company, the transferee needs to be registered as their holder in the company's books. Until these formal requirements have been complied with, the intended transferee does not obtain a legal interest in the assets concerned.

3.65 If, therefore, A undertakes to transfer an asset to B, but does not comply with the formal requirements for a transfer of legal title, A remains the legal owner of the asset concerned, and B obtains no legal proprietary rights in it. If there was a binding contract between A and B to effect the transfer, then B may have a personal claim against A for damages for breach of contract, but he will have no legal proprietary right over the asset.

3.66 This can be particularly important in the context of a secured loan. If C lends money to D, on the basis that D will grant a legal mortgage over an asset which he owns, the legal mortgage will not be effective until the requisite formalities have been complied with. If D goes into insolvency proceedings in the meantime, C's only remedy is a personal claim against D for breach of contract, which will be of no avail in D's insolvency, because it will rank pari passu with all other unsecured claims against D.

3.67 At common law, therefore, fulfilment of the formal requirements for the transfer of title is crucial. Until this has been done, the creditor will not obtain a proprietary interest in the asset but, at best, will have a personal claim against the debtor.

3.68 The position is very different in equity. In some cases, if A has undertaken to transfer an asset to B, equity regards it as being unconscionable for A to retain the asset, and therefore imposes an obligation on A to transfer it to B. What distinguishes the position in equity from that at common law is that this obligation is not just a personal obligation but a proprietary one. As a result, although legal title does not pass until the formalities have been complied with, beneficial title does pass to B as soon as the undertaking has been given. Beneficial title is not as strong as legal title (it can be defeated by someone who acquires the legal title to the asset for value and without notice of the equitable interest) but, crucially, it is a proprietary interest and is therefore effective in A's insolvency.

3.69 In the context of a secured loan, the effect is that, if C had made a loan to D against an undertaking by D to create a mortgage over a particular asset, C obtains an equitable proprietary interest by way of security (ie an equitable mortgage) over the asset even if the formalities for the creation of a legal mortgage have not been complied with. If, therefore, D becomes insolvent before the legal mortgage is completed, the creditor will still have a proprietary interest, and therefore effective security, in D's insolvency.

3.70 The reason why this equitable proprietary interest is created is the maxim that 'equity treats as done that which ought to be done'. If a person ought to transfer an asset, equity will treat it as being transferred, thus granting an equitable proprietary interest to the intended transferee.

3.71 It is not entirely clear in which types of case the maxim that equity will treat as done that which ought to be done will be applied. The starting point is that a distinction is drawn between existing assets and future assets. Although future assets cannot be transferred at common law, they are transferable in equity. Even so, a simple undertaking to transfer future assets, whether outright or by way of security, is ineffective even in equity. What is required is that the intended transferor has entered into a contract under which he is bound to effect the transfer, and that the consideration for that transfer has been paid (ie the consideration is executed, not executory).

3.72 The position with regard to existing assets is more complicated. This is partly because they are also transferable at common law, so that equity did not have a free hand. Equity will give effect to a gift of any type of existing property, even if the steps required for a common law transfer have not been completed, if the debtor has declared himself a trustee of them or, in the case of intangible assets, he has assigned them.[27] If there is a contract to sell land, the beneficial interest will pass immediately to the purchaser on exchange of contracts (even if the price has not been paid in full),[28] but this is not the case with a contract for the sale of goods (even if the price has been paid),[29] and the position is not entirely clear in relation to contracts to sell other assets. Thankfully, the position is clearer where the transfer is by way of security. The principle is the same as in relation to security over future assets – an agreement by the debtor to transfer existing assets of any kind will create an equitable security interest if the debtor is under a binding contract to create the security and the consideration has been executed (ie the debtor has got the money).

3.73 As a result, although the circumstances in which the maxim that equity treats as done that which ought to be done have not finally been determined in all cases, the position with regard to security interests is clear. Whether the assets concerned are existing assets or future assets, and whether they are land,

---

27 *Kekewich v Manning* (1851) 1 De GM&G 176.
28 *Lysaght v Edwards* (1876) 2 Ch D 499 at 506, per Jessel MR.
29 *Re Wait* [1927] 1 Ch 606.

goods or intangibles, the maxim that equity treats as done that which ought to be done will be applied (and an equitable proprietary interest will therefore be transferred to the creditor) if:

- the creditor has undertaken to create the security under a binding contract; and
- the consideration for that contract has been executed.

3.74 In practice, both these criteria will have been satisfied in a secured transaction, and the creditor will therefore obtain an equitable proprietary interest by way of security in the assets concerned.

Creating an equitable mortgage

3.75 The creation of an equitable mortgage over an asset requires the transfer of beneficial title in the asset by way of security. There are various ways in which the beneficial title to the asset can be transferred to the creditor, three of which are particularly important:

- an assignment by way of security;
- a declaration of trust by way of security; and
- an agreement to create a legal mortgage.

3.76 The first method is normally used where the mortgagor cannot transfer legal title and is therefore restricted to an equitable security interest – for instance, because the asset to be mortgaged is one which cannot be transferred at common law or the mortgagor only has an equitable interest in the asset. This is a common means of creating security over intangibles such as contract rights and receivables.

3.77 The other two methods are normally used to create an equitable mortgage in a case where the mortgagor could create a legal mortgage but the parties only intend an equitable mortgage to be created (for instance, because the cost of creating a legal mortgage would outweigh its added benefits). In practice, it is not very common to use either of these methods. In such a case, the creditor would normally take a charge rather than an equitable mortgage.

Assignment by way of security

3.78 The simplest method of transferring the beneficial interest in property is for the debtor to assign it to the creditor. In principle, all that is required is evidence that the debtor intended to effect the assignment, although further formalities are required in relation to particular types of asset. In practice, the most common way to effect an equitable mortgage is by a document under which the debtor assigns the property concerned to the creditor as security for the discharge of a liability.

3.79 Equitable assignments by way of security are frequently used to transfer the beneficial interest in intangible assets which are incapable of being transferred at common law and which, in the absence of statutory intervention, can only, therefore, be assigned in equity. Until the intervention of statute in the late nineteenth century, the only method of assigning most types of intangible was by means of an equitable assignment. Such an assignment can, generally, be made without any formality, although in practice it will be effected by a document.

3.80 Similarly, an equitable interest in property is only capable of being transferred in equity, and an equitable mortgage over such an asset is normally effected by means of an equitable assignment. An assignment of an equitable interest must be made in writing.

Declaration of trust by way of security

3.81 As an alternative to an equitable assignment, it is possible for the debtor to declare itself a trustee of particular property by way of security for a particular liability. This will confer on the creditor a beneficial interest in the property concerned which will cease on discharge of the secured liability. Although there are conceptual distinctions between the rights of an assignee and those of the beneficiary under a bare trust, there is no practical distinction where the transaction is effected by way of security. Both give the creditor an equitable proprietary interest in the asset concerned by way of security. Declarations of trust are sometimes used in financing transactions, but it is rare for security to be created in this way.

Agreement to create a legal mortgage

3.82 It is commonly said that an agreement to create a legal mortgage is itself an equitable mortgage.[30] It is, however, a concept which needs to be treated with some caution.

3.83 Its main importance in practice is in relation to future property. If the debtor agrees to create a legal mortgage over property which he does not yet own, an equitable mortgage will be created as soon as the property concerned becomes owned by the debtor. This is considered in more detail below.

3.84 It is not, however, every agreement to give a legal mortgage which will itself create an equitable mortgage. What is necessary is that the debtor intends the agreement to have immediate effect.[31] Many loan documents contain agreements by the debtor to create security. In most cases, they do not themselves create equitable mortgages over the property to which they relate. This is because it is not usually intended that these documents will themselves create the security. It is normally contemplated that a further document will be entered into which will create the security.[32] For example, in *Williams v Burlington Investments*,[33] C agreed to sell land to D for development, the price being left outstanding. D agreed that, if requested by C, he would enter into a

---

30 See *Eyre v McDowell* (1861) 9 HLC 619.
31 *Tailby v Official Receiver* (1888) 13 App Cas 523 at 543, per Lord Macnaghten; *National Provincial and Union Bank of England v Charnley* [1924] 1 KB 431 at 449–450, per Atkin LJ.
32 *Thames Guaranty Limited v Campbell* [1985] 1 QB 210 at 234, per Slade LJ.
33 (1977) 121 Sol Jo 424.

charge by way of legal mortgage over such part of the land as he still owned when the request was made, to secure the price. The House of Lords held that this agreement did not create an equitable mortgage over the property. It was simply an agreement that, in particular future circumstances, security would be created.

3.85 Where a security document provides that the debtor 'agrees to create' a mortgage over a particular asset, it is always open to the debtor's insolvency officer to argue that the document was not intended to create an immediate equitable mortgage, but was subject to the execution of a further document. This is a particular risk where the property concerned was in existence at the time the agreement was entered into, since it will then be argued that it would have been perfectly possible for the debtor to 'mortgage' rather than 'agree to mortgage' the property concerned. For such evidential reasons, it is preferable for the security document to be expressed to create an immediate security over the property concerned, rather than to be expressed to be an agreement to create security. The documentation should make it clear that:

- immediate security is taken over existing property; and
- immediate security will automatically be taken over future property as soon as it becomes owned by the debtor.

Summary

3.86 Whichever method of creating an equitable mortgage is used, there are two main requirements which have to be satisfied:

- there must be evidence that the debtor intends to transfer beneficial title to the creditor by way of security; and
- the assets which are intended to be secured must be sufficiently identified.

These are recurring themes, which are considered further in this part.

Creating a charge

3.87 What is required to create a charge over an asset is evidence that the debtor intended to give the creditor a proprietary interest in the asset as security for a particular liability. In most cases, this is done very simply, by the debtor executing a document by which he is expressed to charge a particular asset as security for a particular liability.

3.88 As in the case of an equitable mortgage, the main requirement of the creation of a charge is that the debtor intends to create security over identifiable assets. This requirement is considered in more detail later in this part.

Assets which can be the subject of an equitable mortgage or charge

3.89 It has been seen that it is only possible to create a legal mortgage over those types of asset which are recognised as being property, and therefore capable of being transferred, at common law. The principle is the same in equity. It is only possible to create an equitable mortgage or charge over assets which are regarded in equity as being property, and therefore capable of being transferred. The difference is that equity regards most types of asset as capable of being transferred. In particular, intangibles are generally capable of being transferred in equity, subject only to the terms of the intangible itself and the principle that certain limited classes of intangible are incapable of being transferred for public policy reasons. These issues are considered further in part 5 of this chapter (**3.175ff**).

Taking security over future assets

3.90 The other important distinction between equitable and legal security interests is in relation to future property. It has been seen that it is not generally possible to create a legal mortgage over an asset unless the asset is in existence and owned by the mortgagor at the time the mortgage is created. A legal mortgage will not affect after-acquired property unless a 'new act' is performed in relation to it, such as the execution of a new mortgage document or the transfer of possession to the creditor, after the mortgagor has become its legal owner.

3.91 The position is very different in equity:

- Even in equity, it is not possible for a person to create security over an asset which he does not own.
- But, if a debtor enters into a contract to do so, the creditor will obtain an equitable security interest in the asset once it becomes owned by the debtor.
- This security interest is created automatically on the property becoming owned by the debtor, there being no need for any further act by the debtor.

3.92 Many of the important concepts which apply to equitable mortgages and charges generally have been developed in relation to future property and are accordingly discussed in this section. The main issues (the importance of intention and identification, the circumstances in which consideration is required and those cases where formalities are required) are then considered more generally in the later sections of this part.

The principle

3.93 The leading case is the decision of the House of Lords in *Holroyd v Marshall*.[34] D transferred machinery in a mill to T to be held on trust to repay a debt owing by D to C and, thereafter, for D. The trust deed provided that new machinery which was taken into the mill after the execution of the trust would be subject to the same trusts. The trust deed was duly registered under the then-prevailing bills of sale legislation. New machinery was taken into the mill,

---

34 (1861–62) 10 HLC 191.

but was subsequently taken in execution by the sheriff on behalf of a judgment creditor of D. The question arose whether C had an equitable proprietary interest in the machinery taken into the mill after the execution of the trust deed, or whether he only had a personal right against D. If C had a proprietary interest, it would take priority over that of the execution creditor. If, on the other hand, he only had a personal right, it would not bind anyone other than D, and the execution would therefore be effective.

3.94   In the first hearing of the case, Lord Campbell LC held that C only had a personal right in equity to take possession of the new machinery. This decision was overruled by the House of Lords, which held that C did have an equitable proprietary interest in the new machinery, which therefore took priority over the rights of the execution creditor. The principal judgment was given by Lord Westbury LC:[35]

> 'In equity it is not necessary for the alienation of property that there should be a formal deed of conveyance. A contract for valuable consideration, by which it is agreed to make a present transfer of property, passes at once the beneficial interest, provided the contract is one of which a Court of Equity will decree specific performance ... And this is true, not only of contracts relating to real estate, but to contracts relating to personal property, provided that the latter are such as a Court of Equity would direct to be specifically performed.'

He went on to say:[36]

> 'It is quite true that a deed which professes to convey property which is not in existence at the time is as a conveyance void at law, simply because there is nothing to convey. So in equity a contract which engages to transfer property, which is not in existence, cannot operate as an immediate alienation merely because there is nothing to transfer.
>
> But if a vendor or mortgagor agrees to sell or mortgage property, real or personal, of which he is not possessed at the time, and he receives the consideration for the contract, and afterwards becomes possessed of property answering the description in the contract, there is no doubt that a Court of Equity would compel him to perform the contract, and that the contract would, in equity, transfer the beneficial interest to the mortgagee or purchaser immediately on the property being acquired. This, of course, assumes that the supposed contract is one of that class of which a Court of Equity would decree the specific performance. If it be so, then immediately on the acquisition of the property described the vendor or mortgagor would hold it in trust for the purchaser or mortgagee, according to the terms of the contract. For if a contract be in other respects good and fit to be performed, and the consideration has been received, incapacity to perform it at the time of its execution will be no answer when the means of doing so are afterwards obtained.'

---

35   (1861–62) 10 HLC 191 at 209.
36   (1861–62) 10 HLC 191 at 210–211.

3.95   The principle was later described by Lord Macnaghten, in *Tailby v Official Receiver*,[37] in the following terms:

'It has long been settled that future property ... [is] assignable in equity for value. The mode or form of assignment is absolutely immaterial provided the intention of the parties is clear. To effectuate the intention an assignment for value, in terms present and immediate, has always been regarded in equity as a contract binding on the conscience of the assignor and so binding the subject matter of the contract when it comes into existence, if it is of such a nature and so described as to be capable of being ascertained and identified.'

3.96   Although the basic principle is clear, the precise prerequisites of the creation of the equitable interest in future property have created more controversy. There are essentially two prerequisites:

- the debtor must intend to transfer or charge identifiable property; and
- that intention must arise out of a binding contract, the consideration for which has been executed.

Intention and identification

3.97   It is a necessary, but not a sufficient, prerequisite of the creation of an equitable mortgage or charge (whether over existing or future property) that the debtor intends to transfer, or to create a charge over, particular property. As Lord Macnaghten made clear in *Tailby v Official Receiver*, the form of the transaction is immaterial if the intention of the parties is clear. That intention can either be to effect a transfer of beneficial title or to create a proprietary interest by way of a charge. But there are two crucial limits on the principle.

3.98   In the first place, in the words of Lord Macnaghten in *Tailby v Official Receiver*, the intention must be to create a 'present and immediate' mortgage or charge. In other words, it must be the intention of the parties that the creditor is to have a proprietary interest in the asset as soon as it is owned by the debtor, without the necessity for any further act. An example of a case where there was no such present and immediate intention to create a security is *Mornington v Keane*.[38] In that case, D undertook, before a certain date, to secure the payment of an annuity to his wife either by a charge on freehold property in England and Wales or by an investment in funds or by the best means he may have in his power. It was held that, although there was an enforceable undertaking by D, it did not create a charge on his property. It was not intended to do so, but was simply a personal undertaking to create a charge in the future.[39]

3.99   The second requirement is that the intention relates to identifiable property. This requirement is illustrated by another leading case, *Tailby v Official Receiver*.[40] D created a security bill of sale in favour of C over all of his

---

37   (1888) 13 App Cas 523 at 543.
38   (1858) 2 De G&J 292.
39   (1858) 2 De G&J 292 at 313.
40   (1888) 13 App Cas 523.

stock-in-trade, both present and future, on particular premises and over all his present and future book debts. The Court of Appeal held that the security over the book debts was too vague to be effective. This decision was, however, overturned by the House of Lords, who held that the document created a valid assignment by way of security over all present and future book debts of D. They held that the assignment was not too vague or uncertain to be given effect. It was possible to establish the assets to which it related at the time it was necessary to enforce the security. As they pointed out, it is normally easier to identify the subject of security if it relates to all assets, rather than certain assets.

3.100   As far as the width of the assignment was concerned, there had been some concerns in the cases after *Holroyd v Marshall* that a debtor should not be able to assign all of his present and future assets, it being suggested that there was a policy reason for some type of restriction on the scope of assignments of future property, at least in relation to non-corporate debtors. The House of Lords conclusively rejected this approach. The position is stated in typically forthright terms by Lord Macnaghten:[41]

'Between men of full age and competent understanding ought there to be any limit to the freedom of contract but that imposed by positive law or dictated by considerations of morality or public policy? The limit proposed is purely arbitrary, and I think meaningless and unreasonable.'

3.101   There is, therefore, no limit on the extent of the assignment or charge. Nor is it necessary to be able to identify precisely which assets are covered by the security when it is created. All that is required is to be able to identify those assets which fall within the scope of the security when it comes to be enforced.

3.102   But it is still, of course, necessary to identify the subject matter of the security. An example of a case where there was no such identification is *Berrington v Evans*.[42] In that case, D agreed to pay certain debts to certain creditors on a particular day and, in the event of non-payment by that time, 'he hereby engages to sell so much of his estates as shall be found necessary for that purpose'. The Court of Exchequer held that this document did not create an equitable charge for two reasons. In the first place, it was only intended as a personal undertaking by D; it was not intended to create an immediate security interest. Secondly, it was held that it was impossible to identify any particular assets as being the subject of the security.

3.103   In summary, therefore, what is required is that:

●   the debtor intends to transfer an equitable interest or to create a charge over an asset as soon as the debtor becomes its owner; and
●   the asset can be identified at the time the security needs to be enforced.

Contract for executed consideration

3.104   When a person owns property, he is normally able to dispose of it in equity without the requirement for a contract, or any consideration by the

---

41   (1888) 13 App Cas 523 at 545.
42   (1839) 3 Y&C Ex 384.

transferee. In certain cases the disposition must be in writing, but a person may create an equitable assignment over existing property by gift.

3.105 The position is different in relation to future property. *Holroyd v Marshall* and *Tailby v Official Receiver* make it clear that an equitable assignment of future property will only be effective if there is a contract, in other words if there has been consideration for the transferor's promise to effect the transfer.

3.106 That much is straightforward. Thereafter, it becomes more difficult. Lord Westbury, in his speech in *Holroyd v Marshall*, indicates that there are two further requirements which may need to be satisfied in relation to the contract, although whether they are cumulative or alternative is not entirely clear. These are:

- that the contract must be capable of specific performance; and
- that the consideration under the contract must be executed, rather than executory (ie that it has been paid or performed, rather than just promised).

3.107 The requirement that the consideration is executed causes little difficulty in the context of the law of security. Where the transfer is by way of security, rather than absolute, it will always be the case that the consideration for the security is executed. There is no point attempting to enforce security unless there is a secured liability. If the creditor has not made the loan available or otherwise provided the secured credit to the debtor, the security is not required.

3.108 Lord Westbury's other requirement, that the contract be capable of specific performance, has resulted in a great deal of debate. Its necessity was rejected by Lord Macnaghten in *Tailby v Official Receiver*,[43] who denied that the availability of specific performance in any particular case was relevant. He considered that the question was what the parties intended, equity then treating as done that which ought to be done.

3.109 It has already been seen that the maxim that 'equity treats as done that which ought to be done' is of great importance in the context of commercial law because it is the means by which equitable proprietary interests are created. At common law, it is generally not possible to transfer title to assets other than goods simply by agreeing to do so. Some other formality normally needs to be complied with. But it has long been recognised in equity that there are circumstances where it would be unconscionable for the intended transferor to retain an asset which it was intended should be transferred even though the common law formalities for the transfer had not been complied with. In such cases, the transferor ought to make the transfer, equity will treat as done that which ought to be done, and the transferor will accordingly hold the property concerned on trust for the transferee.

3.110 It is sometimes said that the reason why equity treats as done that which ought to be done is because it will decree specific performance of the

---

43   (1888) 13 App Cas 523 at 547–548.

contract, but it is suggested (in common with Lord Macnaghten) that this is not the case. The basic principle is that equity will treat as done that which ought to be done. From this principle there developed two linked, but separate, concepts: a personal remedy (specific performance) and a proprietary right (equitable proprietary interests, such as trusts and assignments).

3.111   The courts will award specific performance of certain types of contract because they are prepared to treat as done that which ought to be done. The main requirement for specific performance of a contract is that it will generally only be granted where damages would be an inadequate remedy, although there are a number of other prerequisites of the remedy. The courts will also declare that, in certain circumstances, a person is the beneficial owner of property which has been agreed to be transferred to him, even though the formal legal requirements for transfer have not been effected. The reason why they will do so is as a result of the same maxim, that equity treats as done that which ought to be done. But the precise requirements of the doctrine are different from those of specific performance. One does not derive from the other; they are different branches of the same tree, the trunk of which is the equitable maxim.

3.112   As a result, it is suggested that the availability of specific performance is not a prerequisite of the creation of an equitable mortgage or charge over a future asset. In the case of an equitable security interest, the key requirement is that there is a contract and that the consideration for the contract is executed: the creditor must have given value to the debtor. This is the type of case with which Lord Westbury was concerned in *Holroyd v Marshall*. In that case, the loan had already been made, the debtor had received his consideration, and the court accordingly held that the assets which he had agreed to transfer by way of security were automatically transferred in equity once they became owned by him. It has been so at least since the time of Lord Eldon in the early nineteenth century.[44] The principle applies regardless of the nature of the property concerned. It extends to personal property, such as goods[45] and intangibles[46] as well as to land.[47]

Summary

3.113   A contract to create security over future property will be effective to create an equitable proprietary interest in that property as soon as it becomes owned by the debtor if:

- the parties have an intention to create an immediate security interest over the property as soon as it comes into the debtor's ownership;
- the property concerned can be identified as falling within the scope of the security when it needs to be enforced; and
- some secured obligations are outstanding.

---

44   *Curtis v Auber* (1820) 1 Jac & W 526 at 531–532, per Lord Eldon LC.
45   *Holroyd v Marshall* (1862) 10 HLC 191.
46   *Tailby v Official Receiver* (1888) 13 App Cas 523.
47   *Metcalf v Archbishop of York* (1836) 1 My & Cr 547 at 556, per Lord Cottenham LC.

3.114 Although the future property becomes the subject of the equitable security interest as soon as it becomes owned by the debtor, until that time there is only a contract, not a proprietary interest. This is made very clear by Sir George Jessel MR in *Collyer v Isaacs*.[48] In relation to after-acquired property, he said:[49]

> 'That assignment, in fact, constituted only a contract to give him the after-acquired chattels. A man cannot, in equity, any more than at law, assign what has no existence. A man can contract to assign property which is to come into existence in the future, and when it has come into existence, equity, treating as done that which ought to be done, fastens upon that property, and the contract to assign thus becomes a complete assignment.'

Creating an equitable mortgage or charge – intention and identification

3.115 The preceding section has shown how important are the intention of the parties to create security and the identification of the secured assets to the creation of an equitable mortgage or charge over future property. These concepts of intention and identification are equally important when taking equitable security over existing assets. Both concepts are central to an understanding of equitable mortgages and charges, and are therefore discussed in more detail in this section.

Intention to create security

3.116 The principal requirement of an equitable mortgage or charge is an intention by the debtor to transfer beneficial title by way of security or to create a charge. As Lord Macnaghten said in *Tailby v Official Receiver*:[50] 'The mode or form of assignment is absolutely immaterial provided the intention of the parties is clear.'

3.117 The question can be stated simply: Did the parties intend the creditor to have an equitable proprietary interest by way of security in the asset concerned? This will normally be clear from the documentation. The debtor will usually be expressed to 'assign' or 'charge' particular property as security for a liability. But an intention to create a proprietary interest can exist even if the parties do not use these terms. In such cases, the role of the court is the usual one of construing the documents in the light of their surrounding circumstances in order to establish the intention of the parties. This has been a particular issue in relation to assignments of intangibles, and is considered further in the context of intangibles in part 5 of this chapter (**3.57ff**). In this part, the way in which the courts approach the question will be illustrated by two contrasting cases.

---

48 (1891) 19 Ch D 342 at 351.
49 This is a very clear statement of the legal position, although the actual decision in *Collyer v Isaacs* is very difficult to reconcile with the later Court of Appeal decision in *Re Lind* [1915] 2 Ch 345.
50 (1888) 13 App Cas 523 at 543.

3.118 In *Re Kent & Sussex Sawmills*,[51] D had entered into contractual arrangements with T as a result of which T was obliged to pay money to D from time to time. D was indebted to C, its bank, and D wrote to T irrevocably authorising T to pay its debts to C. The question arose whether the letter created an equitable mortgage or charge. Wynn-Parry J held that it did. Had it been a simple authority to make the payments into D's bank account with C, there would have been no assignment or charge. But the letter stated that the authority was to be irrevocable without C's consent. In the circumstances, it was held that it was the intention of the parties that C was to obtain a proprietary interest in the debts owing by T, even though there was no express wording creating an assignment or a charge.

3.119 This case can be contrasted with *Swiss Bank v Lloyds Bank*.[52] In that case, the question arose whether C had a charge over certain securities. No formal charge had been created, but C had lent the money to D to acquire the securities. At the time, exchange control consent was required from the Bank of England for the transaction, and one of the terms of the loan agreement between D and C was that D complied with the terms of that consent, which required the securities to be held in a separate account and the repayment of the loan to be made from proceeds of sale of the securities. C argued that the combination of the terms of the loan agreement and the exchange control consent meant that C had an equitable mortgage or charge over the securities. But the Court of Appeal decided that C did not, and their decision was upheld by the House of Lords.

3.120 The principal judgment in the Court of Appeal was given by Buckley LJ, who said that the essence of an equitable security interest is that the debtor confers on the creditor a proprietary interest in an asset, or undertakes in a binding manner to do so, out of which the secured liability is repayable. Whether there is an equitable mortgage or charge depends on the intention of the parties, ascertained from what they have done in the circumstances that then existed; and if, on a proper construction of the documentation, the parties have entered into a transaction the legal effect of which is to create an equitable mortgage or charge, the fact that they may not have realised the consequence is irrelevant.

3.121 In this case, however, the parties did not intend that C should have the right to have the loan repaid out of the securities. All that was intended was that the loan should be repaid in a manner approved by the Bank of England under the exchange control consent; and the Bank of England could have agreed that the loan could be repaid in some other way.

3.122 In the House of Lords, the principal speech was given by Lord Wilberforce. He decided that the requirement of the loan agreement that D complied with the terms of the exchange control consent was intended to operate as a restriction, preventing D from repaying the loan otherwise than

---

51   [1947] Ch 177.
52   [1982] AC 584.

from the securities without the Bank of England's consent. It did not constitute an obligation to repay the loan out of the securities. It was intended to have a negative, rather than a positive, effect.

3.123 It is clear from both judgments that C would have had a charge over the securities if the intention of the parties had been that the loan was to have been repaid out of the securities. An agreement between a debtor and a creditor that the debt is to be paid out of a particular fund is sufficient evidence that the parties intend the fund to be charged with the payment of the debt. A simple authority by D to a third party who owes D money that the third party should pay the money into D's bank account with C is not, of itself, sufficient to show an intention to create a charge.[53] What is needed is a positive agreement that the debt should be paid out of the fund. In the *Kent & Sussex Sawmills* case, this agreement was implied from the fact that the authority to make the payment was expressed to be irrevocable without C's consent. In the *Swiss Bank* case, it was not, because the requirement to repay the loan out of the securities was only negative, not positive.

3.124 The distinctions in some of the cases can be very fine. They are considered further when considering assignments of intangibles in part 5 of this chapter (**3.175ff**). But the principle is clear. It is simply a question of whether the parties intended the creditor to have an equitable proprietary interest by way of security in a particular asset.

3.125 In practice, the implication of an equitable mortgage or charge is unlikely to be of much value in many cases. As will be seen in **CHAPTER 6**, most types of mortgage or charge created by a company are registrable and, if not registered within the 21-day time limit, are, to all intents and purposes, void. Charges created by companies over certain types of property (for instance, securities and contingent rights under contracts) are not registrable and, in those cases, it might be possible for a creditor to establish that he has an implied charge. But in many cases, the creditor will be met with the response that, even if it were possible to imply a charge over the asset concerned, it would be void for non-registration. Indeed, that was the result in the *Kent & Sussex Sawmills* case. Although Wynn-Parry J decided that C did have a charge over the debts owing to D, he went on to decide that the charge was void for non-registration.

3.126 As has been mentioned above, the intention must be to create an immediate security, either over existing assets or, in the case of future assets, once they are owned by the debtor. This requirement will not be satisfied if it is not intended that security will be created until some further document is executed or a further act committed.

---

53   *Palmer v Carey* [1926] AC 703.

Identification

3.127 It is not sufficient that there should be an intention to create security. It is also necessary to establish that that intention relates to identifiable assets.[54] This requirement has already been discussed in relation to future property, but it is applicable in all cases. As has been seen from *Tailby v Official Receiver*,[55] there is no reason why the security should not extend to all present and future assets of a particular type. Equally important, that case establishes that it is not necessary, at the time the charge is created, to be able to identify all of the assets which will become subject to it. All that is necessary is that it is possible to identify those assets which fall within the scope of the security at the time it is to be enforced.

When is consideration necessary?

3.128 In addition to an intention to create security over identifiable property, it is sometimes necessary to establish that the transfer or creation of the proprietary interest concerned is being made for valuable consideration.

3.129 This is not an issue which will normally arise in relation to the creation of equitable mortgages or charges, because the making of the credit available to the debtor will normally constitute sufficient consideration. Even where the credit has been granted before the security is given, fresh consideration is normally given, either in the form of additional credit or by forbearance to demand repayment. But it is nevertheless important to appreciate in which circumstances consideration is required.

3.130 Consideration is required in two cases:

● where the assets mortgaged or charged are future property – ie they are not in existence and owned by the debtor at the time the security is created; and

● where the assets mortgaged or charged are existing property, but there is no immediate transfer, only an agreement to transfer them in the future.

3.131 This is because, in each case, an equitable proprietary interest is only created because of the existence of a binding contract to create it. Where, on the other hand, there is an immediate assignment of existing property, no consideration is required. In such a case, there is no necessity to rely on a contract – a gift of existing property being perfectly effective.[56] There is some uncertainty concerning whether consideration is necessary for an equitable assignment of an existing legal interest in property (as opposed to an equitable assignment of an existing equitable interest), but it is difficult to see why there should be a distinction between the two.[57] In principle, no consideration should be required for an immediate assignment of existing assets, regardless of the nature of those assets.

---

54 *Berrington v Evans* (1839) 3 Y&C Ex 384; *Mornington v Keane* (1858) 2 De G&J 292.
55 (1888) 13 App Cas 523.
56 *Kekewich v Manning* (1851) 1 De GM&G 176; cf *Re Ellenborough* [1903] 1 Ch 697.
57 See the judgment of Windeyer J in the High Court of Australia in *Norman v Federal Commissioner of Taxation* (1963) 109 CLR 9 at 24–34. Although Windeyer J dissented on the facts of this case, his legal analysis was not dissented from by the other members of the court.

Formalities

3.132 Most mortgages and charges created by companies, and many created by individuals, require to be registered under the Companies Act 1985 or the Bills of Sale Acts 1878–1891, respectively. The Bills of Sale Acts 1878–1891 also require mortgages and charges over goods created in writing by individuals to be the subject of further formalities. These requirements are considered in CHAPTER 6. There are also very stringent formal requirements for security given in relation to credit regulated by the Consumer Credit Act 1974.

3.133 Apart from these requirements, all of which have been introduced by statute, there are few formal requirements for the creation of an equitable mortgage or charge. The most important in practice is that contained in the Law of Property (Miscellaneous Provisions) Act 1989. Before that Act was passed, a common method of creating an equitable mortgage over land was to deposit the title deeds for the land with the creditor. This was because the deposit of the title deeds was evidence of an agreement that the creditor was to have a mortgage over the land which was the subject of the title deeds. Although the law generally required contracts for the disposition of interest in land to be made in writing and to be signed by the disponor, one of the exceptions to the requirement for writing was where there was part performance, and the delivery of the deeds was regarded as sufficient part performance for this purpose. The informal oral agreement to create security was therefore effective.

3.134 This position was changed when the Law of Property (Miscellaneous Provisions) Act 1989 came into force. As a result of s 2 of that Act, a contract to dispose of an interest in land (including a mortgage or charge) must be in writing and must be signed by both parties to the contract. In *United Bank of Kuwait v Sahib*,[58] the Court of Appeal decided that: 'By reason of section 2, the mere deposit of title deeds by way of security cannot any longer create a mortgage or charge.'[59]

3.135 This provision has far-reaching effects. It requires all the express terms of the agreement to be in writing, although this would normally have been the case in any event. What is more important is that the new legislation requires both parties to sign the agreement. The old legislation (which was ultimately derived from the Statute of Frauds of 1677) required the person who was disposing of the interest in land to execute the document, but the new legislation requires both parties to do so. This has required a change in practice in relation to the execution of mortgages and charges. It is not normally necessary for a mortgage or charge document to be executed by the creditor. All the obligations contained in it are normally imposed on the debtor, so that it is normally only the debtor who needs to execute it. In the case of security over land, however, it is now necessary for the creditor to execute the document as well. This is the case not only in relation to specific mortgages of land, but also in cases where land is included in more general security, such as in a debenture creating fixed and floating charges over all the assets of a company.

---

58   [1997] Ch 107.
59   [1997] Ch 107 at 141, per Peter Gibson LJ.

3.136 The other formal requirements are all less important in practice. Under s 53(1)(c) of the Law of Property Act 1925, a disposition of an equitable interest must be in writing and must be signed by the person disposing of the interest.[60] Equitable interests do arise in commercial transactions. For example, a debtor who has created a legal mortgage of property only has an equity of redemption; and a mortgage of that is a disposition of an equitable interest. In practice, however, security is invariably taken in writing and is signed by the debtor; and the statutory requirement therefore only reflects the practical reality.

3.137 There are also particular requirements for the taking of security over certain intellectual property rights. For instance, a mortgage or charge over a patent is void unless it is in writing and signed by or on behalf of the debtor.[61] There are similar provisions for registered trade marks and copyright, although in these cases the requirement only seems to extend to mortgages, and not to charges.[62] In practice, of course, security in such a case is invariably taken in writing.

3.138 In theory, however, where the statutory requirements do not apply, the creation of an equitable mortgage or charge need not be in writing. This would be the case, for instance, in the case of a charge created by a debtor over goods or receivables to which he has the legal title.

Summary

3.139 The requirements of an equitable mortgage or charge can be summarised as follows:

- Both an equitable mortgage and a charge require evidence that:
  - the debtor intends to grant the creditor an immediate equitable proprietary interest in an asset by way of security for the discharge of a liability; and
  - the asset can be identified as falling within the security at the time it requires to be enforced.
- A mortgage is normally created by the debtor assigning, declaring a trust over or agreeing to mortgage identifiable assets.
- A charge is normally created by the debtor executing a charge document, but all that is required is evidence of an intention to create a charge over identifiable assets.
- An equitable mortgage and a charge can be created over most types of asset, including future assets.
- There are few formalities for the creation of an equitable mortgage or charge, the most important in practice being the requirement for equitable security over land to be executed by both parties.

---

60 A signature is not a requirement in relation to financial collateral arrangements: see part 5 of this chapter (**3.175ff**).
61 Patents Act 1977, s 30(6), as amended by the Regulatory Reform (Patents) Order 2004, SI 2004/2357, and s 130(1).
62 Trade Marks Act 1994, s 24; Copyright, Designs and Patents Act 1988, s 90(3).

- Most equitable mortgages and charges created by companies, and many equitable mortgages and charges created by individuals, require registration against the debtor to be effective in an insolvency.

Part 4: THE SCOPE OF THE SECURITY

3.140 It is difficult to overestimate the importance of intention in relation to the creation of equitable mortgages and charges. This issue has been discussed in detail in part 3 of this chapter (**3.57**ff). Intention is also crucial to two other issues – the nature of the interest created and the extent of the security; and this is the case for legal mortgages as well as for equitable mortgages and charges. This part considers those two issues.

3.141 When considering the nature of the interest created by the parties, their intention governs:

- whether a transfer of legal or beneficial title to an asset is outright or by way of security; and
- whether a transfer of possession by way of security also involves a transfer of title (and accordingly whether the transferee has a pledge or a mortgage).

3.142 When analysing the extent of the security, the intention of the parties governs:

- the identity of the assets which are the subject of the security (although there are certain limitations on this principle); and
- the scope of the liabilities secured.

The nature of the interest created

Is the transaction outright, or by way of security?

3.143 It has been seen that a legal mortgage requires the title to the asset to be transferred to the creditor. The document creating the transfer will generally make it clear whether the transfer is intended to be outright or by way of security. But, whether or not a transfer is intended to be by way of security or outright ultimately depends on the intention of the parties. The fact that, on the face of it, the transfer appears to be absolute does not prevent it being a mortgage if that was what the parties intended.[63]

3.144 An example of this principle is found in the New Zealand case *Re Universal Management*.[64] In that case, certain receivables were transferred to a bank, and the question arose whether the document creating the transfer was

---

63   *Cripps v Jee* (1793) 4 Bro CC 472.
64   [1983] NZLR 462.

registrable under provisions equivalent to those contained in s 395 of the Companies Act 1985. If the document was a mortgage, it would have been registrable as a mortgage over book debts but, if absolute, it would not.

3.145 The New Zealand Court of Appeal held that the document was a mortgage and, not being registered, was therefore void. Although the transfer was expressed to be absolute, it was clearly given in consideration for a loan, and the court decided that, as a result of the terms of the document itself and the surrounding circumstances of the transaction, it was intended to be given by way of security. The test was clearly stated by Cooke J:[65]

> 'It is common ground that the question is whether in substance the transaction was a sale on the one hand or a mortgage on the other; and that in determining its substance not only the terms of the documents but the surrounding circumstances are relevant.'

Is a transfer of possession also a transfer of title?

3.146 Certain types of asset, particularly goods, are transferable by delivery. If a bill of lading is delivered from one person to another, there are at least three possible interpretations of that action. It could be an outright transfer of title (for instance, a sale or a gift), a transfer of title by way of security (ie a mortgage) or a transfer of possession by way of security (ie a pledge). The intention of the parties, obtained from the documentation and the surrounding circumstances, will establish which type of transaction it was.[66]

The extent of the security

3.147 The requirements for the creation of a mortgage or charge can be compared with the so-called 'three certainties' for the creation of a trust. It is frequently said that there are three requirements for the creation of a valid trust:

- certainty of intention (is there intended to be a trust?);
- certainty of subject matter (which assets are subject to the trust?); and
- certainty of objects (who are the beneficiaries of the trust?).

3.148 In the case of the security interests, the analogous 'certainties' are:

- certainty of intention (is there intended to be a mortgage or charge?);
- certainty of subject matter (which assets are subject to the security?); and
- certainty of objects (which liabilities are secured?).

3.149 Certainty of intention has been discussed in part 3 of this chapter (**3.57ff**). This part concentrates on the other two – the identity of the assets mortgaged or charged and the extent of the liabilities secured by the mortgage or charge.

---

65   [1983] NZLR 462 at 470.
66   *Sewell v Burdick* (1884) 10 App Cas 74.

The secured assets

3.150   The requirement to identify the secured assets is common to all forms of security interest, but it is less of an issue in relation to pledges because of the requirement that the creditor obtains actual or constructive possession of the assets pledged. The pledge cannot, therefore, generally extend beyond the scope of the assets in the possession of the creditor.

3.151   Because possession is not a requirement of a mortgage or a charge, it is crucial that the identity of the assets secured is properly defined. As an example of the type of issue which can arise, a number of cases have considered the question of whether or not a mortgage of an asset includes the proceeds of insurance taken out in respect of that asset.

3.152   The basic principle was stated by Parker J in *Sinnott v Bowden*, in relation to mortgages of land:[67]

'It is, I think, clear that, apart from special contract or the provisions of some statute, a mortgagee has no interest in the moneys payable under a policy of insurance effected by a mortgagor on the mortgaged premises.'

3.153   A mortgage over an asset will normally contain an undertaking by the debtor to insure the asset concerned. It will also normally expressly mortgage or charge the proceeds of insurance. But in the absence of an express or implied mortgage or charge over the insurance proceeds, the creditor will not have security over them. The difficulties of establishing whether there is an implied security interest over insurance proceeds are illustrated by two contrasting cases.

3.154   In *Lees v Whiteley*,[68] D created a security bill of sale over machinery in favour of C to secure a debt owing to C. The bill of sale contained a covenant to insure, but contained no provision for the application of the proceeds of the insurance to repay the debt. The machinery was the subject of a fire, D became bankrupt and C claimed the insurance proceeds. Kindersley V-C said that at first sight it was consistent with natural justice that C should have the insurance proceeds – why else would there be a covenant to insure? If the bill of sale had provided that the insurance proceeds were to be used to restore the machinery, he would have held that there was an implied charge over the insurance proceeds. But, since there was no express or implied covenant that the policy monies were to be applied in payment of the debt, C did not have a charge over the insurance proceeds.[69]

3.155   A charge over insurance proceeds was, however, implied in *Colonial Mutual v ANZ*.[70] It is easier to understand the judgment of the Privy Council

---

67   [1912] 2 Ch 414 at 419.
68   (1866) LR 2 Eq 143.
69   See now Law of Property Act 1925, s 108.
70   [1995] 1 WLR 1140.

in that case in the light of the very clear judgment of the New Zealand Court of Appeal.[71] D had mortgaged land to C. The mortgage contained a clause under which:

- D was required to insure the land; and
- C had the sole right to settle with, and recover from, any insurance company in respect of insurances over the land.

3.156 It was held that C had a charge over the insurance policy and its proceeds. In the Privy Council, Lord Hoffmann said that the purpose of the clause was to ensure that, if the value of the security depreciated, the proceeds would provide a fund to make up the shortfall and, since this purpose could only be achieved if C had a charge over the proceeds, then one was implied.

3.157 How does this case differ from *Lees v Whiteley*? The answer is to be found in the judgment of the New Zealand Court of Appeal. They stressed the importance of the second of the covenants described above, by which C had the sole right to settle with, and recover from, any insurance company. This showed the intention that C should have a proprietary interest in the insurance proceeds.

3.158 There are other examples of the courts placing restrictive interpretations on provisions in charging clauses. A charge over 'book debts' does not extend to bank accounts,[72] even though amounts due from a bank are debts and ought to be written up in the debtor's books.

3.159 Similar problems arise in relation to security over a company's uncalled capital. The courts have declined to regard uncalled capital as being property of a company and, as a result, a security document must specifically refer to uncalled capital if the security is to extend to it.[73] Uncalled capital is of little importance in practice, but it is another example of the need to describe clearly everything which is intended to be the subject of the security.

3.160 It is, therefore, preferable to ensure that the security document expressly mortgages or charges all ancillary rights which might arise in relation to the asset concerned. If an express security interest is not created, the court will only imply one if it is clear from the documents and the surrounding matrix of facts that the parties did intend the creditor to have a proprietary interest over the asset concerned.

3.161 In certain types of case, an express or implied security interest over the ancillary asset is not necessary. In limited circumstances, the creditor will have a security interest over the ancillary asset because he has a security interest over the primary asset. If, for instance, a creditor has security over an asset which is wrongfully sold by the debtor, the creditor clearly has a charge over the proceeds of sale, provided they can be traced in accordance with the normal tracing rules. It is not necessary for the security documents specifically to say

---

71 [1994] 3 NZLR 136.
72 *Re Brightlife* [1987] Ch 200.
73 *Re Russion Spratts Patent* [1898] 2 Ch 149.

this. It follows from the fact that there is a security interest over the asset concerned. A constructive trust is imposed over the proceeds as a result of the wrongful sale by the debtor.[74]

3.162 In one type of case the creditor will have a security interest in the ancillary asset even if the parties had not intended him to do so. If a chattel is taken onto land and becomes a fixture, it becomes part of the land. A mortgage of the land will therefore extend not only to the land itself, but also to fixtures on the land; and this rule not only applies to fixtures which were on the land at the time the mortgage was created, but also to items which subsequently become fixtures.

3.163 An example of how the principle works in practice is *Meux v Jacobs*.[75] D owned a leasehold interest in land. He created an equitable mortgage over it in favour of C. Fixtures were subsequently added to the land and D created a security bill of sale over them in favour of T. There was a dispute between C and T concerning who had the best right to the fixtures. The House of Lords held that C took priority over T in relation to the fixtures. A mortgage of land carries with it fixtures on the property.

3.164 It is important to appreciate that this is not a particular rule relating to mortgages. It is simply an application of a principle of land law that fixtures are part of the land and are therefore transferred with the land. A mortgagee of the land can take advantage of this principle, not only in relation to fixtures on the land at the time the mortgage was created, but also in respect of fixtures subsequently added to the land. The principle applies to mortgages of leaseholds as well as to mortgages of freeholds, and to equitable, mortgages and charges as well as to legal mortgages.

3.165 In summary, the security document should clearly establish the identity of the assets which are to be the subject of the security. A creditor can rely on the principle that security over land will encompass its fixtures and that fixed security over an asset will extend to its proceeds. But, otherwise, a creditor should not assume that security over one particular asset will extend to associated assets. It has been seen that the courts are slow to imply that security over an asset extends to its insurances, even though that would have been the obvious inference to draw. The security document should therefore be drafted to extend not just to the asset which it is contemplated should be the subject of the security, but also to any potential substitute assets and to any rights associated with it.

The secured liabilities

3.166 It is equally important to ensure that the liabilities which are secured are adequately described. Security over valuable assets is worthless to a creditor if it does not secure the intended liabilities. Because the creditor obtains a

---

74 *Re Hallett's Estate* (1880) 13 Ch D 696.
75 (1875) LR 7 HL 481.

security interest, rather than an outright interest, in the secured assets, the security is only as good as the liabilities as it secures.

3.167 In the case of consensual security interests (such as mortgages, charges and pledges) the extent of the secured liability is a matter of the construction of the security document, in the light of the other finance documents and the circumstances which existed at the time the transaction was entered into. In practice, there are two principal types of secured liability. In some cases, security is limited to obligations under a particular facility. In others, it extends to all liabilities from time to time owing by the debtor or a third party to the creditor.

Security for a particular facility

3.168 Mortgages and charges are frequently expressed to secure liabilities under a particular facility. This is particularly common where the facility is syndicated (where the option of an 'all moneys' security is extremely difficult to achieve), but many bilateral facilities are also expressed to secure a particular facility. The most common practical problem with such an arrangement is what happens when the facility is amended or replaced. To what extent will the security be effective to secure the amended or replaced facility? This is ultimately a matter of construction of the security document in the light of the surrounding facts at the time the security was taken. It is very common for the security document to state that it secures the facility as it may be amended or replaced from time to time. But it should not be assumed that this will have the effect that *any* amendment or replacement of the facility will be the subject of the security. The court will construe this expression in the light of the surrounding facts at the time the security was entered into and on the basis of what the parties, at that time, would have contemplated those words as extending to. If the effect of the amendment or replacement of the facility is that, in substance, it has become a different facility, it will no longer be secured.

3.169 This can best be illustrated by an example. An acquisition finance facility is entered into, under which a syndicate of banks agrees to lend the debtor £200 million to finance a particular acquisition. Security is taken for the facility. One year later, the facility is amended. Its amount is increased to £600 million, the increased amount being used for a new acquisition. The security is expressed to secure the original facility agreement 'as amended or replaced from time to time'. The issue is whether the new facility agreement can properly be described as an amendment or variation of the old one. This is ultimately a matter of construction of the document as a whole in the light of the circumstances in which it was entered into, but it is unlikely that a court would regard the new facility as being an amendment or variation of the old one. Its amount has been increased threefold and its purpose has been extended. It is quite likely that a court would decide that, in substance, the new facility was not amendment or replacement of the old facility, but a new, and different, one.

3.170   A recent example of the approach of the courts in such cases is *Triodos Bank v Dobbs*.[76] That was a case concerning a guarantee, but the principles of construction are exactly the same in the case of security documents. Mr Dobbs had guaranteed to a bank the obligations of a company under two loan agreements, by which the company was lent £900,000 to complete the first stage of a particular project. Those loan agreements were replaced by two further loan agreements in 1998 and by another one in 1999. Their effect was to increase the amount of facility from £900,000 to £2,600,000, the purpose of the increase being to finance the second stage of the project. The Court of Appeal held that the guarantee did not extend to the new facilities. Even though the guarantee was expressed to extend to amendments or variations of the existing facility, the new facilities were for a greatly increased amount and for new purposes. In substance, they documented a different facility from that which Mr Dobbs had guaranteed.

3.171   As a result, even if the security is expressed to extend to amendments or replacements of the secured facility, it should not be assumed that this allows the creditor to make more than relatively modest amendments to the facility, such as the rescheduling of repayments. Anything which might be said to change the nature of the facility will lay the creditor open to the argument that, in substance, the amended or replaced facility is a new facility and that the security does not extend to it. Very clear wording in a security document is needed to enable the security to extend to a materially altered facility.

'All moneys' security

3.172   Because of these difficulties, where possible (and particularly where the facility is bilateral), the security should be taken in 'all moneys' form – ie to secure all moneys from time to time owing by the debtor (or by a third party) to the creditor. If the security is not limited to a particular facility, issues concerning amendments and replacement facilities are irrelevant. The security secures all money which is from time to time owing, whatever the nature of the facility concerned.

3.173   But even an 'all moneys' provision is not a panacea. The courts will inevitably construe any ambiguity in favour of the debtor. An example is *Re Quest Cae*.[77] The debtor had granted an 'all moneys' debenture in favour of a creditor. It was expressed to secure all moneys and liabilities 'now or hereafter owing by or incurred by [the debtor] to [the creditor] on any account whatever ...'. After the debtor had gone into receivership, the creditor purchased, at a very substantial discount, loan stock which the debtor had issued to another party. The creditor contented that the debenture secured the repayment of the loan stock. Nourse J held that it did not. He decided that the reference to the moneys and liabilities being incurred 'on any account whatever' could only refer to dealings or transactions between the debtor and the creditor, and that they did not extend to liabilities incurred by the debtor to a third party which were subsequently acquired by the creditor.

---

76   [2005] EWCA Civ 630.
77   [1985] BCLC 266.

3.174 As a result of this decision, it is common for 'all moneys' clauses to make it clear that they extend to liabilities of the debtor which are subsequently acquired by the creditor. What is instructive about *Quest Cae* is that the court would have found it much more difficult to reach the conclusion which it did if there had been no reference to an 'account'. If the debenture had simply secured 'all moneys and obligations from time to time incurred by the debtor to the creditor' it would have been much more difficult to decide that this did not extend to obligations acquired by the creditor from third parties. As is so often the case, the creditor would have been better off by expressing what he wanted in fewer, more general, words.

Part 5: SECURITY OVER INTANGIBLES

3.175 It is difficult to overestimate the importance to creditors of being able to take security over intangibles. Much of the value of companies is tied up in assets such as contracts, receivables, securities and intellectual property. Except in certain limited cases (which are discussed in part 2 of this chapter (**3.25ff**)), the common law has never recognised the assignability of intangibles.[78] The reason for the rule was to avoid 'maintenance', ie to prevent the multiplicity of actions. Because intangibles are incapable of being possessed, and rights over them are therefore ultimately enforced by action, it appears to have been considered that the ability to assign such rights would increase the number of actions. In *Master v Miller*,[79] Buller J described the rule as a 'quaint maxim'[80] and said that: 'The good sense of that rule seems to me to be very questionable.'[81] It nevertheless continues to be the case even today that the basic rule is that intangibles cannot be assigned at common law.

3.176 Since the early seventeenth century, however, the courts of equity recognised that most types of intangible were capable of being assigned in equity.[82] This had an indirect effect on the common law courts, which took notice of the effectiveness of assignments in equity and recognised that, even in the common law courts, an equitable assignee could sue in the assignor's name.[83]

3.177 The disadvantage of an equitable assignment was that, although it gave the assignee the ability to sue to recover the assigned right, the action had to be brought in the name of the assignor, who continued to have the legal right to the intangible concerned. The legislature ultimately intervened and, as a result of s 25(6) of the Judicature Act 1873 (now replaced by s 136 of the Law of

---

78   *Picker v London and County Banking Co* (1887) 18 QBD 515 at 519, per Bowen LJ.

79   (1791) 4 TR 320.

80   (1791) 4 TR 320 at 341.

81   (1791) 4 TR 320 at 340.

82   *Warmstrey v Tanfield* (1628–29) 1 Rep Ch 29.

83   *Master v Miller* (1791) 4 TR 320 at 340, per Buller J; *Norman v Federal Commissioner of Taxation* (1963) 109 CLR 9 at 27, per Windeyer J.

Property Act 1925), the assignee became entitled to sue in his own name if certain conditions were complied with. Such assignments are sometimes described as 'legal assignments' but they will be referred to as 'statutory assignments' in this book. The reason is that the purpose and effect of the legislation was to amend the procedure for the enforcement of equitable assignments, rather than to create a new regime for the transfer of intangibles at common law. In this respect, it can be contrasted with the effect of the Companies Act 1862 and its successors on the transferability of shares and loan stock. The Companies Acts created new forms of property as a result of enabling the incorporation of businesses in a simplified form; and it was recognised that compliance with the requirements of the companies legislation effected a transfer of legal, rather than just beneficial, title to shares and loan stock. This is not the case with most other intangibles.

3.178	The basic principles concerning the creation of an equitable mortgage or charge (which are discussed in part 3 of this chapter (**3.57ff**)) are as applicable to intangibles as they are to any other type of asset. The purpose of this part is to consider certain other issues which are only applicable to intangibles, although the first section explores in a little more detail an issue which was discussed in part 3 but which has been particularly important in practice in relation to intangibles.

3.179	The issues considered in this part are:

•	the creation and effect of equitable assignments and charges over intangibles;

•	the creation and effect of statutory assignments over intangibles;

•	the effect of restrictions on the assignment of intangibles;

•	the effect of an assignment or charge on the counterparty to the intangible;

•	the benefits of giving notice to the counterparty of an assignment or charge of an intangible;

•	rights of set-off against assignees or chargees of intangibles; and

•	the rules concerning financial collateral.

Equitable assignments and charges

3.180	The distinction between the approaches of the courts of equity and the common law courts to the assignment of intangibles was explained by Cozens-Hardy LJ in *Fitzroy v Cave*.[84] At common law, intangibles such as debts were looked on as strictly personal obligations and an assignment of them was regarded merely as an assignment of a right to bring an action in the courts, which was seen to be objectionable from a policy point of view. But the courts of equity took a different view. They saw a debt 'as a piece of property, an asset capable of bring dealt with like any other asset'.[85]

84	[1905] 2 KB 364.
85	[1905] 2 KB 364 at 372.

3.181   The courts of equity have recognised the ability to transfer intangibles from at least the early seventeenth century.[86] The way in which they have approached the question is illustrated by *Row v Dawson*.[87] In that case, C had lent money to D. D was owed money by T, and D directed T to pay the debt to C 'out of the money due to me from' T. D then went bankrupt and there was a dispute between C and D's trustees in bankruptcy as to who was entitled to the money due from T. Lord Hardwicke LC held that C was entitled to the money. Unlike at common law, the assignment of an intangible was possible in equity. Although there were no express words of assignment in the arrangement between D and T, it was an agreement for valuable consideration and it was to be construed as an assignment of that amount of the debt as was necessary to repay the loan due to C. In deciding whether or not a particular transaction amounted to an assignment, the Lord Chancellor said that 'any words will do; no particular words being necessary'.[88]

3.182   In practice, an equitable mortgage of an intangible is normally created by an equitable assignment which is expressed to be by way of security. It is also very common to create charges over intangibles.

Creation of the security – intention and identification

3.183   It has been seen in part 3 of this chapter (**3.57ff**) that two of the key requirements for the creation of a mortgage or charge are:

●   that the debtor intends to create an equitable proprietary interest by way of security over an asset; and
●   that the identity of the secured asset can be identified with sufficient certainty.

3.184   Much of the litigation in the area has concerned intangibles. Indeed, it was in a case concerning receivables that Lord Macnaghten made his famous comment:[89] 'The mode or form of assignment is absolutely immaterial provided the intention of the parties is clear.'

3.185   Two contrasting sets of examples show how these principles of intention and identifiability have been applied in the case of receivables.

3.186   In *Palmer v Carey*,[90] there was an agreement between D and C that, when D bought goods, the purchase price would be payable by C and, when the goods were sold, their proceeds would be paid into C's bank account. The Privy Council held that this did not create an assignment or charge in favour of C. This case can be contrasted with *Re Kent & Sussex Sawmills*,[91] which was discussed in part 3 of this chapter at **3.118**. In that case, D was owed money by

---

86   *Warmstrey v Tanfield* (1628–29) 1 Rep Ch 29.
87   (1749) 1 Ves Sen 331.
88   (1749) 1 Ves Sen 331 at 332.
89   *Tailby v Official Receiver* (1888) 13 App Cas 523 at 543.
90   [1926] AC 703.
91   [1947] Ch 177.

T. He wrote to T, authorising him to pay his debt to C. The authority was expressed to be irrevocable without C's consent. This arrangement was held to create a charge in favour of C.

3.187 What was the distinction between the two cases? *Palmer v Carey* looks like a deliberate attempt to create security, whereas, in the *Kent & Sussex Sawmills* case, there was simply an authority (rather than a direction) to pay C, albeit that it was expressed to be irrevocable without C's consent. It was nevertheless held that the former did not create a security, whereas the latter did.

3.188 In *Percival v Dunn*,[92] D owed money to C and T owed money to D. D requested T to pay C. It was held that this did not constitute an equitable assignment or charge over monies owing by T to D because there was no indication in the request to T that there was a particular fund being assigned or charged. By contrast, in *Brice v Bannester*,[93] D was building a vessel for T, the price being payable in instalments. D owed money to C and therefore directed T to pay C a certain sum out of the moneys due or to become due from T to D. At the time of the direction, nothing was actually owing by T to D. The Court of Appeal nevertheless held that the arrangements created a valid equitable assignment.

3.189 It is unwise to place too much reliance on such cases as precedents. Each case depends on a decision by the court, in the light of the surrounding facts, whether it was the intention of the parties to create security over a particular intangible in that particular case. The analysis can be broken down into two questions:

- Did the parties intend that the creditor should have a proprietary interest by way of security in the debtor's asset?
- Is the asset over which the security is to be taken sufficiently identifiable?

3.190 The first question is simply one of intention. In *Palmer v Carey*, it was decided that, on the facts, there was no such intention, whereas in the *Kent & Sussex Sawmills* case, there was. The second question cannot be entirely divorced from the first, but it does raise a separate issue – whether there is a sufficiently identifiable fund over which the security can operate. In *Brice v Bannester* there was, but in *Percival v Dunn* there was not.

3.191 Although it is possible to create an equitable mortgage or charge over intangibles informally, in practice it is normally done by the execution of a document by the debtor which expressly assigns or charges particular intangibles to secure specified liabilities. This is for two reasons. In the first place, this approach produces much more certainty both as to the existence of the security and as to its terms. Secondly, in practice, the requirement for the registration of most types of security interest created by companies means that an informal arrangement to create security will, in many cases, be ineffective

---

92   (1885) 29 Ch D 128.
93   (1878) 3 QBD 569.

even if there is an intention to create security because it will not have been registered within the 21-day period from its creation. Registration is considered in **CHAPTER 6**.

Notice to the counterparty

3.192 Most intangibles consist of rights against third parties, and are ultimately enforced by legal action against those third parties. The most common type of intangible to form the subject matter of security is rights under contracts. The debtor will have entered into a contract with a third party (in this book, referred to as the 'counterparty') as a result of which the debtor will, or may, receive money. As security for credit granted to the debtor, the creditor will take an equitable mortgage or charge over the debtor's rights under the contract. Subject to the very limited formalities discussed in part 3 of this chapter (**3.57ff**), all that is required to create the assignment or charge is evidence that the debtor intended the creditor to have a proprietary interest in the contract by way of security. That will normally be evidenced by a document executed by the debtor by which he assigns or charges his rights under the contract to the creditor by way of security for a particular liability.

3.193 The equitable proprietary interest of the creditor is complete when this has been done. There is no necessity for the counterparty to be notified of the arrangement. This principle is illustrated in *Gorringe v Irwell India Rubber and Gutta Percha Works*.[94] In that case, D owed money to C and was owed money by T. D accordingly wrote to C that he held at C's disposal an amount of money due from T until the debt had been paid. Neither D nor C notified T of the arrangement. D then went into liquidation, after which C gave notice to T. D's liquidator claimed the monies due from T. The Court of Appeal held that the arrangement created a valid charge over the debt owing by T. Although the words 'assign' or 'charge' were not used, the document showed that there was an intention that C was to have a charge over the debt owing by T. The charge was complete without the necessity for any notice being given to T, and it was therefore effective against D's liquidator.

3.194 The absence of a requirement to give notice to the counterparty is very important in practice. It is common for lenders to take security over their debtors' contractual rights, and it is frequently impracticable to give notice to all the counterparties concerned. As will be seen later in this part, there are substantial advantages to be gained from giving notice, but it is not necessary. A valid equitable proprietary interest is created without the necessity for such a notice, and is therefore effective against an insolvency officer of the debtor.

The effect of an equitable mortgage or charge

3.195 In the case of an equitable mortgage, the creditor obtains beneficial title to the intangible concerned. Where there is a charge, the creditor obtains an equitable proprietary interest in the intangible, but not beneficial title. Both

---

94   (1886) 34 Ch D 128.

are effective in the insolvency of the debtor and both are subject to the same priority rules, which are discussed in **CHAPTER 7**. In each case, the creditor's interest is given by way of security. In the case of an equitable assignment, the intangible must be re-assigned to the debtor once the secured liability has been discharged. Where the creditor has a charge, it automatically terminates on discharge of the secured liability.

3.196   The mortgage or charge can be enforced by the creditor taking over the debtor's rights to the intangible concerned. If the intangible is a debt, the creditor will be entitled to recover it from the counterparty and, for this purpose, to give a good discharge to the counterparty.[95]

3.197   If, however, the creditor wishes to bring legal proceedings against the counterparty, he must ensure that all parties with an interest in the matter are before the court. It is in the nature of a security interest that the debtor retains a reversionary interest in the asset concerned; and it is therefore necessary for the creditor to join the debtor in any proceedings.[96] The same principle applies in relation to an outright assignment of a legal intangible (such as a debt), because the assignor retains legal title. But an equitable assignee can sue in his own name if he has an absolute assignment of an equitable intangible (such as a right under a trust), because the assignor has parted with his whole interest.[97]

3.198   The requirement to join the debtor in any legal proceedings is not a major problem in practice. If the debtor refuses to become involved in the proceedings, he can be joined as a defendant to the proceedings, and the court will compel him to allow his name to be used, subject to an indemnity for costs.[98] It is also common for assignments of contracts and receivables to be taken as part of a debenture over all of a debtor company's assets, in which event any enforcement will be taken by an administrator or receiver as agent for the debtor company, rather than on behalf of the creditor.

3.199   Under an equitable mortgage or charge, therefore, the creditor has the effective right to recover the intangible concerned. The terms of the equitable mortgage or charge will generally given the creditor substantial additional powers, including a power to sell the intangible. Enforcement of security is considered in more detail in **CHAPTER 8**.

Statutory assignments

3.200   The advantage of equitable mortgages and charges is the ease by which they can be created. Their disadvantage is that the debtor needs to be joined in any legal proceedings by the creditor in respect of the intangible concerned.

---

95   *Jones v Farrell* (1857) 1 De G&J 208 at 218, per Lord Cranworth LC. The statement of Chitty LJ in *Durham Brothers v Robertson* [1898] 1 QB 765, that an equitable assignee cannot give a valid discharge unless expressly given the power to do so is inconsistent with the decision in *Jones v Farrell* and would render an equitable assignment of little practical value.
96   *Cator v Croydon Canal Co* (1846) 4 Y&C Ex 593 at 593–594.
97   *Cator v Croydon Canal Co* (1846) 4 Y&C Ex 593 at 593–594.
98   *Crouch v Credit Foncier of England* (1873) LR 8 QB 374 at 380, per Blackburn J.

Although this was not a material disadvantage, when the administration of the common law and equity was fused in the Judicature Act 1873, the legislature took the opportunity to introduce a statutory method of assignment of intangibles which would enable the assignee to bring proceedings in his own name, without joining the assignor. Statutory assignments were introduced by s 25(6) of the Judicature Act 1873, which has since been replaced by s 136 of the Law of Property Act 1925.[99]

3.201 The procedural nature of the legislation has been emphasised in a number of cases. In *Walker v Bradford Old Bank*,[100] Smith J said that the legislation does not 'give new rights, but only affords a new mode of enforcing old rights'. Similarly, in *Marchant v Morton, Down & Co*,[101] Channel J described the legislation as 'merely machinery. It enables an action to be brought by the assignee in his own name in cases where previously he could have sued in the assignee's name, but only where he could so sue'.

3.202 The relevant part of s 136(1) of the Law of Property Act 1925 provides as follows:

'Any absolute assignment by writing under the hand of the assignor (not purporting to be by way of charge only) of any debt or other legal thing in action, of which express notice in writing has been given to the debtor, trustee or other person from whom the assignor would have been entitled to claim such debt or thing in action, is effectual in law (subject to equities having priority over the right of the assignee) to pass and transfer from the date of such notice—

(a) the legal right to such debt or thing in action;
(b) all legal and other remedies for the same; and
(c) the power to give a good discharge for the same without the concurrence of the assignor: ...'

3.203 Before considering the effect of a statutory assignment, it is necessary to consider the prerequisites of the new remedy. There are three issues:

- What types of intangible does the legislation apply to?
- What types of assignment does the legislation apply to?
- What other conditions must be complied with?

Type of intangible

3.204 The Law of Property Act 1925 applies to 'any debt or other legal thing in action'. On the face of it, this might seem to apply only to common law rights, and not to equitable ones, but the courts have construed it more widely. In *Torkington v Magee*,[102] Channell J held that the section needs to be

---

99 There are also particular rules for assignments of life insurance policies which pre-date this legislation: see the Policies of Assurance Act 1867.
100 (1884) 12 QBD 511 at 515.
101 [1901] 2 KB 829 at 832.
102 [1902] 2 KB 427. The decision was overruled, but on a different point, by the Court of Appeal in [1903] 1 KB 644.

construed in the light of the fact that it was initially part of the Judicature Act 1873, a procedural statute combining the administration of law and equity. He decided that a 'debt or other legal chose in action' means a 'debt or right which the common law looks on as not assignable by reason of its being a chose in action, but which a Court of Equity deals with as being assignable'.[103] The purpose of the section was to provide an easier method of enforcement of intangibles which were previously assignable in equity; and it was intended that the statutory remedy would apply to those types of intangible which could be the subject of an equitable assignment. It therefore covers both legal intangibles (such as debts) and equitable intangibles (such as rights under trusts), but not those types of intangible which are transferable at common law, such as shares and debentures of companies.[104]

3.205 The converse is also true. Certain types of intangible are not assignable in equity;[105] and the same restrictions apply to statutory assignments. In the words of Lord Lindley in *Tolhurst v Associated Portland Cement*,[106] the legislation 'has not made contracts assignable which were not assignable in equity before, but it has enabled assigns of assignable contracts to sue upon them in their own names without joining the assignor'.

3.206 It appears that there is one exception to the principle that the statute applies to the same types of intangible as are assignable in equity. It is generally considered (although there is no clear authority on the point) that the statute only applies in respect of intangibles which are existing at the time the assignment is created; and this would seem to follow from the requirement (which is discussed below) that notice of the assignment needs to be given to the counterparty. This can only be done in relation to an existing intangible.

Type of assignment

3.207 In order for the statutory provisions to apply, the assignment must be:

- absolute (not purporting to be by way of charge only); and
- in writing under the hand of the assignor.

3.208 It might have been thought that the requirement for the assignment to be 'absolute' would preclude assignments by way of security, but this is not the way in which the legislation has been construed by the courts. Their approach can be seen in two contrasting cases.

3.209 In *Durham Brothers v Robertson*,[107] D assigned to C his interest in a debt owing by T until D's liability to C had been repaid. The Court of Appeal held that this created a valid equitable assignment, but did not satisfy the requirement of a statutory assignment that it be absolute. The assignment was

103 [1902] 2 KB 427 430–431.
104 [1902] 2 KB 427 at 430.
105 They are discussed later in this part.
106 [1903] AC 414 at 424.
107 [1898] 1 QB 765.

only effective until the secured debt had been repaid. T might not know whom he was to pay and, in any legal proceedings, all the parties therefore needed to be joined.

3.210   A different result was achieved in *Hughes v Pump House Hotel Co.*[108] In that case, as security for an overdraft, D assigned to C all moneys due under a particular building contract. The Court of Appeal held that this was an absolute assignment within the meaning of the statute. The test was whether, on a construction of the document as a whole, the intention was to pass all of D's rights under the contract to C. If so, the assignment was 'absolute' even though it was given by way of security.

3.211   The distinction between an assignment which is absolute and one which is not depends on the effect of the assignment on the counterparty. The purpose of the statute is to enable an assignee to sue in his own name, without joining the assignor. This is only possible if it is clear that the counterparty only has to deal with the assignee, and does not need to involve himself with the assignor. If the assignee obtains the entire right to the intangible concerned, then the debtor is entitled to deal with him alone, and the assignment is absolute. This is the case even if the debtor has an equity of redemption because, until the counterparty receives notice of a re-assignment to the debtor after the secured liability has been repaid, he is entitled to deal with the creditor alone.

3.212   If, by contrast, the debtor automatically becomes entitled to the intangible once the secured liability has been repaid (as would be the case in relation to a charge – where there is no requirement for a re-assignment, the charge automatically determining on discharge of the secured liability), the transfer is not absolute, and therefore will only take effect in equity.

3.213   For the same reason, an assignment of part of a debt will only take effect in equity.[109] Because only part of the debt is assigned, the counterparty cannot safely deal only with the creditor. He must join the debtor in any arrangements.

3.214   These cases again show the procedural nature of a statutory assignment. The effect of a statutory assignment is to enable the assignee to sue in his own name; and the purpose of most of the prerequisites of statutory assignments is to ensure that this can be done without prejudice to the assignor or the counterparty.

Notice to the counterparty

3.215   The other requirement of a statutory assignment is that express notice in writing has been given to the counterparty. The statute does not require the notice to be given by any particular person. Nor is there any requirement as to when it is given. If the other requirements of the section have been satisfied,

---

108   [1902] 2 KB 190.
109   *Re Steel Wing Company* [1921] 1 Ch 349.

notice can be given at any time after the assignment has been created. In such a case, the giving of notice will have the effect of turning the equitable assignment into a statutory one. Nor is there any particular form which the notice has to comply with. The important thing is to ensure that it brings to the debtor with reasonable certainty the fact that he must pay the assignee and not the assignor.[110] In practice, the notice is normally given by the assignor for the obvious reason that he is the person with whom the counterparty has contracted and the counterparty is unlikely to act on an instruction from anyone else.

Registration

3.216 The requirements for the registration of a statutory assignment given by way of security are the same as those for an equitable assignment, and are considered in more detail in CHAPTER 6.

Effect of a statutory assignment

3.217 Like an equitable assignment, a statutory assignment gives the creditor a proprietary interest by way of security in the intangible concerned, and is therefore effective in the insolvency of the debtor. But its effect differs from an equitable assignment in that it transfers to the assignee the 'legal right' to the intangible concerned and 'all legal and other remedies for the same' in addition to a power to give a good discharge without the concurrence of the assignor.

3.218 As has been seen, the purpose of the statute is to enable the assignee to bring proceedings against the counterparty in his own name, without joining the assignor. Although the assignee obtains 'the legal right' to the intangible concerned, this does not mean that he becomes the legal owner of the intangible in the same way as if he had become the legal owner of land or goods. The reference to the 'legal right' to the intangible is a reference to the right to enforce it in the courts without joining the assignor.[111] The distinction is important in relation to priorities, and is discussed further in CHAPTER 7.

3.219 In practice, therefore, the only advantage of taking a statutory assignment rather than an equitable one (assuming that, in each case, notice of the assignment has been given to the counterparty) is that a statutory assignment enables the assignor to sue the counterparty in his own name without joining the assignor. But, in the light of the court's willingness to join a reluctant assignor as a defendant in proceedings by the assignee, this procedural advantage is only of limited value. In most cases, therefore, if notice has been given to the counterparty, it is of little importance whether the assignment is statutory or equitable.

Summary

3.220 In summary, the requirements of a statutory assignment over an intangible are that:

---

110   *Van Lynn Developments v Pelias Construction Co* [1969] 1 QB 607.
111   *Marchant v Morton, Down & Co* [1901] 2 KB 829 at 832, per Channell J.

- the intangible must be existing at the time of the assignment;
- the assignment must be an absolute assignment of the whole intangible (a security assignment meets this requirement if the creditor has the entire right to the benefit of the intangible until redemption);
- the assignment must be in writing and signed by the debtor; and
- written notice of the assignment must be given to the counterparty.

3.221   The effect of a statutory assignment is that:

- the creditor obtains a proprietary interest in the intangible (as he does in the case of an equitable assignment or charge); and
- the creditor can sue the counterparty in his own name, without joining the debtor (which he cannot do in the case of an equitable assignment or charge).

Intangibles which cannot be assigned or charged

3.222   Although most intangibles are capable of being assigned or charged, there are certain types of intangible which cannot. They fall into two categories:

- where there is a public policy reason why they should not be capable of being assigned or charged; and
- where the contract under which the intangible is created prohibits or restricts assignments or charges.

Public policy

3.223   The reason why it is not generally possible to assign intangibles at common law is that the common law courts regarded most intangibles as being rights to sue, and that their assignment would multiply the number of court actions. It has been seen that courts of equity took a different view, regarding intangibles as being items of property, rather than simply being rights to sue. Even in equity, however, the rules against maintenance mean that it is not generally possible to assign what is normally described as a 'bare right of action'. The leading case is *Trendtex Trading Corporation v Credit Suisse*.[112] D was in legal proceedings against T. D owed C money and purported to assign to C its cause of action against T by way of security for its indebtedness. The arrangement was that D and C would share the proceeds of the claim against T. The House of Lords held that the arrangement was void. Although it did not offend against the rules concerning maintenance, it breached the rules concerning champerty.

3.224   Lord Roskill said[113] that the law was now more liberal in its approach to maintenance than it had been previously. Although it is still a fundamental principle of English law that it is not possible to assign a bare right to litigate, such an assignment is valid if the assignee has a genuine commercial interest in

---

112   [1982] AC 679.
113   [1982] AC 679 at 702–703.

the enforcement of the claim or if the assignment of the right to litigate is incidental to the assignment of a right to property. In this case, C did have a genuine commercial interest in the enforcement of the claim and, if it had simply been assigned to C by way of security, it would have been effective. But, because C was not obtaining the full benefit of the amount recovered from T, the arrangement constituted champerty, which, in essence, prevents an assignment being made by which the assignor and assignee divide up the spoils of a claim.

3.225   A straightforward assignment by way of security of a right to litigate is therefore enforceable if the creditor is entitled to all of the proceeds of the claim (subject only to the debtor's equity of redemption). If the assignee is owed money by the assignor, he does have a genuine commercial interest in maximising recoveries from his debtor's counterparties. This should be the case whether or not the right of action being assigned is incidental to some other property right.

3.226   The rules against maintenance and champerty are not the only restrictions on the types of intangible which are capable of being assigned. There is a substantial number of cases where, for public policy reasons, the courts have refused to countenance assignments of particular types of intangible. The most common example is contracts which are 'personal' to the contracting parties. An employment contract, for instance, is personal and it is not possible for the employer to assign the benefit of the employment contract to a third party. Under the general law, an employee cannot be required to work for someone other than the person with whom he has contracted.[114] An employment contract is not, therefore, property of the employer.[115]

3.227   Similarly, there are common law[116] and statutory[117] prohibitions on the ability of public officers, such as those serving in the Armed Forces, to assign or charge their salaries or pensions. None of these restrictions is of any material importance to creditors taking security over intangibles.

Restrictions on assignment

3.228   What is much more important in practice is that most intangibles are created by contract and that contracts frequently contain provisions prohibiting or restricting assignments or charges of the benefit of the contract concerned. Although some debts may arise by statute or in tort, the vast majority of debts over which creditors take security are created by contract. Unlike land or goods, contractual intangibles only exist by virtue of the contract by which they are created. In the case of an intangible created by contract, a provision of the contract restricting the ability of one of the parties

---

114   There are now substantial statutory inroads into this principle, in particular under the Transfer of Undertakings (Protection of Employment) Regulations 1981, SI 1981/1794, reg 5.

115   *Nokes v Doncaster Amalgamated Collieries* [1940] AC 1014.

116   See, for instance, *Aston v Gwinnell* (1827–29) 3 Y&J 136 at 148.

117   See, for instance, the Army Act 1955, s 203(1), by which an assignment or charge is void if it is over the pay or pension payable in respect of service in the Army.

to transfer the benefit of the contract to someone else necessarily affects third parties to the contract, whether or not they are aware of it. The assignee can have no greater rights under the contract than the assignor; and a right created by a contract can only be transferred in accordance with the terms of that contract.

3.229   Although this may seem obvious, there used to be some doubt whether a purported assignee who did not have notice of a restriction on assignment was bound by it. In *Linden Gardens Trust v Lenesta Sludge Disposals*,[118] however, the House of Lords held that a contractual restriction on assignment was effective regardless of whether or not the purported assignee was aware of it. In that case, A was the lessee of part of a building. A entered into a contract with B for B to remove asbestos from the building, the contract providing that '[A] shall not without written consent of [B] assign this contract'. The asbestos was not all removed and A, having assigned the benefit of the lease to C, then issued proceedings against B for negligence. A later assigned to C the right of action against B and any other rights incidental to the leasehold interest.[119]

3.230   The question arose whether the assignment was effective. The House of Lords held that it was not, having been made in breach of the prohibition on assignment contained in the contract. The purported assignment did not, therefore, vest any rights in C. It had been argued by C that the prohibition was void on the ground of public policy, but the House of Lords decided that a party to a contract might have a genuine commercial interest in ensuring that he dealt only with his contracting party, and there were therefore no grounds of public policy for refusing to give effect to the prohibition on assignment.

3.231   The Court of Appeal had considered that, although the prohibition on assignment was effective, it only applied to the right to future performance under the contract, and not to accrued rights to damages for breach of contract in existence at the time of the purported assignment. The House of Lords decided that prohibition could not be construed as applying only to the right to future performance. It extended to all of A's rights under the contract.

The effect of the restriction

3.232   In principle, therefore, it is possible for a contract to provide that it is incapable of being assigned. The prohibition can also extend to the creation of a charge or a trust or of any other proprietary interest in the contract. The effect of any particular contractual provision concerning assignment will depend on its construction. It could be intended:

- to constitute a promise by one party not to assign, breach of which would give rise to a claim to damages and, if sufficiently serious, to terminate the contract; or
- to prevent any purported assignment from having any effect on the other party to the contract.

---

118   [1994] 1 AC 85.
119   The assignment did not contravene the rules against maintenance because the right of action against B was incidental to the leasehold interest now vested in C.

3.233 Although the first alternative is theoretically possible, the second is much more likely. The purpose of the clause is to prevent assignment. This purpose is best achieved by ensuring that any purported assignment is a nullity as far as the other contracting party is concerned. He does not want a claim for damages; he wants to avoid the consequences of assignment.

3.234 If the contract provides that 'the benefit of this contract is not assignable' it is clearly intended to prevent any purported assignment, not to give rise to a claim for damages. Even if the clause is drafted on the basis that one of the contracting parties 'shall not assign' the benefit of the contract, it is still much more likely that the parties intended any purported assignment to be of no effect, rather than that it would simply give rise to a claim for damages against the purported assignor. Indeed, this was exactly how the House of Lords construed a similar clause in the *Linden Gardens* case.

3.235 It is theoretically possible that such a clause might be intended to have both the effects described above – so that the purported assignment is a nullity and would also give rise to a claim for damages. This is, however, an unlikely construction and it is, in any event, difficult to see what loss would be suffered by the other party if the assignment were a nullity.

3.236 In practice, therefore, and subject to the precise terms of the contract concerned, a prohibition on assignment is likely to be construed so that any purported assignment in breach of it is a nullity, but is unlikely, of itself, to give rise to a claim for damages or a power to terminate the contract.

The extent of the restriction

3.237 The extent of the restriction is also a matter of construction, in the context of the contract as a whole and in the light of the matrix of surrounding facts at the time it was entered into. A prohibition on assignment will not necessarily prevent other forms of transfer, such as a charge or a trust. If the clause only prevents assignments of the benefit of the contract, in principle, there is no reason why the benefit of the contract should not be charged in favour of a creditor or held on trust for the creditor by way of security, particularly if no notice of the charge is given to the counterparty, so that he can continue to deal with the party with whom he has contracted.

3.238 If it is intended to prohibit all forms of transfer, the prohibition should make it clear that it extends to any assignment or charge or to the creation of any other type of proprietary interest over all or some of the rights under the contract, in each case whether it is absolute or by way of security.

3.239 There is one further issue which is of particular concern in relation to assignments by way of security. It is clear that a properly drafted prohibition on assignment will mean that, as between the counterparty and the purported assignor, the purported assignment is a nullity. But what is the position as between the assignor and the assignee? The main purpose of an equitable mortgage or charge over the benefit of a contract is to give the creditor priority over the monetary proceeds of the contract in the insolvency of the debtor. If the contract contains a prohibition on assignment, any purported assignment cannot affect the counterparty, and any notice of the purported assignment would be of no effect. But, to the extent that the debtor receives the proceeds of the contract, and they remain identifiable in his hands, is the purported mortgage or charge effective to give the creditor a security interest in the monies, or is that also nullified by the prohibition on assignment?

3.240 The purpose of a prohibition on assignment is to protect the counterparty from having to deal with anyone other than the person with whom he has contracted and to ensure that his rights against the debtor are not adversely affected by an assignment. It would not be contrary to that purpose for identifiable proceeds of the contract, in the hands of the debtor, to be subject to a security interest in favour of the creditor. It is likely that a court would try to construe the prohibition on assignment as being intended to have effect only between the parties to the contract.

3.241 In a different context, this was the conclusion reached by Lightman J and the Court of Appeal in *Don King Productions v Warren*.[120] In that case, A and B entered into a partnership. The partnership agreement provided for the assignment by A to the partnership of the benefit of certain contracts. The contracts were generally for personal services, the assignment of which is not possible as a result of public policy, and many of the contracts also expressly prohibited their assignment. The question arose whether the benefit of these contracts formed part of the partnership assets. Hardly surprisingly, in view of the obvious intention of the parties concerned, it was held that the prohibitions on assignment did not prevent the benefit of the contracts being part of the partnership assets. Lightman J held that the benefit of the agreements was held on trust, there being no prohibition in the contracts of a declaration of trust of the benefit of the contracts. This conclusion was strengthened by the fact that a declaration of trust cannot prejudice the rights of the counterparty.[121]

3.242 The *Don King* case did not involve a mortgage or charge. It nevertheless indicates that the courts are likely to construe prohibitions on assignment as only extending to acts which can prejudice the rights of the counterparty and that a declaration of trust over the proceeds will not affect the counterparty and should therefore be effective.

3.243 Two further questions remain. The first is whether a purported mortgage or charge over the benefit of a contract which is incapable of being mortgaged or charged will automatically take effect as a trust of the benefit of the contract or its proceeds, or whether an express declaration of trust is required. If there is any doubt about the assignability of the contract, it is clearly preferable for there to be an express declaration of trust but, if there is not, will one be implied? A trust was implied on the facts of the *Don King* case, although that did not involve a security arrangement. In principle, a trust ought to be implied on the basis that it gives effect to the intention of the parties to create security in a manner which avoids prejudicing the counterparty. But the position is not free from doubt.

---

120 [2000] Ch 291.
121 [2000] Ch 291 at 321.

3.244 The second question is whether the courts would give effect to a provision of a contract which made it clear that it was intended not only to nullify the effect of an assignment as between the parties to the contract, but also to nullify any arrangements between the debtor and a third party. In the *Linden Gardens* case, the House of Lords held that a prohibition on assignment was not contrary to public policy because a party could have a genuine commercial interest in ensuring that he dealt only with the party with whom he contracted. It is difficult to see what genuine commercial interest the counterparty could have in the way in which the proceeds of the contract are dealt with between his contracting party and a third party. And in principle it is also difficult to see how the terms of a contract between the counterparty and the debtor could affect the ability of the debtor to create security over the proceeds of the contract, which are his assets. But, again, there is no authority on the point.

Restrictions – summary

3.245 The position concerning contractual restrictions on assignment may be summarised as follows:

- A prohibition or restriction on assigning a contractual intangible is effective in accordance with its terms, regardless of whether the purported assignee was aware of the prohibition.
- In construing such a prohibition, a court will consider its purpose, which is likely to be that the counterparty does not wish to have to deal with anyone other than the person with whom he has contracted.
- As a result, a clause which purports to create a charge or a trust over the benefit of the contract is unlikely to offend against a prohibition on assignment if it only affects the monetary proceeds of the contract in the hands of the debtor and therefore does not adversely affect the counterparty.

The effect of an assignment or charge on the counterparty

3.246 When a creditor obtains a mortgage or charge over the debtor's rights against the counterparty, the basic principle is that the creditor obtains no better rights against the counterparty than the debtor. The creditor's rights are derivative (in the sense that they are derived from the debtor's rights), and the counterparty should not, therefore, be adversely affected by the assignment.

3.247 An example of this principle is *Tooth v Hallett*.[122] D, who had entered into a building contract with T, assigned the benefit of the contract to C by way of security. D breached the contract and later became bankrupt. D's trustee in bankruptcy completed the building contract with his own money in a way which was provided for in the contract, and was then paid by T. As a result, nothing further was owing to D under the contract. C requested T to pay him the amount which he had paid to D. The Court of Appeal in Chancery held

---

122 (1869) LR 4 Ch App 242.

that C was in no better position than D; and, since D was not entitled to any further money under the contract, neither was C. In the words of Selwyn LJ:[123]

'The thing, therefore, which was assigned to [C] was not any absolute property of [D], but that which was coming to him under the building contract, and was, therefore, subject to the conditions of that contract ...'

3.248 It is, therefore, clear that the creditor can obtain no more under the assigned contract than the debtor could have obtained. There is, however, a further protection for the counterparty as a result of the principle that the assignee of an intangible takes his interest 'subject to equities'. This has been the position in relation to equitable assignments since at least the early eighteenth century;[124] and statutory assignments are expressed to take effect 'subject to equities having priority over the right of the assignee'.[125] What this means is that if the counterparty has any defences (such as rights of set-off) against the debtor, then he will also be able to enforce them against the creditor. In other words, the counterparty should not be put at a disadvantage as a result of the debtor having assigned the benefit of the contract to the creditor.

3.249 There is a distinction between these two principles. The principle that the creditor obtains no greater rights than the debtor under the contract is an absolute principle, which has no exceptions. If no monies are payable to the debtor under the contract, then nothing is payable to the creditor either. The second principle is rather different. There might be no dispute that money is payable to the debtor under the contract, but the counterparty might have had a defence against the debtor if he had not assigned the benefit of the contract to the creditor. For instance, the counterparty might have a cross-claim against the debtor which, in the absence of the assignment, he would have been able to use as a defence to any claim by the debtor for the payment of the monies due under the contract. In such a case, the counterparty would not be denying that amounts were owing under the contract; he would be accepting that they were owing but setting up a defence, by way of set-off, to their recovery, based on his cross-claim against the debtor.

3.250 The practical importance of the distinction is that the counterparty's right to set up equities such as set-offs and other defences against the creditor is not unlimited. Once the counterparty has received notice of the assignment to the creditor, he is not able to increase the rights which he had at the time the notice was received. If he had a right of set-off against the debtor at the time he received notice of the assignment, he is entitled to enforce it against the creditor. But if he subsequently obtains a right of set-off against the debtor which is unconnected with the assigned contract, he cannot use it as a defence to a claim by the creditor. Set-offs are of particular importance in practice and are considered in more detail below.

3.251 In summary:

---

123 (1869) LR 4 Ch App 242 at 245.
124 *Coles v Jones* (1715) 2 Vern 692.
125 Law of Property Act 1925, s 136(1).

- The creditor's rights under the assigned contract can never be greater than those of the debtor.
- The counterparty is entitled, as against the creditor, to the same defences he would have had against the debtor, but those defences cannot generally be increased once the counterparty has received notice of the assignment.

3.252 The effect of the notice to the counterparty can therefore be very important, and it is considered in the next section.

Notice to the counterparty

3.253 It has been seen that a statutory assignment is not complete until notice in writing has been given to the counterparty, but that an equitable assignment is effective without notice to the counterparty. Even in the case of an equitable assignment, however, there are advantages in giving notice to the counterparty if possible. The three most important in practice are that:

- the priority of interests in many intangibles (particularly contract rights and debts) is affected by the order in which notice is given to the counterparty;
- until the counterparty receives notice of the mortgage or charge, he can obtain a good discharge by paying the debtor; and
- although the creditor takes his interest in the intangible 'subject to equities' (such as rights of set-off), they cannot be increased once notice has been given to the counterparty.

3.254 Priorities are considered in CHAPTER 7. Discharge is discussed in this section. Assignments 'subject to equities' have just been discussed and the particular issues concerning set-off are considered in the next section.

What type of notice is required?

3.255 Notice needs to be given in writing in order to obtain a statutory assignment, or if the mortgage or charge relates to an equitable interest in trust property.[126] Otherwise, there are no formal requirements. In the words of Lord Macnaghten in *William Brandt's Sons & Co v Dunlop Rubber Company*:[127]

'All that is necessary is that the debtor should be given to understand that the debt has been made over by the creditor to some third person. If the debtor ignores such a notice, he does so at his peril.'

Discharge of the counterparty

3.256 Until the counterparty receives notice of the assignment, he has the same rights against the creditor as he had against the debtor.[128] It follows that, until the counterparty has received notice of the assignment, he can obtain a

---

126 Law of Property Act 1925, ss 136(1) and 137(3).
127 [1905] AC 454 at 462.
128 *Norrish v Marshall* (1821) 5 Madd 475 at 481, per Sir John Leech V-C.

good discharge by paying the debtor or by entering into a settlement with the debtor.[129] Indeed, if this were not the case, a debtor could never safely pay his creditor.[130]

3.257 Once the counterparty has received notice of the assignment, however, he must pay the assignee, and will not obtain a good discharge by paying the assignor.[131] If, therefore, the counterparty receives notice of the assignment and nevertheless pays the debtor, he must then pay the creditor again.[132]

Set-off against assignees or chargees

3.258 It has been seen that, even though there has been an assignment of, or charge over, the benefit of the contract, the counterparty is entitled to set up against the creditor any set-offs which he would have had against the debtor until he receives notice of the assignment or charge. Once he receives notice, however, his rights change. The position was explained by James LJ in *Roxburghe v Cox*:[133]

> 'Now an assignee of a chose in action, according to my view of the law, takes subject to all rights of set-off and other defences which were available against the assignor, subject only to this exception, that after notice of an assignment of a chose in action the debtor cannot by payment or otherwise do anything to take away or diminish the rights of the assignee as they stood at the time of the notice.'

3.259 Set-off is discussed in detail in CHAPTER 12. In this context, it is important to distinguish between those rights of the counterparty which are provided for in the assigned contract and those which are not.

3.260 It has been seen that the creditor's rights to an assigned intangible are derivative of those of the debtor and, accordingly, where the intangible is a contract, the creditor's rights are limited in the same way as those of the debtor. If no monies are payable to the debtor under the contract, then they will not be payable to the creditor either. This principle also applies where the contract contains netting provisions (ie where the amount payable under the contract is a net sum derived from various transactions between the parties) and where the contract contains an express right of set-off (ie where it is agreed that cross-claims between the parties will be set off against each other, with only the balance being payable). Because the creditor's rights under the contract cannot exceed those of the debtor, the counterparty is entitled to rely on contractual netting or set-off provisions against the creditor in the same way as he would against the debtor.

3.261 The statement of James LJ referred to above does not apply to such cases. What it does is to describe the limits of the circumstances in which the

---

129 *Stocks v Dobson* (1853) 4 De GM&G 11.
130 *Stocks v Dobson* (1853) 4 De GM&G 11 at 16, per Turner LJ.
131 *William Brandt's Sons & Co v Dunlop Rubber Co Limited* [1905] AC 454.
132 *Jones v Farrell* (1857) 1 De G&J 208.
133 (1880) 17 Ch D 520 at 526.

counterparty can rely on non-contractual rights of set-off against the creditor once he has given notice of the assignment or charge. As will be seen in **CHAPTER 12**, in the absence of insolvency proceedings (for which there are different rules, which are not relevant in this context) there are broadly two circumstances in which one party can set up a cross-claim as a defence to a claim by the other.

3.262 If A is suing B for the payment of money, B can use a monetary cross-claim against A as a defence to A's claim if B's claim against A:

- is for a liquidated or certain amount (a statutory set-off); or
- arises out of the same transaction and is so closely connected with A's claim against B that it would be unfair for A to recover from B without taking B's claim into account (an equitable set-off).[134]

The principle

3.263 There were a number of reported cases concerning set-off against assignees which were decided towards the end of the nineteenth century. Some of the statements in those cases led it to be considered that different rules might apply to set-off against assignees than applied to set-off between the original parties the contract. They indicated that the counterparty might have greater rights of set-off against an assignee than he would have had against the assignor. That would have been a surprising result, and it was rejected by the House of Lords in *Bank of Boston Connecticut v European Grain & Shipping*.[135] In that case, D assigned all of the earnings of a vessel to C by way of security. D chartered the vessel to T under a voyage charterparty and C gave notice of the assignment to T. During the voyage, the vessel was arrested and, as a result, T terminated the charterparty and completed the voyage on another vessel. The charterparty provided for the freight to be prepaid and C, as assignee of D's rights under the contract, sued T for payment of the freight. T denied liability on the basis that the costs of completing the voyage on a different vessel had exceeded the freight payable under the contract.

3.264 On the construction of the charterparty, the House of Lords held that D became entitled to the freight before the termination of the charterparty and that, on normal contractual principles, the termination did not affect the accrued right to freight. If the freight had not been payable under the contract, then C could have had no greater right than D to the freight.

3.265 But T had two further arguments. In the first place, it argued that it had a right, as against D, to set off against the freight the damages recoverable against D for breach of the charterparty and that it therefore had the same right against C. If it had been any other type of contract, T would have been successful on this ground because it would have had an equitable set-off against D, it being unfair for T to have to pay the freight without having the closely connected cross-claim arising under the same contract being taken into

---

134 See part 4 of **CHAPTER 12** (**12.76**ff).
135 [1989] AC 1056.

account. Unfortunately for T, however, there is a special rule which applies to freight, the effect of which is that no such equitable set-offs are available against freight.[136]

3.266 T's second argument was that the late nineteenth-century cases referred to above had the effect that T had a right of set-off against C, even though it did not have one against D. It was contended that T had an independent right of set-off against C as a result of the fact that the claim for freight and the cross-claim for damages for breach of contract flowed out of the same contract and were inseparably connected with each other. The House of Lords also rejected this argument, holding that the nineteenth-century cases were simply examples of cases where the counterparty would have had a right of set-off against the assignee because it had a right of set-off against the assignor.

3.267 It is now clear that the counterparty's rights of set-off against the assignee are not independent rights, but are derived from its rights against the assignor, and that they can therefore be no greater than the rights of set-off which the assignor would have had in the absence of the assignment. The House of Lords approved the judgment of Hobhouse J at first instance,[137] who said:[138]

'The correct principle is that a debtor is entitled to rely upon all defences which would be valid defences if raised against the assignor in respect of the assigned right.'

3.268 Although the counterparty can have no greater rights of set-off against the creditor than he would have had against the debtor, the converse is not true. The counterparty can find himself in a worse position, as regards set-off, against the creditor than he would have been in against the debtor. This is because, as James LJ indicated in *Roxburgh v Cox*,[139] once the counterparty has received notice of the assignment, his rights of set-off crystallise. In accordance with the decision of the House of Lords in *The Bank of Boston Connecticut* case, therefore, it is necessary to establish what rights of set-off the creditor would have had against the assignor at the date he receives notice of the assignment.

3.269 It has been seen that the counterparty would have had a right to set off a cross-claim against the debtor in two principal situations:

● where the cross-claim was liquidated or of a certain amount; or
● where the cross-claim arose out of the same transaction and was so closely connected with it that it would be unfair to allow one to be recovered without taking into account the other.

How have these principles been applied in relation to assignees and chargees?

---

136 See part 4 of **CHAPTER 12** (**12.76ff**). The unfairness of this special rule is apparent from the decision in this case.
137 [1987] 1 Lloyd's Rep 239 at 254–257.
138 [1987] 1 Lloyd's Rep 239 at 257.
139 (1880) 17 Ch D 520.

Application of the principle

3.270   The first principle is illustrated by *Christie v Taunton, Delmard, Lane & Co.*[140] In that case, D charged to C certain shares issued by T. The shares were not fully paid. On 3 November, T made a call on D for payment of part of the nominal value of the shares, the call being payable on 20 November. On 6 November, C gave T notice of the charge and further calls were then made on the shares. Sterling J held that T could set-off against C the amount of the first call. Even though the call was not actually payable before T received notice of the assignment, it had accrued due before that notice had been received. It was a liquidated sum which must become payable at a specified future date, and it was therefore capable of being set off. The later calls could not, however, be set off, because they were not made until after T had received notice of the charge.

3.271   An example of the second principle is *Government of Newfoundland v Newfoundland Railway Co.*[141] In that case, D had contracted to build and maintain a railway for T, in consideration for which T agreed to make certain payments to D. D broke the contract, and T refused to make any further payments. D had assigned part of its rights under the contract to C by way of security, and it was assumed that notice of the assignment had been given to T. Both D and C then sued T for payment under the contract.

3.272   The first question was whether anything was payable under the contract because, if it was not, neither D nor C would be entitled to anything. The Privy Council held that, on the construction of the contract, T did have a liability to make payments to D. T nevertheless argued that it had the right to set off against D its unliquidated claim for damages for breach of contract. C admitted that T could set up the cross-claim as a defence against D, but argued that C was in a different position. It had given notice of its assignment to T and was therefore free of any set-offs which had not then arisen.

3.273   The Privy Council rejected this argument. They held that T's cross-claim against D was 'intertwined in the closest manner'[142] with D's rights against T under the contract and that it was a claim 'flowing out of and inseparably connected with the dealings and transactions which also give rise to the subject of the assignment'.[143] As a result, T had an equitable set-off against D, and C could therefore be in no better position than D.[144]

3.274   If the counterparty cannot rely on either of these two principles, it will not have a right of set-off against the assignee. The types of situation in which this can arise are illustrated in two cases.

3.275   In *Watson v Mid Wales Railway Co*,[145] T owed money to D, which D assigned to C, notice of the assignment then being given to T. After it had

---

140   [1893] 2 Ch 175.
141   (1888) 13 App Cas 199.
142   (1888) 13 App Cas 199 at 212.
143   (1888) 13 App Cas 199 at 213.
144   (1888) 13 App Cas 199 at 210.
145   (1867) LR 2 CP 593.

received the notice, T leased certain premises to D in respect of which D defaulted on the payment of the rent. C sued T on the assigned debt and T claimed to set off the arrears of rent owing by D. The Court of Common Pleas held that no such set-off was available because:

- the cross-claim had arisen after T had received notice of the assignment; and
- it did not arise out of matters connected with the assigned debt.

3.276 A more recent example of a case where a counterparty can be prejudiced by an assignment is provided by *Business Computers v Anglo-African Leasing*.[146] D entered into two transactions with T as a result of which D was owed money for computers bought by T. In a third transaction between D and T, D sold a computer to T and then leased it back. D had created a debenture over all of its present and future assets in favour of its bank, C. A receiver was appointed by C, and notice of the appointment of the receiver was given to T. At that time, T was owed a small amount of money by D. Subsequently, however, the third transaction was terminated and D became liable to pay damages to T for breach of the contract. It was accepted that the monies owing by D to T at the time of the notice of the appointment of the receiver could be set off against the money owing by T to D, but the question arose whether T could also set off the damages claim for breach of the third transaction.

3.277 Templeman J held that T did not have a right of set-off in relation to that amount. The right to damages arose when a contract was terminated, which occurred after T had received notice of the appointment of the receivers. It arose under a separate contract which was not closely connected with the earlier two contracts; and accordingly there was no right of set-off. It is not possible to set off a claim which is contingent at the time the notice of assignment is received unless there is a sufficiently close connection that an equitable set-off is available.

3.278 The position was summarised by Templeman J as follows:[147]

'The result of the relevant authorities is that a debt which accrues due before notice of an assignment is received, whether or not it is payable before that date, or a debt which arises out of the same contract as that which gives rise to the assigned debt, or is closely connected with that contract, may be set-off against the assignee. But a debt which is neither accrued nor connected may not be set-off even though it arises from a contract made before the assignment.'

3.279 This case is also important in showing that, where a floating charge is created, it is notice of the appointment of the receiver (which crystallises the floating charge), rather than notice of the floating charge itself, which is relevant.

---

146 [1977] 1 WLR 578.
147 [1977] 1 WLR 578 at 585.

3.280   There is one case which is difficult to reconcile with the others. In *Stoddart v Union Trust*,[148] A entered into a contract with B to buy a newspaper, part of the consideration remaining outstanding. B assigned the benefit of that contract to C, who gave notice to A. C then sued A for the recovery of the money remaining outstanding under the contract and A's defence was that it was induced to enter into the contract by B's fraud and, as a result, was owed damages in excess of the amount payable under the contract.

3.281   On the face of it, it would seem that there was a sufficiently close connection between the price payable under the contract and the cross-claim for damages that an equitable set-off should have been available. The Court of Appeal, however, held that no set-off was available. The reasoning of the court is not entirely easy to understand. The most convincing judgment was given by Kennedy LJ, who said that the cross-claim did not arise out of the contract but was a personal claim for fraud, behind the contract, but it is difficult to understand the ratio of the case. All members of the Court of Appeal stressed that A did not attempt to rescind the contract for fraud and, if he had done so, he would have succeeded. It is probably therefore best seen as a case where, on the basis of its own particular facts, an equitable set-off was not available. It should certainly not be regarded as a precedent for later cases.

Effect on the counterparty: summary

3.282   Where the benefit of a contract is assigned or charged by a debtor to a creditor, its effect on the counterparty may be summarised as follows:

- Although notice to the counterparty is a prerequisite of a statutory assignment, it is not necessary for the creation of a valid equitable assignment or charge.
- The creditor will, nevertheless, obtain advantages if notice is given to the counterparty. In particular:
  - it will improve his priority position as against third parties;
  - it will prevent the counterparty from being able to get a good discharge by paying the debtor; and
  - it will prevent further rights of set-off being created in favour of the counterparty.
- The creditor's rights against the counterparty are derived from those of the debtor. If no monies are owing to the debtor under the contract, or the counterparty has a contractual netting arrangement or contractual right of set-off against the debtor, the creditor will be in no better position than the debtor.
- If monies are payable under the contract by the counterparty to the debtor, the counterparty will only be able to set off, as against the creditor, a cross-claim which he has against the debtor if he would have been able to do so against the debtor at the time he received notice of the assignment or charge. This will only be the case if:
  - the cross-claim was liquidated at that time (although it need not necessarily have been payable then); or

---

148   [1912] 1 KB 181.

— the cross-claim arises out of the same transaction and is so closely connected with it that it would be unfair for it not to be taken into account.

Financial collateral

3.283 There are special rules for security over financial collateral. These derive from the EU Directive on financial collateral arrangements,[149] which was brought into force in England by the Financial Collateral Arrangements (No 2) Regulations 2003.[150]

3.284 The purpose of the Directive was to 'contribute to the integration and cost-efficiency of the financial market as well as to the stability of the financial system in the Community' by providing an EU-wide regime 'for the provision of securities and cash as collateral under both security interest and title transfer structures'.[151] It would do this by removing obstacles in the way of using cash (by which it meant amounts standing to the credit of accounts) and securities in transactions on the international financial markets, whether they were structured as secured transactions or as outright title transfer arrangements.[152] What lay behind the Directive was a concern that, in some continental European jurisdictions, the effectiveness of such arrangements was in doubt. The purpose of the Directive was therefore to do away with formal requirements for the creation of financial collateral arrangements, to limit the application of insolvency law and to validate close-out netting provisions in relation to them, and generally to enable transactions concerning cash and securities to be effected with greater certainty in the international financial markets.

3.285 Many of the Directive's requirements were already provided for in English law. It already gave effect to transfer of title arrangements (such as repos and stock lending arrangements) in accordance with their terms, without recharacterising them as security arrangements. It also gave effect to bilateral contractual netting arrangements and to set-offs both outside and within insolvency procedures. And it imposed few formal requirements for the creation of security. The main changes which the Directive required to be made to English law concerned the abolition of the requirement to register charges over financial collateral and the disapplication of those provisions of insolvency law which restricted the rights of a creditor with security over financial collateral.

3.286 These modifications to English law were brought into effect in England by the Regulations but, in one respect, they went much further than was required by the Directive. Although the Directive was aimed at transactions in

---

149 Directive 2002/47/EC of the European Parliament and of the Council of 6 June 2002 on financial collateral arrangements.
150 SI 2003/3226.
151 Directive 2002/47/EC, Recital 3.
152 The distinction between secured transactions and outright transfer arrangements is discussed in part 3 of CHAPTER 6 (6.32ff).

the financial markets, and only required its provisions to be applied if at least one of the parties to the arrangement was a body such as a public authority, a central bank, a financial institution subject to prudential supervision or a clearing house,[153] the Regulations are not so restricted. They apply in any transaction unless one or more of the parties is an individual.

Financial collateral arrangement

3.287   The key to the Regulations is the meaning of the expression 'financial collateral arrangement'. A financial collateral arrangement can be either a 'security financial collateral arrangement' or a 'title transfer financial collateral arrangement'. As their names suggest, a security financial collateral arrangement is a transaction concerning financial collateral which is structured as a secured transaction (for instance, by means of a mortgage, charge or pledge), whereas a title transfer financial collateral arrangement is an arrangement which is structured as an outright transfer of financial collateral (such as a repo). The distinction between these two types of arrangement is discussed in part 3 of **CHAPTER 6 (6.32ff)**.

3.288   Both types of financial collateral arrangement have certain features in common. They both require there to be an agreement in writing between parties, none of which is an individual. In both cases, the purpose of the arrangement must be to secure (or, in the case of a title transfer arrangement, to 'cover')[154] obligations owing to one of the parties to the arrangement. And they must both involve 'financial collateral'. This is defined to mean either 'cash' or 'financial instruments'. In this context, cash means money credited to an account or a similar claim for the repayment of money. Financial instruments means shares and equivalent securities, bonds and other debt instruments which are tradable on the capital market, and certain other types of securities.

3.289   Thereafter, the two types of arrangement diverge. As would be expected, it is a requirement of a title transfer financial collateral arrangement that one party transfers outright the legal and beneficial title in financial collateral to the other on the basis that title to equivalent financial collateral will be re-transferred; and it is a requirement of a security financial collateral arrangement that a security interest (such as a mortgage, charge or pledge) is created over the financial collateral. In the case of a security financial collateral arrangement, however, there is a further requirement – the financial collateral must be:

> '... delivered, transferred, held, registered or otherwise designated so as to be in the possession or under the control of the collateral-taker or a person acting on its behalf; any right of the collateral-provider to substitute

---

153   Directive 2002/47/EC, art 1(2).

154   This rather clumsy expression is used because an outright transfer of an asset does not actually 'secure' anything.

equivalent financial collateral or withdraw excess financial collateral shall not prevent the financial collateral being in the possession or under the control of the collateral-taker.'[155]

There is no definition of what is meant by 'possession' (a curious expression to use in the context of intangible assets) or 'control' in the Regulations. The uncertainty creates particular problems in the context of floating charges, but may also be an issue in the case of a fixed charge.

3.290 It will be seen from this discussion that there is a substantial amount of uncertainty about the application of the Regulations. In particular, there are two areas of doubt. The first concerns the meaning of the expressions 'cash' and 'financial instruments' (which are the two constituent elements of financial collateral). It is clear, in broad terms, what types of asset they are intended to apply to but, at the edges, there is uncertainty as to their precise application.

3.291 Even more difficult is to establish what is meant by the requirement that the financial collateral is in the possession or control of the creditor. This is not a requirement of a title transfer financial collateral arrangement but is likely to be a material concern to those relying on security financial collateral arrangements, particularly where the security could be characterised as a floating charge.

3.292 If the asset concerned is not 'financial collateral' or, in the case of a security arrangement, the financial collateral is not in the possession or control of the creditor, the Regulations will not apply. In view of this uncertainty, it is clearly preferable not to rely on the Regulations when structuring a transaction (albeit that they could be helpful in the event the security has to be enforced).

The effect of the Regulations

3.293 Where the Regulations do apply, their effect is:

- to remove formal requirements for the creation of security other than the requirement of writing;
- to remove any requirement for registration under the companies legislation;
- to provide certain additional rights of enforcement;
- to remove many of the provisions of insolvency law which restrict the rights of secured creditors;
- to amend the law concerning netting and set-off in insolvency; and
- to alter the conflict of laws rules concerning cross-border security.

3.294 Each of these matters is considered in the appropriate chapter of this book, but the principal effect of the Regulations can be summarised as follows.

- *Registration*: Charges over shares have never been registrable at Companies House. There has always been some doubt about the

---

155 Financial Collateral Arrangements (No 2) Regulations 2003, SI 2003/3226, reg 3, definition of 'security financial collateral arrangement'.

registrability of charges over bank accounts and over debt securities, and these are now resolved if the transaction is covered by the Regulations. In such a case, no registration is required. But the uncertainty of their application means that, in practice, charges over financial collateral are likely to continue to be registered in the ordinary way, at least in transactions which do not involve the wholesale financial markets (for which the Directive was really intended).

• *Insolvency*: The main effect of the Regulations is likely to be their effect on insolvency law. In cases to which the Regulations do not apply, a secured creditor's power to enforce its security is limited in the debtor's administration. Where the creditor has a floating charge, its rights are further limited in two ways: first, because a floating charge is more vulnerable than a fixed charge to attack under the claw-back provisions in a liquidation or administration of the debtor; and, secondly, because the floating chargee's rights are subject to certain other claims (such as preferential claims and a proportion of unsecured claims). Where the Regulations apply, many of these provisions are not applicable. The Regulations also contain certain other relaxations of insolvency law for the benefit of the secured creditor concerned, although financial collateral continues to be subject to the other claw-back provisions in an insolvency (such as preferences).

These changes will place the holder of security over financial collateral in a materially better position than the holder of security over other types of asset. That might be appropriate in the wholesale financial markets, but it is hard to see why, in any other case, a lender with security over a bank account or securities should be in a better position than one with security over other assets, such as land.

• *Other matters*: The other matters with which the Regulations deal are likely to be of less importance in practice. They do away with certain formalities (which were unlikely to apply in any event), give certain (relatively minor) additional rights of enforcement (which are, again, really only appropriate in the context of the capital markets), alter netting and set-off arrangements in an insolvency to a very limited extent and establish a particular conflict of laws rule which will apply to financial collateral in a cross-border transaction.

Part 6: THE EQUITY OF REDEMPTION

The development of the equity of redemption

3.295 It is in the very nature of a security interest that the debtor is entitled to recover the secured asset on payment of the secured liability. This right is often referred to as an 'equity of redemption' (although, in many cases, it will be a legal, rather than an equitable, right). It constitutes a proprietary interest in the secured asset, although it is, of course, subject to the proprietary interest of the creditor.

3.296   The concept of the equity of redemption was developed in relation to legal mortgages of land, although it now extends to all legal mortgages. Until 1925, a legal mortgage of land was constituted by the transfer of the legal title to the land from the debtor to the creditor. At common law, if the debtor did not repay the secured liabilities on the due date for payment, the creditor became the unencumbered owner of the land, although he was still entitled to pursue the debtor for the unpaid debt. But, if the debtor applied to the Lord Chancellor, he would be given the ability to recover the land on payment of the secured liability, even if that occurred after the due date for payment. This right, which started off as a personal right against the creditor, became a proprietary right because the Lord Chancellor allowed the debtor to redeem not only against the original creditor, but also against anyone else who acquired the land unless he did so for value and without notice of the debtor's right. Unless the creditor had enforced the security by sale (in which event the equity of redemption was transferred to the sale proceeds), the debtor only lost his equity of redemption when the court ordered foreclosure of the mortgage (as to which, see **CHAPTER 8**).[156]

3.297   As Lindley MR said in *Santley v Wilde*:[157] 'The right to redeem is not a personal right, but an equitable estate or interest in the property mortgaged.' Its purpose is to ensure that the debtor continues to have rights in the secured asset after it had been transferred to the creditor, and that those rights are not forfeited simply because the secured liabilities are not paid on time. It is, in essence, a means of restricting the forfeiture of the debtor's rights in the secured asset and, although it cuts across freedom of contract, it is essentially intended to give effect to the underlying substantive bargain between the parties – that the mortgage is a security interest, not an outright one.

3.298   There is less need for intervention by the courts of equity where the security interest consists of an equitable mortgage or charge. In such a case, the debtor retains his legal title to the asset, which he continues to be able to enforce, subject to the creditor's rights. As a result:

● In the case of a legal mortgage, the creditor obtains the legal title to the secured asset (or, if it is land, an equivalent statutory right) whilst the debtor retains an equitable interest in it (or, in the case of land, a legal interest).
● In the case of an equitable mortgage or charge, the creditor obtains an equitable interest in the secured asset, whilst the debtor retains legal title to it.
● In each case, the rights of the debtor and the creditor in the secured asset are proprietary, the debtor's rights being subject to those of the creditor.

Extensions of the principle

3.299   If the courts of equity had stopped there, this principle would have caused no real problems, but it has been extended in two ways, one of which still creates uncertainties in practice.

---

156 The development of the equity of redemption is explained by Viscount Haldane LC in *Kreglinger v New Patagonia Meat and Cold Storage Company* [1914] AC 25 at 35.
157 [1899] 2 Ch 474 at 475.

3.300 The first extension, which is no longer of any practical significance, was to restrict the creditor from taking any 'collateral advantage' of the debtor. For many years, usury legislation was in force which restricted the amount of interest which creditors could charge on loans. The courts of equity extended the usury laws by taking into account not just interest, but any other benefit which the creditor was to obtain from the transaction. They set aside such 'collateral advantages' if they had the effect that the creditor's total benefit from the transaction exceeded the interest to which he was entitled under the usury legislation. The usury legislation was abolished in the middle of the nineteenth century and, as a result, the equitable extension also fell away. As a result, there is now no special equitable rule for mortgages. In the absence of statutory provision (for instance, under Part VIII of the Consumer Credit Act 1974 or under the Insolvency Act 1986[158]), such collateral advantages can only be set aside if they would render the security ineffective in accordance with general equitable principles.[159]

Clogs on the equity of redemption

3.301 The second extension of the principle is still with us, and can cause problems in practice. It is best explained by Lindley MR in *Santley v Wilde*:[160]

'The principle is this: a mortgage is a conveyance of land or an assignment of chattels as a security for the payment of a debt or the discharge of some other obligation for which it is given. This is the idea of a mortgage: and the security is redeemable on the payment or discharge of such debt or obligation, any provision to the contrary notwithstanding ... Any provision inserted to prevent redemption on payment or performance of the debt or obligation for which the security was given is what is meant by a clog or fetter on the equity of redemption and is therefore void. It follows from this, that "once a mortgage always a mortgage" ...'

3.302 Lord Lindley drove the point home in *Bradley v Carritt*,[161] when he said:

'The restoration of the mortgaged property to the mortgagor on performance of the obligation to secure which it was mortgaged is the grand object which Courts of Equity have always steadily kept in view and insisted on, all agreements to the contrary notwithstanding.'

3.303 Most of the cases concern legal mortgages, but the principle also applies to equitable mortgages and charges,[162] including floating charges.[163]

---

158 Sections 244 and 343.
159 *Noakes v Rice* [1902] AC 24 at 33, per Lord Davey; *Kreglinger v New Patagonia Meat and Cold Storage Company* [1914] AC 25.
160 [1899] 2 Ch 474 at 474–475.
161 [1903] AC 253 at 279.
162 *Kreglinger v New Patagonia Meat and Cold Storage Company* [1914] AC 25 at 52, per Lord Parker.
163 [1914] AC 25 at 41, per Viscount Haldane LC; *Knightsbridge Estates v Byrne* [1940] AC 613.

3.304 In spite of Lord Lindley's very clear statements of the principle, there is no doubt that the approach of the courts to this issue has altered over the years. The early cases concerned mortgages of land created by individual landowners, and the judges were very protective of them. The repeal of the usury laws and the increased recognition of the importance of freedom of contract in the nineteenth century led to a series of cases, decided in the 15 years leading up to the First World War, which tested the boundaries of the doctrine. These cases, which ran from *Santley v Wilde*[164] in 1899 to *Kreglinger v New Patagonia Meat and Cold Storage Co*[165] in 1913 saw a retrenchment of the previous doctrine, but there was still a divergence of views as to its scope. This came to a head in *Bradley v Carritt*,[166] in which Lords Lindley and Macnaghten set out their respective views – Lord Lindley for a more limited doctrine, Lord Macnaghten for a more expansive one. On that occasion, Lord Macnaghten's views held sway (by a majority of three to two) but that victory was short-lived. In the *Kreglinger* case[167] in 1913, the House of Lords adopted Lord Lindley's approach in preference to that of Lord Macnaghten. The sentiments which give rise to this approach are explained in a statement of Lord Shand in *Bradley v Carritt*:[168]

> 'My Lords, I confess I think it was unfortunate for the law that the rule, now called a principle, "once a mortgage always a mortgage", with all its consequences, was ever carried further than was necessary for the purpose of relieving borrowers from forfeiture of their property on non-payment of the sum lent on a fixed day.'

3.305 The approach of the courts since the *Kreglinger* case has tended to limit the effect of the doctrine,[169] although there have still been cases where the courts have struck down contractual arrangements as a result of the principle.[170] There have been few recent cases, but it is suggested that there is little doubt that the pendulum continues to swing towards freedom of contract and against debtor protection, at least where the debtor is not a consumer (not least because consumer protection for debtors is now accorded by various statutes, particularly the Consumer Credit Act 1974).

Restrictions on the secured asset after redemption

3.306 As a result, it is not a straightforward exercise to establish the current limits of the principle. One thing is, nevertheless, clear. As Lord Lindley indicated in the two judgments quoted above, any provision which is part of the secured transaction (ie a transaction which involves the creation of a mortgage or charge) and which restricts the debtor's ability to use the secured asset after the security has been redeemed, is ineffective. The effect of this prohibition can be illustrated by two examples.

---

164 [1899] 2 Ch 474.
165 [1914] AC 25.
166 [1903] AC 253.
167 [1914] AC 25.
168 [1903] AC 253 at 262.
169 See, for instance, *Knightsbridge Estates v Byrne* [1940] AC 613.
170 See, for instance, *Lewis v Frank Love* [1961] 1 WLR 261.

3.307 The first involves undertakings by the debtor which are intended to extend beyond the period of the security. In *Noakes v Rice*,[171] a mortgage of a leasehold public house contained an undertaking by the debtor that he would only sell certain beverages if they were purchased from the creditor. The undertaking was expressed to continue not just during the period of the mortgage but throughout the continuance of the term of the debtor's lease of the public house. The House of Lords decided that, once the debtor had redeemed the security, this contractual provision could have no further effect because it was a clog on the debtor's equity of redemption. It would have prevented him from getting back the mortgaged property unencumbered.

3.308 This principle does not apply if the undertaking is contained in a transaction which is, in substance, not part of the secured transaction[172] or if the undertaking does not affect the secured assets (for instance, if it is a personal undertaking by the debtor).[173]

3.309 The second illustration of the principle concerns options to purchase. If, as part of the secured transaction, the creditor is granted an option to purchase the secured asset, the option is void, because it prevents the debtor from recovering the mortgaged asset once the secured liability has been paid. In *Samuel v Jarrah Timber and Wood Paving Corporation*,[174] a corporate debtor borrowed money on the security of its debenture stock, on terms that the creditor would have an option to purchase the debenture stock at an agreed price. The House of Lords decided that the option was void because it 'prevents the mortgagor from getting back his property on paying off what is due on his security'.[175] Their Lordships reached the decision with regret. They clearly thought that a perfectly fair bargain between the parties ought to have been enforceable. But they were bound not to enforce it because it offended against the rule concerning clogs on the equity of redemption. The same approach was taken to an option to purchase the secured asset by Plowman J in *Lewis v Frank Love* in the 1960s.[176]

3.310 This principle does not apply if the option is granted as part of a separate transaction entered into after the secured transaction.[177] Although there are dicta which suggest that the principle does not apply where the mortgage and the option are entered into by separate documents one day apart,[178] it would be unwise to assume that the problem is solved simply by separate documents entered into at different times. The test is whether the mortgage and the option are part of the same transaction, and that is a matter

---

171 [1902] AC 24.
172 *Reeve v Lisle* [1902] AC 461.
173 *Kreglinger v New Patagonia Meat and Cold Storage Company* [1914] AC 25.
174 [1904] AC 323.
175 [1904] AC 323 at 329, per Lord Lindley.
176 [1961] 1 WLR 261.
177 *Reeve v Lyle* [1902] AC 461.
178 *Samuel v Jarrah Timber and Wood Paving Corporation* [1904] AC 323 at 325, per Earl of Halsbury LC.

of substance, rather than one of form.[179] If the transaction is, in substance, a secured transaction, the fact that the option is contained in a separate document entered into on a different day is unlikely to save it. But if, on its true construction, there are two independent transactions, or if the transaction is in substance not a secured transaction at all but (for instance) a conditional sale, the option will be enforceable.[180]

3.311　The safest course is not to combine a secured loan with an option to purchase the subject matter of the security. If the main purpose of the transaction is a purchase, rather than a loan, but it is contemplated that there will be an initial loan, the best course is to structure the transaction as a purchase and to avoid taking security over the subject matter of the purchase.

Postponing redemption

3.312　In spite of the doubts of various judges about the sense of the principle, it has been seen that it is still the case that a provision of a secured transaction will be set aside if its effect is to encumber the secured assets once they have been redeemed by the debtor. This principle only operates if the debtor is able to redeem the security in accordance with its terms.

3.313　The more difficult question is the extent to which the creditor can be forced to accept a redemption in circumstances where it is not provided for in the documentation. There is authority for the proposition that a security interest granted by an individual cannot be irredeemable, and that a provision which prevents the debtor from redeeming for an unreasonable period is also void.[181] There is considerable doubt whether these cases would still be followed, even in relation to an individual debtor, particularly where the loan is made available for a long period and the creditor is unable to accelerate repayment in the absence of an event of default.[182] But, if there is still the vestige of a restriction on the irredeemability of security created by individuals, it is clear from the decision of the House of Lords in *Knightsbridge Estates v Byrne*[183] that, in view of s 193 of the Companies Act 1985,[184] there is no such restriction where the debtor is a company.

Summary

3.314　The position with regard to the debtor's equity of redemption may be summarised as follows:

179　*Kreglinger v New Patagonia Meat and Cold Storage Company* [1914] AC 25 at 39, per Viscount Haldane LC.

180　*Samuel v Jarrah Timber and Wood Paving Corporation* [1904] AC 323 at 328, per Lord Lindley.

181　*Morgan v Jeffreys* [1910] 1 Ch 620, Ch D; *Fairclough v Swan Brewery Company* [1912] AC 565.

182　*Kreglinger v New Patagonia Meat and Cold Storage Company* [1914] AC 25, per Viscount Haldane LC, esp at 38.

183　[1940] AC 613.

184　Although the legislation does not apply to foreign companies, it is unlikely that the court would treat them differently from English companies.

- Where a debtor has created a legal mortgage over an asset, he continues to have an equity of redemption in the asset and its proceeds. The equity of redemption is an equitable proprietary interest enabling the debtor to recover the asset on payment of the secured liabilities, even where the contractual date for redemption has passed. This right over the asset or its proceeds can be enforced until the creditor obtains a court order for foreclosure.
- A provision of a secured transaction which purports to encumber the secured assets after the security has been redeemed is void. In particular, an option for the creditor to purchase the secured assets will be void if it is part of the mortgage transaction. The principle does not apply if, in substance, the transaction is not a secured transaction but a conditional purchase or if, in substance, the option is contained in a separate transaction.
- Where the debtor is a company, a secured loan can be irredeemable, or be granted for a very long period, even though that would effectively prevent the debtor from redeeming. Where the debtor is an individual, there remains doubt whether it is possible to do this.

Chapter 4

FLOATING CHARGES

Part 1: THE DEVELOPMENT OF THE FLOATING CHARGE

Limitations on fixed charges

4.1 It has been seen that equitable mortgages and charges provide a very flexible method of taking security over any type of property. Such security is easy to create. At its simplest, it requires the execution of a document by the debtor and (usually) its registration.

4.2 One particular advantage of an equitable mortgage or charge, as opposed to a legal mortgage, is its ability to extend to after-acquired property. Certain judicial statements in the nineteenth century suggested that, as a matter of public policy, the courts might not allow an individual debtor to charge all of his present and future property, because this would deprive him of any means of subsistence. But this line of argument was roundly dismissed by the House of Lords in *Tailby v Official Receiver*.[1] In that case, it was decided that there was no public policy restriction on the scope of an equitable mortgage or charge.

4.3 In theory, therefore, it was possible for an equitable mortgage or charge to extend to all of a debtor's present and future assets. In the context of a 'normal' equitable mortgage or charge, however, such an approach would have created practical difficulties in relation to assets which the debtor needed to dispose of. A mortgage or charge gives the creditor a proprietary interest in the asset concerned. If the debtor wishes to dispose of it, he must therefore obtain a release from the debtor, failing which the purchaser will acquire the asset concerned subject to the creditor's proprietary interest.[2]

4.4 The problem is particularly acute where security is taken over the assets of a business. An important part of the value of a business lies in its current assets. It would be impracticable to create a 'normal' charge over the stock-in-trade of a business. The debtor requires to sell its stock in order to continue in business, and it is impracticable to obtain a release from the creditor each time an item of stock is to be sold.

---

1   (1888) 13 App Cas 523.
2   Unless he can rely on the bona fide purchaser doctrine or a similar principle. See **CHAPTER 7**.

4.5   Debts create different problems. Unlike stock-in-trade, they do not need to be sold in order for the debtor to make a profit. They are normally collected. But the debtor does normally require the use of the proceeds of debts for the purpose of funding his business. If the debts are charged, and the proceeds paid to the creditor, an important source of funding will be removed.

4.6   For these reasons, although creditors had the theoretical possibility of obtaining an equitable mortgage or charge over all the debtor's future assets, a 'normal' mortgage or charge would only be practicable in circumstances where the assets concerned were unlikely to be disposed of in the ordinary course of the debtor's business. This was the case in relation to the future machinery which was charged in *Holroyd v Marshall*.[3] Fixed assets, such as equipment, are ideally suited to such a mortgage or charge. But current assets, such as stock-in-trade and debts, are not.

4.7   In addition to this practical restriction on the taking of security over all the debtor's future assets, the legislature intervened to protect individual debtors. In the bills of sale legislation, Parliament decided that individuals should not be able to create security over after-acquired goods or, indeed, over any goods other than those specified in the mortgage itself.[4] Although that restriction did not apply to intangibles, the decision of the House of Lords in *Tailby v Official Receiver*[5] that an individual could create a charge over all of his present and future debts led Parliament to require that a general assignment of book debts by an individual be registered as if it were a bill of sale.[6] The legislature had therefore made it impossible in practice for an individual to create security over all of his present and future assets.[7]

The creation of floating charges

4.8   Security created by companies was not affected by the bills of sale legislation,[8] but the practical limitation on the creation of 'normal' charges over all of the company's present and future assets remained. It would, therefore, have been easy for the courts to have set their face against companies granting such general security, either with a view to protecting debtors or in order to protect other creditors from the effect of one creditor obtaining security over all of a debtor's assets.[9] But they did not do so.

4.9   As has been seen in CHAPTER 3, by the nineteenth century a creditor could obtain an equitable charge not only of assets owned by the debtor at the time the charge was created, but also over future assets which were acquired by

---

3   (1861–62) 10 HLC 191. See CHAPTER 3.
4   See part 6 of CHAPTER 6 (**6.130ff**).
5   (1888) 13 App Cas 523.
6   The legislation is now contained in the Insolvency Act 1986, s 344.
7   Although farmers can create agricultural floating charges under the Agricultural Credits Act 1928.
8   *N V Slavenburg's Bank v Intercontinental Natural Resources* [1980] 1 WLR 1076 at 1093–1098.
9   This is broadly what was done by the US courts, the resulting problems having to be cured by legislation.

the debtor, provided they answered the description of the charged assets contained in the charge document. Some doubt about this principle seems to have developed in the mid-nineteenth century but, in *Holroyd v Marshall*[10] in 1862, the House of Lords definitively confirmed that a future asset falling within the description of the charged property did automatically become charged to the creditor once the debtor became the owner of the asset concerned.

4.10 At about the same time, in 1856, the first modern Companies Act provided a cheap and straightforward way of allowing traders to incorporate their businesses.[11] The new companies, looking around for capital, found it not only from those who were prepared to subscribe for equity, but also from those willing to make debt finance available by way of loan stock. If the loan stock was to be secured, the equitable charge provided a straightforward method of enabling the stockholders to take security over both present and future assets of the company. To the extent that they consisted of assets, such as land, which would not be disposed of by the debtor in the ordinary course, that presented no problem. But, where the stockholders wanted to take security over assets, such as stock-in-trade, which required to be disposed of in the ordinary course of a debtor's business, the issue that faced them was the necessity to enable the debtor to continue to operate its business and to sell those assets. The problem was that a chargor of an asset can only transfer it free of the charge with the consent of the chargee; and it was wholly impracticable for creditors to have to approve every sale by the debtor of an item of stock-in-trade.

4.11 Stockholders nevertheless wanted to take security over all of a debtor's present and future assets, and it soon became common for debtors to charge their 'undertakings', ie the entirety of their present and future businesses, to secure issues of loan stock.

4.12 In 1867, a case came before the courts which involved such an arrangement. In *Re Marine Mansions Company*,[12] the debtor company had charged all of its undertaking and assets to secure an issue of debentures. The debtor went into liquidation, and the liquidator contended that the parties could not have intended the charge to extend to all of the debtor's assets, because that would have had the effect of paralysing its business. Page Wood V-C held that the debentureholders did have a valid charge over all of the debtor's assets, although it was not explained how the problem of paralysing the debtor's business was avoided.

4.13 The explanation came 3 years later in *Re Panama, New Zealand and Australian Royal Mail Company*.[13] The debtor company had issued 'mortgage debentures' which contained a charge over its undertaking 'and all sums of money arising therefrom' to secure the payment of principal and interest on loans made by the holders of the debentures. The debtor was wound up, and the debentureholders claimed that they had a charge over all its assets. The

---

10   (1861–62) 10 HLC 191.
11   Joint Stock Companies Act 1856, followed by the Companies Act 1862.
12   (1867) LR 4 Eq 601.
13   (1870) LR 5 Ch App 318.

liquidator contended that the charge was not intended to extend to all of the company's property, but only to the benefit of contracts. The Court of Appeal in Chancery held that the debentureholders did have a charge over all the present and future property of the debtor. The problem of how such an arrangement can avoid paralysing the business of the debtor was solved by Sir G M Giffard LJ. He decided that there was an implied agreement by the debentureholders that the debtor company could carry on its business, and deal with its property, until the debentureholders were entitled to intervene and to enforce their rights under the charge. Although the period of the loan had not expired, the winding up of the company meant that the debentureholders were entitled to intervene and to enforce their rights under the charge.

4.14 What is interesting about the *Panama* case is that, 18 years before *Tailby v Official Receiver*,[14] there was no suggestion by the court that a charge over all of a debtor's present and future assets was ineffective. The court gave effect to the parties' intention to create a charge over all of the debtor's assets by implying an authority by the debentureholders to enable the debtor to carry on business notwithstanding the charge.

4.15 The same conclusion was reached by the Court of Appeal 8 years later in *Re Florence Land and Public Works Company, ex parte Moor*.[15] In that case, the debtor company had issued 'Obligations' to raise money, by which it had bound itself and all its 'estate, property and effects' to repay the debt. On this very slight wording, the Court of Appeal not only implied that the debtor had charged all of its assets, but also implied an authority for the debtor to carry on business in the ordinary course. The security was described by Jessel MR as 'a security on the property of the company as a going concern, subject to the powers of the directors to dispose of the property of the company while carrying on its business in the ordinary course'.[16] The directors' powers to do so would continue until the creditor applied to the court to appoint a receiver or the company went into liquidation.

4.16 In *Re General South American Company*,[17] the court had to consider a more elaborate debenture. The debtor company had charged all of its present and future assets to the debentureholders, and there was an express provision that the debtor was at liberty to continue to use the assets for the purpose of carrying on its business until a default or the debtor was wound up. Malins V-C held that the security was effective. The debtor's authority to deal with its assets was express, rather than implied.

4.17 These few cases established a new type of charge, described by Jessel MR in *Re Colonial Trusts Corporation, ex parte Bradshaw*[18] as a 'floating' charge. It is difficult to overestimate the importance of what was achieved in these cases. The problem of taking security over current assets was solved by the simple expedient of implying a power for the debtor to use them until

---

14   (1888) 13 App Cas 523.
15   (1878) 10 Ch D 530.
16   (1878) 10 Ch D 530 at 540–541.
17   (1876) 2 Ch D 337.
18   (1879) 15 Ch D 465 at 472.

intervention by the creditor. In a handful of cases in the 1870s, the English courts created a simple, elegant and effective answer to the problem of taking security over current assets.

Freedom of contract and proprietary rights

4.18 The consideration by the courts of the express provisions of the charge before them (as was done in *Re General South American Company*) is a recurring theme in cases concerning floating charges. In the cases, there is a tension between two roles which the court is performing. On the one hand, it is setting down rules of law concerning the nature of a floating charge and, on the other, it is construing the particular document in front of it. How is this potential conflict resolved?

4.19 There is no doubt that the principle of freedom of contract underlies much of the thinking of the courts in relation to the floating charge. The very way in which floating charges were created, by implying an authority in favour of the debtor, is symptomatic of an approach in terms of contract. This approach has also informed the view of the courts more recently, when they have had to consider the effectiveness of automatic crystallisation (which is considered in part 4 of this chapter (**4.65ff**)).

4.20 There are, nevertheless, limits to this approach. Although the terms of the floating charge will always be relevant as between the debtor and the creditor, it does not follow that they will necessarily affect third parties. The basic principle is that, if a provision of a floating charge differs from the position under the general law, it will only adversely affect a third party if he has notice of it.

4.21 Although it is created by contract, a floating charge does not only create personal rights. It also creates proprietary rights. As between its parties, the contract is the final arbiter of their personal rights and duties. But, to the extent that proprietary rights are created, the contract can never be the sole determinant of the scope of those rights. It is a distinction which needs to be borne in mind when considering the remaining parts of this chapter.

Debentures

4.22 A floating charge is an essential element in the security available to creditors, but it is rarely taken on its own. It is normally combined with fixed charges over assets which are susceptible to them, such as land and investments. The document which creates these fixed and floating charges over the present and future assets of a debtor company is generally referred to as a 'debenture'. This can create some confusion in practice because a debenture is, in its primary sense, 'a document which either creates a debt or acknowledges it'.[19]

4.23 The reason why the expression 'debenture' is now also used to describe a document creating fixed and floating charges over all of the assets of a

---

19   *Levy v Abercorris Slate & Slab Company* (1887) 37 Ch D 260 at 264, per Chitty J.

company is historical. In most of the early cases concerning floating charges, they were given to secure issues of debentures by the debtor company. As part of its capital-raising exercise, the company issued debt securities, secured over its property. Because they were documents creating or evidencing debts, they were described as 'debentures'. In the twentieth century, floating charges became widely used by banks and, whilst taking over the concept, they also adopted the description 'debenture' for the document creating it. In practice, most debentures of this kind are now taken by banks and other financial institutions to secure loans or other credit facilities made available to corporate debtors.

Structure of this chapter

4.24 The remaining parts of this chapter consider the following questions:

- Part 2 (**4.25ff**) – what is the nature of a floating charge?
- Part 3 (**4.35ff**) – what is the effect of a floating charge before it crystallises?
- Part 4 (**4.65ff**) – when does a floating charge crystallise, and what is its effect?
- Part 5 (**4.79ff**) – what is the distinction between fixed and floating charges?

Part 2: WHAT IS THE NATURE OF A FLOATING CHARGE?

4.25 If defining a fixed charge is difficult,[20] the problems only increase when it comes to defining a floating charge. Once the charge has crystallised (ie once it has ceased to be 'floating'), it becomes a fixed charge, no different in principle from any other fixed charge, although it has certain different effects in insolvency proceedings in relation to the debtor.[21] The problem comes in analysing the nature of a floating charge before it crystallises. There are many descriptions in the cases, and they tend to fall into one of two main types, first identified by Professor Pennington.[22] There are many potential examples, but two sets of contrasting examples will suffice.

4.26 The first two are provided by Lord Macnaghten. In *Governments Stock and Other Securities Investment Co v Manila Railway Co* he said:[23]

'A floating security is an equitable charge on the assets for the time being of a going concern. It attaches to the subject charged in the varying condition in which it happens to be from time to time. It is of the essence of such a

---

20   See part 1 of CHAPTER 3 (**3.1ff**).
21   See part 5 of this chapter (**5.79ff**).
22   Pennington 'The genesis of the floating charge' (1960) 23 MLR 630.
23   [1897] AC 81 at 86.

charge that it remains dormant until the undertaking charged ceases to be a going concern, or until the person in whose favour the charge is created intervenes.'

4.27 A few years later, following a discussion of the uncertainties of this description by Vaughan Williams LJ in *Re Yorkshire Woolcombers Association*,[24] Lord Macnaghten attempted a clarification in *Illingworth v Houldsworth*:[25]

'A specific charge, I think, is one that without more fastens on ascertained and definite property or property capable of being ascertained and defined; a floating charge, on the other hand, is ambulatory and shifting in its nature, hovering over and so to speak floating with the property which it is intended to affect until some event occurs or some act is done which causes it to settle and fasten on the subject of the charge within its reach and grasp.'

4.28 If the concern with the first description was its lack of precision, the second only makes matters worse; it is riddled with metaphors. The important difference between these two descriptions is the contrasting approach to the nature of the floating charge before it crystallises. In the *Manila Railway* case, the security is expressed to attach to the assets concerned, in the varying condition in which they happen to be from time to time, although it remains dormant until it crystallises. In *Illingworth v Houldsworth*, a floating charge was, before crystallisation, expressed to be 'ambulatory and shifting' and 'hovering over' or 'floating with' the debtor's assets until, on crystallisation, it comes to 'settle and fasten' on the assets concerned.

4.29 From the context of Lord Macnaghten's speech in *Illingworth v Houldsworth*, it is difficult to believe that he had changed his view of the nature of a floating charge since deciding the *Manila Railway* case. But commentators have used these two statements to suggest two different analyses of the nature of a floating charge before crystallisation: one indicating that a floating charge is an existing charge on the assets of the company from time to time (albeit with the debtor having a power of disposal), the other suggesting that a floating charge does not attach to any particular assets until crystallisation.

4.30 The distinction is elaborated upon in two further judgments, by different generations of Buckley LJ in the Court of Appeal. In 1910, in *Evans v Rival Granite Quarries*, Buckley LJ said:[26]

'A floating security is not a future security; it is a present security, which presently affects all the assets of the company expressed to be included in it. On the other hand, it is not a specific security; the holder cannot affirm that the assets are specifically mortgaged to him. The assets are mortgaged in such a way that the mortgagor can deal with them without the concurrence of the mortgagee. A floating security is not a specific mortgage of the assets, plus a licence to the mortgagor to dispose of them in the

---

24   [1903] 2 Ch 284 at 291–292.
25   [1904] AC 355 at 358.
26   [1910] 2 KB 979 at 999.

course of his business, but is a floating mortgage applying to every item comprised in the security, but not specifically affecting any item until some event occurs or some act on the part of the mortgagee is done, which causes it to crystallise into a fixed security.'

4.31 Although not expressed in the same metaphorical terms as Lord Macnaghten's speech in *Illingworth v Houldsworth*, this description raises just as many difficulties of interpretation. A floating charge is 'present', but not 'specific'. It 'applies' to the assets concerned from the date of creation, but does not 'specifically affect' them until crystallisation. In place of Lord Macnaghten's metaphors, Buckley LJ has to fall back on distinctions without a difference. An asset is either subject to a charge, or it is not. The chargee either has a personal right against the chargor, or a proprietary one. There can be no halfway house.

4.32 An alternative (and much clearer) view was expressed by a later Buckley LJ in 1978 in *Cretanor Maritime v Irish Marine*:[27]

'[T]he debenture created an immediate equitable charge upon the assets of the [company], wherever situated, subject to a power in the [company], so long as the charge continued to float, to deal with their assets in the course of their business, notwithstanding such charge, as though it did not exist.'

4.33 These contrasting descriptions of a floating charge raise a number of questions. What is the nature of the creditor's interest in an uncrystallised floating charge? Does he have a charge over all the debtor's assets from time to time? If so, in what circumstances can they be disposed of, free from the charge? If not, what type of interest does the creditor have?

4.34 The cases discussed in part 1 of this chapter are clear about the nature of a floating charge – the only distinction from a fixed charge is the debtor's ability to dispose of the charged assets until crystallisation. The judicial pronouncements discussed in this part suggest that the clarity and simplicity of this approach has not been universally accepted. The answers to these questions need to be considered in the light of the way in which the courts have approached the rights of the debtor, the creditor and third parties before crystallisation of the floating charge. This issue is therefore considered further at the end of the next part of this chapter at **4.60ff**.

Part 3: THE POSITION BEFORE CRYSTALLISATION

4.35 Whatever the nature of the creditor's rights before crystallisation, there is no doubt that, as a general principle, the debtor can carry on its business in the normal way notwithstanding the existence of the floating charge. That is the whole purpose of a floating charge. In this context, two main issues arise:

---

27   [1978] 1 WLR 966 at 978.

- Are there any limits on the debtor's ability to carry on its business and dispose of its assets before crystallisation under the general law?
- What is the effect of specific provisions in the debenture restricting the debtor's powers?

As mentioned in part 1, these two questions are distinct, but are often hard to distinguish in the cases.

The debtor's powers under the general law

4.36 Before considering the limits on the debtor's powers to carry on business, it is instructive to look at some examples of what the debtor has been allowed to do before the charge crystallises.

4.37 In the first place, it can sell its assets free from the floating charge, even if the sale is of a material part of its business.[28] The extent of this power can be seen from the decision of the Court of Appeal in *Re Borax Company*.[29] In that case, the debtor intended to sell the whole of its business to another company in consideration for shares and debentures in that company, but would nevertheless continue as a going concern. The Court of Appeal held that the debtor was entitled to effect such a transaction whilst it continued to carry on business, notwithstanding the existence of the floating charge. It was only once it had ceased to be a going concern or the creditor had intervened (for instance, by appointing a receiver) that the debtor's power to dispose of its assets would cease.

4.38 The debtor is also able, before crystallisation, to mortgage or charge its assets in priority to the rights of the floating chargee. In *Re Hamilton's Windsor Ironworks Co, ex parte Pitman & Edwards*,[30] the debtor, which had created a floating charge over all of its assets, subsequently assigned a debt by way of security. Malins V-C held that the subsequent assignment had priority over the floating charge because the floating chargee had authorised the debtor to carry on its business in the ordinary course, and this included raising money and charging its assets in support.

4.39 In addition to being able to dispose of the property the subject of the charge, whether outright or by way of security, the company also has the general power to carry on its business and, for instance, to create rights of set-off which will adversely affect the floating chargee.[31]

4.40 The recurring theme in these cases is that, notwithstanding the existence of the floating charge, the debtor company is entitled to carry on its business 'in the ordinary course' and, accordingly, to dispose of its assets free of the charge and generally enter into transactions without reference to the floating

---

28   *Re H H Vivien & Co* [1900] 2 Ch 654.
29   [1901] 1 Ch 326.
30   (1879) 12 Ch D 707.
31   *Biggerstaff v Rowatt's Wharf* [1896] 2 Ch 93.

chargee and as if the floating charge did not exist. This raises the question whether any actions by the debtor could be said to fall outside the ordinary course of its business.

Transactions in the 'ordinary course of business'

4.41   The first point to note is that a requirement that a transaction must be 'in the ordinary course' has hardly ever been used in the cases as a reason for preventing the debtor from entering into a transaction or deciding that it ranks behind the floating charge. In a number of cases, the floating chargee has objected to proposed actions by the debtor on the basis that they fall outside the ordinary course of its business, but the courts have generally been reluctant to declare actions by the creditor to fall outside the scope of the ordinary course of its business. A good example is the decision of the Court of Appeal in *Re Borax Company*,[32] discussed at **4.37**. The sale of all the debtor's business is within the ordinary course of that business, provided that the company continues to be a going concern.

4.42   The important point is that the debtor continues to be a going concern. In *Willmott v London Celluloid Company*,[33] the debtor entered into a debenture which created a floating charge over all of its assets and which expressly allowed it to deal with the charged property in the ordinary course of its business. The question arose whether a payment made by the company was in the ordinary course of business. The Court of Appeal held that it was. The importance of the case is that Cotton LJ made it clear[34] that, in considering whether or not the transaction concerned was in the ordinary course of business, the only relevant question was whether the company had stopped business. If it had not, the transaction was necessarily in the ordinary course of business, even if it was unusual and even if the company was then insolvent.

4.43   It will be seen, in part 4 of this chapter (**4.65**ff), that one of the circumstances in which a floating charge crystallises is if the debtor stops business. The effect of the *Willmott* case is, therefore, that until crystallisation, *any* transaction by the company will be within the ordinary course of its business. In the words of Somer J in the New Zealand Court of Appeal in *Julius Harper v F W Hagedorn*,[35] the effect of the *Willmott* case is 'to afford the words 'in the ordinary course of business' a temporal construction'.

4.44   The courts have not always adopted this approach. Particular problems have been caused by the relationship between floating chargees and execution creditors. There has been some suggestion in the cases that an execution is not in the ordinary course of business. An example of this approach is *Davey & Co v Williamson & Sons*,[36] a decision of the Queen's Bench Divisional Court in 1898. In that case, the debtor company had created a floating charge over all of

---

32   [1901] 1 Ch 326.
33   (1886) 34 Ch D 147.
34   (1886) 34 Ch D 147 at 151.
35   [1991] 1 NZLR 530 at 543.
36   [1898] 2 QB 194.

its assets, and its goods were subsequently seized in execution on behalf of a judgment creditor. The court held that the floating chargee was entitled to the goods because the execution was not a dealing by the company in the ordinary course of business. Indeed, it was not a dealing by the company at all, but a compulsory legal process.

4.45   The flaws in this reasoning are manifest. It is not the execution which has been authorised, but the contracting of debts by the debtor company. There is no doubt that the debtor company is entitled to incur credit; and a failure to repay can ultimately result in a judgment creditor obtaining execution against the debtor's assets. The floating chargee should not be allowed to argue that, although the company can incur credit, it cannot allow execution to be suffered against its assets. The authority to incur credit must carry with it an acceptance of the consequences of doing so.

4.46   The approach in *Davey v Williamson* did not last very long. In 1910, in *Evans v Rival Granite Quarries*,[37] the Court of Appeal refused to accept it. Fletcher Moulton LJ described *Davey v Williamson* as 'a very peculiar case',[38] and believed that it was wrongly decided if the mere existence of the floating charge was sufficient to prevent an execution. Buckley LJ[39] considered that, on its facts, the business of the debtor company in *Davey v Williamson* had ceased, and that the floating charge had crystallised. Either way, it is now clear that an execution is not outside the ordinary course of business of the company. Priorities between a floating chargee and an execution creditor are, however, still complex, and are considered further in part 8 of CHAPTER 7 (7.234ff).

4.47   Are there any circumstances in which a transaction entered into by the debtor before crystallisation will fall outside the scope of its authority to deal with its assets in the ordinary course of business? The 'temporal' approach adopted in the *Willmott* case suggests that, unless fraud is involved, practically all transactions carried out by the debtor will be in the ordinary course of business.

4.48   It is possible to conceive of transactions which fall outside the scope of the debtor's authority to carry on its business, but they will be extremely limited. If the floating chargee can apply to court quickly enough, he should be able to obtain an injunction to prevent such a transaction from proceeding.[40] If it has been effected before the floating chargee becomes aware of it, in principle, a transaction outside the scope of the company's authority should, if the person dealing with the company has notice of it, be sufficient to prevent that person from obtaining title to the assets concerned free from the floating charge.

4.49   It should be stressed, however, that the circumstances in which the floating chargee will be able to intervene before crystallisation are extremely

---

37   [1910] 2 KB 979.
38   [1910] 2 KB 979 at 997.
39   [1910] 2 KB 979 at 1000–1001.
40   In *Hubbuck v Helms* (1887) 56 LJ Ch 536, the same result was achieved by the appointment of a receiver.

limited. Except in the case of fraud, the debtor's authority to deal with its assets extends to practically all transactions entered into by the debtor.

Express restrictions

4.50 A modern floating charge will invariably contain an express provision authorising the debtor company to deal with its assets in certain ways and preventing it from doing so in others. As has been mentioned above, the courts frequently refer to the specific provisions of the floating charge concerned. By way of example, this was done by the New Zealand Court of Appeal in the *Julius Harper* case[41] and by the Queen's Bench Divisional Court in *Davey v Williamson*.[42]

4.51 Where the authority simply mirrors that under the general law, it may not be necessary to distinguish between the express authority and that which the general law allows. An express authority to deal with the debtor's assets 'in the ordinary course of its business' will, in principle, be given the same broad interpretation described above although, because the expression has to be interpreted in the light of the debenture as a whole and the surrounding matrix of facts, it may, as a matter of contractual construction, be given a narrower meaning.[43]

4.52 Most floating charges restrict the authority of the debtor further. It is, for instance, common for floating charges to restrict dealings by the debtor to those 'in the ordinary course of its trading' – in the expectation that the ordinary course of trading is a more restricted concept than the ordinary course of business. Such an approach is often coupled with specific restrictions on the debtor entering into particular types of transaction, such as the sale of a material part of its business. In addition, a floating charge will invariably contain a restriction on the debtor creating any type of security interest over its assets without the consent of the floating chargee.

4.53 Such express restrictions are the direct result of the width of the authority given to the debtor under the general law to deal with its assets until crystallisation. Although the company needs to be able to sell its current assets in order to continue in business, it is unlikely to need to sell its entire business (as happened in *Re Borax Company*[44]) or even a material part of its business (as in *Re H H Vivien & Co*[45]). Restrictions on material disposals, and the limitation of the debtor's authority to transactions in the ordinary course of trading, are intended to plug the perceived gaps left by the general law.

4.54 More importantly, although the debtor needs to be able to dispose of assets outright in order to continue its business, the creditor will normally want to control dispositions by way of security, particularly where they would rank

---

41   *Julius Harper v F W Hagedorn* [1991] 1 NZLR 530.
42   *Davey & Co v Williamson & Sons* [1898] 2 QB 194.
43   For an example of such a case, see *Ashborder v Green Gas Power* [2004] EWHC 1517.
44   [1901] 1 Ch 326.
45   [1900] 2 Ch 654.

ahead of the floating charge. Hence the (normally very widely drawn) prohibition on the creation of any security, invariably (if inelegantly and inaccurately) known as a 'negative pledge'.

4.55 There is no doubt that, as a matter of contract between the debtor and the creditor, such provisions are effective. But, to what extent do they affect third parties? Hardly surprisingly, the courts have decided that such provisions only affect third parties if they are aware of them. A person who deals with a debtor which has created a floating charge is entitled to assume that the debtor has the authority afforded by the general law to a debtor which has created a floating charge. If the authority of the debtor is, in fact, limited by the terms of the floating charge, a person dealing with the company will only be affected by it if he is aware of it. Such an approach is consistent with the approach of the courts to restrictions on the apparent or usual authority of agents.

4.56 An example of the approach of the courts is *Re Castell & Brown*.[46] The debtor company had issued debentures which contained a floating charge over all of its present and future property. It also contained a restriction on the debtor creating any mortgage or charge on its land in priority to the floating charge. The debtor borrowed money from its bank, which obtained an equitable mortgage over land owned by the debtor. The bank was not aware of the debentures, let alone of the restriction in them.

4.57 Romer J held that the bank's mortgage took priority over the floating charge. Although the floating charge was created before the bank's mortgage, it was in the nature of a floating charge that the debtor was authorised to deal with its property as if it had not been encumbered. The bank was entitled to rely on this general authority notwithstanding the express restriction in the debentures because the bank was not aware of the restriction.

4.58 In practice, as far as third parties are concerned, the most important restriction in a floating charge is the negative pledge, which is considered in more detail in part 8 of CHAPTER 7 (**7.203ff**).

Effect of a floating charge before crystallisation

4.59 The effect of the floating charge before crystallisation can be summarised as follows:

- Under the general law, in the absence of fraud, the debtor has the authority to enter into practically any type of transaction before the floating charge crystallises, and any interests created over its property as a result will take priority over the floating charge.
- Most floating charges contain restrictions on the debtor's authority. They are effective as between the debtor and the creditor, but will only affect third parties who are aware of them.

---

46   [1898] 1 Ch 315.

The nature of a floating charge

4.60 It is now possible to return to the question debated in part 2 of this chapter (**4.25**ff): what is the nature of a floating charge before crystallisation? It was seen, in part 2, that there have been two approaches to the question. One saw the floating charge as creating an immediate proprietary interest over all of the debtor's assets from time to time, but subject to an authority in favour of the debtor to dispose of those assets in the ordinary course of business. The other is more difficult to describe without the use of metaphors. It sees a floating charge as not affecting particular assets of the company until crystallisation although, in some sense, it does create an 'immediate' charge over the debtor's assets generally.

4.61 The problem with the former approach is that the courts have generally regarded the authority of the company as extending to all dispositions of assets before crystallisation. Problems have arisen where (as, for instance, in *Davey v Williamson*[47]) the courts have attempted to restrict the authority of the company on the basis that the action concerned was not in the 'ordinary course of business'. As has been seen, this approach has been rejected, with the effect that the courts do not, in practice, examine the nature of the transaction in order to see whether it is, or is not, 'ordinary'.

4.62 The latter approach, however, suffers from even more problems. The nature of an existing security over the debtor's assets which does not affect particular assets is by no means easy to grasp. It is too dependent on metaphor to be a reliable guide. Either the creditor has a proprietary interest in all of the debtor's assets from time to time, or he does not. It is also inconsistent with those cases which establish that a floating charge creates an interest in the land owned by the company before crystallisation.[48] More importantly in practice, if the floating chargee does not have a proprietary interest in the assets of the company from time to time, why does a subsequent fixed chargee, with notice of a negative pledge, take his interest subject to that of the floating chargee?[49] Nor is it the case that the only assets which are the subject of the floating charge are those which exist at the date of crystallisation. Assets which become owned by the company after the crystallisation are also subject to the crystallised floating charge.[50]

4.63 Theories about the nature of floating charges are much less important than the effect of floating charges in practice. But, as will be seen from part 5 of this chapter (**4.79**ff), it has become important in practice to distinguish between fixed and floating charges, and an understanding of the conceptual nature of a floating charge is important in drawing the distinction. The position is by no means free from doubt, and no one analysis can accommodate all the dicta in all the cases. But the actual decisions in the cases and the principles which underlie them suggest that the following is the correct analysis:

---

47   *Davey & Co v Williamson & Sons* [1898] 2 QB 194.
48   *Driver v Broad* [1893] 1 QB 744.
49   See *English and Scottish Mercantile Investment Co v Brunton* [1892] 2 QB 700, discussed further in part 8 of **CHAPTER 7** (**7.234**ff).
50   *N W Robbie & Co v Witney Warehouse Co* [1963] 1 WLR 1324.

- Until crystallisation of a floating charge, the creditor has a proprietary interest in the assets of the company from time to time.
- The creditor's proprietary interest is, however, an extremely precarious one. The debtor is entitled to carry on its business and dispose of its assets and, unless fraudulent, practically any disposition or action by the debtor will bind the floating chargee, regardless of whether or not the transaction is 'ordinary' in the context of that debtor's business.
- The debtor will be bound by express restrictions in the floating charge, but a third party will only be affected by them if he is aware of them.

4.64   This approach is, it is suggested, consistent with the decisions in the authorities, although not with all of the dicta in all of the cases (which are themselves irreconcilable). It is also entirely consistent with the decision of Sir G M Giffard LJ in the case which first created the floating charge, *Re Panama, New Zealand, and Australian Royal Mail Company*.[51] It will be recalled that, in that case, a charge over the debtor's undertaking was construed as a charge over all of its present and future property, but subject to an implied authority for the company to carry on business, and deal with its property, until the creditor was entitled to intervene. Despite all the subsequent elaborations, that case continues to encapsulate the essential simplicity of the concept of the floating charge – a charge which contains an authority to deal with the charged property.

Part 4: CRYSTALLISATION, AND ITS EFFECT

4.65   From the time of the very earliest cases in the 1870s, it was clear that the authority of the debtor to continue to deal with its assets terminated in two circumstances: when the debtor stopped business; and when the creditor intervened. More recent cases have added a third: when the floating charge so provides.

Stopping business

4.66   It is inherent in the very nature of a floating charge that the debtor's authority to deal with its assets will cease when it ceases business. This is because the reason why the debtor has the authority is to enable it to continue in business. Once that business has ceased, it has no further need for the authority.

4.67   The clearest example of a case where a company has ceased business is where it has gone into liquidation. In *Re Panama, New Zealand and Australian Royal Mail Company*,[52] it was decided that the floating chargee was entitled to

---

51   (1870) LR 5 Ch App 318.
52   (1870) LR 5 Ch App 318.

enforce the security in a liquidation of the debtor company, even though it had no contractual power to intervene under the charge document because the period of the loan had not yet expired.

4.68 It is possible for a company to cease business without going into liquidation, although it is rare for this to be done in practice without the company entering into some form of insolvency procedure.[53] Although an administrator has the power to carry on the company's business, it is likely that administration of the debtor will also crystallise the charge – the nature of the administrator's power to carry on business being very different from that of its board of directors. In theory, the charge will also crystallise if it is possible to identify a point in time, before liquidation or administration, at which the company's business has ceased.[54]

Intervention by the creditor

4.69 A floating charge will also crystallise if the floating chargee intervenes. In the words of Lord Macnaghten in *Governments Stock and Other Securities Investment Co v Manila Railway Co*:[55]

> 'It is of the essence of ... [a floating] charge that it remains dormant until the undertaking charged ceases to be a going concern, or until the person in whose favour the charge is created intervenes.'

4.70 In the absence of express wording in the charge document, the basic method of enforcement of a charge (whether fixed or floating) is for the chargee to apply to the court for the appointment of a receiver.[56] This was the common form of intervention when the floating charge was first developed. The limited nature of a chargee's rights of enforcement, however, led to the insertion of express powers of enforcement in the charge document. Charges (whether fixed or floating) now invariably contain detailed provisions providing when the creditor can enforce and how the enforcement is to be effected. In practice, floating charges are invariably enforced by the appointment of a receiver or an administrator over the charged assets, and the floating charge will normally, therefore, crystallise on the appointment of the receiver or administrator. Enforcement is considered in detail in CHAPTER 8.

Express crystallisation

4.71 The elaboration of the express terms of floating charge documents, particularly in the last 50 years, has led to a third method of crystallisation. There has been an increasing tendency for provisions to be inserted into debentures which provide expressly for the crystallisation of the floating charge in particular circumstances. There are two common types of approach. The

---

53 Not least because of the fiduciary duties of the directors of the company and their potential liability for wrongful trading under the Insolvency Act 1986, s 214.
54 *Hubbuck v Helms* (1887) 56 LJ Ch 536 at 539, per Sterling J.
55 [1897] AC 81 at 86.
56 See CHAPTER 8.

first is for the floating chargee to be given the power to deliver a notice to the debtor crystallising the floating charge over the assets which are the subject of the notice. The alternative approach is to provide for the automatic crystallisation of the floating charge on the happening of certain events. Those events frequently include (a) the creation of another charge by the debtor in favour of a third party and (b) the commencement of an execution against the assets of the debtor. The essential purpose of such provisions is to give the floating chargee priority over third parties dealing with the debtor. In the first type of case, the floating chargee can crystallise the floating charge in whole or in part without appointing a receiver. In the latter case, the crystallisation happens automatically on the happening of events which are likely to prejudice the floating chargee.

4.72 A power for the creditor to crystallise the floating charge by notice might be of value in a limited number of cases, although, in practice, a receiver or administrator can be appointed very quickly. Automatic crystallisation, on the other hand, is more problematical. It is extremely doubtful that it will assist the chargee's priority position in practice[57] and it has the serious disadvantage of enabling the floating charge to crystallise without the creditor being aware of it,[58] thus creating uncertainty.

4.73 There was initially some doubt concerning whether such clauses were effective, it being suggested that there were public policy reasons why they should not be.[59] But it now seems clear, at least in England and Australasia, that they are effective, the reasoning being that it is simply a matter of contract between the debtor and the creditor when the floating charge should crystallise.[60] It is nevertheless doubtful whether an automatic crystallisation clause will affect a third party who is not aware of it. It has been seen in part 3 of this chapter (**4.35ff**) that a person dealing with the debtor company will not be adversely affected by a provision of the floating charge which restricts the debtor company's authority to deal with its assets unless that person is aware of the restriction. The same line of reasoning would suggest that a third party will not be adversely affected by an automatic crystallisation clause unless he is aware of it.

4.74 Although such provisions are generally seen as a relatively recent phenomenon, their effectiveness was established towards the end of the nineteenth century in *Re Horne & Hellard*.[61] In that case, a debenture created a floating charge 'until default in payment' of principal and interest under the debenture. The debtor company contracted to sell land, and the purchaser asked for evidence that there was no default in the payment of principal and interest under the debentures. It was held that the purchaser was entitled to

---

57   Crystallisation will normally happen too late – after the problem has occurred.
58   As happened in *Dovey Enterprises v Guardian Assurance Public* [1993] 1 NZLR 540.
59   Particularly in Canada. See *R v Consolidated Churchill Copper Corporation* [1978] 5 WWR 652.
60   *Re Brightlife Limited* [1987] Ch 200; *Covacich v Riordan* [1994] 2 NZLR 502.
61   (1885) 29 Ch D 736.

reasonable evidence that there had been no such default because the floating charge would have crystallised on such a default, without the appointment of a receiver being necessary.

When a charge crystallises: summary

4.75 In summary, therefore, there are three circumstances in which a floating charge crystallises:

- if the debtor company ceases business (which will normally be when it enters into liquidation or administration);
- if the creditor intervenes (normally by the appointment of a receiver or administrator); or
- if some other event occurs which the charge document provides is to crystallise the floating charge (which will normally either be a notice by the creditor or the happening of a specified event).

4.76 In practice, most floating charges crystallise on the appointment of a receiver or administrator.

The effect of crystallisation

4.77 Once a floating charge crystallises, it becomes a fixed charge over the assets owned by the debtor company at the time of crystallisation, and over any other assets subsequently acquired by the company.[62] As has been seen, the difference between fixed and floating charges is that, in the latter case, the company has an authority to dispose of its assets. That authority ceases on crystallisation, and the charge therefore becomes a fixed charge.

4.78 Statute has, however, introduced a distinction between fixed charges and floating charges in an insolvency and, for this purpose, a crystallised floating charge is considered as a floating charge, not a fixed charge.[63] This issue is considered further in the following part of this chapter.

Part 5: THE DISTINCTION BETWEEN FIXED AND FLOATING CHARGES

Why is the distinction important?

4.79 Until the end of the nineteenth century, there was no reason to draw elaborate distinctions between fixed and floating charges. The only difference between them related to the authority of the debtor to deal with its assets and

---

62   *N W Robbie & Co v Witney Warehouse Co* [1963] 1 WLR 1324.
63   Insolvency Act 1986, s 251.

therefore the priority of subsequent dispositions. If the charge over an asset was floating, a person acquiring an interest in the asset would take free of the floating charge because the debtor had been authorised by the creditor to deal with the asset free from the floating charge. If the charge was fixed, the person acquiring the interest would only take free of the fixed charge if the creditor specifically released it. The only question was whether the debtor had the authority to dispose of the asset concerned free from the charge; and it did not matter whether that authority was general or specific.

4.80 It has been the intervention of statute since the end of the nineteenth century which has required the courts to draw a distinction between fixed and floating charges. There are five principal reasons why the distinction is now important. In broad terms, they all relate to the effectiveness or priority of a floating charge in the insolvency of the debtor.

4.81 The first relates to the requirement to register company charges, failing which they are rendered void in the debtor's insolvency. Fixed charges are only registrable if they are taken over one of the categories of asset described in s 396(1) of the Companies Act 1985. The list extends to most types of land and chattels, but does not cover all types of intangible. Floating charges, on the other hand, are registrable regardless of the type of asset over which they are created.[64]

4.82 Secondly, a floating charge is more vulnerable to be set aside in a liquidation or administration of the debtor than a fixed charge. A fixed charge created by a debtor to secure its own indebtedness can generally only be set aside on insolvency if it amounts to a preference. In practice, this will rarely be the case unless the creditor is connected with the debtor.[65] A floating charge is more vulnerable. Broadly, a floating charge created within the year before the beginning of the insolvency will be set aside if the debtor was insolvent at the time it was given, except to the extent that new money or other new value was made available to the debtor at or after the time the floating charge was granted.[66]

4.83 Thirdly, the rights of preferential creditors to receive payment in an insolvency in priority to other unsecured creditors was, at the end of the nineteenth century, extended to give them priority also over floating charges (but not over fixed charges).[67] As a result of the Enterprise Act 2002, which abolished Crown preference, preferential claims are now largely restricted to claims by employees.[68]

4.84 Fourthly, the abolition of Crown preference was accompanied by an arrangement (referred to in this book as the unsecured creditors' lifeboat) by which unsecured creditors have been given certain limited rights of priority

---

64 Companies Act 1985, s 396(1)(a)–(e) and (g)–(j) for fixed charges, and s 396(1)(f) for floating charges. See **CHAPTER 6**.
65 Insolvency Act 1986, s 239; *Re M C Bacon* [1990] BCLC 324. See **CHAPTER 9**.
66 Insolvency Act 1986, s 245. See **CHAPTER 9**.
67 Preferential Payments in Bankruptcy Amendment Act 1897.
68 Enterprise Act 2002, s 251; Insolvency Act 1986, ss 40, 175 and 386 and Sch 6. See **CHAPTER 9**.

over floating charges (but not over fixed charges). As a result, a certain percentage of floating charge realisations (broadly, 20 per cent), up to a maximum amount of £600,000, has to be set aside for unsecured creditors.[69]

4.85 Finally, an administrator is entitled to use floating charge assets (but not fixed charge assets) in the administration, and can pay his expenses out of them.[70]

4.86 It can be seen that these legislative provisions fall into two broad categories, both of which become relevant in the debtor's insolvency. The effect of the first two provisions is to make a floating charge more vulnerable to be set aside in the debtor's insolvency than a fixed charge. The effect of the last three is, in practice, even more important. They enable certain persons to use floating charge assets in priority to the floating chargee even though those persons have no proprietary interest in the assets concerned, and the floating chargee does.

4.87 In the past, the reason why creditors have attempted to obtain fixed charge security has largely been because of concerns about preferential creditors reducing, or even obliterating, the value of the floating charge assets. That is still an issue (and it now extends to the unsecured creditors' lifeboat as well as to preferential claims) but, in many cases, the concern now is more likely to be the ability of an administrator to use floating charge assets for the purpose of running the debtor's business and paying his expenses. The creditor will obtain a floating charge over the proceeds of the assets, but the administrator may well trade at a loss and his expenses are likely to be substantial, in which event the value of the floating charge assets will diminish rapidly. This concern has increased since the Enterprise Act 2002 has come into force, because many companies which would previously have gone into administrative receivership will now go into administration.[71]

4.88 These disadvantages of a floating charge should not, however, be taken out of context. There is no doubt that the ability to obtain a floating charge over all of the debtor's present and future assets is a material advantage for a creditor, and it is not available in all legal systems. These statutory limitations are the price which has to be paid for the ability to obtain security over all of the debtor's assets and to be able to enforce it by the appointment of a receiver or administrator.

What is the distinction?

4.89 In theory, the distinction between fixed and floating charges is straightforward. The only difference is that a debtor which has created a floating charge has a prospective general authority to deal with its assets free from the charge before crystallisation, whereas a debtor which has created a

---

69   Enterprise Act 2002, s 252; Insolvency Act 1986, s 176A; Insolvency Act 1986 (Prescribed Part) Order 2003. See CHAPTER 9.
70   Insolvency Act 1986, Sch B1, paras 70 and 99(3)(b). See CHAPTER 9.
71   As a result of the Enterprise Act 2002, s 250, inserting ss 72A–72H into the Insolvency Act 1986. See CHAPTER 8.

fixed charge requires the specific authority of the creditor each time it wishes to deal with the asset concerned. In the words of Lord Millett in *Re Brumark Investments (Agnew v Commissioner of Inland Revenue)*:[72] 'The company's freedom to deal with the charged assets without the consent of the holder of the charge ... is what makes it a floating charge.' After crystallisation, there is no difference at all.

4.90   The distinction is easy to state, but much more difficult to apply in practice. The problem is in deciding how much 'freedom to deal with the charged assets' is consistent with a fixed charge. At one extreme, a charge over land, the documentation of which provides that the debtor has no authority to dispose of the land (whether outright or by way of security) without the express permission of the chargee, is clearly a fixed charge. At the other extreme, a charge over the undertaking of the debtor, the documentation of which gives the debtor the authority to dispose of its assets (whether outright or by way of security) as if the charge did not exist, is clearly a floating charge. But these are extreme cases. In practice, most charges fall somewhere on the axis between them. At some point along that axis, a line has to be drawn between fixed and floating charges, but it is by no means easy to decide where that line should be drawn. Some examples will illustrate the problem.

4.91   Because, under the general law, the debtor company has an extremely wide authority to dispose of its floating charge assets, practically all floating charges contain express restrictions on the ability of the debtor to do certain things with the charged assets, such as create other fixed or floating charges over them. It has been seen that they are effective to bind third parties if they have notice of them. But it has never been suggested that these restrictions on the debtor's authority to carry on its business have the effect of converting the floating charge into a fixed charge.

4.92   Conversely, the ability of the debtor to deal with the charged assets in a limited way will not turn a purported fixed charge into a floating charge. An example is a fixed charge over land which has the benefit of a lease. Generally, until the creditor enforces the charge, the debtor is entitled to the rental income. It is only on enforcement that the creditor becomes entitled to the rents. There is no doubt that the creditor has a fixed charge in these circumstances, even though the debtor has the benefit of the charged asset until enforcement.

4.93   What these examples show is that a floating charge remains a floating charge even though restrictions are imposed on the debtor's authority to use the charged assets, and that a fixed charge can remain a fixed charge even if the debtor has some authority to use the charged assets until enforcement. The test therefore has to be stated in broad terms: a charge is a floating charge if the debtor has, in a practical, commercial sense, the authority to deal with the assets concerned as if the charge did not exist; and a charge is a fixed charge if the debtor does not have that authority.

4.94   This is, necessarily, a very imprecise test; and it is one on which two different tribunals can legitimately draw a different conclusion. Case-law can

---

72   [2001] 2 AC 710 at [34].

indicate which particular types of transaction fall which side of the line, but it is ultimately a question of fact in each case whether the debtor is able to deal with the asset concerned as if the charge did not exist.

4.95 The application of this test in practice has led to much debate, particularly in relation to the ability of lenders to take fixed security over all of a company's debts. That debate has now largely been settled, and discussion has moved on to the question of the amount of control required by a debtor to take security in more structured financial transactions, such as asset and project financings and securitisations. The remainder of this chapter will consider the availability of fixed security in relation to charges over debts generally before briefly considering security in structured transactions.

Charges over debts generally

4.96 The result of the legislative inroads into floating charges has been to encourage creditors to structure their transactions in such a way as to try to create fixed charges over assets over which it would be more natural to take a floating charge. In practice, the most common type of current asset over which creditors try to obtain fixed security is debts owing to the company. A significant proportion of the wealth of a company can be tied up in its debts. If a creditor can take a fixed charge over them, he will be able to obtain the full value of those debts, rather than taking second place behind preferential creditors, the 'unsecured creditors' lifeboat' and the expenses of an administrator. As a result, most of the cases concerning the distinction between fixed and floating charges concern general charges over debts.

4.97 Before considering the cases, it is important to appreciate what is meant by an authority to deal with assets such as debts. Since it is the badge of a floating charge that the debtor has a general authority to deal with its assets and release them from the charge until crystallisation, it is necessary to consider the types of action which are required in order to release the assets concerned from the charge.

4.98 When considering tangibles, such as goods, it is relatively straightforward to describe what is meant by an authority to release the charge. It involves the granting by the creditor to the debtor of an authority to dispose of the goods in question and use the proceeds of the disposal in the chargor's business. Because of the nature of intangibles, an authority to release debts must be of a different nature. Unlike goods, debts are not normally disposed of – they are collected. Accordingly, an authority to release a charge over debts involves the creditor giving the debtor an authority to collect the debts and to use the proceeds of the collection in the debtor's business.

The Yorkshire Woolcombers case

4.99   The question of a creditor's ability to obtain a fixed charge over debts generally was considered in *Re Yorkshire Woolcombers Association*,[73] which was affirmed by the House of Lords in *Illingworth v Houldsworth*.[74] In that case, the debtor company assigned its present and future debts to trustees by way of security under a deed which provided that the trustees could at any time require the company to give notice to the debtors and could appoint a receiver. It was found that it was implicit (although not explicit) in the deed that the debtor was entitled to carry on trading and to receive its debts and use their proceeds for the purpose of its business.

4.100   At first instance, Farwell J held that the charge was a floating charge, rather than a fixed charge. He said:[75]

'A charge on all book debts which may now be, or at any time hereafter become charged or assigned, leaving the mortgagor or assignor free to deal with them as he pleases until the mortgagee or assignee intervenes, is not a specific charge, and cannot be ...'

4.101   The Court of Appeal unanimously upheld the decision of Farwell J. The deed created a floating charge because it was the intention of the parties that the debtor should be able to deal with the debts, and to dispose of them, until the trustees intervened. Romer LJ gave a description of a floating charge which is almost invariably cited in later cases. He said:[76]

'I certainly do not intend to attempt to give an exact definition of the term "floating charge", nor am I prepared to say that there will not be a floating charge ... which does not contain all the three characteristics that I am about to mention, but I certainly think that if a charge has the three characteristics that I am about to mention it is a floating charge. (1) If it is a charge on a class of assets of a company present and future; (2) if that class is one which, in the ordinary course of the business of the company, would be changing from time to time; and (3) if you find that by the charge it is contemplated that, until some future step is taken by or on behalf of those interested in the charge, the company may carry on its business in the ordinary way as far as concerns the particular class of assets I am dealing with ...'

4.102   The House of Lords unanimously upheld the decision of the Court of Appeal, deciding that the deed showed an intention by the parties that the debts should be capable of being used by the company, and therefore to carry on business in the normal way; and that the security was therefore a floating charge.

4.103   The decision in the *Yorkshire Woolcombers* case seemed to have decided the issue conclusively. If the debtor is free to use the proceeds of the debts, the

---

73   [1903] 2 Ch 284.
74   [1904] AC 355.
75   [1903] 2 Ch 284 at 289.
76   [1903] 2 Ch 284 at 295.

charge will be a floating charge. In practice, debtors will almost invariably require to use the proceeds of their debts for the purpose of carrying on their businesses. Charges over debts will, therefore, almost invariably be floating charges.

Later developments

4.104 There the matter lay until, in the late 1960s, banks looked round to find ways of increasing the value of their security by obtaining a fixed charge over their customers' debts. The problem was obvious: how to give the creditor sufficient control over the debts that it could be said to have a fixed charge over them. The lead was taken by Barclays Bank. It produced a charge document which purported to provide such control by requiring the debtor to pay the proceeds of its debts into its account with the bank and by preventing it from dealing with them in any other way. This approach found favour with Slade J in *Siebe Gorman & Co. v Barclays Bank*,[77] who decided that it created a fixed charge.

4.105 The problem with this approach was that it was only available where the creditor concerned was the company's clearing bank, and was therefore not generally available to other banks, let alone to creditors other than banks. There was also concern that the case had been wrongly decided: a requirement to pay the proceeds of debts into the debtor's account with the bank should only be effective if the account was blocked and where, as in practically all cases, the debtor was entitled to draw on the account, the bank's control was illusory. In reality, it was argued, the debtor did have the ability to carry on its business as if the charge did not exist. What else would it do but pay its debts into its clearing bank account, on which it would then draw?

4.106 This led to a different approach being adopted by some creditors, particularly those which were not clearing banks and who could therefore not rely on *Siebe Gorman*. They purported to divide debts into two separate assets: the receivable due from the debtor, and the proceeds of that receivable, which would normally constitute a credit balance at the debtor's bank. Institutions such as 3i purported to take a fixed charge over the receivables, but only a floating charge over the proceeds in the debtor's bank account. That approach also met with favour, this time by the Court of Appeal in *Re New Bullas Trading*.[78]

4.107 Significant doubts were, however, also expressed about the correctness of that decision. Although a debt and its proceeds are separate assets, it does not follow that the debtor's power to use the proceeds is irrelevant in characterising the nature of the charge over the debt. The only value in a debt is in its proceeds; and it is inconceivable that a person would lend money against debts in circumstances where they did not have a charge over the proceeds. Since the question at issue is whether the debtor has, in practice, the ability to

---

77   [1979] 2 Lloyd's Rep 142.
78   [1994] 1 BCLC 485.

deal with the charged asset in the ordinary course of its business, it was argued that the answer to that question must ultimately depend on whether the debtor is able to deal with the proceeds.

The Brumark case

4.108 These various questions were considered by the Privy Council in *Re Brumark Investments (Agnew v Commissioner of Inland Revenue)*[79] in 2001, which became the most important case on the issue since the *Yorkshire Woolcombers* case almost a century earlier. The debtor had purported to create a fixed charge over its debts in favour of its bank. The proceeds of the debts were, however, generally excluded from the fixed charge, and were expressed to be the subject of a floating charge. The charge therefore adopted the approach which had found favour with the Court of Appeal in the *New Bullas* case. The New Zealand Court of Appeal nevertheless held that the charge was floating, rather than fixed, and refused to follow the *New Bullas* case. This decision was unanimously approved by a very strong Privy Council, their opinion being given by Lord Millett.

4.109 Like the New Zealand Court of Appeal, the Privy Council considered that *New Bullas* was wrongly decided. Introducing some much-needed common sense into a debate which was becoming increasingly artificial, Lord Millett held that, whilst a debt and its proceeds are two separate assets, any attempt, in this context, to separate them makes no commercial sense.[80] If the debtor is free to use the proceeds of the debts, the creditor cannot have a fixed charge on the debts themselves. It is the extent of the debtor's right to use the proceeds of the debt which is determinative of the nature of the charge over the debt.

4.110 Lord Millett confirmed that the key question is[81]:

'... the intention that the company should be free to deal with the charged assets and withdraw them from the security without the consent of the holder of the charge; or, to put the question another way, whether the charged assets were intended to be under the control of the company or of the charge holder.'

The Spectrum Plus case

4.111 Although *Brumark* contained an authoritative opinion of a strong court, it suffered from two limitations. In the first place, the court was concerned with a *New Bullas* form of debenture and therefore did not deal directly with the issues raised in *Siebe Gorman*. Even more importantly, as a decision of the Privy Council, it was not binding in England.

4.112 As a result, a test case was commenced in the English courts to establish, once and for all, the limits of the ability of a creditor to obtain a fixed

---

79   [2001] 2 AC 710.
80   [2001] 2 AC 710 at [46].
81   [2001] 2 AC 710 at [32].

charge over debts generally. In 2005, the House of Lords gave judgment in *National Westminster Bank v Spectrum Plus*.[82] The importance of the decision was recognised in the fact that the House of Lords fielded a seven-member panel. The case involved a debenture in substantially the same form as that in the *Siebe Gorman* case. The debtor company was prevented from disposing of its debts and was required to pay their proceeds into its account with the creditor bank, but there was no restriction on the ability of the debtor to draw on that account in the ordinary way. The House of Lords unanimously decided that, although the charge over debts was expressed to be a fixed charge, it was in fact a floating charge because the debtor remained free to use their proceeds. They overruled the *Siebe Gorman* decision and, for good measure, confirmed (for the reasons given in *Brumark*) that the *New Bullas* case was also incorrectly decided.

4.113   The principal speech was given by Lord Scott. He regarded the critical point as being that the debtor could continue to draw on the account and therefore to use the proceeds of the charged debts.[83] *Siebe Gorman* had been wrongly decided. What is important is 'the commercial nature and substance of the arrangement', rather than 'a formalistic analysis'.[84] He also confirmed that it made no difference if the security was taken by means of an assignment, rather than a charge. The key question, in each case, was whether the debtor had control of the proceeds of the debts.[85]

Summary

4.114   The effect of *Brumark* and *Spectrum Plus* is as follows:

• It is conceptually possible to create a fixed charge over all the present and future debts of a company. But, if the company remains free to use the proceeds of the debts and to remove them from the security until it is enforced, the charge will be a floating charge even if it is described as a fixed charge.

• Accordingly, the normal form of clearing bank debenture under which the company:
   – is prohibited from disposing of its debts;
   – is required to pay the proceeds of the debts into its account with the chargee bank; and
   – is in fact able to draw on the account in the ordinary way,

 constitutes a floating charge over the debts.

• In addition, if a debenture purports to:
   – divide the debts from their proceeds;
   – create a fixed charge over the debts; and
   – create a floating charge over the proceeds,

82   [2005] 2 AC 680.
83   [2005] 2 AC 680 at [117].
84   [2005] 2 AC 680 at [116].
85   [2005] 2 AC 680 at [107].

the charge over the debts will be a floating charge. If the security over the proceeds is floating, so it is over the debts.

- In deciding whether the charge is fixed or floating, what is important is the commercial nature and substance of the arrangement and what happens in practice, not just what the document says.

- The position is the same if, instead of the company creating a charge over the debts, it assigns them by way of security.

Examples of fixed charges over debts generally

4.115　In spite of *Brumark* and *Spectrum Plus*, there are still types of case where it is possible to obtain a fixed charge over debts. Three examples can illustrate the position.

4.116　In the first type of case, the creditor will take a charge over debts and give notice to the counterparty requiring them to be paid to the creditor. There is no doubt that this will create an effective fixed charge, even over future debts, although it is only practicable in a minority of cases.

4.117　Alternatively, the creditor can take a charge over debts and require the debtor to collect them on his behalf and pay them to the creditor. As Lord Millett pointed out in the *Brumark* case:[86] 'The fact that the [debtor] was free to collect the book debts was not inconsistent with the fixed nature of the charge, because the [debtor] was not collecting them for its own benefit but for the account of the [creditor].'

4.118　Thirdly, a bank can take a charge over debts and require their proceeds to be paid into an account with the bank which is blocked, so that withdrawals can only be made from it with the approval of the bank. In such a case, the bank will have a fixed charge over the book debts because it controls their proceeds. Such an approach was held to be effective by the Irish Supreme Court in *Re Keenan Brothers*.[87] In that case, the bank purported to take a fixed charge over debts and required the company to pay them into an account designated by the bank and not to withdraw them without the bank's consent. Because the company was in serious financial difficulties, the bank did actually control the account. No withdrawal could be made from it without the counter-signature of a bank official. The charge was held to be fixed.

4.119　But these types of arrangement will only assist in exceptional cases. In most cases where a lender is taking a charge over debts generally, the company will require the use of their proceeds in its business, failing which it will simply need to borrow more money; and the charge will therefore be a floating charge.

86　[2001] 2 AC 710 at [18].
87　[1986] BCLC 242.

Structured transactions

4.120 *Spectrum Plus*[88] is as important for what it did not decide as for what it did. Although it is now clear that a purported fixed charge over debts generally will be recharacterised as floating where the debtor controls their proceeds, it is less clear when a creditor will obtain a fixed charge in a more structured transaction. Most of the cases have involved transactions where the creditor has made no real attempt to control the proceeds of the charged debts. In more structured transactions, such as asset finance or project finance transactions or securitisations, the creditor will always obtain some degree of control over the proceeds of charged or assigned debts, but there is at present no clear authority concerning the extent of control which is required in order to enable the charge to be regarded as fixed.

4.121 It has been seen that the test is whether the debtor is, in a practical, commercial sense, able to deal with the proceeds of the debts as if the charge did not exist. In *Brumark*[89] and *Spectrum Plus*, this question clearly had to be answered in the affirmative. In more structured transactions, it is more likely to be answered in the negative.

4.122 Two examples illustrate the issue. The first example involves a debtor which owns a vessel which it has leased. The debtor charges the vessel and the benefit of the lease to a creditor. If the creditor requires the lease rentals to be paid into a blocked account which are only capable of being drawn on to repay the loan, the charge will clearly be fixed. But, in practice, it is normally the case that the debtor will have some rights over the rentals, and the question then arises whether those rights are such that it can effectively use the rentals as if the charge did not exist. This is a particular problem where the creditor allows the debtor to use the lease rentals until the creditor wishes to enforce the security, although the *Atlantic Computers*[90] and *Atlantic Medical*[91] cases suggest that such arrangements create a fixed charge.

4.123 Those cases have been severely criticised on the basis that they are impossible to reconcile with the basic principle that a charge is a floating charge if the debtor is able to use the asset in the ordinary course of its business before enforcement. Nevertheless, in the equivalent case of a charge over land which has been leased, the fact that the debtor is able to receive the rents until enforcement does not affect the fixed nature of the creditor's charge over the land. Once a charge over the land is enforced, it carries with it the right to receive the rents. It may be that a similar approach should be taken to leased goods.

4.124 The second example involves a debtor which is a project company and which has charged (or assigned by way of security) the benefit of its principal contract to the creditor financing the project. In some cases the proceeds of the contract may be paid into a blocked account under the complete control of the

---

88   *National Westminster Bank v Spectrum Plus* [2005] 2 AC 680.
89   *Re Brumark Investments (Agnew v Commissioner of Inland Revenue)* [2001] 2 AC 710.
90   *Re Atlantic Computer Systems* [1992] Ch 505.
91   *Re Atlantic Medical* [1993] BCLC 386.

creditor, in which event it is likely that security will be fixed. But is often the case that the creditor will have contractual obligations to make amounts available to the debtor or that the debtor may have certain limited drawing rights on the account. It is not clear when the rights of the debtor over the account will become sufficiently extensive that it can be said to have the general authority to use the proceeds in the ordinary course of its business but, in many cases, the creditor will have a significant amount of control over the proceeds, albeit that it will fall short of complete control.

4.125 The courts have yet to grapple with the issue of the degree of control which is necessary in order to constitute the charge as fixed. The test is whether the debtor can, in a broad commercial sense, deal with the asset concerned as if the charge did not exist. The nature of a structured finance transaction is very far removed from the type of general security with which the courts have so far been concerned. Although we await a definitive decision, there is much to be said for the proposition that, in many structured transactions, the degree of control which is exercised by the creditor, although by no means absolute, should be sufficient to ensure that the charge is fixed.

CREATING SECURITY

Chapter 5

CREATION

Part 1: INTRODUCTION

5.1 A creditor has three main concerns when taking security:

- Is it effective in the debtor's insolvency?
- Will it have priority over other proprietary interests in the same asset?
- Will it be enforceable on default by the debtor?

5.2 This chapter, and **CHAPTER 6**, are concerned with the first of these issues – is the security effective in the debtor's insolvency? Priority issues are considered in **CHAPTER 7** and enforcement in **CHAPTERS 8** and **9**.

5.3 The previous three chapters have described the three main types of consensual security interest available to a creditor. It has been seen that the creditor has the choice of a pledge, a mortgage or a charge. The purpose of this chapter is to consider, in the light of those three types of security interest, the practical choices open to a creditor and the steps he needs to take to obtain effective security.

5.4 For the purposes of this chapter, pledges can be disposed of quickly. Their main value in commercial transactions is to enable short-term security to be taken over bills of lading when financing international trade transactions. In most financings, the main choice available to a creditor is between a mortgage and a charge.

5.5 There are three prerequisites of the creation of an effective mortgage:

- the transfer to the creditor of legal or beneficial title to the asset concerned (depending on whether the mortgage is to be legal or equitable), subject to the debtor's equity of redemption;
- the execution of a document creating or evidencing the mortgage (although a document is not always required in theory, it is in practice); and
- registration against the debtor, if required, under the Companies Act 1985 or the Bills of Sale Acts 1878–1891.

5.6 The prerequisites of the creation of an effective charge are:

- the execution of a document creating the charge (again, a document is not always required, but is invariably taken in practice); and

- registration against the debtor, if required under the Companies Act 1985 or the Bills of Sale Acts 1878–1891.

5.7 If these steps are complied with, the security is effective not only against the debtor whilst it remains solvent, but also in the event that the debtor goes into insolvency proceedings, such as liquidation, administration or bankruptcy. This is because the mortgage or charge creates a proprietary interest in the secured asset, which binds the debtor's insolvency officer as much as it binds the debtor itself.

5.8 It has been seen in CHAPTER **3** that there is no practical distinction between an equitable mortgage and an equitable fixed charge so that, in reality, the choice available to a creditor is between:

- a legal mortgage; and
- an equitable mortgage or charge.

5.9 For the purpose of the creation of security which is effective in the insolvency of the debtor, there is no distinction between the two. They both create proprietary interests which are effective in the debtor's insolvency. The distinction is only of any material relevance in a priority dispute between the creditor and another person claiming a proprietary interest in the secured asset (which is considered in CHAPTER **7**).

5.10 When deciding whether to create a legal mortgage or a charge, the parties have to weigh up the advantages and disadvantages of each. In some cases, the decision is straightforward. There are some types of asset (most intangibles and all future assets) which cannot be the subject of a legal mortgage. In the case of other types of asset, the priority advantages of a legal mortgage need to be weighed against the fact that it is generally quicker and easier to create a charge than a legal mortgage.

5.11 There are two other matters which concern a creditor taking security over an asset:

- What is the value of the asset, particularly on enforcement?
- Is the debtor bound by the transaction by which the security is created?

5.12 The first issue is, of course, of great practical importance. Much of the time taken by creditors and their lawyers in relation to secured transactions is spent evaluating the secured assets. In the case of land, for instance, the creditor would expect to obtain a certificate as to the title to the land. Similarly, a creditor obtaining security over a major piece of equipment will be concerned about its physical state and any contracts connected with it (such as leases or charterparties). Where the secured asset is a contract, the creditor will want to know what the debtor's rights are under the contract and the circumstances in which those rights can be lost.

5.13 These issues go to the value of the asset rather than to the way in which security is taken over it, and it is beyond the scope of this chapter to consider them. For the most part, they are not specific to the law of security, but are general matters of land law and personal property law. But their importance in practice should not be ignored.

5.14 Whether or not the debtor is bound by the transaction also depends on general legal considerations, in this case deriving from areas of law such as company law, equity, the law of contract and the law of agency. Although they are not peculiar to the law of security, they are of practical importance and, because they do go to the validity of the security, they are considered briefly in this chapter.

5.15 The remaining parts of this chapter therefore consider the following issues:

- Part 2 (**5.17**ff) – how can the creditor ensure that the debtor is bound by the secured transaction?
- Part 3 (**5.46**ff) – in the case of a mortgage, how is title to the secured assets transferred to the creditor?
- Part 4 (**5.57**ff) – in the case of a mortgage or charge, what documentation is required?

5.16 The other key requirement of the creation of effective security is that, in many cases, registration is required at a debtor registry, either under the Companies Act 1985 or under the Bills of Sale Acts 1878–1891. This topic deserves a chapter to itself, and is considered in CHAPTER 6.

Part 2: IS THE DEBTOR BOUND BY THE SECURED TRANSACTION?

5.17 Whether a debtor is bound by a transaction encompasses two main issues – whether he has validly entered into the transaction, and whether it can be set aside. Particularly where the debtor is a company, it is helpful to divide the first of these questions into two – does the debtor have the capacity to enter into the transaction, and do those persons who have purported to enter into it on behalf of the debtor have the authority to do so? This part will accordingly consider three separate issues:

- capacity;
- authority; and
- setting aside transactions (particularly for breach of fiduciary duty).

Capacity

5.18 Capacity is no longer an issue of much practical importance in English law. As far as individuals are concerned, there are now very few limitations on the capacity of an individual. The reduction in the age of contractual consent to 18 has reduced the number of problems concerning minors. As a result, the two main limitations on capacity of an individual are bankruptcy and mental incapacity.

5.19 As far as companies incorporated under the English Companies Acts are concerned, there is now very little left of the old rule that a company only had the capacity to do that which was authorised by its memorandum of association. By the middle of the twentieth century, the proliferation of objects in companies' memoranda of association and the introduction of provisions which turned every power in a memorandum into a main object meant that there were very few cases in practice of incapacity of companies. Since 1972, there have been various statutory attempts to limit, and then to abolish, restrictions on a company's capacity. Despite some false starts, this has now been achieved by s 35 of the Companies Act 1985, which provides that:

> 'The validity of an act done by a company shall not be called into question on the ground of lack of capacity by reason of anything in the company's memorandum.'

5.20   As a result, capacity is no longer an issue in relation to companies incorporated under the Companies Acts.[1] It may, nevertheless, be a problem in relation to other types of debtor, including those which are incorporated or resident abroad. Even in relation to English companies, it still continues to be the practice of lawyers advising lenders in financing transactions (particularly if they are secured) to check the debtor's memorandum of association and, if it does not contain appropriate provisions, to require the objects clause in the memorandum to be altered by special resolution before the transaction is effected.

Authority

5.21   Where the debtor is an English company, of more importance in practice is to ensure that those persons who have purported to enter into the transaction on its behalf have the authority to do so. In most cases, the body which will have the authority to do so is the company's board of directors. The company will only be bound if those acting on its behalf had the authority to do so. If they did not have the authority, the transaction does not bind the company, although it can be ratified by the company.

5.22   Even if the persons who are purporting to act on behalf of the debtor company do not have the actual authority to do so, the debtor will nevertheless be bound by their actions if it has conferred on them the apparent (or, as it is sometimes called, ostensible) authority to do so. This will be the case if the debtor has held out those who purport to enter into the transaction as having the authority to do so on its behalf. This general principle of the law of agency is reflected in company law by the rule in *Turquand's* case,[2] which establishes that persons dealing with a company are entitled to assume that the requirements of its internal corporate governance have been complied with.

5.23   There is now statutory recognition of this principle in s 35A(1) of the Companies Act 1985:

---

1   The issue will be completely abolished when the Company Law Reform Bill, published in 2005, comes into force.
2   *Royal British Bank v Turquand* (1856) 6 E&B 327.

'In favour of a person dealing with a company in good faith, the power of the board of directors to bind the company, or authorise others to do so, shall be deemed to be free of any limitation under the company's constitution.'

5.24 The legislation makes it clear that the person dealing with the company is presumed to have acted in good faith unless the contrary is proved and that he will not be regarded as not acting in good faith 'by reason only of his knowing that an act is beyond the powers of directors under the company's constitution'.[3] In most day-to-day transactions with companies, persons dealing with a company rely on these common law and statutory protections. In financing transactions, however, particularly when they are secured, it is the general practice of the lawyers acting on behalf of the lenders to check that the persons who have entered into the transaction on behalf of the company did, in fact, have the authority to do so. This is because there are limits on the common law and statutory protections (such as the requirement that the creditor acted in good faith), which might throw doubt on their application in any particular case.

5.25 The result is that the lawyers acting for the lenders will take steps to establish whether the transaction has, in fact, been authorised by the company. In doing so, a number of issues need to be considered, including the following:

- Who are the directors of the company?
- Does the board of directors have the authority to enter into the transaction? This is established by reference to the company's articles of association. It will normally give the board of directors wide powers to manage the company's business.[4] In some cases, there will be a specific provision concerning borrowing powers, which may contain limitations on the amount of borrowings.[5]
- Has the board of directors properly exercised its authority to enter into the transaction? This will require an appropriate board resolution passed by the requisite number of directors in accordance with the company's articles of association. It is often the case that some of the company's directors are interested in the transaction (for instance, because they are directors of other companies in the group which are guaranteeing the transaction), in which event it needs to be established whether (and, if so, on what terms) interested directors are entitled to be counted in a quorum and to vote on the resolution.

5.26 The other matter which can affect the authority of the board of directors is the commencement of insolvency proceedings. If the company goes into liquidation or administration, the authority of the board to bind the company is terminated and replaced by that of the insolvency officer

---

3   Companies Act 1985, s 35A(2)(b).
4   See, for instance, art 70 of Table A to the Companies Act 1985 and art 80 of Table A to the Companies Act 1948.
5   This is particularly likely in the case of companies listed on The Stock Exchange, but may also be the case with companies which have adopted Table A to the Companies Act 1948 – see art 79.

concerned.[6] In addition, if a petition is presented for the compulsory winding up of a company, and a winding up order is ultimately made, the liquidation dates back to the date of the presentation of the petition (which is quite likely to have happened a month of two before the order is made), and any disposition of the company's property entered into in the meantime is void unless the court validates it.[7]

5.27 Where the debtor is incorporated outside England, advice will be required on these issues from lawyers in the appropriate jurisdiction.

Can the transaction be set aside?

5.28 There are various ways in which a security arrangement which has been duly entered into by the debtor is capable of being set aside. Such circumstances include mistake, misrepresentation, duress, fraud, undue influence and illegality. Most of these arise under general principles of the law of contract and will not be discussed here. In practice, the most likely circumstances in which a security transaction will be set aside is where the security has been created by a company and its directors have acted in breach of fiduciary duty when entering into the transaction.

Breach of fiduciary duty

5.29 The directors of an English company have a collective fiduciary duty, when deciding how to exercise their powers, to do so in the best interests of the company.[8] If the directors of the debtor company commit a breach of that duty and the person dealing with the company enters into the transaction with (actual or constructive) notice of that breach of duty, then:

- although the transaction is valid at common law, it is voidable in equity;
- if it still executory, it can be set aside at the instance of the company (normally by a liquidator or administrator), subject to the normal limitations on the right of rescission;
- the company can trace into the hands of the person dealing with the company any money paid or property transferred to him under the transaction, subject to the normal limitations on equitable tracing; and
- the person dealing with the company may also be personally liable to the company as a constructive trustee for the benefits he has received under the transaction.[9]

5.30 The problem is particularly likely to arise where the company guarantees the obligations of another company in the same group (or an associated company) to a lender, or creates a third party charge over its property. The directors must act in what they consider to be the interests of *their* company

---

6   Insolvency Act 1986, ss 91(2) and 103 and Sch B1, para 64.
7   Insolvency Act 1986, s 127.
8   *Re Smith and Fawcett* [1942] Ch 304.
9   *Rolled Steel Products (Holdings) v British Steel Corporation* [1986] Ch 246.

and not simply in the interests of the group as a whole.[10] Frequently, the interests of the company will coincide with those of the group. This will often be the case where guarantees are given by subsidiaries to secure facilities to their ultimate parent company which acts as the group's banker. If, on the other hand, a subsidiary is guaranteeing fellow subsidiaries (especially if the fellow subsidiaries are in a different sub-group) or if the guarantee is of a facility which will not be used for the purpose of funding the existing group (for instance, an acquisition finance facility), the directors may find it more difficult to establish why they consider the giving of the guarantee to be in the best interests of their company.

5.31 It is important to put this issue in context. The directors' duty is to act in what *they* consider to be the interests of the company. If they do, the transaction will only be set aside if no reasonable board of directors could have reached the same conclusion. The court will not substitute its own judgment for that of the directors but, if challenged, the board must show that they honestly believed that their actions were entered into for the benefit of the company and that they had reasonable grounds for their belief.[11]

5.32 If the directors have acted in breach of duty and the lender has actual or constructive notice of this fact, the company can avoid the transaction and recover any benefits conferred under it. This problem is particularly acute for lenders, since, as a result of their relationship with the company, they may have sufficient information about the company to give them constructive notice of such an irregularity.

5.33 The problem can be avoided in two ways:

- by attempting to ensure the directors do not commit a breach of duty; or
- by obtaining from the company (as beneficiary of the duty) an affirmation of any potential breach of duty by the directors.

5.34 Where there is any doubt about whether the transaction is in the company's interests (and particularly where security is given for the liabilities of another person), the board minutes of the company will need to explain why the directors consider that it is in the interests of the company to enter into the transaction. In many cases, there will be sufficient reasons why the transaction will benefit the company that the likelihood of the transaction being set aside will be extremely remote. It will only be set aside if the company (acting normally through its liquidator or administrator) can prove either that the directors did not honestly believe that the transaction was in the company's interests or that no reasonable board of directors could have considered that it was.

Affirmation

5.35 In some cases, however, doubt will remain about the possibility of there being a breach of duty, in which event the company's shareholders (who will

---

10   *Charterbridge Corporation v Lloyds Bank* [1970] Ch 62 at 74.
11   *Colin Gwyer & Associates v London Wharf (Limehouse)* [2002] EWHC 2748 (ch) at [72]– [90].

often be another group company) will be asked to affirm the transaction so that it will not amount to a breach of fiduciary duty. In this context, various issues need to be borne in mind:

- The affirmation will only be effective if the shareholders have possession of all material information concerning the transaction.[12]

- Where a shareholder is also a company, its directors must have authority to give the affirmation and must not themselves be acting in breach of duty in giving it.

- If there is any possibility that the transaction might be regarded as a 'fraud on the minority' (for example, if it involves expropriation of the company's property – as in the case of a guarantee not given in the interests of the company), the shareholders' consent must be unanimous.[13]

- Where the company is insolvent or is likely to become insolvent as a result of the transaction, even the unanimous consent of the shareholders is unlikely to validate the transaction.

Company in financial difficulties

5.36 The final point requires some elaboration, since it is of considerable importance in practice. Directors owe their fiduciary duties to the company, rather than to individual shareholders or creditors of the company. Whilst the company is solvent, what this means is that the directors owe their duties to the shareholders of the company as a class.[14] If, however, the company is insolvent, it is its creditors, rather than its shareholders, who are interested in its affairs. The actions of the directors in such a case will affect the company's creditors more than it its shareholders. For this reason, where the company is insolvent, 'the company' to which the directors owe their duties encompasses its creditors.[15]

5.37 In *West Mercia Safetyware v Dodd*[16] a payment was made by the company for the benefit of its shareholder at a time when it was insolvent. The Court of Appeal held that the transfer was made in breach of fiduciary duty to the company and accordingly that the amount should be repaid to the company. Dillon LJ approved the decision of Street CJ in *Kinsela v Russell Kinsela*[17] to the effect that, where a company is insolvent, directors must consider the interests of creditors, and that shareholder confirmation is therefore ineffective to waive a breach of duty.

---

12 *Winthrop Investments v Winns* [1975] 2 NSWLR 666.
13 *Parke v Daily News* [1962] 1 Ch 927.
14 *Greenhalgh v Arderne Cinemas* [1951] Ch 286 at 291.
15 *Walker v Wimborne* (1976) 137 CLR 1.
16 [1988] BCLC 250.
17 (1986) 4 NSWLR 722.

5.38 There is authority in New Zealand that this is also the case where the company is in danger of becoming insolvent as a result of entering into the transaction, even if it is not actually insolvent at the time. In *Nicholson v Permakraft (NZ)*,[18] Cooke J said:[19]

'The duties of directors are owed to the company. On the facts of particular cases this may require the directors to consider *inter alia* the interests of creditors. For instance, creditors are entitled to consideration, in my opinion, if the company is insolvent, or near-insolvent, or of doubtful solvency, or if a contemplated payment or other course of action would jeopardise its solvency.'

5.39 As a result, if the company is insolvent or in financial difficulties at the time the transaction is entered into, or it becomes so as a result of the transaction, it is not open to the company's shareholders to affirm a potential breach of fiduciary duty by the directors. The affirmation has to be effected by the 'company', which would also require the involvement of its creditors.

5.40 Particular problems arise where the transaction open to attack will result in a contingent liability (for instance, under a guarantee). For accounting purposes, a contingent liability will only appear on the company's balance sheet if it is likely to mature but, as Cooke J pointed out in *Nicholson v Permakraft*[19], for the purpose of establishing the nature of the directors' duties, insolvency is not tested solely by reference to financial statements. The question is whether, in fact, the company was in financial difficulties at the time of, or as a result of, the transaction. In the case of a guarantee, difficult problems are involved in deciding how likely the contingency is to occur. If, for instance, the company gives a guarantee to a bank of the obligations of its parent company which is in financial difficulties, the likelihood is that the guarantee will be called and the contingent liability should probably be taken into account. If, however, the parent company is solvent and there is no real likelihood of the guarantee being called in the foreseeable future, it might be justifiable to discount the contingent liability substantially.

5.41 An example of security being set aside in this way is *Rolled Steel Products (Holdings) v British Steel Corporation*.[20] In that case, an individual directly or indirectly owned the share capital of two companies, A and B. A owed a substantial amount of money to C, which had been guaranteed by the individual shareholder. A was insolvent, but B appeared to have net assets. B executed a guarantee and supporting debenture in favour of C to secure A's liability to C. C eventually appointed a receiver of B under the guarantee and debenture.

5.42 The documentation was approved at a board meeting at which there was no quorum. The individual shareholder, who was interested in the transaction (because he had given a personal guarantee of the secured debt), had not disclosed his interest as required by the company's articles of association.

---

18   [1985] 1 NZLR 242.
19   [1985] 1 NZLR 242 at 249.
20   [1986] Ch 246.

5.43 The Court of Appeal held that C could not rely on the guarantee and debenture. The documentation had not been properly authorised by the directors. The directors had also acted in breach of fiduciary duty in purporting to enter into the documentation, and C knew this to be the case.

5.44 It was not clear whether B's shareholders had purported to affirm the transaction but, for technical reasons, it was not open to C to plead this point. It nevertheless seems clear from the cases referred to above that the problem could not have been solved simply by a shareholders' affirmation if B had been rendered insolvent, or at risk of insolvency, as a result of entering into the guarantee.

Summary

5.45 The position may be summarised as follows:

- It is necessary to check that the debtor has the capacity to enter into the transaction concerned. This will not be an issue in relation to companies incorporated under the English Companies Acts, because previous limitations on their capacity have effectively been abolished.

- Although a person dealing with a company is normally entitled to assume that the company's internal procedures have been complied with, there are limitations on this principle. In particular, the protection will not be available if that person has not acted in good faith. As a result, it is common in financing transactions (particularly where they are secured) for the lenders' lawyers to check the authority of those purporting to enter into the transaction on behalf of the company. This is a relatively straightforward exercise.

- Of much more difficulty is that a transaction with a creditor can be set aside if it was entered into in breach of fiduciary duty by the directors of the debtor company and the creditor had actual or constructive notice of that fact. In practice, this is a particular problem where the debtor is entering into a guarantee (whether secured or not) or into third party security. Because of the amount of information which a lender is likely to have about the company, and because shareholder affirmation may not solve the problem where the debtor is in financial difficulties as a result of the transaction, it is important to ensure that the debtor's directors have good reasons for entering into the transaction and that they are properly minuted.

Part 3: CREATING A MORTGAGE – TRANSFERRING TITLE

5.46 It has been seen in CHAPTER 3 that the transfer of title to the secured asset (whether legal or beneficial) is a requirement of both a legal, and an equitable, mortgage. The purpose of this part is to put the issues raised in

CHAPTER **3** in a practical context, by briefly considering what is involved in transferring title to the principal types of asset over which mortgages are taken in commercial transactions.

Goods

5.47   In many cases, it is as straightforward to take a legal mortgage over goods as an equitable mortgage or charge. This is because the transfer of title to most types of goods can be effected by the execution of a document by the debtor. In the document (which may be described as a mortgage or, in some cases, as a bill of sale), the debtor will transfer title to the creditor by way of security for the payment of the secured liabilities. The only difference from the creation of a charge is that the security document will be expressed to transfer legal title to the goods, rather than to create a charge over them. The advantage of obtaining a legal mortgage, as opposed to an equitable mortgage or charge, is in relation to priorities over third parties who might obtain an interest in the goods. Priorities are considered in CHAPTER **7**.

5.48   There are special requirements for ships. In most cases, the transfer of legal title to a ship registered in Great Britain will require the registration of the mortgage in the British ship registry. Although there is no equivalent title register in relation to aircraft, mortgages of aircraft are also registrable, and registration of them gives the creditor priority advantages. Paradoxically, the most common type of goods over which legal mortgages are created in practice is ships and aircraft – the very assets which require the most formalities for the creation of a legal mortgage. Apart from ships and aircraft, legal mortgages are sometimes taken over major items of capital equipment, in which event all that is required is a document which transfers legal title. It is relatively rare for an equitable mortgage to be taken over goods. In those cases where it is not cost-effective to take a legal mortgage, it is more common to take a fixed charge if the goods are unlikely to be sold in the course of the debtor's business, or a floating charge if they are.

Land

5.49   A legal mortgage of land is created by a charge by way of legal mortgage, which does not effect a transfer of the land to the creditor, but gives the creditor a legal interest in the land, and rights which are equivalent to those which he would have had if the land had been transferred to him. In practice, therefore, the choice for a creditor is either to obtain a charge by way of legal mortgage, or to take an equitable mortgage or charge. Where the debtor's interest in the land is registrable (which is the case in relation to all freehold interests and most leasehold interests in registered land[21]), the creditor's interest will need to be registered at the Land Registry in order to constitute a legal interest.

---

21   The principal exception being leases for 7 years or less.

5.50 Where the debtor has valuable land (particularly if it is freehold land or land with a long, valuable lease), it is common for a creditor to take a charge by way of legal mortgage and register it at the Land Registry. If, on the other hand, the land owned by the debtor is of little value (particularly if it has a large number of leasehold properties which have little premium value, for instance, because they are let at rack rents), it is common for the creditor simply to take an equitable mortgage or charge because, on a cost-benefit analysis, the time and expense involved in registering the security at the Land Registry outweighs the (priority) benefits of doing so. The creation of an equitable mortgage or charge requires the parties to execute a deed, but does not require registration at the Land Registry.

Registered shares

5.51 The common law recognises the transfer of shares. Where, as in most cases, there is a register of shareholders, legal title is transferred by removing the name of the debtor from the share register and replacing it with that of the creditor, or his nominee. A legal mortgage gives the creditor certain priority rights, but they are used relatively infrequently in practice, most lenders taking a charge, rather than going to the trouble and expense of being entered on the register of members. In the case of shares, concerns about potential liability of the lender for pension deficits has recently made it even less likely that lenders will wish to become the legal owner of shares. This is because the pensions legislation might require a creditor who controls the exercise of voting rights in relation to shares of a company to contribute to the pension deficit of its group.[22]

Legal mortgages generally

5.52 Except in the case of goods other than ships and aircraft, the creation of a legal mortgage normally requires something to be done other than the execution of a document. In the case of land, ships and aircraft, registration is required at an asset registry. In the case of shares, registration is required in the share register kept by the company whose shares are being mortgaged. When deciding whether to take a legal mortgage, or an equitable mortgage or charge, the creditor has to weigh up the additional cost of obtaining a legal mortgage against the (mainly priority) advantages which it will obtain from doing so. The result is that, in practice, most legal mortgages are taken over freehold land, valuable leases of land, ships, aircraft and other valuable items of capital equipment. In most other cases, the creditor will settle for an equitable mortgage or charge.

Contract rights and receivables

5.53 Apart from shares, the common law does not generally recognise intangibles as being property. As a result, the choice for a creditor who is taking

---

22 Pensions Act 2004, ss 38–51.

security over contract rights and receivables is between a statutory assignment and an equitable assignment or charge. A statutory assignment or an equitable assignment will transfer to the creditor the beneficial title to the asset, subject to redemption. A charge will give the creditor an equitable proprietary interest by way of security. There is no practical difference between an equitable assignment and a charge. The only advantage of a statutory assignment is that it gives the creditor the ability to sue the counterparty in his own name, although this is of little practical significance.

5.54 Apart from the ability to sue in the creditor's own name, the advantage of a statutory assignment over an equitable assignment or charge is that written notice has to be given of a statutory assignment and therefore the creditor will obtain greater rights against the counterparty (who can no longer obtain a good discharge by paying the debtor and whose rights of set-off are thereby restricted) and also against third parties who claim an interest in the asset (as a result of the priority rules). But it should be borne in mind that an equitable assignee or chargee can also give notice (although it is not a requirement of a valid equitable assignment or charge), in which event these benefits can be obtained by an equitable assignee or chargee as well.

5.55 The real issue, therefore, for the creditor is not whether he takes a statutory assignment or a charge, but whether he gives notice to the counterparty. Whether or not he does so ultimately depends on commercial considerations. Giving notice can provide the creditor with significant advantages but it is not practical to do so in all cases. Where security is taken over a particular contract, or a small number of contracts, it is common for notice to be given. Where security is taken over a large number of contracts or receivables, it is less likely that this will be done. The question is a commercial one, rather than a legal one – is it commercially practicable for notice to be given?

Equitable assignments and charges generally

5.56 The other major advantage of an equitable assignment or a charge is that, unlike a legal mortgage, it is not only available over more types of asset (particularly intangibles), but can also be taken over future assets. As a result, in a commercial transaction, it is rare for a legal mortgage to be taken in isolation. Because it will only extend to existing land, goods or securities, it will very commonly be linked with an equitable assignment or charge over future assets of those descriptions which are subsequently acquired by the debtor. Legal mortgages can be taken in isolation from other types of security, but they are commonly just one part of a security package. In a debenture, for instance, a legal mortgage will be taken over land currently owned by the debtor, and fixed and floating charges will be taken over all other present and future assets of the debtor.

Part 4: DOCUMENTING MORTGAGES AND CHARGES

5.57 In practice, a secured transaction will require to be documented, whatever its nature, but the documentation can serve two different purposes. In some cases it will create the security, and in others it will evidence it.

5.58 In the case of a pledge and of certain types of legal mortgage, the security is created by the delivery of, or by the transfer of title to, an asset, rather than by the execution of a document by the debtor. In cases of this type, the purpose of the documentation is to evidence the transaction – to set out the terms on which the security has been granted. But, where the security consists of an equitable mortgage or charge (and in those cases where legal title to goods can be transferred by a document), the security is actually created by the execution by the debtor of the security documentation.

5.59 The purpose of this part is to consider some of the key provisions of a security document. It is beyond the scope of this part to consider the detailed terms of security documents, but it will briefly describe some of the key provisions. The three most important provisions of any security document are those which describe the secured assets, the secured liabilities and the creditor's powers of enforcement. Other key provisions include a set-off clause and a further assurance clause.

Secured assets

5.60 One of the most important provisions of any security document is to describe the identity of the secured assets. Security over all of the present and future assets of a company is easy to describe, but it is more difficult where the security is only intended to extend to some of the debtor's assets or where (as is normally the case when the creditor takes a debenture from a company) only some of the company's assets are intended to be the subject of a fixed charge, the others being subject to a floating charge.

5.61 What is required is that the assets which are the subject of the charge can be identified when the security requires to be enforced. Although it should not generally be difficult to describe the secured assets as they exist at the time the security is created, it is necessary to consider how the identity of the assets might change during the period of the security, and to ensure that they are covered by the description of the secured assets. For instance, equipment might be replaced, or a deposit might be transferred. It is important to ensure that the replacement asset and the transferred asset are sufficiently described that the security extends to them.

5.62 It has been seen in CHAPTER 3 that it is not necessarily the case that security over an asset will extend to connected assets. If, for instance, security is taken over equipment, it is important to ensure that it expressly extends to the insurances of that equipment and to warranties given in relation to it. Even more importantly, where an asset has contractual rights associated with it (for instance, a vessel which is the subject of a charterparty or a lease), it is necessary to ensure that the security is taken not just over the asset, but also over the associated contractual rights. Because there is no general legal proposition that security over an asset extends to all rights associated with it, it is essential to ensure that they are specifically made the subject of the security.

5.63 Particular problems occur where the secured assets consist of some only of the assets of a particular class (for instance, certain goods of a particular type). The security will only be effective if, on enforcement, the creditor is able to establish which of the relevant assets are the subject of the security.

5.64 Where the security is taken by way of a charge, the documentation will need to make it clear whether the charge is fixed or floating. In many cases, it will be expressed to be fixed over some assets and floating over others. Where the security is taken by way of floating charge, it is important to ensure that there are appropriate restrictions on the authority of the debtor company to deal with the floating charge assets. It has been seen in CHAPTER 4 that the general authority of the debtor to deal with its floating charge assets is very wide. As a result, the floating charge will normally contain very stringent restrictions on the creation of other security interests and also some restrictions on material outright disposals (whilst continuing to enable the company to dispose of its assets outright in the ordinary course of its trading).

Secured liabilities

5.65 The provision which describes which liabilities are secured is as important as that which describes the secured assets. It does not matter how many assets are secured if there are no secured liabilities.

5.66 In practice, the choice in most security documents is between securing all monies from time to time owing by the debtor (or a third party) to the creditor or securing only those monies from time to time owing under a particular facility agreement. The issues raised by these two formulations are discussed in part 4 of CHAPTER 3 (**3.140**ff). It is clearly preferable to use an 'all monies' clause where possible, particularly where the facility is bilateral. In a syndicated facility, it is not generally practicable to do so, in which event the secured liabilities will need to be restricted to a particular facility. In such a case, the definition of the secured facility should be drafted as widely as possible in order to encompass variations to it.

5.67 Particular problems arise where the security is being given to secure the liabilities of a third party. This will be done either by the chargor entering into a guarantee of the principal debtor's obligations and then granting security in respect of that guarantee or by the chargor creating security for the obligations of the principal debtor. The problems involved in enforcing guarantees and indemnities are discussed in CHAPTER 11. For this purpose, it is sufficient to say that the courts are very protective of guarantors and that the security document needs to contain provisions which contract out of these protections. This is the case whether the document is drafted as a secured guarantee or as a third party charge. What is important is not the form of the document, but its substance – that the chargor is creating security for someone else's obligations.

Enforcement

5.68 After those provisions describing the secured assets and the secured liabilities, the enforcement clause is the most important clause in any security document. A secured creditor has few implied powers of enforcement which are of much use in practice. As a result, it is crucial that the security document explains when and how the security is to be enforced. In view of the potential liabilities of secured creditors (or of receivers on their behalf) when enforcing security, it is also common for security documents to limit liability and to require indemnities. Enforcement is considered in detail in CHAPTER 8.

Other provisions

5.69 Most security documents contain a contractual set-off provision. Such a provision can be extremely useful where the debtor holds deposit accounts or current accounts with the secured creditor. Set-off is considered in detail in CHAPTER 12.

5.70 Most security documents will also contain a further assurance clause. This will require the debtor to take further steps to perfect the security if required, for instance, by executing other documents, giving notices or effecting registrations. Where security is taken over future assets, it may require the debtor to notify the creditor of material acquisitions. It will also frequently require the debtor to provide other documentation which might be required on enforcement. In the case of a share charge, for instance, it is likely to require the debtor to provide the creditor with the share certificates to the charged shares, as well as a signed blank stock transfer form in relation to those shares.

5.71 A security document is likely to contain a number of undertakings by the debtor relating to the charged assets. These are, of course, purely personal obligations, enforceable as a matter of contract. They do not confer any proprietary right on the creditor. They are, nevertheless, a useful means of trying to ensure that the creditor does what is necessary to protect the value of the secured assets.

5.72 Even in a purely domestic transaction, a security document will normally contain a law and jurisdiction clause. Cross-border issues are considered in CHAPTER 13.

Execution

5.73 A security interest is created by the debtor and, as a result, the basic principle is that it only needs to be executed by the debtor. There are, however, two circumstances in which it will be necessary for the creditor to execute it. The first is where the security is taken over land. As has been seen in part 3 of CHAPTER 3 (3.57ff), a mortgage or charge over land must be executed by both the creditor and the debtor. This is the case not just in relation to mortgages and charges over land, but also to debentures which secure land in addition to other assets. The other circumstance is where the security document contains undertakings by the creditor, although it is not often the case that a security document will contain such undertakings. It would be more common for undertakings by the creditor to be contained in the underlying facility documentation.

5.74 It is frequently the case that security documents are executed as deeds. Although there is no harm in doing so, a deed is only required if the secured assets include land.

Chapter 6

REGISTRATION

Part 1: INTRODUCTION

6.1 Both at common law and in equity, security was effective without the necessity for any registration, but the intervention of legislation has had the effect that registration is now seen in practice as being the hallmark of security. Registration is not required in all cases, but most security taken from companies is registered.

6.2 Registration requirements fall into two distinct categories:

- registration against the debtor; and
- registration against the asset.

Registration against the debtor

6.3 It has been seen how few formalities are required in order to create an equitable mortgage or charge. The main requirement is that the parties have evinced an intention that a security interest be created over an identifiable asset. There are many cases in which the courts have had to consider whether or not a particular informal arrangement between a debtor and a creditor had the effect of conferring an equitable mortgage or charge on the creditor. A number of them are discussed in **CHAPTER 3**. But it is instructive that most of these cases were decided before the advent of the requirement to register mortgages and charges. Similar cases are still possible now, but the scope of their application is much diminished because the registration requirement generally forces the parties to decide, at the time the transaction is entered into, whether it constitutes a security interest.

6.4 An example of the effect of the registration requirement on informal security arrangements can be seen in relation to reservation of title clauses. It is common for sellers of goods to attempt to reserve title to those goods until payment. A provision of this kind is perfectly effective. The seller is reserving title to an asset he owns, rather than taking security over the buyer's asset.[1] In many cases, however, the seller is aware that the buyer will need to sub-sell the

---

[1] *Armour v Thyssen Edelstahlwerke* [1991] 2 AC 339; *Clough Mill v Martin* [1985] 1 WLR 111.

goods before paying the seller, and it is often implicit (if not explicit) in such arrangements that the buyer is authorised to sub-sell the goods. In such cases, the courts may be willing to imply into the reservation of title clause (if it is not expressed) a requirement that the proceeds of the sub-sale be held on trust for the seller. But this will not assist the seller. His rights under the trust will normally be by way of security for payment of the purchase price; and the trust will therefore constitute a charge. If the buyer is a company, a charge created by it over its right to payment from the sub-buyer will constitute a charge over book debts and will therefore be registrable under s 396(1)(e) of the Companies Act 1985.[2] It is not the practice for reservation of title clauses to be registered under the Companies Act and the effect is that, although the courts might be willing to imply a charge in favour of the seller, it will be void for non-registration in most circumstances.

6.5   There is, however, one recent development which pulls in the opposite direction. The Financial Collateral Directive[3] removes the requirement to register security over financial collateral, and therefore gives scope, in such cases, for the implication of a charge. The Financial Collateral Directive is discussed in part 5 of **CHAPTER 3 (3.175ff)** and is considered further in part 3 of this chapter **(6.32ff)**.

6.6   The first attempt to provide for a registration system against debtors was the Bills of Sale Act 1854. The current legislation is now contained in the Bills of Sale Acts 1878–1891 (the Bills of Sale Acts). These Acts do not apply to companies and, at the turn of the twentieth century, the registration requirement was extended to companies by the Companies Act 1900. It is now contained in the Companies Act 1985 (the Companies Act).

6.7   The legislation in relation to individuals and companies has, however, remained distinct, and they have a number of very different features, of which two are particularly important. In the first place, the registration requirements in the Companies Act have much wider application than those in the Bills of Sale Acts. The Bills of Sale Acts only apply to security over goods, although the insolvency legislation has extended their effect to general assignments of book debts. In contrast, most types of mortgage or charge created by companies are registrable under the Companies Act, although there are exceptions to this basic principle. The other important distinction concerns the requirements of the legislation. The Companies Act provides a registration system, but it does not attempt to regulate the form or nature of security created by companies. The Bills of Sale Acts, by contrast, do not restrict themselves to requiring the registration of security bills of sale created by individuals. They also govern the form of the security and the extent of the assets to which it can extend.

6.8   The purpose of the registration systems contained in both sets of legislation is to provide a means by which persons dealing with the debtor can

2   *Compaq Computer v Abercorn Group* [1993] BCLC 602.
3   Directive 2002/47/EC of the European Parliament and of the Council of 6 June 2002 on financial collateral arrangements, brought into force in England by the Financial Collateral Arrangements (No 2) Regulations 2003, SI 2003/3226.

discover what security has been created by the debtor.[4] There was a concern that the ability of a debtor to create security relatively informally not only over existing assets, but also over future ones, could result in those dealing with the debtor being misled about his finances. Assets in his possession, and assets which he subsequently acquires, could be the subject of security in favour of a third party without that fact being apparent to the outside world. Where the security concerned was created by means of a pledge, this was not generally an issue because it would be the creditor, rather than the debtor, which would be in possession of the assets concerned. But in the case of a non-possessory security, such as a mortgage or charge, there was a concern that credit could be provided to the debtor on the assumption that he was the unencumbered owner of assets which were, in fact, the subject of security. For this reason, the registration requirement applies to mortgages and charges, but not to pledges.

Registration against the asset

6.9   Registration systems in respect of assets have existed for longer than those against debtors, but the most important registration systems were developed in the twentieth century. They fall into three main categories:

- *Land.* Most land is now registered at the Land Registry or requires to be registered as soon as it is next transferred. All material freehold and leasehold interests in registered land require to be registered.
- *Goods.* Unlike land, most goods are not the subject of asset registers. The two main exceptions are ships and aircraft, which share the characteristics of being both valuable and likely to move outside the jurisdiction of the English courts.
- *Intangibles.* Certain types of intellectual property are registrable, such as patents and registered trade marks, but most types of intangible asset (such as contract rights and receivables) are not the subject of asset registries.

6.10   These registration systems have certain features in common. In the first place, they only exist in relation to assets which are sufficiently valuable to warrant the cost of a registration system. Secondly, they are not intended primarily as systems for the registration of security. They are primarily registers of ownership. They were established to provide a clear record of the identity of those persons who have proprietary rights in the asset concerned, whether outright or by way of security. They are concerned with clarifying the rights over the assets concerned, making transfers easier (particularly in relation to land), and providing systems which are compatible with those in other jurisdictions where the assets concerned are likely to move between jurisdictions (such as ships and aircraft) or to have international ramifications (such as patents and registered trade marks).

6.11   This leads to the third characteristic which they have in common, and which distinguishes them from registration systems against the debtor. The

---

4   Those requirements of the Bills of Sale Acts which prescribe the form and extent of security have another purpose – to protect individual debtors from their creditors. As such, they are the precursor of the current consumer credit legislation.

purpose of debtor registration systems is to provide a means of informing third parties of the existence of the security concerned. Failure to register results in the security being ineffective for most practical purposes. If the security is not registered against the debtor, it is of little value. By contrast, asset registration systems provide a means of giving priority to those who register. Generally speaking, a mortgage or charge over an asset which is the subject of such a registration system will take priority over mortgages or charges registered subsequently and also over registrable, but unregistered, security. There is therefore a powerful incentive for the creditor to register at the asset registry concerned, but it is not compulsory. Failure to register will not render the security void, it will simply put it at a disadvantage in a priority dispute against a third party. As far as the debtor and its insolvency officer are concerned, however, the security remains effective even if it is not registered at the asset registry concerned. It will still be effective in the debtor's insolvency.

6.12 For this reason, the asset registration systems are discussed in CHAPTER 7, which considers priorities. This chapter will concentrate on registration against the debtor, starting with companies, and then briefly considering individuals and other non-corporate debtors.

Structure of this chapter

6.13 When considering the company registration system, the rest of this chapter discusses the following matters:

* Part 2 (**6.16**ff) – which types of company the system applies to.
* Part 3 (**6.32**ff) – which types of security require registration.
* Part 4 (**6.102**ff) – how registration is effected and what is its effect.
* Part 5 (**6.120**ff) – the effect of non-registration.

Part 6 (**6.130**ff) discusses registration under the bills of sale legislation.

6.14 The registration systems do not draw a distinction between mortgages and charges. For the purpose of company registration, the expression 'charge' is used to include a mortgage; and the same approach will be adopted in this chapter.

6.15 Finally, it should be mentioned that the requirements for the registration of charges at Companies House are likely to change in the next few years. The precise nature of the changes is not clear, but a brief discussion of proposals for reform is contained in CHAPTER 1.

Part 2: COMPANIES REGISTRY – TO WHICH COMPANIES DOES IT APPLY?

6.16 The Companies Act 1985 requires the registration of charges created by two types of company:

- companies incorporated under the UK companies legislation which are registered in England and Wales (referred to in this chapter as 'English companies'); and
- companies which are incorporated outside Great Britain (known in the legislation as 'oversea companies').

6.17 Charges created by UK companies which are registered in Scotland are registrable in Scotland,[5] but not in England.

6.18 Where the company is registered in England and Wales, s 395 of the Companies Act 1985 requires the registration of charges created by it if they are of the type described in s 396. This is the case regardless of where the assets concerned are situated.

6.19 The registration requirements in respect of companies which are incorporated outside Great Britain are more limited. Under s 409 of the Companies Act 1985, charges created by an oversea company are registrable if:

- they are of the type described in s 396;
- the company has an established place of business in England and Wales; and
- the mortgage or charge relates to property in England and Wales.

6.20 As a result, both s 395 and s 409 only apply to the extent that the charge concerned is of the type described in s 396. This requirement is considered in part 3 of this chapter (**6.32ff**). This part considers the additional requirements of registration in respect of oversea companies.

Established place of business in England and Wales

6.21 The requirement that the company has an established place of business in England and Wales has caused a great deal of difficulty in practice.

6.22 The purpose of the registration requirement is to provide a means whereby third parties can discover what security a company has created. Where the company concerned is registered in England and Wales, this is easy to achieve. Every English company has its own registered number, and it is a straightforward matter to search at Companies House for charges created by the company concerned.

6.23 Part XXIII of the Companies Act 1985 requires companies incorporated outside Great Britain which establish a place of business in Great Britain to register under the Companies Act. The company is given an identifying number and is required to send various documents to Companies House and to register charges created by it over property in England and Wales (and in Scotland). The purpose of the extension of the registration requirement to oversea companies must have been to require those companies which had registered as oversea companies under the Companies Act to register charges created over

---

5   Companies Act 1985, s 410.

property in England and Wales in the same way as English companies had to register their charges. Persons dealing with the company would then have been able to search the register in the same way as if it were an English company.

6.24 Unfortunately, s 409 does not require registration of charges by oversea companies only where they have registered under Part XXIII. It requires registration where they have 'an established place of business in England and Wales'. It is possible for a company to have an established place of business in England and Wales without having registered under Part XXIII. The company concerned might not be aware of the requirement, it might ignore it or it might not yet have got round to it. Indeed, it might not be clear whether it ought to register – whether or not a company does have an established place of business is a complex issue on which different judges can have different views.[6] But it is clear that the registration requirement applies to oversea companies which, in fact, have an established place of business in England and Wales even if they have not registered under Part XXIII. This was decided in *N V Slavenburg's Bank v Intercontinental Natural Resources*.[7]

6.25 In the *Slavenburg* case, the company concerned was incorporated in Bermuda. A bank had taken security over its assets, and the company went into liquidation in Bermuda. The company had not registered under the Companies Act 1985 but, for the purpose of the proceedings, it was assumed that the company did have an established place of business in England and Wales. Lloyd J held that the security should have been registered and, since it had not been, it was void against the Bermudan liquidators.[8] The legislation applied if the company had a place of business in England, regardless of whether it had complied with its statutory requirement to register under Part XXIII of the Companies Act 1985. The legislation required the delivery of the charge document and the prescribed particulars within the 21-day time limit. Provided this was done, the charge would be effective even though it was not actually registered. Since this had not been done in this case, the security was void against the Bermudan liquidator.

6.26 The relevant date for establishing whether or not the company concerned has an established place of business in England and Wales is the date on which the charge is created. This was established by Lloyd J in the *Slavenburg* case and confirmed by the Court of Appeal in *Re Oriel*.[9] It follows that, if a company has an established place of business in England and Wales at the time the charge is created, the charge will be registrable even if the company later ceases to have an established place of business. Conversely, the charge will not require registration if the company did not have an established place of business at the time the charge was created, even though it subsequently acquired one.

---

6   See *Re Oriel Limited* [1986] 1 WLR 180.
7   [1980] 1 WLR 1076.
8   This was the position under English law. Whether the requirement would be recognised in Bermuda is a different matter. See **CHAPTER 13**.
9   [1986] 1 WLR 180.

6.27   Whether or not a company has an established place of business is not a straightforward question. In *Re Oriel*,[10] the Court of Appeal decided that a company can carry on business in England and Wales without having an established place of business there. In order for the company to have an established place of business, it must not only have some 'more or less permanent location' associated with the company, but must conduct business from it with some degree of regularity so that there is a degree of recognisability that the place concerned is a location of the company's business.

6.28   Such a test is difficult enough to apply when the facts are clear. In most cases, the creditor concerned will not be confident that he has all the necessary facts to make an informed decision and, even if he did, he might find that, in hindsight, a judge disagreed. For that reason, creditors tend to err on the side of caution and to attempt to register charges created by oversea companies if there is any connection at all with England and Wales.

Secured assets in England and Wales

6.29   The other requirement for registration is that the charge concerned is 'on property in England and Wales'. It is not clear from s 409 of the Companies Act 1985 whether the property must be in England and Wales at the time the charge is created, or whether the section will apply if property within England and Wales subsequently becomes subject to the charge. The cautious view is to assume that the section will apply in respect of property which is in England and Wales at the time the creditor enforces the security, whether or not it was there at the time it was created. For this reason, where security is taken over movables, it is common to assume that they might come within the jurisdiction and that the charge should therefore be registered. This is particularly the case where the asset concerned is likely to move between jurisdictions, such as in the case of ships and aircraft.

6.30   Problems can also arise where the security is taken over intangibles. It is notoriously difficult to establish with any precision where intangible assets are situated.[11] The only conclusion which can be drawn with any degree of certainty is that security created by an oversea company over foreign land does not need to be registered in England.

Summary

6.31   In summary, where the company is registered in England and Wales, the charge will be registrable if it is of a type described in part 3 of this chapter (**6.32ff**). Where the company is incorporated outside Great Britain, there are two additional requirements for registration: that it has an established place of business in England and Wales and that the property is situated in England and Wales. In practice, it is difficult for a creditor to establish whether or not these requirements are present in any particular case. Whether or not the company

---

10   [1986] 1 WLR 180.
11   This issue is discussed in **CHAPTER 13**.

has an established place of business is a difficult factual question which the creditor may not feel competent to decide. In the case of movables, the creditor can never be sure that the assets will not subsequently be moved into England and Wales. Where the charged assets are intangibles, it is difficult in many cases to establish where they are situated with any degree of precision. For these reasons, it is common to attempt to register charges against oversea companies if there is any possibility that the charged assets might be situated in England and Wales before the security is discharged.

Part 3: COMPANIES REGISTRY – WHAT TYPES OF SECURITY REQUIRE REGISTRATION?

6.32   If the debtor creating the security is a company to which the legislation applies, what types of security created by that company are registrable? There are essentially three requirements:

- the security must be a 'charge';
- it must be 'created by the company'; and
- it must fall within one of the categories listed in s 396(1) of the Companies Act 1985.

It must be a charge

6.33   The legislation applies to 'charges', which includes mortgages.[12] The nature of mortgages and charges is discussed in CHAPTER 3.

Pledges

6.34   It does not apply to pledges.[13] The bills of sale legislation does not apply to pledges, and the companies legislation has followed suit. The purpose of the registration system is to provide a means of giving notice of the creation of security to those dealing with a debtor. The mischief at which the legislation is directed is the creation of security by a debtor who retains possession of the assets concerned and the consequent possibility of misleading third parties into thinking that the debtor is the outright owner of those assets. In the case of a pledge, it is the creditor, not the debtor, who has the possession of the goods concerned. This issue is discussed in more detail in part 5 of CHAPTER 2 (**2.62ff**).

---

12   Companies Act 1985, s 396(4).
13   Section 396(2) of the Companies Act 1985 specifically exempts the deposit of a negotiable instrument, but this simply confirms what is the case anyway – that a pledge is not registrable.

Quasi-security

6.35 The expression quasi-security is the term frequently (if inelegantly and with a lack of precision[14]) given to transactions which have the same economic effect as the creation of security. They fall into two types, neither of which is registrable under the companies legislation or the bills of sale legislation.

6.36 The first type of case involves a debtor who wishes to acquire an asset, but cannot pay for it. He may borrow money from a bank, use it to buy the asset and charge the asset to the bank as security for the loan. Alternatively, he may agree with the bank that it will buy the asset and then make it available to the debtor under a conditional sale or hire-purchase agreement, or under a lease. Both transactions can be structured so that they have the same economic effect but, in the first type of case, a charge is created which will generally require registration, whereas in the second type of case, no charge is created and no registration is required. In the latter case, the creditor retains the ownership of the asset concerned, and the debtor only obtains possessory rights over the asset. The debtor can never be said to have created a charge because he never has any rights over the asset which he can charge. The creditor is relying on his pre-existing ownership of the asset, not on a charge created by the debtor over its assets.

6.37 The other type of case involves an asset which is already owned by the debtor, but which he wants to raise money on. He may borrow money from a bank, secured by a charge over the asset. Alternatively, if the asset is land or equipment, he may sell it to the bank and take it back on conditional sale, hire-purchase or lease; or, if the asset consists of receivables, he may sell them to the bank on discounted terms, and on the basis that the bank will have recourse to him if they are not paid. Again, both transactions can be structured to produce the same economic effect and, again, in the first type of case a charge is created, whereas in the second, it is not. This case is, however, different from the first type of case. There the debtor never obtained an interest in the asset concerned. Here, the debtor does have a pre-existing interest in the asset which he transfers to the creditor. In this case, the reason why this does not create a charge is that the transfer is outright (ie by way of sale) rather than by way of security.

6.38 In neither case (though for different reasons) does the debtor create a charge over his property. In the first case, he does not have property to charge. In the second case, he sells the property, rather than charging it.

6.39 English law does not recharacterise transactions on the basis of their economic effect. In some jurisdictions (most notably the United States, and those jurisdictions which have adopted its approach to secured transactions), a transaction will be recharacterised as a secured transaction, even if it is not structured as one, if its economic effect is the same. In jurisdictions of this type, transactions of the kind described above are recharacterised as secured

---

14   As Lord Simon said in *National Westminster Bank v Halesowen Presswork and Assemblies* [1972] AC 785 at 808: 'quasi-anything gives uncertain guidance in the law.'

transactions, and therefore subject to the same requirements (including any necessary registrations) as would have been the case if they had been structured as secured transactions.

6.40 This is not the position in England. As Staughton LJ said in *Welsh Development Agency v Export Finance Company* (normally referred to as the '*Exfinco* case')[15]: 'Statute law in this country, when it enacts rules to be applied to particular transactions, is in general referring to the legal nature of a transaction and not to its economic effect.' And as Lord Devlin said in *Chow Yoong Hong v Choong Fah Rubber Manufactory*:[16]

> 'There are many ways of raising cash besides borrowing ... If in form it is not a loan, it is not to the point to say that its object was to raise money ... or that the parties could have produced the same result more conveniently by borrowing and lending money.'

6.41 It is not the task of an English court to rewrite parties' contracts. To do so, in the words of Lord Wilberforce in *Lloyds & Scottish Finance v Cyril Lord Carpet Sales*:[17] 'would be to impose upon the parties a form of transaction totally different from that which they had selected ... and which there is no evidence whatever that either of them desired.'

6.42 This basic principle is subject to two exceptions.[18] They are clearly described by Staughton LJ in the *Exfinco* case. After describing the basic principle, he said:[19]

> 'There are in my opinion two routes by which this principle can be overcome. The first, which I will call the external route, is to show that the written document does not represent the agreement of the parties. It may, if one wishes, then be called a sham, a cloak or a device. The second is the internal route, when one looks only at the written agreement, in order to ascertain from its terms whether it amounts to a transaction of the legal nature which the parties ascribe to it.'

6.43 The external route is only available if the document produced by the parties does not represent their real intention. It was described by Diplock LJ in *Snook v London and West Riding Investments*.[20] He explained a 'sham' as follows:

> 'I apprehend that, if it has any meaning in law, it means acts done or documents executed by the parties to the "sham" which are intended by them to give to third parties or to the court the appearance of creating between the parties legal rights and obligations different from the actual legal rights and obligations (if any) which the parties intend to create ... for

---

15 [1992] BCLC 148.
16 [1962] AC 209 at 216–217.
17 [1992] BCLC 609 at 615.
18 The courts have adopted a more interventionist approach in taxation cases, but this approach has not been adopted in other cases.
19 [1992] BCLC 148 at 186.
20 [1967] 2 QB 786 at 802.

acts or documents to be a "sham", with whatever legal consequences follow from this, all the parties thereto must have a common intention that the acts or documents are not to create the legal rights and obligations which they give the appearance of creating.'

6.44 Of much more importance in practice is the internal route. The approach of the courts in this respect is described by Lord Watson in *McEntire v Crossley Brothers*:[21]

'The duty of a Court is to examine every part of the agreement, every stipulation which it contains, and to consider their mutual bearing upon each other; but it is entirely beyond the function of a Court to discard the plain meaning of any term in the agreement unless there can be found within its four corners other language and other stipulations which necessarily deprive such term of its primary significance.'

6.45 As has been seen in CHAPTER 4, if the parties describe a charge as being fixed, but the terms of the charge do not give the creditor sufficient control over the assets concerned, the court will recharacterise the charge as being floating. In such a case, the court is not rewriting the parties' agreement. It is giving effect to their agreement (which is that the creditor will not control the relevant assets) and establishing that the parties have themselves mis-described the nature of the security.

6.46 In the context of financial transactions which could have been structured as secured loans, but were not, the courts will not recharacterise them if they represent the parties' agreement and, in the light of normal principles of contractual construction, the agreement does not involve a secured loan. As a result, transactions such as finance leases, sale and lease-back arrangements, and sales of receivables are given effect in accordance with their terms, and are not recharacterised as secured loans. There are many cases in the books in which this has been done, but two will illustrate how transactions can be structured in such a way as to avoid the creation of a registrable charge.

6.47 The first example is a sale and lease-back. A debtor which has a valuable asset and requires money can borrow money on the security of a charge over the asset. Such a charge is generally registrable. Alternatively, the debtor could sell the asset to a finance company and take it back on lease. It would receive the sale proceeds from the finance house (which would be the equivalent of the principal amount of a loan) and would then pay lease rentals throughout the period of the lease (which would, in aggregate, be equivalent to the amount of a loan plus interest). If the asset had any residual value at the end of the lease period, the debtor could have an option to reacquire it for a price equal to its value at that time.

6.48 If properly structured, such an arrangement can provide the debtor and the creditor with economically equivalent rights to those which they would have obtained if they had entered into a secured loan. But the legal structure is

---

21 [1895] AC 457 at 467.

different. The debtor does not charge the asset to the creditor to secure a loan. It sells the asset to the creditor and takes a lease back of it. Although these transactions can have the same economic effect, they do not have the same legal consequences. In the case of a charge, the creditor does not become the outright owner of the asset – the debtor retains an equity of redemption. In the case of a sale and lease-back, the creditor does become the absolute owner of the asset – the debtor has no equity of redemption, but must rely on its rights as lessee and any contractual right it may have against the creditor to repurchase the asset.

6.49 The courts will not recharacterise a sale and lease-back as a loan merely because it has the same economic effect. In *Yorkshire Railway Wagon Company v Maclure*,[22] the debtor company's power to borrow under its constitution was exhausted. Because it needed money, but could not borrow, it sold its rolling-stock to a finance house and agreed to take it back on hire purchase over a 5-year period at a rental which would provide the finance house, at the end of the 5-year period, with an amount equal to the purchase price plus interest over that 5-year period. The debtor had an option to repurchase at the end of the period at a nominal price.

6.50 At first instance, Kay J held that this arrangement was a disguised borrowing, put in place to avoid the restriction on borrowings in the company's constitution. This decision was overturned by the Court of Appeal, who held that it was perfectly proper for the company to enter into a transaction the legal effect of which did not amount to borrowing, even though its economic effect was substantially the same. The debtor wanted to borrow money, found that it could not, and therefore entered into a different legal transaction with the same commercial effect. The parties intended the transaction to operate as a sale and lease-back and it could not be recharacterised as a secured loan.

6.51 The important point is that the parties intended to enter into a sale and lease-back. The documents provided for this and the parties intended to comply with them. As Lindley LJ stated in the Court of Appeal, he would have held that the transaction was a secured borrowing if the documents had merely been drawn up to cloak the real intention of the parties. But, since the documents reflected the intention of the parties, the fact that they produced the same economic effect as secured borrowing did not alter the legal effect, which was a sale and lease-back, not a borrowing.

6.52 The second example involves the purchase of debts. A company's debts can be one of its most valuable assets. If it requires money, it can borrow against a charge over its debts. Such a charge is registrable. But it is common for companies to sell their debts to finance houses, rather than charge them. The company will sell debts for a purchase price equal to a percentage of the face value of the debt concerned. In some cases, notice of the arrangement will be given to the counterparty but, frequently, the company will collect the debts on behalf of the finance house. The terms of the arrangement will normally provide that the debtor company is responsible for failure by the counterparty to pay; and the economic effect of the arrangements will be equivalent to a loan

---

22   (1882) 21 Ch D 309.

having been made by the finance company to the debtor company. But if such arrangements are properly structured as a purchase of the debts, rather than a charge over them, they will not be registrable.

6.53 The approach of the courts in such cases can be seen from the decision of the House of Lords in *Lloyds & Scottish Finance v Cyril Lord Carpets Sales*.[23] The debtor company entered into a block discounting agreement under which a finance company bought its debts. The debtor subsequently went into liquidation and the liquidator argued that the agreement was unworkable and was widely departed from in practice and that the arrangements between the parties therefore amounted to a charge over the debtor's book debts which was void for non-registration. The House of Lords held that the transaction was a sale of debts, and not a charge over them. Although there were a number of departures from the terms of the agreement, in substance the parties intended the agreement to be carried out. Although commercially, and in its economic result, block discounting does not differ from lending money, its legal effect is different.

6.54 In an appropriate case, however, the court can recharacterise a transaction – not because it performs the same function as another type of transaction, but because the label given to it by the parties does not represent its true legal nature. An example is *Orion Finance v Crown Financial Management*.[24] A let goods to B on hire-purchase, which were then leased to C. The terms of the hire-purchase agreement required B to assign the lease rentals to A by way of security for the payment of rentals under the hire-purchase agreement. In fact, the form of the assignment executed by B over the lease rentals was in outright form – not by way of security. Notwithstanding this, the Court of Appeal decided that the assignment was by way of security for the payment of rentals due under the hire-purchase agreement and therefore constituted a registrable charge. The court reviewed the terms of the transaction as a whole and decided that, although the parties had described the assignment as being outright, it was intended to be by way of security. In other words, the parties had given the document the wrong label.

6.55 In the words of Millet LJ:[25]

'Once the documents are accepted as genuinely representing the transaction into which the parties have entered, its proper legal characterisation is a matter of construction of the documents. This does not mean that the terms which the parties have adopted are necessarily determinative. The substance of the parties' agreement must be found in the language which they have used; but the categorisation of a document is determined by the legal effect which it is intended to have, and if when properly construed the effect of the document as a whole is inconsistent with the terminology which the parties have used, then their ill-chosen language must yield to the substance.'

---

23 [1992] BCLC 609.
24 [1996] 2 BCLC 78.
25 [1996] 2 BCLC 78 at 84.

Summary

6.56 In summary, the legislation applies to mortgages and charges, but not to pledges or to transactions which have the same economic effect but which are structured differently.

It must be created by the company

6.57 The requirement to register only occurs if the charge is created by the company concerned. It does not, therefore, apply to security, such as liens, which are created by operation of law. In *London and Cheshire Insurance Company v Laplagrene Property Company*,[26] a company which owned land sold it to a purchaser, but did not require all of the purchase price to be paid on completion. Although the land was transferred to the purchaser, the vendor retained an equitable lien over the land to secure the remaining purchase price. Such a lien arises by operation of law, without the necessity for any agreement by the parties. Brightman J held that it was not registrable. Because the lien arose by operation of law, it was not created by the company.

6.58 The same principle applies to other types of lien created by operation of law, whether they arise at common law or in equity. Liens are discussed in CHAPTER 10.

6.59 Under s 400 of the Companies Act 1985, a company which acquires property which is the subject of a charge has an obligation to register it if it would have been registrable had the charge been created by the company. Failure to comply with this provision results in default fines, but does not invalidate the charge, and is therefore not of concern to the creditor.

It must fall within one of the categories listed in s 396(1)

6.60 The requirement to register does not extend to all types of charge. Since the requirement was introduced in 1900, the categories of registrable charge have been extended piecemeal, and they are now contained in s 396(1) of the Companies Act 1985. A charge created by the company is only registrable if it falls within one of the categories listed in s 396(1). They are categorised in two different ways:

- by reference to the type of charge concerned; and
- by reference to the type of asset charged.

The type of charge

6.61 Section 396(1) of the Companies Act 1985 requires two types of charge to be registered regardless of the assets which are the subject of the charge. They are:

---

26 [1971] 1 Ch 499.

- a floating charge on the company's undertaking or property; and
- a charge for the purpose of securing any issue of debentures.

A floating charge

6.62 The requirement to register applies to 'a floating charge on the company's undertaking or property' (s 396(1)(f)). It applies not only where there is a floating charge over all of the company's assets (ie its 'undertaking'), but also where a floating charge is created on certain of its assets (ie its 'property'). It will apply not only where the charge is expressed to be a floating charge, but also where the court construes a purported fixed charge as a floating charge. The circumstances in which the court will do this are discussed in part 5 of **CHAPTER 4 (4.79ff)**.

A charge to secure an issue of debentures

6.63 It has been seen in **CHAPTER 4** that the floating charge developed in cases where the company concerned had charged its assets to secure an issue of debentures. All floating charges are registrable, regardless of the nature of the obligation which they secure, but the legislation also requires any type of charge, whether fixed or floating, to be registered if it is 'for the purpose of securing an issue of debentures' (s 396(1)(a)). In its broadest sense, a debenture has been described, by Chitty J in *Levy v Abercorris Slate & Slab Company*,[27] as 'a document which either creates a debt or acknowledges it'. In *Lemon v Austin Friars Investment Trust*,[28] the Court of Appeal indicated that it was impossible to give an exhaustive definition of a debenture, although its primary feature was that it was an acknowledgement of indebtedness. In that case, it was decided that a contingent debt instrument issued by a company, which was only payable out of profits, was a debenture.

6.64 The provision only applies if there is an 'issue of debentures' and, in *Automobile Association (Canterbury) v Australasian Secured Deposits*,[29] Richmond J, in the New Zealand Court of Appeal, decided that the ordinary natural meaning of these words meant that it did not apply to a single debenture but only to 'a number of debentures issued at a particular time or so connected together in some way as to form a collective group'.[30]

6.65 The requirement to register such charges was first imposed at the turn of the twentieth century and it would seem that what was intended to be covered was issues of transferable debt securities by companies, such as secured loan stock, which were common at the time. Security granted for a loan agreement or other facility of a similar kind does not require registration under this head (although it may well do so under another head). This is for two reasons. In the first place, a loan agreement is not, in ordinary usage, a debenture. Although a

---

27 (1887) 37 Ch D 260 at 264.
28 [1926] Ch 1.
29 [1973] 1 NZLR 417.
30 [1973] 1 NZLR 417 at 424.

loan agreement evidences indebtedness, it is suggested that the key requirement of a debenture is that it is a transferable debt security issued by a company. Loan agreements are assignable, but are not transferable at common law on a register held by the company in the way that debt securities are. In any event, it would be a rare case where a number of loan agreements would be entered into as part of one transaction so that they could be described as an 'issue' of debentures.

6.66 For these reasons, it is suggested that this head is restricted to issues of transferable debt securities by companies.

The type of asset

6.67 Most of the provisions of s 396(1) of the Companies Act 1985 require charges to be registered by reference to the nature of the asset charged, rather than the nature of the charge itself. They require most charges over land or goods to be registered but only charges over certain types of intangible.

Land

6.68 Section 396(1)(d) requires a charge to be registered if it is 'a charge on land (wherever situated) or any interest in it, but not including a charge for any rent or other periodical sum issuing out of the land'.

Goods

6.69 Under s 396(1)(c) a charge is registrable if it is 'created or evidenced by an instrument which, if executed by an individual, would require registration as a bill of sale'. Most written charges over goods in England (other than ship mortgages and registered aircraft mortgages) constitute registrable bills of sale and, if created by a company, are therefore registrable under the Companies Act 1985. The relevant provisions are considered in part 6 of this chapter (**6.130ff**).

6.70 In addition, s 396(1)(h) requires a registration of 'a charge on a ship or aircraft, or any share in a ship'. Although mortgages over ships and aircraft are generally exempted from the requirement to register under the Bills of Sale Acts, when granted by companies they are nevertheless required to be registered under s 396(1)(h).

6.71 As a result, all charges over ships and aircraft created by companies are registrable. In addition, most written charges created by companies over other goods are registrable if the goods are in England. In practice, all charges over goods are registered.

Intangibles

6.72 There are only very limited exceptions to the principle that charges over land and goods require registration. The position is very different where intangible assets are concerned. The requirement to register only applies to three types of intangible:

- uncalled share capital and calls;
- goodwill and intellectual property; and
- book debts.

Uncalled share capital and calls

6.73 Section 396(1)(b) requires the registration of 'a charge on uncalled share capital of the company' and s 396(1)(g) requires the registration of 'a charge on calls made but not paid'.

6.74 Security over uncalled capital has caused problems in practice. A general charge over all of a company's 'property' does not include its uncalled capital, because the courts have declined to regard uncalled capital as being the 'property' of the company.[31] In order to take security over uncalled capital, therefore, it is necessary specifically to refer to it in the charge document. General words are insufficient.

6.75 This is less of a problem now than it was in the nineteenth century. In the early years of the companies legislation (during the latter half of the nineteenth century), it was common for companies to have uncalled capital, which would be capable of being called up by the company if needed, for instance on a liquidation. It is now very rare for companies to have uncalled share capital, it being the practice for shares to be paid up in full when they are issued. It is, therefore, unlikely that a charge will be required to extend to uncalled share capital or to calls which have been made but not yet paid. But if there is such security, it requires to be registered.

Goodwill and intellectual property

6.76 Section 396(1)(j) requires the registration of 'a charge on goodwill, or on any intellectual property'. Goodwill cannot exist independently of the company's business. A debenture over all of a company's present and future property will necessarily include its goodwill. It is common to take a fixed, rather than a floating, charge over goodwill but it is only of value when sold with the business to which it relates.

6.77 Certain types of intellectual property, on the other hand, are capable of existing separately from the business of the company and can be sold separately. For this purpose, s 396(3A) defines intellectual property as '(a) any patent, trade mark, ... registered design, copyright or design right; (b) any licence under or in respect of any such right'.

Book debts

6.78 Section 396(1)(e) requires the registration of 'a charge on book debts of the company'. The meaning of the expression 'book debts' has caused a great deal of uncertainty in practice. The starting point in any discussion of its

---

31   *Re Russian Spratts Patent* [1898] 2 Ch 149.

meaning is the decision of the Court of Common Pleas in *Shipley v Marshall*,[32] in which the court had to consider the meaning of the expression 'book debts' for the purpose of the Bankruptcy Act 1861. In that case, a saddler had a side-line in buying and selling copyrights of newspapers. He contracted to sell the copyright in a newspaper, the price being payable in instalments. The question arose whether the rights under the contract were 'book debts' even though they had not been entered into the books of his trade as a saddler. The Court of Common Pleas held that the rights under the contract were book debts. They held that it was not necessary that the debts were actually written up in his books. All that was required was that there were debts 'in respect of which entries could be made in the ordinary course of his business'[33] or which 'are commonly entered in books'.[34]

6.79   The test laid down in *Shipley v Marshall* has been used in the cases concerning the registration of charges. Although the test is easy enough to state, it is more difficult to apply in practice, as can be seen from two contrasting first instance decisions in the 1960s.

6.80   In *Independent Automatic Sales v Knowles and Foster*,[35] D was the owner of goods which were the subject of hire-purchase agreements. D charged its rights under the hire-purchase agreements to C to secure finance provided by C. The charge was not registered under the Companies Act. Buckley J held that D's rights under the hire-purchase agreements were book debts and that the charge ought to have been registered. He expressed the test as follows:[36]

> '*Shipley v Marshall*, I think, establishes that, if it can be said of a debt arising in the course of a business and due or growing due to the proprietor of that business that such a debt would or could in the ordinary course of such a business be entered in well-kept books relating to that business, that debt can properly be called a book-debt whether it is in fact entered into the books of the business or not.'

6.81   Buckley J decided that the charge over D's rights under the hire-purchase agreements included the right to receive rental payments which were book debts. He also went on to decide that, even if there had been no book debts in existence at the time the charge was created (ie because the charge, at that stage, only extended to future contracts), the charge would still have been registrable. The book debts need not be in existence at the time the charge is executed. The section applies where book debts arise in the future, even if there are no existing ones at the time the charge is created.

6.82   This case needs to be contrasted with the decision of Pennycuick J 5 years later in *Paul & Frank v Discount Bank (Overseas)*.[37] In that case, as a result of transactions entered into with an overseas customer, D had the benefit of an ECGD policy, under which he was entitled to claim against the Export

---

32   (1863) 14 CB NS 566.
33   (1863) 14 CB NS 566 at 572, per Williams J.
34   (1863) 14 CB NS 566 at 573, per Byles J.
35   [1962] 1 WLR 974.
36   [1962] 1 WLR 974 at 983.
37   [1967] Ch 348.

Credits Guarantee Department of the Board of Trade a certain percentage of the amounts due under its contract with the overseas counterparty in certain events, which included the insolvency of the counterparty and its failure to pay within a particular period. D charged the ECGD policy to C to secure finance. The charge was not registered, and the question arose whether it should have been.

6.83 Pennycuick J held that it was not registrable. On the basis of expert accountancy evidence, he found that, at the date the charge was executed, the ECGD policy ought not to have been entered in D's books. Whilst the liability remained contingent, it ought not to be written up in D's books. It might never become payable, and it would clearly be misleading for it to be entered as a debt in such a case.

6.84 Pennycuick J decided that book debts are 'such debts as are commonly entered in books'[38] and the question to be asked was whether it is the practice that they should be entered in well-kept books. Hence the importance of the expert accountancy evidence. He also decided that the relevant date for establishing whether or not the asset charged is a book debt is the date of the creation of the charge. It is only if the asset is a book debt at that date that it requires to be registered. The ECGD policy was clearly not a book debt at the date of the creation of the charge, and the charge over it was therefore not registrable.

6.85 On the face of it, this would seem to conflict with the approach of Buckley J in the *Independent Automatic Sales* case, in which he held that the section applied to future book debts as well as to existing book debts. Pennycuick J, however, distinguished the two cases. If there was an existing contract at the date the charge was created, and there was no book debt then in existence, the charge is not registrable merely because a book debt may ultimately result from that contract,[39] but:

'... if a charge ... covers future debts, in the sense of debts under a future contract which, when that contract comes to be made, will constitute book debts, e.g. an ordinary contract for the sale of goods on credit, I see no reason why [s 396(1)(e)] should not be fairly applicable to the charge; and that, I think, is all that Buckley J says.'

6.86 In *Contemporary Cottages (NZ) v Margin Traders*,[40] Thorp J had difficulty in reconciling the *Independent Automatic Sales* case with the *Paul & Frank* case. He thought that there was a basic conflict between the proposition that registration may be required of a debt not existing at the time the charge is created and the proposition that the test is the character of the property charged at the date of its creation; and he preferred the approach of Buckley J to that of Pennycuick J.

6.87 It is, nevertheless, suggested that the approaches of Buckley J and Pennycuick J are reconcilable:

38   [1967] Ch 348 at 361.
39   [1967] Ch 348 at 363.
40   [1981] 2 NZLR 114.

- It is necessary to draw a distinction between existing assets (ie those which exist at the time the charge is created) and future assets (ie those which do not, but which subsequently fall within the scope of the charge).
- It is also necessary to draw a distinction between:
  - present debts (ie debts which are presently payable);
  - future debts (ie debts which must become payable in the future); and
  - contingent debts (ie debts the payment of which is contingent on the happening of some uncertain future event).
- Present and future debts ought to be written up in a company's books. Contingent debts ought not – to do so would be contrary to the basic accounting principle of prudence.
- The question of whether or not an asset is a book debt is to be tested at the date of the creation of the charge.
- If, at the time the charge is created, it extends to existing assets, it will be registrable if they are present debts or future debts, but not if they are contingent debts.
- If, at the time the charge is created, it extends to future assets, they will be registrable if, when they fall within the scope of the charge, they will be present debts or future debts but not if, at the time they fall within the scope of the charge, they will be contingent debts.

6.88 Particular problems have arisen in relation to charges over bank accounts. In *Re Brightlife*,[41] Hoffmann J decided that a document which charged 'book debts' did not extend to a bank account; and this was followed by the Northern Ireland Court of Appeal in *Northern Bank v Ross*.[42] Would this reasoning be applied when construing s 396(1)(e)? The point was left open by Lord Hoffmann in *Re Bank of Credit and Commerce International SA (No 8)*,[43] although he appeared to be in favour of the view that a charge over a bank account is not registrable as a charge over a book debt.

6.89 The reason for the distinction is that, in the accounts of a company, a credit balance or deposit is described as 'cash at bank' rather than a 'trade or other debtor'. There are, however, doubts about this approach. The money standing to the credit of a bank account is clearly a 'debt' and it ought to be written up in the company's books. The fact that it appears in those books under a different heading to trade or other debtors may not, therefore, be conclusive that it is not a 'book debt'. It may be the requirement for it to be contained in the company's accounts, rather than the precise heading under which it appears, which is the relevant criterion.

6.90 The scope of the expression 'book debts' is, therefore, extremely unclear. The uncertainty is not helped by the fact that the issue is not a purely legal one, but also involves accounting practices, which can change over time. In the words of Thorp J in *Contemporary Cottages (NZ) v Margin Traders*:[44]

---

41 [1987] Ch 200.
42 [1991] BCLC 504.
43 [1998] AC 214.
44 [1981] 2 NZLR 114 at 121.

'It is ... an inevitable consequence of the circumstance, accepted in all the cases, that the definition [of "book debts"] involves not only legal principle but the application of such principle to the varied accounting practices adopted by different trades, that any definition will be relatively imprecise and likely to involve difficulties in application to trades in which accounting practices are not uniform.'

Intangible assets generally

6.91 Where does that leave the creditor who has taken a charge over intangibles? If the charge is, or might be construed as, a floating charge, it is clearly registrable. If not, it is clearly registrable if it is a charge over uncalled share capital or calls, goodwill or intellectual property. If it is none of those things, it will be registrable if it is a charge over a book debt. There is substantial uncertainty about the meaning of the expression which is caused by some disagreement about the legal principle and also by the fact that accounting practices can change.

6.92 There are certain types of asset which are clearly not book debts. Shares are the most obvious example. It is also clear that contingent rights under contracts such as insurance policies are not book debts. Further than that, it is difficult to go. In practice, it is frequently the case that all charges created by companies are registered out of abundant caution. This is the case even in relation to charges over shares. When taken as part of a fixed and floating charge debenture, the charge over shares will be registered in the same way as charges over the other assets which are the subject of the debenture. It is, however, common for stand-alone charges over shares to be registered, even though there is no doubt that they are not registrable. (There may be certain priority advantages from doing so, which are discussed in CHAPTER 7.)

6.93 It is impossible to justify the present requirements of s 396(1). There is no logic in the requirement that a charge over the benefit of a hire-purchase contract should be registered, but a charge over rights under an insurance contract need not. And why should all floating charges be registered, but only certain types of fixed charge? The position is not helped by the substantial difficulties of interpretation of parts of s 396(1), particularly the meaning of the expression 'book debts'. These uncertainties, and the natural caution of those taking security, has led to most types of security being registered in any event.

Financial collateral

6.94 Since 2003, there have been particular rules in place in relation to financial collateral. They are described in part 5 of CHAPTER 3 (**3.175ff**). Under reg 4(4) of the Financial Collateral Arrangements (No 2) Regulations 2003:[45]

'Section 395 of the Companies Act 1985 (certain charges void if not registered) shall not apply (if it would otherwise do so) in relation to a

---

45   SI 2003/3226.

security financial collateral arrangement or any charge created or otherwise arising under a security financial collateral arrangement.'

6.95 There is considerable doubt about the precise meaning of the expression 'security financial collateral arrangement'. In the context of the registration of charges, the abolition of the requirement to register applies if:

- the security agreement is in writing, and none of its parties is an individual;
- the security is over cash (ie money credited to an account or a similar claim for the repayment of money) or financial instruments (ie shares and equivalent securities, bonds and other debt instruments which are tradable on the capital market, and certain other types of securities); and
- the financial collateral is 'delivered, transferred, held, registered or otherwise designated so as to be in the possession or under the control' of the creditor or someone acting on its behalf. There is no definition of what is meant by possession or control, except that the ability of the debtor to substitute equivalent assets or to withdraw excess assets from the security does not prevent it being in possession or under the control of the creditor.

6.96 Except perhaps in the context of the wholesale financial markets (for which these arrangements are really intended), the uncertainties involved in establishing whether a particular transaction is a security financial collateral arrangement means that the safest course is to continue to register all security taken from companies.

Charges which are not registrable

6.97 If a charge does not fall within any of the heads of s 396(1) of the Companies Act 1985, it is not registrable. It has been seen that most charges over land and goods are registrable, but that it is not every charge over an intangible which requires registration. In particular, there are three types of intangible asset, which are commonly the subject of a charge, which do (or may) not require registration if the charge is fixed, rather than floating.

6.98 In the first place, it is clear that a fixed charge over shares is not registrable because it does not fall within any of the heads of charge described in s 396(1). Secondly, a charge over contingent rights under a contract (for instance, rights under an insurance policy) is not registrable, again because it does not fall within any of the heads of charge described in s 396(1). Finally, but more debatably, a fixed charge over a bank account may not be registrable, either because it is not a charge over a book debt or because, even if it is, it constitutes a security financial collateral arrangement.

6.99 It is, nevertheless, the practice (at least outside the scope of the wholesale financial markets) to register all of these types of charge. In part, this is out of abundant caution – in view of the uncertainty surrounding the meaning of the expression 'book debts' and the precise scope of a financial collateral arrangement. Equally importantly, there may well be other advantages gained from registration. Lenders almost invariably search the register before lending, and the registration of a charge is therefore likely to bring it to the notice of a potential subsequent lender and thereby protect the priority position of the existing lender. This issue is discussed further in CHAPTER 7.

Summary

6.100 In summary, there is a requirement to register security at Companies House if:

- the debtor is:
    - a company registered in England and Wales; or
    - a company incorporated outside Great Britain which has an established place of business in England Wales and the charge is created over property in England and Wales;
- the security constitutes a mortgage or a charge;
- the security is created by the company;
- the security is of a type described in s 396(1), which covers all floating charges, most fixed charges over land and goods and certain types of fixed charge over intangibles; and
- the transaction is not a financial collateral arrangement.

6.101 In practice, because of the uncertainties involved in some of these concepts, most mortgages and charges created by a company are registered:

- regardless of the nature of the secured asset; and
- regardless of where the company is incorporated unless:
    - it is incorporated in Scotland; or
    - it is incorporated outside Great Britain and there can be no doubt that the secured asset will not be situated in England at any time during the continuance of the charge.

Part 4: COMPANIES REGISTRY – REGISTRATION AND ITS EFFECT

The process of registration

6.102 If a charge created by a company is registrable, s 395(1) of the Companies Act 1985 describes what is required:

'... the prescribed particulars of the charge together with the instrument (if any) by which the charge is created or evidenced [must be] delivered to or received by the Registrar of Companies for registration in the manner required by [Chapter 1 of Part XII of the Companies Act 1985] within 21 days after the date of the charge's creation.'

6.103 The procedure is relatively straightforward. The original of the charge document and particulars of the charge must be delivered within 21 days after the charge has been created. In most cases, it must be the original charge which is delivered to the Registrar, not a copy, although a verified copy may be substituted in the case of a charge created out of the United Kingdom over property situated outside the United Kingdom.[46]

6.104 In addition to delivering the charge document, there must also be delivered the 'prescribed particulars' of the charge in the form contained in the Companies (Forms) Regulations 1985,[47] normally known as a Form 395. This form requires the person lodging it to provide brief particulars of certain matters including the identities of the chargor and the chargee, the date of the creation of the charge, the amount secured and the identity of the property charged.

6.105 The charge document and the particulars need to be delivered to the Registrar of Companies within 21 days after the date of the charge's creation, although there are provisions which extend the time limit in the case of charges created out of the United Kingdom over property situated outside the United Kingdom.[48] There are also particular requirements for the registration of charges securing issues of debentures.[49]

6.106 For the purpose of deciding whether the statutory requirements have been complied with, it is necessary to establish when the charge was created. Unless it is held in escrow, a charge over existing property is normally created at the time the charge document is executed (or, if it is a deed, when it has been executed and delivered). If the charge extends to existing and future assets, the charge over all of the assets which it covers is created when the charge document is executed (and, if necessary, delivered). It is not necessary to register a new charge every time a new asset falls within the scope of the charge.

6.107 If, on the other hand, at the time the charge document is executed, there are no existing assets covered by it, it is arguable that the charge is only created when an asset falling within the description of the charged assets comes into existence. A purported charge over a non-existent asset is only an agreement to create a charge. The charge is not actually created until there is a charged asset.[50] The alternative view[51] is that, for the purpose of the registration requirement, the charge is created at the time it is executed even if there are then no existing assets subject to it. In view of the uncertainty on the point, it is preferable to ensure that, at the time the charge is executed, there are at least some existing assets to which it extends. If, for instance, security is to be taken over the moneys standing to the credit of an account, but those moneys are not due to be paid until some time in the future, the deposit of a nominal amount in the account at the time the charge is executed will avoid any

---

46 Companies Act 1985, s 398(1).
47 SI 1985/854.
48 Companies Act 1985, s 398(2).
49 Companies Act 1985, s 397.
50 See the judgment of Jessel MR in *Collyer v Isaacs* (1881) 19 Ch D 342 at 351, referred to in part 3 of CHAPTER 3 (3.57ff).
51 Accepted by Buckley J in *Independent Automatic Sales v Knowles & Foster* [1962] 1 WLR 974 at 985.

questions as to whether the charge is actually created at the date of its execution, and thereby provide certainty as to the period within which registration needs to be effected.

6.108 Although it is the company which has the duty to comply with these provisions,[52] in practice it is invariably the creditor, or its solicitors, who do so because of the importance to the creditor of ensuring due registration.

6.109 The Registrar of Companies has a duty to keep a register of charges, which is open to inspection by any person.[53] In practice, it is possible to search not only that register, but also copies of the Forms 395 submitted in respect of each charge.

The certificate of registration

6.110 When a charge has been registered, the Registrar of Companies has a duty to issue a certificate of registration. Under s 401(2) of the Companies Act 1985, that certificate 'is conclusive evidence that the requirements of [Chapter 1 of Part XII of the Companies Act 1985] as to registration have been satisfied'. This provision is extremely important in practice because it gives creditors certainty that the statutory requirements have been complied with, and that their charge will not be invalidated for non-registration.

6.111 An example of the approach of the courts to the construction of this provision is the decision of the Court of Appeal in *National Provincial and Union Bank of England v Charnley*.[54] In that case, the company had charged its leasehold factory to a creditor and had created a floating charge over the plant in the factory. The prescribed particulars delivered to the Registrar of Companies did not mention the plant. In execution of a judgment against the company, the sheriff seized some of the plant on the premises. The bank claimed that it had a charge over them, and therefore the execution could only be effected subject to the bank's charge. The execution creditor contended that the charge did not cover the plant because the registered particulars did not mention them. The Registrar of Companies had issued a certificate of registration.

6.112 The Court of Appeal held that the certificate of registration was conclusive evidence that the charge had been duly registered, even though the particulars were incomplete and even though the entry by the Registrar in the register was, as a result, defective. Having established that the charge was effective, they went on to decide that, when construing the effect of the charge, it was necessary to look at the charge document itself, and not at the registered particulars. This was the case even though it was the bank, not the company, which had submitted the incorrect particulars. As Atkin LJ said, the purpose of the conclusive certificate is to match the obligation to register charges with a protection for the creditor concerned that the statutory requirements had been

---

52   Companies Act 1985, s 399.
53   Companies Act 1985, s 401.
54   [1924] 1 KB 431.

complied with. The conclusive certificate provided certainty for those dealing with the company that the requirements had been complied with, and avoided any subsequent argument that the procedures had not properly been complied with. The importance of certainty in commercial transactions was more important than the fact that the creditor had misstated the extent of the charge in the prescribed particulars, although Atkin LJ considered that the position would be different if the creditor had intentionally abstained from mentioning part of the security (ie if fraud were involved).

6.113 In the *Charnley* case, the creditor had misstated the extent of the charged assets. In *Re Mechanisations (Eaglescliffe)*,[55] the same principle was applied where the amount secured by the charge had been misstated. The extent to which this principle is taken by the courts is illustrated by the decision of the Court of Appeal in *Re C L Nye*.[56] In that case, the company had created security in favour of a bank. It sent an executed, but undated, charge to the bank's solicitor on 28 February. The charge was then lost and was not found until 18 June. The bank's solicitor dated the charge on 18 June and lodged it within 21 days of that date. The company went into liquidation on 16 July and the Registrar subsequently issued a certificate of registration. The company's liquidator claimed rectification of the register on the basis that the charge had not, in fact, been registered within 21 days of its creation.

6.114 At first instance, Plowman J held that the charge had been created on 28 February, that the reason why the certificate of registration had been issued was the misstatement by the bank's solicitors in the prescribed particulars, and that the bank could not take advantage of its own wrong. His decision was, however, overruled by the Court of Appeal. They assumed that the charge had been created on 9 March (which was the date when the bank made funds available to the company on the basis of the charge). As a result, therefore, the relevant documents had, in fact, been lodged with the Registrar of Companies outside the 21-day period for registration. They nevertheless held that the whole purpose of the certificate was to give certainty and that 'conclusive' meant what it said. Even though the mistake was caused by the misstatement of the bank's solicitors, the fact that the Registrar had issued the certificate meant that there could be no room to argue that the charge had not validly been registered. In the words of Harman LJ:[57] 'The certificate is no less conclusive as to date than as to amount and to hold otherwise would frustrate the whole purpose of the legislature.'

6.115 The position would have been different in the case of fraud, however. Russell LJ considered that, in such a case, although the charge would have been valid because of the conclusive nature of the certificate of registration, a personal claim would have been available against the bank.

6.116 It is difficult to emphasise too strongly the importance of the certificate of registration as providing certainty that the registration requirements have been complied with. In the absence of fraud, once the certificate of registration

---

55 [1966] Ch 20.
56 [1971] Ch 442.
57 [1971] Ch 442 at 470.

has been provided, no challenge can be made to the charge on the basis of failure to register. This is, however, in stark contrast to the position which pertains in relation to oversea companies which have not registered under Part XXIII of the Companies Act 1985. It has been seen in part 2 of this chapter (**6.16ff**) that a charge created by a company incorporated outside Great Britain over property in England and Wales is registrable if the company has an established place of business in England and Wales, even though it has not registered under the Companies Act 1985. As a result of the decision of Lloyd J in *N V Slavenburg Bank v Intercontinental Natural Resources*,[58] the Registrar of Companies has established what is known as a 'Slavenburg register', in which he places copies of documents sent to him in respect of charges created by oversea companies which it is considered might have an established place of business in England and Wales even though they have not registered under Part XXIII of the Companies Act 1985. The Slavenburg register serves no useful purpose because it cannot be easily searched, but it is necessary in order to demonstrate, if the occasion should arise, that the charge and the relevant prescribed particulars were delivered to the Registrar of Companies within the 21-day period. Because there can be no actual registration against a company which is not registered in England and Wales and has not registered a place of business in England and Wales, the Registrar does not produce a conclusive certificate of registration, but simply writes to the creditor concerned confirming receipt of documents on a particular day. The benefits of the conclusive certificate are not, therefore, available in relation to Slavenburg registrations.

The effect of registration

6.117 What is the effect of registration? Its primary effect is negative, rather than positive – the charge is not void if it is registered in time. But it can also have an important effect on priorities because it is a means of giving notice of a security interest. This aspect is considered further in CHAPTER 7.

The release and transfer of charges

6.118 Once a charge has been registered, it will only be removed from the register if the Registrar receives a statutory declaration by the company that the secured liability has been discharged or the secured property released from the charge.[59] The statutory declaration has to be in Form 403(a) or (b) and is made on behalf of the company, normally by a director or the secretary. Because it is not necessary for the creditor to be a party to the statutory declaration, it is theoretically possible for the company to deliver a Form 403 to the Registrar of Companies in circumstances where the charge has not, in fact, been released. This will not affect the validity of the charge, because the creditor will have received a certificate of registration which is conclusive evidence that the requirements of the Companies Act 1985 concerning registration have been complied with. But it would mislead those searching the register into believing

---

58   [1980] 1 WLR 1076.
59   Companies Act 1985, s 403.

that the charge concerned had been released. It is not, therefore, possible to take the register at face value. Charges which appear to have been released may not necessarily have been.

6.119   As far as English law is concerned, there are no provisions in the Companies Act 1985 dealing with the transfer of registered charges (although there are such provisions in Scotland). The details of the chargee may not, therefore, be accurate. The chargee may have transferred the secured liability and the charge to a third party, and there is no provision in the legislation for amending the identity of the chargee.

Part 5: COMPANIES REGISTRY – THE EFFECT OF NON-REGISTRATION

6.120   Under s 395(1) of the Companies Act 1985, if the charge and the prescribed particulars are not delivered to the Registrar of Companies within 21 days after the charge has been created, the charge is 'so far as any security on the company's property or undertaking is conferred by the charge, void against the liquidator or administrator and any creditor of the company'.

6.121   Once the company has gone into liquidation or administration (or into an equivalent insolvency procedure in a foreign jurisdiction[60]), the charge is void and the creditor concerned will rank as unsecured.[61] Before liquidation or administration, however, the position is rather more complicated. The security is expressed to be void against 'any creditor' of the company. In establishing what this means, it is necessary to distinguish between secured and unsecured creditors. In essence, the courts have decided that it means secured creditors, but not unsecured creditors.

6.122   As far as a secured creditor is concerned, the security created by an unregistered charge will be void against him, even if he is aware of the existence of the unregistered charge and even though the company is not in liquidation or administration. An example of the effect of the section is provided by the decision of the Court of Appeal in *Re Monolithic Building Company*.[62] The company had created a mortgage over land in favour of A, which was not registered under the Companies Act. The company then created a floating charge over all of its assets in favour of B, who was aware of the mortgage in favour of A. The floating charge was registered. The company was not in liquidation, but the question arose whether A or B had priority. At first instance, Astbury J held that, since B had notice of A's mortgage, he could not take advantage of its non-registration and accordingly that A took priority.

---

60   *NV Slavenburg's Bank v Intercontinental Natural Resources* [1980] 1 WLR 1076.
61   This is what s 395(1) says although, in *Smith v Bridgend County Borough Council* [2002] 1 AC 336, the Court of Appeal had some difficulty with the concept, and it required the House of Lords to put them right.
62   [1915] 1 Ch 643.

The decision was, however, overruled by the Court of Appeal. They held that A had priority. The section meant what it said. Because A's charge was unregistered, it was void against B, who was a creditor with a registered charge over the property. The fact that B had notice of the earlier mortgage was irrelevant.

6.123 Failure to register can, therefore, have an indirect effect on priorities. If it has not been registered, it will be void against a subsequent registered charge even if the subsequent chargee has notice of the unregistered charge. But, until the company goes into liquidation or administration, neither the company nor any unsecured creditor is able to challenge the effectiveness of an unregistered charge.[63] The approach of the courts to unsecured creditors is best seen in relation to applications for late registration, which are considered at the end of this part.

6.124 In theory, therefore, an unregistered charge is still of some value to the creditor concerned. If there is no subsequent encumbrancer over the assets concerned, and if he can enforce it before insolvency proceedings commence, he will be able to retain the benefit of the security.[64] But this will only be the case where the creditor has completed the enforcement of the charge before liquidation or administration intervene.[65] In practice, therefore, creditors should assume that an unregistered charge is of little practical value.

6.125 Although the security created by an unregistered charge is void, the liability secured by the charge becomes immediately payable when the charge becomes void (ie after the expiry of the 21-day period).[66] This is important when considering the options available to a creditor who discovers that his charge has not been registered. He has two options:

- to take a new charge and register it within the 21-day period; or
- to apply for late registration under s 404.

6.126 Since the secured debt becomes repayable, there is an incentive for the debtor to co-operate with the creditor in putting in place a new security document and ensuring that it is registered in time. This is the most common response to the problem.

6.127 The alternative is to apply to court for late registration. Section 404 applies if the court is satisfied that the omission to register a charge within the 21-day period 'was accidental, or due to inadvertence or to some other sufficient cause, or is not of a nature to prejudice the position of creditors or shareholders of the company, or that on any other grounds it is just and equitable to grant relief'. In such a case, the court may order that the time for registration is extended on such terms and conditions as seem to the court just and expedient.

---

63   *Re Ehrmann Brothers* [1906] 2 Ch 697.
64   *N V Slavenburg's Bank v International Natural Resources* [1980] 1 WLR 1076.
65   *N V Slavenburg's Bank v International Natural Resources* [1980] 1 WLR 1076.
66   Companies Act 1985, s 395(2).

6.128   The approach of the courts to such cases is illustrated by the judgment of Lord Brightman in *Re Ashpurton Estates*.[67] The position can be summarised as follows:

- When the court extends the time for registration, the order will normally contain a proviso that it is without prejudice to the rights of parties acquired during the period between the date of the creation of the charge and the date of its actual registration.[68]

- This order will protect a third party who obtains a proprietary interest in assets which are the subject of the unregistered charge before the charge is registered.[69]

- But the order will not protect unsecured creditors of the company.[70] It is not generally appropriate for the order to attempt to protect unsecured creditors whilst the company is a going concern. Because an unsecured creditor is always exposed to the risk that the company will create security over its assets, it would not be appropriate, in a normal case, to attempt to protect unsecured creditors where the company is not in liquidation or administration.

- However, once a company has gone into liquidation, the rights of its creditors then crystallise and should be protected. This is normally done by the court refusing to extend the time for registration once the company is in liquidation.[71]

- The imminence of liquidation is also a good reason to refuse to extend the time for registration in the absence of exceptional circumstances.[72]

- It would seem that administration should be treated in the same way as liquidation for these purposes.[73]

- The court has a discretion whether or not to extend the time for registration and, if so, the terms on which it should do so, and the principles described above may be diverted from in exceptional cases.[74]

6.129   In many cases, it will be quicker and cheaper for the creditor to take new security, and register it in time, rather than to apply for late registration of the existing security. Because the effect of non-registration is to make the secured liabilities immediately payable, the company will have the incentive, at least where it is solvent, to accede to such a request. Where the company is insolvent, the company may refuse to grant the new security. If it does grant new security in such a case, there may be grounds for its avoidance in a subsequent liquidation or administration as a result of the claw-back provisions considered in **CHAPTER 9**. But it would also be difficult to obtain a

---

67   [1983] Ch 110.
68   This form of order was introduced by Buckley J in *Re Joplin Brewery Company* [1902] 1 Ch 79. The current form of the normal order is explained by Templeman J in *Watson v Duff Morgan & Vermont (Holdings)* [1974] 1 WLR 450.
69   *Re Ehrmann Brothers* [1906] 2 Ch 697.
70   *Re Ehrmann Brothers* [1906] 2 Ch 697.
71   *Re S Abrahams & Sons* [1902] 1 Ch 695.
72   *Re Ashpurton Estates* [1983] Ch 110.
73   *Re Barrow Borough Transport* [1990] Ch 227.
74   *Re Ashpurton Estates* [1983] Ch 110.

late registration order where the company was insolvent. In many cases, therefore, re-execution of the security will be a better option than applying to the court for late registration.

Part 6: REGISTRATION UNDER THE BILLS OF SALE ACTS

6.130 The position with regard to the registration of charges against individuals and other non-corporate debtors is very different from that which applies in relation to companies. The requirement to register only applies to mortgages or charges over goods and to general assignments of book debts by way of security.

6.131 A bill of sale is a document which transfers title to goods, either outright or by way of security. The purpose of the first Bills of Sale Act, in 1854, was to prevent potential frauds by owners of goods who transferred title to them, but retained possession of them. The concern was that, because the transferor retained possession of the goods, third parties would be induced to grant credit to the transferor on the assumption that he owned the goods whereas, in fact, they were owned by the transferee. The answer to the problem was to require the registration of such bills of sale.

6.132 Subsequent legislation distinguished between absolute bills of sale and those given by way of security. In the latter case, the legislation, in addition to requiring registration of the bill of sale, also had the objective of protecting debtors by requiring various formalities for the execution of bills of sale given by way of security.[75] The purpose of this aspect of the bills of sale legislation is therefore the same as that which underlies the Consumer Credit Act 1974 – consumer protection.

6.133 The current legislation is contained in the Bills of Sale Acts 1878–1891. The Bills of Sale Act 1878 (the '1878 Act') governs absolute bills of sale. The Bills of Sale Act (1878) Amendment Act 1882 (the '1882 Act') governs security bills of sale. It is therefore the 1882 Act which is most important in relation to mortgages and charges of goods, although that Act does incorporate certain provisions of the 1878 Act by reference. The 1882 Act regulates the form of mortgages and charges over goods, it provides for their registration, and it restricts their scope.

To what types of debtor do the Bills of Sale Acts apply?

6.134 The Bills of Sale Acts apply to bills of sale created by individuals and other non-corporate debtors, but not to those created by companies. The

---

75 See the speech of Lord Herschell in *Manchester, Sheffield & Lincolnshire Railway Company v North Central Wagon Company* (1888) 13 App Cas 554 at 560.

registration of mortgages and charges over goods created by companies is provided for in the Companies Act 1985. Section 17 of the 1882 Act provides that it does not apply to 'any debentures issued by any ... incorporated company, and secured upon the capital stock or goods, chattels, and effects of such company'. In *N V Slavenburg's Bank v Intercontinental Natural Resources*,[76] Lloyd J confirmed that the Act did not apply to security over goods created by companies, wherever they are incorporated.

To what types of security do the Bills of Sale Acts apply?

6.135   The 1882 Act applies to 'bills of sale' which are given by way of security for the payment of money.[77] The expression 'bill of sale' is defined in s 4 of the 1878 Act to include:

● 'bills of sale, assignments, transfers, declarations of trust without transfer, inventories of goods with receipt thereto attached, or receipts for purchase moneys of goods, and other assurances of personal chattels';
● 'powers of attorney, authorities, or licences to take possession of personal chattels as security for any debt'; and
● 'any agreement, whether intended or not to be followed by the execution of any other instrument, by which a right in equity to any personal chattels, or to any charge or security thereon, shall be conferred'.

6.136   The first two categories (with certain minor differences) were contained in the first Bills of Sale Act in 1854. The third category was added by the 1878 Act; and this distinction needs to be borne in mind when considering the relevance of some of the earlier cases.

6.137   The first category includes documents which were regarded as bills of sale at common law, together with certain similar documents. At common law, a bill of sale is a document by which the property in goods is transferred.[78] In principle, a legal mortgage falls within this definition, as was accepted by the Court of Appeal in *Ex parte Hubbard*.[79] It has also been decided that an equitable mortgage and an equitable charge over existing goods are 'assurances of personal chattels' within this category.[80] But a document is not a bill of sale if it simply records the terms of an agreement by which possession is transferred, rather than title.[81] It does not, therefore, extend to pledges of goods, even if the parties have entered into a document recording the terms of the pledge, because the creditor's interest under the pledge is obtained by the delivery of possession, rather than by the execution of a document.[82]

6.138   The second category of documents has been very narrowly construed by the courts. It only applies to documents given as security for debts in their

---

76   [1980] 1 WLR 1076 at 1093–1098, per Lloyd J.
77   1882 Act, s 3.
78   *Allsop v Day* (1861) 7 H&N 457.
79   (1886) 17 QBD 690.
80   *Ex parte Mackay* (1873) LR 8 Ch App 643; *Edwards v Edwards* (1876) 2 Ch D 291.
81   *Charlesworth v Mills* [1892] AC 231.
82   *Ex parte Hubbard* (1886) 17 QBD 690.

technical sense, and not as security for claims for damages.[83] The third category is much wider and clearly covers equitable mortgages and charges over present and future goods.

6.139 The legislation only applies to documents. It does not apply if the charge is created orally, even if it is evidenced by a document.[84] In practice, of course, charges over goods (as over any other type of asset) are invariably created by a document, so this is not a material limitation.

6.140 Certain types of document are excluded from the definition of 'bill of sale',[85] the most material being:

- 'bills of sale of goods in foreign parts or at sea' and charges over certain imported goods;
- 'transfers or assignments of any ship or vessel or any share thereof' and mortgages of aircraft which are registered in the UK aircraft registry;
- 'transfers of goods in the ordinary course of business of any trade or calling'; and
- 'bills of lading ... or any other documents used in the ordinary course of business as proof of the possession or control of goods, or authorising or purporting to authorise, either by endorsement or by delivery, the possessor of such document to transfer or receive goods thereby represented'.

6.141 Security over goods abroad is therefore excluded from the scope of the 1882 Act, although it is not clear when their location is to be tested. Mortgages of ships and aircraft are also generally excluded, although they are required to be registered if created by a company.[86] The other exceptions extend to documents used in the ordinary course of business and documents, like bills of lading, used as proof of the possession or control of goods. It has been seen in CHAPTER 2 that they apply to trust receipts used in relation to pledges over bills of lading.[87] They are, however, unlikely to be of much relevance in relation to mortgages or charges of goods, because they are more concerned with commercial, rather than financing, transactions.

6.142 The 1882 Act only applies to bills of sale given in relation to 'personal chattels'. These are also defined in s 4 of the 1874 Act to mean 'goods, furniture, and other articles capable of complete transfer by delivery', subject to certain minor exclusions. It also applies to fixtures if they are mortgaged or charged separately from the land to which they are affixed, although the Act does not generally apply to mortgages of land which also extend to fixtures on the land.

6.143 In essence, therefore, the 1882 Act applies to most written mortgages and charges over goods in England created by persons other than companies,

---

83   *Ex parte Newitt, re Garrud* (1881) 16 Ch D 522.
84   *Newlove v Shrewsbury* (1888) 21 QBD 41.
85   1878 Act, s 4; Bills of Sale Act 1890, s 1 (substituted by Bills of Sale Act 1891, s 1); Mortgaging of Aircraft Order 1972, SI 1972/1268, art 16(1).
86   Companies Act 1985, s 396(1)(h). See part 3 of this chapter (**6.32ff**).
87   *Re David Allester Limited* [1922] 2 Ch 211.

except mortgages over ships and most aircraft mortgages. As has been seen in part 3 of this chapter (**6.32**ff), the definitions contained in the Bills of Sale Acts are also relevant when considering mortgages or charges over goods created by companies. This is because, under s 396(1)(c) of the Companies Act 1985, a mortgage or charge is registrable if it is 'created or evidenced by an instrument which, if executed by an individual, would require registration as a bill of sale'.[88]

Requirements of the 1882 Act

6.144   A mortgage or charge over goods which is governed by the 1882 Act must comply with a number of requirements, the purpose of which is twofold – to protect the debtor from the creditor[89] and to protect third parties dealing with the debtor.

6.145   Protection of debtors is achieved in two ways. In the first place, a security bill of sale must be in the form of the Schedule to the 1882 Act[90] and all the goods comprised in it must be described in a schedule to the bill of sale.[91] In addition, the security will not extend to any assets of which the debtor was not the true owner at the time of the execution of the security document.[92] It follows, therefore, that a mortgage of goods given by an individual is restricted to existing goods identified in the schedule, and not to any future goods. It is for this reason that it is not practicable for an individual to create a floating charge over all his present and future assets.

6.146   Secondly, the Act also places restrictions on the ability of the creditor to enforce the security. He can only take possession of the goods in the circumstances described in s 7 of the 1882 Act, although these include payment default, certain other breaches of the bill of sale, bankruptcy and execution.

6.147   The other purpose of the bills of sale legislation is to provide a means by which third parties can be made aware of the creation of security over goods which is not accompanied by possession. Under s 8 of the 1882 Act, the security must generally be registered within 7 days after its execution, failing which it will be void. The registration procedure is contained in the 1878 Act and is significantly more cumbersome than the registration procedure under the Companies Act. The document needs to be attested by a solicitor, who has to state that he has explained the effect of the document to the debtor.[93] An affidavit also has to be sworn concerning the execution of the document and

---

88   For the difficulties which can still be encountered in interpreting the definition sections, see *Re Cosslett (Contractors)* [1998] Ch 495, discussed in (1997) 11 JIBFL 530.

89   In this respect, its purpose is similar to the Victorian legislation regulating pawnbrokers. That legislation was concerned with pledges, the Bills of Sale legislation with mortgages and charges.

90   1882 Act, s 9.

91   1882 Act, s 4.

92   1882 Act, s 5.

93   1878 Act, s 10(1).

that, together with the bill of sale, needs to be registered at the High Court.[94] The registration also has to be renewed every 5 years.[95]

General assignments of book debts

6.148 In addition, under s 344 of the Insolvency Act 1986, a general assignment of existing or future book debts, or any class of them, by a person engaged in any business, is void against his trustee in bankruptcy as regards any debts which were not paid before the presentation of a bankruptcy petition unless the assignment is registered under the Bills of Sale Act 1878. The expression 'assignment' includes a mortgage or charge, but a 'general assignment' does not include an assignment of book debts due at the date of the assignment from specified debtors or of debts becoming due under specified contracts or assignments of book debts included in a business transfer.

The effect of the bills of sale legislation in practice

6.149 The effect of the bills of sale legislation has been that mortgages and charges over goods are rarely taken from individuals. Their limitation to existing scheduled goods, their restrictions on enforcement and their onerous formal requirements mean that it is rarely cost-effective to take such security. In practice, therefore, security granted by individuals over chattels normally takes the form of a pledge. Where the secured loan is for £25,000 or less, a pledge of goods given by an individual must comply with the Consumer Credit Act 1974 but, although exacting, the requirements of the consumer credit legislation are less onerous than the requirements of the Bills of Sale Acts. A mortgage or charge created by an individual over goods will, if the amount of the loan falls within the consumer credit legislation's threshold, be regulated both by the consumer credit legislation and by the bills of sale legislation.

---

94 1878 Act, s 10(2).
95 1878 Act, s 11.

PRIORITY OF SECURITY

Chapter 7

PRIORITIES

Part 1: INTRODUCTION

7.1   When a creditor takes security, he needs to be assured not only that the security will be effective against the debtor even if he is the subject of insolvency proceedings, but also that the security will take priority over other proprietary interests in the assets concerned.

7.2   The first requirement is satisfied by the creditor obtaining an effective mortgage, charge or pledge in accordance with the principles discussed in the previous chapters. As has been seen in **CHAPTER 5**, it can be a relatively straightforward process.

7.3   The second requirement is much more difficult – hence the length of this chapter. The creditor will wish to ensure not only that there are no existing proprietary interests in the secured asset, but also that his security will rank ahead of any proprietary interests created subsequently. As far as existing proprietary interests are concerned, the creditor can protect himself to some extent by making appropriate inquiries, including the searching of any registers of relevant security interests. If he fails to discover an existing proprietary interest, his security will frequently (although not inevitably) rank behind the existing interest.

7.4   But what about interests which are created in the future? The law could have approached this question on the basis that the debtor, having once created a proprietary interest over the asset concerned, could only deal with the asset subject to that interest; and that any person acquiring an interest in the asset subsequently would get no better rights over it than the debtor. This principle is the basis of the maxim 'the first in time is the first in law'. It is the starting point in any discussion of priorities, but it is by no means universally adopted. It is subject to very many qualifications.

7.5   One qualification arises from the peculiarity of common law systems (as opposed to modern civil law systems) that they recognise two different types of proprietary interest – legal and equitable. It has been seen that the common law is more restrictive than equity as regards the creation of security. A legal mortgage or a pledge can only be created over an existing asset. It depends upon the transfer of legal title or possession to assets the transfer of which is recognised at common law. It is not, therefore, generally available in relation to intangibles. Equity, on the other hand, has extended the class of assets capable of being the subject of security and has simplified the procedure for the creation of security. Equitable mortgages and charges can be created very easily over all types of present and future asset.

7.6 If the advantage of equitable security interests is the ease of their creation, their disadvantage is that they are generally less effective against third parties than legal security interests. Equitable proprietary interests developed out of a purely personal right – the right of a person with an equitable claim to apply to the Lord Chancellor for an injunction to prevent someone else from taking advantage of his common law rights. The Lord Chancellor would give effect to the equitable claim if the conscience of the holder of the common law right was affected by the rights of the person with the equitable claim. If, for instance, in consideration for a loan made to him by a creditor, a debtor had agreed to create security over an asset, the debtor would be bound, in conscience, to grant the security and an equitable proprietary interest would be created over the asset in favour of the creditor. That interest would not just affect the debtor. It would bind anyone whose conscience was affected by it, for instance, a transferee of the asset who was aware of it or a person who received it as a gift. But it would not bind a person who acquired the legal title to the asset for value and without notice of it. The courts of equity recognised that a legal interest was a stronger right than an equitable one and, in these circumstances, the conscience of the legal owner would not be affected by the earlier equitable right. Hence the development of the principle that a bona fide purchaser of a legal estate for value without notice of a prior equitable interest will take free of that interest.

7.7 In practice, this principle is now of less importance than it used to be as a result of requirements for the registration of security interests. In part, this is because asset registries (such as those for land, ships and aircraft) provide for an alternative system of priorities based on the time of registration. But, even where the asset concerned is not of a type which is the subject of an asset register, the requirement for registration against the debtor of most types of mortgage or charge created by a company has had the effect that it is now much easier for a potential secured creditor to establish whether or not there are existing equitable (or, indeed, legal) security interests. A subsequent secured creditor is, as a result, much more likely to have notice of earlier security interests. The bona fide purchaser principle nevertheless remains of importance, particularly in relation to the priority of security over shares. If a secured creditor has only an equitable interest in shares, it will not necessarily take priority over a later legal interest.

7.8 The principle that the first in time has priority therefore gives way to the principle that law takes precedence over equity. Both principles are, however, subject to a third, overriding, principle. They only apply if 'the equities are equal'. If it would be inequitable to apply either principle, it will not be applied. The breadth of this third principle means that its application to the facts of any particular case can be difficult to predict.

7.9 An analysis of priority issues therefore starts with three basic principles:

- If the equities are equal, the first in time has priority.

- If the equities are equal, a person with a legal interest may take priority over a person with an equitable interest.
- If the equities are not equal, priority goes to the person with the better equity.

7.10   The first principle is subject to the second; and both are subject to the third.

7.11   There have, however, been a number of other developments over the last two centuries, which have substantially affected these three principles. In practice, five are particularly important:

- the rule in *Dearle v Hall*;[1]
- the rules concerning tacking further advances;
- the advent of the floating charge;
- the purchase money security interest; and
- the introduction of debtor and asset registries.

7.12   During the nineteenth century, a principle (now known as the rule in *Dearle v Hall*) developed regulating the priority of proprietary interests in debts and certain other intangibles, the effect of which was that priority depended, not on the date of creation of the interest concerned, but on the date on which notice of the interest was given to the person who owed the debt or controlled the intangible concerned. This rule developed from the principle described above that the first in time rule will not apply if the equities are not equal, but it soon took on a life of its own and developed into a quite separate rule.

7.13   There were two other case-law developments in the nineteenth century which substantially affected the priority question. The first related to what has become known as 'tacking further advances'. The earlier priority principles were developed at a time when a security interest normally secured a particular loan made available by the creditor at the time the security was created. During the nineteenth century, the courts had to consider whether the same rules would apply even where further monies were lent by the creditor after the creation of the security; and they developed a principle which restricted the priority of such 'further advances'. The development of the floating charge from the 1860s also required further priority principles to be developed in order to take account of the requirement for the debtor to carry on its business in the ordinary course and to dispose of assets free from the floating charge.

7.14   A further case-law development, this time in the twentieth century, led to the creation of the principle that a 'purchase money security interest' (to use the American expression) would generally take priority over earlier security interests. In essence, the effect of this principle was that a person who has funded the acquisition of an asset by the debtor ought to have priority over the debtor's earlier secured creditors.

7.15   Finally, and most importantly, statutory intervention in the nineteenth and twentieth centuries required the registration of many types of security

---

1   *Dearle v Hall; Loveridge v Cooper* (1823, 1827, 1828) 3 Russ 1.

interest either against the asset concerned or against the debtor. This has had a far-reaching impact on priority rules in three main ways:

- by providing that, in certain cases, priority depends on the date of registration;
- by making unregistered security interests void in many cases; and
- by giving third parties a means to discover the existence of earlier security interests.

7.16 These principles only apply where there are competing proprietary interests in a particular asset. They do not apply where only one creditor has a proprietary interest and the other has a personal claim against the debtor. For instance, an unsecured creditor who has lent on the basis only of a negative pledge can never be involved in a priority dispute with a secured creditor because he does not have a proprietary interest in an asset of the debtor.

7.17 There are also particular rules which govern the effectiveness of 'mere equities' against persons other than those by whom they were created. These are referred to in part 3 of this chapter (**7.48ff**).

7.18 The following parts of this chapter will first consider the 'first in time' principle and then the various exceptions mentioned above and it will then discuss the way in which these priority rules work in practice. This chapter is divided into the following parts:

- Part 2 (**7.19ff**) – the 'first in time' principle.
- Part 3 (**7.48ff**) – legal and equitable interests.
- Part 4 (**7.97ff**) – unequal equities.
- Part 5 (**7.151ff**) – the rule in *Dearle v Hall*.
- Part 6 (**7.190ff**) – the purchase money security interest.
- Part 7 (**7.203ff**) – tacking further advances.
- Part 8 (**7.234ff**) – floating charges.
- Part 9 (**7.251ff**) – registration.
- Part 10 (**7.296ff**) – priorities in practice.

Part 2: THE 'FIRST IN TIME' PRINCIPLE

The principle

7.19 The concept that a person who obtains a proprietary interest in an asset will take priority over all subsequent proprietary interests in the asset is the basic principle on which all the other principles are premised and to which they are all exceptions. It is the basic principle for two obvious reasons. In the first place, in the absence of a compelling argument to the contrary, it is only fair that a person who has a proprietary interest in an asset should take priority over those who subsequently acquire such an interest. There is also a conceptual reason: that a person cannot give to another more than he has. If the debtor's right to the asset is subject to a proprietary right of a third party then, in principle, so should the claim of any person who derives his rights from the debtor.

7.20   There is no doubt that the principle that a person cannot give what he does not have is the basic position at common law, often referred to in its Latin form nemo dat quod non habet.[2] It is also the case in equity, although equity judges have sometimes been more influenced by the conduct of the parties than the time of creation of their interests.[3] Nevertheless, in *Phillips v Phillips*,[4] Lord Westbury LC said:

> 'I take it to be a clear proposition that every conveyance of an equitable interest is an innocent conveyance, that is to say, the grant of a person entitled merely in equity passes only that which he is justly entitled to and no more.'

7.21   Accordingly, if a debtor creates a mortgage over his property, and then sells the property, the purchaser will, in principle, only obtain what the debtor had. He acquires the property subject to the mortgage. It is for this reason that a person who has reserved title to goods in the hands of the debtor is entitled to recover them from a receiver appointed under a debenture. It is also the basis of the priority of a purchase money security interest, which is described in part 6 of this chapter (**7.190ff**).

7.22   The principles discussed in the remaining parts of this chapter are all exceptions from this basic principle, but there are two types of case where the exceptions do not generally apply:

- where the person with the later interest has notice of the earlier one; and
- where the person with the later interest does not give value.

Notice

7.23   The first exception is obvious. The principles which have been developed to give priority to subsequent purchasers or secured creditors are intended to protect those who acquire their interest in ignorance of the existence of the earlier interest. They do not generally apply if the later purchaser or secured creditor had notice of the earlier interest at the time he obtained his own interest.

7.24   The question of whether or not a person has notice of an earlier interest is relevant in a number of different contexts. It will be seen that the absence of such notice is a necessary pre-requisite of the ability of a person with legal title to an asset to take priority over an earlier equitable interest. It is also relevant to the application of the rule in *Dearle v Hall*[5] and to the priority of floating

---

2   If, for instance, a seller sells goods to a buyer, the buyer generally acquires no better title than the seller: Sale of Goods Act 1979, s 21(1).

3   See part 4 of this chapter (**7.97ff**).

4   (1861) 4 De G F & J 208 at 215.

5   *Dearle v Hall; Loveridge v Cooper* (1823, 1827, 1828) 3 Russ 1.

charges. In short, notice of an earlier interest in an asset generally prevents a person with a later interest in that asset from using one of the exceptions to the first in time rule to take priority over the person with the earlier interest.

7.25 The one possible exception to this principle is where the interest concerned is registered at an asset registry, in which event it may take priority over an earlier registrable but unregistered interest even if the holder of the later interest had notice of it. This issue is discussed in part 9 of this chapter (**7.251**ff). But, subject to this possible exception, a person who has notice of an earlier proprietary interest in an asset will take subject to it. Hence its importance in practice.

7.26 There is much written on the doctrine of notice; and there are many cases in the books, not all of which are easy to reconcile. Ultimately, however, whether or not one person has notice of the interest of another is a matter of fact, to be determined in relation to the circumstances of a particular case. The dangers of too much citation of authority in this area were forcibly urged by Sir Horace Davey QC in *The London Joint Stock Bank v Simmons*,[6] where he is reported to have said:[7]

> 'A decision ought to be cited only for some proposition of law, and never as a decision upon facts or as a reason why a ... judge ... should decide similar facts in a similar way.'

7.27 This concern was echoed in the speech of Lord Halsbury LC who said:[8]

> '[I]f ... the question is one which is to be determined upon the facts of the case, no one case can be an authority for another.'

7.28 What is important is to establish the principles to be applied, rather than to spend too much time considering how they were applied on the particular facts of cases long since decided.

7.29 Notice falls into three main categories. It may be actual, constructive, or deemed by statute.

Actual notice

7.30 There is little that needs to be said about actual notice, except to point out that a person will have actual notice of a matter not only if he is aware of it, but also if he deliberately tries to avoid becoming aware of it (for instance, like Lord Nelson, by 'turning a blind eye').

Constructive notice

7.31 Constructive notice is much more difficult to define. It developed in cases involving land, and many of the decisions on the subject are inextricably

---

6   [1892] AC 201.
7   [1892] AC 201 at 203.
8   [1892] AC 201 at 208.

tied up with the conveyancing practices of the times. Those cases are of limited value now, even where land is involved.

7.32 There has been an understandable reluctance, particularly on the part of common law judges, to extend the doctrine of constructive notice to commercial transactions.[9] An example of this approach is the decision of the Court of Appeal in *The English and Scottish Mercantile Investment Company v Brunton*.[10] The question which arose in that case was whether a person had constructive notice of a prohibition on creating charges contained in a floating charge debenture. The person concerned knew of the existence of the debenture, but not of the prohibition. The Court of Appeal held that he did not have constructive notice of the prohibition because, although such restrictions were contained in some debentures, they were by no means universal. The approach of many judges to the question of constructive notice is epitomised by the judgment of Lord Esher MR in that case, who described it as a dangerous doctrine which the courts should not extend.

7.33 But there is no doubt that constructive notice is relevant to priority issues, whether they arise in relation to mortgages of land or in relation to other more 'commercial' transactions. Although there is a reluctance on the part of the courts to extend the doctrine, there is no question that it still exists. In a different context, Lord Browne-Wilkinson re-stated the importance of the doctrine of notice in *Barclays Bank v O'Brien*:[11]

> 'The doctrine of notice lies at the heart of equity. Given that there are two innocent parties, each enjoying rights, the earlier right prevails against the later right if the acquirer of the later right knows of the earlier right (actual notice) or would have discovered it had he taken proper steps (constructive notice). In particular, if the party asserting that he takes free of the earlier rights of another knows of certain facts which put him on inquiry as to the possible existence of the rights of that other and he fails to make such inquiry or take such other steps as are reasonable to verify whether such earlier right does or does not exist, he will have constructive notice of the earlier right and take subject to it.'

7.34 In *Macmillan v Bishopsgate Investment Trust (No 3)*,[12] Millett J also stressed the importance of constructive notice, describing it as 'notice of such facts as he would have discovered if he had taken proper measures to investigate them'.[13]

7.35 A clear description of what is meant by 'constructive notice' is to be found in s 199(1) of the Law of Property Act 1925. This is couched in negative terms: it is intended to restrict the scope of constructive notice as it was previously applied in the case of land. But, if taken as a positive statement of the circumstances in which constructive notice will arise, it does express very clearly the nature of the concept. It provides that:

---

9   See Lindley LJ's comments in *Manchester Trust v Furness* [1895] 2 QB 539 at 545.
10   [1892] 2 QB 700.
11   [1994] 1 AC 180 at 195–196.
12   [1995] 1 WLR 978.
13   [1995] 1 WLR 978 at 1000.

'A purchaser shall not be prejudicially affected by notice of—

(i) ...

(ii) any other instrument or matter or any fact or thing unless—

    (a) it is within his own knowledge, or would have come to his knowledge if such inquiries and inspections had been made as ought reasonably to have been made by him; or

    (b) in the same transaction with respect to which a question of notice to the purchaser arises, it has come to the knowledge of his counsel, as such, or of his solicitor or other agent, as such, or would have come to the knowledge of his solicitor or other agent, as such, if such inquiries and inspections had been made as ought reasonably to have been made by the solicitor or other agent.'

7.36   This section shows that there are two circumstances in which a person will have constructive notice of a matter. The first is where the matter would have come to his knowledge if he had made such inquiries 'as ought reasonably to have been made' by him. The second is where the matter is known, or ought reasonably to have been known, to his agent in the transaction concerned.

7.37   What inquiries ought reasonably to be made? As Lindley LJ made clear in *Bailey v Barnes*,[14] what is reasonable depends on what is usually done by men of business under similar circumstances. It is therefore necessary to look at the particular transaction with a view to deciding:

- what inquiries the person concerned ought reasonably to have made; and
- if he had made them, what matters he would have become aware of.

7.38   The dangers of citing cases for the purpose of deciding such matters of fact has already been adverted to. There is little point citing cases concerning procedures in relation to unregistered land in the nineteenth century when considering what is reasonable to be investigated in relation to other forms of property in the twenty-first.

7.39   It is the nature of the whole transaction which has to be considered in order to establish whether or not particular inquiries ought to have been undertaken. The nature of the asset concerned is important, but so is the type of transaction and the amount involved. What is reasonable to be undertaken by a mortgagee may differ from that by an outright purchaser. What is reasonable in relation to a major financing transaction may be different where the amounts involved are much smaller. And practices change: what is reasonable now may be very different from what would have been reasonable 50 years ago. The test is clear, but its application to any particular set of facts must necessarily be imprecise, because it will depend on the particular circumstances of the transaction concerned.

7.40   In commercial transactions, the person entering into the transaction will normally be a corporation, rather than an individual. Whether or not the corporation has knowledge can depend on the knowledge of individuals acting

---

14   [1894] 1 Ch 25 at 34–35.

on its behalf. It will have knowledge of matters which are known to those of its officers, employees and agents who are involved in effecting the transaction concerned. This is simply a matter of normal agency principles. In addition, a company will have the knowledge of those persons who can properly be described as 'the directing mind and will' of the company concerned, whether or not they are involved in the transaction.[15]

Notice by registration

7.41   Registration can affect notice in one of two ways. In the first place, certain statutes give deemed notice to all the world of the registration of certain matters.[16] More importantly in practice, other statutes (for instance, the Companies Act 1985), although they do not provide for deemed notice, may result in a person obtaining actual notice of a matter (because the person concerned searched the register and discovered its existence) or constructive notice of it (if, in the particular circumstances of the transaction concerned, that person ought to have searched the register and, if he had, would have discovered the matter in question). These issues are considered in more detail in part 9 of this chapter (**7.251**ff).

Value

7.42   The exceptions to the first in time principle also assume that the person with the subsequent interest has given value for his interest. It does not matter whether he is an outright purchaser or the holder of a security interest. What is important is that he has given value. If he has not, he is described as a 'volunteer' and will not be able to take priority over an earlier proprietary interest in the asset concerned.

7.43   In commercial transactions, the most common example of a volunteer is a judgment creditor who obtains execution against the assets of the debtor. In one sense, an execution creditor will have given value to the debtor. He might, for instance, have lent money to the debtor, or have provided goods or services to him, and is now claiming payment. But he did not bargain for security over the debtor's asset. He is an unsecured creditor who is trying to obtain security after the event. He is a volunteer because he has not provided consideration for the execution itself. As Chadwick J said in *United Bank of Kuwait v Sahib*:[17]

> 'In seeking a charging order, a judgment creditor is concerned to obtain whatever security he can in respect of credit already given to the debtor; he is not at all in the same position as one who is deciding whether to give credit against the security which he is offered.'

7.44   This was said in the context of a charging order, but the concept applies to all forms of execution of judgments. An execution creditor is, therefore, only

---

15   *El Ajou v Dollar Land Holdings (No 1)* [1994] 2 All ER 685.
16   See, for instance, Law of Property Act 1925, s 198.
17   [1997] Ch 107 at 119.

entitled to what the judgment debtor can honestly give him. He can be in no better position than the debtor and therefore takes the debtor's property subject to all existing proprietary interests.[18]

7.45 As a general principle, therefore, a creditor who is executing judgment over an asset of the debtor will only obtain priority over a third party claiming an interest in the asset concerned if he obtains his proprietary interest in the asset before the third party does (although this principle is subject to one exception where the priority dispute is with a floating chargee – this is considered in part 8 of this chapter (**7.234**ff)). In the case of execution against goods under a writ of fieri facias, the sheriff who executes against the goods obtains a limited proprietary interest when the writ is delivered to the sheriff to be executed[19] and a more general one when the goods are seized in execution.[20] In the case of execution against debts by a third party debt order, the execution creditor obtains a proprietary interest in the debt concerned when the interim order is served on the person who owes the debt.[21] In the case of charging orders against land and other assets, the execution creditor obtains a proprietary interest in the asset concerned when the interim order is made.[22]

Interests created at the same time

7.46 The first in time principle assumes that the two proprietary interests concerned were created in sequence. If two security interests are executed on the same day, the court will inquire which was in fact executed first but, if there is anything in the documents to show that they were intended to rank pari passu or in reverse order, the court will presume that the documents were executed in such order as to give effect to the intention of the parties.[23]

Summary

7.47 In summary:

- The first in time principle is the starting point in any consideration of priorities.

- The principles discussed in the following parts of this chapter are all exceptions to this basic principle.

- In general, a person cannot rely on any of these exceptions to take priority over an earlier interest if:

   – he had notice of the earlier interest at the time he obtained his own interest; or

   – he did not give value for his interest.

---

18   *Re General Horticultural Company, ex parte Whitehouse* (1886) 32 Ch D 512.
19   *Payne v Drewe* (1804) 4 East 523.
20   *Wilbraham v Snow* (1670) 2 Wms Saund 47; *Slater v Pinder* (1872) LR 7 Exch 95.
21   *N Joachimson v Swiss Bank Corporation* [1921] 3 KB 110 at 131, per Atkin LJ.
22   Charging Orders Act 1979, s 3(4).
23   *Gartside v Silkstone and Dodworth Coal and Iron Co* (1882) 21 Ch D 762 at 767–768, per Fry J.

Part 3: LEGAL AND EQUITABLE INTERESTS

Legal interests: the bona fide purchaser principle

7.48 The principle that the first in time takes priority is subject to the principle that, in a dispute between an equitable and a legal interest, the legal interest will take priority if certain criteria are satisfied, even if the legal interest is created after the equitable one. A person who obtains a legal interest in the asset concerned for valuable consideration and without notice of an earlier equitable interest obtains, in the words of James LJ in *Pilcher v Rawlins*,[24] 'an absolute, unqualified, unanswerable defence' to that equitable interest.

7.49 Although the principle was developed in relation to land, its application in that context has been severely circumscribed by the registration requirements for land which are discussed in part 9 of this chapter (**7.251ff**). In practice, therefore, it is now of more relevance in relation to goods and shares. An example of its application in relation to goods is provided by *Joseph v Lyons*.[25] A created an equitable mortgage over after-acquired goods in favour of B. (The mortgage had to be equitable because it was over future property.) Before B took possession of the goods, A pledged some of them to C who had no notice of B's equitable mortgage. The Court of Appeal held that C had priority over B. B had obtained beneficial title by way of security, but not legal title, to the goods. Legal title was retained by A, who was therefore able to grant C a legal interest in the goods, rather than just an equitable one, by way of pledge. Since C took his legal interest for value and without notice of B's equitable mortgage, he took free of it.

The requirements

7.50 A person who acquires a proprietary interest in an asset can only take priority over an earlier equitable interest under this principle if three conditions are satisfied:

- he must be a 'purchaser for value';
- he must take his interest in good faith and without notice of the earlier equitable interest; and
- he must obtain a legal interest in the asset concerned.

7.51 In order to be a 'purchaser for value', the person concerned need not be the outright purchaser of the asset concerned. It is sufficient if he has obtained a mortgage or pledge, provided that he has given value for it. The principle will not, however, apply where the person concerned is a volunteer. This will therefore preclude a person from relying on the principle if he is claiming by means of a gift. More importantly, as has been discussed in part 2 of this chapter (**7.19ff**), the principle does not apply to an execution creditor.

---

24   (1871) LR 7 Ch App 259 at 269.
25   (1884) 15 QBD 280.

7.52 The second criterion is that the purchaser must obtain his interest in good faith and without notice of the earlier equitable interest. The requirement for 'good faith' adds little to the necessity that the person concerned should not have notice of the prior equitable interest. The concept of notice is discussed in part 2 of this chapter (**7.19ff**).

7.53 The third criterion is that the person concerned must obtain a legal interest in the asset concerned. It may consist of the legal title to the asset concerned, either under an outright purchase or by way of a legal mortgage. Alternatively, as has been seen from *Joseph v Lyons*,[26] it is sufficient for the person concerned to obtain a possessory legal interest under a pledge.

7.54 In most cases, the person relying on the principle will obtain a legal mortgage or a pledge at the time credit is given to the debtor. There are, however, two extensions to the principle. The first is that a person can rely on the principle, even where he does not have the legal title, if he has the best right to it. The second is the doctrine of 'tacking the legal estate'.

The best right to the legal estate

7.55 A person can rely on the principle not only where he acquires the legal title to the asset concerned, but also where he has the best right to it. If he is entitled to have the legal title transferred to him, he will be treated in the same way as if he had the legal title. This is as a result of the equitable maxim that 'equity treats as done that which ought to be done'.

7.56 The principle was explained by Stirling LJ in *Taylor v London and County Banking Company*[27] as follows:

'Now, a purchaser for value without notice is entitled to the benefit of a legal title, not merely where he has actually got it in, but where he has a better title or right to call for it ... It has accordingly been held that if a purchaser for value takes an equitable title only, or omits to get in an outstanding legal estate, and a subsequent purchaser for value without notice procures, at the time of his purchase, the person in whom the legal title is vested to declare himself a trustee for him, or even to join as party in a conveyance of the equitable interest (although he may not formally convey or declare a trust of the legal estate), still the subsequent purchaser gains priority.'

7.57 The most common example of the use of this doctrine is where the legal owner of the asset concerned holds it on trust for the creditor. When a creditor takes a legal mortgage over shares, it is common for the legal title to the shares to be vested, not in the creditor itself, but in a nominee company in the same group as the creditor. Although the creditor is not the legal owner of the shares, there will be a declaration of trust in favour of the creditor, who therefore has the best right to call for the legal estate, and is treated as if it were the owner of the legal estate for the purpose of this principle.

---

26 (1884) 15 QBD 280.
27 [1901] 2 Ch 231 at 262–263; and see *Wilkes v Bodington* (1707) 2 Vern 599.

Tacking the legal estate

7.58   The second extension of the bona fide purchaser doctrine is more controversial and much more complicated. It was established by Sir Matthew Hale in *Marsh v Lee*[28] in 1670, and was apparently described by him as tacking tabula in naufragio.[29] It will be described here as 'tacking the legal estate', in order to differentiate it from 'tacking further advances', which is discussed in part 7 of this chapter (**7.203ff**).

The basic principle

7.59   The principle is clearly (if somewhat optimistically, in the light of the opening words) described by Lord Selborne LC in *Blackwood v The London Chartered Bank of Australia*:[30]

> 'There is nothing more familiar than the doctrine of equity that a man, who has *bona fide* paid money without notice of any other title, though at the time of the payment he, as purchaser, gets nothing but an equitable title, may afterwards get in a legal title, if he can, and may hold it; though during the interval between the payment and the getting in the legal title he may have had notice of some prior dealing inconsistent with the good faith of the dealing with himself.'

7.60   The doctrine was originally established in relation to mortgages of land. As a result of s 94(3) of the Law of Property Act 1925, it has been abolished in relation to mortgages of land. It is, however, still applicable to mortgages of other assets, and is particularly important in practice in relation to security over shares. It also continues to apply in relation to outright transfers of (as opposed to mortgages over) land.

7.61   At its simplest, the effect of the doctrine is that the creditor does not have to obtain his legal interest at the time he provides credit to the debtor. If he only takes an equitable mortgage or charge and, at that time, has no notice of a prior equitable interest, he can, having discovered the existence of the equitable interest, then proceed to obtain the legal title and, if he does so, is entitled to rely on the bona fide purchaser principle in order to take priority. Although he has notice of the earlier equitable interest at the time he obtains the legal title, he did not have notice at the time he took his original equitable mortgage or charge, and that is sufficient.

7.62   An example of the use of the doctrine is *Blackwood v The London Chartered Bank of Australia*.[31] In that case, A granted successive equitable mortgages of property to B and C. C took his equitable mortgage without notice of B's interest and then applied to be registered as the legal owner of the property. Before he obtained the registration, he found out about B's interest.

---

28   (1670) 2 Ventr 337.
29   Ie a plank in a shipwreck.
30   (1874) LR 5 PC 92 at 111.
31   (1874) LR 5 PC 92.

He was subsequently registered as the legal owner of the property. The Privy Council decided that C had priority over B. C had obtained legal title to the asset and, although he had done so at a time when he was aware of B's interest, he had obtained his equitable interest without notice.

7.63   The result is that a creditor who obtains an equitable mortgage or charge is able to take priority over an earlier equitable interest if:

- he took his equitable interest without notice of the earlier equitable interest; and
- he subsequently converts his equitable security into a legal mortgage by acquiring the legal title to the asset concerned,

and this is the case even if he became aware of the earlier equitable interest before he obtained legal title to the asset.

The extended principle

7.64   The doctrine extends even further. In *Marsh v Lee*,[32] Sir Matthew Hale CB postulated three subsequent mortgages over the same property:

- a legal mortgage in favour of A;
- a second equitable mortgage in favour of B; and
- a third equitable mortgage in favour of C.

He decided that if:

- at the time he took his equitable mortgage, C did not have notice of B's interest; and
- C then bought A's mortgage, thereby obtaining the legal title to the property,

C would have priority over B's mortgage not only in respect of money lent under A's mortgage, but also in respect of money lent under his own.[33]

7.65   This is a significant extension to the doctrine as applied in the *Blackwood* case. In that case, the later mortgagee obtained priority because he converted his equitable mortgage into a legal mortgage. In *Marsh v Lee*, C did not convert his mortgage into a legal mortgage. He obtained the legal title to the property concerned, but he did this in his capacity as the purchaser of A's mortgage. The legal title was held to secure A's mortgage, not C's mortgage. C was nevertheless given priority over B not only in respect of A's mortgage, but also in respect of his own. The result is curious. It is one thing to give a person priority if he is able to convert his equitable mortgage into a legal one. It is another matter to give him priority simply because he happens to become the legal owner of the property as a result of acquiring a legal mortgage which secures a completely different debt.

---

32   (1670) 2 Ventr 337.
33   The doctrine only applies to the extent that the mortgages are over the same property. If, for instance, only part of the property had been mortgaged to A, C would only take priority in relation to that part.

7.66   Subsequent cases[34] cast doubt on the reasons for the doctrine and suggested that it created hardship for the intermediate equitable mortgagee. Although it soon became clear that the courts were reluctant to extend the doctrine, they continued to apply it, albeit subject to certain exceptions.

7.67   The effect of the extended doctrine is that there is another circumstance in which an equitable mortgagee can take priority over an earlier equitable interest of which he did not have notice at the time he acquired his equitable mortgage. If the later mortgagee can acquire a legal mortgage which was created before the equitable interest, he can thereby take priority over the equitable interest. This is the case even though the acquisition of the earlier legal mortgage does not convert his equitable mortgage into a legal one. The mere acquisition of the legal title, albeit for a different purpose, is sufficient.

7.68   The doctrine does not only apply where the person who acquires the legal estate is a mortgagee. It also applies to outright purchasers. In *Bailey v Barnes*,[35] A had mortgaged property to B. B exercised his power of sale under the mortgage and sold the property to C at an undervalue. C then mortgaged the property to D, and sold his equity of redemption to E. When E discovered what had happened, he paid off D's mortgage and acquired the legal title. There was therefore a priority dispute between A (who had the equitable right to have the undervalue transaction set aside) and E (who had acquired his equitable interest without notice of A's interest but, on discovering the facts, had obtained legal title to the property). The Court of Appeal decided that the doctrine of tacking the legal estate applied to E, as a purchaser. E was now the legal owner of the property and, since he had acquired his beneficial interest before he had notice of A's interest, he took priority over A. Lindley LJ regarded the reasoning as technical and unsatisfactory but decided that the law was settled on the point.

When is notice relevant?

7.69   The relevant time for determining whether or not a creditor has notice of the earlier equitable interest is the time when the creditor obtains his equitable mortgage or charge[36] or, if later, when he makes the credit available to the debtor.[37] If the creditor had actual or constructive notice of the earlier equitable interest at that time, he will be unable to take advantage of the doctrine. But if he did not have notice at that time, it does not matter that he became aware of the earlier equitable interest before he obtained the legal interest in the property concerned. Indeed, as Lord Hardwicke LC said in *Wortley v Birkhead*,[38] it is the fact that he has now received notice of the earlier equitable interest, that requires him to obtain the legal title.

---

34   See, for instance, *Brace v Duchess of Marlborough* (1728) 2 P Wms 491.
35   [1894] 1 Ch 25.
36   *Wortley v Birkhead* (1754) 2 Ves Sen 571.
37   *Earl of Sheffield v The London Joint Stock Bank Limited* (1888) 13 App Cas 333.
38   (1754) 2 Ves Sen 571 at 574.

Statutory restriction of the doctrine

7.70   The doctrine of tacking the legal estate was established in 1670 but, from at least the early eighteenth century, it was being criticised as creating hardship; and a number of subsequent judgments expressed doubts about the good sense of the doctrine. These criticisms led to the restriction of the doctrine by s 94(3) of the Law of Property Act 1925. Section 94 modifies the rules concerning the tacking of further advances, which are considered in part 7 of this chapter (**7.203**ff). Section 94(3) then provides that 'save in regard to the making of further advances as aforesaid, the right to tack is hereby abolished'.

7.71   On the face of it, this section appears to constitute a complete abolition of the doctrine of tacking the legal estate. It is, however, more limited in its effect. Although the Law of Property Act 1925 does contain some provisions which apply to assets other than land, s 94 is contained in a part of the Act which deals entirely with mortgages and charges over land. Indeed, s 94(4) provides that 'this section applies to mortgages of land ..., but not to [charges over registered land]'.

7.72   In view of these provisions, it seems clear that it only abolishes the doctrine in relation to mortgages and charges over land; and that it therefore continues to apply in respect of security over other assets. This was certainly the approach adopted by Millett J in *Macmillan v Bishopsgate Investment Trust (No 3)*.[39] Nor is the doctrine abolished in relation to purchasers (as opposed to mortgagees or chargees) of land.[40] The doctrine has proved to be particularly important in practice in relation to mortgages of shares.

Shares

7.73   It has been seen that shares are one of the few types of intangible the transfer of which is recognised at common law. It is therefore possible for a creditor to obtain a legal mortgage of shares and thereby obtain priority over an earlier equitable interest of which he was not aware when he took the legal mortgage.

7.74   In applying this principle, it is important to establish at what stage a person becomes the legal owner of shares in a company. This issue was considered by the House of Lords in *SociétéGénérale de Paris v Walker*.[41] A had charged his shares in a company to B by depositing the share certificate and a signed blank transfer form with B. A then fraudulently executed a new blank stock transfer form and delivered it to C by way of security, saying that he had lost the share certificate. C notified the company of his interest and delivered the stock transfer form to it. The House of Lords held that B took priority. He was first in time, and C had not displaced that priority because he had not acquired the legal title to the shares. The delivery of the stock transfer form to the company was insufficient to obtain legal title.

---

39   [1995] 1 WLR 978.
40   *McCarthy & Stone v Julian S Hodge & Co* [1971] 1 WLR 1547 at 1556, per Foster J.
41   (1885) 11 App Cas 20.

7.75 C would have become the legal owner once he had been registered as the holder of the shares in the company's register of members. The Earl of Selborne also left open the possibility that legal title might be obtained at an earlier stage if all necessary conditions had been fulfilled in order to give him 'a present, absolute, unconditional right to have the transfer registered'.[42]

7.76 The circumstances in which a person will have a present, absolute, unconditional right to be registered will depend on the articles of association of the company concerned. Where, as is commonly the case with a private company, the board of directors has a discretion to refuse to register transfers, he will only have that right once the board has approved the transfer and all that is required is the physical act of amending the register. If, on the other hand, the articles do not require board approval for transfers, it would seem that the proposed transferee will have such a right once all steps have been taken by himself and the transferor as are sufficient to enable the transferee to require the company to complete the transfer.

7.77 The ultimate question is whether the transferee has the right to require the company to register the transfer. If he does, he has the legal right to the shares albeit that he is not entered in the books of the company. If not, he only has an equitable interest in the shares.

7.78 Two contrasting cases illustrate how these principles work in practice. In *Ireland v Hart*,[43] A was the registered holder of shares, which he held on trust for B. A borrowed money from C against a charge over the shares, giving C a blank stock transfer form and the share certificate. C had no notice of the trust. C later completed the stock transfer form and delivered it to the company for registration. Before the board had approved the registration, B obtained an interim injunction to prevent C becoming registered.

7.79 Joyce J held that B had priority over C. As between two equitable interests, the first in time will take priority. The latter can obtain priority if he acquires the legal title to the shares for value without notice of the earlier interest. In this case, C had not become the registered holder of the shares. Nor did he have 'a present, absolute, unconditional right' to be registered. The board had not approved the transfer and he had no right to require the company to register it.

7.80 If, however, the creditor does become the legal owner of the shares, he is entitled to take priority over an earlier equitable interest if he acquired an equitable interest in the shares before having notice of the earlier equitable interest; and this is the case even if he has become aware of that interest at the time he becomes the legal owner. In *Dodds v Hills*,[44] A was the registered holder of shares in a company, and held them on trust for B. A borrowed money from C, securing the loan by a charge over the shares and delivering to C a signed blank stock transfer form and the share certificates. C had no notice of B's interest in the shares. A then went bankrupt and B informed C of the trust. C

---

42   (1885) 11 App Cas 20 at 29.
43   [1902] 1 Ch 522.
44   (1865) 2 H & M 424.

then completed the stock transfer form and sent it and the share certificate to the company secretary for registration; and the shares were then registered in C's name. C claimed priority over B. B argued that, because C had notice of B's equitable interest when he sent the shares for registration, he could not use his legal title to defeat T's equitable interest.

7.81 Page Wood V-C held that C took priority over B. He had acquired the legal title to the shares without any breach of trust on anyone's part and the equities were therefore equal. C was accordingly entitled to take priority over B because, at the time he took his equitable charge over the shares, he did not have notice of B's equitable interest.

7.82 The facts of *Ireland v Hart* and *Dodds v Hills* were very similar. The crucial distinction was that, in *Ireland v Hart*, the creditor was unable to get on the company's register of members whereas in *Dodds v Hills* he was. Priority can therefore depend on the speed of action of the parties concerned. Can the person with the later equitable interest become the legal owner of the shares before the person with the earlier equitable interest obtains an injunction to prevent him from doing so?

7.83 A recent example of the application of these principles can be found in the decision of Millett J in *Macmillan v Bishopsgate Investment Trust (No 3)*.[45] The decision in that case was affirmed by the Court of Appeal on different grounds,[46] but the case contains an illuminating discussion by Millett J of these issues which summarises the position with regard to security over shares:

- In order to rely on the bona fide purchaser principle, it must generally be established that the purchaser did not have notice of the prior equitable interest at the time he acquired the legal title.
- In order to acquire legal title to shares, it is necessary either to be entered on the company's register of members or to have a present, absolute, unconditional right to have the transfer registered.
- There are, however, two exceptions to the requirement that the purchaser must obtain the legal title before he has notice.
- The first exception is that the purchaser need not himself hold the legal title provided it is held by another person as nominee for him.
- The second exception is where the purchaser can tack the legal estate without a breach of trust by the legal owner. An equitable mortgagee with the share certificate and a signed blank stock transfer form is in a position to obtain registration without further recourse to the legal owner. If he does become the legal owner, he will take priority over an earlier equitable interest if he did not have notice of it at the time he acquired his equitable mortgage.

Are the equities equal?

7.84 The principal exception to the bona fide purchaser doctrine is that, like the 'first in time' principle, it is subject to the requirement that 'the equities are

---

45 [1995] 1 WLR 978 at 999–1005.
46 [1996] 1 WLR 387. See **CHAPTER 13**.

equal'. If the equities are not equal, the person with the better equity will take priority. In *Rooper v Harrison*,[47] Page Wood V-C said that the principle that the person who obtains the legal interest in the asset concerned takes priority over an earlier equitable interest does not apply if the person with the earlier equitable interest has a superior equity. Priority of time is an insufficient equity for this purpose, but the conduct of the legal owner may require him to be postponed. As Lindley LJ said in *Bailey v Barnes*,[48] 'equality' does not mean equality in time. 'Equality means the non-existence of any circumstance which affects the conduct of one of the rival claimants, and makes it less meritorious than that of the other.'[49] These issues are considered in part 4 of this chapter (**7.97ff**).

7.85 In *Harpham v Shacklock*,[50] Sir George Jessel MR said, in a passage which is frequently repeated in later cases, that the bona fide purchaser doctrine does not apply where the creditor acquires the legal estate from a person who commits a breach of trust in transferring it to him. Although this is often described as an independent rule, it is probably better seen as an example of the overriding principle that the doctrine will only apply if the equities are equal. It was certainly put in this way by Lord Macnaghten in *Taylor v Russell*.[51] He indicated that the question was whether a person who obtained the legal estate had acted inequitably in doing so or there was some equity which prevented him from relying on his legal title.

Equitable interests

7.86 It has been seen that the acquisition of the legal title to an asset can enable a creditor with a later security to obtain priority over the holder of an earlier equitable interest over the same asset. The principle only applies where the first interest is equitable and the second is legal. Where the dispute is between two legal interests or between two equitable interests, the first in time rule will apply in the absence of one of the other exceptions which are described later in this chapter. If, for instance, there are two equitable mortgages of property, the mere fact that the second mortgagee took his interest for value and without notice of the earlier interest will not assist him in obtaining priority.[52]

7.87 The distinction is well illustrated in *Cave v Cave*.[53] In that case, A had a beneficial interest under a trust of certain property. The trustee wrongfully transferred the property to B, who then:

- mortgaged it by way of legal mortgage to C; and
- subsequently created an equitable mortgage in favour of D.

---

47   (1855) 2 K & J 86.
48   [1894] Ch 25.
49   [1894] Ch 25 at 36.
50   (1881) 19 Ch D 207 at 214.
51   [1892] AC 244.
52   *Phillips v Phillips* (1861) 4 De GF&J 208.
53   (1880) 15 Ch D 639.

7.88 Both C and D took their interests for value and without notice of the trust. Fry J held that:

- C had acquired the legal title to the property and therefore took free of A's equitable interest; but
- D only obtained an equitable interest and therefore took subject to A's earlier equitable interest.

7.89 Unless he can rely on one of the other exceptions to the first in time principle discussed in the succeeding parts of this chapter, a person who acquires an equitable interest for value will not take priority over an earlier equitable interest merely because he had no notice of it when he acquired his own interest.

Equities

7.90 The position is different, however, where the earlier right is an 'equity' as opposed to an equitable interest. If a person acquires an equitable interest in property for value and without notice of an existing equity, he will take free of it.[54]

7.91 The expression 'equity', when used to describe a right conferred by a court of equity, is used in a number of different senses. It is sometimes used as a synonym for an equitable interest. In relation to priority disputes, it is frequently used (as in the expression 'if the equities are equal') to signify a weighing of the conduct of the parties in dispute. In this context, however, an 'equity' means a proprietary right conferred by a court of equity which is of lesser value than an equitable interest. It is frequently accompanied by the diminutive epithet 'mere', in an attempt to emphasise its lowly position in the pantheon of proprietary interests.

7.92 An equity of this type is a proprietary interest, in the sense that it can affect third parties. It is not only exercisable against the person whose actions initially led to its creation – it can also be exercised against third parties in an appropriate case. But it is not as far-reaching as an equitable interest. Unlike an equitable interest, it cannot be enforced against a person who obtains a subsequent proprietary interest in the property concerned in good faith and without notice of the equity, even if that interest is only equitable.

7.93 It is beyond the scope of this chapter to consider in detail the types of equity which can arise. In the context of security, there are two important equities:

- a right of set-off; and
- the right to have an agreement set aside as a result of a vitiating factor such as fraud, mistake or misrepresentation.

7.94 Set-offs are particularly important in relation to security over debts and are discussed in part 5 of **CHAPTER 3** (**3.175ff**). An example of the latter type of

---

54 *Phillips v Phillips* (1861) 4 De GF&J 208; *Cave v Cave* (1880) 15 Ch D 639.

equity is found in *Latec Investments v Hotel Terrigal*.[55] In that case, A had mortgaged property to B. B wrongfully sold the property at an undervalue to C, an associated company. C then created a floating charge in favour of D, who took for value and without notice of the wrongdoing. If the property had remained with C, A would have been entitled to have the transaction set aside, and the question arose whether it was entitled to do so as against D. The High Court of Australia held that it was not. A's right to have the transaction set aside could not be enforced against D, who had acquired an equitable interest for value and without notice of the facts which gave rise to A's right.

7.95 The judgments of the members of the High Court of Australia contain elaborate discussions of the distinction between equitable interests and equities, and show how difficult it can be in many cases to draw a distinction between them. There are subtle differences of approach between various members of the court concerning the distinction. As a matter of principle, however, it is clear that, if an equitable right is properly described as an 'equity', it will be defeated by a bona fide purchaser for value without notice even if he only obtains an equitable interest in the property concerned.

Summary

7.96 In summary:

- A person who acquires legal title to an asset for value and without notice of an earlier equitable interest will take free of it.
- This is also the case if that person is not the legal owner but has the best right to obtain the legal title or if he is subsequently able to tack the legal estate.
- Successive equitable interests (and successive legal interests) rank in order of creation.
- An equity is postponed to a person who acquires a legal or equitable interest in the asset concerned for value and without notice.
- These principles are subject to the exceptions discussed in the following parts of this chapter.

Part 4: UNEQUAL EQUITIES

The principle

7.97 Both the principle that an earlier interest takes priority over a later one and the principle that a legal interest can take priority over an earlier equitable interest are expressed only to apply where 'the equities are equal'. They will apply, in other words, unless it would be inequitable to abide by them.

---

55   (1965) 113 CLR 265.

7.98   This sounds like a recipe for uncertainty, and it is certainly the case that it is difficult to reconcile all of the cases. Two very different approaches can be seen in the cases. These contrasting approaches can be illustrated by comparing the decision of Kindersley V-C in *Rice v Rice*[56] in 1853, with that of Lord Westbury LC in *Phillips v Phillips*,[57] 8 years later.

7.99   In *Rice v Rice*, B transferred land to A by way of sale without receiving the purchase price and therefore had an equitable lien to secure the price. A nevertheless obtained the deeds and deposited them with C by way of an equitable mortgage. A priority dispute arose between B and C, each of whom had equitable interests. It was held that C took priority.

7.100   Kindersley V-C was at pains to stress that, as between equitable interests, the rule was not that the first in time prevails but that: 'As between persons having only equitable interests, if their equities are *in all other respects* equal, priority of time gives the better equity.'[58] Priority of time is the last question to be considered. The court will first see if there is any other ground to prefer one claimant over the other and, if a better ground can be found, priority of time is immaterial. In considering the parties' equities, the court will consider the nature and condition of their equitable interests, the circumstances and manner of their acquisition, and the whole conduct of each party with respect to the matter. The court will consider these matters on the basis of 'broad principles of right and justice'.[59] He summarised the position as follows:

> '... in all cases of contest between persons having equitable interests the conduct of the parties and all the circumstances must be taken into consideration, in order to determine which has the better equity.'[60]

7.101   When he applied these principles to the priority dispute between B and C, Kindersley V-C decided that:

- there was no material distinction between B's equitable lien and C's equitable mortgage, even though one was created by agreement and the other by operation of law; but
- by allowing A to retain the deeds, B had enabled A to persuade C that the land was unencumbered, and C therefore had a better equity than B; and
- as a result, it was unnecessary to consider who was first in time.

7.102   It will be seen that this approach gives very great weight to the conduct of the parties in establishing their priorities, and makes the first in time principle a matter of last resort – only relevant if there is no other basis on which the rights of the matter can be decided.

7.103   A very different approach was adopted by Lord Westbury LC in *Phillips v Phillips*.[61] In reverting to what he described as 'elementary principles', Lord Westbury said:

---

56   (1853) 2 Drew 73.
57   (1861) 4 De GF&J 208.
58   (1853) 2 Drew 73 at 78 (emphasis in the original).
59   (1853) 2 Drew 73 at 78–79.
60   (1853) 2 Drew 73 at 83.
61   (1861) 4 De GF&J 208.

'I take it to be a clear proposition that every conveyance of an equitable interest is an innocent conveyance, that is to say, the grant of a person entitled merely in equity passes only that which he is justly entitled to and no more.'[62]

7.104 He went on to deny the relevance of the absence of notice by the second encumbrancer:

'[I]t is quite immaterial whether the subsequent incumbrancers at the time when they took their securities and paid their money had notice of the first encumbrance or not.'[63]

7.105 The starting point, for Lord Westbury, was the inability of a person to grant a second equitable interest otherwise than subject to the existing equitable interest. What was important was therefore the time of creation of the interests, rather than the conduct of the parties.

7.106 The approach of Kindersley V-C was followed in a number of nineteenth-century cases. More recently, however, it is Lord Westbury's approach which appears more accurately to reflect the way in which the courts now deal with the issue. As between two equitable interests, the court will assume that the first in time will take priority unless there is a good reason why he should not. The actual decision in *Rice v Rice* is entirely consistent with this approach. Although, in that case, B was the first in time, there was a very good reason why he should be postponed to C. He had enabled A to create a subsequent mortgage by allowing him to retain the title deeds to the property concerned. The difference in approach should not be overestimated. The result may be the same. What differs is the starting point.

Four types of case

7.107 Before discussing the nature of the conduct which is required to postpone a creditor who would otherwise have priority, it is useful to consider the possible types of priority dispute which can arise between two parties. There are four possibilities:

- a first equitable interest followed by a second equitable interest;
- a first legal interest followed by a second legal interest;
- a first legal interest followed by a second equitable interest;
- a first equitable interest followed by a second legal interest.

7.108 Successive equitable interests are quite common. In such a case, the first in time will take priority, but he will be postponed if his conduct is such that it would be inequitable to give him priority.

7.109 Successive legal interests are rare. This used to be because of the difficulty of creating two legal interests over the same asset. In principle, it is only possible for one person to obtain the legal title to an asset. If one

---

62   (1861) 4 De GF&J 208 at 215.
63   (1861) 4 De GF&J 208 at 215–216.

mortgagee has the legal title, any other mortgage must necessarily be equitable. Since the 1925 property legislation, it is possible to create subsequent charges by way of legal mortgage over land, but priority disputes in relation to land are now, more often than not, governed by the rules concerning registration, which are discussed in part 9 of this chapter (**7.251**ff). As a result, it is unlikely that many problems will arise in practice in relation to successive legal interests.

7.110 In the third type of case, where a legal interest is followed by an equitable one, the person with the first interest will have a double advantage, having both a legal interest and priority in time, but he will nevertheless be postponed to the subsequent equitable interest if it would be inequitable to allow him to retain that priority.

7.111 The position is rather different in relation to the fourth type of case: an equitable interest followed by a legal one. In principle, the later legal interest will take priority over the earlier equitable one if it was taken for value and without notice of the earlier equitable interest, but the owner of the earlier equitable interest may regain priority if the conduct of the owner of the legal interest was such that it would be inequitable to allow him to rely on his legal title.

When are the equities unequal?

7.112 In what circumstances will it be inequitable for a person to take advantage of the priority which the law would otherwise accord him? *Rice v Rice*[64] shows that the courts adopt a broad view of the nature of the circumstances which are necessary, but there are two main criteria – notice and conduct.

7.113 The first criterion is notice. In the first three types of case described above, the person with the earlier interest will take priority unless it would be inequitable to allow him to do so. If the person with the later interest had notice of the earlier one at the time he took his interest, there can be no question of the person with the earlier interest losing priority. It cannot be inequitable to rely on an interest of which the other person was aware when he acquired his interest. This is not an issue in the fourth type of case because the later legal owner will only take priority if he did not have notice of the earlier equitable interest. In short, therefore, it is only possible for a person to have the better equity if he did not have notice of the competing interest at the time he took his own interest.

7.114 The second criterion is even more important – the conduct of the parties in relation to the security, particularly the conduct of the person who would otherwise have priority. The key question is to identify what types of conduct are sufficient to make it inequitable for that person to retain his priority. Where there are two contenders for priority, the overriding consideration is whether the conduct of one of them has enabled the debtor to persuade the other that the secured asset is unencumbered – for instance, by

---

64   (1853) 2 Drew 73.

allowing him to retain the title documents relating to the asset. In the cases, whether conduct of this kind is sufficient to postpone one of the contenders for priority depends on whether that person was fraudulent or negligent or whether he has given the debtor the authority to create prior security.

Fraud

7.115 It goes without saying that the fraud of one party (in its primary common law sense of dishonesty) is sufficient to prevent him from relying on what would otherwise be his priority. In the words of Denning LJ, 'Fraud unravels everything'.[65]

Negligence

7.116 The circumstances in which the negligence of a secured creditor will postpone him are, in contrast, much more difficult to describe. The cases are by no means consistent. They used to require what has been variously described as 'negligence amounting to fraud' or 'gross negligence', although later cases indicate that simple negligence can be sufficient. The words of Fry J in *Cave v Cave*[66] are apposite, although used in a slightly different context: 'Criticisms upon old cases lie many strata deep, and eminent Lord Chancellors have expressed diametrically opposed conclusions upon the same question.'

7.117 The starting point is to consider how the courts have approached the issue in three different types of case:

- where there are two successive equitable interests;
- where there is a legal interest followed by an equitable interest; and
- where there is an equitable interest followed by a legal interest which was taken without notice of the earlier equitable interest.

Two successive equitable interests

7.118 If there are two successive equitable interests, and the second had notice of the first at the time he acquired his interest, there is no reason to displace the principle that the first in time will take priority. But, if the owner of the second interest is unaware of the first, he will take priority if the negligence of the first has enabled the debtor to allow the subsequent equitable interest to be created.

7.119 As has been seen, in *Rice v Rice*[67] the second creditor took priority over the first, even though he was later in time, because the first creditor had allowed the debtor to retain the title deeds to the property concerned and thereby gave the debtor the opportunity to create the second mortgage.

---

65   *Lazarus Estates v Beasley* [1956] 1 QB 702 at 712.
66   (1880) 15 Ch D 639 at 646.
67   (1853) 2 Drew 73.

7.120   The same approach can be seen in the decision of the High Court of Australia in *Heid v Reliance Finance Corporation*.[68] The facts of the case were very similar to those in *Rice v Rice*. B sold property to A on the basis that most of the purchase price was to be left outstanding, and for which B accordingly had an unpaid vendor's lien. The transfer nevertheless acknowledged payment of the full price and A obtained the title deeds. A then created an equitable mortgage in favour of C, who did not have notice of B's lien.

7.121   The High Court of Australia held that C had priority over B. B's conduct in acknowledging receipt of the purchase price and 'arming' A with the 'indicia of title' was sufficient to postpone him to C. The judgment of Mason and Deane JJ contains an interesting discussion of the theory, and is reminiscent of the approach in *Rice v Rice*. The overriding question was who had the better equity, bearing in mind the conduct of both parties. In this case, the fact that B had acknowledged receipt of the purchase price and had left the transfer documents with A was sufficient evidence of negligence by B that he should be postponed. C therefore took priority because he had the better equity.

7.122   The same principle has been applied where the first interest is an equitable mortgage, rather than an equitable lien. In *Farrand v Yorkshire Banking Co*,[69] A created an equitable mortgage in favour of B, who did not take the title deeds. A then created a further equitable mortgage by deposit of the title deeds with C, who did not have notice of the mortgage in favour of B. North J held that C took priority because B had allowed A to keep the deeds and therefore to effect the fraud. Although C's interest was created later than B's interest, the equities were not equal and C had priority. In the words of North J:[70]

> 'Of course, one equity is always prior to the other in date, and the expression "equal equities" does not refer to equality in date. When equities are equal in other respects the earlier in date is preferred, but, when equities are not equal, then the priority of date is easily got over, at any rate, as between equitable encumbrancers.'

7.123   Whether or not the actions of the person with the earlier equitable interest are sufficient to postpone him is a matter of fact in each case, but allowing the mortgagor to retain the title deeds is powerful evidence of sufficient negligence to postpone him.

7.124   This will not be the case, however, where the conduct of the later mortgagee is such that he ought to be postponed. In *National Provincial Bank of England v Jackson*,[71] A and B both had a beneficial interest in property. B effectively allowed A wrongfully to create an equitable mortgage over it in favour of C by deposit of the title deeds. A told C that B was the joint owner of the property with A, but that none of the money raised on the mortgage would

---

68   (1983) 154 CLR 326.
69   (1888) 40 Ch D 182.
70   (1888) 40 Ch D 182 at 188.
71   (1886) 33 Ch D 1.

go to B. This statement was inconsistent with the title deeds deposited with C. The Court of Appeal held that C was put on inquiry by A's statements and, had C made the proper inquiry in relation to the deeds, B's fraud would have been discovered. Both B and C had equitable interests in the property. But for C's failure to inquire, C would have had the better equity on the basis that A had allowed B to create the mortgage. But C's failure to inquire, having been put on inquiry, was sufficient negligence that he should be postponed to B.

7.125 In summary, as between the holders of two successive equitable interests, the negligence of the first in relation to the transaction will postpone him to the second unless the second was himself negligent, in which event their mutual negligence cancels each other out, leaving the first in time to take priority.

Legal interest followed by equitable interest

7.126 Where there is a legal interest followed by an equitable interest, the holder of the legal interest has both time and the law on his side. Some cases suggest that he will therefore only be postponed to the later equitable interest if his conduct is particularly bad, in other words, that the conduct which is required to postpone him is greater than would be required if he only had an equitable interest. Other cases indicate that there is no difference between this type of case and the case where there are two competing equitable interests; and that all that is required to postpone the owner of the earlier legal interest is that his negligence in relation to the arrangement has allowed the subsequent equitable mortgage to be created.

7.127 The approach of the courts can be seen by contrasting two cases. In *Northern Counties of England Fire Insurance Company v Whipp*,[72] A created a legal mortgage of his land in favour of B and gave B the deeds. B was a company, of which A was the manager, and A had the keys to the safe where the deeds were kept. A wrongfully obtained the deeds and delivered them to C under an equitable mortgage. C took his mortgage without notice of B's legal mortgage. C argued that B had been negligent in enabling A to recover the deeds and that B was therefore postponed to C. B relied on the fact that it was first in time. The Court of Appeal decided that B had priority over C. The actual decision is clearly correct. It is difficult to conclude that B was negligent simply in allowing the deeds to remain in its safe. It was not a case where the owner was deliberately allowed to retain the deeds; and the decision in the case is therefore consistent with the view that, if B had been negligent in relation to the deeds, he would have been postponed.

7.128 The judgment of the Court of Appeal, however, proceeds on the assumption that a legal owner will not be postponed merely because he was negligent in relation to the deeds. It indicated that the holder of a prior legal interest will only be postponed to a subsequent equitable one if:

- he had assisted in the fraud which led to the creation of the equitable interest; or

---

72 (1884) 26 Ch D 482.

- he had constituted the owner his agent for the purpose of the creation of the later equitable interest.

7.129   The question of authority is considered later in this part. For present purposes, what is important is the requirement that the holder of the earlier legal interest should have assisted in the fraud which led to the creation of the equitable interest. Taken by itself, this would materially restrict the circumstances in which a legal owner could be postponed to a later equitable interest, but the court went on to indicate that an omission by him to use ordinary care in relation to the deeds may be sufficient evidence that he has assisted in a fraud. Such an approach is unsatisfactory for two reasons. In the first place, it is clearly not the case that an omission to use ordinary care in relation to deeds is evidence that the person concerned has assisted in a fraud. It is evidence of negligence, but not of fraud. Secondly, it is difficult to see why negligent conduct of a holder of an equitable mortgage should have any different effect from negligence by the holder of a legal mortgage.

7.130   The *Whipp* case can be contrasted with *Walker v Linom*.[73] In that case, trustees held the legal estate in land subject to a trust under which B was a beneficiary. The land had been conveyed to them by A, who had retained the conveyance and was accordingly wrongfully able to create an equitable mortgage in favour of C by delivery of the title deeds. C had no notice of the trust. Parker J decided that the question was whether the trustees' rights as legal owners were postponed to C's equitable mortgage. He held that the trustees were postponed, even though they had both the legal title and the earlier interest. They ought to have obtained all of the deeds and, by not doing so, had allowed A to create the equitable mortgage in favour of C.

7.131   Parker J decided that it was not necessary, in order to postpone the trustees, that they should have been guilty of a fraud. Although in the *Whipp* case, it was indicated that fraud was necessary, later cases had established that this was no longer the case. He said:[74]

> 'In my opinion any conduct on the part of the holder of the legal estate in relation to the deeds which would make it inequitable for him to rely on his legal estate against a prior equitable estate of which he had no notice ought also to be sufficient to postpone him to a subsequent equitable estate the creation of which has only been rendered possible by the possession of deeds which but for such conduct would have passed into the possession of the owner of the legal estate.'

7.132   On this basis, the test is the same as in the third category of case, to which it is now necessary to turn.

Equitable interest followed by legal interest without notice

7.133   The third type of case arises where a person obtains a legal interest in property for value and without notice of an earlier equitable interest. If the

---

73   [1907] 2 Ch 104.
74   [1907] 2 Ch 104 at 114.

equities are equal, the legal owner will take priority, but in what circumstances will his negligence prevent the equities being equal and therefore postpone him? In this case, one party has the benefit of being first in time and the other the benefit of the legal title.

7.134 The approach of the courts to this type of case can again be seen by contrasting two cases. In *Oliver v Hinton*,[75] A had obtained an equitable mortgage over property by deposit of title deeds. B then purchased the legal title to the land without notice of A's mortgage. When his agent inquired for the deeds, he was told that they also related to other property and therefore would not be handed over. The question arose whether B was entitled to priority over A on the basis that he had acquired legal title to the property for value and without notice of the equitable mortgage.

7.135 The Court of Appeal held that A took priority over B. This decision was not based on B having constructive notice of A's interest but on the basis that a legal estate only prevailed over an earlier equitable interest if the equities were equal, and here they were not. Lindley MR held that it was not necessary to establish fraud on the part of the legal owner, in order to postpone him. He could be postponed if he had committed 'such gross negligence as would render it unjust to deprive the prior incumbrancer of his priority'.[76] On the facts, they found that B had been grossly negligent by allowing himself to be fobbed off by an excuse that the deeds related to other property.

7.136 In contrast, in *Hudston v Viney*,[77] A created an equitable mortgage in favour of B and a subsequent legal mortgage in favour of C, who took without notice of B's equitable interest. C did not properly investigate A's title and Eve J found that there had been some negligence by C but insufficient to prevent him from relying on his legal estate. He decided that the effect of *Oliver v Hinton* was that what was needed in order to postpone the legal owner was 'carelessness of so aggravated a nature as to amount to the neglect of precautions which the ordinarily reasonable man would have observed and to indicate an attitude of mental indifference to obvious risks'.[78]

7.137 Although it is clear that fraud is not necessary to postpone the holder of the legal title in such a case, what has been required by the courts is what they describe as 'gross' negligence, although the reference by Eve J in *Hudston v Viney* to failure to carry out the ordinary precautions which a reasonable man ought to have performed looks very like a description of simple negligence. In the third type of case, unlike the other two, it would have been possible to have reached the same conclusion on the basis that the subsequent legal encumbrancer had been put on inquiry of, or had constructive notice of, the earlier equitable interest, but this was not the way in which the cases were approached.

---

75 [1899] 2 Ch 264.
76 [1899] 2 Ch 264 at 274.
77 [1921] 1 Ch 98.
78 [1921] 1 Ch 98 at 104.

Summary

7.138 In reviewing the cases, it has been seen that there has been no consistency in the approach of the courts in establishing the standard of misconduct which is required in order to postpone a person who would otherwise take priority. The tests proposed range from 'negligence amounting to fraud' through 'gross negligence' to simple 'negligence'.

7.139 There are some suggestions in the cases that the degree of negligence required of a party varies depending on the strength of his claim (for instance, that it requires greater negligence to postpone a legal, than an equitable, interest). Such an approach could be justified on the basis that the stronger the right which is being taken away, the greater the misconduct should be. It would, however, be misconceived. It is very difficult in practice to establish gradations of negligence. The problem with the use of an expression such as 'gross negligence' is that it is difficult to establish the degree of care which is required beyond that which is required to prove simple negligence. The person concerned has either acted unreasonably in all the circumstances or he has not. Gross negligence has, with some justification, been described as negligence 'with the addition of a vituperative epithet'.[79]

7.140 Ultimately, the only meaningful question is whether:

- the conduct of the person who would otherwise be entitled to priority is such that he has enabled the other interest to be created; and
- in the light of all of the facts of the case, the conduct concerned was unreasonable in all the circumstances.

7.141 Most of the cases in this area have involved land, and there have been very few cases since the 1925 property legislation, largely because of the growing significance of the date of registration in relation to priority issues concerning land. Such issues continue to be relevant, however, in relation to other assets,[80] and can still be of relevance in relation to land where there are unregistered interests. The absence of many recent cases means that it is difficult to establish precisely which approach will be taken by the courts, but the growth of the concept of negligence during the twentieth century makes it likely that the issue will ultimately become one of simple negligence.

7.142 It is therefore suggested that, in a priority dispute between A and B in which A would otherwise have priority over B, A will be postponed to B if:

- A's conduct has enabled B to take his interest without knowledge of A's interest; and
- in all the circumstances (which include the conduct of both parties and the nature of the transaction), A's conduct was unreasonable.

---

79 Rolfe B in *Wilson v Brett* (1843) 11 M&W 113 at 116.
80 Unless the assets are intangibles to which the rule in *Dearle v Hall; Loveridge v Cooper* (1823, 1827, 1828) 3 Russ 1 applies, as is explained in part 5 of this chapter (**7.151**ff).

Authority

7.143 In addition to fraud and negligence, there is one other type of conduct which the cases establish can postpone a person who would otherwise have priority. If the creditor has authorised the debtor to create mortgages which rank ahead of the creditor's mortgage, the later mortgage will clearly take priority over the earlier one. This is the basis on which floating charges are postponed to later fixed charges (which is discussed in part 8 of this chapter (**7.234ff**)).

7.144 Where the creditor has actually authorised the debtor to create the mortgage concerned (either expressly or by implication) there is no doubt that the later mortgage will take priority. The problems arise where the debtor exceeds his authority. If, for instance, he is authorised to create a prior mortgage of a particular type, but in fact creates a mortgage of a type which falls outside the scope of that authority, will the later mortgage still take priority? The answer depends on basic principles of agency law. Even though the debtor does not have actual authority to create a prior mortgage of the type concerned, it will still take priority over the earlier mortgage if the debtor is held out by the creditor as having general authority to create mortgages. In such a case, the person obtaining the later mortgage is entitled to assume that his mortgage falls within the criteria imposed by the creditor unless he has notice to the contrary.

7.145 An example of such a case is *Perry Herrick v Attwood*.[81] In that case, A created a legal mortgage in favour of B, but B allowed A to retain the deeds in order to create a mortgage in favour of a particular person to secure a particular debt, it being agreed that the later mortgage would rank in priority to B's mortgage. In fact, A used the deeds to create a mortgage for a larger amount in favour of a different person. Lord Cranworth LC held that the later mortgage took priority over B's mortgage even though A had exceeded his authority. B had left A with the deeds with the intention of raising money and was not entitled to complain if he raised more than he was entitled to. This case was followed by the House of Lords in *Brocklesby v The Temperance Permanent Building Society*,[82] where it was explained as being based on agency law. The mortgagee had held out the owner as having authority to create mortgages and could not complain if his agent did more than he was actually authorised to do.

7.146 A clear explanation of this line of authority is found in the judgment of Farwell J in *Rimmer v Webster*.[83] In that case, A, who was the legal owner of a bond, allowed B to become the registered holder of the bond as a result of misrepresentations by B. B then borrowed money by creating an equitable mortgage over the bond in favour of C. Farwell J held that, even though A had an earlier legal interest, he was postponed to C's later equitable interest because he had given B the indicia of title and C was not aware of the actual limitation on B's authority. As Farwell J said:[84]

---

81 (1857) 2 De G & J 21.
82 [1895] AC 173.
83 [1902] 2 Ch 163.
84 [1902] 2 Ch 163 at 173.

'[When] the owner is found to have given the vendor or borrower the means of representing himself as the beneficial owner, the case forms one of actual authority apparently equivalent to absolute ownership, and involving the right to deal with the property as owner, and any limitations on this generality must be proved to have been brought to the knowledge of the purchaser or mortgagee.'

7.147   It is for the same reason that a possessory lien will normally rank in priority to a mortgage even if the mortgage prohibits the creation of such liens. If, for instance, a mortgagee of goods allows the debtor to remain in possession of them, he will almost inevitably be holding out the debtor as having the authority to have the goods repaired and thereby to enable a repairer's lien to be created, which will rank in priority to the mortgage unless the repairer is aware of a restriction on the debtor's authority.[85]

Summary

7.148   It is impossible to reconcile all the cases which consider the circumstances in which a person who would otherwise have priority will be postponed because the equities are unequal. The courts will consider the conduct of both the secured creditors concerned in relation to their security. It is suggested that the creditor who would otherwise have priority will lose it in three circumstances:

● if he was fraudulent;
● if he gave the debtor actual or apparent authority to create the prior security; or
● if his conduct was unreasonable in the circumstances and it misled the other creditor into thinking the asset concerned was unencumbered.

7.149   In spite of the width of the principle, there are few cases in practice where it is ever likely to arise, as can be seen from the dearth of recent cases concerning it. The requirement to register most mortgages and charges created by companies means that, in practice, the risks of a subsequent chargee being unaware of the existence of an earlier charge is less likely to arise than previously. And, as will be seen in the next part of this chapter, the principle does not apply where the asset concerned is an intangible to which the rule in *Dearle v Hall*[86] applies.

7.150   The principle is therefore restricted to security over land and goods and over those types of intangible to which the rule in *Dearle v Hall* does not apply (such as shares and certain types of intellectual property). In practice, it is the continued possession of title documents by the debtor which has created most problems. As far as land is concerned, the ubiquity of land registration has meant that the possession of title deeds is now of much less importance than it was in the nineteenth century. Goods and shares are very rarely the subject of title documents. As a result, the principle is most likely to be relevant in cases

---

85   See, for instance, *Williams v Allsup* (1861) 10 CB NS 417 and part 2 of chapter 10 (**10.17ff**).
86   *Dearle v Hall; Loveridge v Cooper* (1823, 1827, 1828) 3 Russ 1.

where one creditor has given the debtor actual or apparent authority to deal with the asset as if it were unencumbered – a principle which is seen most frequently in relation to floating charges, and which is discussed in part 8 of this chapter (**7.234ff**).

Part 5: THE RULE IN *DEARLE V HALL*[87]

7.151   It has been seen that, in a priority dispute between two holders of equitable interests, the basic principle is that the first in time will take priority unless the equities are unequal. During the nineteenth century, however, a different rule developed in relation to the priority of interests in trust funds, and that rule was then extended to other intangibles which consist of the right to receive money from a third party, the most important examples of which are contract rights and debts. The rule, which is subject to various exceptions, is that the first person to give notice of his interest to the trustee of the fund or the person who owes the debt will take priority, regardless of when his interest was actually created.

7.152   The rule can be illustrated by two examples. It developed in relation to assignments of rights under trusts. A is a beneficiary under a trust. He assigns or charges that interest first to B, and then to C. (It does not matter whether it is an assignment or a charge or whether the interest created is outright or by way of security: the same rule applies.) B does not give notice of his interest to the trustees of the trust fund, but C does. Subject to certain exceptions, C will take priority over B even though his interest was created after B's.

7.153   Although the rule initially developed in relation to interests in trust funds, it was subsequently extended to assignments and charges of contract rights and debts, and this is where it has become most important in commercial practice. A is owed a debt by T. He assigns or charges it first to B and then to C. C gives notice to T before B does. Subject to certain exceptions, C will take priority over B, even though his interest was created after B's.

7.154   Stated in such bald terms, the reason for the rule is difficult to understand, and a discussion of the way in which the rule developed is necessary in order to obtain a proper understanding of the rule.

The development of the rule

7.155   The rule was developed in the twin cases of *Dearle v Hall* and *Loveridge v Cooper*.[88] The facts of each case were similar. In essence, they involved the following:

- A owned a beneficial interest in a trust fund.

---

87   *Dearle v Hall; Loveridge v Cooper* (1823, 1827, 1828) 3 Russ 1.
88   (1823, 1827, 1828) 3 Russ 1.

- A assigned it to B as security for a debt, but B did not give notice to the trustees of the fund.
- A then agreed to sell it to C outright. C's solicitor made inquiries of the trustees but, because they had not received notice from B, they were not aware of, and therefore did not mention the existence of, the assignment in favour of B.
- A then assigned his interest in the fund to C absolutely in consideration for the payment of the purchase price.
- C then gave notice of the assignment to the trustees.
- B subsequently gave notice to the trustees.

7.156   The question then arose as to whether B or C had priority in respect of the trust fund. Both interests were necessarily equitable and B accordingly claimed that he took priority because his equitable interest was created before C's. C said that he took priority because he gave notice first. B should have given notice and, by failing to do so, had allowed A to commit a fraud on C.

7.157   The case first came before Plumer MR, who held that C had priority over B. He gave two reasons for this decision. The first was based on the principle (discussed in part 4 of this chapter (**7.97ff**)) that the first in time will only take priority if the equities are equal. By failing to give notice, B had negligently allowed A to commit a fraud on C. In these circumstances, the equities were not equal and therefore C was entitled to priority. The other reason was that the giving of notice was tantamount to taking possession of the trust fund and, by failing to perfect his title, B was responsible for the consequences, which were that A had been enabled to commit a fraud on C.

7.158   The case then went on appeal to the Lord Chancellor. B argued that the 'first in time' principle is only overridden in cases of fraud or gross negligence, and that C could get no more than A was properly able to give him. C, on the other hand, argued that the equities were not equal, that B should have given notice to the trustees and that his negligence in failing to do so had enabled A to commit a fraud on C.

7.159   Lord Lyndhurst LC upheld the decision of Plumer MR that C was entitled to priority. He agreed that B's neglect had enabled A to commit a fraud on C, but he placed more reliance on the second ground of Plumer MR's decision. By failing to give notice, B had effectively allowed A to remain in apparent possession of the trust fund; and he was not, therefore, entitled to rely on an assignment of which he had not given notice.

7.160   The first ground of the decision, that C had priority because the equities were unequal, is entirely consistent with the principles discussed in part 4 of this chapter (**7.97ff**). The other ground is more puzzling. It seems to be based on the doctrine of reputed ownership, which used to apply in the bankruptcy of individuals to prevent a secured creditor from relying on his security if the assets which were the subject of the security remained in the apparent possession of the debtor. The rule never applied to companies, and has subsequently been abolished in relation to individuals; and it certainly never applied outside bankruptcy.

7.161 Nevertheless, the case can easily be seen as a straightforward example of a situation where the holder of a later interest took priority over the holder of an earlier interest because the conduct of the former meant that the equities were not equal. Later cases, however, turned it into an absolute rule (although subject to certain exceptions) that the first to give notice takes priority.

7.162 Seven years later, in *Foster v Cockerell*,[89] the House of Lords had to consider a case where the person with the second interest had not made any inquiries of the trustees when taking his interest, although he did then give notice to the trustees of that interest. The House of Lords held that he was still entitled to priority because the holder of the first interest had, by failing to give notice of trustees, enabled the owner of the trust fund to commit a fraud. Subsequent cases went even further in establishing the absolute nature of the rule. It applies even if the holder of the first interest was not negligent in failing to give notice, for instance, because he was not aware of it[90] or because there was no one to whom notice could be given.[91]

7.163 The effect of the rule was reviewed and explained by the House of Lords in *Ward v Duncombe*.[92] The House of Lords decided that the rule that notice determines priority of dealings applied regardless of the conduct of the competing assignees. Lord Macnaghten said:[93] 'I am inclined to think that the rule in *Dearle v Hall* has on the whole produced at least as much injustice as it has prevented.' But the existence and effect of the rule was, nevertheless, acknowledged.

7.164 In summary, the rule initially developed as an example of the principle that the first in time will not take priority if the equities are unequal. Subsequent developments have frozen it in aspic, turning it into an absolute rule (although subject to certain exceptions) that the first person to give notice takes priority whether or not the holder of the first interest was negligent in failing to give notice, and regardless of the conduct of the parties.

Exceptions to the rule

7.165 There are three main exceptions to the rule, one of which is an apparent, rather than a real, one.

7.166 The first exception is that the holder of a later interest cannot take priority over the holder of an earlier interest by giving notice first if, at the time he took his interest, he had notice of the existence of the earlier interest.[94] It would clearly be unjust if this were not the case. But, so long as the holder of the later interest does not have notice of the earlier interest at the time the later interest is created, the fact that he subsequently becomes aware of the earlier

---

89 (1835) 3 Cl & Fin 456.
90 *Re Lake, ex parte Cavendish* [1903] 1 KB 151.
91 *Re Dallas* [1904] 2 Ch 385.
92 (1893) AC 369.
93 (1893) AC 369 at 393.
94 *Re A D Holmes* (1885) 29 Ch D 786.

interest before he has given notice does not prevent him from giving notice first, and thereby obtaining priority. At Cotton LJ said in *Mutual Life Assurance Society v Langley*:[95] 'It is not a question of what a man knows when he does that which will better or perfect his security, but what he knows at the time when he took his security and paid his money.'

7.167   In this context, as in all others, notice includes constructive notice. If, therefore, the holder of the later interest ought reasonably to have been aware of the existence of the earlier interest at the time the later interest was created, he will not be able to take priority by giving notice first even though he was not actually aware of the existence of the earlier interest. In *Spencer v Clarke*,[96] A created a mortgage over his insurance policy in favour of B, handing B the policy. A then created another mortgage over the policy in favour of C. C gave notice to the insurance company, but B did not. Hall V-C held that C had constructive notice of B's interest at the time he took his own interest. He had been put on inquiry by being fobbed off about the policy document and could not, therefore, take priority by giving notice first.

7.168   The second exception to the rule is that it does not apply to volunteers, such as execution creditors. It has been seen in part 2 of this chapter (**7.19ff**) that a volunteer, such as an execution creditor, is only entitled to receive what the owner can honestly deal with. If the owner has already created a proprietary interest in the asset, the execution creditor will therefore take the asset subject to that interest, regardless of whether or not he was aware of it and regardless of whether or not he gave notice first.[97]

7.169   By way of example, A is owed a debt by T, and charges it to B. B does not give notice to T. C subsequently obtains judgment against A and proceeds to execute that judgment by obtaining a third party debt order against T, which is then served on T. Although C has given notice of his interest to T before B has done so, B will still take priority. C has not given value for the execution. He is a volunteer and he is therefore in no better position than A. He is only entitled to the debt to the extent that A can honestly deal with it.

7.170   The third exception is an apparent one, rather than a real one. It has been seen, in **CHAPTER 3**, that a mortgage or charge over a debt creates a valid proprietary interest whether or not notice is given to the counterparty.[98] Such a mortgage or charge is, therefore, valid against an insolvency officer of the debtor even if notice has not been given to the counterparty.[99] It follows that, even if the insolvency officer gives notice of his appointment before the owner of the interest has done so, the proprietary interest will still be effective in the insolvency.

---

95   (1886) 32 Ch D 460 at 468. It has been seen in part 3 of this chapter (**7.48ff**) that the same reasoning has justified the doctrine of tacking the legal estate.

96   (1878) 9 Ch D 137.

97   *Re General Horticultural Company, ex parte Whitehouse* (1886) 32 Ch D 512.

98   *Gorringe v Irwell India Rubber and Gutta Percha Works* (1886) 34 Ch D 128.

99   *Gorringe v Irwell India Rubber and Gutta Percha Works* (1886) 34 Ch D 128.

7.171   To take an example: A, who is an individual, is owed money by T. A charges that debt to B. B does not give notice to T. A then subsequently becomes bankrupt and his trustee in bankruptcy gives notice of his appointment to T. B's charge is still effective against the trustee in bankruptcy, regardless of the fact that the trustee gave notice first.[100]

When does the rule apply?

7.172   When considering the circumstances in which the rule in *Dearle v Hall*[101] applies it is necessary to distinguish between two issues:

- Which types of asset does it apply to?
- Which types of transfer does it apply to?

Which types of asset?

7.173   The rule initially applied to equitable assignments and charges of equitable interests in personal property. By s 137(1) of the Law of Property Act 1925, it was extended to dealings in equitable interests in land. It now applies, therefore, to dealings in equitable interests in all types of asset. Where, therefore, the debtor is not the legal owner, but only the beneficial owner of property, it is the rule in *Dearle v Hall* which will regulate the priority of the dealings with that equitable interest. The first to give notice to the trustee will, subject to the exceptions described above, take priority. This can be of importance in commercial practice. The debtor may only have an equitable interest if it has already created a legal interest in the assets concerned or where the legal title to the assets is held by an intermediary.

7.174   Even more importantly in practice, the rule also applies to assignments and charges of debts and other monetary amounts owing to the debtor. This is the case even if the debtor is their legal owner.[102] In such a case, the person to whom notice must be given is the person who owes the amount concerned.

7.175   The rule does not, however, apply to all types of intangible. In particular, it does not apply to transfers of the legal title to shares. As has been seen in **CHAPTER 3**, the common law recognises the transfer of shares. It is, therefore, possible to create a legal mortgage over shares by transferring title to the mortgagee. It is not possible to enter notice of any trust on the register of members of a company, and the company's registrar has no duty to accept any such notice.[103] Because of this provision (which has been a part of the companies legislation since the first Companies Act in 1862), it was decided by the Earl of Selborne in *Société Générale de Paris v Walker*[104] that the rule in *Dearle v Hall* did not apply to security over shares in companies incorporated under the Companies Acts. This was because any such notice would be

---

100   *Re Wallis, ex parte Jenks* [1902] 1 KB 719.
101   *Dearle v Hall; Loveridge v Cooper* (1823, 1827, 1828) 3 Russ 1.
102   *Marchant v Morton Down & Co* [1901] 2 KB 829.
103   Companies Act 1985, s 360.
104   (1885) 11 App Cas 20.

inoperative to affect the company concerned. Security over shares therefore depends on the first in time principle and the bona fide purchaser principle, as varied by the exceptions discussed in the following parts of this chapter.

Which types of transfer?

7.176   The rule applies to all types of dealing in equitable interests and debts, whether they are by way of outright equitable assignment, equitable mortgage or charge or, indeed, by means of a statutory assignment under s 136 of the Law of Property Act 1925.[105] As has been seen in **CHAPTER 3**, a statutory assignment gives the assignee a procedural advantage over an equitable assignment, but it was not intended to alter its substance or the priority rules. A statutory assignee does not obtain a legal interest sufficient to bring into play the bona fide purchaser rule. Whether the interest created is equitable or statutory, the rule in *Dearle v Hall* will apply.

What amounts to notice?

7.177   When considering what is meant by 'notice' in the context of the rule in *Dearle v Hall*,[106] there are two principal issues – to whom must notice be given; and how must it be given?

7.178   In the case of dealings with equitable interests, the notice must be given to the person who holds the legal title to the asset in question. If, therefore, the debtor is entitled to a beneficial interest under a trust, notice of a dealing with that beneficial interest must be given to the trustees.[107] In the case of a debt or other monetary amount owing to the debtor (a receivable), the notice must be given to the person who owes the receivable (the counterparty).

7.179   As far as the form of the notice is concerned, with one exception which is referred to below, there is no requirement concerning the form of the notice or, indeed, the person who must give it. All that is necessary is that the trustees or the counterparty become aware of the assignment. They must, however, actually receive notice; constructive notice is insufficient. In *Lloyd v Banks*,[108] Lord Cairns LC said that what is required is:[109]

> '[P]roof that the mind of the trustee has in some way been brought to an intelligent apprehension of the nature of the incumbrance which has come upon the property, so that a reasonable man, or an ordinary man of business, would act upon the information and would regulate his conduct by it in the execution of the trust.'

---

105 *E Pfeiffer v Arbuthnot Factors* [1988] 1 WLR 150.
106 *Dearle v Hall; Loveridge v Cooper* (1823, 1827, 1828) 3 Russ 1.
107 There is a great deal of authority concerning what happens if notice is given to some only of a number of trustees. In practice, of course, if there is more than one trustee, it is prudent to give notice to them all.
108 (1867–68) LR 3 Ch App 488.
109 (1867–68) LR 3 Ch App 488 at 490–491.

7.180   The exception referred to above relates to notices given in respect of dealings in equitable interests. Section 137(3) of the Law of Property Act 1925 provides that:

> 'A notice, otherwise than in writing, given to, or received by, a trustee ... as respects any dealing with an equitable interest in real or personal property, shall not affect the priority of competing claims of purchasers in that equitable interest.'

7.181   In the case of dealings with equitable interests, written notice must therefore be given to the trustees. There is no such requirement in relation to the notice to be given to the counterparty in respect of a receivable. In practice, however, it is usual for notices to be given in writing for obvious evidential reasons. It is also usually the case in practice that the notice is given by the debtor (ie the assignor or chargor) rather than the creditor (ie the assignee or chargee). This is because the counterparty or trustee will want evidence that the assignment or charge has actually been created before it pays money to the putative assignee or chargee; and the best way to provide that evidence is for the debtor (who, as far as the counterparty or trustee is concerned, is the owner of the asset) to tell the counterparty or trustee that it has assigned or charged the asset to the creditor.

7.182   In financial transactions, it is common, when notice is given to the counterparty, to request the counterparty to acknowledge receipt of the notice. An acknowledgement is not necessary – all that is required is evidence that the counterparty has received the notice; but an acknowledgement is useful in evidential terms. It is also common for the acknowledgement to contain certain confirmations and undertakings by the counterparty, for instance, that the assigned contract remains in force, that the counterparty is not aware of any breaches of it, that he has not received notice of any other interest in it and that he will make the payments under it to the creditor without set-off or deduction. It is not always practicable to expect the counterparty to give such an undertaking, but it is common to do so where the assigned contract is a material one. Where the undertaking contains promises by the counterparty to do certain things, or to refrain from doing them, it is important to ensure either that there is consideration for those promises, or that they are given by way of a deed.

7.183   Where more than one notice is received on the same day, they will rank in order of the actual time at which they were received; and, if they were received simultaneously, they will rank in order of their dates of creation.[110]

7.184   There is one further peculiarity, which results from a series of cases, described as the 'army agents' cases[111] in the latter part of the nineteenth century. The cases all involved money payable by the army to retired officers in respect of the resignation of their commissions. A typical example is *Johnstone v Cox*.[112] In that case, army agents received money for the account of B, a

---

110   *Calisher v Forbes* (1871) LR 7 Ch App 109.
111   They were described in this way by Vaughan Williams LJ in *Re Dallas* [1904] 2 Ch 385 at 407.
112   (1880) 16 Ch D 571.

retiring army officer, on 29 March. B's retirement was gazetted on the evening of 16 May, at which time he then became entitled to the money. B had previously assigned this money to three different assignees, C, D and E. C had given notice to the army agents some years earlier and did so again on 29 March and on 21 May. D gave notice to the army agents on 17 May and on each succeeding day. E had given notice to the army agents earlier in the year and did so again on 29 March and on every subsequent day, including 17 May.

7.185 Bacon V-C held that B only became entitled to the money when his retirement was gazetted. Until that time, therefore, there was no asset which was capable of being assigned. He went on to decide that no notice given before then could affect the matter, so that the notices given before the opening of business on 17 May were of no effect. Since D and E had each given notice simultaneously on 17 May, they were entitled to priority over C, whose only effective notice had been given on 21 May. As between D and E, because their notices were simultaneous, their rights would rank in order of creation. This decision was affirmed by the Court of Appeal.

7.186 The result is rather curious. Even if the receivable did not exist until the opening of business on 17 May, the counterparty was, at that time, aware of all three assignments and, on the basis of *Lloyd v Banks*,[113] even if the prior notices would have had no effect until 17 May, the army agents would have been aware of all three notices simultaneously, in which event all three should have ranked in order of creation. It nevertheless appears to be the effect of the army agent cases and of *Re Dallas*[114] that no notice received by the counterparty before the receivable exists will have any effect. This principle would only seem to apply where the assignment only extends to future assets – not where the assignment is over both present and future assets.

Summary

7.187 The rule in *Dearle v Hall*[115] may be summarised as follows:

- It applies if:
    - the debtor is the legal owner of a receivable or a contract right; or
    - the debtor is the beneficial (but not the legal) owner of any type of asset.
- It governs the priority of competing proprietary interests in such assets, whether those interests are:
    - outright or by way of security;
    - equitable or statutory; or
    - by way of assignment, charge or other form of transfer.
- Where there are competing proprietary interests in such an asset, the first to give notice of his interest to the party who owes the receivable or contract right (or, in the case of an equitable interest, to the holder of the legal title), will take priority.

---

113 (1868) LR 3 Ch App 488.
114 [1904] 2 Ch 385, explained in *Ipswich Permanent Money Club v Arthy* [1920] 2 Ch 257.
115 *Dearle v Hall; Loveridge v Cooper* (1823, 1827, 1828) 3 Russ 1.

- The rule does not give priority to the holder of a later interest over the holder of an earlier one if the holder of the later interest:
  - is a volunteer (for instance, an execution creditor); or
  - had actual or constructive notice of the earlier proprietary interest at the time he took his interest (but he can rely on the rule if he subsequently becomes aware of the other interest and then gives notice).
- Where the asset concerned consists of an equitable interest, the notice must be given in writing. Where the asset is a future asset, it would seem that notice must be given after the asset has come into existence, although this is not necessary where it consists of both existing and future assets. Otherwise, there are no formalities required in giving notice.
- The rule in *Dearle v Hall* is not otherwise affected by the conduct of the parties. Although it developed as an example of the principle that the court must weigh the 'equities' of the case, it is now clear that it is an absolute rule, which is not affected by other equities.

7.188   It can be seen that the rule in *Dearle v Hall* plays a very similar role to the bona fide purchaser rule. The latter rule only applies to assets which can be transferred at common law and does not, therefore, apply to the types of asset which the rule in *Dearle v Hall* applies to. In the case of assets such as goods and shares, a person who has gone to the trouble of obtaining a legal interest will take priority over an earlier equitable interest if he does so for value and without notice of the earlier equitable interest. In the case of debts, contract rights and equitable interests, the bona fide purchaser rule can have no application because the common law does not recognise the transfer of such assets, but the rule in *Dearle v Hall* achieves a similar result. If the subsequent assignee takes the trouble to give notice to the counterparty or legal owner of the asset, and he does so for value and without notice of the earlier assignment, he will take priority.

7.189   It is not a coincidence that the exceptions to the bona fide purchaser rule are the same as those to the rule in *Dearle v Hall*. Neither can be relied upon by volunteers. Neither can be relied upon by a person who had notice of an earlier interest at the time he took his interest, but both allow such a person to take priority if he obtained legal title or gave notice having subsequently become aware of the earlier interest. And the requirement to register most types of mortgage or charge created by a company has, in practice, reduced the importance of both principles and thereby given greater prominence to the first in time principle.

Part 6: THE PURCHASE MONEY SECURITY INTEREST

7.190   The starting point in any priority dispute is that the debtor cannot give more than he has. If he has created a proprietary interest in the asset concerned in favour of one person, then he can only transfer it to a second person subject to the existing interest. Although it has been seen that there are a number of exceptions from this principle (including the bona fide purchaser principle discussed in part 3 of this chapter (**7.48**ff), the principle that the conduct of the parties can affect priorities discussed in part 4 of this chapter (**7.97**ff) and the rule in *Dearle v Hall*[116] discussed in part 5 of this chapter (**7.151**ff)), the starting point is still that the debtor cannot give more than he actually has.

7.191　The principle is, in practice, applied more rigorously where the debtor never has the full legal and beneficial ownership of the asset concerned, but only obtains a more limited interest. If, for instance, a seller of goods sells them to a purchaser on the basis that the seller retains title until payment, a security interest created by the purchaser over his assets will not affect the goods to which the seller has reserved title. They do not belong to the debtor, but to the seller. The debtor cannot charge assets which he does not own.

7.192　This principle is also the basis of the purchase money security interest. An example will explain what this means. A has created a fixed charge over all of his present and future land in favour of B. A wishes to acquire further land, and agrees with C that C will provide the finance for the acquisition on the basis that he obtains a first fixed charge over the land. A accordingly buys the land with C's money and charges it to C. In practice, C is likely to be aware of B's security, and an agreement will therefore be reached between the parties concerning their respective priorities. But if this is not the case, who takes priority?

7.193　On one analysis, it can be argued that, before he can charge the land to C, it must first be acquired by A. Having been acquired by A, it automatically becomes subject to B's fixed charge, with the effect that C's interest is created after B's and therefore ranks behind it. The alternative analysis is that A is only able to acquire the land because it has been funded by C. The acquisition of the land, the making of the loan and the granting of security in favour of C are all part of a single transaction. It is not realistically possible to separate the acquisition from the security. When A acquires the land, therefore, he does so subject to C's charge. All that B can obtain is a charge over A's equity of redemption.

7.194　Neither line of argument is obviously correct, as a matter of logic. The transaction is susceptible to being analysed in either way and, indeed, different courts have, on different occasions, adopted each of these analyses. After a certain amount of indecision, however, the courts have come down firmly in favour of the second analysis, not least because this could be regarded as producing the fairer outcome. If C has made available the purchase price for the land, it would be a windfall for B to obtain a charge over it without recognising that it could only have been acquired with C's money. And even if C takes priority over B, B still has the benefit of a charge over the equity of redemption of the property.

7.195　As has been mentioned above, the cases on this subject have not adopted a uniform approach. The first two cases to consider the issue, *Wilson v Kelland*[117] in 1910 and *Re Connolly Brothers Limited (No 2)*[118] in 1912 each

---

116　*Dearle v Hall; Loveridge v Cooper* (1823, 1827, 1828) 3 Russ 1.
117　[1910] 2 Ch 306.

adopted the second line of argument set out above, deciding that the acquisition of the property and the secured loan were all part of one transaction, so that all that was charged to the existing secured creditor was the equity of redemption.

7.196   In the *Connolly Brothers* case, A had created a floating charge over its assets in favour of B which contained a restriction on the creation of prior charges. A wanted to acquire a further asset, and borrowed money from C to do so on the basis that she would obtain a mortgage over it. The Court of Appeal held that C took priority over B because A had never acquired the asset unencumbered. All it acquired was an equity of redemption and it could therefore grant no more to B. The case is a curious one. B only had a floating charge over the asset concerned, and C did not have notice of the restriction on the creation of prior charges. As a result C would, in any event, have acquired priority over B in accordance with the priority principles concerning floating charges which are discussed in part 8 of this chapter (**7.234ff**).[119]

7.197   This case was distinguished by the Court of Appeal in 1954 in *Church of England Building Society v Piskor*.[120] A agreed to buy land, to be financed by B. A was let into possession of the land before completion and purported to grant a tenancy to C. The Court of Appeal held that the transfer of the land to A and the charge to B were not one indivisible transaction. For a moment of time A obtained the legal estate in the land before he could execute the charge in favour of B and, during that period, C obtained an interest in the land under the purported tenancy. In the words of Evershed MR:[121]

'[I]n one sense the transaction was one transaction; but it is equally true to say that it consists necessarily of certain defined steps which must take place in a certain defined order, if the result intended is eventually to be achieved. That seems to me not an artificiality, but a necessary result of the law and of the conveyancing practice which was involved.'

7.198   The Privy Council subsequently distinguished *Piskor* and followed *Connolly Brothers* in *Security Trust Company v Royal Bank of Canada*,[122] thus leaving the law in doubt.

7.199   The doubt was resolved by the House of Lords in *Abbey National Building Society v Cann*[123] in 1991. The question in that case was whether a person in occupation of the land took priority over a mortgage as a result of certain provisions of the land registration legislation. In order to decide this point, the House of Lords had to consider whether the purchase of the

---

118   [1912] 2 Ch 25.
119   In *Abbey National Building Society v Cann* [1991] AC 56, Lord Oliver said at 91, that 'the debentures in *Re Connolly* were duly registered and [C] clearly had constructive notice of their terms'. The relevant principles concerning constructive notice of such restrictions are considered in part 9 of this chapter (**7.251ff**), but it is difficult to see how this statement can be justified.
120   [1954] 1 Ch 553.
121   [1954] 1 Ch 553 at 561.
122   [1976] AC 503.
123   [1991] AC 56.

property and the secured loan made to finance the transaction were one transaction or not. They decided to follow the reasoning in the *Connolly Brothers* and *Security Trust Company* cases and they overruled the decision of the Court of Appeal in the *Piskor* case. In the words of Lord Oliver:[124]

> 'Of course, as a matter of legal theory, a person cannot charge a legal estate that he does not have, so that there is an attractive legal logic in the ratio in *Piskor's* case. Nevertheless, I cannot help feeling that it flies in the face of reality. The reality is that, in the vast majority of cases, the acquisition of the legal estate and the charge are not only precisely simultaneous but indissolubly bound together.'

7.200   The House of Lords has, therefore, laid the controversy to rest. They have decided that the acquisition of the property and the secured loan are effectively one transaction. Although neither the *Piskor* case nor the *Abbey National* case involved mortgages, the principle is now clear. It can be described as follows.

7.201   If:

- A charges its future property of a particular description in favour of B by way of equitable mortgage or fixed charge; and
- A then acquires further property of that description as a result of a loan from C and creates a charge over the land in favour of C at the time it is acquired,

then:

- the acquisition of the property and the charge in favour of C will be considered to be one transaction, as a result of which:
- A is unable to charge more than his equity of redemption in favour of B, with the effect that:
- C will take priority over B.

7.202   It is important to see this principle in context. It is effectively an extension of the first in time principle – a means of deciding who is first in time where one creditor has a general fixed charge over future assets and another finances a particular future asset. As a result of *Abbey National Building Society v Cann*, the latter will be regarded as being the first in time. But, like the first in time principle, it can be overridden by the exceptions discussed above and in the remaining parts of this chapter. In practice, the creditor claiming a purchase money security interest is likely to have notice of the other security interest and, as a result, would not be able to take priority. It will be a rare case where the purchase money security interest is likely to provide the answer to a priority dispute.

Part 7: TACKING FURTHER ADVANCES

7.203   The discussion of priorities in the earlier parts of this chapter has assumed that, once one security interest has priority over another, it will retain

---

124   [1991] AC 56 at 92.

that priority in relation to all liabilities secured by it. Where the security is given to secure credit given at the time it is entered into, that is correct, but the issue becomes more complicated where the security secures credit made available after the security has been granted, such as a revolving credit facility or an overdraft.

7.204 The early cases on priorities assumed that a security interest was granted to secure credit granted at the time the security was entered into. Typically, the creditor would lend money to the debtor and the security would secure the repayment of that money together with interest. During the nineteenth century, however, it became more common for security interests to be granted for the purpose of securing bank facilities under which the credit was not all made available at the time the security interest was entered into. The most typical example, which is still extremely common, is security granted to a bank to secure the repayment of an overdraft. Provided the customer keeps within the overdraft limit, he is able to borrow money from the bank from time to time; and amounts paid by him to the bank in reduction of outstandings will increase the amount available to be borrowed in the future. During the nineteenth century, therefore, it became more common for security interests to secure not only money lent at the time the security interest was created, but also money to be lent in the future. The most flexible arrangement involved the security extending to secure all money from time to time owing by the customer to the bank.

7.205 But the question then arose what would happen if the customer created a further security interest, in favour of a different creditor, after he had created such security in favour of his bank. Would the bank continue to have priority in respect of advances made after the new security interest had been created?

Gordon v Graham

7.206 Early in the eighteenth century, this question had been answered in the affirmative. In *Gordon v Graham*,[125] A created a mortgage in favour of B to secure present and future indebtedness. A then created a second mortgage in favour of C for a fixed amount of money. C was aware of the first mortgage. B, with knowledge of C's mortgage, continued to lend money to A, and the question arose whether his security took priority over C's mortgage in respect of the money lent after he became aware of C's mortgage. Lord Cowper LC held that B had priority over C for all of the money which he had lent.

7.207 Such an approach has a great deal to commend it. B's security interest was created before C's. It secured future indebtedness. Before lending, C was able to discover the terms of B's security. B was therefore able to retain his priority over C in respect of all money secured by the mortgage, regardless of when it was lent.

---

125   (1716) 2 Eq Cas Abr 598.

Hopkinson v Rolt

7.208 The issue appeared to be settled, but the increase of lending on overdraft in the nineteenth century led to a challenge to this principle in *Hopkinson v Rolt*.[126] A created a mortgage in favour of his bank, B, to secure all monies from time to time lent by B, subject to a limit as to principal amount. He then created a second equitable mortgage in favour of C, his father-in-law, to secure amounts which C had to pay on behalf of A. C was aware of the mortgage in favour of B. With notice of the second mortgage in favour of C, B continued to advance further money to A. A went bankrupt and the question arose whether B had priority for the money advanced by it after it was aware of C's mortgage.

7.209 By a majority, the House of Lords overruled *Gordon v Graham*[127] and held that C had priority over B in respect of those advances. Lord Campbell LC and Lord Chelmsford considered that *Gordon v Graham* had been misreported and that it was not actually authority for what was stated in the report. Lord Campbell said that *Gordon v Graham* was contrary to principle and had been criticised in later cases and text books. The first mortgagee had no obligation to make further advances and, if he was not happy with his security, he need not lend once he had notice of the later security. He is not, therefore, injured by being subordinated with respect to future advances. Lord Chelmsford took a similar approach, arguing that the mortgagor would otherwise be prevented from raising further secured finance because the first mortgagee might lend further money.

7.210 Lord Cranworth gave a dissenting speech, taking the view that *Gordon v Graham* had been properly reported and that the rule which it propounds 'is a convenient rule, causing injustice to no one'.[128] One of the problems which Lord Cranworth thought would be caused by the new rule was that there would be difficulty in sorting out who takes priority where both mortgages secure future advances. This point was specifically considered by Lord Chelmsford,[129] who took the view that, in such a case, the advances would have priority in the order in which they were made.

7.211 The effect of *Hopkinson v Rolt* was that a first mortgagee whose security covered future advances was unable to rely on the priority which he had obtained by being first in time. Although his priority in respect of further advances would not be affected merely by the creation of a later mortgage, once he had notice of it any further advances made by him would rank behind the later mortgage. And if both mortgages secured further advances, there would have to be an analysis of when each advance was made in order to determine its priority.

7.212 The rule makes very little commercial sense. The argument that the first mortgagee need not lend once he has notice of the second mortgage is matched

---

126 (1861) 9 HLC 514.
127 (1716) 2 Eq Cas Abr 598.
128 (1861) 9 HLC 514 at 548.
129 (1861) 9 HLC 514 at 553.

by the contrary argument that the second mortgagee need not lend if he is unhappy with the terms of the first mortgage. Since the first mortgage is already in place, what is the utility of penalising the first mortgagee? Lord Chelmsford's concern that the effect of *Gordon v Graham* was that the mortgagor would be prevented from obtaining further secured finance is avoided if the second mortgagee enters into a priority agreement with the first. If the first mortgagee will not consent, the debtor will have to refinance. The balance of convenience would seem to lie with allowing the existing mortgage to continue to secure that which it was supposed to secure.

7.213 There have been subsequent attempts to find a conceptual basis for the new rule, most particularly by Lord Blackburn in *The Bradford Banking Company v Henry Briggs, Son & Co*[130] and by Lindley MR in *West v Williams*.[131] Their approach was as follows:

- A mortgagor, acting honestly, cannot give more than he has got.
- If a mortgagor creates a first mortgage in favour of A to secure further advances, the security is only created in respect of the further advances once they are actually made.
- The mortgagor is able to mortgage his equity of redemption to B to secure a fixed sum advanced at the time the mortgage is created.
- Once he has done so, the mortgagor can no longer grant further security to A except subject to B's security.
- This includes securing the further advances to A which have not yet been made, because they are not yet the subject of the security, not having been made.
- Until A becomes aware of B's interest, he can continue to assume that the mortgagor has not created any further mortgages.
- But once A becomes aware of B's interest, he is in the same position as the mortgagor: he cannot properly allow future advances to be secured in priority to B's mortgage.

7.214 This reasoning is dependent on the assumption that a security interest can only secure monies which have actually been advanced and that, before they have, the security is ineffective. In one sense that is, of course, perfectly correct. On enforcement, the security will only be effective to the extent that monies have actually been advanced. But it does not necessarily follow that a mortgagor only has priority in respect of monies which have actually been advanced before he becomes aware of a later mortgage over the same assets. There is no logical reason why, as between two mortgages, priority should not be given in respect of all the monies secured by the first, rather than those which are actually owing at the time the first mortgagee obtains notice that the second mortgage is created.

7.215 It is therefore suggested that there are good commercial reasons why the rule in *Gordon v Graham* is preferable, and that there is no logical reason why it was wrong. The decision of the House of Lords in *Hopkinson v Rolt* has nevertheless settled the matter. A secured creditor is only entitled to rely on the

---

130   (1886) 12 App Cas 29.
131   [1899] 1 Ch 132.

priority of his security interest to the extent that the money secured by the security interest has been made available to the debtor at the time the creditor receives notice of a subsequent security interest over the same assets. In this context, it is suggested that notice means actual notice. There is no indication in the case that it should be given a wider meaning.

West v Williams

7.216 In *Hopkinson v Rolt*,[132] the first mortgagee had no obligation to lend further money to the debtor, and the House of Lords stressed the fact that the first mortgagee could protect itself by simply refusing to lend further money to the debtor until it was comfortable with its security. In *West v Williams*,[133] the question arose as to what would happen if the first mortgagee had an obligation to lend further money when it received notice of a second mortgage. In that case, A had a beneficial interest under a trust. A created an equitable mortgage in favour of B, of which no notice was given to the trustees. A then created a second equitable mortgage in favour of C to secure all moneys from time to time owing to C, and C agreed to lend certain further money to A. C was not aware of B's mortgage. C gave notice to the trustees before B did and C then discovered the existence of B's mortgage.

7.217 In a priority dispute between B and C, B admitted that, as a result of the rule in *Dearle v Hall*,[134] C, who had given notice to the trustees first, had general priority over B for all monies lent until C became aware of B's mortgage. The question was whether C also had priority in respect of the further advances which it had an obligation to make to A. Kekewich J held that C had priority for the future advances which it had a duty to lend, taking the view that, because there was an obligation to make further advances, *Hopkinson v Rolt* did not apply. His decision was overruled by the Court of Appeal. They decided that the creation of the second mortgage released the first mortgagee from his agreement to make further advances because the mortgagor had prevented himself from giving the first mortgagee the agreed security.

The problem of overdrafts

7.218 It is very common for future advances to be made in the form of drawings on overdrafts. Particular practical problems are caused in relation to overdrafts by the rule in *Clayton's Case*.[135] Where there are debit and credit entries on an unbroken current account, there is a presumption that payments to the credit of the account are used to repay earlier debits before later ones. This is a rule of presumption, and is overridden by contrary agreement between the parties. It also assumes that neither the debtor, when paying the credit into

---

132 (1861) 9 HLC 514.
133 [1899] 1 Ch 132.
134 *Dearle v Hall; Loveridge v Cooper* (1823, 1827, 1828) 3 Russ 1.
135 *Devaynes v Noble, Clayton's Case* (1815–16) 1 Mer 572.

the account, or the creditor, when receiving it, specifically appropriated it to the repayment of any particular liability. The rule is often described as 'first in, first out' or 'FIFO'.

7.219 The rule in *Clayton's Case*, when combined with the effect of *Hopkinson v Rolt*,[136] can create problems for banks. The problem is best explained by an example. A is a customer of a bank, B. B has granted A an overdraft facility of £100. The facility is fully drawn. A then creates a subsequent mortgage in favour of C to secure a loan of £50 made by C at the same time; and C gives notice of the mortgage to B. A then pays a cheque for £60 into the account and subsequently pays in a further cheque for £40. He then draws £100 from the account. At the end of the transaction, £100 remains owing by A to B. What is the effect of these arrangements as regards the respective priorities of B and C?

7.220 As a result of *Hopkinson v Rolt*, B is entitled to priority in respect of advances made to A before it receives notice of C's mortgage, but not in respect of advances made afterwards. It had made an advance of £100 by the time it received notice of C's mortgage and, had there been no further debits or credits to the account, B would have been secured in respect of that amount in priority to C. In fact, B continues to be owed £100. The amount of the overdraft is now the same as it was at the time he received notice. But the effect of *Clayton's Case* is that the credits of £60 and £40 received into the account have discharged the £100 which was owing at the time B received notice of C's mortgage. When the further £100 was drawn by A, it therefore represented new money lent by B after it had received notice of C's mortgage. The £100 owing to B therefore ranks behind the £50 owing to C even though the actual amount of the overdraft is the same as it was before B received notice of C's mortgage.

7.221 The effect of *Clayton's Case* is illustrated by the decision of the House of Lords in *Deeley v Lloyds Bank*.[137] In that case, A mortgaged land to B, a bank, to secure an overdraft on A's current account and then, subsequently, to C, his sister, to secure a loan. After B had notice of C's mortgage, B continued to operate the current account in the normal way. B subsequently realised the security and the question arose who had priority. The House of Lords held that *Clayton's Case* applied and that the payments into the account had discharged all indebtedness owing by A to B at the time B received notice of C's mortgage. Accordingly, C had priority over B.

7.222 In the absence of a specific appropriation of a payment by the debtor or (failing him) by the creditor, *Clayton's Case* applies where there is an unbroken current account. It is a presumption of fact which may be rebutted by evidence to show that it was not the intention of the parties to apply it, but there was no such evidence in this case. It is therefore the normal practice for banks who receive notice of a subsequent charge to close their accounts with the customer and to open new ones, which are then operated on a credit basis. This ensures that the amount lent at the time notice is received is not reduced

---

136   (1861) 9 HLC 514.
137   [1912] AC 756.

by subsequent credits to the account. In the *Deeley case*, the manager of the branch concerned had failed to comply with the bank's rule to that effect.

7.223   If the bank does close the current account and open a new one, it will be protected from the effect of *Clayton's Case*. But *Clayton's Case* is only a rule of presumption. It gives way to evidence of a contrary intention, and it is common for security documents specifically to provide that, even if the creditor does not close the existing account and open a new one, it will be deemed to have done so, with the effect that future credits to the account will not go to discharge the debt incurred at the time notice was received. Such a clause is effective to establish the intention of the parties that *Clayton's Case* should not apply.

Statutory modifications

7.224   The rule in *Hopkinson v Rolt*[138] continues to apply in relation to security over goods and intangibles, but it has been amended in relation to security over land – in the case of unregistered land by s 94 of the Law of Property Act 1925 and, in the case of registered land, by s 49 of the Land Registration Act 2002.

7.225   They both acknowledge the basic principle in *Hopkinson v Rolt* that a secured creditor's priority is only affected once he has received notice of the existence of a subsequent charge, and that the first creditor is at risk if he lends money once he has received that notice, but they give the first creditor a greater ability to tack further advances even when he has notice of a subsequent charge.

7.226   In *West v Williams*,[139] it was decided that notice of a subsequent charge released the first chargee from any obligation to make further advances. Where the security is over land, this decision is reversed. If the creditor does have an obligation to lend further money, it will remain in force, and money lent under it will rank ahead of a later charge even if the first chargee has notice of it if, in the case of registered land, the obligation to do so is noted on the land register[140] or, in the case of unregistered land, the security document imposes the obligation to do so.[141] In practice, however, it is debatable whether this change is of much significance. In most cases, the first mortgage will contain a prohibition on the creation of other mortgages, and a breach of that provision is likely to be an event of default and therefore to enable the first mortgagee to decline to make any further advances. If so, the creditor will not have an obligation to lend further money and the position will be the same as it is under *West v Williams* – further advances will rank behind the later mortgage.

7.227   There is, however, a further exception in relation to registered land. If the debtor and the first chargee have agreed a maximum amount for which the

138   (1861) 9 HLC 514.
139   [1899] 1 Ch 132.
140   Land Registration Act 2002, s 49(3).
141   Law of Property Act 1925, s 94(1)(c).

charge is security, and that amount is entered on the land register, the first chargee can make advances up to that maximum amount in priority to a subsequent charge even where he has received notice of it at the time those further advances are made.[142]

7.228   The legislation also clarifies what is meant by 'notice' for this purpose when the assets concerned consist of land. In relation to registered land, s 49(2) of the Land Registration Act 2002 and r 107 of the Land Registration Rules 2003[143] establish the various ways in which a creditor will receive notice of a subsequent charge for this purpose. Registration is not sufficient – steps have to be taken by the subsequent chargee to make the earlier chargee aware of the charge, but actual receipt of notice is not required. In relation to unregistered land, s 94(2) of the Law of Property Act 1925 establishes that, where a charge is made expressly for securing a current account or other further advances, the chargee is not deemed to have notice of another charge merely by reason that it was registered as a land charge if it was not so registered when the original charge was created or when the chargee last searched the land charges register.

7.229   The Land Registration Act 2002 and the Land Charges Act 1972 also make it clear (as is the case in relation to other assets), that the priority rules can be varied by agreement between the two chargees.[144]

7.230   In summary, once the secured creditor has received notice of another security interest over the same asset, he is at risk if he lends further money. The only safe way to do so is if he reaches an agreement with the subsequent secured creditor or, in the case of registered land, if he has agreed a maximum amount to be secured, which is noted on the land register.

Conclusion

7.231   This section is called 'tacking further advances', because that is the expression normally used. It would be more accurate to describe it as 'restrictions on tacking further advances'. The rule is restrictive, not permissive. It does not allow a creditor to increase the extent of the obligations secured by his mortgage. On the contrary, it restricts his ability to rely on the mortgage to secure the obligations which the mortgage purports to secure.

7.232   The basic principle is that a secured creditor can only rely on the priority of his security to the extent that it secures credit made available by him before he receives notice that any subsequent security interest has been created over the property concerned. Having received such notice, he should not make any further advances until he has entered into a priority agreement with the second mortgagee which he is comfortable preserves the value of his security or unless the secured assets are registered land and he has registered a maximum amount for which the charge is security. In the case of security over property

---

142   Land Registration Act 2002, s 49(4).

143   SI 2003/1417.

144   Law of Property Act 1925, s 94(1)(a); Land Registration Act 2002, s 49(6).

other than land, this is the case even if he has an obligation to make further advances, because that obligation is discharged by the creation of the subsequent security. In the case of security over land, he will have priority in respect of advances which he has an obligation to make, but the documentation should be carefully considered in order to see whether, in fact, there is an obligation to make them or whether (which is more likely) the fact of the second mortgage having been created has discharged that obligation.

7.233   There is one final point to be made. A secured creditor can only tack further advances if they are secured by the mortgage. It is, therefore, crucial to ensure that the mortgage does cover all liabilities, whether present or future, which are intended to be secured. If the mortgage does not secure future advances, there is no possibility whatsoever that they will have priority over a subsequent mortgagee.

Part 8: FLOATING CHARGES

The general principle – the debtor's authority to deal with its assets

7.234   The nature of floating charges is discussed in CHAPTER 4. Before crystallisation, the creditor has a proprietary interest in the assets of the debtor. That interest is, however, precarious, in the sense that it is capable of being overridden by the actions of the debtor. Until the floating charge crystallises, the debtor is given the authority by the creditor to dispose of its assets free of the floating charge. In *Re Panama, New Zealand, and Australian Royal Mail Company*,[145] Sir G M Giffard LJ decided that, where the floating charge had not crystallised, it was the parties' implied intention that the debtor should be free to carry on its business, and deal with its property, notwithstanding the existence of the floating charge.

7.235   The effect of this principle on priority disputes is illustrated by *Re Hamilton's Windsor Ironworks, ex parte Pitman & Edwards*.[146] The debtor company had charged all of its assets to A and had then assigned a debt to B by way of security. B was aware of A's security. Malins V-C held that B nevertheless took priority. In a priority dispute between two fixed security interests, the person holding the second interest would normally take his interest subject to that of the first. But the security granted to A over all of the debtor's assets was a floating charge, and the debtor company accordingly had the authority to carry on its business, raise money and charge its property free from the floating charge.

---

145   (1870) LR 5 Ch App 318.
146   (1879) 12 Ch D 707.

7.236 The same approach was adopted by North J in *Wheatley v Silkstone and Haigh Moor Coal Co.*[147] In that case, the floating charge was expressed to be a 'first charge'. It was nevertheless held that the debtor had the authority to create prior fixed charges because it cannot have been intended to stop the debtor company from carrying on business and creating fixed security for borrowings.

7.237 Until crystallisation, therefore, the general principle is that the debtor is entitled to deal with the charged assets, and thereby to dispose of them absolutely or to create security over them ranking ahead of the floating charge. The reason is straightforward – the debtor has been given the creditor's authority to do so.

Express restrictions on the debtor's authority

7.238 It soon occurred to creditors that this gave the debtor an extremely broad authority which the creditor might want to restrict. It is not generally practicable to restrict outright disposals, at least of stock-in-trade, because they are necessary in order to enable the debtor's business to continue. But a creditor which has the benefit of a floating charge is likely to want to restrict the debtor company from creating other security over its assets, at least if that security would rank ahead of, or rateably with, the floating charge. The practice accordingly developed by which floating charges contained restrictions on the authority of the debtor company to create fixed charges.

7.239 The approach of the courts to such restrictions was to apply basic agency principles to them. They decided that such a restriction was only effective against a third party dealing with the debtor if he had notice of it. This is because:

- under the general law, a floating charge gives the debtor the authority to dispose of its assets and to create charges ranking in priority to the floating charge; and
- a third party dealing with the debtor is entitled to rely on the apparent authority of the debtor to do so unless he has been made aware of a restriction on that authority.

7.240 This approach is illustrated by *Re Castell & Brown.*[148] In that case, the debtor company created a floating charge in favour of A over all of its present and future property. The floating charge contained a restriction on the debtor company creating any mortgage or charge on its land in priority to the floating charge. The debtor company then borrowed money from B, a bank, which obtained an equitable mortgage over the debtor company's land. The bank was not aware of the existence of the floating charge. Romer J held that B had priority over A. Although A's floating charge was created before B's fixed charge, the floating charge authorised the debtor company to deal with its property as if it had not been encumbered and the restriction on this authority could not affect B because he was not aware of it.

---

147 (1885) 29 Ch D 715.
148 [1898] 1 Ch 315.

7.241 In that case, the fixed chargee was unaware of the floating charge, but later authority establishes that the same principle applies even if he is aware of the floating charge, so long as it he not aware of the restriction. In *The English and Scottish Mercantile Investment Company v Brunton*,[149] the debtor company had created a floating charge in favour of A, which contained a prohibition on creating charges ranking in priority to the floating charge. The company then assigned a debt to B to secure a loan. B was aware of the existence of the floating charge, but not of the prohibition. The Court of Appeal held that B took priority over A.

7.242 It is clear from the decision of the Court of Appeal in the *Brunton* case that, if B had been aware of the prohibition, he would have taken his fixed charge subject to the floating charge. This is because the floating charge creates a proprietary interest in the debtor company's assets before crystallisation, albeit that it can be overridden as a result of the debtor's authority to deal with its assets before crystallisation. A person dealing with the debtor company can rely on that authority until he has notice to the contrary but, once he does have such notice, he can no longer rely on the debtor's authority to create prior-ranking charges. As a result, the charges will rank in accordance with the normal principles, in which event the floating charge, being first in time, will take priority.

7.243 It is therefore important to consider in what circumstances a person dealing with the debtor will have notice of a restriction contained in the floating charge. The concept of notice is considered in part 2 of this chapter (**7.19ff**). The requirement for the registration of floating charges at Companies House is an important means by which persons dealing with the company can become aware of the existence of a floating charge and of restrictions on the authority of the debtor company. Because these issues are inextricably tied up with the way in which the registration systems work, they will be considered further in part 9 of this chapter (**7.251ff**).

Implied restrictions on the debtor's authority

7.244 In addition to any express restrictions contained in the floating charge, there are three implied restrictions on the ability of the debtor company to dispose of its assets free from the floating charge.

Crystallisation

7.245 The first is that the debtor's authority to deal with its assets ceases on crystallisation of the floating charge. Crystallisation is considered in part 4 of CHAPTER 4 (**4.65ff**). Although there is no clear authority on the point, it would be consistent with the agency principles discussed above that a third party should only be affected by the crystallisation of a floating charge once he has actual or constructive notice of it. In practice, a floating charge normally crystallises on appointment of a receiver or administrator. The appointment of

---

149 [1892] 2 QB 700.

a receiver or administrator is an event which requires registration at Companies House and requires to be noted on the debtor company's letterhead. In practice, it soon becomes apparent to persons dealing with the debtor company that a receiver or administrator has been appointed. This would not necessarily be so if the creditor were to rely on automatic crystallisation or on crystallisation by notice, in which event it would be incumbent on the creditor to make the crystallisation clear to persons dealing with the company.

Subsequent floating charge over the same assets

7.246   The second implied restriction on the authority of the debtor company is that it does not have the authority to create a second floating charge which ranks in priority to an earlier floating charge if the second floating charge is created over the same assets as are the subject of the earlier floating charge. In *Re Benjamin Cope & Sons*,[150] the debtor company created an 'issue of debentures', which was secured by a floating charge and which contained no specific restrictions on further charges. The company later created a 'second issue of debentures', which were also secured by a floating charge over all of its assets. The question arose concerning the priority of the two issues of debentures. Sargant J held that the first issue of debentures took priority over the second issue. Although the debtor company had the authority to create fixed charges ranking ahead of the floating charge, it did not have the authority to create a prior floating charge over the same assets.

7.247   This principle does not, however, extend to a case where the second floating charge is only created over part of the assets which are the subject of the first floating charge. In such a case, the second floating charge will rank ahead of the earlier floating charge.[151] This is because, in the absence of an express restriction, the debtor does have the authority to create such a floating charge in priority to the first floating charge.

Execution creditors

7.248   The third implied restriction on the authority of the debtor company relates to execution creditors. In principle, an execution creditor who has obtained a proprietary interest in the debtor company's assets ought to take priority over an uncrystallised floating charge. As has been seen in part 3 of **CHAPTER 4** (**4.35ff**), there were some suggestions in the earlier cases that the debtor's authority does not extend to allowing execution to be created over its assets.[152] But this approach was decisively rejected by the Court of Appeal in *Evans v Rival Granite Quarries*,[153] who decided that the debtor did have the authority to enter into transactions the result of which might result in execution being levied against its assets. But they went on to decide that the execution creditor would only take priority if he had completed the execution by the time the floating charge had crystallised.

---

150   [1914] 1 Ch 800.
151   *Re Automatic Bottle Makers* [1926] 1 Ch 412.
152   See, for instance, *Davey & Co v Williamson & Sons* [1898] 2 QB 194.
153   [1910] 2 KB 979.

7.249 The result is curious. An execution creditor obtains a proprietary interest in the debtor's assets before the execution has been completed. In the case of execution against goods under a writ of fieri facias, the sheriff obtains a limited proprietary interest in the goods once the writ has been delivered to the sheriff to be executed,[154] and a more general proprietary interest once they have been seized in execution.[155] In the case of a third party debt order, the execution creditor obtains a proprietary interest when the interim order is served on the person who owes the debt[156]. In the case of a charging order, a proprietary interest is obtained when the interim order is made.[157] In contrast, execution is only completed, in the case of a writ of fieri facias, by the sale of the seized goods, in the case of a third party debt order, by payment of the debt the subject of the order and, in the case of a charging order, when the court process is completed. The effect of this rule is, therefore, to give the floating chargee the ability, once he has discovered the existence of an execution, to crystallise the floating charge before it is completed, and thereby deprive the execution creditor of the fruits of his execution.[158]

Summary

7.250 The priority position concerning floating charges may be summarised as follows:

- The basic principle is that a debtor company which has created a floating charge has the authority to dispose of its assets and to create security ranking ahead of the floating charge.
- A person obtaining a proprietary interest from the debtor company cannot rely on that authority, and will therefore rank behind the floating charge, if:
  - the floating charge has crystallised; or
  - the floating charge contains a restriction on the authority of the debtor company to create that proprietary interest,

  and, in each case, that person had actual or constructive notice of that fact.
- A floating chargee does not have the authority to create a prior ranking floating charge over substantially the same assets.
- An execution creditor will only obtain priority over the holder of a floating charge if the execution is completed before crystallisation of the floating charge.

Part 9: REGISTRATION

7.251 The development of systems for the registration of mortgages and charges during the nineteenth and twentieth centuries has had a profound effect

---

154 *Payne v Drewe* (1804) 4 East 523.
155 *Wilbraham v Snow* (1845) 2 Wms Saund 47; *Slater v Pinder* (1872) LR 7 Exch 95.
156 *N Joachimson v Swiss Bank Corporation* [1921] 3 KB 110 at 131, per Atkin LJ.
157 Charging Orders Act 1979, s 3(4).
158 See, generally, Calnan 'Priorities Between Execution Creditors and Floating Chargees' (1982) 10 NZULR 111.

on priorities. The registration systems have not abolished the principles discussed in the earlier parts of this chapter, but they have substantially modified them in practice in a number of ways.

7.252 As has been seen in CHAPTER 6, there are two distinct types of registration system for mortgages and charges. Their effects on priorities are very different. Registration can be effected:

● against the debtor; or
● against the asset.

7.253 The requirement for registration against the debtor depends on the type of debtor concerned. In relation to companies, registration is governed by the Companies Act 1985. Registration against individuals is governed by the Bills of Sale Acts 1878–1891. Most mortgages and charges created by companies, and some mortgages and charges created by individuals, are registrable against the debtor concerned. Registration against the debtor is discussed in CHAPTER 6.

7.254 Registration against assets is of more limited scope. Asset registries are primarily registries of ownership and of other rights (such as security interests) which affect ownership. They exist only where the asset concerned is sufficiently valuable to warrant the cost of a registration system or where there are international ramifications which justify their costs of establishment. As a result, there are asset registers for:

● land;
● ships and aircraft; and
● certain intellectual property rights, such as patents and registered trade marks.

7.255 If security is created over an asset of a type which is not the subject of an asset register, the only registration required is against the debtor. If security is created over an asset which is the subject of an asset register, the security is registrable both in the relevant debtor register and in the relevant asset register.

7.256 These two types of registration system have had three different effects on priorities.

7.257 The asset registries have had the most direct effect on priorities. They establish separate systems for the priority of registrable interests over the assets concerned. They provide for the priority of registered interests to be governed, not by their dates of creation, but by their dates of registration in the asset register. They also provide for registered interests to take priority over registrable, but unregistered interests.

7.258 The effect of the debtor registries on priorities is more indirect. In the first place, they make unregistered interests void in most respects, and thereby effectively give priority to registered interests over registrable, but unregistered ones. More importantly in practice, registration at a debtor registry can also affect issues concerning notice. The fact that a security interest is registered will make it more likely that a person dealing with the debtor will become aware of it. But they do not directly affect priorities, which are still ultimately dependant on the date of creation of the security (and the exceptions from that principle), not on its date of registration.

7.259 It is also important to draw one further distinction between the debtor registries and the asset registries. The effect of failure to register in a debtor registry is, as has been seen in CHAPTER 6, effectively to render the security void, not only in the context of a priority dispute, but also against the insolvency officer of the debtor. Failure to register in the debtor registry will, therefore, make the security largely worthless. The position is different at the asset registries. Failure to register at an asset registry will affect the priority of the unregistered security, but it does not affect the validity of the security, even in the insolvency of the debtor. Registration in both registers is important to provide maximum protection for the secured creditor, but the failure to register at a debtor registry has more serious effects than a failure to register at an asset registry.

7.260 This part will first consider the effect of the asset registries on questions of priority, and will then discuss the effect of the debtor registries on these questions.

Asset registries

7.261 Most asset registries deal with priorities in broadly the same way. In particular, they ascribe priority between two registered interests by date of registration, rather than by date of creation; and, where there is a priority dispute between a registered interest and an unregistered, but registrable one, the registered interest takes priority. A number of them also have procedures to enable a person taking a registrable interest to issue a priority notice in advance, the effect of which is that the priority of the interest, if it is actually registered within the priority period, will date back to the date the priority notice was issued.

Registered land

7.262 Once a legal mortgage of registered land is registered at the land registry, it will, in general, take priority over:

- all later registered interests in the land (whether outright or by way of security); and
- all unregistered interests in the land (whether outright or by way of security and whether created before or after the legal mortgage) other than overriding interests (ie interests in the land which are effective without the necessity for registration – such as short leases and rights of persons in actual occupation of the land),

but it will rank behind all earlier registered interests in the land.[159]

---

159 Land Registration Act 2002, ss 28–30 and 48, and Sch 3.

7.263 For the purpose of priority, an entry on the register has effect from the time the application is made for registration.[160] Provision is also made for priority notices, by which a person intending to take a registered mortgage is able to make an official search of the register, thereby establishing whether there are any other registered mortgages on the title and obtaining a priority period. If an application for entry on the register is made during the priority period, the mortgage will take priority over any entry made in the register during that period.[161]

Unregistered land

7.264 Unregistered land is now of much less importance in practice than registered land, not least because most transactions in relation to unregistered land (including first mortgages) will trigger first registration of the title to the land. There are provisions for the registration of mortgages of unregistered land, although they are less sophisticated than those which apply in relation to registered land.

7.265 If a lender has a legal or equitable mortgage or a charge over the legal estate to unregistered land, and has obtained the title deeds to the land, the transaction is not registrable. The fact that the creditor holds the title deeds is considered to be sufficient protection. If, however, a creditor has a legal or equitable mortgage or a charge over the legal estate to unregistered land but has not obtained the title deeds (in practice this will be because it is a second or subsequent mortgage or charge), the security can be registered as a Class C land charge under the Land Charges Act 1972.[162] Under s 97 of the Law of Property Act 1925, registered land charges rank in order of registration. There is also a curious provision in s 4(5) of the Land Charges Act 1972 which renders such a land charge void against a purchaser unless it is registered before completion of the purchase. There is potential here for conflict with the priority rule in the Law of Property Act 1925 described above, although it does not appear to have created any problems in practice.

7.266 The Land Charges Act 1972 also contains provision for priority notices, which enable the effect of the registration to date back to the date of the priority notice.[163]

Beneficial interests in land

7.267 These provisions only apply where security is taken over the legal title to land, whether it is registered or unregistered. If security is taken over a beneficial interest in land, it has been seen in part 5 of this chapter (**7.151ff**) that priority is determined by application of the rule in *Dearle v Hall*.[164]

---

160 Land Registration Act 2002, s 74.
161 Land Registration Act 2002, s 72.
162 Land Charges Act 1972, ss 2(1) and 4.
163 Land Charges Act 1972, s 11.
164 *Dearle v Hall; Loveridge v Cooper* (1823, 1827, 1828) 3 Russ 1.

Ships

7.268   The title to British ships is registrable in the British Ship Register, and mortgages of registered ships are also registrable at that registry if they are in the prescribed form.[165] The priority of registered mortgages is regulated by para 8 of Sch 1 to the Merchant Shipping Act 1995. Paragraph 8(1) provides that:

> 'Where two or more mortgages are registered in respect of the same ship or share, the priority of the mortgagees between themselves shall [subject to the rules concerning priority notices, which are discussed below], be determined by the order in which the mortgages were registered (and not by reference to any other matter).'

7.269   Although the legislation is only expressed to regulate priority between registered mortgages, it has been construed so as to give priority to a registered mortgage over an earlier unregistered mortgage.[166] An intending mortgagee can issue a priority notice to the Registrar and, if the mortgage is registered within the priority period, its priority dates back to the date of the priority notice.[167]

7.270   It would seem that the date of registration of the mortgage is absolutely determinative of the priority of the mortgage over other registered or unregistered mortgages or charges. Paragraph 8(1) of Sch 1 to the Merchant Shipping Act 1995 provides that priority between mortgages is determined by the order of registration 'and not by reference to any other matter'. Although it is arguable that, in the case of fraud (ie deliberate dishonesty), this principle may be departed from, in all other cases it would seem to be absolute. As a result, the holder of a registered mortgage will take priority over an earlier unregistered one even if he is aware of it at the time he takes his mortgage.[168] It would also seem to follow that the restrictions on the tacking of further advances will not apply to a registered ship mortgage.[169]

7.271   Ship mortgages generally rank behind maritime liens (such as those for seamen's wages, collision damage and salvage)[170] and also behind possessory liens.[171]

---

165   Merchant Shipping Act 1995, Sch 1, para 7(2).
166   *Coombes v Mansfield* (1855) 3 Drew 193; *Black v Williams* [1895] 1 Ch 408. In the latter case, the competing unregistered charge was a floating charge, and so would have ranked behind the registered ship mortgage in any event; but this was not the reason given for the decision.
167   Merchant Shipping Act 1995, Sch 1, para 8(2); Merchant Shipping (Registration of Ships) Regulations 1993, SI 1993/3138, reg 59.
168   *Coombes v Mansfield* (1855) 3 Drew 193; *Black v Williams* [1895] 1 Ch 408.
169   The contrary conclusion was reached in *The Benwell Tower* (1895) 8 Asp MLC 13, but the wording of the relevant provision is now different – 'and not by reference to any other matter'.
170   See, generally, *Harmer v Bell, The Bold Buccleugh* (1852) 7 Moo PCC 267.
171   *Williams v Allsup* (1861) 10 CB (NS) 417.

Aircraft

7.272   Mortgages of aircraft registered in the United Kingdom are registrable under the Mortgaging of Aircraft Order 1972.[172] Under art 14:

- registered aircraft mortgages 'shall as between themselves have priority according to the times at which they were respectively entered in the Register'; and
- a registered aircraft mortgage has priority over any unregistered mortgage or charge of the aircraft.

7.273   An intending mortgagee can have a priority notice registered and, if the mortgage is registered within the priority period, its priority will relate back to the date the priority notice was registered.[173]

7.274   Article 14(4) provides that: 'The priorities provided for by the preceding provisions of this article shall have effect notwithstanding any express, implied or constructive notice affecting the mortgagee.' This provision is not as widely drawn as the equivalent for registered ship mortgages.[174] It nevertheless makes it clear that even actual notice of a prior unregistered interest will not postpone a registered mortgagee. As far as tacking further advances is concerned, the Schedules to the Mortgaging of Aircraft Order enable the mortgagee to specify whether further advances are to be made, which suggests that the rules concerning tacking in relation to aircraft are likely to be the same as those in relation to land – ie that further advances can be tacked if there is an obligation to make them which is noted on the register.

7.275   Registration of a mortgage does not give the mortgagee priority over possessory liens or statutory rights of detention of the aircraft.[175]

7.276   Mortgages of aircraft (and also conditional sales and leases of them) are the subject of the Cape Town Convention on International Interests in Mobile Equipment and the supporting Protocol on Matters Specific to Aircraft Equipment. The Convention and the Aircraft Protocol will come into effect on 1 March 2006 in those countries which have ratified it. It will provide for the registration of such interests at an international registry, and for priorities to be dependent on the date of registration. The United Kingdom has not yet ratified it, but is expected to do so.

Intellectual property

7.277   Some intellectual property is registrable. By way of example, where security is taken over a patent or an application for a patent, a registered mortgage or charge will take priority over an unregistered one (and over any other unregistered, but registrable disposition), unless the registered mortgagee

---

172 SI 1972/1268.
173 Mortgaging of Aircraft Order 1972, SI 1972/1268, art 14(2).
174 See Merchant Shipping Act 1995, Sch 1, para 8(1).
175 Mortgaging of Aircraft Order 1972, SI 1972/1268, art 14(5).

or chargee knew of the earlier transaction.[176] Similarly, a mortgage or charge of a registered trade mark is ineffective against a person acquiring a conflicting interest in it in ignorance of the mortgage or charge until an application has been made for registration of the mortgage or charge.[177]

7.278   It will be seen that the effect of registration of security over these types of intellectual property is different from that for ships and aircraft. The register does not purport to be conclusive. A registered interest will take priority over an earlier unregistered one, but only if the holder of the registered interest did not know of the earlier transaction. The potential unfairness of the other systems (that a person might be able to take priority by registering first even if he was aware of an unregistered earlier interest) does not exist where patents and registered trade marks are concerned.

Notice of earlier interest

7.279   Where a registered mortgage is taken over a patent or patent application or over a registered trade mark, it has been seen that the fact of registration will not give priority over an earlier unregistered interest if the registered mortgagee knew of the existence of the earlier interest. But the position is different where land, goods and aircraft are concerned. They all provide that a registered interest will rank ahead of a registrable, but unregistered interest, as well as over any subsequently registered interest. In relation to ships and aircraft, this point is driven home in the legislation. In the case of ships, priority is expressed to be determined by the order of registration 'and not by reference to any other matter'.[178] In the case of aircraft, the priority of a registered mortgage is expressed to have effect 'notwithstanding any express, implied or constructive notice affecting the mortgagee'.[179]

7.280   The legislation either expressly (in the case of ships and aircraft) or impliedly (in the case of land) gives priority to a registered mortgagee even if he was aware of an earlier unregistered interest at the time he paid his money. In spite of this, there must be room for doubt as to the outcome if it could be established that a person deliberately took advantage of the legislation. There is an equitable principle that a statutory provision should not be used to commit a fraud.[180] It is at least arguable that, in such a case, even if the legal mortgagee did take priority, he would hold the benefit of the prior mortgage on constructive trust for the person with the earlier interest or be liable to account for the benefit received in a personal claim in equity. It would be prudent for a creditor who becomes aware of an earlier unregistered interest before lending his money to enter into a priority agreement with the owner of the earlier interest, rather than relying on getting registered first and thereby taking priority.

---

176 Patents Act 1977, s 33.
177 Trade Marks Act 1994, s 25. As its name suggests, there is a register of registered designs, but it does not expressly deal with priorities: see the Registered Designs Act 1949, s 19.
178 Merchant Shipping Act 1995, Sch 1, para 8(1).
179 Mortgaging of Aircraft Order 1972, SI 1972/1268, art 14(4).
180 *Rochefoucauld v Boustead* [1897] 1 Ch 196.

Debtor registries

7.281 The effect of non-registration under the Companies Act 1985 and the Bills of Sale Acts 1878–1891 is to render the security void for most purposes. This is discussed in part 5 of **CHAPTER 6 (6.120ff)**.

7.282 Of more importance in practice is the effect of registration on the doctrine of notice. A register exists of most mortgages and charges created by companies. Intending lenders are able to search the register in order to discover whether the company has already created security. An intended secured lender will usually search the register and thereby discover the existence of any existing security. But what if he does not? Will he have constructive notice of its contents? Neither statute deals specifically with the question. In principle, it is suggested that the position is as follows.

7.283 Because there is no statutory provision that registration under the Companies Act 1985 or the Bills of Sale Acts 1878–1891 is deemed to constitute actual notice, the mere fact of registration will not, of itself, mean that all persons dealing with the debtor are deemed to have notice of what is registered. The purpose of the system is to enable persons dealing with the debtor to find out about security it has created. It is not implicit in such a system that every person dealing with the debtor is to be deemed to have notice of what is registered.

7.284 Registration can, however, be of relevance in establishing constructive notice. It was seen, in part 2 of this chapter **(7.19ff)**, that a person will have constructive notice of matters which would have come to his knowledge if he had made such inquires as he ought reasonably to have made. The question, in this context, is whether a person dealing with the debtor ought reasonably to have searched the register. This is not a question which can be answered in the abstract. It can only be answered by reference to the circumstances of a particular transaction.

7.285 For example, a bank taking a fixed and floating charge debenture over the assets of a company would be expected, in accordance with normal practice, to conduct a company search in order to see whether any security was registered against the debtor. If it failed to do so, a court might easily reach the conclusion that it had failed to do that which it ought reasonably to have done, and was therefore fixed with constructive notice of what it would have found if it had searched the register.

7.286 At the other end of the spectrum is a case where an individual is buying a second-hand motor car from a debtor company, in circumstances where a bank has a fixed charge over the debtor's fleet of motor cars. It is extremely unlikely that a court would decide that the individual in such a case ought reasonably to have searched the register of the company in order to establish whether or not a bank had a fixed charge over the asset concerned.

7.287 In each case, it is necessary to consider the nature of the transaction (for instance, whether it is a security transaction or an outright purchase), the nature of the asset concerned, the amounts involved in the transaction and any other relevant circumstances. Only when this has been done is it possible to establish whether or not the person concerned ought reasonably to have searched the register.

7.288 In principle, therefore, it is suggested that:

- a person dealing with the debtor will not automatically be deemed to have notice of the contents of the charges register of the debtor concerned; but
- if, in the circumstances of the particular transaction, he ought reasonably to have searched the register, he will have constructive notice of the contents of the charges register at the time he ought to have searched.

7.289 The position has been considered in principle because there is a dearth of case-law authority on the issue. There is, however, one case which does consider the issue, and which is frequently cited as authority for the proposition that registration of charges at Companies House is notice to the whole world of the existence of those charges. In *Wilson v Kelland*,[181] the question arose whether a person dealing with a debtor company had constructive notice of a registered floating charge. As it turned out, a decision on the point was not required, but Eve J nevertheless gave his view on the point. He said:[182]

> 'I should have been prepared to hold that the particulars registered in this case ... amounted to constructive notice of a charge affecting the property but not of any special provisions contained in that charge restricting the company from dealing with their property in the usual manner when the subsisting charge is a floating security.'

7.290 *Wilson v Kelland* is often taken as authority for the proposition that the registration of a charge gives constructive notice of the existence of the charge to anyone dealing with the company. Since a conclusion on this point was not necessary for the decision of the case, the statement is not of binding authority. In any event, it is suggested that all Eve J was saying was that, on the facts of the particular case concerned, B ought reasonably to have searched the register. His statement cannot be authority for the proposition that everyone dealing with a debtor has notice of all charges registered against it.

7.291 That case does, however, raise another issue which is particularly important in practice, which is the extent to which a person dealing with the debtor can obtain constructive notice of a restriction on the authority of the debtor to deal with assets the subject of a floating charge. It has been seen in part 8 of this chapter (**7.234ff**) that such a restriction is only effective against a person dealing with the company if he had notice of it. In *Wilson v Kelland*, Eve J held that such a person would not have constructive notice of such a restriction simply because the floating charge had been registered. Although it is not clear from the judgment why he took this view, it is generally assumed that there is a distinction between those matters which are required to be registered and those which are not. In the case of registration under the Companies Act, what needs to be registered, in addition to details of the

---

181   [1910] 2 Ch 306.
182   [1910] 2 Ch 306 at 313.

parties concerned, are descriptions of the assets charged and the liabilities which are secured by the charge. There is no requirement to register any restrictions on the authority of the debtor to deal with the charged assets.

7.292 In practice, it is invariably the case that details of any such restriction are entered on the form sent to the Registrar and therefore appear on the company's register. Because, however, they are not prescribed particulars, it is generally considered, relying on *Wilson v Kelland*, that a person dealing with the company will not have constructive notice of the restrictions, even if he ought to have searched the register, because he should only have constructive notice of matters which require to be registered, not of matters which do not.

7.293 It is, therefore, unlikely that a person dealing with the debtor will have constructive notice of a restriction on the debtor's authority which is registered at Companies House, even if he ought reasonably to have searched the register. That is not to say that there is no point in registering such restrictions. On the contrary, it is important to do so because of the likelihood that persons dealing with the debtor will, in fact, conduct a search and will therefore discover the existence of the restriction. In other words, they will obtain actual, rather than constructive, notice of it.

7.294 In summary, it is suggested that:

- Registration of a charge under the Companies Act 1985 or the Bills of Sale Acts 1878–1891 does not constitute deemed notice to all the world of the existence of the charge.
- A person dealing with the debtor will have constructive notice of such a registered charge if, in the circumstances of the transaction concerned, he ought reasonably to have searched the register and, had he done so, he would have discovered the existence of the charge.
- A person dealing with the debtor will not have constructive notice of matters which do not require to be registered, such as restrictions on dealings by the debtor, even if they are in fact registered. But he may obtain actual notice of them if he does in fact search the register.

7.295 There is one final point. The creditor has 21 days within which to lodge the charge and the particulars of the charge with the Registrar of Companies. The Registrar then has to check the particulars and enter them on the register. There will, therefore, inevitably be a delay between the creation of the charge and its appearance on the register. If a person dealing with the company ought reasonably to search the register, he will only have constructive notice of what actually appeared on the register at the time he ought to have searched. He will not, for instance, have constructive notice of a charge which has already been created but details of which do not yet appear on the register. There is, therefore, an incentive on those registering charges to do so as soon as practicable in order to reduce the amount of time before details of the charge appear on the register.

Part 10: PRIORITIES IN PRACTICE

7.296 The earlier parts of this chapter have considered the various principles which govern the priority of security. The purpose of this part is to put those principles into context, and briefly to discuss how priority issues should be dealt with in practice. The problem is approached in five stages.

First step

7.297   There are two preliminary matters to be considered. The first is that, in a priority dispute with an owner, a secured creditor is likely to come second. The question in such a case is whether the debtor is able to grant a proprietary interest over the asset concerned to the creditor. If the debtor only has a limited interest in the asset, he cannot create security over anything more than that limited interest. A buyer of goods which have been purchased on reservation of title cannot charge them to a lender. The buyer does not obtain either legal or beneficial title to the goods, and therefore has nothing which he can charge to the lender. Similarly, a lessee of goods cannot charge them because he has only a limited possessory interest in them. The first question is therefore to establish what rights the debtor has in the asset concerned.

7.298   The second question (which is in some senses the converse of the first) is to establish whether the lender has itself obtained a proprietary interest in the asset. It is only if it has done so that any question of priorities arises. If, for instance, the creditor has lent simply on the basis of a negative pledge, with nothing more, he will have no proprietary interest in the debtor's assets, and therefore no question of priorities can ever arise.

Second step

7.299   The next step is to consider the nature of the asset over which security is being taken in order to establish the correct priority rules to apply. It has been seen, in the preceding parts of this chapter, that the way in which the priority principles operate is often dependent on the nature of the asset concerned. The discussion in this section will concentrate on three types of asset:

- registered land, ships and aircraft;
- other goods and shares; and
- contract rights, debts and equitable interests.

7.300   Priorities in relation to registered land, ships and aircraft are relatively straightforward. Registered interests rank by date of registration and generally take priority over unregistered interests, even if they were created earlier. There are limitations on this principle, but they are relatively modest. In the case of land, overriding interests take priority over registered interests, but the categories of overriding interests have been materially reduced as a result of the Land Registration Act 2002. As far as ships and aircraft are concerned, possessory liens will normally rank in priority, as will most maritime liens (in the case of ships) and statutory rights of detention (in the case of aircraft).

7.301   The position is more complicated where the assets concerned consist of shares, or of goods other than registered ships and aircraft. Here, the starting point is that priorities depend on the date of creation of the interest concerned, but that principle is subject to the bona fide purchaser principle, and it will not apply if the equities are not equal. In relation to these types of asset, obtaining legal title can give a creditor a material advantage if he can also establish that he took his interest for value and without notice of an earlier equitable interest. The key limitation on this principle is notice. The fact that charges over goods are registrable means that, in practice, a subsequent lender is likely to have actual notice of an earlier charge and, even if he has not searched, he will be treated as if he has if, in the circumstances, he ought to have done so. Registration therefore means that the bona fide purchaser rule is of much less importance in practice than it used to be. But it can still be relevant, particularly in relation to security over shares. Because fixed charges over shares are not registrable, it is still possible, in practice, for a creditor taking a legal mortgage over shares to take priority over an earlier equitable interest; and the ability to tack the legal estate means that a creditor who takes an equitable interest in the shares without notice of an earlier equitable interest, but then manages to obtain the legal title to the shares, can take priority.

7.302 In theory, both the first in time principle and the bona fide purchaser principle only apply if the equities are equal, and it is open to one of the parties to argue that the conduct of the other ought to postpone him. This is not an argument which is likely to carry much weight any longer in practice. It tends to have been used in circumstances where one creditor has enabled the debtor to retain title documents and thereby commit a fraud on another creditor; and neither shares nor goods are generally the subject of title documents.

7.303 In practice, therefore, as far as shares and goods other than registered ships and aircraft are concerned, the first in time principle is likely to be of paramount importance, although there are limited circumstances where the bona fide purchaser principle can give priority to a later legal mortgagee. A possessory lien over goods will usually rank in priority to a mortgage or charge.

7.304 The third category of assets is contract rights and debts (and also equitable interests in any type of asset). Here, the basic priority rule is the rule in *Dearle v Hall*,[183] and the starting point is that the first person to give notice to the counterparty or trustee will take priority. Again, one of the key determinants of priority is likely to be notice. A person cannot take priority under the rule in *Dearle v Hall* if, at the time he obtained his interest, he had notice of an earlier interest in the same asset. Where the debtor is a company, security over assets of this kind is generally registrable (and invariably registered), with the effect that a person who searches the register is likely to obtain actual notice of the existence of an earlier interest and, if he does not, will obtain constructive notice of it if, in the circumstances, he ought to have searched. It has been seen that, where the rule in *Dearle v Hall* applies, there is no requirement to weigh up the equities between the parties.

7.305 In short, although the basic principle is that priorities are determined by the order in which notices are received by the counterparty or trustee, it is quite difficult in practice for a creditor to take advantage of this in order to take priority over an interest created earlier in time. In many cases, such a

---

183 *Dearle v Hall; Loveridge v Cooper* (1823, 1827, 1828) 3 Russ 1.

creditor will have either actual or constructive notice of the earlier interest, and will therefore be unable to take advantage of the fact that he has given notice first.

Third step

7.306 Having established the basic priority position in relation to the particular asset concerned, it is then necessary to consider the various ways in which that basic priority position can be affected. There are three ways in which this can be done. They concern:

- purchase money security interests;
- floating charges; and
- tacking further advances.

7.307 Where a creditor finances the acquisition of a new asset by the debtor, his security will rank ahead of an earlier general charge created by the debtor over future assets of that type. In practice, however, the creditor who finances the asset is likely to obtain either actual or constructive notice of the earlier security (since in most cases it will be registered), and it is therefore unlikely that this principle will have any material effect on the outcome of a priority dispute.

7.308 Of much more importance in practice, the rules for floating charges are completely different from those for fixed charges. A floating chargee will rank behind a later fixed charge unless the fixed chargee had notice, at the time he took his interest, that the debtor's authority to create such an interest was restricted or that the floating charge had crystallised. In many cases, a subsequent creditor will search the register and discover the existence of the restriction but, because it is not a prescribed particular, he is unlikely to obtain constructive notice of it. As a result, it is still quite possible for a subsequent fixed chargee to take priority over an earlier floating charge.

7.309 The rules concerning tacking further advances can also affect the priority of a secured creditor. Even though one security interest ranks ahead of another, finance made available after the creditor becomes aware of a later security interest over the same asset will rank behind that later security in most cases. Unless the asset consists of registered land and a maximum amount of lending has been noted on the land register, a creditor should assume that any money lent after he has received notice of a subsequent mortgage over the same asset will rank behind that mortgage. In practice, therefore, a creditor who receives notice of a subsequent mortgage should not lend any more money until he is comfortable that he has an appropriate priority agreement with the other mortgagee.

Fourth step

7.310 The discussion so far has concerned priorities between secured creditors. Where there is a priority dispute between a creditor with fixed security and an execution creditor, the execution creditor will only take priority if his interest is created before that of the secured creditor. Because he is a volunteer, he cannot take advantage of any of the exceptions to the first in time principle. Where the security consists of a floating charge, the execution creditor will take priority if he completes his execution before the floating charge crystallises.

Fifth step

7.311 Finally, the complexity of the rules concerning priorities and the fact that they often depend on matters of fact (such as the presence or absence of notice), means that, in practice, a secured creditor who is aware that another creditor has, or will obtain, security over the same asset is likely to enter into a priority agreement with that person. The great advantage of a priority agreement is that it will establish with certainty who takes priority, and to what extent.

ENFORCING SECURITY

Chapter 8

ENFORCEMENT

Part 1: INTRODUCTION

8.1 If the two most important things to get right when taking security are ensuring that it is effective in the debtor's insolvency and that it takes priority over third parties, the third is to ensure that the creditor can enforce the security when he needs to do so. A security interest is not complete in itself. It is not an end. It is a means to an end – the repayment of the secured liability.

8.2 Perhaps the most important feature of the enforcement of security under English law is that the creditor is generally able to enforce the security himself, without the necessity to go to court. That is in marked contrast with many other jurisdictions (particularly civil law jurisdictions). And what is just as important in practice is that the creditor's power to do so generally continues even if the debtor is the subject of insolvency proceedings. In many other jurisdictions (including some other common law countries), a creditor's power to enforce his security is curtailed during insolvency proceedings. Until recently, English law did not restrict a creditor's ability to enforce his security in the debtor's insolvency proceedings. Over the last 20 years, however, insolvency legislation has had a major impact on a creditor's ability to do so, particularly as a result of the introduction of administration in the Insolvency Act 1986 and the curtailment of administrative receivership in the Enterprise Act 2002. These issues are considered further in this chapter and in the following one.

8.3 There is one important respect in which the power of enforcement is of a different nature from the other two key aspects of the law of security mentioned above. Whether a creditor obtains rights over the asset concerned which are effective in the debtor's insolvency, and whether those rights are effective against third parties who have an interest in the asset, are matters which are determined by the law of property. The ease of creation of equitable proprietary interests by agreement between the parties has tended to blur the distinction between the contractual elements and the proprietary ones; but, regardless of the intentions of the parties, a proprietary interest will only be created if the relevant requirements of the law of property have been complied with. Whether valid security has been created, and its priority over other security interests, is not just a matter of concern to the debtor and the creditor. It also affects third parties, which is why it is not just the province of the law of contract but also of the law of property.

8.4   Enforcement is different. When and how the security is enforced is largely a matter for agreement between the debtor and the creditor. In the absence of enforcement provisions in the security document, the law does provide default remedies for the creditor if the security needs to be enforced. But security documents invariably contain detailed enforcement provisions, and they are generally effective as matters of contract between the debtor and the creditor. The result is that the ability of the creditor to enforce the security largely depends on the construction of the security document concerned, rather than on general legal principles. The parties can decide when and how the security is to be enforced and the courts do not generally interfere with that agreement.

8.5   That is not to say that the underlying law relating to enforcement is unimportant. Although a security document can create its own regime for enforcement, it will frequently cross-refer to the default rules under the general law, particularly to the implied powers contained in the Law of Property Act 1925 and in the Insolvency Act 1986. It is therefore necessary to understand the default rules in order to appreciate what security documents are intending to achieve.

The development of enforcement powers over land

8.6   Like so much else in English law, it is impossible to understand these default powers except in the context of the nature of security interests as they have developed historically. In the abstract, many of the rules seem rather curious. Perhaps they are, from the perspective of the twenty-first century. But they can only be understood by appreciating how and why they developed.

8.7   In this respect, the development of the creditor's enforcement powers has features in common with the development of the priority rules discussed in **CHAPTER 7**. Both sets of principles were developed at a time when much wealth was tied up in land, security over chattels was frequently taken by way of pledge, and intangibles were nothing like as important as they are today. Most of the cases on enforcement powers therefore involve security over land. There are fewer cases in relation to other assets and, even now, it is by no means clear the extent to which all the principles which were developed in relation to land are also applicable to other assets.

8.8   As with priorities, therefore, it is necessary to start with the nature of security over land before the 1925 property legislation.[1] A legal mortgage of land was effected by a transfer of land to the creditor, on terms that the creditor would re-transfer it to the debtor if the loan was repaid by a certain date. At common law, if the loan was not repaid by that date, the debtor had no further rights over the land. But equity stepped in to allow the debtor to get the land back by repaying the loan, even though he had no legal right to do so. This right to redeem the land in equity became known as the 'equity of redemption'. It is discussed in part 6 of **CHAPTER 3 (3.295ff)**.

---

1   It is not just the forms of action which rule us from their graves.

8.9   The fundamental right of a mortgagee at common law was not so much to get the debt paid, as to get the land if it was not. The debtor accordingly had a real interest in repaying the secured debt on time because of the severe consequence of failing to do so. Equity stepped in to prevent the land being taken away from him without giving him a reasonable chance of paying the secured debt, even after the contractual date for payment. As a result, the creditor could not simply rely on the terms of the security document to keep the land. He had to apply to the court for the 'foreclosure' of the debtor's equity of redemption. In doing this, he was asking the court to allow him to keep the land free from the equitable rights of the debtor.

8.10   The right of foreclosure was the creditor's ultimate remedy. Short of that, his other principal remedy was the right of possession. Because, under a legal mortgage, the creditor was the legal owner of the land, he was entitled to go into possession. But, because his interest was only a security interest, the purpose of the possession was only to enable the secured debt to be repaid. If, for instance, the land was subject to tenancies, the creditor could collect the rent and apply it in reduction of the secured debt. Alternatively, he could use the land himself and apply the notional occupational rent in discharge of the secured debt.

8.11   The two main remedies of the creditor under a legal mortgage were, therefore, possession and, ultimately, foreclosure. Sale of the mortgaged property was not, generally, an option. The remedies of foreclosure and possession were available to the creditor if he had a legal mortgage. They were also available if the creditor had an equitable mortgage, provided that it contained an agreement to create a legal mortgage. This was because equity would treat as done that which ought to be done, and would force the debtor to create the legal mortgage if he were unwilling to do so. But they were not available in relation to equitable charges. If the creditor only had a charge, he was neither the legal nor the beneficial owner of the land. Since foreclosure was simply a process for allowing the creditor to keep land in an unencumbered form which he already owned in an encumbered form, it could not be used by an equitable chargee, who had neither legal nor beneficial title to the land. For the same reason, in the absence of a specific provision in the security document, a chargee was not entitled to possession of the land.

8.12   A chargee therefore needed a different remedy. This was achieved by allowing him to apply to the court for the charged property to be sold, and for the proceeds to be applied in payment of the secured debt and for any balance to be paid to the debtor. Alternatively, if the creditor wanted rights equivalent to possession, he could apply to the court for the appointment of a receiver of the income of the land.

8.13   Two different systems for the enforcement of security over land had therefore developed. One enabled the creditor to go into possession and to foreclose, but not, generally, to sell the land. The other allowed the creditor to apply to the court for the land to be sold or for the appointment of a receiver of the income of the land.

8.14   These powers of the creditor were capable of being increased by agreement and, during the nineteenth century, the practice became more common for security documents to include an express power of sale by the creditor. In the case of an equitable charge, the benefit of such a provision was to avoid the necessity to apply to the court for the sale to be effected. It was even more advantageous in relation to a legal mortgage because, in the absence of such an express provision, the court would not generally order the sale of the property concerned. This practice led to legislation (Lord Cranworth's Act of 1860) which implied powers of sale and receivership, subject to certain conditions, into mortgages and charges. These implied powers were extended by the Conveyancing Act 1881 and are now contained in the Law of Property Act 1925. In relation to any mortgage or charge over land which was created by deed, the creditor therefore had implied powers of sale and to appoint a receiver of income. These powers could be exercised without application to the court and, in the case of a legal mortgage, they avoided the necessity for relying on the rights of foreclosure and possession.

Enforcement powers over businesses

8.15 The other important development in the nineteenth century was, as a result of the creation of the floating charge in the 1860s, to enable a creditor to take security over all of the present and future assets of a corporate debtor. In the absence of specific powers of enforcement in the floating charge, the creditor's principal remedy was to apply to the court for the appointment of a receiver and manager of the charged assets. Such a receiver and manager served a very different purpose from a receiver of the income of land. His function was not simply to collect rent, but to sell the charged assets. And because these would often be realised more advantageously if they were sold as a going concern, he was also given the power to continue the company's business for the purpose of effecting a sale as a going concern. The ultimate remedy of the floating chargee was the same as the fixed chargee's – to have the charged property sold. The difference lay in the way in which this object was to be achieved. In the case of a fixed charge over land, it was effected simply by giving the creditor the ability to have the land sold. Where a business was concerned, however, this would be insufficient if the business was to be sold as a going concern. It was therefore necessary for the court to appoint a receiver and manager whose primary function was to sell the charged property but who was entitled to run the business in the meantime for the purpose of effecting the sale.

8.16 The advantages to the creditor of such an approach are manifest. He is likely to get a better price where the business is sold as a going concern than he would if it was sold on break-up basis. It therefore soon became the practice in floating charges for the creditor to be given an express power to appoint a receiver and manager, thus avoiding the necessity to apply to the court.

8.17 By these processes, the nature of the creditor's powers of enforcement has been totally reinvented. Foreclosure and possession are still available, at least in relation to legal (and some equitable) mortgages, but are rarely used in practice. It is still possible for a creditor to apply to the court for sale, for the appointment of a receiver of income or for the appointment of a receiver and manager, but the limitations on a number of these powers and the time and expense involved in an application to court mean that they are hardly ever used.

Although (at least in relation to security over land) there are now implied statutory powers of sale and of the appointment of a receiver of income, these powers are only capable of being enforced subject to restrictive conditions and are not sufficiently wide to enable the creditor to appoint a receiver and manager to carry on the debtor's business and then to sell it.

8.18 For these reasons, it is invariably the practice for express powers of enforcement to be contained in the security document, or at least for the implied powers to be extended. A debenture over the present and future assets of a corporate debtor will contain express powers for the appointment of a receiver, and it has generally been the case that enforcement of such security has been effected by the appointment of a receiver. In the case of other types of security, other remedies (such as the power to enter into possession of, and sell, the assets) may be appropriate, but receivership is still the preferred method of enforcement in most cases, not least because it enables the enforcement to be carried out by professionals and without the necessity for the creditor to assume the liabilities which he might incur if he enforced the security himself.

8.19 Since the Enterprise Act 2002 came into force in September 2003, the power of a creditor to appoint a receiver over all or substantially all of the assets of a corporate debtor (such a person being referred to in the legislation as an 'administrative receiver'), has been severely curtailed. A creditor can now only appoint an administrative receiver in limited circumstances. In those cases where it cannot, the creditor has been given a statutory power to appoint an administrator of the debtor company under the Insolvency Act 1986. In practice, such an administrator will have broadly the same powers as a receiver, although these are contained in the statute, rather than in the security document itself. As a result of these legislative changes, administration is likely to become the principal method of enforcing security over businesses, although receivership will continue to be of importance in some cases.

Enforcement powers over other assets

8.20 It cannot necessarily be assumed that the powers of a creditor in relation to security over land are replicated where goods or intangibles are involved. Pledges over goods are straightforward. As has been seen in part 6 of CHAPTER 2 (**2.73ff**), a pledgee has the power to sell the pledged goods if default is made in paying the secured debt, and this can be done without the necessity for application to the court. Even in the case of pledges, however, it is normal to give the creditor express powers of enforcement, in order to ensure that it is clear both when and how the security can be enforced. A pledgee does not, however, have legal title to the goods concerned, and cannot, therefore, foreclose.

8.21 There is little authority in relation to the implied powers of a legal mortgagee of goods. In principle, they should be similar to those in relation to legal mortgages of land, although the mortgagee may, in addition, have an implied power of sale similar to that of a pledgee. Because of the uncertainty, it is invariably the case that the mortgage will contain express powers of enforcement.

8.22   As far as security over intangibles is concerned, the position becomes even less clear. Except in the case of those limited types of intangible which are transferable at common law (such as shares), it is not possible to obtain a legal mortgage over intangibles. The security will, therefore, normally consist of an equitable mortgage or charge. Where the security is taken over receivables, the basic remedy of the creditor is to give notice to the counterparty to pay them directly to the creditor. Alternatively, the creditor could apply to the court for the appointment of a receiver. But the creditor will, in practice, also want a power to sell the receivables and this needs to be expressed in the security document, which should also contain a power to appoint a receiver out of court.

8.23   It is important to tailor the enforcement powers in a security document to the nature of the property charged. In the case of a debenture over all of the debtor's assets, there should always be an express power to appoint a receiver and manager or an administrator. In other cases, it will nearly always be appropriate for there to be a power to appoint a receiver, but it may not always be appropriate to use that power. In relation to security over a receivable, for instance, the creditor may simply wish to require the counterparty to pay the creditor direct. Where the security is taken over a credit balance with the creditor himself, he will wish to enforce the security by applying that credit balance in discharge of an equivalent amount of the secured debt. What is important is to ensure that the security document gives the creditor all express powers which he needs in order to enforce the security in the most beneficial way. It is unwise to rely on the powers of a secured creditor under the general law.

The position of the debtor

8.24   There are two parties to a security document, and the position also needs to be seen from the point of view of the debtor. Until enforcement, what are his rights in relation to the property concerned? In the case of a legal mortgage, the creditor is, on the face of it, entitled to possession because he has title but, in practice, it is generally agreed that he will not enter into possession until default. The security document will, however, normally restrict the powers of the mortgagor to deal with the property concerned without the approval of the mortgagee. The extent of those restrictions is a matter for agreement. But there are certain limitations on the powers of the mortgagor which result from the nature of a legal mortgage itself. Because the creditor becomes the legal owner of the property, any lease created by the debtor after the mortgage has been created will be ineffective to bind the mortgagee unless he has expressly or impliedly consented to it. The Law of Property Act 1925 gives the debtor certain implied powers to create leases, but these are normally contracted out of.

8.25   The position of the debtor before enforcement is, therefore, ultimately a question to be decided by agreement with the creditor. In many cases, in the absence of agreement, the debtor will be able to do things which might prejudice the creditor. In other cases, the nature of a legal mortgage, even after the 1925 property legislation, means that the debtor will, in the absence of any specific provision, be prevented from doing certain things merely as a result of having entered into the mortgage. It is therefore important, from the point of view of both parties, to ensure that the security document properly regulates the powers of the creditor and the debtor in relation to the charged property.

The structure of this chapter

8.26 The next part of this chapter considers when the creditor is entitled to exercise his powers of enforcement. The following parts consider the powers of the creditor under the general law. They are considered in ascending order of importance, starting with foreclosure, working through possession and sale and finishing with receivership and administration. It then considers the responsibilities of a creditor, receiver or administrator when exercising his powers and it concludes with a discussion of powers of enforcement in practice. This chapter is accordingly divided into the following parts:

- Part 2 (**8.27ff**) – when can the creditor exercise his powers?
- Part 3 (**8.52ff**) – foreclosure.
- Part 4 (**8.66ff**) – possession.
- Part 5 (**8.82ff**) – sale.
- Part 6 (**8.103ff**) – receivership.
- Part 7 (**8.148ff**) – administration.
- Part 8 (**8.173ff**) – liabilities of the creditor, receiver and administrator.
- Part 9 (**8.221ff**) – enforcement in practice.

Part 2: WHEN CAN THE CREDITOR EXERCISE HIS POWERS?

8.27 Because the creditor's powers of enforcement are normally expressly provided for in the security document, the circumstances in which he is entitled to exercise those powers normally depends on the construction of that document and on the other documents which govern the relationship between the debtor and the creditor, such as the facility agreement. It is nevertheless necessary briefly to consider when the creditor can exercise his rights if he is relying on his implied powers of enforcement. This depends on the nature of the power concerned.

Implied enforcement powers

8.28 Generally, the creditor's implied powers of enforcement are only available once the secured debt has become payable to the creditor. The creditor can therefore apply to the court for a foreclosure order, for the sale of the property concerned or for the appointment of a receiver if the secured liability has become payable.[2] The creditor's implied power to sell the property or to appoint a receiver of its income under the Law of Property Act 1925 are also exercisable once the secured debt has become payable, subject to certain limitations.[3]

8.29 The right of a legal mortgagee to obtain possession of the mortgaged property is different. Because the creditor is the legal owner of the property, he has the right to possession unless it is expressly or impliedly excluded by the terms of the mortgage. Although a mortgagee will rarely rely on this implied right of possession, it can be useful where the mortgage document is defective as far as the creditor's powers are concerned. Its availability has been reaffirmed in *Western Bank v Schindler*.[4] In that case, the Court of Appeal confirmed that a legal mortgagee's right to possession of the mortgaged property arose as soon as the mortgage was entered into unless it was expressly or impliedly limited by the terms of the documentation, and that it therefore arises even before default in payment by the debtor. But, until the power of sale is exercisable, 'the right to possession can only be exercised to protect the security, not as a means of enforcing it'.[5]

8.30 Unless it is excluded, therefore (and it can be excluded impliedly, as well as expressly), the right to possession can be used to protect the security even before the secured debt becomes payable. It is also possible for the creditor to apply to the court for the appointment of a receiver of income in circumstances where the value of the secured property is diminishing, even though the secured debt is not then payable.[6]

8.31 In summary, the creditor's power to apply to the court for foreclosure or sale, or to exercise the implied powers to sell or appoint a receiver under the Law of Property Act 1925, are only available once the secured liability has become payable. But, unless expressly or impliedly excluded, the power of a legal mortgagee to take possession is available before default, as is a creditor's power to apply to the court to appoint a receiver if it is necessary to preserve the value of the security.

Express enforcement powers

8.32 If, as is normally the case, the creditor's powers of enforcement are provided for expressly in the security document, it is a matter of construction of that document when they arise.[7] In practice, they are likely to be exercisable when the secured debt has become payable. In most cases, therefore, the creditor's first question will be whether the secured liability is payable. This will

---

2   *Burrowes v Malloy* (1845) 8 I Eq R 482. This assumes that the creditor has such an implied power. Whether he does is considered in the following parts of this chapter.
3   Law of Property Act 1925, s 101(1)(i) and (iii), although these are subject to s 103.
4   [1977] Ch 1.
5   [1977] Ch 1 at 10, per Buckley LJ.
6   *Burrowes v Malloy* (1845) 8 I Eq R 482.
7   *Twentieth Century Banking Corporation Limited v Wilkinson* [1977] Ch 99 at 105, per Templeman J.

normally depend, not on the security documents, but on the document (such as a loan agreement) which evidences the terms of the underlying transaction by which the creditor has made credit available to the debtor.

8.33 One question which frequently arises is whether the secured liability is payable automatically, or whether it is necessary for the creditor to demand repayment before it becomes payable. This depends on the terms of the documentation concerned. It will sometimes provide that, on the happening of a certain event, the debtor is under a liability to pay the creditor. This is likely to be the case, for instance, on expiry of the term of the loan. More frequently, the documentation will provide that, on the happening of the event concerned, the creditor will have the option to require payment of the secured liability by serving a demand on the debtor. This is normally (but not always) the case if there is an event of default. In such a case, the secured debt will only become payable once the demand has been made.

8.34 In practice, a creditor who is about to enforce security will, in any event, want to make formal demand on the debtor for payment of the secured liability, not only to prevent any argument by the debtor that there was an express or implied obligation to do so, but also to make sure that the debtor is fully aware of what is happening.

8.35 A further question for the creditor is to establish if there are any other requirements in the security or facility documentation which need to be complied with before the security can be enforced. Security documents commonly provide that the security can be enforced once the secured debt has become payable, without the requirement for any notice to the debtor or any other formality. In particular cases, however, the security document might provide that it cannot be enforced until notice has been given to the debtor, and it may also give a period of grace within which the security cannot be enforced.

8.36 Finally, the creditor will want to ensure that any relevant statutory provisions have been complied with. There are few statutory requirements, but the Insolvency Act 1986 does contain certain formal provisions which need to be complied with in relation to the appointment of receivers.[8]

Administration

8.37 One effect of the Enterprise Act 2002 has been to increase the importance of statutory provisions in the enforcement of security. The restriction on a secured creditor's ability to appoint an administrative receiver (ie a receiver over all or substantially all of the debtor's assets), and the consequent ability of the creditor to appoint an administrator in cases where he could previously have appointed an administrative receiver, will have the effect that the most common method of enforcing security over a business will be to appoint an administrator. Unlike the appointment of a receiver, this is a statutory procedure, the requirements of which cannot be contracted out of. These requirements are considered in part 7 of this chapter (**8.148ff**).

---

8   See, for instance, Insolvency Act 1986, s 33.

Giving the debtor time to pay

8.38 In addition to complying with the terms of the relevant finance documents, the debtor must also be given sufficient time to enable him to effect the repayment before the creditor enforces his security.[9] The purpose of this requirement is to enable the debtor to get the money from a source already available to him (for example, a bank account in credit or an established line of credit on which he can draw). He will not be given time to raise funds from elsewhere, only to effect the mechanics of repayment.[10]

8.39 Whether or not he has been given sufficient time depends on the circumstances of the transaction.[11] There are five factors which have been particularly important in the cases in establishing whether or not the debtor has been given sufficient time to pay:

* What does the documentation say about the issue? A demand will clearly be invalid if the creditor does not comply with the terms of the documentation. But, even where the requirement is to pay 'immediately upon demand'[12] or 'instantly on demand, and without any delay on any pretence whatsoever',[13] the courts will imply that the debtor must be given a reasonable time to effect the repayment.

* On whom was the demand served? If it is not served on an officer of the debtor who has the authority to obtain the funds and effect the repayment, the period required to effect repayment will be longer than it would have been if demand had been served on someone with that authority.[14]

* How specific and accurate was the demand? If a demand is made for 'all monies due' to the creditor, or for more than the amount owing to the creditor, the debtor will be given longer to effect the repayment than if the demand were precise.[15]

* What discussions have taken place between the parties beforehand? If the creditor has been negotiating for some time with the debtor to have the loan repaid, and the debtor is aware that it is only a matter of time before a formal demand is made, the period of that formal demand can be very short.[16]

* Most importantly, what is the financial position of the debtor? If the debtor is insolvent or in such a difficult financial position that it is unable to repay, very little time will be required between the making of the demand and the enforcement of the security because the debtor will not be able to pay in any event.[17]

---

9   *Massey v Sladen* (1868) LR 4 Exch 13.
10   *Bank of Baroda v Panessar* [1987] Ch 335.
11   *ANZ v Gibson* [1982] 2 NZLR 513; [1986] 1 NZLR 556.
12   *Toms v Wilson* (1862) 4 B&S 442.
13   *Massey v Sladen* (1868) LR 4 Exch 13.
14   *Massey v Sladen* (1868) LR 4 Exch 13.
15   *Massey v Sladen* (1868) LR 4 Exch 13.
16   *Cripps v Wickenden* [1973] 1 WLR 944.
17   *Cripps v Wickenden* [1973] 1 WLR 944; *Bank of Baroda v Panessar* [1987] Ch 335.

8.40　Three examples illustrate how these principles operate in practice. In *Massey v Sladen*,[18] a security bill of sale provided by an individual debtor stated that the loan should be repaid 'instantly on demand, and without any delay on any pretence whatsoever'. It also provided that the demand could be made either personally on the debtor 'or by giving or leaving a verbal or written notice to or for him at his present or last-known place of business, ... so nevertheless that a demand be in fact made'. The creditor made demand for payment on the debtor but, earlier on the same day, the creditor's solicitor had already made a demand at the debtor's place of business on the debtor's son, who had been left in charge of the business, and the creditor had immediately taken possession of the debtor's chattels. The debtor sued the creditor in trespass for wrongful seizure of the goods and it was held that his claim succeeded.

8.41　The court held that, on a proper construction of the bill of sale, the words 'instantly on demand' and 'without any delay on any pretence whatsoever' must be construed to give the debtor a reasonable time to pay. Since the debtor himself did not hear of the demand until after the seizure had taken place, he had had no opportunity of complying with it. In the words of Pigott B:

> 'It is not necessary to define what time ought to elapse between the notice and the seizure. It must be a question of the circumstances and relations of the parties, and it would be difficult, perhaps impossible, to lay down any rule of law on the subject, except that the interval must be a reasonable one.'

Cleasby B also relied on the unspecific nature of the demand in deciding that insufficient time had been given to the debtor to comply with it.[19]

8.42　*Massey v Sladen* illustrates the first three principles described above. It shows that even a very stringently worded document will not prevent the court from implying that the debtor must be given a reasonable time to effect the repayment; that the less specific the demand the greater the time that will be required; and that, if demand is not served on a person who can actually effect the repayment, further time will be required.

8.43　The second example is *Cripps v Wickenden*.[20] The debtor company had created a debenture in favour of the bank. The financial position of the debtor deteriorated, and there were refinancing proposals which broke down. On 6 August, the bank accordingly wrote to the debtor indicating that, in the absence of additional finance, the only alternative would be for the bank to appoint a receiver. On 8 August, the bank made demand on the company's chairman at about 11 am and appointed receivers at about 12 noon. The receivers quickly managed to sell assets sufficient to repay the bank's overdraft. Goff J held that the appointment of the receivers was valid. He made it clear

---

18　(1868) LR 4 Exch 13.
19　Some doubt was cast on this approach by the Court of Exchequer in *Wharlton v Kirkwood* (1873) WR 93, but it was followed by the Privy Council in *Moore v Shelley* (1883) 8 App Cas 285.
20　[1973] 1 WLR 944.

that all the creditor had to do was 'to give the debtor time to get [the money] from some convenient place, not to negotiate a deal which he hopes will produce the money'.[21]

8.44 It is not entirely clear whether the debtor was insolvent, but it was clearly in financial difficulties. In the words of Goff J:[22]

'It is abundantly plain that [the debtor] had not got the money and had no convenient place to which they could go to get it ... In my judgement therefore, the plaintiffs cannot object on the ground that they were not given time to find the money or that the interval of time between 11 o'clock or shortly before, when the demand was made, and 12 o'clock or later, when the receiver was appointed, was too short.'

8.45 If *Massey v Sladen* illustrates the first three principles described above, *Cripps v Wickenden* illustrates the last two. The debtor was well aware of the fact that the bank had run out of patience. It was also clear that the company simply did not have the money with which to repay the loan. In those circumstances, a gap of one hour between the making of the demand and enforcement was sufficient.

8.46 The leading modern case is *Bank of Baroda v Panessar*.[23] The debtor company had executed a debenture in favour of the bank. The debtor had repeatedly exceeded its overdraft limit, and was insolvent. The bank eventually decided to recall its money, and demand was served on the company's premises at about 10 am. A receiver was appointed at about 11 am. The demand was very brief. It simply demanded 'all monies due to us under the powers contained in [the debenture]'. It was alleged that the appointment of the receiver was invalid, first because a proper demand had not been served and, secondly, because insufficient opportunity had been given to the debtor to repay the monies demanded.

8.47 Walton J held that the receiver had been validly appointed. On the first point, he decided that it was not necessary for the demand to specify the amount owing. On the second point, he held that the debtor was only entitled to 'a reasonable opportunity of implementing whatever reasonable mechanics of payment he may need to employ to discharge the debt'.[24] In this case, although the demand was not specific, the fact that the company was insolvent, and therefore unable to repay the bank, meant that a period of one hour between making demand and enforcement was sufficient.

8.48 In spite of the decisions in *Cripps v Wickenden* and *Bank of Baroda v Panessar*, the dangers of the creditor giving the debtor insufficient time to effect the repayment are manifest. If, for instance, a receiver is wrongfully appointed, he will be liable in damages for trespass or wrongful interference with goods and may also become liable in equity as an intermeddler. The creditor might

---

21   [1973] 1 WLR 944 at 955.
22   [1973] 1 WLR 944 at 955.
23   [1987] Ch 335.
24   [1987] Ch 335 at 348.

find itself liable for the acts of the receiver either under an express indemnity or as a result of s 34 of the Insolvency Act 1986. The potential damages could be substantial – not just the difference between the sale price of assets sold by the receivers and the value which could have been obtained outside receivership, but also the loss suffered by the company as a result of an unnecessary receivership.

8.49 Notwithstanding the *Bank of Baroda* case, secured creditors should not assume that in every case they will be able to give just one hour's notice having made a general demand for payment of all monies due. If the company is clearly insolvent, their position is unlikely to be capable of being challenged. If, however, there is doubt about solvency and the ability to raise funds, they might find themselves with an argument on their hands. In addition to complying scrupulously with the terms of the documentation, a secured lender would therefore be well advised:

- to make specific demand for an amount which is clearly due (and, if in doubt, to under-demand – it always being possible to demand the balance subsequently);
- to ensure not only that the demand is made strictly in accordance with the documents but also that the directors of the company are made aware of it in sufficient time to enable them to have effected repayment if the debtor had the ability to do so; and
- to consider the financial position of the debtor and the terms of its recent discussions with the debtor before deciding how long to give it to effect repayment.

Nature of the rights

8.50 It should, finally, be mentioned that a secured creditor is generally entitled to exercise all of his rights at the same time, unless they are contradictory. He can, for instance, sue the debtor in personal proceedings for recovery of the debt whilst, at the same time, enforcing his security by receivership or sale or by applying to the court for relief.[25]

8.51 If his rights are enforceable, the creditor is entitled to exercise them regardless of the consequences. In relation to the appointment of a receiver, in *Re Potters Oils*,[26] Hoffmann J said:

'The [creditor] is under no duty to refrain from exercising his rights merely because to exercise them may cause loss to the [debtor] or its unsecured creditors. He owes a duty of care to the [debtor] but this duty is qualified by being subordinated to the protection of his own interests.'

Part 3: FORECLOSURE

8.52 In common parlance, if a debtor gets into financial difficulties, a creditor will often be said to 'foreclose' on the mortgage. In practice, although

---

25 *China and South Sea Bank v Tan Soon Gin* [1990] 1 AC 536.
26 [1986] 1 WLR 201 at 206.

the remedy of foreclosure was initially one of the creditor's principal remedies, it has long since ceased to play an important part in the methods of enforcement of a secured creditor. But the expression continues in popular usage long after the concept has ceased to play a role in legal practice.

What is foreclosure?

8.53   Foreclosure does what its name suggests – it shuts out the debtor from the mortgaged property. Whilst the mortgage continues, the debtor has an equity of redemption – the ability to get his property back on payment of the secured liability.[27] Foreclosure bars that remedy. It makes the creditor the absolute owner of the property. On foreclosure, the debtor ceases to have any further rights to it. Indeed, as well as shutting out the rights of the debtor, it also bars the rights of anyone who has a subsequent security interest in the property concerned.

How is foreclosure effected?

8.54   At common law, the rights of the debtor to recover property which had been mortgaged to the creditor depended on the terms of the mortgage. If the debtor did not repay the secured debt at the required time, he no longer had any rights to the property. In equity, however, the debtor continued to have the right to recover the property on payment of the secured indebtedness. The only way in which the creditor could extinguish the debtor's equity of redemption was to apply to the court for an order that the debtor no longer had the right to redeem. As Sir George Jessel MR said in *Carter v Wake*,[28] a legal mortgagee can foreclose because he is the legal owner of the property concerned and the court can simply remove its own stop on him cancelling the equity of redemption. And as Warrington J said in *Re Farnol Eades Ervine & Co*:[29]

> 'Foreclosure is done by the order of the court, not by any person. In the strict legal sense it is nothing more than the destruction of the equity of redemption which has previously existed.'

8.55   The creditor's right to apply to the court for foreclosure arises once the secured liability has become repayable. If the creditor wants to foreclose, he will make an application to the court to do so. The court will require an account to be taken of the amount of the secured indebtedness and will give the debtor a period of time (normally 6 months) to repay it, failing which it will make a foreclosure order absolute. This will have the effect of barring the debtor's equity of redemption and the rights of any subsequent encumbrancers, and will therefore make the creditor the absolute owner of the property concerned.[30]

8.56   Since 2003, there have been particular rules in relation to financial collateral. The nature of financial collateral is discussed in part 5 of **CHAPTER 3**

---

27   The equity of redemption is discussed in part 6 of **CHAPTER 3** (**3.295**ff).
28   (1877) 4 Ch D 605.
29   [1915] 1 Ch 22 at 24.
30   *Platt v Mendel* (1884) 27 Ch D 246.

(**3.175**ff). For this purpose, the important point is that a creditor with a legal or equitable mortgage which arises under a security financial collateral arrangement and which allows the creditor to 'appropriate' the secured assets is effective without the need for a foreclosure order from the courts.[31]

What are the effects of foreclosure?

8.57   Once the foreclosure order has been made, the creditor becomes the absolute owner of the property concerned free, not only of the debtor's equity of redemption, but also of the rights of any persons with security over the property concerned which rank behind those of the creditor. But foreclosure is not a one-way street. It does have one material disadvantage for the creditor – it effectively prevents the creditor from bringing a claim against the debtor to recover the secured debt. This is not because the debt ceases to exist once there has been foreclosure, but because the creditor is only entitled to sue to recover the debt if he allows the foreclosure to be re-opened.

8.58   The effect was explained in *Lockhart v Hardy*.[32] In that case, the creditor foreclosed on the mortgage and then sold the property concerned for less than the amount of the secured debt. The sale was a perfectly proper sale and the creditor attempted to recover the difference between the amount of secured debt and the sale price of the property concerned from the debtor. It was held that the creditor could not recover the balance from the debtor.

8.59   The principle was stated by Lord Langdale MR. If the creditor sues the debtor for payment, and receives payment only in part, he can still foreclose for the balance. If he forecloses first, he can still sue the debtor, but that then allows the debtor to redeem the mortgage – in other words it opens up the foreclosure. Once, however, the creditor has put it out of his power to allow the debtor to redeem, for instance, by selling the property, he can no longer sue for the unpaid debt. In practice, therefore, foreclosure makes it very difficult for the creditor thereafter to recover the unpaid amount of the debt from the debtor.

What types of security does foreclosure apply to?

8.60   The paradigm case for foreclosure is a legal mortgage of land, although the principle also applies to legal mortgages of goods, and also of shares.[33] It is also available where there is an equitable mortgage if it contains an agreement to create a legal one. Equity will treat as done that which ought to be done and will therefore require the debtor to create a legal mortgage.[34] The right to foreclose in such a case is only available if the asset concerned is one which is capable of being the subject of a legal mortgage. In addition to land and goods,

---

31   Financial Collateral Arrangements (No 2) Regulations 2003, SI 2003/3226, reg 17.
32   (1846) 9 Beav 349.
33   *General Credit and Discount Company v Glegg* (1883) 22 Ch D 549.
34   *Cox v Toole* (1855) 20 Beav 145; *James v James* (1873) LR 16 Eq 153.

the right of foreclosure is therefore also available in relation to an equitable mortgage of shares where there is an agreement to create a legal mortgage over them.[35]

8.61   Foreclosure is, however, only available where the creditor either has legal title or is entitled to it. It is not, therefore, available in relation to a pledge, even though it is a common law interest, because, although the creditor has possession and 'special property' in the goods, he does not have legal title to them. In the words of Sir George Jessel MR, 'his equitable rights cannot exceed his legal title'.[36] Nor can a creditor foreclose if he has an equitable charge or an equitable mortgage which does not contain an agreement by the debtor to create a legal mortgage.[37]

8.62   In summary, therefore, if the creditor has legal title to the property concerned or the right to obtain the legal title, he will be entitled to foreclose. If not (whether because his security is only a simple charge or the property concerned is not capable of being the subject of a legal mortgage), he will have a right of sale, but not a right to foreclose. In the absence of specific powers in the document concerned, the courts appear to have regarded foreclosure and sale as being irreconcilable, in the sense that the creditor had the right to one or the other, but not, generally, to both. This rigid distinction has, however, been amended by statute. Under s 91(2) of the Law of Property Act 1925, the court is entitled to order the property concerned to be sold in a foreclosure action.

Why would a creditor want to foreclose?

8.63   It has been seen that the advantage of foreclosure is that the creditor becomes the absolute owner of the property concerned, but its disadvantage is that the creditor is effectively unable to recover the balance of the secured indebtedness. If, therefore, the property is worth less than the outstanding balance of the secured indebtedness, there is little point in the creditor foreclosing.

8.64   The theoretical advantage of foreclosure, from the point of view of the creditor, is his ability to become the absolute owner of the property in circumstances where it is worth more than the secured indebtedness. But, in such a case, it ought to be possible for the mortgagee to refinance the security in order to avoid the loss of his equity of redemption. Indeed, under s 91(2) of the Law of Property Act 1925, if the creditor does apply for a foreclosure order, it is open to the debtor to request that the property be sold. Although the court has a discretion whether or not to accede to such a request, it will inevitably do so where the value of the property is in excess of the secured indebtedness because foreclosure would penalise the debtor.

8.65   For all these reasons, foreclosure is of little practical value to a secured creditor.

---

35   *Harrold v Plenty* [1901] 2 Ch 314.
36   *Carter v Wake* (1877) 4 Ch D 605 at 606.
37   *Re Owen* [1894] 3 Ch 220.

Part 4: POSSESSION

8.66 Along with foreclosure, the right to possession of the mortgaged property was the creditor's other main remedy if it had a legal mortgage. The remedy was particularly important in relation to land. If the land was the subject of tenancies, the mortgagee could go into possession and collect the rents. Alternatively, he could use the land himself and pay an occupational rent for it by way of set-off against the secured indebtedness.

Going into possession

8.67 As has been seen in part 2 of this chapter (**8.27ff**), in the absence of agreement to the contrary, the creditor is entitled to possession as soon as the mortgage is created although, in practice, his right to take possession is now normally postponed until the secured indebtedness has become repayable.

8.68 If the creditor has a legal mortgage, he can enter into possession simply because he is the legal owner. He does not require the involvement of the court. When he goes into possession, the mortgagee is entitled to the property as it is at the time, including future rents. He is also entitled to rent which has not yet been paid, even if it relates to the period before he took possession.[38] He is entitled to them because he is the legal owner. As Sir George Jessel said in *Cockburn v Edwards*,[39] 'the mortgagee receives rents which are his own, subject, of course, to the right of redemption …'.

8.69 Although the creditor is entitled to everything to which the debtor was previously entitled, the creditor does not have the same rights as an absolute owner would have to dispose of the property or create interests in it. Rights of sale are considered in part 5 of this chapter (**8.82ff**), and will not, therefore, be discussed here. As far as the granting of leases over the land is concerned, the creditor does not have an absolute right to grant them once he is in possession; and the debtor, whilst he is in possession, is the subject of similar restrictions. Once the mortgage has been created, the position under the general law was that, unless the debtor had an express or implied power to create leases, any lease which he did create after the mortgage had been created would bind him, but would not bind the creditor;[40] and the creditor, once he has gone into possession, did not have the ability to create leases in the absence of express or implied authority to do so.[41] The position has, however, been altered by statute. Section 99 of the Law of Property Act 1925 contains provisions which apply in the absence of agreement to the contrary and which give each of the debtor and the creditor, whilst they are in possession, the ability to create leases of certain types subject to certain conditions. In practice, these provisions are invariably overridden by the express terms of the mortgage. The debtor's right to grant leases is normally limited (the extent of the limitation depending on

---

38   *Moss v Gallimore* (1779) 1 Doug 279.
39   (1881) 18 Ch D 449 at 457.
40   *Dudley and District Benefit Building Society v Emerson* [1949] 1 Ch 707.
41   *Hungerford v Clay* (1795) 9 Mod 1.

the nature of the mortgagor's business), whereas the creditor is normally given wide powers to create leases once the mortgage is being enforced.

Duties of a mortgagee in possession

8.70   The right of a mortgagee in possession to appropriate the income of the property carries with it certain responsibilities. The relationship between these rights and responsibilities is clearly expressed by Sir John Romilly MR in *Chaplin v Young*:[42]

> 'In the case of a mortgagee of the business, if he enters into possession, he becomes the owner of the business, and he stands exactly, as regards his powers, in the place of the mortgagor, and, accordingly, he is accountable to the owner of the equity of redemption for everything which he either has received or might have received, or ought to have received, while he continued in such possession.'

8.71   The reason why this duty is imposed on the mortgagee, and the nature of that duty, are explained by Rigby LJ in *Gaskell v Gosling*.[43] He described the position as follows. If the debtor was left in possession, he was entitled to the income from, and use of, the property for his own purposes without having to account for it to the creditor. If the creditor wanted the income of the property, therefore, he had to go into possession. He continued:[44]

> 'This entry into possession by a mortgagee was always considered a strong assertion of his legal rights, since he did not come under any obligation to account to the mortgagor except in a suit for redemption. He was accordingly treated with exceptional severity in a suit for redemption and made to account, not only for what he actually received, but for what he might without wilful default have received.'

8.72   As Rigby LJ explained, this was a particular problem if he was a second mortgagee, since he might, at any time, be removed by the first mortgagee. And it also created risks where he was a mortgagee of a business and was therefore 'subject to the vicissitudes of commercial business'.[45]

8.73   The strong rights of the creditor were therefore matched by equally strong responsibilities. The creditor could go into possession and receive the income from the property without any obligation to account for it until the debtor applied to the court to redeem the property or the creditor applied to the court to foreclose the equity of redemption. But once that accounting took place, the creditor had to account not only for what he had received but for what he ought to have received. The extent of that liability is considered in part 8 of this chapter (**8.173**ff), which discusses the duties and liabilities of creditors, receivers and administrators.

---

42   (1863) 33 Beav 330 at 337–338.
43   [1896] 1 QB 669 at 691–693. It was a dissenting judgment, but was upheld on appeal by the House of Lords in *Gosling v Gaskell* [1897] AC 575.
44   [1896] 1 QB 669 at 691.
45   [1896] 1 QB 669 at 691.

What types of security does it apply to?

8.74 As with foreclosure, the paradigm security which affords the creditor a right of possession is a legal mortgage.[46] If the rule concerning possession were to be consistent with that relating to foreclosure (and it should be consistent, because the right to possess and the right to foreclose both depend on legal title), the creditor ought also to have a right to possession where he has an equitable mortgage which contains an obligation by the debtor to create a legal mortgage on request. It would appear, however, that this is not the case, and that an equitable mortgagee, like a chargee, has no right to possession unless the document concerned makes express provision for it,[47] an outcome which has been rightly criticised.[48]

8.75 In practice, this problem is normally avoided because the security document will contain an express power for the creditor to enter into possession of the property concerned on default. In the absence of such power, a creditor with an equitable mortgage or charge has the right to apply to the court for the appointment of a receiver of the income of the property concerned.[49]

Statutory restrictions on taking possession

8.76 It has been seen that, unless it is excluded, a legal mortgagee has the right to take possession of the mortgaged property at any time after the mortgage has been created. In other cases (and usually in the case of legal mortgages as well), the security document normally contains an express power for the mortgagee to take possession on default by the debtor. In commercial transactions, this power is generally capable of being exercised in accordance with the terms of the security documents. But there are statutory restrictions on the ability of a creditor to take possession of the property concerned in certain transactions of a consumer nature. The purpose of these statutory provisions is to protect the debtor.

8.77 The most important statutory restriction on taking possession is contained in s 36 of the Administration of Justice Act 1970, as amended by s 8 of the Administration of Justice Act 1973. The purpose of these provisions is to limit the ability of creditors to evict debtors from their homes. They apply where there is a mortgage or charge over a dwelling-house; and they broadly give the court the power to delay the creditor from obtaining possession if the debtor is likely to pay what is required to be paid under the mortgage or charge within a reasonable period. For this purpose, the creditor is not, generally, able to increase the amount payable in excess of that which would have been expected to have been paid if there had not been a default by the debtor.

---

46 *Western Bank v Schindler* [1977] Ch 1.
47 *Vacuum Oil Company v Ellis* [1914] 1 KB 693 at 703, per Buckley LJ.
48 *Wade* (1955) 71 LQR 204.
49 *Vacuum Oil Company Limited v Ellis* [1914] 1 KB 693.

8.78 As Griffiths LJ said in *Bank of Scotland v Grimes*,[50] the purpose of these statutory provisions is obvious:

> 'It is the intention of both sections to give a measure of relief to those people who find themselves in temporary financial difficulties, unable to meet their commitments under their mortgage and in danger of losing their homes.'

8.79 In addition, where the debtor is an individual and the amount financed is less than £25,000, Part VIII of the Consumer Credit Act 1974 limits the creditor's powers of enforcement in various ways, for instance, by requiring a court order to enforce a mortgage of land[51] and by regulating the creditor's power to enforce a pledge.[52]

8.80 Of less importance in practice, but with a similar aim in mind, s 7 of the Bills of Sale Act 1878 (Amendment Act) 1882 restricts the circumstances in which a creditor can take possession of goods which are the subject of a security bill of sale granted by an individual. As would be expected, there is no similar restriction in relation to mortgages or charges over goods created by companies.

Taking possession in practice

8.81 In consumer transactions, the creditor's power to take possession is normally exercised as a precursor to a sale, in order to ensure that the sale can be effected with vacant possession. In commercial transactions, the creditor's power to take possession is hardly used at all, except in the most straightforward transactions. The creditor will normally appoint a receiver or an administrator, rather than enter into possession himself; and the receiver or administrator will have the power not only to collect income, but also to sell. The reluctance of creditors to enter into possession results partly from concerns as to liability as mortgagees in possession and partly because the creditor rarely has the resources necessary to do so. The appointment of a receiver or administrator avoids these problems as far as the mortgagee is concerned, although it raises issues as to the liability of receivers and administrators, which are discussed in part 8 of this chapter (**8.173ff**).

Part 5: SALE

8.82 It has been seen that the primary remedies of a creditor who has a legal mortgage were foreclosure and possession. In the absence of express provision, a power of sale (whether by application to the court or otherwise) was not

---

50   [1985] QB 1179 at 1190.
51   Consumer Credit Act 1974, s 126.
52   Consumer Credit Act 1974, s 121. The monetary limit is likely to be removed in the near future.

generally available to a legal mortgagee. If the value of the property concerned was lower than the amount of the secured indebtedness, taking possession would be unlikely to assist the creditor (not least because the income was unlikely to be sufficient to meet interest accruing on the secured indebtedness), and foreclosure would effectively prevent the debt from being recovered.

8.83 On the other hand, an equitable chargee did have the ability to apply to the court for an order that the property be sold. Indeed, along with the power to apply to the court for the appointment of a receiver, this was his primary remedy. In some respects, therefore, it could be said that an equitable chargee was in a better position than a legal mortgagee, and this dichotomy led to the inclusion of express powers of sale in mortgages and charges. The increase in the use of express powers of sale in the nineteenth century led to their being implied by statute, first in Lord Cranworth's Act of 1860, subsequently in the Conveyancing Act 1881 and now in the Law of Property Act 1925. The implied power of sale in the Law of Property Act 1925 is still frequently relied on in security documents, although it is invariably extended by removing the restrictions contained in that Act.

8.84 Before considering express powers of sale, it is therefore necessary to consider when such a power is implied, first, under the general law and, secondly, by statute.

When is a power of sale implied under the general law?

8.85 It has been seen in part 3 of this chapter (**8.52ff**) that, where there was a legal mortgage of land or an equitable mortgage which contained a power to take a legal mortgage, the creditor was entitled to apply to the court for foreclosure and was, correspondingly, not entitled either to sell the property or to request the court to sell it.[53] In the case of security over land, therefore, there was a clear distinction between those securities which carried the right to the legal title and those which did not. In the former case, the creditor could apply for foreclosure. In the latter, he could apply for sale. But he could not have both.

8.86 The position in relation to security over goods is rather different. In many cases, such security was effected by means of a pledge, in which event the creditor was entitled to sell the goods concerned on default by the debtor, without the necessity to apply to the court.[54] Legal mortgages of goods ought, in principle, to be subject to the same rules as legal mortgages over land, with the effect that the creditor under a legal mortgage of goods ought not, in the absence of an express power to do so, be able to sell the goods or to apply to the court to do so, his remedy being foreclosure and possession. In *Re Morritt, ex parte Official Receiver*,[55] however, three members of a very strong Court of Appeal (Cotton, Lindley and Bowen LJJ – the court, in that case, consisting of six judges), decided that, although there was little authority, a legal mortgagee

---

53   *Cox v Toole* (1855) 20 Beav. 145.
54   See part 6 of **CHAPTER 2** (**2.73ff**).
55   (1886) 18 QBD 222.

of goods has an implied power of sale at common law, but only once he has entered into possession. The case was treated as analogous to that of a pledge. Lord Esher MR and Lopes LJ did not have to consider this issue but Fry LJ, dissenting on this point, was of the opinion that a mortgage of goods was different from a pledge and that the creditor could only sell the goods if there was an express power to do so in the mortgage document. *Re Morritt* is accordingly authority for the proposition that a legal mortgagee of goods does have an implied power of sale under the general law, irrespective of any statutory provision.

8.87   As far as intangibles are concerned, very few are capable of being the subject of a legal mortgage. Shares and similar securities are exceptions and, where a legal mortgage is created over them, the normal remedy of foreclosure is available. The courts have, however, been more willing to allow a sale of securities than of land. This is because their value can fluctuate markedly, so that it may be necessary for a sale to be effected before their value has diminished too greatly. Accordingly, where the value of the assets concerned is capable of fluctuating, it would appear that the creditor with a mortgage or charge over them has a power of sale on default, even without applying to the court.[56]

8.88   Where security is taken over intangibles which are incapable of being the subject of a legal mortgage (for instance, receivables), the creditor does not have the right to foreclose and is accordingly entitled to apply to the court for an order of sale.

8.89   It will be seen from this brief description that the circumstances in which the creditor has an implied power of sale are by no means clear. In some cases (such as a legal mortgage of land), he will generally have no power of sale at all, even by application to the court. In a second category of cases (for instance, an equitable charge), the creditor will be able to apply to the court for an order that the property be sold. In yet another category of cases (such as mortgages or charges of goods or securities which fluctuate in value), the creditor may be able to sell on default by the debtor without the necessity to apply to the court. It was these inconsistencies and uncertainties which led to an attempt to regularise the position by statute.

The statutory power of sale

8.90   Sections 101 and 103 of the Law of Property Act 1925 give the creditor a power of sale in the case of a mortgage or charge which is made by deed. The power arises when the secured indebtedness has become payable, and it enables the creditor to sell the property concerned privately or by auction, and without the necessity to apply to the court.[57] The circumstances in which the creditor can enforce this power are, however, restricted by s 103. This prevents the creditor from exercising his power of sale except in one of three circumstances:

---

56   *Tucker v Wilson* (1714) 1 P Wms 261; *Lockwood v Ewer* (1742) 2 Atk 303.
57   Law of Property Act 1925, s 101(1)(i).

- where principal is in arrears for 3 months after notice requiring payment has been served on the debtor;
- where interest is in arrears for 2 months; or
- where the debtor has committed some other breach of the mortgage document.

8.91 It is invariably the case that the restrictions contained in s 103 are excluded in security documents.

8.92 What is less clear is the types of security to which these powers relate. Section 101 applies to a mortgage which is made by deed, and s 205(1)(xvi) defines 'mortgage' to include a charge on any property, and defines 'property' to include both land and personal property.

8.93 In *Re Morritt, ex parte Official Receiver*,[58] the Court of Appeal had to consider whether ss 19 and 20 of the Conveyancing Act 1881 (which were the precursors of ss 101 and 103 of the Law of Property Act 1925) applied to mortgages of goods. All six members of the court held that they did because of the equivalent definitions to those referred to above. The result is surprising. The primary purpose of the Act is to modernise land law. It does, incidentally, have some provisions which deal with intangibles, but none with goods. The structure of the Act indicates that at least the first three Parts are intended to deal only with land; and the provisions relating to mortgages are contained in Part III. Nevertheless, the decision of a very strong Court of Appeal in *Re Morritt* has established that it does apply to security over goods, when made by deed.

8.94 The same logic would indicate that the statutory provisions also extend to security over intangibles. Nevertheless, the absence of clear authority in relation to intangibles means that it is preferable not to rely on the implied power of sale under the Law of Property Act 1925 in the case of security over intangibles.

Express powers of sale

8.95 Express powers of sale in security documents became very common during the nineteenth century[59] and they are ubiquitous in modern security documents. Since the introduction of implied statutory powers in 1860, it is also common for security documents to rely on the implied statutory power of sale (now contained in s 101 of the Law of Property Act 1925), but to exclude the restrictions (now contained in s 103).

Where there is more than one mortgagee

8.96 It will sometimes be the case that the debtor has created more than one security interest over the property concerned, in which event the powers of the various mortgagees need to be established.

---

58 (1886) 18 QBD 222.
59 *Clarke v Panopticon* (1857) 4 Drew 26 at 30, per Kindersley V-C.

8.97   Each creditor needs to consider whether his security has become enforceable and whether his power of sale has arisen. If the first mortgagee exercises his powers, the subsequent mortgagees will be unable to do so themselves. When the first mortgagee sells, this will have the effect not only of barring the debtor's equity of redemption in the property, but will also override the interests of the subsequent mortgagees in the property.[60] The rights of the subsequent mortgagees are transferred to the sale proceeds. After the first mortgagee's secured debt has been paid, any surplus proceeds are held on trust by him for the subsequent mortgagees in accordance with their priorities. If there is sufficient to repay them all, the balance is then paid to the debtor.

8.98   Although the subsequent mortgagees are unable to prevent the first mortgagee from exercising his powers, they do have the benefit of the proceeds of sale. Accordingly, they have an interest in ensuring that the first mortgagee obtains the market value of the property when he sells, and they therefore have the same rights as the debtor in this respect. This issue is discussed in part 8 of this chapter (**8.173ff**).

8.99   If the first mortgagee decides not to enforce his security, it is open to the second mortgagee to do so but, in the absence of an agreement with the first mortgagee, the second mortgagee is only able to sell subject to the first mortgage. This will be a disadvantage because a purchaser will normally want to acquire the property unencumbered. The rights of a subsequent mortgagee are therefore doubly precarious. Not only does he rank behind the first mortgagee, but his powers of enforcement are, in practice, more limited. This is one reason why it is common for there to be a priority agreement between the various mortgagees which not only regulates priorities but also establishes the basis on which the various securities will be enforced.

The effect of a sale

8.100   Once the creditor has entered into a contract to sell the property, the debtor's right to redeem is extinguished. In *Property & Bloodstock v Emerton*,[61] a debtor mortgaged a leasehold interest in land to his creditor. The creditor's power of sale became enforceable, and he contracted to sell the land to a purchaser, conditionally on the landlord's consent (which was required for the sale). After the contract had been entered into, the debtor tendered the full amount of the secured indebtedness to the creditor and claimed the right to redeem. The Court of Appeal held that he could not do so. Whilst the contract subsisted, it barred the debtor's right to redemption. And this was the case even though the contract was conditional. If the condition was fulfilled, the contract of sale would be completed. If not, the contract would be terminated, and the debtor would have the right to redeem. But, whilst the contract subsisted, the debtor's right to redeem was barred.

---

60   Law of Property Act 1925, s 104(1) expressly provides for this where the sale is made under that Act.

61   [1968] Ch 94.

8.101 The debtor's equity of redemption is a proprietary interest in the charged property, rather than simply a personal right against the creditor. The debtor loses his right to redeem on sale, but it does not follow that he thereby loses all of his proprietary rights arising out of his equity of redemption. If the net sale proceeds exceed the amount of the secured indebtedness owing to the creditor, the balance is held on trust for the debtor by the creditor. The existence of the trust follows logically from the fact that the debtor has a proprietary interest in the property as a result of his equity of redemption. Once the equity of redemption is barred, the debtor's proprietary interest is transferred to any balance of the net sale proceeds after the creditor has been repaid. This has always been the case in equity,[62] and it is recognised in s 105 of the Law of Property Act 1925 in relation to sales effected under the implied powers contained under that Act.

Duties of the creditor when selling

8.102 In the same way that a mortgagee owes duties to the debtor when he goes into possession of the property, he also owes duties when he sells the property (and the former is frequently a precursor of the latter). The duties of a mortgagee when selling are discussed in part 8 of this chapter (**8.173ff**), at the same time as the other principal liabilities of the mortgagee, a receiver and an administrator are considered.

Part 6: RECEIVERSHIP

8.103 Receivership is worthy of a book of its own, and has achieved a number. It cannot be treated in detail here, but the law of security cannot be properly understood without some explanation of how security is normally enforced; and receivership (and its offshoot, administration) is by far the most popular method of enforcement of security in commercial transactions.

8.104 Receivership has a long history. Courts of equity have, for a very long time, had jurisdiction to appoint receivers of property, and they have done so in a number of different circumstances. One of those circumstances is where a creditor has security over property and needs someone to be appointed to look after the property and receive its income.

8.105 It has been seen that the power of a mortgagee to take possession of the mortgaged property is matched by a corresponding duty – he is strictly accountable to the debtor when he goes into possession. One way of avoiding this liability was for the creditor to request the debtor to appoint a receiver to collect the income of the property and to pay it to the mortgagee. If the debtor would not agree to do so, the creditor could apply to the court for the appointment of a receiver of the income of the property, and the court could

---

62   *Charles v Jones* (1887) 35 Ch D 544.

(at least in the case of an equitable mortgage) accede to the request if the secured indebtedness was then payable. Indeed, the court could appoint a receiver even before the secured indebtedness became payable if the property was at risk.

8.106 The ability of the creditor to apply to court for the appointment of a receiver was even more important where the creditor's security consisted of a charge rather than a mortgage. In the absence of an express power of enforcement in the charge, the creditor's sole remedy was to apply to court.

8.107 In order to avoid the necessity to obtain the agreement of the debtor or the assistance of the court, it became common for security documents to give the creditor the power to appoint a receiver himself. The prevalence of this practice led to such a power being implied as a result of Lord Cranworth's Act of 1860, which was followed by the Conveyancing Act 1881. This implied power to appoint a receiver is now contained in the Law of Property Act 1925.

8.108 It is no coincidence that the person who was appointed (whether by the debtor, the creditor or the court) was described as a receiver. That was his job – to receive the income of the property. The modern idea that a receiver runs the business of a company is a later development, the impetus for which was the development of the floating charge during the second half of the nineteenth century. Where security was given over a business, rather than simply over property, the court would appoint a receiver and manager of the business whose function was not just to collect the income of the business, but to sell it; and, in order to be able to sell it as a going concern, to manage it in the meantime. In the same way that express powers to appoint a receiver of income were introduced into security documents during the early part of the nineteenth century, it soon became apparent that an express power to appoint a receiver and manager was preferable to having to apply to the court, with the potential delay and expense that involved. It therefore became the practice for debentures to contain express powers for the appointment of receivers and managers, and to give them very wide powers to manage and sell the debtor's business.

How is a receiver appointed?

8.109 It is still possible to apply to the court for the appointment of a receiver if the security document concerned does not contain an appropriate power for the creditor to do so. Historically, the jurisdiction of courts of equity to appoint receivers was normally only exercised in favour of equitable mortgagees and chargees, rather than in favour of creditors with legal mortgages. This was because the legal mortgagee was entitled to take possession or foreclose. In *Berney v Sewell*,[63] Lord Eldon LC said that a legal mortgagee was not entitled to the appointment of a receiver, because he could take possession; and that an equitable mortgagee was entitled to a receiver unless a prior mortgagee was already in possession. Where the mortgaged

---

63   (1820) 1 Jac & W 647.

assets included the goodwill of the business, the court also had the power to appoint the receiver as a manager to sell the business as a going concern.[64]

8.110 The High Court now has a very wide power to appoint a receiver under the Supreme Court Act 1981. Section 39 of that Act gives the High Court the power to appoint a receiver 'in all cases in which it appears to the court to be just and convenient to do so'. The power can be exercised either unconditionally or on such terms and conditions as the court thinks just.[65] As a result, the High Court now has the jurisdiction to appoint a receiver on the application of any mortgagee or chargee if the court considers it just and convenient to do so. Although the jurisdiction is now unlimited, and it would seem that there is no longer any restriction by reference to the nature of the security document itself (so that a legal mortgagee should have the same right as an equitable mortgagee or chargee), the discretion of the court must be exercised judicially and it is likely that the creditor will still need to establish either that the secured indebtedness has become payable or that there is some risk to the property concerned.[66]

8.111 Most receivers are, however, appointed by the creditor under powers contained in a security document, so that the court is not involved in the process. Under s 101(1)(iii) of the Law of Property Act 1925, where the mortgage or charge is made by deed the creditor has an implied power to appoint a receiver of the income of the property concerned once the secured indebtedness is payable. Section 109 elaborates on this power, and restricts its use to circumstances where the creditor is entitled to exercise his power of sale.

8.112 There is no doubt that the implied power to appoint a receiver of income extends to mortgages and charges over land. As with the implied power of sale, however, it is not clear to what extent it is also applicable to security over goods or intangibles. The part of the Act in which the power is contained is devoted to security over land, and it might therefore have been thought that it only applied to security over land. It has been seen, in part 5 of this chapter (**8.82ff**), that the power of sale has been extended to mortgages over chattels,[67] but the ability to appoint a receiver under these implied powers is sufficiently uncertain that it is preferable not to rely on it.

8.113 Fixed and floating charge debentures invariably contain express powers to appoint receivers. This is partly because the exercise of implied powers under the Law of Property Act 1925 is restricted by s 103 of that Act, partly because the implied power under the Law of Property Act 1925 is restricted to the appointment of a receiver of income and partly because of uncertainty as to the extent of the power. The debenture will therefore contain an express power to appoint a receiver and manager of the property and will include provisions concerning the powers of the receiver and manager.

---

64   *Whitley v Challis* [1892] 1 Ch 64 at 69–70, per Lindley LJ.
65   Supreme Court Act 1981, s 37(2).
66   See *Parker v Camden London Borough Council* [1986] Ch 162, for a general discussion of the courts' jurisdiction under this section.
67   *Re Morritt, ex parte Official Receiver* (1886) 18 QBD 222.

What is the receiver's status?

Receiver appointed by the court

8.114   In those comparatively rare cases where the receiver is appointed by the court, he is an officer of the court, rather than an agent of either the debtor or the creditor. The disadvantages of his being so are illustrated in *Re Newdigate Colliery*.[68] In that case, the debtor company owned a colliery and had entered into forward contracts for the sale of coal. It had created a floating charge over all of its assets, and a receiver was appointed by the court on the application of the holders of the floating charge. Shortly after his appointment, the receiver applied to the court for liberty to disregard the contracts, which would have enabled him to sell the coal on the spot market at higher prices.

8.115   If the receiver had been appointed by the creditor under a power contained in the debenture, this is exactly what he would have done. Although the debtor company was bound by the contract, the receiver would not have been and would have been at liberty to disregard them. This would have led to claims for breach of contract being provable against the company in its ultimate liquidation, but would have increased the value of the charged assets as far as the debentureholders were concerned.

8.116   The court nevertheless refused to allow their receiver to disregard the contracts. As an officer of the court, he had an obligation to act fairly between the debtor and the creditor. During the course of the argument, Buckley LJ asked counsel for the receiver the following question:[69]

> 'The Court has by its officer at the instance of the mortgagees taken charge of the mortgaged business. Ought not the Court to act as an honourable man would?',

clearly anticipating that the answer was 'Yes'. During his judgment, he went on to say:[70]

> 'It is the duty of the judge who has taken control of the assets to deal with those assets with due regard to the interests of everybody concerned, and not to advance the interests of one of the persons concerned at the expense of the other.'

Receiver appointed by the creditor

8.117   A receiver appointed by the court is therefore more constrained in his actions than he would be if he were appointed by the creditor under a power contained in the security document. By contrast, a receiver appointed by the creditor is entitled (and, indeed, would be expected) to disregard contracts which were not in the interests of the creditor. The remedy of the other

---

68   [1912] 1 Ch 468.
69   [1912] 1 Ch 468 at 469.
70   [1912] 1 Ch 468 at 478.

contracting party is to claim damages against the company, thus increasing its unsecured liabilities, but the value of the assets is thereby increased, thus benefiting the secured creditor.[71]

8.118   The status of a receiver appointed by the creditor depends on the terms of the document under which he was appointed. It will almost invariably provide that he acts as the agent of the debtor. The reason why this is so was explained by Rigby LJ in *Gaskell v Gosling*.[72] Because of the (potentially severe) liabilities which could be incurred by a mortgagee in possession, it became common for the creditor to request the debtor to appoint a receiver of the income of the property for the purpose of paying it to the creditor. It then became common for the security document itself to contain a provision enabling the creditor to appoint the receiver himself, but the receiver continued to be expressed to act as agent for the debtor. The powers of receivers were gradually extended, but the receiver continued to act as the agent of the debtor, even though appointed by the creditor. When these powers came to be implied by statute, the legislation followed suit. Section 109(2) of the Law of Property Act 1925 provides that a receiver appointed under the powers conferred by the Act 'shall be deemed to be the agent of the mortgagor; and the mortgagor shall be solely responsible for the receiver's acts or defaults unless the mortgagee otherwise provides'.

8.119   This arrangement has major advantages for the creditor. He is not himself in possession of the property, and cannot be liable as a mortgagee in possession. Nor is he liable for the acts of the receiver, who is the agent of the debtor, not of the creditor. The mortgagee will only be liable for the actions of the receiver if the security document so provides (which, in practice, it never will) or if the actions of the creditor are such that he constitutes the receiver as his agent by his conduct, for instance, by interfering to such an extent in the conduct of the receivership that the receiver is effectively acting as his agent, rather than as an independent person. It is expected that the creditor will keep a close eye on the receiver and, so long as the receiver retains the ultimate responsibility for acting, it is unlikely that the receiver will become the creditor's agent. (The creditor may, of course, have a duty to indemnify the receiver against losses. Contractual indemnities are sometimes given to receivers.)

What are the receiver's powers?

8.120   Where the receiver is appointed by the court, his powers will depend on the order under which he was appointed. He will normally have the power to collect the income of the property which is the subject of the security, and to pay the net proceeds to the creditor. If the security includes the goodwill of the business, the receiver may also be given power to carry on the business of the company with a view to its sale.

---

71   *Airlines Airspares v Handley Page* [1970] Ch 193.
72   [1896] 1 QB 669.

8.121 Where the receiver is appointed by the creditor under a security document, his powers will be set out in that document, which will normally give him very broad powers to deal with the assets which are the subject of the charge. In most cases, the receiver will be appointed under a fixed and floating charge debenture which will have created security over all of the present and future assets of the company. In such a case, the debenture will invariably give the receiver broad powers to carry on the business of the company and to sell it as a going concern. Although the company will continue to have a board of directors, the receiver will effectively take over all of their powers except to the extent of any assets which fall outside the scope of the charge.[73] This process was acknowledged in the Insolvency Act 1986 which, in Sch 1, gives receivers very wide implied powers to deal with the assets of the company where security is taken over all, or substantially all, of the company's assets.[74]

What is the effect of liquidation on the receiver's status and powers?

8.122 The position of the receiver becomes more complicated if the debtor company goes into liquidation, which it is quite likely to do during the course of the receivership. The effect of the liquidation of the debtor is also explained in the judgment of Rigby LJ in *Gaskell v Gosling*.[75] If the debtor goes into liquidation, the liquidator cannot revoke the appointment of the receiver, because he is acting as a receiver of property which has been charged to the creditor. The creditor has a proprietary interest in the assets concerned, and the receiver can therefore continue to deal with them. But the effect of the liquidation is to prevent the company from carrying on business and the receiver cannot, therefore, create debts as agent for the company which would be provable in the liquidation. The liquidation therefore halts the receiver's agency for the company. He can no longer bind the company in the sense of creating new contractual obligations by which it will be bound.

Who is liable on the receiver's contracts?

8.123 If, on liquidation, the receiver can no longer bind the debtor to new contracts, who is bound by contracts entered into by the receiver after liquidation? This question was discussed in *Gosling v Gaskell*.[76] In that case, the debtor company created a floating charge over all of its assets in favour of trustees for debentureholders. The floating charge gave the trustees power to appoint a receiver, who was expressed to act as agent for the debtor company. The trustees appointed a receiver and the company then went into compulsory liquidation. The receiver nevertheless continued to carry on business and ordered goods from a supplier. The supplier sued the trustees for payment of the price. The Court of Appeal held that the trustees were liable, although Rigby LJ gave a dissenting judgment which has been discussed above. On

---

73   *Newhart Developments v Co-operative Commercial Bank* [1978] QB 814.
74   Insolvency Act 1986, ss 29(2) and 42.
75   [1896] 1 QB 669.
76   [1896] 1 QB 669; [1897] AC 575.

appeal, the House of Lords unanimously overruled the decision of the Court of Appeal, preferring the reasoning of Rigby LJ. They assumed that, on liquidation of the debtor company, the receiver would cease to act as agent for the debtor, but they held that the mere fact that the receiver was no longer agent for the debtor did not make him agent for the creditor. The trustees were not, therefore, liable for the actions of the receiver.

8.124 If the debtor is not liable for the receiver's actions, and nor is the creditor, the obvious conclusion is that the receiver himself must be liable. This issue was adverted to in some of the judgments in *Gosling v Gaskell*, but was not decided, because it was not necessary in that case. In *Thomas v Todd*,[77] however, it did have to be decided. In that case, the debtor company had created a floating charge over all of its assets, and the debenture provided that a receiver appointed by the creditor would be the agent of the debtor. A receiver was appointed and, after the debtor company went into voluntary liquidation, the receiver entered into a contract with a supplier. The supplier claimed payment under the contract from the receiver and Wright J held that the receiver was liable. The principle that the authority of the receiver to bind the debtor ceases on compulsory liquidation also applied in a voluntary liquidation. In both cases, the company ceases to carry on its business and it is only the liquidator who can bind the company thereafter. There was no doubt, however, that a contract had been created. The debtor was not liable and therefore the receiver must himself be liable.

8.125 That appears to settle the issue but, when dealing with liability under contracts, it is unwise to assume that there are immutable rules which will apply in all circumstances – particularly because these days receivers invariably contract out of personal liability. The question of who is liable on a contract is ultimately a matter of fact, to be decided in relation to the individual circumstances of the case in question. In this context, the only immutable rule is that, after liquidation, the receiver can no longer bind the company to new contracts. The effect of contracts entered into by him thereafter depends on the intention of the parties in the light of the documents and the surrounding circumstances. But there are certain basic principles which assist in deciding who, if anyone, is liable.

8.126 First, if the receiver is expressed in the security document to act as the agent of the debtor, it is unlikely that, if the company is in liquidation, he will therefore be acting as agent for the creditor. *Gosling v Gaskell* establishes that the mere fact of the liquidation does not have this effect, and it would seem that clear evidence is needed in order to establish that a person who was previously acting as agent for the debtor has now become the agent of the creditor.

8.127 Secondly, if the receiver purports to enter into a contract after the debtor has gone into liquidation, and neither the debtor nor the creditor is liable on that contract, there are only two possibilities – first, that the receiver is liable and, secondly, that there is no contract. It is a general principle of the law of contract that the court will attempt to give effect to a purported contract, at least where made in a commercial context, and the second alternative is

---

77 [1926] 2 KB 511.

therefore unattractive. But the first also has its problems. In practice, receivers take great efforts to ensure that those dealing with them realise that they are not personally liable on the contracts that they enter into. In *Thomas v Todd*, the receiver did not do this, but, in most cases today, it will be clear to the person dealing with the receiver that the receiver is not assuming personal liability.

8.128 This creates something of a logical conundrum – there is probably a contract, but there appears to be only one party to it. The way to resolve the conundrum is to acknowledge that a contract has been entered into, and therefore there must be a way in which the person dealing with the receiver can get paid, whilst at the same time recognising that it was not intended that the receiver should be personally liable. This can be achieved by deciding that the receiver is bound by the contract, but only to the extent that there are assets available to him in the receivership to satisfy the liability. This approach has the merit of recognising that a contract has been created but also acknowledges that the person dealing with the receiver will normally realise that he is not accepting liability to the extent of putting his own assets at risk. It also has the advantage that it produces the same commercial effect before, and after, liquidation. Before liquidation, the receiver acts as agent for the company, and the person dealing with the receiver will expect to be paid from the assets in the hands of the receiver. A claim against an insolvent debtor will be of no value to him, and he will therefore expect to be paid by the receiver out of the assets in his hands. If this is the case before receivership, there is much commercial sense in applying the same principle afterwards.

8.129 That is not to say that a receiver will never be personally liable on contracts he enters into. His liability depends on the facts of the particular case concerned. But in most cases it will be clear to the person dealing with the receiver that he is not to be personally liable. To acknowledge that the person dealing with the receiver will only be paid out of the assets available to the receiver steers a path between the two extremes of there being no liability by anyone (which the court is unlikely to countenance) and the receiver being liable to the full extent of his individual personal assets (which, in most cases, will clearly not be the intention of the parties).

What are the receiver's powers of sale?

8.130 It has been seen how the liquidation of the debtor affects liability on contracts made by the receiver. But how does it affect his authority to deal with the assets which are the subject of the security? This issue had to be resolved in *Sowman v David Samuel Trust*.[78] The debtor had created a floating charge in favour of a creditor. It contained the usual power to appoint a receiver, who would act as the debtor's agent. The creditor appointed a receiver, and the debtor then went into liquidation. The receiver contracted to sell land which was charged under the debenture, but the Land Registry questioned his ability to do so. The problem was expressed in the following way by Goulding J:

---

78   [1978] 1 WLR 22.

- The debenture provided, as usual, that the receiver would act as agent for the debtor.
- Any sale by the receiver was therefore as agent for the debtor.
- The liquidation of the debtor determined the receiver's agency.
- How, then, could the receiver exercise his power of sale after liquidation?

8.131 Goulding J held that the receiver continued to have the power to sell the debtor's land after liquidation. Having considered the judgment of Rigby LJ in *Gosling v Gaskell*, he said:[79]

'Winding up deprives the receiver ... of power to bind the company personally by acting as its agent. It does not in the least affect his powers to hold and dispose of the company's property comprised in the debenture, including his power to use the company's name for that purpose, for such powers are given by the disposition of the company's property which it made (in equity) by the debenture itself. That disposition is binding on the company and on those claiming through it, as well in liquidation as before liquidation ...'

8.132 This conclusion follows from the nature of a security interest. The debenture creates a proprietary interest in favour of the secured creditor. In a liquidation of the debtor, the secured creditor is therefore entitled to remove the assets charged to him and to deal with them without reference to the liquidation. If he can do this, then so can a receiver. Although, for the purpose of creating new contracts, the receiver acts as agent for the company before liquidation, when dealing with the assets which are the subject of the charge the receiver does not need to rely on any agency, but simply on the fact that he is enforcing a document which, before the liquidation, created a proprietary interest in favour of the creditor.

What are the receiver's liabilities?

8.133 The potential liabilities of a receiver are considered in part 8 of this chapter (**8.173ff**).

Limitations on administrative receivership

8.134 When it reported on insolvency law in 1982, the Cork Committee[80] described receivership (justifiably, if perhaps with a little hyperbole) as being 'of outstanding benefit to the general public and to society as a whole'.[81] Twenty years later, receivership was all but abolished by the Enterprise Act 2002. It is the purpose of this section to consider how this came about and what its practical implications are likely to be.

---

79 [1978] 1 WLR 22 at 30.
80 *Insolvency Law and Practice*: Report of the Review Committee, Cmnd 8558 (1982).
81 *Insolvency Law and Practice*: Report of the Review Committee, Cmnd 8558 (1982) para 495.

Why has administrative receivership been restricted?

8.135 Until recently, receivership has been by far the most popular method of enforcing security granted by companies over their businesses. The reason for its popularity with secured creditors has already been explained. But, for this purpose, what is more important is that the popularity of receivership led to a change in the way that insolvency law was structured. Until 1986, liquidation was the only formal insolvency procedure available in respect of companies. But in practice, where a company had created a fixed and floating charge debenture over its assets, it was more likely to go into receivership, rather than liquidation. The benefit of a receivership over a liquidation was that the receiver was able to continue to run the business of the company with a view to selling the profitable parts as a going concern. This had two material advantages: first, the likelihood of increased returns for creditors (primarily the secured creditor which had appointed the receiver) because the value of the business as a going concern was often likely to be greater than the value of its individual parts on a break-up basis; and, secondly, because the result was often to preserve the company's business (or at least the profitable parts of that business) for the benefit of its employees, customers, suppliers and the economy generally.

8.136 From the point of view of insolvency law, however, receivership suffered from one major disadvantage – it was only available where the company had created security over its assets. It was this which led the Cork Committee to recommend a new insolvency procedure – administration – which was brought into law by the Insolvency Act 1986. Its purpose was to enable the benefits of receivership to become available to companies which had not created security over their assets. Where the company had created security over all, or substantially all, of its assets in favour of a creditor, that creditor could appoint a receiver (from now on known as an 'administrative receiver') to enforce the security. Where the company had not created such security, or where an administrative receiver was not appointed, the company or a creditor could request the court to appoint an administrator. The receiver and the administrator had broadly the same powers. Their role was, essentially, to continue the (profitable parts of) the company's business with a view to a sale as a going concern. The main difference between the role of the administrative receiver and that of the administrator was the identity of the person to whom proceeds were paid – the secured creditor in the case of an administrative receivership, creditors generally in the case of an administration.

8.137 This duality of procedure reflected the underlying commercial realities. Where all or most of the company's assets were charged, the secured creditor had the main interest in them and was therefore able to appoint an administrative receiver to realise them. If no one had security over all or most of the company's assets, a wider class of persons was interested in the assets and the company or a creditor could therefore request the court to appoint an administrator.

8.138 Despite this, in the early 2000s, the government decided that administration was preferable to administrative receivership and that administrative receivership should be abolished. Its reasoning was muddled. It was largely based on two ideas. The first was that administration was fairer than receivership because, in an administration, it was the general creditors who got paid, whereas, in an administrative receivership, it was the secured creditor. The premise is correct, but the conclusion is wrong. The reason why the secured creditor scoops the pool in an administrative receivership is not because it is a receiver, rather than an administrator, who has been appointed, but because the creditor concerned has security over the company's assets and therefore ranks ahead of unsecured creditors.

8.139 The other reason for preferring administration to receivership was the idea that the company was more likely to be rescued in an administration than in a receivership. This was also untrue. In the vast majority of cases, the outcome of an administration is the same as a receivership – the sale of the profitable parts of the company's business as a going concern.

8.140 It was nevertheless decided that administrative receivership should be abolished, and replaced by administration. Last-minute lobbying by certain interest groups led the government to agree that there should be a number of exceptions from the prohibition on the appointment of an administrative receiver – principally in relation to major capital markets transactions and project finance transactions – the government being persuaded that, in such cases, it was important that the secured creditors should be entitled to continue to appoint an administrative receiver.

8.141 The result is unnecessary complexity. In some cases, a secured creditor can continue to appoint an administrative receiver. In others, he cannot, and is instead given the ability to appoint an administrator. The use of administration as a procedure for enforcing security is discussed in the following part of this chapter (**8.148ff**), which will also consider whether there is likely to be any material difference between administrative receivership and administration in this context. This section considers the circumstances in which an administrative receiver can continue to be appointed.

When can an administrative receiver be appointed?

8.142 The basic principle is contained in s 72A(1) of the Insolvency Act 1986, by which: 'The holder of a qualifying floating charge in respect of a company's property may not appoint an administrative receiver of the company.' A person is 'the holder of a qualifying floating charge in respect of the company's property' if:

- he has security over the whole, or substantially the whole, of the company's property;
- that security includes a floating charge; and
- the floating charge contains a power to appoint an administrative receiver or an administrator.[82]

8.143 The prohibition therefore applies in the normal case where a secured creditor takes a fixed and floating charge debenture over all of the present and

---

82   Insolvency Act 1986, s 72A(3) and Sch B1, para 14.

future assets of the debtor. It does not apply if the floating charge does not contain a power to appoint an administrator or an administrative receiver but, in practice, a floating charge is of little practical value without such a provision because it would be necessary to apply to the court for it to be enforced.

8.144 The prohibition only applies to the appointment of an administrative receiver – not to a receiver over one or more assets of the company which do not constitute the whole or substantially the whole of its assets. But the position of a non-administrative receiver is more precarious than that of an administrative receiver and, in practice, he can be removed by an administrator of the company.[83]

8.145 The prohibition on the appointment of an administrative receiver is subject to two types of qualification. The first is that it does not apply to a floating charge created before 15 September 2003 (which was the date the new legislation was brought into force).[84] The other limitation is that the prohibition does not apply to certain types of financing. They are set out in ss 72B–72H and Sch 2A to the Insolvency Act 1986. These statutory provisions are complex and, when considering whether or not a particular transaction falls within them, there is no alternative to a detailed review of them. All that can be done here is to indicate the main scope of the exceptions. They fall into four main categories – project finance, capital markets transactions, financial markets and registered social landlords:

- The first exception concerns project finance transactions. The transaction must involve a 'project' (which is not defined) and must give the secured creditor 'step-in rights' (ie rights to assume responsibility for the project independently of appointing an administrative receiver).[85] The transaction must normally involve indebtedness of at least £50 million, but this requirement does not apply to public-private partnership projects (where the resources for the project are provided partly by the public and partly by private persons) or to utility projects (projects involving regulated industries such as water, energy, telecoms and railways).[86]
- The second exception relates to capital market transactions. These require indebtedness of at least £50 million and for the arrangement to involve the use of the capital markets.[87]
- There are also specific exceptions for the financial markets[88] and for registered social landlords.[89]

8.146 Why it is considered that there is such a fundamental difference between (say) an acquisition finance transaction and a project finance transaction that they require different methods of enforcement has yet to be satisfactorily explained.

---

83   Insolvency Act 1986, Sch B1, para 41.
84   Insolvency Act 1986, s 72A(4)(a) and Insolvency Act 1986, Section 72A (Appointed Date) Order 2003, SI 2003/2095.
85   Insolvency Act 1986, s 72E and Sch 2A, paras 6 and 7; *Feetum v Cabvision* [2005] EWCA Civ 1601.
86   Insolvency Act 1986, ss 72C and 72D and Sch 2A, paras 6, 7 and 10.
87   Insolvency Act 1986, s 72B and Sch 2A, paras 1, 2 and 3.
88   Insolvency Act 1986, s 72F.
89   Insolvency Act 1986, s 72G.

8.147 If the creditor can appoint an administrative receiver, it is important for him to do so quickly if there is any possibility that an administrator might be appointed. A person who is intending to appoint an administrator must give notice to any creditor who is entitled to appoint an administrative receiver, and this gives the creditor a short period of time (normally 5 days, although in some cases it may be fewer) within which to appoint an administrative receiver. If this is done, an administrator cannot be appointed but, if the secured creditor fails to act in time, an administrator can be appointed, in which event the creditor loses the opportunity to appoint an administrative receiver.[90]

Part 7: ADMINISTRATION

8.148 The restriction on the ability of a secured creditor to appoint an administrative receiver is matched by a new power to appoint an administrator instead. As a result, the administration procedure now serves two very different purposes:

- 'Old-style' administrations continue to be available to debtors in circumstances where the company is insolvent or close to insolvency in order to try to find some means of rescuing the company or its business.
- 'New-style' administrations are a means for a creditor with security over all of the company's assets to enforce that security.

8.149 Old-style administrations are an alternative to liquidation, whereas new-style administrations are an alternative to administrative receivership. The problem with the legislation is that it has to fit two very different processes into one procedure.

8.150 As yet, there is very little authority which examines in any detail the way in which an administrator appointed by a secured creditor must act. It is beyond the scope of this chapter to consider the issue in detail but, in view of the likelihood that administration will become the most common form of enforcement of security over businesses, it is necessary to consider how it is likely to work in practice. This part considers three issues:

- Who can appoint an administrator?
- How is an administrator appointed?
- The role and duties of an administrator.

Who can appoint an administrator?

8.151 Before the Enterprise Act 2002 became law, administrators could only be appointed by the court. The new procedure enables administrators to be appointed either by filing certain documents with the court or by obtaining a court order. In practice, the former procedure is likely to be used in most cases

---

90   Insolvency Act 1986, Sch B1, paras 12, 15, 26 and 28.

because it is simpler, quicker and cheaper. A secured creditor (like any other creditor) can apply to court for an administration order to be made, but there is a special procedure which enables creditors who could previously have appointed an administrative receiver to appoint an administrator out of court, the purpose of which is to compensate them for no longer being able to appoint an administrative receiver in most cases. The debtor can also take advantage of this new expedited procedure.

8.152   A secured creditor can appoint an administrator out of court if he is 'the holder of a qualifying floating charge in respect of a company's property'. This requires that:

- he has security over the whole, or substantially the whole, of the company's property;
- the security includes a floating charge; and
- the floating charge contains a power to appoint an administrator or an administrative receiver.[91]

8.153   The floating charge must be enforceable,[92] and, if the appointment of the administrator turns out to have been invalid, the court may order the creditor to indemnify the administrator.[93]

8.154   As an alternative to an appointment out of court, a creditor (whether secured or unsecured) can apply to the court for an administration order in respect of a company.[94] It is normally a requirement of a making of an administration order that the company is, or is likely to become, unable to pay its debts[95] but, where the application is made by the holder of a qualifying floating charge in respect of the company's property, that requirement does not apply if the creditor could have appointed an administrator out of court.[96]

8.155   There are certain limitations on a company going into administration. It cannot do so if it is already in administration or in liquidation[97] or if it is in administrative receivership.[98] In addition, an administrator cannot be appointed out of court if the company is in provisional liquidation.[99]

8.156   The secured creditor is unlikely to be too concerned about the restriction on appointing an administrator if an administrative receiver is in office. As has been seen in the previous part of this chapter (**8.103ff**), administrative receivership is now only available in limited circumstances. Nor should the fact that an administrator cannot be appointed if the company is already in administration create a problem in practice. If the debtor wishes to appoint an administrator out of court, it must notify the secured creditor,

---

91   Insolvency Act 1986, Sch B1, para 14.
92   Insolvency Act 1986, Sch B1, para 16.
93   Insolvency Act 1986, Sch B1, para 21.
94   Insolvency Act 1986, Sch B1, paras 10–13.
95   Insolvency Act 1986, Sch B1, para 11(a).
96   Insolvency Act 1986, Sch B1, para 35.
97   Insolvency Act 1986, Sch B1, paras 7 and 8.
98   Insolvency Act 1986, Sch B1, paras 39 and 17.
99   Insolvency Act 1986, Sch B1, para 17.

which can then appoint its own administrator before the company's appointment takes effect.[100] If there is an application to court to appoint an administrator, the creditor must be notified and can appoint his own administrator before the court hearing[101] or can (generally) have his nominee appointed by the court.[102]

8.157 Liquidation is more of a problem. If the company is in compulsory liquidation or provisional liquidation, the secured creditor can apply to the court for an administration order (although the making of the order is discretionary).[103] But, where the company goes into voluntary liquidation, although the voluntary liquidator can apply to the court for an administration order, the secured creditor cannot force him to do so.[104] As a result, it is theoretically possible for the debtor to stymie the secured creditor's ability to appoint an administrator by passing a resolution to wind up first. Any such action by the directors of the debtor is quite likely to constitute a breach of fiduciary duty (because of the damage which it will do to the rights of creditors by preventing the company from continuing to trade), and the secured creditor might be able to persuade the voluntary liquidator to apply for an administration order where there is a reasonable prospect of saving the company's business. But it is, nevertheless, an unsatisfactory state of affairs for the secured creditor.

8.158 In summary, a secured creditor can appoint an administrator in broadly the same cases in which he could previously have appointed an administrative receiver. Where he cannot appoint the latter as a result of the new restrictions, he will be able to appoint the former. But appointing an administrator will not be as straightforward as appointing an administrative receiver in cases where the debtor is already in some form of insolvency procedure. In most cases, this should not create a material practical problem (although it will increase costs, because an application to court will normally be required) but there is a concern that the secured creditor could be left without appropriate remedy if the company were to enter into voluntary liquidation before the secured creditor appointed an administrator.

How is an administrator appointed?

8.159 It has been seen that the way in which a receiver is appointed will depend on the terms of the security document under which the appointment is made. Generally, all that will be required is the delivery of a written notice to the debtor. Conversely, the ability to appoint an administrator is given by statute and the procedure depends on the statute, not on the security document. The procedure is contained in para 18 of Sch B1 to the Insolvency Act 1986:

- The creditor must file certain documents in court, including a statutory declaration that the floating charge is enforceable (which he must

---

100 Insolvency Act 1986, Sch B1, paras 7, 22, 26 and 28.
101 Insolvency Act 1986, Sch B1, paras 7 and 12.
102 Insolvency Act 1986, Sch B1, para 36.
103 Insolvency Act 1986, Sch B1, paras 8, 17 and 37.
104 Insolvency Act 1986, Sch B1, paras 8 and 38.

reasonably believe to be true – and he may have to indemnify the administrator against an invalid appointment[105]).

- The intended administrator must confirm that, in his opinion, the purpose of the administration is reasonably likely to be achieved.
- Where there is a prior secured creditor with a floating charge, a period of notice must be given to that person unless his consent is obtained.[106]
- In the unlikely event that an application is made to the court for an appointment of administrator, the procedure will necessarily be more complex.[107]

8.160 In practice, the procedure for the appointment of an administrator is unlikely to be significantly more onerous than that for the appointment of an administrative receiver.

The role and duties of an administrator

8.161 The purpose of an administration and the duties of an administrator are set out in paras 3–5 of Sch B1 to the Insolvency Act 1986. They are particularly important, and need to be set out in full:

'**3**(1) the administrator of a company must perform his functions with the objective of—
  (a) rescuing the company as a going concern, or
  (b) achieving a better result for the company's creditors as a whole than would be likely if the company were wound up (without first being in administration), or
  (c) realising property in order to make a distribution to one or more secured or preferential creditors.

(2) Subject to sub-paragraph (4), the administrator of a company must perform his functions in the interests of the company's creditors as a whole.

(3) The administrator must perform his functions with the objective specified in sub-paragraph (1)(a) unless he thinks either—
  (a) that it is not reasonably practicable to achieve that objective, or
  (b) that the objective specified in sub-paragraph (1)(b) would achieve a better result for the company's creditors as a whole.

(4) The administrator may perform his functions with the objectives specified in sub-paragraph (1)(c) only if—
  (a) he thinks that it is not reasonably practicable to achieve either of the objectives specified in sub-paragraph (1)(a) and (b), and
  (b) he does not unnecessarily harm the interests of the creditors of the company as a whole.

4 The administrator of a company must perform his functions as quickly and efficiently as is reasonably practicable.

---

105 Insolvency Act 1986, Sch B1, para 21.
106 Insolvency Act 1986, Sch B1, para 15.
107 Insolvency Act 1986, Sch B1, paras 10–13.

5 An administrator is an officer of the court (whether or not he is appointed by the court).'

8.162 The objective is clear. The administrator has three levels of duty. Initially, his duty is to rescue the company as a corporate entity in the interests of all of its creditors. If he cannot do that, his duty is to achieve a better result than a liquidation which, in practice, will mean to continue the company's business and to sell it as a going concern for the benefit of those creditors entitled to the proceeds of sale. Finally, if even that is not achievable, his duty is to sell the assets on a break-up basis for the best price he can get for them for the benefit of those creditors entitled to the proceeds.

8.163 This sounds straightforward, but these provisions leave a number of important questions unanswered. The first is how long an administrator will be expected to try to save the company as a corporate entity. In practice, if there was any real possibility of saving the company, it would have happened before the company went into administration. Other than in very exceptional circumstances, *companies* which go into administration are not saved. The benefit of administration is that some or all of the company's *business* can be saved (by selling it as a going concern to a third party), but it is very rare for the company itself to survive. The administrator will carry on the business for a period, sell it for the best price he can obtain and distribute the proceeds to those creditors who are entitled. In practice, therefore, it is likely to take the administrator very little time to decide that he cannot achieve the primary objective.

8.164 The second question concerns the speed at which the administrator will be able to operate. He has very broad powers to do anything necessary or expedient for the management of the company's affairs, business and property.[108] He also now has the power to make distributions to creditors (although distributions to unsecured creditors require court approval).[109] He also has the benefit of a moratorium on creditor action (including action by secured creditors).[110] But these broad powers are accompanied by a duty to obtain the views of creditors; and this could create the potential for a conflict. The administrator must make a statement of the proposals for achieving the purpose of the administration,[111] send them to the creditors, convene a meeting of creditors and then exercise his powers in accordance with any proposals approved at a creditors meeting.[112] It would seem that creditors can only vote to the extent that they are unsecured.[113]

8.165 A creditors meeting is not required if the administrator thinks there is no money for unsecured creditors or he cannot rescue the company as a going

---

108 Insolvency Act 1986, Sch B1, paras 59–64 and 66.
109 Insolvency Act 1986, Sch B1, para 65.
110 Insolvency Act 1986, Sch B1, paras 43 and 44.
111 Insolvency Act 1986, Sch B1, para 49.
112 Insolvency Act 1986, Sch B1, para 68.
113 Insolvency Act 1986, Sch B1, para 50(3) and Insolvency Rules 1986, SI 1985/1925, r 2.24.

concern or achieve a better realisation than on a liquidation, but creditors representing 10 per cent of unsecured liabilities can require one to be held.[114]

8.166 The administrator is required to perform his functions as quickly and as efficiently as is reasonably practicable,[115] and it is normally imperative for him to make decisions quickly. He will quite likely trade at a loss, and will have limited funding. It is, therefore, inevitable that he will need to sell the business quickly in the interests of creditors. This sits uneasily with the idea that the administrator will make proposals to creditors, which they will then vote on, particularly where the vote is taken of unsecured creditors who may have no real economic interest in the outcome. In many cases, by the time that has happened, the opportunity to sell the company's business at the best price will have gone.

8.167 The administrator clearly has the power to sell before the creditors meeting has been held. In practice, an administrator is likely to carry the major creditors with him by informal discussions, rather than to delay the sale until the creditors meeting has been held. In most cases, only by doing so will he be able to maximise value for creditors.

8.168 The third question concerns the administrator's duties. An administrator is an officer of the court, even if he is not appointed by the court.[116] It has been seen, in part 6 of this chapter (**8.103**ff), that, because a court-appointed receiver is an officer of the court, he cannot simply procure that the company breaches its contracts because that would be of benefit to the secured creditor.[117] A receiver appointed out of court is in a very different position. He can (and will be expected to) maximise value for the secured creditor by procuring that the company breaches contracts. There is some first instance authority for the proposition that an administrator, as an officer of the court, is under a similar limitation to a court-appointed receiver,[118] although it is impossible to establish from the cases either the conceptual basis for the limitation or the extent of its application. It is possible that similar limitations might be imposed on an administrator appointed by a secured creditor.

8.169 This could have very serious consequences for two reasons. In the first place, the vagueness of the judgments in the cases produces a great deal of uncertainty about the circumstances in which an administrator might have a duty to procure that the company complies with a pre-existing contract. Secondly, and equally importantly, the suggestion that an administrator must procure that the company complies with contracts entered into before the administration runs totally contrary to the basic principle of insolvency law that a creditor with a proprietary interest (such as a secured creditor) can continue to enforce his rights in the debtor's insolvency, but that a creditor with only personal contractual rights cannot force the company to perform them

---

114 Insolvency Act 1986, Sch B1, para 52.
115 Insolvency Act 1986, Sch B1, para 4.
116 Insolvency Act 1986, Sch B1, para 5.
117 *Re Newdigate Colliery* [1912] 1 Ch 468.
118 *Astor Chemical v Synthetic Technology* [1990] BCC 97; *Land Rover Group v UPF (UK)* [2003] 2 BCLC 222.

and must be content with a claim for damages which can be proved in the insolvency. To suggest that an administrator has to procure that an insolvent company complies with its personal (as opposed to proprietary) obligations cuts across that clear principle.

8.170 In summary, the powers and duties of an administrator appointed by a secured creditor can be described as follows:

- The administrator has very broad powers to deal with the company's assets.
- The primary duty of the administrator is to save the company as a corporate entity but, in practice, this is hardly ever likely to be achievable.
- In practice, the main duty of an administrator will be to achieve a better realisation than on a liquidation, by continuing the (profitable parts of) the company's business and selling it as a going concern.
- Although the administrator has a duty to convene a meeting of creditors, the need to act quickly in the interests of creditors is likely to mean that he will need to sell the company's business before the creditors meeting is held.
- The extent to which an administrator, as an officer of the court, has an obligation to procure that the company continues some pre-existing contracts is unclear. In principle, he should be free to continue, or not to continue, contracts depending on his assessment of the best outcome for those creditors who are entitled to the proceeds of sale of the business.

8.171 The final question is whether there will be any material difference between an administrative receivership and an administration where the appointment is made by a secured creditor. It would be surprising if there were. They both perform the same function. They both control a fund for the benefit of other persons. The duties which they owe those persons must depend on the extent of their interests in the fund. It cannot make any difference if the person in control of the fund is called an administrator, rather than a receiver. His primary duty will be to the person with the main interest in the fund, but his duties will extend to others if they have a real interest in it.

8.172 If a secured creditor has security over all of the company's assets, the duties of the person in control of the assets (whether he is called a receiver or an administrator) will primarily be to serve the interests of that secured creditor. It is only if there is a likelihood of recovery by unsecured creditors that their interests become relevant. If there is, the administrator will owe them duties. But so does a receiver, albeit indirectly. If there are potential surplus assets, the receiver owes duties to those entitled to the surplus. What is important is not the procedure, or the title of the person in control of the fund, but the substantive rights of those interested in the fund. Those substantive rights are not altered by the Enterprise Act 2002 and therefore the essential qualities of the duties owed by the person in control of the fund should not alter as a result of the change in procedure.

Part 8: LIABILITIES OF THE CREDITOR, RECEIVER AND ADMINISTRATOR

8.173 For the same reason that security cannot properly be understood without an understanding of how it is enforced, a creditor who is proposing to take security needs to understand the nature of the liabilities which can be incurred on enforcement, and how they can be avoided. This is self-evidently the case where the creditor himself can incur the liability, but it is also important where the liability can be incurred by others, such as receivers, not least because the effectiveness of the enforcement system depends on there being a body of insolvency accountants prepared to take on such appointments.

8.174 It is beyond the scope of this chapter to consider all the potential liabilities which they face. There is, however, one issue which has been particularly important in practice and which has provoked a wide diversity of judicial views. What is the standard of responsibility of a creditor, a receiver or an administrator when enforcing security?

8.175 The issue does not arise in all types of case. Where the enforcement is effected by the court, for instance on a judicial sale, the responsibility for the enforcement is taken by the court, and there is therefore no room for the debtor to complain of misconduct. It is common, for example, for ship mortgages to be enforced by arresting the vessel and procuring a judicial sale.

8.176 The problem arises when the creditor, a receiver or an administrator enforces the security, either by going into possession or by selling the property concerned. In such cases, his actions (or inactions) can materially affect the financial position of the debtor, and, indeed, that of subsequent mortgagees. For this reason, the courts have always recognised that the creditor and a receiver owe duties to the debtor and to subsequent mortgagees; and there is no doubt that administrators will owe similar duties. The problem has been to establish the precise extent of those duties. The approach of the courts has not been consistent. One of the problems has been a perceived distinction between the approach of the equity judges and that of the common law judges. These distinctions are often more apparent than actual, but it is true to say that there has been a tendency for common law concepts, particularly the imposition of a duty of care in negligence, to subsume some equitable concepts, although there has undoubtedly been a fight-back by equity judges, first in Australia and later in England.

8.177 It has been seen that, apart from foreclosure (where the issue does not arise), the initial principal remedy of a legal mortgagee was to take possession of the mortgaged property, and it is in this context that the duties of the mortgagee to the debtor were first worked out. When powers of sale became more common in mortgages in the nineteenth century, the issue then shifted to the scope of the responsibility of the mortgagee when exercising his power of sale, and this is a question which has exercised the courts from the end of the nineteenth century until the present day.

8.178 From the late nineteenth century until very recently, the growth of receivership as the enforcement procedure of choice in most commercial transactions has resulted in another shift of emphasis – from the responsibilities of mortgagees to those of receivers. A receiver will normally run the business of the debtor company, as well as eventually selling it. The courts have had to grapple with the question of the extent to which the receiver is in the same position as a mortgagee, or whether his role requires a different standard of care. The restriction of administrative receivership in the Enterprise Act 2002 will require the courts to consider whether administrators (who will take over from administrative receivers) will be in any different position from receivers when enforcing security.

8.179 The next four sections will therefore consider, first, the duty of a mortgagee in possession; secondly, the duty of a mortgagee when exercising his power of sale; thirdly, the duties of a receiver in those circumstances; and, finally, the duties of an administrator in those circumstances.

Duty of mortgagee in possession

8.180 It was seen in part 4 of this chapter (**8.66**ff) that, when a mortgagee went into possession, he became the owner of the income of the property. He was only under a duty to account to the debtor when he brought an action against the debtor for foreclosure or the debtor brought an action against him for redemption. But, in those circumstances, the creditor was liable not only for what he actually received, but also for what he might without wilful default have received.

8.181 Although this test has constantly been reiterated by the courts, the precise nature of the duty has fluctuated from case to case. A typical example of the approach of the equity courts in relation to the duty of a mortgagee of land is given by Lord Erskine LC in *Hughes v Williams*:[119]

> 'I do not mean to say, that, to charge a mortgagee in possession, actual fraud is necessary. It is sufficient, if there is plain, obvious, and gross negligence, by not making use of facts within his knowledge: so as to give the mortgagor the full benefit, that the mortgagee, in possession of the estate of the mortgagor ought to give him.'

He went on to say[120] that the mortgagee 'is not bound to engage in adventures and speculations for the benefit of the mortgagor; but is liable only for wilful default'.

8.182 This requirement of 'plain, obvious, and gross negligence' could, nevertheless, amount to little more in practice than simple negligence. In *Williams v Price*,[121] T owed a debt to D, on which D obtained judgment. D owed money to C, and assigned the judgment debt to C by way of security. D alleged that C had failed to execute the judgment properly and expeditiously, with the effect that he could no longer do so because T was insolvent. Sir John Leach V-C assigned the case to a Master to take an account, saying that C, having taken possession of the judgment debt, was chargeable 'not only with what he actually receives, but with what he might have received but for his wilful default or neglect'.[122]

---

119 (1806) 12 Ves Jun 493 at 494.
120 (1806) 12 Ves Jun 493 at 496.
121 (1824) 1 Sim & St 581.
122 (1824) 1 Sim & St at 587.

8.183   It may not be entirely coincidental that this latter case involved security over an intangible, rather than over land. It is certainly the case that, where goods are concerned, the courts have tended to be more willing to set standards by reference to simple negligence than they have in relation to land. In *Johnson v Diprose*,[123] for instance, D gave C a security bill of sale over certain goods. On default by D, C seized the goods, and they were damaged when being removed from D's premises as a result of the negligence of C's employees. The case concerned a claim for wrongful interference with the goods but, in the course of the discussion of that issue, the Court of Appeal had no doubt that D could redeem the goods on payment of the amount of the secured indebtedness less an amount equal to the loss suffered by D as a result of C's negligent dealing with the goods.

8.184   It is therefore not a straightforward matter to describe the duty of the mortgagee in possession. Two trends are discernible. First, the courts have been less willing to introduce the concept of simple negligence in cases involving land (traditionally the province of equity judges) than they have where goods are involved (which are more frequently dealt with by common law judges). And secondly, the later cases tend to place more reliance on the requirement for simple negligence than the earlier cases. This is only to be expected in the context of the growth of the tort of negligence in the twentieth century.

8.185   Recent cases on the issue are few, not least because of the reluctance of mortgagees to enter into possession when there is the alternative of receivership. But the issue is an important one, not least because the approach which the courts take to a mortgagee in possession must have a bearing on the similar issue of the extent of the liability of a receiver. Any conclusion in this area must be tentative but it is suggested that a mortgagee would now be liable for simple negligence, not least because the flexibility of the concept of negligence means that the standard of care required varies depending on the circumstances. The ultimate test is what it is reasonable for the particular person concerned to have done in the particular circumstances.

8.186   Indeed, as the Court of Appeal made clear in *Bompas v King*,[124] the nature of the security and the terms of the document are also crucial in determining what the mortgagee is entitled to do, and the extent of his potential liability. Security documents normally contain provisions under which the secured creditor contracts out of liability for his actions (or inaction), and they frequently make specific reference to contracting out of the duty of a mortgagee in possession. But the well-known difficulty of contracting out of liability for negligence means that the effect of such provisions is not always clear-cut. Contracting out of these duties is considered further in part 9 of this chapter (**8.221**ff).

Duty of mortgagee on sale

8.187   It has been seen that the insertion of an express power of sale in security documents became common during the nineteenth century. There were

---

123   [1893] 1 QB 512.
124   (1886) 33 Ch D 279.

a number of conflicting statements made by judges during the nineteenth century concerning the extent of the creditor's duty on sale, but an authoritative decision of the Court of Appeal in 1888 appeared to have settled the position. In *Farrar v Farrars*,[125] the debtor mortgaged property to three individual creditors. The creditors went into possession and, having been unable to sell the property elsewhere, sold it to a company in which one of them was interested. The debtor tried to get the sale set aside, but failed.

8.188 The judgments of Chitty J at first instance and of Lindley LJ, giving the judgment of the Court of Appeal, contain clear statements about the scope of the creditor's duty when selling the mortgaged property:

- The creditor, when exercising his power of sale, is not a trustee of the power. It is part of his security, and he can therefore exercise it in his own interests. He is not exercising it on behalf of the debtor.

- The creditor can sell the property when he wants to do so, the debtor having no right to require the creditor to wait for better times before selling. The creditor has the right to have his debt repaid in accordance with the terms of the bargain between the debtor and the creditor, and without regard to the then existing conditions of the market. The creditor does not have to run the risk of postponing the sale.

- But when the creditor does sell, he must act fairly and in good faith, and must take reasonable steps to obtain a proper price.

- The creditor cannot sell the property to himself, either alone or with others, or to a trustee for himself or to someone employed by him in the conduct of the sale. Chitty J regarded such a case as being one where there could be no independent bargain between the parties, although Lindley LJ saw it as being a case where, in reality, there was no sale at all, the power of sale not having been properly exercised. Whichever is the true reason for the principle, it is clear that, where there is such a sale, the court will set it aside regardless of the good faith of the parties or the sufficiency of the price.

- The last principle does not apply where the creditor sells to a company formed by him, or in which he has an interest. Not only is the company a separate legal entity, but it is beneficially entitled to its assets, its shareholders having no beneficial interest in them. Such a sale is, therefore, permissible provided that there is real, honest and independent bargaining between the parties and it can be shown that the creditor's interest in the company did not affect the terms of the sale. In short, in such a case, it is up to the creditor and the purchasing company to show that the transaction was entered into in good faith, that there was a real and independent bargain, and that a proper price was paid.

8.189 Chitty J found as a fact that there was an honest and independent bargain between the creditors and the purchasing company and that the sale should not, therefore, be set aside. His decision was affirmed by the Court of Appeal. Notwithstanding its suspicious appearance, the purchasing company had proved that the transaction was thoroughly honest and fair.

---

125 (1888) 40 Ch D 395.

8.190   That analysis of the responsibility of a creditor when exercising his power of sale is as correct today as it was when it was first formulated. Careless statements in later cases, however, have meant that a degree of uncertainty was introduced concerning the accuracy of the analysis in the *Farrar* case. It was not until the 1970s that the analysis was finally confirmed in England. In Australia, there is still some doubt about the precise responsibility of a creditor in such a case.

8.191   The problem was caused by statements of the members of the Court of Appeal and the House of Lords in *Kennedy v De Trafford*.[126] The facts of that case are relatively unimportant, but various statements, none of which was necessary for the decision in the case, have cast a shadow over all subsequent discussions of the liability of a creditor when selling. On the facts of the case, the creditors, when selling, had acted in a proper and businesslike manner and the sale was not set aside. But, commenting on the decision in the *Farrar* case, Lindley LJ, in the Court of Appeal, said that a creditor, when selling, can look after his own interests first, but not solely, but cannot fraudulently or wilfully or recklessly sacrifice the property of the debtor. In the House of Lords, Lord Herschell said that, if the creditor exercises his power of sale in good faith, without any intention of dealing unfairly with the debtor, it would be very difficult indeed, if not impossible, to establish a breach of duty to the debtor. He indicated that it would be very difficult to define exhaustively all that would be included in the words 'good faith'; and he went on to say that, if the creditor must take reasonable precautions in the exercise of his power of sale, he had done so on the facts of the case. Lord Macnaghten agreed with Lord Herschell that, when exercising the power of sale, the creditor need only act in good faith.

8.192   It seems clear from the discussion in *Kennedy v De Trafford* that the creditor had complied with the requirements laid down in the *Farrar* case, but there is no doubt that the statements of Lindley LJ in the Court of Appeal and of Lords Herschell and Macnaghten in the House of Lords created doubt as to one of those requirements – the creditor's duty to ensure that, when he does sell, he takes reasonable steps to obtain a proper price.

8.193   The uncertainty which this created can be illustrated by two cases, decided at around the same time, which approached the question in very different ways. In *McHugh v Union Bank of Canada*,[127] the Privy Council (on appeal from Canada) had to consider the basis on which an account should be taken between the debtor and the creditor. They saw no difficulty in allowing the debtor an amount for the loss suffered by him as a result of the negligence of the creditor when preparing for a sale of the property. The debtor was entitled to assume that the creditor would obtain a fair value for the property sold. This seems to have been accepted by all sides. It was certainly not argued in the Privy Council, although it may be significant that the property concerned consisted of goods, rather than land. It has been seen, in the cases concerning

---

126   [1896] 1 Ch 762; [1897] AC 180.
127   [1913] AC 299.

the responsibility of a mortgagee in possession, that the courts have tended to be more willing to accept a standard of care based on negligence when dealing with goods.

8.194 By contrast, the High Court of Australia in *Pendlebury v The Colonial Mutual Life Assurance Society*[128] took a very different view, at about the same time, of the responsibility of the creditor when selling. Although Barton J accepted that the creditor had a duty to take reasonable precautions to obtain a fair price for the property sold, the other members of the court, Griffith CJ and Isaacs J, saw the test in terms of a subjective duty of good faith, rather than an objective obligation to take reasonable care to obtain a fair price at the time the sale was conducted.

8.195 There are two significant features of the decision in the *Pendlebury* case. In the first place, the court did set aside the sale by the creditor, on the basis that the creditor had disregarded the debtor's interests by not advertising the sale properly and therefore not taking proper steps to obtain a fair price. The result, therefore, would have been the same whichever test had been adopted.

8.196 The other interesting feature of the case is the reason why the majority of the court were not prepared to accept that there was an objective duty of care in carrying out the sale. Their concern was that to impose such a general duty of care might require the creditor to delay the sale if the market was inauspicious. But in the *Farrar* case, it was not suggested that the creditor owed a general duty of care in relation to the timing of the sale. It was made clear, in that case, that the power of sale could be exercised by the creditor in his own interests, when he wanted to do so, and that the duty of care only related to obtaining the proper price at the time the sale actually took place. The judgments of the majority in the *Pendlebury* case are perfectly consistent with this approach.

8.197 The approach in the *Farrar* case was affirmed by the Court of Appeal in *Cuckmere Brick Company v Mutual Finance*,[129] which has now become the leading English case on the subject. D owned land with planning permission for 100 flats. It was charged to C. D later obtained planning permission for 35 houses. Before the development of the land had commenced, C went into possession and auctioned the land. The advertisements for the auction mentioned the later planning permission (for the 35 houses) but failed to mention the earlier planning permission (for the 100 flats). D notified C of this omission and asked for the auction to be delayed, but C nevertheless went ahead and the land was sold. D claimed an accounting with the creditor on the basis of the true value of the property.

8.198 Plowman J decided that the failure to advertise properly was a breach of duty by C, and ordered an accounting based on the real value of the property. The Court of Appeal varied the form of the order, but agreed with the substance of it. They decided that:

---

128 (1912) 13 CLR 676.
129 [1971] Ch 949.

- C owed a duty to take reasonable care to obtain a proper price or the market value of the property; and
- (by a majority) on the facts, C was in breach of that duty.

8.199 The Court of Appeal recognised the ambiguity of the creditor's position when selling. He is acting in his own interests, but does owe responsibilities to the debtor. All three members of the Court of Appeal regarded the statements of Lord Herschell and Lord Macnaghten in *Kennedy v De Trafford* as being unnecessary for the decision in that case and as therefore not weakening the earlier cases, such as the *Farrar* case. The liability of the creditor was reaffirmed in very much the same terms as it had been stated in the *Farrar* case. A creditor is not a trustee of the power of sale. The creditor can exercise it for his own purposes whenever he chooses to do so even if the time is not propitious and the market is likely to improve. He can give preference to his own interests over those of the debtor but he must act in good faith and he must take reasonable care to obtain the proper price for the land (or what Salmon LJ described as the 'true market value') when he decides to sell.

8.200 The *Cuckmere Brick* case has been strongly criticised, particularly in Australia, for having laid down a duty of care in relation to sales by mortgagees. These criticisms frequently stem from the belief that the *Cuckmere Brick* case introduces a common law liability in negligence into a relationship which had previously been the responsibility of courts of equity. Salmon LJ referred to the 'neighbour' principle in *Donoghue v Stephenson*[130] as a justification for imposing a duty of care. He considered the debtor and creditor to be 'neighbours' in the sense that actions by the creditor in relation to the debtor's property could clearly damage the debtor. A number of the Australian commentators consider that this approach is wrong in principle, and that the courts should be looking, not to common law concepts of negligence, but to the way in which courts of equity approach the issue – by reference to concepts of good faith, rather than negligence.

8.201 There is something in this criticism, and the Privy Council, in *Downsview Nominees v First City Corporation*[131] and the Court of Appeal, in *Parker-Tweedale v Dunbar Bank*,[132] have made it clear that the common law concept of negligence has not subsumed all of the earlier equity jurisprudence. But that is only part of the story. As Cross LJ indicated in the *Cuckmere Brick* case, the courts of equity impose a duty of care on mortgagees in possession, and it would be curious if that duty were to cease at the moment of sale. Indeed, in the *Farrar* case, experienced equity judges had no difficulty in accepting the imposition of a duty to take care to obtain the proper price for the property concerned when it was actually sold. To assume that the courts of equity would not impose a duty of care in an appropriate case, and would only act if there had been bad faith, is simply not the case. The correct position is well summarised by Richmond J in the New Zealand Court of Appeal in *Alexandre v New Zealand Breweries*,[133] when he said:[134]

---

130 [1932] AC 562.
131 [1993] AC 295.
132 [1991] Ch 12.
133 [1974] 1 NZLR 497.

'... [w]hether in any particular case there has been a breach of that duty should I think be judged in a realistic way and with ample regard to the fact that a power of sale is given to a mortgagee to enable him to obtain repayment of his advance.'

8.202 The test of the creditor's duty when selling the charged asset, which was established in the *Farrar* case, has now been confirmed, at least in England, as the guiding principle. The other issue which the *Farrar* case dealt with – the responsibility of a creditor when he sells to a company in which he has an interest – has also been followed, in this case by the Privy Council in *Tse Kwong Lam v Wong Chit Sen*.[135] The creditor sold the mortgaged property to a company in which he was the principal mover. The sale was effected by auction, the reserve set by the creditor was equal to the price which his company had decided to pay for it, and that company was the only bidder.

8.203 The Privy Council confirmed that, where the seller and buyer are connected, the onus of proof shifts to the creditor and the purchasing company to prove that the transaction had been entered into in good faith and that the creditor had taken reasonable precautions to get the best price reasonably obtainable at the time. Lord Templeman, delivering the opinion of the Privy Council, made it clear that, in such a case, the circumstances surrounding the sale would be closely examined by the court and that there was a heavy onus on the creditor to show that the sale was proper.

8.204 On the facts of the case, it was decided that the creditor had not taken sufficient precautions to obtain the best price at the time of sale. In such circumstances, the court would normally set aside the sale but it was not prepared to do so in this case because of the extreme delay of the debtor in bringing the proceedings. In the account between the debtor and the creditor, it therefore allowed the debtor the true market value of the property at the time of the sale, rather than the price actually paid by the purchasing company.

8.205 The creditor's duty on a sale is therefore twofold – to act in good faith and to take reasonable steps to obtain the proper price for the property concerned. Security documents frequently purport to absolve creditors from liability when exercising their powers but, in practice, it is very difficult for a creditor to contract out of these two duties. It is, in practice, almost impossible to contract out of a duty of good faith, and similar considerations apply to a duty to take reasonable care. In *Bishop v Bonham*,[136] the security document contained a standard provision by which the creditor was given authority to sell on such terms as he thought fit. The Court of Appeal decided that these words did not absolve the creditor from liability for negligent acts. They were only intended to give a discretion to the creditor within the ambit of the usual duty to take reasonable care. Unless the document makes it absolutely clear that the creditor is not to be liable for his own negligence, such general words will not be sufficient to contract out of that liability.

---

134 [1974] 1 NZLR 497 at 501–502.
135 [1983] 1 WLR 1349.
136 [1988] 1 WLR 742.

Duty of a receiver

8.206 In principle, and subject to one exception, the duties of a receiver when taking possession of the charged assets and selling them should be the same as those of the creditor. It would make no commercial sense for the rules to be any different. The risks to the debtor are just the same if enforcement is effected through a receiver as if the creditor has himself enforced the security.

8.207 The exception concerns the duty to account of a mortgagee in possession. It has been seen that the creditor has no general duty to account to the debtor until the creditor claims foreclosure or the debtor claims redemption. A receiver is not subject to the same procedures, but there is no reason why the basic duty of a mortgagee in possession (which is to take reasonable care in relation to the assets concerned) should not also apply to a receiver. Indeed, the standards of care imposed on a receiver may well be higher than those imposed on a creditor. Receivers are professionals, paid to do a job on behalf of creditors. The standards which a court will expect from them are likely to be greater than those which were required of an individual mortgagee going into possession of land 200 years ago.

8.208 This principle sits very uneasily with the decision of the Privy Council (on appeal from New Zealand) in *Downsview Nominees v First City Corporation*.[137] In that case, the debtor company had created two debentures over its assets. The second debentureholder appointed a receiver and the first debentureholder then followed suit, not in order to enforce the security, but simply to frustrate the receivership under the second debenture. The holder of the second debenture offered to buy out the first debentureholder for an amount equal to the secured debt, but was refused. The first debentureholder's receiver traded the business of the debtor company, and made losses. Since it was found that the receivership was instigated for improper purposes and was conducted in bad faith, it was hardly surprising that the Privy Council decided that the receiver and the first debentureholder were liable to the second debentureholder for the loss suffered as a result. A subsequent debentureholder is as much entitled to recovery for the loss suffered as a result of the improper actions of a receiver, as would be the debtor company itself.

8.209 The case is therefore authority for the proposition that a receiver will be liable to the debtor or a subsequent encumbrancer if he exercises his powers for a purpose other than to preserve and realise the creditor's security. Even though the receiver is acting as agent for the debtor, he still owes duties to the debtor and to subsequent encumbrancers. In this case, the receiver and his debentureholder were liable because the powers conferred on the receiver were not exercised in good faith for the purpose of obtaining repayment of the secured debt.

8.210 Unfortunately, the opinion of Lord Templeman also contains a number of statements, not necessary for the decision in the case, which suggest that receivers owe more limited duties than creditors who enforce the security themselves. Lord Templeman said that a general duty of care by the creditor or

---

137 [1993] AC 295.

a receiver to the debtor or a subsequent mortgagee was inconsistent with the creditor's rights, which are to receive repayment of the secured debt. If the creditor enters into possession, he is liable on the basis of wilful default. If the creditor exercises a power of sale in good faith to protect his security, he is not liable to the debtor even if he might have got more, subject only to taking reasonable steps to obtain a proper price for the property when he actually decides to sell. A receiver owes the same duty as a mortgagee on sale but, that apart, the receiver has no general duty of care in dealing with the creditor's assets. He can trade the business or close it down and sell the assets, and his actions cannot be impeached if they are taken in good faith while protecting the creditor, even though they are disadvantageous to the debtor.

8.211 As a general statement of the duties of a receiver, this is difficult to reconcile with both principle and authority. It is correct to say that the receiver is appointed primarily to protect the interests of the creditor, and that he therefore owes no general duty of care in favour of the debtor. The receiver is entitled to do things for the benefit of the creditor which do not benefit the debtor or, indeed, which positively disadvantage him. But it cannot be the case that the debtor is worse off if a receiver is appointed to enforce the security than if the creditor had done it himself. Such a distinction flies in the face of commercial logic and common sense.

8.212 The problem with the statements in the *Downsview* case is the denial of any duty, other than one of good faith, in conducting the receivership, with the one exception of obtaining market value when the property is sold. Such an approach is inconsistent with the responsibility of a mortgagee in possession. Although it has been seen that there is some doubt concerning the precise extent of that duty, on balance it is suggested that a mortgagee in possession is liable if he does not take reasonable care to deal with the assets which he has taken away from the debtor. In any particular case, it may not be an easy task to establish whether or not that duty has been complied with, but to restrict the receiver's duty to one to act in good faith, regardless of the reasonableness of his actions, is inconsistent with the courts' approach to mortgagees in possession and fails to acknowledge that receivers are professionals and should be liable if they fail to take reasonable care.

8.213 The important thing about liability in negligence is that the standard of care required depends on the circumstances of the case. A receiver is acting for the creditor, not the debtor. He has limited information when he takes over as receiver and has to act very quickly and take decisions which may, in hindsight, be incorrect. The primary object of his powers is to get the secured debt repaid. These are not reasons for denying that a duty of care exists, simply for accepting that the standard of care of a receiver has to be judged by reference to the circumstances within which he operates and the purpose for which his powers have been granted. As Richardson J said in the New Zealand Court of Appeal[138] (in a passage with which Lord Templeman disagreed), 'the extent of the receiver's duty of care must be measured in relation to the primary objective of the receivership which is to enforce the security'.

---

138 [1990] 3 NZLR 265 at 276.

8.214   Lord Templeman's statements concerning the liability of a receiver in such a case were not necessary for his decision and, it is suggested, are inconsistent both with principle and with authority. Indeed, it is significant that, at about the same time, Sir Nicholas Browne-Wilkinson V-C, in *Knight v Lawrence*,[139] had no difficulty in finding that a receiver was liable in negligence to the debtor for failing to trigger rent reviews which would have increased the value of the charged assets. The mere fact that it is difficult to establish the precise extent of the receiver's liability does not mean that such liability does not exist in an appropriate case.

8.215   The most authoritative recent decision on this point is the judgment of the Court of Appeal in *Medforth v Blake*.[140] It rejects the *Downsview* approach. The debtor claimed that the receivers had been negligent in the conduct of the receivership. The case was tried on a preliminary issue – whether or not receivers did owe a duty of care. Counsel for the receivers argued that, when carrying on the debtor's business, the receiver owes no duty to the debtor except to act in good faith. This proposition was roundly rejected by the Court of Appeal. In a thoughtful judgment, which considered the earlier cases, including the *Downsview* case, Sir Richard Scott V-C said:[141]

> 'In my judgment, in principle and on the authorities, the following propositions can be stated. (1) A receiver managing mortgaged property owes duties to the mortgagor and anyone else with an interest in the equity of redemption. (2) The duties include, but are not necessarily confined to, a duty of good faith. (3) The extent and scope of any duty additional to that of good faith will depend on the facts and circumstances of the particular case. (4) In exercising his powers of management the primary duty of the receiver is to try and bring about a situation in which interest on a secured debt can be paid and the debt itself repaid. (5) Subject to that primary duty, the receiver owes a duty to manage the property with due diligence. (6) Due diligence does not oblige the receiver to continue to carry on a business on the mortgaged premises previously carried on by the mortgagor. (7) If the receiver does carry on a business on the mortgaged premises, due diligence requires reasonable steps to be taken in order to try to do so profitably.'

8.216   In summary, a receiver does owe a duty of care to take reasonable steps to obtain the best recoveries from the receivership. This duty is primarily owed to the secured creditor concerned, because he has the most to lose from the negligence of the receiver. But the receiver also owes a duty to subsequent encumbrancers and to the debtor company itself if they can establish that the negligent actions of the receiver caused them loss (for instance, because he ought to have recovered sufficient to repay the secured creditor in full and to have provided a surplus for them). In establishing whether the receiver is in breach of duty, full account needs to be taken of the facts that he will normally need to act quickly on the basis of limited information, and that the decision to

---

139   [1993] BCLC 215.
140   [2000] Ch 86.
141   [2000] Ch 86 at 102.

continue to trade (and, if so, for how long) must be taken by the receiver in the light of his primary responsibility to repay the secured creditor as soon as practicable.

Duty of an administrator

8.217   It would be curious if the duties of an administrator appointed to enforce a debenture were any different from those of a receiver appointed to do the same thing. The duties of an administrator are discussed in part 7 of this chapter (**8.148**ff). As has been seen, he has a duty to try to save the company as a going concern although, in practice, this is very unlikely to be feasible. In most cases, his duty will be to obtain the best price he can on a sale of the company's business, and to continue to trade in the meantime for the purpose of enabling this to be done – which is exactly what a receiver has to do.

8.218   In doing so, he 'must perform his functions in the interests of the company's creditors as a whole'.[142] Is it likely that this requirement will have the effect that the duties of an administrator when enforcing security are materially different to those of a receiver? It is suggested that it will not. It has been seen that a receiver does not only owe duties to his appointing creditor. He owes duties to subsequent encumbrancers and to the debtor itself if he ought reasonably to have recovered sufficient to pay off the secured creditor. An administrator is in the same position. Both administrators and receivers control a fund for the benefit of certain persons. The duties which they owe to those persons depend on the extent of their interests in the fund.

8.219   In short, it is suggested that there will be no material difference between the duties of an administrator or of an administrative receiver appointed to enforce security.

Summary

8.220   The duties of a secured creditor, a receiver and an administrator may be summarised as follows:

- When he goes into possession of the debtor's assets, he can sell them immediately. He has no duty to delay a sale if that might realise more value. The secured creditor is entitled to have the secured debt repaid.
- If he does decide to sell the debtor's assets, he owes a duty of care to subsequent encumbrancers and the debtor to obtain the market value of the assets concerned at the time they are sold.
- Whilst he continues in possession of the debtor's assets, he owes a duty of care to subsequent encumbrancers and the debtor to act reasonably in all the circumstances.
- In essence, the courts have recognised that powers of enforcement are provided for the benefit of the secured creditor in order to enable his liability to be repaid. The creditor, receiver or administrator can therefore

---

142   Insolvency Act 1986, Sch B1, para 3(2).

exercise them in the creditor's own interests, although subject to certain safeguards to protect the interests of the debtor. In practice, this means that the creditor can enforce, or decline to enforce, his security when he wants to do so and in his own interests. Timing issues are in his control, but once the creditor, receiver or administrator has decided to exercise his powers, he must do so in a reasonable manner.

Part 9: ENFORCEMENT IN PRACTICE

8.221 Foreclosure is hardly ever used by a secured creditor in practice. Nor is the right of possession, except in the context of obtaining vacant possession before a sale. The power of sale is still important in consumer cases, but is used relatively infrequently in commercial cases. By far the most important remedy in commercial cases has been receivership. In the future, this is likely to be overtaken by administration, although receivership will still be used in some types of case.

8.222 It is crucial for the security document to contain appropriate express enforcement powers. The implied powers of enforcement are inadequate, partly because they depend on the nature of the security involved, partly because their precise extent is unclear and partly because the implied powers in the Law of Property Act 1925 are only exercisable in limited circumstances. In addition, the power to appoint an administrator under a debenture is only available if the debenture contains an appropriate power.

8.223 The security document needs to explain when and how the security can be enforced. A debenture over all of the assets of a company should contain a power to appoint an administrator or an administrative receiver. It is prudent to give the secured creditor this flexibility because it may not always be clear at the outset whether it is possible in any particular case to appoint an administrative receiver. Administration is a statutory enforcement procedure, and the powers and duties of an administrator are set out in the Insolvency Act 1986. The statute also contains implied powers of an administrative receiver, although it is common to extend these by giving authority for an administrative receiver to do anything which the debtor could have done were it not in insolvency proceedings.

8.224 Where the security document is not a debenture, it is important to tailor the enforcement powers to the type of asset which is the subject of the security. It will almost invariably be appropriate to give the secured creditor the power to appoint a receiver over the secured assets; and the receiver will need to be given extensive powers to manage and sell the assets concerned. Otherwise, the nature of the enforcement power depends on the asset concerned. If security is taken over accounts with the secured creditor, an express right of application or set-off is required. Where the security is taken over debts or contract rights, the secured creditor will need the ability to give notice to the counterparty to make payments directly to the secured creditor.

8.225   The security document will also normally contain certain protections for the secured creditor and for any administrative or other receiver. The creditor is able to rely on these provisions because he is a party to the security document. A receiver is not, but he can be given the benefit of such provisions under the Contracts (Rights of Third Parties) Act 1999. Most commercial documents exclude the application of that Act, and it is accordingly necessary to ensure that it is not excluded to the extent necessary to give the receiver the appropriate rights.

8.226   A security document will normally contain two types of protective provision. One will exclude the liability of the creditor or a receiver in respect of his actions, although this does not normally extend to liability in negligence. It is debatable how much effect such a clause is likely to have in practice, because it is unlikely that the creditor or receiver would have a liability stricter than one in negligence, but, at the very least, such a clause can clarify the extent of his liability. The other common form of provision is an indemnity by the debtor in favour of the secured creditor and receiver in respect of any liability they may suffer in relation to the enforcement otherwise than as a result of their own negligence.

Chapter 9

THE EFFECT OF INSOLVENCY

Part 1: INTRODUCTION

9.1   The reason why a creditor takes security is to protect himself against the insolvency of his debtor. There is little point in having security which is effective whilst the debtor is able to pay his debts in full but not when he cannot do so. English law recognises this and, as a general principle, the insolvency of the debtor does not affect the validity or enforceability of security. There are, however, exceptions from this principle which derive from insolvency legislation. It is the purpose of this chapter to examine those exceptions.

9.2   There are three. In the first place, insolvency legislation has for a very long time enabled security to be set aside in certain circumstances if it is taken in the period immediately before the debtor enters into insolvency proceedings. These procedures are described in this chapter as 'claw-back' procedures. Secondly, in recent years, insolvency legislation has limited a creditor's right to enforce his security during certain types of insolvency proceedings, particularly in administration. This restriction is described in this chapter as a 'moratorium'. Finally, where the debtor is insolvent, a floating chargee is postponed to certain other creditors of the debtor.

9.3   Before looking at these limitations on the rights of a secured creditor in more detail, it is first necessary to appreciate what is meant by the 'insolvency' of a debtor. The expression 'insolvency' is used in two different senses – one reflecting the factual nature of the debtor's financial condition, the other denoting a change in the debtor's legal status.

9.4   In the first sense, to say that a debtor is insolvent establishes the state of his finances. In this sense, a debtor is insolvent either if he is unable to pay his debts as they fall due or if the amount of his liabilities exceeds that of his assets. The test is the same for both companies and individuals, the debtor being insolvent if either of these tests is satisfied. The fact that a debtor is insolvent in this factual sense does not automatically affect his legal status. Nor does it necessarily require him to enter into some form of insolvency procedure.

9.5   In its other sense, insolvency signifies that the debtor is the subject of an insolvency procedure, such as liquidation, administration or bankruptcy. In this sense, the legal status of the debtor has changed. He is no longer the master of his own fortunes and normally an insolvency officer (such as a liquidator, administrator or trustee in bankruptcy) will be appointed to manage his affairs. It is normally insolvency in this sense which triggers the procedures described in this chapter.

Insolvency procedures

9.6 Where the debtor is a company, the ultimate form of insolvency procedure is liquidation. A liquidation can be either voluntary (in the sense that it is instigated by the debtor itself) or compulsory (in which event, it can be instigated by third parties and the court is involved). The purpose of a liquidation is to close down the debtor's business, sell its assets and pay the net proceeds to its creditors rateably in proportion to their debts.

9.7 Since the first Companies Act in 1862, liquidation has been the ultimate method of dealing with the affairs of an insolvent company. But it has one major drawback – the inability of the company to continue trading in liquidation. As a result, once a company has gone into liquidation, its business cannot normally be saved and its assets have to be sold on a break-up basis. If the company had a viable business, this not only prejudices creditors (who will probably receive a smaller dividend than they could have achieved if the business were sold as a going concern) but also adversely affects employees and others (such as suppliers and customers) who are relying on the continuance of the business.

9.8 Where the debtor had created a fixed and floating charge debenture over its assets, this problem was avoided by the debentureholder appointing a receiver over the company's assets, with the receiver being given the power to continue the company's business and to sell it as a going concern. If the receiver was able to sell some or all of the debtor's business as a going concern, the result was not only to increase the net proceeds available for creditors (particularly the debentureholder) but also to preserve the employment of those employees who were needed in the continuing business. Receivership is not, strictly speaking, an insolvency procedure at all. It is instituted by one creditor for his own benefit and is not a collective procedure intended to benefit all the creditors. In practice, however, it has been far more successful than liquidation in maximising recoveries for (secured) creditors and in preserving businesses and employment. Receivership is discussed in part 6 of **CHAPTER 8** **(8.103ff)**.

9.9 Receivership is only available where a creditor has security over the assets of the debtor and is prepared to enforce it. As a result, the Insolvency Act 1986 introduced a new form of insolvency procedure – administration – the purpose of which was to provide the benefits of receivership to those companies which had not created security over their assets. Initially, administration was only available by order of the court, but the Enterprise Act 2002 has now enabled an administrator to be appointed out of court simply by the debtor filing certain documents with the court.

9.10 As has been seen in part 6 of **CHAPTER 8** **(8.103ff)**, the Enterprise Act 2002 made another fundamental change to insolvency procedures – restricting the availability of administrative receivership (ie receivership over all or substantially all of the debtor's assets) and replacing it by administration. The new administration procedure is therefore available not only to the debtor, but also to a creditor which has taken a fixed and floating charge debenture over all (or substantially all) of the debtor's assets. Administration in this latter sense is discussed in part 7 of **CHAPTER 8 (8.148ff)**.

9.11 The purpose of administration is not to bury the debtor, but to save it. In that respect, it resembles a receivership rather than a liquidation. The administrator takes over the control of the debtor's affairs from its board of directors with a view to saving its business. In practice, the debtor company itself is very rarely saved, in the sense of surviving as a viable legal entity. In most cases, the business (or its profitable parts) is sold in broadly the same way as it would be sold by a receiver.

9.12 As an alternative to liquidation or administration, a debtor company can try to enter into an arrangement with its creditors which will enable it to continue trading. Such an arrangement might, for instance, involve the creditors agreeing to accept partial payment of their debts if all other creditors agree likewise. The nature of the arrangement is ultimately a matter for agreement between the company and the creditors concerned. There is no set formula. Such an arrangement can be effected under two different procedures – either by means of a scheme of arrangement under s 425 of the Companies Act 1985 or by a company voluntary arrangement under Part I of the Insolvency Act 1986. There are differences between these two procedures, but they have two features in common. In the first place, they require a percentage of the creditors concerned (broadly three-quarters) to agree to the arrangement with the debtor company. And secondly, they both have a mechanism for dissenting creditors to have the arrangement overturned. In the case of schemes of arrangement under the Companies Act 1985, this is done by requiring the court to sanction the scheme and enabling creditors to oppose it. Where there is a company voluntary arrangement under the Insolvency Act 1986, there is no requirement for a court sanction but dissenting creditors can apply to the court within a limited period after the arrangement has been effected.

9.13 The debtor company will often need a breathing space in order to put proposals to creditors without the threat of legal proceedings, and a scheme of arrangement or a company voluntary arrangement is often used in tandem with an administration because an administration carries with it a moratorium on creditors' claims. In the case of certain small companies, the Insolvency Act 2000 introduced a procedure by which the debtor company itself can obtain a moratorium on creditors' claims for a short period whilst putting proposals for a company voluntary arrangement to its creditors, although this procedure is rarely used in practice.

9.14 Where the debtor is an individual, the two main insolvency procedures are bankruptcy and individual voluntary arrangements. A bankruptcy is similar to a liquidation, in the sense that it is the ultimate form of insolvency procedure available in relation to individuals. But because bankruptcy concerns natural persons, there are differences between the bankruptcy of individuals and the liquidation of companies. In the case of a company, the ultimate effect of a liquidation is the dissolution of the debtor company, but the effect of bankruptcy on individuals is less drastic. The trustee in bankruptcy will perform equivalent functions to a liquidator by collecting in the assets of the bankrupt, selling them, and paying the net proceeds to creditors rateably in accordance with their debts. Whilst the debtor remains bankrupt, he is subject to disabilities but, after a (relatively short) period, he will obtain a discharge from his bankruptcy, the effect of which is essentially to allow him to continue a normal life, freed from the debts which were capable of being proved in the bankruptcy.

9.15 The other main insolvency procedure for individuals, the individual voluntary arrangement, is, as its name suggests, very similar to a company voluntary arrangement, the purpose of which is to try to avoid the bankruptcy of the debtor concerned.

The effect of insolvency procedures

9.16 The fact that a debtor is insolvent in a factual sense does not affect his legal status. This chapter is therefore mainly concerned with the effect of insolvency procedures on a creditor's security. There are three ways in which security can be affected. Insolvency procedures can invalidate the security or prevent its enforcement. They can also give priority to other creditors over assets which are the subject of a floating charge.

Validity

9.17 In general terms, the fact that the debtor is the subject of insolvency proceedings does not affect the validity of security previously granted by it. The whole purpose of security is to enable the creditor to be repaid if the debtor becomes insolvent. Insolvency law does, however, make provision for setting aside transactions which were entered into shortly before the insolvency proceedings started. An example is the setting aside of preferences, which has long been a part of law of bankruptcy and of company liquidation. There are now a number of such procedures, and they operate not only in bankruptcy and liquidation, but also in the administration of a company. They are considered in part 2 of this chapter (**9.23ff**).

9.18 In some respects, creditors are better off now than they used to be. For many years, the 'reputed ownership' doctrine in bankruptcy meant that certain types of security (particularly over goods) were vulnerable in a bankruptcy if the creditor had not taken possession of them. A mortgage or charge over goods was, as a result, capable of being set aside unless the creditor had taken possession. That principle never applied to companies, and was abolished in relation to individuals by the Insolvency Act 1986. In place of reputed ownership are the rules requiring the registration of mortgages and charges, which are discussed in CHAPTER 6. A charge which is registrable under the Companies Act 1985 but has not been registered is void against a liquidator or administrator of the debtor company.

Enforceability

9.19 It has been seen in CHAPTER 8 that, subject to certain constraints aimed mainly at creditors dealing with consumers, a creditor is generally entitled to enforce his security in accordance with its terms and does not require the involvement of the court to do so. In principle, the position is exactly the same if the debtor is the subject of insolvency proceedings. If a company is in liquidation, or an individual is bankrupt, the creditor does not require the consent of the liquidator or trustee in bankruptcy in order to enforce his security. The creditor has a proprietary interest in the property concerned which takes it outside the scope of the bankruptcy or liquidation. As a result, the liquidator or trustee in bankruptcy is unable to interfere with it, provided that the security has validly been created and is incapable of being set aside under the claw-back provisions described in part 2 of this chapter (**9.23ff**).

9.20   Where the debtor is a company, however, there are two circumstances in which the ability of the creditor to enforce the security is affected by insolvency procedures. The first is where the debtor company goes into administration. The second is where a moratorium is imposed because a small company is proposing to enter into a voluntary arrangement. These limitations on enforcement are considered in part 3 of this chapter (**9.79ff**).

Floating charges

9.21   It has been seen in part 5 of **CHAPTER 4** (**4.79ff**) that insolvency legislation has drawn a distinction between fixed and floating charges for certain purposes. The most important distinction is that floating chargees are postponed to certain other creditors of the debtor. In some cases, this only happens if an insolvency procedure is commenced against the debtor. In other cases, the floating chargee is postponed if the security is enforced, regardless of whether the debtor is in insolvency proceedings. These issues are discussed in part 4 of this chapter (**9.98ff**).

The structure of this chapter

9.22   The rest of this chapter is divided into the following parts:

- Part 2 (**9.23ff**) – claw-back procedures.
- Part 3 (**9.79ff**) – the moratorium on secured creditors' rights.
- Part 4 (**9.98ff**) – postponing floating charges.

Part 2: CLAW-BACK

9.23   Insolvency legislation has always catered for the setting aside of transactions which are intended to defraud creditors. The scope of these provisions has gradually been widened, and the Insolvency Act 1986 now enables the court to set aside transactions, even if they were not made with the intention of defrauding creditors, if their effect is to prejudice the debtor's general body of creditors. Prejudice can take one of two forms – either by reducing the value of the debtor's assets (for instance, a transaction at an undervalue) or by giving some creditors an advantage over the others (for instance, a preference). It is not all such transactions, however, which can be set aside on the debtor's insolvency. A transaction can only be set aside if certain criteria are satisfied, one of which is that the transaction took place during the period leading up to the insolvency proceedings. The period depends on the provision concerned. In the case of companies, it can extend up to 2 years before the debtor's liquidation or administration. In the case of individuals it can extend up to 5 years before the bankruptcy.

9.24 Where the debtor is a company, there are three principal provisions of the Insolvency Act 1986 under which such transactions are capable of being set aside. They are:

- transactions at an undervalue (s 238);
- voidable preferences (s 239); and
- floating charges (s 245).

9.25 There are equivalent provisions for individuals in respect of transactions at an undervalue (s 339) and preferences (s 340).[1] There is no equivalent for individuals of the floating charge section which applies to companies. As has been seen in **CHAPTER 4**, the provisions of the bills of sale legislation effectively prevent individuals from creating floating charges.

9.26 These provisions all apply where the debtor company has gone into liquidation or administration or the individual debtor has been made bankrupt. The Insolvency Act 1986 also contains a provision by which transactions defrauding creditors can be set aside (s 423). It applies even if the debtor is not in insolvency proceedings, but it is of much less importance in practice in commercial transactions.

9.27 The following is a summary of the effect of these provisions, but they are complex and there is no alternative to reading their precise terms.

Transactions at an undervalue

9.28 A transaction entered into by a debtor which has gone into liquidation, administration or bankruptcy can be set aside if:[2]

- it is a transaction at an undervalue (for instance, a gift or a transaction for a consideration the value of which, in monetary terms, is significantly less than the value of the consideration provided by the debtor);
- the transaction took place:
  - where the debtor is a company, within 2 years before commencement of its liquidation or administration; or
  - where the debtor is an individual, within 5 years before the commencement of his bankruptcy; and
- the debtor was insolvent at the time of the transaction, or became insolvent as a result of the transaction (although insolvency is presumed

---

1   In the case of bankruptcy, there are also provisions to allow the trustee in bankruptcy to recover excessive pension contributions: Insolvency Act 1986, ss 342A–342F.
2   Insolvency Act 1986, ss 238, 240, 339 and 341.

if the transaction is with a person connected or associated with the debtor and, where the debtor is an individual, it does not need to be proved if the transaction took place within 2 years before the commencement of bankruptcy).

9.29 Where the debtor is a company, there is a defence if it can be shown that:

- the debtor entered into the transaction in good faith and for the purpose of carrying on its business; and
- when it did so, there were reasonable grounds for believing that the transaction would benefit the company.

9.30 If these three requirements are established and the defence is not available, the court has a wide discretion to make such order as it thinks fit in order to restore the position to that which it was before the transaction took place.[3]

9.31 In essence, therefore, the liquidator, administrator or trustee in bankruptcy needs to establish two things:

- first, that the transaction took place within the requisite period before the insolvency commenced and (in most cases) that the debtor was insolvent at that time or became insolvent as a result of the transaction; and
- secondly, that the debtor effectively gave away some of its assets, either by receiving no consideration for them or by receiving less than they were worth.

9.32 Even if both these prerequisites are established, where the debtor is a company the transaction will not be set aside if it can be justified as benefiting the debtor.

9.33 The application of this provision to security was considered in *Re M C Bacon*.[4] In that case, the debtor company had an overdraft facility with its clearing bank. The facility was unsecured but, when the debtor got into financial difficulties, the bank required the debtor to grant it a fixed and floating charge debenture to secure the overdraft. Four months later, the debtor went into liquidation and the liquidator applied to have the debenture set aside as a transaction at an undervalue.

9.34 Millet J dismissed the application, saying.[5]

'In my judgment, the applicant's claim to characterise the granting of the bank's debenture as a transaction at an undervalue is misconceived. The mere creation of a security over a company's assets does not deplete them and does not come within [s 238(4)]. By charging its assets the company appropriates them to meet the liabilities due to the secured creditor and adversely affects the rights of other creditors in the event of insolvency. But it does not deplete its assets or diminish their value. It retains the right to

---

3   Insolvency Act 1986, s 241.
4   [1990] BCLC 324.
5   [1990] BCLC 324 at 340–341.

redeem and the right to sell or remortgage the charged assets. All it loses is the ability to apply the proceeds otherwise than in satisfaction of the secured debt. That is not something capable of valuation in monetary terms and is not customarily disposed of for value.'

9.35 It follows that, where a debtor creates security over its own assets to secure its own liability, that security can never be set aside as a transaction at an undervalue. If balance sheets of the debtor were to be drawn up before and after the security had been created, the amount of the assets and liabilities of the debtor would remain the same, as would the balancing figure (ie the amount of its net assets or its net liabilities). The fact that some of the debtor's liabilities would now have priority over the others does not alter the fact that the amount of debtor's assets and liabilities has not altered. The purpose of setting aside transactions at an undervalue is to stop the debtor entering into transactions under which it loses value. No value is lost by the creation of the security.

9.36 That is not to say that this provision is entirely without effect in relation to security. It does apply to guarantees and to third party security. If, for instance, a person guarantees someone else's obligation, the guarantee is likely to constitute a transaction at an undervalue. In most cases, the guarantor obtains no equivalent monetary benefit for the granting of the guarantee. The value, in monetary terms, of a guarantee will normally be significantly more than the value (if any) provided to the guarantor.

9.37 If a guarantee is entered into by an individual within the relevant period before his bankruptcy, the trustee in bankruptcy will therefore have strong grounds for contending that it should be set aside. Where the debtor is a company, however, the position of the liquidator or administrator is more difficult because the guarantee will not be set aside if it can be established that the guarantor entered into the guarantee in good faith and for the purpose of carrying on its business and, when it did so, there were reasonable grounds for believing that the transaction would benefit the company. Where, for instance, the guarantor is a member of a group of companies which enters into a composite guarantee to secure the liabilities of its parent company, the guarantee will not be set aside if it can be established that (subjectively) the guarantor's directors acted in good faith and (objectively) there were reasonable grounds for believing that it would benefit from the transaction.

9.38 The circumstances in which a guarantee given by a corporate debtor are capable of being set aside as a transaction at an undervalue are, therefore, very similar to those in which it can be set aside as a result of breach of fiduciary duty by the directors of the company as a result of lack of 'commercial benefit', which is discussed in part 2 of **CHAPTER 5 (5.17ff)**. The main distinction between the two remedies is that the statutory remedy has a time limit of 2 years, whereas the equitable remedy is not limited in time.[6]

9.39 In summary, although the undervalue provisions will not assist a liquidator, administrator or trustee in bankruptcy where the security is given by

---

6   It is, of course, subject to the normal limitation rules.

the debtor to secure his own liabilities, they may well be of value where there is a guarantee or third party charge involved, although it will be easier for a trustee in bankruptcy to take advantage of these provisions than a liquidator or administrator.

Preferences

9.40 The undervalue provisions of the Insolvency Act 1986 were introduced in the 1985 insolvency legislation, which was the precursor of the Insolvency Act 1986. Preference provisions have been part of insolvency law for a long time but were substantially amended by the 1985 legislation, with the effect that the cases decided under the previous legislation are of no assistance in construing the current provisions.

9.41 A transaction entered into by a debtor which has gone into liquidation, administration or bankruptcy can be set aside as a preference if:[7]

- the debtor has done something, or has suffered something to be done, which has had the effect of putting a creditor (including a contingent creditor, such as a guarantor) into a better position than he would have been in if the thing had not been done;
- it was done within 6 months before the commencement of the insolvency (or, in the case of certain persons connected with the debtor, within 2 years before that date);
- the debtor was insolvent at the time or became insolvent as a result of the transaction; and
- the debtor was influenced in giving the preference by a desire to put the creditor in a better position than he would have been in if the thing had not been done (this is presumed in the case of certain persons connected with the debtor).

9.42 It will be seen that certain of the requirements are very similar to those which apply in relation to transactions at an undervalue. In order for the preference provision to apply, the debtor must have been insolvent at the time the transaction was effected, or have become insolvent as a result of the transaction, and the transaction must have occurred within the relevant period, which is generally briefer than in relation to an undervalue transaction. The difference between the two provisions is that the undervalue provision deals with cases where the debtor has lost value and the transaction has therefore prejudiced all creditors, whereas the preference provision deals with cases where value has been shifted from all creditors to some creditors. In the first type of case, all creditors suffer; in the second, some creditors benefit at the expense of others.

9.43 What needs to be shown in order to set aside a transaction as a preference is that something has happened which has put the creditor into a better position than he would otherwise have been in, and that the debtor either did it itself or (having the ability to stop it) allowed it to happen. Very many

---

7   Insolvency Act 1986, ss 239, 240, 340 and 341.

transactions carried out by the debtor in the period immediately before the insolvency proceedings start will have the effect of putting one creditor at an advantage. At its simplest, any payment made to a creditor will have this effect. The provision is not intended to set aside all such transactions. The scope of its operation is limited by providing that the transaction will only be set aside if the debtor was influenced in giving the preference by a desire to put the creditor in a better position than he would have been in if the thing had not been done, although this is presumed in the case of certain connected persons.

9.44 It is this final requirement which is likely to restrict the operation of the preference provisions in most cases. A good example of its likely effect on security is provided by *Re M C Bacon*,[8] which was considered at **9.33ff**. The debtor company had an overdraft facility with its clearing bank. The facility was unsecured but, when the debtor got into financial difficulties, the bank required it to grant a fixed and floating charge debenture. Four months later, the debtor went into insolvent liquidation. It has been seen that the liquidator's application to have the security set aside as a transaction at an undervalue failed. He also applied to have it set aside as a voidable preference, and this application also failed.

9.45 Millet J decided that, in considering whether the debtor was influenced by a 'desire' to put the creditor in a better position, it is necessary to look at his subjective wishes. After stating that a person can choose the lesser of two evils without desiring either of them, he went on to say that:[9]

'Under the new regime a transaction will not be set aside as a voidable preference unless the company positively wished to improve the creditor's position in the event of its own insolvent liquidation ... But the mere presence of the requisite desire will not be sufficient by itself. It must have influenced the decision to enter into the transaction ... That requirement is satisfied if it was one of the factors which operated on the minds of those who made the decision. It need not have been the only factor or even the decisive one.'

9.46 In the case itself, the debtor's directors had no desire to put the bank in a better position. They believed that the debtor could be pulled round and, since the bank required the debenture as a condition of continuing its facilities (which were repayable on demand), they had no choice but to accede to the bank's request. In the words of one of the directors:[10] 'It was viewed as a simple decision. Either we gave the bank a debenture or they called in the overdraft.'

9.47 Where there is a connection between the debtor and the creditor, a desire to give the preference is normally presumed, in the absence of evidence to the contrary. Even if it were not presumed, it may not be too difficult for the insolvency officer to establish that such a desire existed as a result of the connection between the parties. But where, as in the normal case, the parties are

8   [1990] BCLC 324.
9   [1990] BCLC 324 at 336.
10   [1990] BCLC 324 at 337.

not connected, it will be very difficult for the insolvency officer to establish that the debtor had a subjective desire to prefer the creditor. Why should he want to do so? In nearly all cases, he will be giving the security not because he really wants to do so but simply because he has no choice. If there is no security provided, the creditor will withdraw its facility. This assumes that the creditor is able to do so but, in practice, the section will only operate if the debtor is insolvent at the time, and, even if the debt is not payable on demand, there will probably have been an event of default, enabling the creditor to withdraw the facility. In practice, therefore, the preference provision is of little concern to a creditor which is not connected with the debtor.

9.48   Where the granting of the facility is conditional on the creation of the security, and the security is created before the facility is made available, no question of a voidable preference arises in any event. The person making the facility available does not become an actual creditor until after the money has been lent, by which time the security is already in place. He has not been put in a better position as a result of granting the security because he has not yet lent the money. The purpose of the provision is to prevent existing creditors being treated more favourably than others, not to prescribe the basis on which new credit can be made available.

9.49   The provision is of more concern where the creditor has initially made available an unsecured facility and then wants to take security when the debtor gets into financial difficulties, or where insufficient security was taken at the outset and the creditor later wants to increase his security. In such a case, the person providing the facilities is already a creditor and the granting of security clearly puts him in a better position than he would otherwise have been in. But, even in this type of case, it is unlikely that the debtor will have the requisite desire to prefer the creditor. If the parties are not connected, it is difficult to see why he should have such a desire. In most cases, he will simply want to keep the facility and, if the only way of doing so is to provide security, then he will do so because he has to, not because he desires to prefer the creditor. In the words of Millet J,[11] 'It was the price he had to pay for the bank's continued support'.

Floating charges

9.50   As has been mentioned earlier, because individuals cannot generally create floating charges, the provision which restricts the rights of holders of floating charges only applies in the liquidation or administration of a debtor company. The enthusiasm of courts of equity for the creation of the floating charge has been matched by a desire by the legislature to put floating charges firmly in their place. This is a tendency which manifested itself quite early in the life of floating charges when it was decided, at the end of the nineteenth century, that preferential debts should rank ahead of the rights of creditors under floating charges. The tendency to regard floating charges as somehow inferior to fixed charges increased during the twentieth century and can be seen very clearly in a number of provisions of the Insolvency Act 1986.[12] A number

---

11   [1990] BCLC 324 at 338.
12   See part 5 of **CHAPTER 4 (4.65ff)**.

of those provisions are discussed in part 4 of this chapter (**9.98ff**). In this context, the important one is s 245 of the Insolvency Act 1986, which limits the effectiveness of certain floating charges in a liquidation or administration of the debtor. Unlike the undervalue provision, which was new in 1986, and the preference provision, which was substantially amended in 1986, the floating charge provision, although modified, is in substantially the same form as its precursors, and the earlier case-law is therefore of relevance in construing the current provision.

9.51   A floating charge created by a debtor company will be invalid in its liquidation or administration:[13]

- if it was created:
    - in favour of a connected person, within 2 years before the commencement of the insolvency proceedings; or
    - in favour of any other person, within one year before the commencement of the insolvency proceedings if the company was insolvent at the time or became insolvent as a result of the transaction,
- except to the extent of the value of the consideration for the creation of the charge (which may consist of money paid, goods or services supplied or debts discharged) at the time of, or after the creation of, the charge.

9.52   Unlike the other two provisions which have just been discussed, there is only one requirement for setting aside the floating charge – that it was created within the relevant period before the insolvency proceedings started. If that is the case, the security is automatically invalid except to the extent that consideration is provided after the charge has been created. There is, however, one type of case in which the provision does not apply – where the floating charge concerned arises under a security financial collateral arrangement.[14] Financial collateral is discussed in part 5 of **CHAPTER 3** (**3.175ff**).

9.53   If the floating charge is created within the relevant period in order to secure existing indebtedness, it will be invalid. If it is created within the relevant period to secure finance made available after it was created, it will be valid. If, as will frequently be the case, it is created within the relevant period to secure both existing indebtedness and new money, it will secure only the new money, and not the existing indebtedness.

9.54   The rule in *Clayton's Case*[15] can work to assist the creditor. In *Re Yeovil Glove Company*,[16] the debtor had an overdraft facility from its clearing bank, which was partially secured. The debtor got into financial difficulties, and the bank threatened to demand repayment of the overdraft unless further security was provided. The debtor accordingly created a floating charge over its assets in favour of the bank. At that time, the amount of the overdraft was approximately £67,500. After the charge had been created, the accounts of the

---

13   Insolvency Act 1986, s 245.
14   Financial Collateral Arrangements (No 2) Regulations 2003, SI 2003/3226, reg 10(5).
15   (1815–16) 1 Mer 572, discussed in part 7 of **CHAPTER 7** (**7.203ff**).
16   [1965] Ch 148.

debtor continued to be operated in the normal way. Seven months later, the bank appointed a receiver over the debtor's assets. At that time, the overdraft was at approximately the same level as when the floating charge was created. In the meantime, however, the debtor's accounts had been operated in the normal way and, during the period between the creation of the floating charge and the receivership, approximately £110,000 had been paid into the account and an equivalent amount had been debited to it.

9.55 Just within one year after the floating charge was created, a petition was presented for the compulsory liquidation of the debtor, and a winding-up order was subsequently made. The company was insolvent at the time the floating charge was created. The floating charge had therefore been created within the relevant time prescribed by the predecessor of s 245. The liquidator accordingly applied to the court to have the floating charge set aside. The bank argued that it had provided approximately £110,000 of new money after the creation of the floating charge and, therefore, that the charge was effective to secure the full amount of the overdraft. The liquidator argued that the amount of the overdraft had not changed between the date of the creation of the charge and the receivership; and, therefore, that no new money had really been provided.

9.56 The Court of Appeal decided in favour of the bank. The debtor's account with the bank was an unbroken current account. As a result of the rule in *Clayton's Case*, the payments into the account were to be applied in repayment of earlier debits before later ones. £110,000 had been paid into the account after the creation of the floating charge, which was more than sufficient to repay the £67,500 owing at the time the charge was created. The amount owing at the date of the receivership was, therefore, all new money which had been advanced after the date of the creation of the charge.

9.57 The Court of Appeal were clearly troubled by the conclusion. In the words of Harman LJ:[17] 'This would seem largely to nullify the effect of the section in the case of a company having at the date of the charge a largely overdrawn account with its bank, and which continues to trade subsequently.' But they could see no way round *Clayton's Case*. The fact that the amount of the overdraft did not alter to any material extent did not affect the conclusion that the amount owing at the date of the receivership represented money advanced by the bank after the date that the charge was created.

9.58 Although, in *Re Yeovil Glove*, the courts were not prepared to ignore *Clayton's Case* on the basis that the bank had not, in substance, increased its facility, the courts have been prepared to adopt a substance test when establishing whether a company has actually received value from a payment made to it. The principle was explained by Mummery J in *Re Fairway Magazines*:[18]

'The question in each case is whether, in all the circumstances, the payment is in substance to the company for its benefit. If the effect of a payment,

---

17   [1965] Ch 148 at 173.
18   [1992] BCC 924 at 932.

which is in form made to the company, is merely to substitute a secured debt for an unsecured debt, then the payment is not in substance a payment to the company.'

9.59   The most obvious abuse which this construction of the legislation avoids is where an unsecured creditor advances funds to the debtor on a secured basis for the purpose of repaying the existing unsecured indebtedness. Such a transaction will be ineffective. In substance, no new monies will have been advanced.

9.60   In *Re Fairway Magazines*,[19] this principle was applied where the secured loan received from the creditor was used, not to repay an existing loan made by the creditor, but to repay indebtedness which he had guaranteed. The court found that, in substance, the money paid by the creditor was not available to the debtor to use as it liked, but had to be used to reduce a liability which the creditor had guaranteed. As a result, no new money had been advanced for the purpose of the section.

9.61   It can be seen, therefore, that the courts have adopted two different approaches to the construction of this provision. In some cases, they are prepared to look at the substance of the transaction in order to see whether the debtor has really received new money. In others, they adopt a more literal approach.

9.62   In one important respect, the approach of the courts has changed over the years. It has been seen that the security is valid to the extent of the value of new consideration given by the creditor at the time of, or after the creation of, the charge. In cases considering the predecessor of s 245, the courts were prepared to take a very liberal view of what was meant by the words 'at the time of'. Where the debtor had promised to create the floating charge, the fact that it was not executed until some days after the monies were advanced did not prevent the courts from deciding that the monies were advanced at the time of the creation of the debenture. In one case, the courts were prepared to decide that the security was valid where the money was advanced more than 50 days before the security was actually executed.[20]

9.63   This approach was altered by the decision of the Court of Appeal in *Power v Sharp Investments*.[21] A creditor had provided finance to a debtor. In February, the debtor resolved to approach the creditor for further finance, to be secured by a fixed and floating charge debenture. The creditor advanced the money in April, May and June and on 16 July, but the debenture was only executed on 24 July. The question at issue was whether this money had been paid to the debtor 'at the same time as, or after, the creation of the charge'. The creditor argued, on the basis of the earlier authorities, that this test had been complied with. The Court of Appeal, however, rejected the earlier approach in favour of a strict test. In the words of Sir Christopher Slade:[22]

---

19   [1992] BCC 924.
20   *Re F and E Stanton* [1929] 1 Ch 180.
21   [1994] 1 BCLC 111. Also known as *Re Shoe Lace*.
22   [1994] 1 BCLC 111 at 123.

'I do not, for my part, see how the relevant temporal requirements of the exemption contained in ... s 245 ... can be satisfied if the making of the advance precedes the formal execution of the debenture by any time whatsoever, unless the interval is so short that it can be regarded as de minimis – for example a "coffee-break".'

9.64

He went on to say:[23]

'In a case where no presently existing charge has been created by any agreement or company resolution preceding the execution of the formal debenture, then, in my judgment, no monies paid before the execution of the debenture will qualify for the exemption under the subsection, unless the interval between payment and execution is so short that it can be regarded as minimal and payment and execution can be regarded as contemporaneous.'[24]

9.65 The courts' change of tack on the question of when the consideration needs to be provided is of great importance in practice. It can often be the case that money is ready to be advanced, and is required, before the parties are in a position to execute the security. *Power v Sharp* shows how important it is to ensure that this does not happen; and that the money is only advanced once the security has been executed.

Connected persons

9.66 It has been seen that a number of the claw-back provisions treat persons who are connected with the debtor more harshly than outsiders. There are detailed definitions of connected persons in s 249 and of associates in s 435 of the Insolvency Act 1986. These provisions are complicated, and there is no point in summarising them here. Suffice it to say that a connection arises where, for instance, the person dealing with the debtor is a relative and, if the debtor is a company, where the person is a director or shadow director of the company, or its controlling shareholder.

Transactions defrauding creditors

9.67 A transaction entered into by a debtor can be set aside if:[25]

- it is a transaction at an undervalue; and
- it was entered into for the purpose of putting assets beyond the reach of a person who may make a claim against the debtor or otherwise prejudicing his interests.

---

23   [1994] 1 BCLC 111 at 123.
24   Although Nolan LJ might have adopted a less rigorous approach, Ralph Gibson LJ agreed with the strict approach of Sir Christopher Slade.
25   Insolvency Act 1986, ss 423–425.

9.68   It is not necessary for the debtor to be in insolvency proceedings – the victim of the transaction can apply to the court himself. Nor is there any time limit. For this purpose, the expression 'transaction at an undervalue' has been given an extremely wide meaning by the courts.[26] But the provision only applies if the debtor had the purpose of putting assets beyond the reach of a claimant or otherwise prejudicing his interests and, for that reason, it is of little practical significance in relation to commercial transactions.

Remedies

9.69   If any of these claw-back provisions is applicable to a transaction, the courts have very wide statutory powers to make such orders as they think fit to restore the position to that which existed before the transaction was entered into.[27]

Conclusion

9.70   There are certain themes which connect the various claw-back provisions of the Insolvency Act 1986. In the first place, they generally only apply where the debtor is insolvent at the time the transaction is entered into or as a result of the transaction. In this context, the debtor is insolvent either if he is unable to pay his debts as they fall due (the 'cash flow' test) or if the value of his liabilities exceeds that of his assets (the 'balance sheet' test). But there is not always a requirement for the debtor to be insolvent at that time. It is not required where a floating charge is given to a connected person or where an individual enters into a transaction at an undervalue within the 2-year period before his bankruptcy. Nor is it required in the case of a transaction defrauding creditors.

9.71   Secondly, all of the provisions (other than that concerning transactions defrauding creditors) have time limits, stretching from 6 months to 2 years in the case of companies, and from 6 months to 5 years in the case of individuals. The different time limits reflect the perceived significance of the transactions concerned. It comes as no surprise that the time limits for transactions at an undervalue are the longest – the effect of such a transaction is that the debtor loses value to the detriment of all of its creditors.

9.72   This leads on to the third general principle – that the provisions only apply if the effect of the transaction is to prejudice the debtor's general body of creditors. There are essentially two ways in which this can be done:

- by the debtor losing value (for instance, by entering into a transaction at an undervalue or a transaction defrauding creditors); or
- by some creditors being advantaged over the others (for instance, by the debtor giving a preference or creating a floating charge).

---

26   *Agricultural Mortgage Corporation v Woodward* [1995] 1 BCLC 1. The provision which it replaced had no such requirement.
27   Insolvency Act 1986, ss 241, 342 and 425.

9.73 In the first case, it is all creditors who suffer. In the latter, one group of creditors loses out to another, although the debtor itself does not lose value.

9.74 Fourthly, although the provisions are broadly objective, there is one important subjective element in relation to preferences. The requirement that the debtor must have a desire to put the creditor in a better position means that the preference provisions are of little value where the creditor is not connected with the debtor.

9.75 Fifthly, it is important not to forget that, in the case of corporate debtors, a claim for breach of fiduciary duty can be at least as effective as a claim under the statutory provisions, and is subject to no time limits other than the usual limitation periods. In that respect, a claim for breach of fiduciary duty can have advantages over a claim under the statutory provisions.

9.76 Finally, what effect do these provisions have on the rights of secured creditors in practice? In relation to what might be described as a normal financing transaction, they have no effect at all. If the debtor is solvent and is borrowing money from an unconnected creditor who takes security from the debtor before the facility is made available, none of the claw-back provisions will affect the creditor's rights. Security given by the debtor to secure its own obligations cannot constitute a transaction at an undervalue. The floating charge will be effective because it will be securing new money. And the security will not constitute a preference because the beneficiary of the security will not have been a creditor at the time the security was entered into. In any event, the provisions generally only apply if the debtor was insolvent at the time of the transaction or as a result of it. For all these reasons, the claw-back provisions are of little concern to a creditor in such a case.

9.77 The danger occurs where the creditor has lent on an unsecured (or insufficiently secured) basis and wakes up to the need for security (or additional security) when the debtor is in financial difficulties. In such a case, a floating charge will be vulnerable, although a creditor lending on a current account will be assisted by the rule in *Clayton's Case*.[28] But it will be very difficult for the debtor's insolvency officer successfully to attack fixed charges because of the difficulty of establishing that the debtor desired to prefer the creditor.

9.78 The most vulnerable types of security are guarantees and third party charges, which can be set aside as transactions at an undervalue if they are created in the period before the commencement of the insolvency proceedings. Where the debtor is an individual, this can be a particularly potent weapon. In the case of corporate debtors, however, the undervalue provision is less far-reaching for two reasons. In the first place, there is an additional defence available for a corporate guarantor, and the issue will often resolve itself into whether there were reasonable grounds for believing that the transaction would benefit the guarantor – a question on which there is scope for much difference of opinion. The other reason why the statutory provision is of less importance in relation to corporate guarantors is that the statutory remedy broadly matches the scope of the existing equitable remedy for breach of fiduciary duty.

---

28   (1815–16) 1 Mer 572.

But there is no doubt that, whether the attack comes in the form of the statute or in equity, the most vulnerable part of the creditor's security will be that given by third parties.

Part 3: MORATORIUM

9.79   If a creditor has security which cannot be set aside under the claw-back provisions discussed in part 2 of this chapter (**9.23ff**), he is entitled to enforce his security even if the debtor is bankrupt or in liquidation – the assets the subject of the security falling outside the powers of the trustee in bankruptcy or liquidator. By contrast, if the debtor is a company and goes into administration, the creditor's rights of enforcement are curtailed; and there are similar restrictions if a small company proposes to go into a voluntary arrangement. Neither of these restrictions applies if the security arises under a financial collateral arrangement.[29] Financial collateral arrangements are discussed in part 5 of CHAPTER 3 (**3.175ff**).

Administration

9.80   The restrictions on the rights of creditors in an administration cannot be understood without a brief discussion of the purpose of administration. As Sir Nicholas Browne-Wilkinson V-C made clear, in *Bristol Airport v Powdrill*,[30] when considering the limitations on the rights of secured creditors in an administration, it is necessary to do so in the light of the purpose of the administration procedure.

9.81   The primary purpose of administration is to save the company or its business. This can be effected either by returning the company to solvency (which is very rare) or, more likely, by enabling the debtor's business (or, at least, its profitable parts) to be sold as a going concern. Either way, the creditors should obtain more than they would have received in a liquidation, and a business will have been preserved, with consequent benefits for all those involved with it, including its employees. Administration is intended to give the debtor company a breathing space within which to enable this to be achieved.

9.82   As a result, during the administration, creditors and others who have dealt with the company are prevented from enforcing their rights against the company without permission. From the point of a view of a secured creditor, the important limitation is contained in para 43 of Sch B1 to the Insolvency Act 1986 which provides that, whilst the company is in administration:

'(2) No step may be taken to enforce security over the company's property except—

---

29   Financial Collateral Arrangements (No 2) Regulations 2003, SI 2003/3226, reg 8(1)(a), (3)(a) and (5).

30   [1990] Ch 744 at 758–759. Also known as *Re Paramount Airways (No 1)*.

(a)　with the consent of the administrator, or

(b)　with the permission of the court.

(3) No step may be taken to repossess goods in the company's possession under a hire-purchase agreement except—

(a)　with the consent of the administrator, or

(b)　with the permission of the court.

...

6(A) An administrative receiver of the company may not be appointed.'

9.83　'Security' means 'any mortgage, charge, lien or other security'.[31] It therefore covers all types of security which can be held by a creditor, whether granted by the debtor or whether arising under the general law. Pledges are not specifically mentioned, but must be included in the expression 'other security'. The expression 'hire-purchase agreement' includes a conditional sale agreement, a chattel leasing agreement and a retention of title agreement.[32]

9.84　During the administration, therefore, a secured creditor is prevented from taking any steps to enforce his security unless he obtains the agreement of the administrator or the court. And it is not just secured creditors who are put into this position. An owner of goods which are in the company's possession under a hire-purchase, conditional sale, chattel leasing or retention of title agreement is subject to a similar restriction, being unable to repossess the goods without the agreement of the administrator or the court.

9.85　It is clear why the moratorium is required. It was discussed by Sir Nicholas Browne-Wilkinson V-C in *Bristol Airport v Powdrill*.[33] The purpose of administration is to enable the administrator, as an officer of the court, to try to save the debtor company's business. It is of the essence of an administration that the business will continue, either to enable the company to survive or (more likely) to enable all or part of the business to be sold. The administrator therefore requires the use of the debtor company's property free from interference by creditors. And the courts have construed these restrictions broadly, with a view to ensuring that the administrator has sufficient powers to carry out his statutory objective.

9.86　As Millet J made clear in *Barclays Mercantile Business Finance v Sibec Developments*,[34] the creditor's substantive rights are not affected by these provisions. They impose a moratorium on their exercise, but do not destroy the rights themselves. Although this may be of little immediate comfort to a creditor prevented from enforcing his security, Millet J made it clear that administrators, as officers of the court, will be liable to pay compensation to a creditor if they wrongfully retain property which they ought not to have retained, for instance, for use as a bargaining counter against the creditor

---

31　Insolvency Act 1986, s 248(b)(i).
32　Insolvency Act 1986, Sch B1, para 111(1).
33　[1990] Ch 744 at 758–759.
34　[1992] 1 WLR 1253.

concerned. In such a case, the creditor can apply to the court for the possession of the assets concerned and for compensation against the administrators for the loss suffered in the meantime.

9.87   The leading example of the approach of the courts to the moratorium is the decision of the Court of Appeal in *Re Atlantic Computer Systems*.[35] That was a case involving leases of goods, rather than security, but it contains the most extensive discussion of the way in which administrators should exercise their powers. Lessors had leased goods to the debtor company, which had then sub-leased them to end users. The debtor went into administration and the lessors applied to the court either to be able to repossess the goods or, if they could not, to require the administrators to pay rent for them in accordance with the terms of the leases.

9.88   At first instance, Ferris J held that, if the administrators used the lessors' assets, they had an obligation to pay for them, not on the basis of any particular provision of the Insolvency Act 1986 but 'upon the fact that this is an ordinary consequence of the use of property belonging to another'.[36]

9.89   The Court of Appeal disagreed. The lessor is not entitled to payment for the goods simply because they are being used by the administrator. An administration is intended to be an interim and temporary regime, a breathing space whilst the company tries to sort itself out. The mere fact that the administrator uses assets leased to the company does not require him to pay for them as an expense of the administration. In the words of Nicholls LJ:[37]

> 'Parliament must have intended, for instance, that, in appropriate circumstances, and for a strictly limited period, such a lessor or owner of goods might not be given leave [to take possession of the goods] if giving leave would cause disruption and loss out of all proportion to the loss which the lessor or the owner of goods would suffer if leave were refused. Indeed, Parliament must have intended that when exercising its discretion the courts should have due regard to the property rights of those concerned. But Parliament must also have intended that the courts should have regard to all the other circumstances, such as the consequences which the grant or refusal of leave would have, the financial position of the company, the period for which the administration order is expected to remain in force, the end result sought to be achieved, and the prospects of that result being achieved.

> If this flexible approach is right, there is no room in administrations for the application of a rigid principle that, if land or goods in the company's possession under an existing lease or hire-purchase agreement are used for the purposes of an administration, the continuing rent or hire charges will rank automatically as expenses of the administration and as such be payable by the administrator ahead (so it would seem) of the pre-administration creditors. Nor, even, for a principle that leave to take proceedings will be granted as of course. Such rigid principles would be

---

35   [1992] Ch 505.
36   [1992] Ch 505 at 519.
37   [1992] Ch 505 at 528.

inconsistent with the flexibility that, by giving the court a wide discretion, Parliament must have intended to should apply.'

9.90 Having carried palm tree justice as far as they could, the court was concerned that it would be swamped by applications by lessors, and it therefore established a requirement that the administrator must act reasonably and properly. Nicholls LJ went on to say:[38]

> 'An administrator is an officer of the court. He can be expected to make his decision speedily, so far as he can do so. He may be able at least to make an interim decision, such as agreeing to pay the current rents for the time being. The administrator should also make his decision responsibly. His power to give or withhold consent was not intended to be used as a bargaining counter in a negotiation in which the administrator has regard only to the interests of the unsecured creditors ... A similar approach should be adopted by the administrator when secured creditors seek his consent to enforce their security.'

9.91 In the circumstances of the case, the court allowed the lessors to recover their goods, and also directed the administrators to pay the sub-lease rentals received by the debtor company in respect of the property leased by the lessors. The lessors, therefore, broadly obtained what they required, which was to repossess the goods concerned and to obtain some compensation for the period during which the goods were in the possession of the administrators.

9.92 What is unfortunate about the decision is that no clear principles were laid down concerning the rights of the creditor either to the property or to payment for it. It had been argued by the lessors that the administrators could not simply expropriate the lessors' assets without compensation: they could not use the assets without paying for them. But this argument was rejected by the court. There is, therefore, no duty on the administrator either to deliver up or pay for the assets concerned. The creditor's ultimate right is to apply to the court and for the court to require the administrator to act reasonably.

9.93 It is possible that, as a result of the changes to the Insolvency Rules brought about by the passing of the Enterprise Act 2002, an administrator is now bound to pay the contractual hire for goods which he uses. Rule 2.67 of the Insolvency Rules 1986[39] provides for the payment of expenses of the administration in a particular order, the first head of which is 'expenses properly incurred by the administrator in performing his functions in the administration of the company'. It would seem that the effect of this provision is to remove any element of discretion, and to require the administrator to pay the expenses incurred in performing his functions in priority to other amounts.[40]

9.94 A secured creditor is in a weaker position than a lessor. He does not own the assets concerned, and is not entitled to their income until he enforces his

---

38   [1992] Ch 505 at 529.
39   SI 1986/1925.
40   See Anderson 'Administration Expenses' (2003) 19 IL&P 206.

security. Since he is prevented from enforcing his security, he has no right to the income, which can continue to be used by the administrator. The only protection for the secured creditor is the requirement that the administrator acts reasonably and, ultimately, his ability to apply to court if he is suffering loss as a result of the actions of the administrator.

9.95 The problem with this is that the secured creditor is ultimately at the mercy of the court. Recognising this, the Court of Appeal in the *Atlantic Computer Systems* case made some general observations concerning the circumstances in which secured creditors would be given leave by the court to exercise their rights.[41] They include the following:

- The purpose of the prohibition on exercise of security rights is to assist the debtor company, under the management of the administrator, to achieve the purpose for which the administration order was made. If the exercise of those rights is unlikely to impede the achievement of that purpose, the creditor should normally be able to exercise them.
- The court has to balance the legitimate interests of the secured creditor and those of the general body of creditors of the debtor. The purpose of the court's power to allow the secured creditor to exercise those rights is to enable the court to intervene where it would be inequitable for the prohibition to apply.
- In carrying out the balancing exercise, great importance will normally be given to the proprietary right of the secured creditor. The underlying principle is that an administration for the benefit of unsecured creditors should not be conducted at the expense of secured creditor, except to the extent where this is unavoidable; and, even then, this will usually be acceptable only to a strictly limited extent.
- The secured creditor should normally be entitled to enforce his security if he will suffer significant loss if he is unable to do so. But if substantially greater loss would be caused to others by the secured creditor enforcing his rights, that may shift the balance in favour of refusing to allow the secured creditor to enforce the security. The court will look at all the circumstances when establishing the respective losses of the secured creditor and the general body of unsecured creditors, but one important consideration will often be whether the secured creditor is fully secured. If he is, a delay in enforcement is likely to be less prejudicial than in cases where his security is insufficient.

9.96 It will be seen that these principles are as uncertain in their application as the rest of the judgment. Little wonder, then, that secured creditors are wary of administration.

Small company voluntary arrangement

9.97 Certain small companies are able to obtain a moratorium without entering into administration if they are proposing to enter into a voluntary arrangement. The requirements are complicated and are set out in Sch A1 to

---

41   [1992] Ch 505 at 542–544.

the Insolvency Act 1986.[42] The nature of the moratorium is substantially the same as that in an administration. These provisions have not been used frequently. Because it is no longer necessary to get a court order to enter into administration, it is now much easier, quicker and cheaper for a company to go into administration than it used to be. As a result, these provisions are unlikely to be of much significance in practice.

Part 4: FLOATING CHARGES

9.98 It has been seen, in part 5 of **CHAPTER 4 (4.65ff)**, that the legislature has required a distinction to be drawn between fixed and floating charges. There are five principal ways in which legislation treats floating charges less favourably than fixed charges. In broad terms, they all relate to the effectiveness or priority of a floating charge in the insolvency of the debtor.

9.99 The first relates to the registrability of charges at Companies House. Although there are certain types of fixed charge which do not require registration at Companies House, all floating charges require to be registered, failing which they will be void in the liquidation or administration of the debtor.[43]

9.100 The second concerns claw-back. The claw-back provisions treat floating chargees more harshly than fixed chargees. Section 245 of the Insolvency Act 1986 contains specific provisions which are only applicable to floating charges. As a result, it is easier to set aside a floating charge than a fixed charge in the liquidation or administration of the debtor.[44]

9.101 The other three cases in which floating charges are treated less favourably than fixed charges are concerned with priorities. They are more important in practice than the other two. They allow certain persons who have claims against the debtor to rank in priority to a floating chargee (though not to a fixed chargee). In two of these cases, priority is given to unsecured creditors of the debtor company whose claims arose before the insolvency proceedings. In the other case, priority is given to claims which are created after the debtor has entered into insolvency proceedings. It is the purpose of this part to consider these three cases. They concern:

- preferential creditors;
- the unsecured creditors' lifeboat; and
- expenses of certain insolvency proceedings.

9.102 The right of these persons to take priority over a floating chargee all arise if the debtor is subject to insolvency proceedings, although some have

---

42 Insolvency Act 1986, Sch A1, paras 1–7. The relevant moratorium is contained in para 12(1)(g).
43 See part 3 of **CHAPTER 6 (6.32ff)**.
44 See part 2 of this chapter (**9.23ff**).

wider application. The position is complicated further by the Financial Collateral Arrangements (No 2) Regulations 2003,[45] which disapply some (but not all) of these provisions if the floating charge arises under a financial collateral arrangement. Financial collateral arrangements are discussed in part 5 of CHAPTER 3 (**3.175ff**).

Preferential creditors

9.103 Preferential creditors take priority over a creditor with a floating charge if:

- the debtor is in liquidation[46] or administration;[47] or
- the creditor enforces the floating charge by appointing a receiver[48] or an administrator[49] or by doing so himself.[50]

9.104 If the floating charge arises under a financial collateral arrangement, the priority given to preferential creditors does not apply if the creditor himself enforces the floating charge,[51] but preferential creditors continue to take priority in a liquidation, administration or receivership.

9.105 The categories of preferential creditor have fluctuated over the years. When they were first established, at the end of the nineteenth century, they were restricted to claims of employees against the debtor company. They were subsequently extended to include a number of claims by the Crown, particularly in respect of taxation. The categories of preferential claim were narrowed in 1986, and were further reduced in 2003 as a result of the Enterprise Act 2002. As a result, the categories of preferential claim have largely come full circle. The principal types of preferential claim now consist of claims by employees and contributions to pension schemes.[52]

The unsecured creditors' lifeboat

9.106 The quid pro quo for the reduction of preferential claims in the Enterprise Act 2002 was the launching of the unsecured creditors' lifeboat – by which a certain percentage of unsecured claims is to be paid in priority to a creditor with a floating charge. The priority is given if the debtor company is in liquidation, provisional liquidation, administration or receivership. In such cases, unsecured creditors are entitled to a certain percentage of floating charge

---

45   SI 2003/3226.
46   Insolvency Act 1986, s 175(2)(b).
47   Insolvency Act 1986, Sch B1, para 65(2).
48   Insolvency Act 1986, s 40.
49   Insolvency Act 1986, Sch B1, para 65(2).
50   Companies Act 1985, s 196.
51   Financial Collateral Arrangements (No 2) Regulations 2003, SI 2003/3226, reg 10(6).
52   Insolvency Act 1986, s 386 and Sch 6.

realisations (broadly 20 per cent) up to a maximum of £600,000.[53] This priority does not apply if the floating charge arises under a financial collateral arrangement.[54]

Expenses of certain insolvency proceedings

9.107   The basic principle in insolvency proceedings is that the expenses of those proceedings are not payable out of assets which are the subject of security. This has recently been confirmed by the House of Lords in the *Leyland Daf* case.[55] Because the secured creditor has a proprietary interest in the secured assets, they are not available to the debtor, and cannot therefore be used by the debtor's insolvency officer to pay his expenses. There are, however, statutory inroads into this principle which apply where the debtor company goes into administration or where a small company proposes a voluntary arrangement. There are also proposals to allow a liquidator to use floating charge assets.

9.108   The most important inroad into the principle occurs in administrations. An administrator has a very limited power to sell assets which are the subject of a fixed charge, but he has a wide power to use assets which are the subject of a floating charge and to pay his expenses out of them.

9.108   The court has the power to enable an administrator to sell assets which are the subject of a fixed charge, but only if the court thinks that the disposal of the property would be likely to promote the purpose of the administration and, even then, only on the basis that the net sale proceeds are paid to the secured creditor. Indeed, if the proceeds are less than the market value of the property concerned, the administrator must pay the balance to the secured creditor. A secured creditor has little to fear from this provision.[56]

9.110   In contrast, where the assets concerned are the subject of a floating charge, the creditor's rights are much more precarious. The administrator may 'dispose of or take action relating to property which is subject to a floating charge as if it were not subject to the charge'.[57] There is no requirement for the administrator to apply to the court. The only safeguard for the secured creditor is that he will have the same priority in respect of assets acquired with floating charge assets as he had over the floating charge assets.[58] As a result, the floating chargee effectively runs the risk of the administrator trading at a loss – a state of affairs which in practice is quite likely to be the case.

---

53   Insolvency Act 1986, s 176A; Insolvency Act 1986 (Prescribed Part) Order 2003, SI 2003/2097.
54   Financial Collateral Arrangements (No 2) Regulations 2003, SI 2003/3226, reg 10(3).
55   *Buchler v Talbot* [2004] AC 298.
56   Insolvency Act 1986, Sch B1, para 71.
57   Insolvency Act 1986, Sch B1, para 70(1).
58   Insolvency Act 1986, Sch B1, para 70(2) and (3).

9.111 Even more importantly, the remuneration and expenses of an administrator are payable out of floating charge assets.[59] The expenses of an administrator can be significant, particularly if he has to borrow money to continue trading. They are all payable in priority to the floating chargee. The floating chargee's only safeguard is that the administrator is an officer of the court and the chargee will therefore be able to challenge the amount of those expenses if they were incurred improperly or unreasonably.

9.112 Where a small company proposes to go into a voluntary arrangement, the company has a similar power to sell fixed charge assets and to use floating charge assets, although there is no equivalent of the ability to pay expenses out of floating charge assets.[60] There are also proposals to allow a liquidator to have his expenses paid out of floating charge assets, although the precise extent of this power is not yet clear.[61]

9.113 Where the floating charge arises under a financial collateral arrangement, neither an administrator nor a company proposing a voluntary arrangement has power to sell or use assets which are the subject of the security,[62] although an administrator can still pay his expenses out of floating charge assets even where the security does arise under a financial collateral arrangement.

Conclusion

9.114 Claw-back provisions are an occupational hazard for secured creditors. A secured creditor has to accept that his security might be set aside if it is taken from a third party or it secures money already lent at the time the security is taken.

9.115 Of more concern is the effect of administration. If the debtor company goes into administration, the secured creditor may not enforce his security without the consent of the administrator or the court. Although he retains the security, he loses the flexibility to realise it at what he considers to be the best time. In addition, to the extent that his security consists of a floating charge, the assets concerned can be used by the administrator and the administrator can pay his expenses out of their proceeds. The secured creditor's main defence is his ability to challenge what the administrator has done on the basis that it is improper or unreasonable.

9.116 Before the coming into force of the Enterprise Act 2002, the main protection for a creditor with security over all of the debtor's assets was that he could prevent the appointment of an administrator by appointing his own administrative receiver first. It has been seen, in part 6 of **CHAPTER 8 (8.103ff)**, that the ability to appoint an administrative receiver has been abolished except

---

59 Insolvency Act 1986, Sch B1, para 99(3) and (4).
60 Insolvency Act 1986, Sch A1, para 20.
61 Company Law Reform Bill (introduced in 2005), cl 868.
62 Financial Collateral Arrangements (No 2) Regulations 2003, SI 2003/3226, reg 8(1)(b), (3)(b) and (5).

in limited cases. In these exceptional cases, it is still open to a secured creditor to appoint an administrative receiver before the company goes into administration, and thereby prevent the administration from happening.[63] But, in cases where an administrative receiver can no longer be appointed, the only protection for the secured creditor is that he can generally appoint the administrator himself.

9.117 There are nevertheless advantages in a secured creditor taking a debenture over all of the debtor company's assets. Even of he cannot appoint an administrative receiver, he will generally be able to appoint his own administrator. In contrast, a creditor who has security only over a specific asset or assets can have an administrator foist upon him. They both owe the same duties, but the creditor is likely to feel more comfortable with his own choice of administrator.

---

63   Insolvency Act 1986, Sch B1, paras 12, 15, 26 and 28.

SECURITY ARISING BY OPERATION OF LAW

Chapter 10

LIENS

Part 1: INTRODUCTION

What is a lien?

10.1   The expression 'lien' is used in a number of different senses. In this chapter, it is used in its primary sense of a security interest created by operation of law. Earlier chapters have considered how the parties can create security by agreement – by means of a mortgage, charge or pledge. This chapter is concerned primarily with how security arises without the necessity for any agreement.

10.2   In this sense, liens are very diverse. The absence of any requirement for intention by the debtor to create the security means that it is difficult to find a connecting thread. This problem is particularly acute in relation to equitable liens. There is one feature which underlies all legal liens – the requirement for the creditor to obtain and retain possession of the asset concerned – but there is no equivalent feature which links the various types of equitable lien or, indeed, which links legal and equitable liens. Apart from the fact that they are both created by operation of law, there are no similarities between legal and equitable liens. They are completely different types of security.

10.3   Although, in its primary sense, the expression 'lien' denotes a security interest created by operation of law, it is used in at least three other senses, and it is important in practice to establish in which sense the expression is being used in any particular transaction.

10.4   First, there is the 'contractual lien'. Although liens arise by operation of law, there is no reason why the debtor should not extend the security by contract. It is common to extend legal liens in this way by expanding their scope or by increasing the available remedies. When this is done, the resulting security is akin to a pledge. It is more difficult in practice to extend equitable liens. The way in which liens can be altered by agreement is considered later in this chapter.

10.5   The second example of the way in which the expression 'lien' is used in a different sense is the 'bankers' lien'. Strictly speaking, a bankers' lien is not a lien at all: it is a right of set-off. A lien gives a creditor a proprietary interest in an asset by way of security for a particular monetary liability. A right of set-off, on the other hand, enables the creditor to apply an amount owing by him to the debtor in discharge of an equivalent amount owing by the debtor to him. Like liens, rights of set-off are created by operation of law, and can be extended by contract. But, unlike liens, a right of set-off does not give the creditor a proprietary interest in any asset of the debtor. Rights of set-off are discussed in CHAPTER 12. For this purpose, it is important to appreciate that the expression 'lien' is sometimes used to mean a right of set-off.

10.6   Finally, the expression 'lien' is sometimes used as an alternative description for a security interest. Particularly in the United States, it is frequently used to describe a security interest created by agreement between the parties, such as a mortgage or charge. There is a tendency in general parlance, and sometimes in judicial pronouncements, to use the expressions 'mortgage', 'charge', 'pledge' and 'lien' interchangeably. It is, therefore, particularly important to understand in what sense the expression is being used in any particular transaction.

10.7   In this chapter, the expression lien will be used in its primary sense of a security interest created by operation of law. This chapter will, however, also consider contractual liens, not only because they are commonly used in practice, but also because they tend to be used in the same contexts as liens arising by operation of law. Liens tend to arise by operation of law in commercial, rather than financial, transactions, for instance, where goods are being held, delivered or repaired. In such a context, it is common for liens to be extended by contract. In a financial transaction, on the other hand, such as a secured loan, it is rare for the financier to rely on a lien. If he requires security, he will take a pledge, mortgage or charge, rather than a contractual lien.

Types of lien

10.8   Liens fall into three main categories, depending on the way in which they are created. They are:

- legal liens;
- equitable liens; and
- statutory liens.

10.9   Legal liens depend on possession. They arise in particular types of transaction in which a creditor has obtained possession of his debtor's asset. Because of the requirement for the creditor to obtain, and retain, possession of the asset concerned, a lien is very similar to a pledge. The main distinction is that a pledge is created by the agreement of the parties, and a lien by operation of law, although the distinction is blurred when a contractual lien is used to extend by contract the security which arises by operation of law. A further important distinction is that, where the creditor has a pledge, he is entitled to sell the asset concerned on default by the debtor. This is not the case where the creditor has a lien. He has no such right of sale – only a right to detain the asset until the secured liability has been paid.

10.10   Legal liens are themselves subdivided into two further subcategories – particular liens and general liens. They arise in different circumstances, and they also have different effects. Where a creditor has a particular lien, he is only entitled to retain possession of the asset concerned until he has been paid the debt which is referable to that asset. But, if a creditor has a general lien on an asset, he is entitled to retain it until he has been paid all monies owing to him by the debtor. The distinction therefore relates to the scope of the liabilities which are secured by the lien.

10.11   Equitable liens are much more difficult to categorise than legal liens. In the case of a legal lien, the requirement that the creditor has possession of the asset concerned unifies the concept. A legal lien can only be created over assets which can be transferred by delivery, such as goods. And it only arises where the creditor has possession of them. The circumstances in which legal liens can be created are therefore circumscribed by their nature.

10.12   There is no such inherent limitation on equitable liens. They are not founded on possession. The expression 'equitable lien' is simply a generic description for those circumstances in which courts of equity will create a proprietary interest by way of security without the requirement for any agreement between the parties. An equitable lien is, in effect, a charge created by operation of law. An equitable lien can be created over any type of property, whether or not it is capable of being rendered into possession, and is available whether or not the creditor has possession of the asset. Its potential scope is, therefore, much wider than that of a legal lien. Its most common manifestation in practice has been the right of an unpaid seller of land to security over the land for the unpaid price. But this is just one example of the diverse situations in which equitable liens are created, and it is difficult to find any guiding principle for their creation, other than the wish of the court concerned to give the creditor a proprietary interest, and therefore give him priority, in the debtor's insolvency.

10.13   Statutory liens arise in a variety of different circumstances. In many cases, they are simply statutory formulations of liens which have previously been recognised at common law. For instance, the legal lien of an unpaid seller of goods is now contained in the Sale of Goods Act 1979, and the legal lien of a marine insurance broker over the policy is now contained in the Marine Insurance Act 1906. In other cases, statutory liens are created in order to give a creditor a right to detain an asset in circumstances where it would not have arisen at common law, for instance, the right of an airport to detain aircraft under s 88 of the Civil Aviation Act 1982. Even in this latter type of case, however, statutory liens are normally created to secure the rights of creditors in possession of assets, and therefore have more in common with legal liens than equitable ones. They will not be treated separately in this chapter.

10.14   Liens are not registrable under the Companies Act 1985 or under the Bills of Sale Acts 1878–1891. There are two reasons for this. The first applies to all liens other than contractual liens. They arise by operation of law rather than being created by the debtor, and it is only security created by the debtor which is registrable.[1] Indeed, there would be no point in having security created by operation of law if it were only effective if registered. The second only applies

---

1   See part 3 of **CHAPTER 6** (**6.32ff**).

to legal liens. They are possessory security interests, and interests of that type are not registrable, even if they are extended by contract.[2]

The importance of liens

10.15   The importance of liens in practice is that they give some small measure of protection to trade creditors in the debtor's insolvency. Although, in theory, equitable liens extend over a much broader class of assets than legal liens and are available in wider circumstances, in practice it is legal liens which are more important, and they tend to benefit trade creditors. From the point of view of financial creditors who have taken security over the debtor's assets, the importance of legal liens is that they will generally rank ahead of the financial creditor's security for the reasons discussed in part 2 of this chapter (**10.17**ff).

10.16   Part 2 of this chapter (**10.17**ff) considers legal liens, and part 3 (**10.79**ff), equitable liens.

Part 2: LEGAL LIENS

What is a legal lien?

10.17   A legal lien is created in certain types of case in which a creditor has possession of his debtor's asset. It gives the creditor the right to retain the asset until payment. It is created by operation of law, although it may be extended by contract; and it does not require registration to be effective. In the words of Sir William Grant MR in *Gladstone v Birley*:[3]

> 'Lien, in its proper sense, is a right which the law gives. But it is usual to speak of lien by contract, though that be more in the nature of an agreement for a pledge. Taken either way, however, the question always is, whether there be a right to detain the goods till a given demand shall be satisfied.'

10.18   Legal liens are either particular or general. The distinction was described by Heath J in *Houghton v Matthews*:[4]

> 'There are two species of liens known to the law, namely, particular liens and general liens. Particular liens are where persons claim a right to retain goods in respect of labour or money expended upon them; and those liens are favoured in law. General liens are claimed in respect of a general balance of account; and these are founded in custom only, and are therefore to be taken strictly.'

---

2   See part 5 of CHAPTER **2** (**2.62**ff).
3   (1816–17) 2 Mer 401 at 404.
4   (1803) 3 Bos & Pul 485 at 494.

10.19 After a discussion of the circumstances in which particular liens and general liens arise, this part of this chapter will then consider the requirement of possession, the effect of agreement and the enforcement of legal liens.

Particular liens

10.20 Particular liens arise in two types of case. In *Majeau Carrying Co v Coastal Rutile*,[5] Stephen J, in the High Court of Australia, described the two classes as follows:

- Where a person, such as an inn-keeper or a common carrier, has a quasi-public calling which imposes on him certain duties to the public in relation to goods, he is entitled to a lien over the goods to recompense him for that duty.
- Where a person improves goods by his skill and labour, he is entitled to a lien on the goods for the cost of the improvement.

In both cases, the lien only extends to secure the liability incurred in relation to the goods in question.

10.21 The first type of case arises where a person is obliged to receive goods. For instance, a common carrier has a general duty to carry goods delivered to him. Similarly, the proprietor of an hotel is obliged to accommodate travellers and their luggage. The duty to do so arises under the general law, although it is now frequently regulated by statute. In such cases, the person who has an obligation to receive the goods is given the benefit of a lien over them for the payment of his costs in relation to them. In the case of a common carrier, this will be the cost of carriage. In the case of an hotel, it will be the cost of accommodating the owner. The lien is the quid pro quo for the obligation.

10.22 An example of a case in which such a lien has been created is *Robins & Co v Gray*.[6] In that case, a commercial traveller, who worked for a sewing machine manufacturer, had sewing machines delivered to him at the inn at which he was staying. The inn-keeper knew that they belonged to his employer. The commercial traveller left without paying his bill and the inn-keeper claimed a lien on his luggage, including the sewing machines, to secure the cost of his accommodation. The Court of Appeal held that the inn-keeper had a lien over all of the luggage, including the sewing machines, even though he knew the sewing machines belonged to a third party. The reason was that the inn-keeper had a duty under the general law to take in all of the traveller's luggage and, because the duty extended to all of the luggage, so did the lien.

10.23 The more common type of case in which a particular lien arises is where a person improves goods in his possession. In *Scarfe v Morgan*,[7] Parke B said:

'[W]here a bailee has expended his labour and skill in the improvement of a chattel delivered to him, he has a lien for his charge in that respect ... And

---

5   (1973) 129 CLR 48 at 54.
6   [1895] 2 QB 501.
7   (1838) 4 M & W 270 at 283.

all such specific liens, being consistent with the principles of natural equity, are favoured by the law, which is construed liberally in such cases.'

10.24   Particular liens of this kind are created whenever the person in possession of goods has improved them. The lien extends to secure the costs of the improvement, but not any other liability owing by the debtor to the creditor. The comment in the judgment of Baron Parke that particular liens are 'construed liberally' is intended to distinguish particular liens from general liens where, it will be seen, the courts are more restrictive.

10.25   The lien only arises where the goods concerned have been improved by the creditor, and not where he has merely maintained them. The distinction between improvement and maintenance of goods is sometimes difficult to draw. In the case of animals, for instance, a person who breaks in a horse or a vet who cures an animal is entitled to a lien,[8] but someone who simply feeds animals has no lien.[9] As well as being difficult to draw, the distinction is also hard to justify. As Pennycuick J indicated in *Re Southern Livestock Producers*,[10] it is difficult to see why a lien should not be available where the creditor's work has prevented the goods from deteriorating. That is as much a benefit to the debtor as an improvement.

10.26   It is, nevertheless, still necessary to draw the distinction. In *Hatton v Car Maintenance Co*,[11] D's car was maintained by C and garaged at C's premises. Sargant J held that C did not have a lien over the car because he had not improved it, but had only maintained it.

General liens

10.27   Particular liens arise in those cases where the common law recognised that it was appropriate for a creditor to be able to take advantage of the fact that he was in possession of the debtor's goods. This was the case either because he had improved the goods or, if he had not, because he had an obligation in relation to them which was imposed by the general law.

10.28   General liens, on the other hand, derive from mercantile custom. In *Bock v Gorrissen*,[12] Lord Campbell LC said:

'The law of England does not favour general liens, and I apprehend that a general lien can only be claimed as arising from dealings in a particular trade or line of business, such as wharfingers, factors and bankers, in which the custom of a general lien has been judicially proved and acknowledged, or upon express evidence being given that, according to the established custom in some other trade or line of business, a general lien is claimed and allowed.'

---

8   *Scarfe v Morgan* (1838) 4 M & W 270.
9   *Re Southern Livestock Producers* [1964] 1 WLR 24.
10   [1964] 1 WLR 24 at 28.
11   [1915] 1 Ch 621.
12   (1860) 2 de G F & J 434 at 443.

10.29 Like a particular lien, a general lien only arises if the creditor has possession of the goods concerned. Unlike a particular lien, however, a general lien gives the creditor the right to retain the goods until he has been paid all monies owing to him by the debtor, whether or not they are connected with the goods concerned.

10.30 The fact that a general lien secures the general balance of the debtor's account, rather than just the debt attributable to the goods concerned, has led to a reluctance on the part of the courts to extend general liens. As Le Blanc J said in *Rushforth v Hadfield*,[13] general liens are a great inconvenience because they give a particular advantage to one person on a bankruptcy and therefore offend against pari passu distribution. The same thing could be said, of course, about particular liens, but the courts appear to be more willing to accept particular liens because they only secure liabilities in relation to the asset over which the lien is held.

10.31 Although general liens arise from mercantile custom, in some cases the custom is so well known that judicial notice has been taken of it.[14] In such cases, it is no longer necessary to prove the custom, which has now become part of the general law. Examples of occupations in which the law recognises a general lien are bankers,[15] stockbrokers,[16] and solicitors.[17]

10.32 Although the courts lean against the creation of general liens, it is still possible to prove that a custom has developed in a particular trade or business that the creditor is entitled to a general lien. As Stephen J said in *Majeau Carrying Co v Coastal Rutile*,[18] rigorous proof is needed in such a case because of the reluctance of the courts to accept general liens. But it is possible to establish that a lien exists as a result of mercantile custom if it can be shown that it is certain and unambiguous, reasonable, of long standing and notorious, so that those dealing in that trade or business know that they are contracting on the basis of it.

Possession

10.33 The basis of a legal lien is that the creditor is in possession of the debtor's goods.[19] The discussion of possession in this part will focus on the following requirements:

- The creditor must obtain possession of the goods.
- He must retain possession of the goods.
- The possession must be lawful.
- He must have the right to continued possession.

---

13 (1805) 6 East 519 at 528 and 529.
14 *Majeau Carrying Co v Coastal Rutile* (1973) 129 CLR 48.
15 *Brandao v Barnett* (1846) 12 Cl & Fin 787.
16 *Jones v Peppercorne* (1858) Johns 430.
17 *Wilkins v Carmichael* (1779) 1 Doug 101 at 104, per Lord Mansfield.
18 (1973) 129 CLR 48 at 55.
19 A lien may, like a pledge, extend to documents of title to goods or intangibles. In this chapter, the expression 'goods' is used to describe any asset which is transferable by delivery.

Obtaining possession

10.34   The first requirement is for the creditor to obtain actual possession of the goods before the debtor enters into insolvency proceedings.[20]

Retaining possession

10.35   In order to retain his rights under a lien, the creditor must retain possession of the goods.[21] An example of the requirement for continued possession is *Pennington v Reliance Motor Works*.[22] In that case, A owned a car and arranged for B to make certain improvements to it. B subcontracted the work to C without A's knowledge. C did the work and then re-delivered the car to B, who re-delivered it to A. A paid B the price for the work done, but B did not pay C. In ignorance of C's involvement, A then sent the car to C for repairs and C claimed a lien on it for the work which had been done for B. McCardie J held that A had not authorised the delivery of the car to C and therefore that C had no lien. He also went on to decide that, even if B had been given the authority to deliver the car to C, C had returned the car to B and had therefore lost any lien which he might otherwise have had. The fact that C had subsequently obtained possession again under a different transaction did not assist him.

10.36   In relation to pledges, it has been seen, in part 4 of CHAPTER 2 (**2.45ff**), that the creditor can re-deliver the asset to the debtor for certain limited purposes without losing his pledge. In that chapter, it was suggested that such a re-delivery would only suffice to preserve the pledge if it was made for the limited purpose of selling the assets concerned and paying the proceeds to the creditor. The justification for this principle was considered to be that, in such a case, the debtor only obtained very limited rights to the asset for the purpose of realising the pledged asset, with the effect that legal possession remained in the creditor.

10.37   In principle, such an exception should not be available in relation to a lien because the creditor has no power to sell the assets concerned. Any re-delivery to the debtor should, therefore, extinguish the lien. There is, nevertheless, some authority for the proposition that this may not always be the case and that, in certain circumstances, a re-delivery to the debtor for a limited purpose might be sufficient to preserve the lien.

10.38   In *Albemarle Supply Co v Hind and Co*,[23] the Court of Appeal held that the lien of a garage proprietor over taxis garaged with him was not affected by his allowing the taxis to be taken out for hire during the day 'in pawn'. It is by

---

20   *Nichols v Clent* (1817) 3 Price 547. Constructive possession can be sufficient in the case of a pledge, but not in the case of a lien – see *Tappenden v Artus* [1964] 2 QB 185 at 195.

21   In the case of a pledge, the creditor may re-pledge the goods with a third party and still retain his pledge, even though he has given possession to the third party, but his is not the case with a lien because it is personal to the creditor. See *Donald v Suckling* (1866) LR 1 QB 585, discussed in part 4 of CHAPTER 2 (**2.45ff**).

22   [1923] 1 KB 127.

23   [1928] 1 KB 307.

no means easy to reconcile this case with the principle that the creditor must retain possession of the asset concerned. Although the asset was re-delivered to the debtor for a limited purpose, the purpose concerned was one which benefited the debtor. The case is nevertheless authority for the proposition that a re-delivery of the asset to the debtor for a limited purpose might not destroy the creditor's lien, although the circumstances in which this will be the case are unclear.

Lawful possession

10.39 It is axiomatic that a person cannot generally create a proprietary interest over an asset unless he owns it or has the authority of the owner to create the interest. The common law recognises certain limited exceptions to this principle, mainly in the context of outright transfers.[24] As has been seen in **CHAPTER 7**, courts of equity have adopted a more liberal approach to this issue when considering the priority of security interests, but the basic principle remains: in order to create an effective security interest, the debtor must either own the asset or have the owner's authority to create the security.

10.40 This principle applies to all types of security interest but it has been of particular importance in practice in relation to the creation of liens. The problem normally arises where an owner of goods has bailed them to the debtor under a hire-purchase agreement or chattel lease and the debtor has delivered the goods for repair. The question is whether the repairer has a lien over the goods even though they were not owned by the debtor. In principle, the repairer will obtain a lien if the owner has authorised the debtor to effect the repairs. Although he may not have envisaged that a lien would be created, by authorising the debtor to have the goods repaired he is necessarily enabling the creation of the lien if the debtor fails to pay for the repairs.

10.41 The position is therefore straightforward where there is an express authorisation by the creditor for the goods to be repaired. But what if the agreement between the owner and the debtor is silent on the point? In that case, the court needs to construe the agreement in the context of the surrounding facts at the time it was entered into in order to establish whether the owner has impliedly authorised the debtor to create a lien. This is a question of fact in each case but, where the purpose of the bailment is to enable the debtor to use the goods concerned, it is normally easy for the court to imply a power for the debtor to have the goods repaired.

10.42 The agreement between the owner and the debtor will, however, frequently provide that the debtor is not entitled to do anything with the goods which will result in the creation of a lien. In such a case, as between the owner and the debtor, the debtor will have no authority to deliver the goods for repair if a lien would be created as a result. If the debtor does allow a lien to be created, he will be in breach of contract with the owner. But it does not necessarily follow that the repairer will not have a lien. Although the debtor does not have actual authority (whether express or implied) to deliver the goods

---

24 See, for instance, ss 21–26 of the Sale of Goods Act 1979.

for repair and thereby allow the lien to be created, he might still, on ordinary principles of agency law, have been given apparent (or ostensible) authority to do so.

10.43 Whether he has such apparent authority will depend on whether the owner has held him out to third parties as being able to do so, and this is a matter of fact in each case. If the repairer is aware of the restriction on the powers of the debtor he will not be entitled to rely on any apparent authority of the debtor to deliver the goods for repair. But if the repairer is not aware of the terms of the agreement between the owner and the debtor, the fact that the owner has allowed the debtor to use the goods might, in an appropriate case, clothe the debtor with the apparent authority to deal with the goods in the normal way and to have them repaired. Some examples from the decided cases show how the courts have approached the problem of implied and apparent authority in practice.

10.44 The most important case is the decision of the Court of Appeal in *Tappenden v Artus*.[25] In that case, A owned a van which he allowed B to use. It broke down, and C (a garage proprietor) repaired it. A then determined B's right to use the van and demanded its return from C. The Court of Appeal held that C was entitled to a lien over the van against A.

10.45 The importance of this case lies in the judgment of Diplock LJ, which clearly explains the nature of legal liens and, in particular, examines the circumstances in which a non-owner of goods can validly create a lien. The starting point is that a lien is the right to continue in existing actual possession of goods and can only be exercised if possession was lawful when the lien was created. If, therefore, the debtor is not the owner of the goods, the question is whether the owner has authorised the debtor to deliver the goods to the creditor. Such authority may be express, implied or apparent. Where the authority is express, no problems are likely to arise. Whether or not there is implied authority will depend on whether the giving of the possession to the creditor was 'reasonably incidental to the [debtor's] reasonable use of the goods'.[26] In general terms, the debtor is impliedly entitled to use the goods for all reasonable purposes incidental to his contract with the owner and, in establishing the debtor's implied authority, it is necessary to understand what is the purpose of the bailment. On the facts of the case, it was decided that it was reasonably incidental to the debtor's use of the van that he should be able to have it repaired in order to ensure that it was roadworthy; and the creditor accordingly had a lien on the van.

10.46 The circumstances of the arrangement between the owner and the debtor may, however, be such that the debtor does not have implied authority to deliver the goods for repair. *Pennington v Reliance Motor Works* has already been discussed.[27] A owned a car and arranged for B to make certain improvements to it. B subcontracted the work to C without A's knowledge. C did the work and re-delivered the car to B, who then delivered it to A. A paid B,

---

25   [1964] 2 QB 185.
26   [1964] 2 QB 185 at 198.
27   [1923] 1 KB 127. See **10.35**.

but B did not pay C. In ignorance of C's involvement, A subsequently sent the car to C for repairs, and C claimed a lien for the work done by B. It has been seen that, by losing possession of the car, C was unable to claim a lien. But McCardie J decided that there was another reason why C did not have a lien. A had arranged for B to do the work on the car, and had not envisaged that anyone else would be involved. He had not impliedly authorised B to deliver the car to C and therefore C was not in lawful possession.

10.47 Even if the debtor does not have actual authority (whether express or implied) to deliver the goods to the creditor, he may still have apparent (or ostensible) authority to do so. In *Tappenden v Artus*,[28] it has been seen that the debtor had implied authority. Diplock LJ nevertheless considered the circumstances in which the debtor would be clothed with apparent authority. If there is a restriction in the contract between the owner and the debtor which prevents the debtor from having actual authority, the creditor can nevertheless rely on the debtor's apparent authority if the owner has held out the debtor as having the necessary authority. In appropriate circumstances, allowing the debtor to use the goods may be sufficient, so long as the creditor was unaware of the restriction in the contract.

10.48 An example of this approach is found in the decision of the Court of Appeal in *Albemarle Supply Company v Hind and Company*,[29] which has already been discussed. In that case, A let taxis to B on hire-purchase, the agreement providing that B could not create liens or part with possession of the taxis without A's consent. B garaged the taxis with C. The Court of Appeal held that A had held out B as having the authority to use the taxis and, therefore, to garage them and create liens. The limit on that authority had not been communicated to C, who was not, therefore, bound by it. The fact that C knew that the taxis were let to B on hire-purchase, and that B was not the owner of them, did not matter. The owner had held out the debtor as having sufficient authority.

10.49 But it cannot necessarily be assumed that the debtor has apparent authority to deliver goods to the creditor merely because he is in possession of them. If the debtor had stolen the goods, for instance, he would not have any actual or apparent authority from the owner. Indeed, even if the debtor was initially lawfully in possession of the goods and had actual or apparent authority to deliver them to a third party, his authority might be revoked by the termination of the contract under which he was in possession of the goods. If, for instance, the owner lets the goods to the debtor on hire-purchase and then lawfully terminates the hire-purchase agreement, the decision of the Divisional Court in *Bowmaker v Wycombe Motors*,[30] indicates that the debtor will no longer have actual or apparent authority to deliver the goods to the creditor, because his right to lawful use of the goods has been terminated. This is a puzzling decision. The debtor was originally in lawful possession of the goods and, although the termination of his right to use them would also have terminated any actual authority to deliver them to a third party, it is difficult to

---

28   [1964] 2 QB 185.
29   [1928] 1 KB 307. See **10.38**.
30   [1946] 1 KB 505.

see why it would also have terminated his apparent authority to do so. The owner had not re-taken possession from the debtor and it is difficult to see why, until he had done so, he was not holding out the debtor as having the authority to deliver the goods for repair.

10.50   The contrasting decisions in the *Albemarle* and *Bowmaker* cases reflect the tension which has always existed between the conflicting desires of the courts to protect the rights of owners of goods and also to give effect to commercial transactions entered into in good faith. The problem is the same as that discussed in CHAPTER 7 – which of two innocent people should suffer as a result of the misconduct of a third. As a result, it is by no means easy to establish the precise extent of the apparent authority of the debtor in a case where he has lawfully been put in possession of goods under an agreement which has subsequently been terminated. Although the *Bowmaker* case would indicate that a lien will not be created in such circumstances, the breadth of the doctrine of apparent authority is such that an alternative analysis in a subsequent case must be a real possibility.

10.51   In addition to relying on the owner giving the debtor actual or apparent authority to enter into the transaction as a result of which the lien is created, a creditor is able to rely on the exceptions to the nemo dat principle[31] in an appropriate case. In the case of negotiable instruments, for instance, a person who obtains an interest in them without notice of a defect in title will obtain a right effective against the true owner if his interest was obtained in good faith and for value. So, for instance, in *Brandao v Barnett*,[32] A was the owner of Exchequer bills which B, as his agent, delivered to C, a banker. C believed B to be the owner and claimed a lien on the bills. As will be seen subsequently, the House of Lords held that C did not have a lien on them but they made it clear that, in principle, a lien could have been created in favour of C even though the Exchequer bills belonged to A. They were negotiable instruments and C could therefore obtain a lien on them if he took them in good faith and for value.

10.52   In summary, the creditor will only obtain a lien if he has lawful possession of the goods concerned. If the debtor is not their owner, the creditor will therefore need to establish that:

●   the debtor has the actual or apparent authority of the owner to enter into the transaction as a result of which the lien has been created; or

●   one of the (limited) exceptions to the nemo dat rule applies.

The right to continued possession

10.53   As Lord Denman CJ said in *Forth v Simpson*,[33] 'it is essential to a lien that the party claiming it should have had the right of continued possession'. In that case, a racehorse trainer was held not to have a lien where the contract

---

31   Ie the principle discussed in CHAPTER 7, that a person cannot grant a greater interest in an asset than he has himself.

32   (1846) 12 Cl & Fin 787.

33   (1849) 13 QB 680 at 684.

allowed the owner to require the horse to run at any race he chose. As a result, the trainer did not have the right to continued possession.

10.54 A more recent example of this principle is provided by *Hatton v Car Maintenance Co.*[34] In that case, A owned a car which was maintained by B and garaged at B's premises. Sargant J held that B did not have a lien because he had not improved the car, but had only maintained it. But he went on to decide that, in any event, B would not have had a lien because A had the right to remove the car at any time, and this right was inconsistent with a lien. B did not have the right to continued possession.

10.55 The principle may also explain the curious case of *Brandao v Barnett.*[35] Exchequer bills had been delivered to a banker. They were held in a tin box and, from time to time, they were taken out of the box and given to the banker in order to receive interest on them and exchange them for other Exchequer bills. The depositor ran up debts with the banker and then went bankrupt, and the banker claimed a lien on the Exchequer bills. The House of Lords held that no lien had been created. Although, under the general law, a banker has a general lien on securities deposited with him, that principle only applies where they are deposited with him as a banker. In this case, the securities had been deposited for a special purpose.

10.56 This case is sometimes taken to be authority for the proposition that no lien is created where assets are deposited for a special purpose. The difficulty with this approach is to understand what is meant by a 'special purpose' in this context. There is always a purpose behind the delivery of assets to someone who might subsequently claim a lien on them. In what circumstances is that purpose sufficiently 'special' to negate the creation of a lien?[36] It is suggested that the reason why there was no lien in *Brandao v Barnett* is that the special purpose for which the securities had been deposited had the effect that the bank did not have the right to continued possession of them. They were deposited for safe keeping, and the depositor could therefore remove them at any time. (In practice, it is very common for the banker's general lien to be extended by contract to include items which are deposited for safe custody. This can be done either by extending the bank's general lien by contract, or by creating a pledge.)

10.57 This principle also explains why, in order for a lien to exist over goods, the secured debt must be payable before the creditor has an obligation to re-deliver the goods to the debtor. In *Fisher v Smith,*[37] Lord Selborne said:

'If the contract is to deliver goods at a certain time, or to deliver them whenever demanded, it will be inconsistent with that contract to refuse to deliver them (the proper time having arrived) upon the ground of any lien for a price, which by agreement was not then payable.'

---

34   [1915] 1 Ch 621.
35   (1846) 12 Cl & Fin 787.
36   A similar problem arises in relation to rights of set-off. See part 3 of **CHAPTER 12 (12.39ff)**.
37   (1878) 4 App Cas 1 at 12.

10.58   An example of the application of this principle in practice is provided by *Crawshay v Homfray*.[38] In that case, A owned goods which were held by B, a wharfinger. Before A went bankrupt, he sold the goods to C. Under the arrangements between A and B, wharfage was only payable at a later date, whether or not the goods were removed. The Court of King's Bench held that B did not have a lien. A was entitled to possession of the goods immediately, but the payment in respect of them was only due at a later date. Such an arrangement was inconsistent with any right of the wharfinger to retain the goods until he had received payment.

10.59   In summary, the creditor must not only retain possession of the goods, but must also have the right to continued possession. In particular, he will not have a lien if he has to deliver up the goods before the secured debt becomes payable.

The effect of agreement

10.60   Although legal liens are created by operation of law, they can be altered by contract between the debtor and the creditor. The agreement can either extend the scope of a lien arising under the general law, or it can exclude the creation of a lien.

Extending the lien

10.61   It is common for persons such as carriers and warehousemen to extend their liens by contract. This can be done specifically in a contract with the debtor but is more commonly done in standard contract terms. Such provisions are perfectly effective provided that they are properly incorporated into the terms of the relevant contracts.

10.62   These contractual arrangements can have various effects. At its simplest, the contract can extend the enforcement rights of the creditor by giving him a power of sale over the goods on default by the debtor. As will be seen below, under the general law creditors do not have a power of sale, and it is common for such a power to be granted by contract.

10.63   The contract can also extend the scope of a legal lien, either by increasing the extent of the secured liabilities (for instance, turning a particular lien into a general lien) or by extending the ambit of the assets which are the subject of the lien (for instance, by extending the lien to goods held for safe custody). Indeed, there is no reason why the contract cannot create a lien in favour of a creditor who is not entitled to any type of lien under the general law (for instance, someone who maintains, rather than improves, goods belonging to another).

10.64   There is, nevertheless, one important limitation on the practical ability of the creditor to extend legal liens by contract. In practice, contractual liens

---

38   (1820) 4 B & Ald 50.

over goods are not registered under the Companies Act 1985 or the Bills of Sale Acts 1878–1891. It has been seen that liens which arise by operation of law are not registrable because they are not created by the debtor. But, to the extent that the lien is created by contract (whether by creating a lien where one would not otherwise exist or by extending the scope of an existing lien), it *is* created by the debtor. A contractual lien will therefore only fall outside the requirement to register if the creditor's security is possessory. In this respect, a contractual lien is in exactly the same position as a pledge. It is effective without registration only because the creditor has possession of the goods.

10.65 The reason why pledges are not registrable is considered in part 5 of CHAPTER 2 (**2.62**ff). The same reasoning applies in the case of contractual liens, so long as the creditor retains possession of the goods. In the case of individual debtors, the House of Lords has confirmed in *Great Eastern Railway Company v Lord's Trustee*[39] that a possessory contractual lien containing a power of sale is not registrable under the bills of sale legislation because the security depends on the creditor's possession of the goods. Similarly, in *Waitomo Wools (NZ) v Nelsons (NZ)*,[40] the New Zealand Court of Appeal confirmed that a possessory contractual lien was not registrable under the equivalent of s 396(1)(c) of the Companies Act 1985. That case is an example of one where the creditor extended the scope of the liabilities secured by a particular lien, thus turning it into a general lien. The creditor had scoured wool for the debtor, and had not been paid. When the debtor went into receivership, the creditor had in its possession wool belonging to the debtor which it had not yet scoured. It had already delivered to the debtor the wool which had been scoured. Under the general law, the creditor would only have had a particular lien over the remaining wool if it had improved it. Since it had not done so, it claimed a lien on the basis of a contractual arrangement with the debtor. The New Zealand Court of Appeal held that the contractual arrangement was effective to give the creditor a contractual general lien over the unscoured wool; and it decided that the contractual lien was not registrable because the registration provisions of the Companies Act did not apply to possessory security interests, such as legal liens.

10.66 Unless contractual liens are registered, therefore (which in practice, they are not), they will only be effective to the extent that they extend to goods in the possession of the creditor. Subject to that point, the existence and extent of a contractual lien is dependent on the terms of the contract concerned.

Excluding the lien

10.67 It is rare for a contract expressly to exclude a lien which would otherwise arise, but the terms of the contract may be impliedly inconsistent with the existence of a lien. As Parke B indicated in *Scarfe v Morgan*,[41] a lien will not exist if it is inconsistent with the terms of the contract.

---

39 [1909] AC 109.
40 [1974] 1 NZLR 484.
41 (1838) 4 M & W 270.

10.68   It has been seen that the delivery of goods for a special purpose, such as safe-keeping, can prevent the creation of a lien because the creditor does not have the right to continued possession of the goods. An alternative way of analysing such cases is that the special purpose is inconsistent with the existence of the lien. In *Walker v Birch*,[42] D deposited goods for sale with C, C promising to pay the proceeds of the sale to D. D went bankrupt, and C claimed a lien on the unsold goods. C was a factor and would therefore, under the general law, have been entitled to a general lien over the goods in his possession. The Court of King's Bench decided, however, that C did not have a lien. A lien can be negatived by express or implied agreement to the contrary, and the requirement that the proceeds be delivered to D was inconsistent with a lien. The reasoning behind the decision appears to be that the goods were delivered for the particular purpose of being sold and the proceeds being paid to D. That purpose failed because D became bankrupt and C accordingly had a duty to return the goods to D which was inconsistent with the establishment of a lien.

10.69   A lien will, therefore, be excluded not only where the parties expressly or impliedly agree that there should be no lien, but also where the agreement is inconsistent with a lien because, for instance, the creditor does not have a right to the continued possession of the goods.

10.70   It is sometimes suggested that a lien is also negatived where the creditor is given other security by the debtor, the argument being that the express terms of the security are all that the parties would have intended.[43] But this is not always the case, as can be seen from *Jones v Peppercorne*.[44] In that case, A owned bearer bonds and deposited them with B, his banker, for safe custody. B wrongfully deposited them with C, a stockbroker, to secure a loan. C sold the securities and repaid the loan but claimed a lien over the balance of the sale price to secure further indebtedness owing by B. Page Wood V-C held that C had a lien to secure the balance of the general account. Evidence was adduced of a practice on the Stock Exchange that brokers had a general lien over securities held by them and also a power of sale. A argued that B had pledged the securities with C to secure the loan and that the express pledge (which was limited to securing the loan) was inconsistent with a general lien. Page Wood V-C decided that the pledge was not inconsistent with the existence of a general lien.[45]

10.71   It is not, therefore, the case that the taking of additional security, even over the same assets which are the subject of a lien, is necessarily inconsistent with the existence of the lien. The true principle was stated by Lindley LJ in *Re Taylor, Stileman & Underwood*:[46]

---

42   (1795) 6 TR 258.
43   *Re Leith's Estate* (1866) LR 1 PC 296 at 305, per Lord Westbury.
44   (1858) Johns 430.
45   The result is, however, inconsistent with the 'special purpose' cases concerning rights of set-off which are discussed in part 3 of **CHAPTER 12 (12.39ff)**.
46   [1891] 1 Ch 590 at 597.

'Whether a lien is waived or not by taking a security depends upon the intention expressed or to be inferred from the position of the parties and all the circumstances of the case.'

10.72 In practice, where additional security is taken, it is best for the security document expressly to provide that it does not exclude any other security which might otherwise exist, including a lien. It is common for security documents to contain such a provision, which makes it clear that the parties do not intend the express security to override the lien arising by operation of law.

Enforcement

10.73 The remedy of a creditor who has a lien over goods is to retain possession of them until the secured liability has been paid. It is, therefore, a self-help remedy, which does not require the intervention of the courts, although it provides a good defence to a claim by the debtor for the return of the goods.[47]

10.74 In the absence of a contractual power to do so, the creditor has no power to sell the goods which are the subject of a legal lien. Nor, in most cases, does he have the ability to apply to the court for an order for sale. In *Thames Iron Works Co v Patent Derrick Co*,[48] a shipbuilder had a lien over the vessel which he had built to secure the balance of the purchase price. He applied to the court for an order to sell the vessel, but Page Wood V-C refused an order of sale. He described a lien as 'passive', enabling the creditor to retain the possession of the asset until he is paid. The creditor cannot generally sell the asset himself and nor will the court order its sale even if the cost of keeping it is great. It will be seen in part 3 of this chapter (**10.79ff**) that the position is different where the lien is equitable.

10.75 The court does now have the ability to order the sale of goods which are perishable or which it is otherwise desirable to sell quickly.[49] In addition, in the case of certain types of lien, there are now statutory provisions authorising the sale of the assets concerned. For instance, where an unpaid seller of goods has a lien, he is, by statute, entitled to re-sell the goods in certain circumstances.[50]

10.76 It is very common for the contract between a debtor and a creditor to give the creditor an express power to sell the goods on default. Such a provision effectively turns the lien into a pledge. Although the security is, at least in part, created by the debtor rather than arising by operation of law, as has been seen it does not require to be registered under the bills of sale legislation or the companies legislation. As a possessory security interest, it is not registrable.[51]

---

47   *Tappenden v Artus* [1964] 2 QB 185.
48   (1860) 1 John & H 93.
49   Civil Procedure Rules, r 25.1(1)(c)(v); *Larner v Fawcett* [1950] 2 All ER 727.
50   Sale of Goods Act 1979, ss 39(1)(c) and 48.
51   *Re Hamlet International* [1999] 2 BCLC 506.

10.77　Like any other form of security interest, a legal lien is enforceable in the debtor's insolvency except in those cases where a moratorium is imposed on the exercise of the rights of secured creditors. As has been seen in CHAPTER 9, this is the case only in relation to administrations and where a small company is trying to effect a voluntary arrangement. The effect of the moratorium is to prevent the creditor from enforcing the lien except in the circumstances described in CHAPTER 9. The effect of these arrangements is not to extinguish the lien, but simply to prevent it being exercised for a period.

10.78　The Insolvency Act 1986 also contains provisions which are peculiar to liens and which apply where a corporate debtor goes into liquidation, administration or provisional liquidation, or an individual becomes bankrupt. In such cases, a lien over the books, papers or other records of the debtor is unenforceable to the extent that its enforcement would deny possession of them to the insolvency officer concerned. The purpose of these provisions is to enable the insolvency officer to have the information necessary to carry out his job, and it is expressly stated not to apply to 'a lien on documents which give a title to property and are held as such'.[52]

Part 3: EQUITABLE LIENS

What is an equitable lien?

10.79　Equitable liens are much more difficult to describe than legal liens. It has been seen that it is the requirement that the creditor is in possession of goods which is the unifying feature of legal liens. Possession of the asset concerned is not a requirement of equitable liens, and they have no corresponding defining characteristic. It is difficult to disagree with the comment of Gibbs CJ in the High Court of Australia in *Hewett v Court*[53] who said: 'It would be difficult, if not impossible, to state a general principle which would cover the diversity of cases in which an equitable lien has been held to be created.'

10.80　Although the circumstances in which an equitable lien is created are not as easy to describe as in the case of a legal lien, its nature is clear. An equitable lien is:

- a proprietary interest,
- by way of security,
- of a non-consensual nature,
- which is created in equity.

10.81　The first three characteristics are common to both equitable and legal liens, although their significance differs depending on whether the lien concerned is legal or equitable.

52　Insolvency Act 1986, ss 246(3) and 349(2).
53　(1983) 149 CLR 639 at 645.

Proprietary interest

10.82 The first characteristic of an equitable lien is that it creates a proprietary interest over the asset concerned. In this sense, a lien is no different from a charge. Although a lien is created by operation of law, and a charge is created consensually, their effect is the same. This was recognised by Slade J in *Re Bond Worth*,[54] when he described an equitable lien as a species of equitable charge arising by implication of law. As a result, an equitable lien, like an equitable charge, is effective in the debtor's insolvency proceedings.[55] It also means that an equitable lien is effective not only against the person over whose asset it is created, but also against transferees of that asset, subject to the normal equitable rules concerning priorities.

10.83 A number of cases[56] suggest that an equitable lien is only available against a transferee of the asset if he has notice of the lien. This is a convenient shorthand, and is correct in many cases, but transferee will also take subject to the lien if he is a volunteer (ie he has not given consideration for the transfer). The true principle is explained in *Rice v Rice*,[57] where it was made clear that the same priority rules apply to an equitable lien as apply to any other type of equitable proprietary interest. An equitable lien is more vulnerable against a transferee than a legal lien because the priority rules (which are discussed in CHAPTER 7) are generally more favourable to holders of legal interests than to holders of equitable ones.

Security interest

10.84 The second feature of an equitable lien is that it is created by way of security for a monetary obligation. In this sense, also, a lien is indistinguishable from a charge. It is this feature of an equitable lien which distinguishes it from a constructive trust. Both arise in equity by operation of law. Both create a proprietary interest over an asset. What distinguishes them is that an equitable lien is created by way of security for the payment of a monetary obligation, whereas a constructive trust gives the beneficiary an outright proprietary interest in the asset concerned.

Non-consensual interest

10.85 What distinguishes an equitable lien from an equitable mortgage or charge is that a lien arises by operation of law, whereas a mortgage or charge is created consensually, as a result of the intention of the parties. It is not a requirement of the creation of a lien that the debtor should intend to create it, although the converse is true – a lien will not exist if the parties have expressly or impliedly contracted out of it.

---

54 [1980] Ch 228 at 250–251.
55 *London and Cheshire Insurance Co v Laplagrene Property Co* [1971] Ch 499.
56 See, for instance, Lord Eldon in *Mackreth v Symmons* (1808) 15 Ves Jun 329.
57 (1853) 2 Drew 73.

10.86   There are suggestions in some of the cases that whether or not an equitable lien exists can depend, at least to some extent, on the intention of the parties.[58] The preponderance of authority, however,[59] establishes that an equitable lien arises without any requirement for the intention of the parties to create one.

10.87   The fact that equitable liens arise by operation of law is particularly important in practice, because it means that they are effective without the necessity to be registered under the companies legislation or the bills of sale legislation. As has been seen in part 3 of **CHAPTER 6 (6.32**ff), the requirement to register only arises if the security concerned is created by the debtor.[60] Because a lien is created by operation of law, not as a result of any express or implied intention on the part of the debtor, it is not registrable. As Harman LJ said in *Capital Finance Co v Stokes*,[61] in relation to an unpaid vendor's lien: 'Such a lien arises in the ordinary course in favour of a vendor who has not received the purchase money, and it is the creature of the law and does not depend upon contract or possession.' Relying on this statement, Brightman J has held, in *London and Cheshire Insurance Co v Laplagrene Property Co*, that an equitable lien is not registrable under the companies legislation.[62]

Equitable interest

10.88   As an equitable interest, an equitable lien is distinct from a common law lien in a number of respects, some of which have already been discussed. The importance of the concept of possession at common law is not matched in equity; and, like all equitable interests, equitable liens rank lower down the pecking order in terms of priorities than legal interests. The circumstances in which equitable liens arise have also been influenced by their development in the Chancery courts. Cases concerning equitable liens frequently involve land (which, although not the exclusive province of the Chancery courts, was heavily influenced by equitable concepts) as well as trusts and intangible property (both of which were mainly the province of the Chancery courts). It therefore comes as no surprise that the cases involving equitable liens are most frequently concerned with land, intangibles and interests in trusts. The equitable nature of the proprietary interest is, therefore, relevant to the types of property over which it has been created.

The structure of this part

10.89   The difficulty of establishing the circumstances in which the law creates equitable liens has already been adverted to. There is a great deal of uncertainty about the circumstances in which equitable liens are created, and it is not

---

58   *Re Albert Life Assurance Co* (1870) LR 11 Eq 164 at 178–179, per Bacon V-C; *Dansk Rekylriffel Syndikat v Snell* [1908] 2 Ch 127 at 136, per Neville J.
59   See, for instance, *Mackreth v Symmons* (1808) 15 Ves Jun 329.
60   This is explicit in the Companies Act 1985, s 395(1). It is implicit in the bills of sale legislation.
61   [1969] 1 Ch 261 at 278.
62   [1971] Ch 499 at 514.

possible to be definitive about the precise extent of their application. The rest of this chapter will discuss the following matters:

- *Contracts of sale.* In practice, this has been the most important type of case in which equitable liens have been created. They arise in relation to contracts of sale in favour of an unpaid vendor and of a purchaser, although the land registration system means that such liens are now of little practical importance.
- *Subrogation.* Equitable liens which arise by subrogation are particularly important in the context of two types of commercial contract – contracts of insurance and contracts of guarantee – but there is uncertainty about the precise extent of the doctrine.
- *Salvage.* This is of most importance in relation to maritime cases, but examples do exist in other areas of law, particularly in relation to those who manage the affairs of insolvent companies.
- *False cases.* Some so-called equitable liens are, in reality, explicable on other grounds.
- *Losing the lien.* In what circumstances will an equitable lien be lost?
- *Remedies.* What are the remedies of a creditor who has an equitable lien?
- *A conceptual basis for equitable liens.* Is it possible to establish any guidelines concerning the circumstances in which equitable liens are imposed?

Contracts of sale

Unpaid vendor's lien

10.90   Where a vendor transfers property to a purchaser under a contract of sale, the vendor may have an equitable lien over the property to secure the payment of the price and of certain other liabilities owing in respect of the contract.

10.91   The main application of the principle is in relation to contracts for the sale of land. The leading case is *Mackreth v Symmons*.[63] In that case, Lord Eldon reviewed the earlier authorities and confirmed that, when a vendor sells land but does not receive the full purchase price, he has an equitable lien over the land to secure the payment of the price. Lord Eldon described the principle as follows: '[A] person, having got the estate of another, shall not, as between them, keep it, and not pay the consideration.'[64]

10.92   As well as securing the purchase price under the contract, the lien also extends to other amounts payable under the contract, such as interest. The lien exists even if the transfer of the land incorrectly expresses the purchase price to have been paid in full, and even though the purchaser has become the legal owner of the land.

---

63   (1808) 15 Ves Jun 329.
64   (1808) 15 Ves Jun 329 at 340.

10.93   A more recent example of the incidence of an unpaid vendor's lien is *London and Cheshire Insurance Co v Laplagrene Property Co.*[65] The vendor sold land to the purchaser for a price which was never paid. Even though the transfer contained an acknowledgement of receipt of the purchase price, it was held that the vendor had a lien over the land to secure the payment of the purchase price. Because it arose by operation of law, the lien was not registrable under the Companies Act 1985.

10.94   The main issue for consideration in the case was whether the lien took priority over a charge by way of legal mortgage over the land which was registered at the Land Registry. The chargee had no notice of the lien. On the particular facts of the case, it was held that the lien did take priority over the charge because the vendor was in actual occupation of the land and the lien was accordingly an 'overriding interest', which was effective even against a registered interest in the land. This is unlikely to be the case very often and, in practice, the extension of land registration means that unpaid vendors' liens in relation to land will be of much less importance in the future than they have been in the past.

10.95   Most of the reported cases concerning unpaid vendors' liens involve sales of land. The lien does, however, extend to certain other types of property. It certainly applies to the sale by a beneficiary of his beneficial interest in trust property. In *Re Stucley*,[66] the vendor sold his beneficial interest in a trust to the trustee of that trust for a price which was never paid. The trustee died, and the question arose whether his executors were bound to pay the purchase price out of the beneficial interest which had been sold. The Court of Appeal held that they were. All three members of the court decided that the unpaid vendor's lien was not restricted to sales of land, although two members of the court were careful to state that it did not apply in every case of a sale of personal property. Stirling LJ decided that the unpaid vendor's lien:

> '… extends, at any rate in some cases, to a sale of personal estate, and in my opinion to all cases in which the property sold is of such a nature as that the Court will decree specific performance of the contract for the purchase of it.'[67]

10.96   Cozens-Hardy LJ said:

> 'I see no reason in principle why the doctrine should not apply to every case of personal property in which the Court of Equity assumes jurisdiction over the subject-matter of the sale.'[68]

10.97   It is clear, therefore, that an unpaid vendor's lien is available where the asset sold is the beneficial interest in a trust. It is also clear that an equitable unpaid vendor's lien is not available in relation to sales of goods. As Atkin LJ made clear in *Re Wait*,[69] the Sale of Goods Act 1979 is a code. It contains a

65   [1971] Ch 499.
66   [1906] 1 Ch 67, following *Davies v Thomas* [1900] 2 Ch 462.
67   [1906] 1 Ch 67 at 79–80.
68   [1906] 1 Ch 67 at 84.
69   [1927] 1 Ch 606 at 638.

statutory restatement[70] of the common law rules concerning liens (which, like all common law liens, are based on possession), and there is no room for equitable principles in relation to simple contracts for the sale of goods. But it is not at all clear whether the lien extends to the sale of intangibles other than a beneficial interest under a trust.

10.98 In *Langen & Wind v Bell*,[71] Brightman J held that an unpaid vendor's lien was available where the assets sold were shares in a private company, but the only authority cited was *Re Stuckley*. An unpaid vendor's lien has also been held to exist in relation to the sale of a patent. In *Dansk Rekylriffel Syndikat v Snell*,[72] Neville J held that the vendor of patents had an unpaid vendor's lien over them to secure the unpaid purchase price, but the reasoning in the case is unsatisfactory. The judge indicated that the lien depended on the intention of the parties to the transaction, which runs contrary to the essential nature of a lien – which is that it is created by operation of law without the necessity for the parties to intend it to be created.

10.99 In considering the types of asset other than land over which an equitable unpaid vendor's lien arises, two things are clear – it does arise in the case of sales of beneficial interests, and it does not arise in the case of sales of goods. Beyond this, there is considerable doubt. There is some authority for the proposition that it applies to sales of shares in private companies and to sales of patents, but the authorities are at first instance and are not entirely satisfactory.

10.100 In practice, if a person is proposing to sell an asset without receiving the purchase price in full, he should either retain title to the asset until payment in full (which is now commonly done in relation to goods) or, having transferred title to the purchaser, should take a charge from the purchaser to secure the purchase price and, if appropriate, make sure that it is registered not only in the appropriate debtor registry but also in any relevant asset registry.

Purchaser's lien

10.101 A person who has entered into a contract to buy property and has paid some or all of the purchase price (for instance, by means of a deposit) may have an equitable lien over the property to secure repayment of that amount in the event that the contract is not completed through no fault of his own.

10.102 An example of the application of this principle in relation to contracts for the sale of land is *Whitbread & Co v Watt*.[73] The purchaser agreed to buy land from the vendor and paid a deposit on signing the contract, the balance to be paid on completion. Completion was conditional on certain things being done to the land within a particular period. Whilst the contract remained executory, the vendor mortgaged the land and the mortgagees, in exercise of

---

70 Sale of Goods Act 1979, s 39.
71 [1972] Ch 685.
72 [1908] 2 Ch 127.
73 [1902] 1 Ch 835.

their power of sale, sold it to a Mr Watt, who had notice of the contract with the purchaser. Because the conditions for completion of the contract were not fulfilled, the purchaser rescinded the contract in accordance with its terms and claimed repayment of the deposit. The Court of Appeal decided that the purchaser had a lien over the land to secure the repayment of the deposit, and that it was effective against Mr Watt, who had acquired the land with notice of the contract which gave rise to the lien.

10.103   It is, doubtful whether the purchaser's lien is anything more than a recognition of the fact that, in a contract for the sale of land, the beneficial interest in the land passes to the purchaser at the time of the contract.[74] The imposition of an equitable lien in such a case does not, therefore, involve the creation of a proprietary interest in favour of the buyer. All the lien does is to establish that the buyer's equitable proprietary interest survives the termination of the contract and secures the repayment of the deposit. This was certainly the view of the House of Lords in *Rose v Watson*.[75] In that case, Lord Cranworth said:[76]

> 'There can be no doubt, I apprehend, that when a purchaser has paid his purchase-money, though he has got no conveyance, the vendor becomes a trustee for him of the legal estate, and he is, in equity, considered as the owner of the estate. When, instead of paying the whole of his purchase-money, he pays a part of it, it would seem to follow, as a necessary corollary, that, to the extent to which he has paid his purchase-money, to that extent the vendor is a trustee for him; in other words, that he acquires a lien, exactly in the same way as if upon the payment of part of the purchase-money the vendor had executed a mortgage to him of the estate to that extent.'

10.104   There is no doubt that the purchaser of land obtains a beneficial interest at the time the contract is entered into. It is equally clear that this is not the case in relation to sales of goods, in respect of which the rules contained in the Sale of Goods Act 1979 concerning the passing of property are a complete code.[77] It is debatable whether the principle applies to intangibles. Although there is some evidence that the purchaser's lien can apply in relation to intangibles, it needs to be treated with caution. In principle, a purchaser's lien should be available in the same types of case as a vendor's lien, but it has been seen that there is doubt concerning the extent of an unpaid vendor's lien where the asset sold is an intangible. As a result, a purchaser of an asset other than land who pays the purchase price, or some of it, before obtaining legal title to the asset concerned, is best advised to take specific security from the vendor.

Other types of contract

10.105   In England, unpaid vendors' and purchasers' liens have not been extended beyond contracts of sale. In Australia, however, an important

---

74   *Lysaght v Edwards* (1876) 2 Ch D 499.
75   (1864) 10 HLC 672.
76   (1864) 10 HLC 672 at 683–684.
77   See *Re Wait* [1927] 1 Ch 606.

judgment of the High Court has extended the concept to contracts for work, labour and materials. In *Hewett v Court*,[78] a builder of pre-fabricated houses agreed to construct a house for a customer and to deliver it to the customer's land. The price was to be paid in instalments, and the contract provided that the house remained the property of the builder until the price had been paid in full. The builder became insolvent and allowed the customer to take the unfinished house on payment of the value of the work done. The builder then went into liquidation, and the liquidator contended that this transaction constituted a voidable preference. The customer asserted an equitable lien over the house to secure the progress payments under the contract and, on this basis, argued that the transaction did not constitute a preference because the customer obtained no more than he was entitled to under the lien.

10.106 By a majority of three to two, the High Court of Australia decided that the customer did have an equitable lien over the house and accordingly that the transaction with the builder was not a preference. All five judges decided that the contract was one for work, labour and materials and not for the sale of goods. Accordingly, they did not have to consider whether, in Australia, an equitable interest could pass under a sale contract in advance of the legal property.[79]

10.107 Gibbs CJ appears to have founded the existence of the lien on some form of implied term in the contract, notwithstanding that the contract expressly provided that property did not pass until payment of the purchase price in full. Murphy J reached his decision with very little citation of authority, apparently on the basis that it was necessary as a consumer protection measure. Deane J decided that the lien arose as a matter of law as a result of the fact that the builder had received moneys payable in relation to the house, that the house was specifically appropriated to the contract and that it would be unconscionable or unfair of the builder to sell the house without repaying the customer's advance. Wilson and Dawson JJ dissented. They decided that the house had not been appropriated to the contract; nor was the contract one which would be specifically enforced. They said: 'The insolvency of the company is no reason of itself for placing the appellants in a secured position so as to achieve an advantage over other creditors.'[80]

10.108 It is unlikely that this case would be followed in England. Although liens clearly exist in relation to contracts for the sale of land, and may exist in relation to contracts for the sale of certain other types of asset, they are now anomalous and are unlikely to be extended. In any event, It is open to parties to a contract to provide for property to pass at a particular time. In *Hewett v Court*, the contract provided that the house would remain the property of the builder until the price had been paid in full, and the lien granted to the contractor was inconsistent with that express term.

Conclusion

10.109 The liens of unpaid vendors and purchasers can best be seen as default rules which, in the absence of contrary intention, establish the

---

78 (1983) 149 CLR 639.
79 In England, it is clear from *Re Wait* [1927] 1 Ch 606 that it does not.
80 (1983) 149 CLR 639 at 658.

respective proprietary interests of vendors and purchasers in relation to contracts for the sale of land and of certain other types of asset.

10.110   In the case of a contract for the sale of land:

- beneficial title passes to the purchaser on exchange of contracts and, accordingly, if the contract is rescinded otherwise than as a result of the fault of the purchaser, the purchaser's proprietary interest secures the repayment of the deposit; and
- the vendor retains an equitable proprietary interest in the land by way of security until the purchase price has been paid in full.

10.111   These principles only apply in the absence of contrary intention. They do not apply to contracts for the sale of goods, but the extent to which they apply to contracts for the sale of other types of asset is by no means clear.

10.112   The effect of land registration is that such liens are of much less importance in practice in relation to contracts for the sale of land than they used to be. When this is added to the doubt that exists as to whether such liens apply to contracts for the sale of intangibles, the moral is clear – express provision should be made either for the retention of title by the vendor or for the creation of security.

Subrogation

10.113   In commercial transactions, the law of subrogation has been of particular importance in relation to contracts of guarantee and contracts of insurance. The precise limits of the doctrine of subrogation are not clear. The decision of the House of Lords in *Banque Financière de la Citév Parc (Battersea)*[81] has opened up the possibility of the considerable extension of the doctrine, although the conceptual basis of that decision is difficult to discern and the extent of its application in other cases is uncertain. This part of this chapter will concentrate on subrogation in the context of guarantees and insurance, in part because of the importance of these types of contract in commercial transactions but also because they illustrate the two different ways in which rights of subrogation are used to create security interests which arise by operation of law.

10.114   The application of the doctrine of subrogation to contracts of guarantee is discussed in part 5 of **CHAPTER 11 (11.140**ff). If the guarantor pays the creditor in full, the effect of subrogation is to transfer the personal and proprietary rights previously owned by the creditor to the guarantor.[82] If, therefore, the creditor had taken security from the debtor, payment by the guarantor in discharge of the debtor's obligation to the creditor results in the transfer by operation of law of the benefit of the security from the creditor to the guarantor. The debtor is in no worse position than it was before. The effect of the subrogation is to transfer, rather than create, a proprietary interest.

---

81   [1999] AC 221.
82   For an example of its application see *Duncan, Fox, & Co v The North and South Wales Bank* (1880) 6 App Cas 1.

10.115 The effect of the doctrine of subrogation in relation to contracts of insurance is very different. It is best illustrated by the decision of the House of Lords in *Lord Napier & Ettrick v Hunter*.[83] In that case, the insurers had paid the insureds, and the insureds' solicitors then received money from third parties in reduction of their clients' insured loss. As a result, the insurers were entitled to repayment by the insureds to the extent that they had been overpaid. But the House of Lords went further. It imposed an equitable lien in favour of the insurers over the moneys held by the insureds' solicitors to secure the insureds' obligation to repay the insurers, even though it was not provided for in the contract of insurance. The House of Lords left open the question whether such a lien would also have existed over the insureds' right to payment from the third parties before it had been collected by them.

10.116 Lord Browne-Wilkinson justified the decision on the basis of the maxim that equity treats as done that which ought to be done. He decided that the insureds must repay the insurer 'out of the moneys received in reduction of the loss'.[84] It is a surprising decision. Equity treats as done that which ought to be done, but what ought to have been done in this case? It was clearly necessary to require the insureds to repay the insurer because the insureds would otherwise have recovered more than their loss. But there was no reason to require them to do so out of the very moneys received from the third parties. This case is nevertheless authority for the proposition that an equitable lien will be imposed in favour of insurers in these circumstances, even though the contract of insurance makes no reference to it.

10.117 The effect of the doctrine of subrogation therefore depends on the circumstances in which it is used. In the case of a contract of guarantee, it does not create a proprietary interest by operation of law – what it does is to transfer it from the creditor to the guarantor. The effect of the doctrine in relation to contracts of insurance is to create a new proprietary interest by operation of law.

Salvage

10.118 Liens have always played an important part in maritime law, although it is beyond the scope of this chapter to consider them in any detail. In practice, their importance in the law of security is that the rights of mortgagees and chargees of vessels rank behind many maritime liens. Maritime liens arise in various circumstances – for instance, to secure liability for damage done by a ship, to secure the wages of the master and seamen of the ship and to secure the cost of salvage services rendered in respect of a ship. There are also various statutory liens imposed in relation to ships and aircraft, which are particularly important in practice in relation to aircraft.

10.119 Most maritime liens arise in circumstances which are particular to maritime law, and which are not duplicated in other areas of the law. The main exception to this principle is the law of salvage, where there are some

---

83   [1993] AC 713.
84   [1993] AC 713 at 752.

similarities between maritime law and other areas of the law, although even here, the link is tenuous. The maritime lien for salvage attaches to a ship in respect of the rendering of salvage services or, in certain circumstances, the saving of life from a ship. A lien is imposed in such a case because the vessel is in danger and there is accordingly a need to take immediate action, without there being sufficient time to reach an agreement with the ship's owners as to the terms on which the salvage will be effected.

10.120   Cases of salvage are rare in non-maritime circumstances but they have arisen in relation to cases involving the management of insolvent estates. The courts have a variety of statutory and inherent powers to appoint persons to manage insolvent estates. These include statutory powers to appoint liquidators or provisional liquidators of companies and an inherent power to appoint a receiver.[85] When these powers are exercised, the proper remuneration and expenses of the officers appointed are payable out of the assets which they are managing, and they have an equitable proprietary interest in the assets by way of security.[86]

10.121   Such cases do not lay down any general principle because they can be seen simply as examples of the courts' general power to regulate the affairs of estates within their control. But the creation of such a proprietary interest is not limited to cases where the person concerned was appointed by the court. In *Re Berkeley Applegate*,[87] a liquidator of a company in creditors' voluntary liquidation (ie one in which there was no court involvement) was faced with a situation where the bulk of the assets under his control were held on trust, and he had insufficient funds to pay his remuneration and expenses out of the company's free assets. The court decided that the work had to be done, and that the liquidator was entitled to have his reasonable remuneration and expenses paid out of the trust fund to the extent that they were incurred in relation to the administration of the fund.

10.122   Outside the area of maritime law, salvage cases rarely arise in practice, and their application is subject to two limitations. In the first place, before there can be any question of his claim being proprietary, the claimant must establish that he is entitled to recover the expenditure incurred by him under general restitutionary principles. In most cases, expenditure incurred by one person in relation to another's asset without that person's consent will not be recoverable, even by means of a personal claim. He can only recover if his actions are not officious and the owner has benefited as a result.[88] The types of circumstance in which this will be the case are where there is an imminent danger to the asset (as in the case of maritime salvage) or it is impracticable for the claimant to get the consent of all the owners of the asset (as in the *Berkeley Applegate* case).

---

85   Insolvency Act 1986, ss 125 and 135; *Hopkins v Worcester and Birmingham Canal* (1868) LR 6 Eq 437.

86   *Bertrand v Davies* (1862) 31 Beav 429 at 436; *Re Exchange Securities & Commodities (No 2)* [1985] BCLC 392.

87   [1989] Ch 32.

88   *Falcke v Scottish Imperial Insurance Co* (1886) 34 Ch D 234.

10.123 Secondly, the expenditure must have been incurred in relation to the defendant's asset, and there must be a good reason why the claimant should have a proprietary right rather than a mere personal one.[89] In the *Berkeley Applegate* case, for instance, a personal claim would have been impracticable because of the large number of beneficiaries involved and, in any event, recourse needed to be limited to the value of the fund. A proprietary, rather than a person, right was therefore the only practicable solution.

False cases

10.124 Equitable liens are created in other types of case, but they are of less importance in practice and they arise in circumstances which, when properly examined, do not involve the imposition of a security interest over a person's assets. This can be illustrated by three examples.

Trustee's lien

10.125 As Lindley LJ said in *Re Beddoe*:[90] '[A] trustee is entitled as of right to full indemnity out of his trust estate against all his costs, charges, and expenses properly incurred.' He also has a lien on the trust assets to secure that indemnity.[91] Although the trustee's right is described as a lien, it is not an example of a case where the law imposes a proprietary interest by way of security over the assets of another person. The trustee is already the legal owner of the assets concerned. Although he has a duty to hold them on behalf of the beneficiaries of the trust, it does not follow that he has no interest whatsoever in the assets. He is entitled to recover his proper expenses in acting as trustee and, in order to do so, he can exercise his legal rights as owner of the assets. The effect of the trustee's lien is not to create a proprietary interest which did not previously exist, but to regulate the existing proprietary rights of the trustee and the beneficiaries in those assets.

Partner's lien

10.126 The same can be said of a partner's lien. On dissolution of a partnership, each partner has a lien on the firm's surplus assets. In *Re Bourne*,[92] Fletcher Moulton LJ said[93] 'I doubt whether "lien" is the word which best describes his right', but the expression is frequently used and it is clear that a partner's lien is a proprietary interest which binds third parties with notice of it.[94] Nevertheless, like a trustee's lien, a partner's lien does not involve the imposition of a proprietary interest over someone else's assets. The partners are

---

89   *Falcke v Scottish Imperial Insurance Co* (1886) 34 Ch D 234.
90   [1893] 1 Ch 547 at 558.
91   *Re Leslie* (1888) 23 Ch D 552.
92   [1906] 2 Ch 427.
93   [1906] 2 Ch 427 at 434.
94   *Cavander v Bulteel* (1873) LR 9 Ch App 79.

the owners of the partnership assets, and the lien simply establishes the extent of their respective interests in the surplus assets of the partnership once creditors have been paid.

Consensual arrangements

10.127   A third example of the use of the expression 'lien' to mean something other than the imposition of a proprietary interest by way of security relates to the creation of consensual interests. In some cases, the expression 'equitable lien' is used to describe a consensual security interest, such as a charge.[95] In *Legard v Hodges*,[96] for instance, a contract to charge future property was expressed to create a lien over that property. In this context, the expression 'lien' was used to describe a consensual security interest. This is often the case in the United States, where the expression 'lien' is given a wider meaning than it has in England. For the sake of clarity, however, as Slade J indicated in *Re Bond Worth*,[97] it is better to restrict the use of the word 'lien' to non-consensual security interests.

Losing the lien

10.128   It has been seen that a legal lien is lost if the creditor loses possession of the asset concerned. Since possession is not a requirement of an equitable lien, no such principle applies in relation to equitable liens. Like any other equitable interest, an equitable lien may rank behind another proprietary interest in the asset concerned in accordance with the normal priority rules which are discussed in **CHAPTER 7**. In such a case, the lien is not lost although, in practice, the result may be little different.

10.129   The main circumstance in which an equitable lien is lost is where the express or implied intention of the parties is that the creditor should not have a lien. This principle applies to all liens – although they are created by operation of law, they give way to contrary intention. In the case of equitable liens, the most difficult question is whether they are lost if the creditor takes other security. In the leading case of *Mackreth v Symmons*, Lord Eldon LC said:[98]

> 'It does not however appear to me a violent conclusion, as between vendor and vendee, that notwithstanding a mortgage the lien should subsist. The principle has been carried this length; that the lien exists; unless an intention, and a manifest intention, that it shall not exist, appears.'

10.130   In spite of this statement, and a number of similar statements in early cases, the more recent cases on equitable liens suggest that it is difficult for a creditor to deny that the lien has been lost if he has purported to take consensual security over the asset concerned. This was the case in *Capital*

---

95   *Re Crossman* [1939] 2 All ER 530.
96   (1792) 1 Ves Jun 477.
97   [1980] Ch 228 at 250–251.
98   (1808) 15 Ves Jun 329 at 341.

Finance v Stokes[99] even though the security purported to be taken by the creditor was in fact void for non-registration – a puzzling decision.

10.131 Nevertheless, the principle is clear that the lien will only be lost if the taking of the other security evinces an intention to release the lien. Most modern security documents contain provisions which provide that the security is in addition to, and without prejudice to, any other security to which the creditor is entitled. In practice, the question of whether or not the taking of other security does evince an intention that there should be no lien can be difficult to resolve, depending as it does on the precise facts of the case. If a creditor is to avoid losing the benefit of an equitable lien, the security document ought to contain such a provision.

Remedies

10.132 In *Rose v Watson*,[100] Lord Cranworth said,[101] in relation to a purchaser's lien, that the purchaser 'acquires a lien, exactly in the same way as if upon the payment of part of the purchase-money the vendor had executed a mortgage to him of the estate to that extent'. Similarly, in *Re Bond Worth*,[102] Slade J described an equitable lien as an equitable charge created by implication of law. It follows that the remedies of a lienee are the same as those of an equitable chargee.

10.133 **CHAPTER 8** contains a discussion of the remedies of chargees. Under the general law, a chargee has two remedies – to apply to the court for an order either to sell the property or to appoint a receiver of it. In *Munns v Isle of Wight Railway Company*,[103] Sir G M Giffard LJ held that a lienee was entitled to the same remedies.

10.134 It is common for chargees to extend the scope of their remedies in the charge document. It is also common for persons with common law liens (such as carriers) to extend the scope of their common law lien by agreement and, in particular, to amplify the very limited remedies available to the holder of a legal lien.[104] Such an approach is practicable in relation to legal liens because, being dependent on possession of the asset concerned, any consensual security interest created over the same assets will be effective without registration under the companies legislation or the bills of sale legislation.

10.135 In one respect, the remedies of an equitable lienee are greater than those of a legal lienee. The implied powers of an equitable lienee (to apply to the court for an order for sale or for the appointment of a receiver) are wider than those of a legal lienee (who simply has the right to retain possession of the asset until payment). But it is more difficult for an equitable lienee to extend his

---

99   [1969] 1 Ch 261.
100 (1864) 10 HLC 672.
101 (1864) 10 HLC 672 at 684.
102 [1980] Ch 228 at 251.
103 (1870) 5 Ch App 414.
104 See part 2 of this chapter (**10.17ff**).

powers by agreement. Since an equitable lien is not based on possession, a contractual extension of the powers of an equitable lienee will involve the creation of a consensual charge over the property. Unless the asset concerned is of a type over which a charge does not require registration, any such contractual extension of the powers of an equitable lienee will be ineffective unless the contractual arrangement is registered under the companies legislation or the bills of sale legislation. To this extent, the position of an equitable lienee is more limited than that of a legal lienee.

A conceptual basis for equitable liens

10.136   An equitable lien is a charge which is created by operation of law, rather than consensually. It has been seen that the conceptual basis of a consensual charge is the maxim that equity treats as done that which ought to be done. If the debtor contracts to create security over an identifiable asset, and the intention is to create that security immediately, equity will treat as done that which ought to be done and will give the creditor an equitable proprietary interest in the assets concerned. Although Lord Browne-Wilkinson indicated, in *Lord Napier & Ettrick v Hunter*,[105] that this was also the basis of the equitable lien imposed in insurance contracts by way of subrogation, it is difficult to apply the same concept to cases such as salvage or the unpaid vendor's lien. To take the unpaid vendor's lien as an example, the application of the maxim would require the court to decide that the purchaser ought to hold the asset for the benefit of the vendor until such time as the price has been paid in full. In circumstances where the vendor has voluntarily transferred the asset to the purchaser, it is difficult to see why this should be the case. In reality, what the purchaser ought to do is to pay the price. There seems little justification for suggesting that his obligation is in fact to hold the property for the benefit of the vendor.

10.137   It is therefore difficult to see the maxim that equity treats as done that which ought to be done as providing the underlying conceptual basis for equitable liens. There are, nevertheless, some principles which can be drawn out of the apparently random circumstances in which equitable liens are imposed.

- In the first place, the unpaid vendor's lien and the purchaser's lien can be seen as underlying default rules which establish the respective rights of vendors and purchasers in relation to contracts of sale. The results which this produces may seem rather curious, and it is particularly unfortunate that different rules apply to different types of asset, but they can ultimately be seen as establishing those rules which, in the absence of agreement to the contrary, determine the respective proprietary rights of the parties to a contract of sale.
- Secondly, It has been seen that a number of so-called equitable liens do not, in fact, involve the imposition by the law of security interests, either because they are examples of consensual security interests or because, like a trustee's lien, they do not involve the imposition of a proprietary right, but simply regulate existing proprietary rights. The right of subrogation

---

105   [1993] AC 713 at 752.

of a guarantor can be seen in a similar light. It does not involve the creation of a new proprietary interest by way of security, simply its transfer from one person to another.

- Of the other types of equitable lien which have been discussed, that leaves only salvage cases and the rights of subrogation of an insurer. It has been seen that the latter is said to be based on the maxim that equity treats as done that which ought to be done (although it is difficult to see why that should be the case). As for salvage rights, they are rare in the non-maritime context, and involve cases where there are compelling reasons why something needs to be done in relation to an asset, it is not practicable to obtain the consent of the owners of the asset and a proprietary remedy is appropriate.

10.138 Unlike legal liens, there is no single conceptual basis for the creation of equitable liens. What can be said, after putting on one side those cases which do not involve the imposition of a proprietary interest by way of security, is that there are relatively few cases where the law will impose such a proprietary interest. If contracts of sale are explicable as default rules for the passing of title, the main examples of the imposition of such proprietary interests concern the right of subrogation in contracts of insurance (which perhaps is best seen as an anomalous case) and the very limited example of salvage in a non-maritime context. There is less to equitable liens than meets the eye.

ALTERNATIVES TO SECURITY

Chapter 11

GUARANTEES AND INDEMNITIES

PART 1: INTRODUCTION

11.1   There are two ways in which a creditor can protect himself against the insolvency of his debtor. One is by taking security – in the sense of obtaining a proprietary interest over an asset out of which the creditor can be paid if the debtor defaults. This book is primarily concerned with security in this sense. The other way is for the creditor to persuade someone else to assume responsibility for the debtor's obligation. If he does so, the creditor has an alternative source of recovery if the debtor becomes insolvent. These two methods can be combined if the creditor takes security for his claim against the third party. Indeed, one of the most common types of security in financial transactions is a composite guarantee and debenture – by which a group of companies borrow money and secure it by cross-guarantees and fixed and floating charges over all of their assets.

11.2   This chapter is concerned with the rights which a creditor can obtain from persons other than the debtor. It assumes that there is a liability owing by one person (the debtor or 'D') to another person (the creditor or 'C') and that a third person (the guarantor or 'G') assumes an obligation to discharge it.

11.3   There are three principal ways in which this can be achieved.[1] The most obvious method is for the creditor to obtain a guarantee – by which the third party guarantees the performance of the debtor's obligation to the creditor. This is the most common method, and much of this chapter is concerned with the issues which arise in relation to guarantees. In the cases, a guarantee is frequently described as a 'contract of suretyship', the guarantor as a 'surety' and the debtor as the 'principal'.

11.4   As an alternative to taking a guarantee, the creditor can take an indemnity – by which the third party agrees to indemnify the creditor against any loss which the creditor suffers as a result of entering into a transaction with the debtor. Subject to the precise terms of the documents concerned, the commercial effect of these two types of transaction is frequently the same; and it is common in practice for documents described as 'guarantees' also to contain an indemnity.

---

1   There are others, such as using a letter of credit, but they are used less frequently.

11.5   The third way is for the creditor to take what is commonly known as a 'third party charge' – by which the third party creates security over his assets to secure the discharge of liabilities owing by the debtor to the creditor. In such a case, the third party does not have any personal obligation to the creditor, but the creditor is entitled to utilise the charged assets in discharge of the debtor's liability.

11.6   Guarantees have always caused problems for creditors, and the reason is not far to seek. The guarantor will usually obtain no commensurate benefit for undertaking to be liable for another person's debt. The courts and the legislature have therefore intervened to protect him. These protections assume a number of different guises but they are all based on the fundamental premise that the guarantor does not obtain any real benefit from giving the guarantee.

11.7   Some of these protections are statutory. Since the Statute of Frauds in 1677, there have been certain formalities required to create a guarantee which are not required for most other types of commercial contract. More recently, the Insolvency Act 1986 has enabled guarantees and similar transactions to be set aside in certain cases in the insolvency of the guarantor.

11.8   It is intervention by the courts, however, which has caused the most problems in relation to the enforcement of guarantees; and many of these problems extend to indemnities and third party charges. In outline, there are four main areas of concern:

- Because the liability of a guarantor is 'secondary' to that of the debtor, if the creditor is unable to recover from the debtor for any reason, he will generally be unable to recover from the guarantor.
- Many actions by the creditor will discharge the guarantor's liability, either absolutely or in part. This is frequently the case even if the actions of the creditor do not, in fact, materially prejudice the interests of the guarantor.
- A guarantor has various rights against the creditor, the debtor and co-guarantors in the event that payment is made under the guarantee; and these rights can sometimes conflict with those of the creditor.
- A guarantee is more likely to be set aside than most other types of transaction. Where the guarantor is an individual, the most common instance of such a case is as a result of the doctrine of undue influence. Where the guarantor is a company, the absence of 'commercial benefit' can create material problems as a result of the operation of the principles concerning directors' fiduciary duties.

11.9   A further problem is that the relevant case-law goes back at least as far as the early seventeenth century. There is a lot of case-law on guarantees and not all of it is easy to reconcile. This is hardly surprising in view of the shifts in judicial attitudes over a 400-year period. A number of very artificial distinctions have arisen as a result of the way in which cases have been distinguished.

11.10   From the creditor's point of view, the most important consideration is that a guarantee is a contract, and that it is therefore possible for many of these problems to be overcome by the terms of the contract concerned. Indeed, most forms of guarantee used in financial transactions contract out of most of the restrictions on the rights of guarantors outlined above. But this does not mean that it is unnecessary to understand the underlying rules. When drafting or negotiating a guarantee, it is vital to understand the default rules in order to ensure that the guarantee does meet the requirements of the creditor and that clauses amended during negotiations do not inadvertently prevent the guarantee from being enforceable as a result of a case decided 200 years ago.

11.11   The rest of this chapter is divided into the following parts:

• Part 2 (**11.12ff**) – the nature of guarantees and indemnities.
• Part 3 (**11.31ff**) – creation and construction.
• Part 4 (**11.83ff**) – discharge by conduct of the creditor.
• Part 5 (**11.140ff**) – the guarantor's rights.
• Part 6 (**11.168ff**) – using guarantees in practice.

PART 2: THE NATURE OF GUARANTEES AND INDEMNITIES

11.12   If a creditor wants to make a third party personally liable for the debtor's obligations, he has a choice of taking a guarantee or an indemnity. There is a great deal of case-law on the difference between guarantees and indemnities. This part discusses the nature of a contract of guarantee, and then how it differs from a contract of indemnity.

The nature of a guarantee

11.13   The best starting point for understanding the nature of a guarantee is the decision of the House of Lords in *Moschi v Lep Air Services*.[2] G guaranteed the payment by D of a sum payable to C in instalments. D did not pay the early instalments in full and C therefore accepted D's repudiatory breach of contract and sued G under the guarantee. The guarantee said nothing about what would happen on a termination of the contract by breach – it simply guaranteed the payment of the instalments. G accordingly argued that his liability was discharged by the termination of the contract – he was only liable to pay the instalments, not damages for breach of contract. The House of Lords unanimously rejected this argument and held that C was entitled to recover from G.

11.14   Lord Diplock's judgment is particularly important because he examined the nature of contracts of guarantee. He analysed a guarantee as being a promise by the guarantor to the creditor by which the guarantor accepts liability for the failure by the debtor to perform an obligation of any kind to the creditor. The nature of the guarantor's obligation under the

---

2   [1973] AC 331.

guarantee is to procure that the debtor performs his obligation to the creditor. Since the guarantor's obligation is not to pay money to the creditor, but to ensure that the debtor performs his obligation, it follows that the creditor's remedy against the guarantor is for damages for breach of contract, even where the debtor's obligation to the creditor was to pay money.[3] If, therefore, the debtor fails to perform, the creditor can recover from the guarantor as damages whatever the creditor could have recovered from the debtor as a consequence of that failure – the measure of the debtor's liability to the creditor being also the measure of the guarantor's liability to the creditor.[4]

11.15 Applying this reasoning to the facts of the case, Lord Diplock decided that, when C accepted D's repudiatory breach of the principal contract, D's primary obligation to perform the contract was replaced by a secondary obligation to pay damages. G's obligation was not to pay the instalments but to procure their payment by D. G's failure to procure performance by D made G liable for his own secondary obligation to C to pay damages for failure to procure D's performance. Accordingly, the fact that the instalments were no longer payable, and that all that was left was the damages claim, did not release G.

11.16 The other important aspect of the decision of the House of Lords in the *Moschi case* is that they made it clear that the law of guarantees is part of the law of contract and that the guarantor's liability is therefore ultimately a matter of construction of the particular contract concerned. In the words of Lord Diplock,[5] where there is a guarantee:

> '[I]t is open to the parties expressly to exclude or vary any of their mutual rights or obligations which would otherwise result ... Every case must depend upon the true construction of the actual words in which the promise is expressed.'

11.17 There are many definitions of guarantees in the cases,[6] but its principal features may be summarised as follows:

- It is a contract and therefore (apart from special rules such as the Statute of Frauds 1677), subject to the normal rules for creating, construing and enforcing contracts.
- The key feature of a contract of guarantee is that one person accepts liability for the failure of another to perform an obligation. The guarantor's liability does not replace that of the debtor. The guarantor's liability is secondary to that of the debtor.

The distinction between guarantees and indemnities

11.18 An indemnity creates a different type of liability from a guarantee. An indemnity is an undertaking by one person to make good loss to another. The

---

3   This is why a claim under a guarantee used to be an action in special assumpsit, rather than in indebitatus assumpsit: *Mines v Sculthorpe* (1809) 2 Camp 215.

4   In *Sunbird Plaza v Maloney* (1988) 166 CLR 245 at 255–256, Mason CJ in the High Court of Australia rejected this approach and said that the guarantor could be sued in debt for the amount payable by the debtor.

5   [1973] AC 331 at 349.

6   A number are collected in *Re Conley* [1938] 2 All ER 127.

loss can arise as a result of a transaction with the indemnifier or as a result of a transaction with a third party. It is the latter type of indemnity with which this chapter is concerned. The indemnifier agrees to indemnify the creditor in respect of loss suffered by him as a result of a transaction with the debtor.

11.19   In commercial terms, there is no real distinction between:

- a person guaranteeing to a creditor the obligations of his debtor under a particular contract; and
- a person agreeing to indemnify the creditor against loss suffered by him as a result of entering into that contract with the debtor.

11.20   The creditor is protecting the same interest in each case, but a distinction is drawn between them in the cases. The principal characteristic of a guarantee is that it imposes on the guarantor a secondary liability – ancillary to that of the debtor. An indemnity, on the other hand, creates a primary obligation. It is not secondary to, or dependent on, the obligation of anyone else.

11.21   The distinction arose as a result of the passing of the Statute of Frauds in 1677. It required a guarantee to be in writing and to be signed by the guarantor, failing which it was unenforceable. In an attempt to give effect to contracts which they considered ought to be enforceable, the courts developed a distinction between contracts of guarantee (which created secondary obligations) and contracts of indemnity (which created primary obligations). Although guarantees were caught by the Statute of Frauds 1677, indemnities were not.

11.22   The problem with this approach was that it created artificial distinctions between two types of contract which were, in essence, doing the same thing. The effect of the cases is best summed up by Harman LJ in *Yeoman Credit v Latter*,[7] where he said that the distinction between guarantees and indemnities:

'... seems to me a most barren controversy. It dates back, of course, to the Statute of Frauds, and has raised many hair-splitting distinctions of exactly that kind which brings the law into hatred, ridicule and contempt by the public.'

11.23   Although the distinction between guarantees and indemnities grew up as a result of the Statute of Frauds 1677, in practice, it is now of more importance when deciding whether the third party is liable to a creditor even if the debtor is not. The point is illustrated by two contrasting cases.

11.24   In *Yeoman Credit v Latter*,[8] G agreed to indemnify C against loss arising out of a hire-purchase agreement between C and D. D was a minor and was therefore not liable under the hire-purchase agreement.[9] D failed to pay the

---

7   [1961] 1 WLR 828 at 835.
8   [1961] 1 WLR 828.
9   Under the law at the time, a minor was not liable on this type of contract. See now the Minors' Contracts Act 1987.

instalments under the hire-purchase agreement and C sued G under the indemnity. The Court of Appeal held that, since the contract was an indemnity, not a guarantee, the fact that D was not liable under the hire-purchase agreement did not affect G's liability. The contract provided for G to indemnify C against loss arising out of the hire-purchase agreement, 'loss' being defined in the agreement to include the loss actually suffered by C. Since G's indemnity was an independent obligation – not dependent on D owing an obligation to C – C was entitled to recover its loss against G even though it could not have done so against D.

11.25   This can be compared with what would have happened if the contract had been a guarantee. In *Coutts & Co v Browne-Lecky*,[10] C granted an overdraft to D, who was a minor. The overdraft was guaranteed by G. Oliver J held that, because was D was a minor, and was therefore not liable on the overdraft, neither could G be liable in respect of a debt 'which is no debt at all'.[11] Because a guarantee is a secondary obligation, and is therefore dependent on there being a primary obligation, the absence of a valid primary obligation is fatal to a claim under the guarantee.[12]

11.26   In this context, the distinction between a primary and a secondary liability is not at all easy to grasp. Where the promise is given in respect of a contract entered into with a third party, the liability of the promisor is, at least in one sense, always secondary. As between the promisor and the debtor, the debtor is primarily liable and the promisor will therefore be entitled to recover from the debtor any amounts paid to the creditor. The distinction is in the relationship between the promisor and the creditor. What the cases show is that an indemnity is, as between the promisor and the creditor, a primary obligation and is therefore not dependent on the effectiveness of the debtor's obligation.

11.27   The real question is whether the promisor has agreed to be liable even if the debtor is not. A guarantor promises to perform the debtor's obligation if the debtor does not. An indemnifier is liable in any event. This is the approach adopted by Fisher J in *Heald v O'Connor*.[13] In that case, it was held that a guarantee of an obligation which was void (because it constituted unlawful financial assistance) was also invalid. Fisher J made the following comment:[14]

> 'It seems to me that the only true distinction [between the cases concerning guarantees and indemnities] is one of construction. Did the guarantor undertake to pay only those sums which the principal debtor could lawfully be called upon to pay but had not duly paid, or did he promise to pay those sums which the principal debtor had promised to pay but had not paid whether the principal debtor could lawfully be called upon to pay them or not?'

---

10   [1947] KB 104.
11   [1947] KB 104 at 108.
12   The actual decision in this case would now be different as a result of the Minors' Contracts Act 1987, s 2, but the principle remains valid.
13   [1971] 1 WLR 497.
14   [1971] 1 WLR 497 at 506.

11.28 This approach brings us back to the underlying concept that guarantees and indemnities are both contracts and that the role of the court, when considering any contract, is to establish the intention of the parties. The distinction between guarantees and indemnities can be understood once it is appreciated that what needs to be established is whether the parties intended the promisor to be liable whether or not the debtor was liable. If so, it is an indemnity. If not, it is a guarantee.

11.29 In practice, most guarantees given in financial transactions contain an indemnity, the purpose of which is to ensure that it is clear that the parties' intention is that the guarantor is liable to repay everything which the debtor has received from the creditor, even if the debtor is not itself liable to repay it.

11.30 Apart from this distinction, and that relating to the Statute of Frauds 1677, there is no material difference between a guarantee and an indemnity given in respect of a third party's obligation. The protections which the courts have developed for guarantors are equally applicable to such indemnifiers. Both types of contract involve one person taking responsibility for the obligations of another, usually without receiving any commensurate benefit; and the reasons for intervention are accordingly the same in both cases.

Part 3: CREATION AND CONSTRUCTION

11.31 This part considers how guarantees are created and construed. It first considers the formalities required to create a guarantee. It then discusses some problems of construction of guarantees and of comfort letters. Finally, it considers the circumstances in which a guarantee can be set aside as a result of a vitiating factor – particularly undue influence.

Formalities

11.32 Both guarantees and indemnities have the usual requirements for the creation of a contract, such as the requirement for consideration. In the case of guarantees, there is an additional requirement. They must comply with the Statute of Frauds 1677, as amended. Section 4 provides that:

'No action shall be brought ... whereby to charge the defendant upon any special promise to answer for the debt default or miscarriages of another person ... unless the agreement upon which such action shall be brought or some memorandum or note thereof shall be in writing and signed by the party to be charged therewith or some other person thereunto by him lawfully authorised.'[15]

11.33 A guarantee is a 'special promise to answer for the debt default or miscarriages of another person' – the guarantor undertaking to accept liability

---

15   The spelling has been modernised.

for a failure to perform an obligation of another person.[16] But, for the reasons discussed in part 2 of this chapter (**11.12ff**), the Statute of Frauds 1677 does not apply to indemnities.[17]

11.34   The Statute imposes two requirements on a guarantee:

●   It must be in writing or there must be a memorandum of it in writing.
●   It, or the memorandum, must be signed by the guarantor or his agent.

11.35   The memorandum must contain all the material terms of the guarantee,[18] but the consideration for the guarantee no longer needs to be stated.[19] A guarantee which does not comply with the Statute of Frauds 1677 is not void, but it is unenforceable. It can therefore be used as a defence, but cannot found an action in the courts.[20]

11.36   The Statute of Frauds 1677 can still cause problems in practice, as can be seen from the recent *Actionstrength* case.[21] D had agreed to build a factory for G, in connection with which C had agreed to provide labour to D. C alleged that it had complained to G about late payment by D and that G had entered into an oral agreement with C to persuade D to pay, failing which G would pay C itself. C sued G on the alleged oral agreement. G denied that it had made the agreement, but also applied to have the claim struck out on the basis that, even if it had, the oral agreement was a guarantee which would be unenforceable under s 4 of the Statute of Frauds 1677. The House of Lords gave judgment for G. Although they were concerned that C's commercial expectations could have been defeated, they were bound to give effect to the Statute.

11.37   In financial transactions, where guarantees are invariably in writing, the Statute of Frauds 1677 is of little practical significance, but the *Actionstrength* case shows that it can still create problems in non-financial cases where the requirements of commercial practice make it impracticable to record every contractual undertaking in writing. The requirement for the guarantee to be signed by the guarantor can also create practical problems, not least in international trade transactions where undertakings may still be sent by means of communication which cannot carry a signature.

Principles of construction

11.38   There are a lot of cases involving the construction of guarantees and indemnities, not all of which are easy to reconcile. To the extent that the cases involve the construction of a particular document, rather than laying down a point of law, they need to be treated with caution. There are a number of indications in the cases that guarantees must be construed strictly in favour of the guarantor, but this probably only means that, because most guarantees are

---

16   See *Moschi v Lep Air Services* [1973] AC 331 at 347–348, per Lord Diplock.
17   *Lakeman v Mountstephen* (1874) LR 7 HL 17.
18   *Holmes v Mitchell* (1859) 7 CB NS 361 at 370, per Williams J.
19   Mercantile Law Amendment Act 1856, s 3.
20   *Lavery v Turley* (1860) 6 H & N 239.
21   *Actionstrength v International Glass Engineering* [2003] AC 541.

drafted by the creditor, any ambiguity will be construed contra proferentem – against the creditor and in favour of the guarantor.[22]

11.39   In consumer contracts, there will doubtless continue to be a tendency for courts to bend over backwards to construe guarantees in favour of guarantors, but there is no justification for such an approach in relation to commercial contracts. The fact that a guarantor obtains no obvious benefit from the guarantee has undoubtedly been a factor which has influenced courts when construing guarantees,[23] but the modern approach to guarantees in commercial transactions is to treat them as contracts, like any other, and to construe them, as any other contract, in the light of the surrounding matrix of facts and from the point of view of the businessmen entering into them.[24] It is nevertheless clear that there are competing pressures on courts when they construe guarantees. On the one hand, they should be given a reasonable business meaning, like any other commercial contract. On the other, they will be construed strictly against the creditor, with any ambiguity being decided in favour of the guarantor.

11.40   An example of the problems which can arise concerns guarantees which are expressed to secure all amounts from time to time owing by the debtor to the creditor. These 'all monies' clauses will be construed as only extending to liabilities arising out of transactions between the debtor and the creditor (and therefore not covering debts acquired by the creditor from third parties) in the absence of very clear wording to the contrary,[25] although this tendency can also be seen in relation to security documents, and not just to guarantees.[26]

11.41   Although in general terms modern courts will construe commercial guarantees in the same way as any other commercial document, there can be little doubt that not only will ambiguities be construed against the creditor, but the court will require the creditor to prove that the rights which he seeks are clearly established by the guarantee. This makes it even more important than usual for the document to be drafted as simply and clearly as possible. Some of the particular problems of construction which have arisen in practice are discussed in the following sections of this part.

When is the guarantor liable?

11.42   It has been seen that the obligation of a guarantor is to procure that the debtor performs his obligations. It is for this reason that the creditor is

---

22   *Eastern Counties Building Society v Russell* [1947] 2 All ER 734.
23   *Blest v Brown* (1862) 4 De G F & J 367 at 376, per Lord Westbury LC.
24   *Hyundai Shipbuilding & Heavy Industries Co v Pournaras* [1978] 2 Lloyd's Rep 502.
25   *Re Clark's Refrigerated Transport* [1982] VR 989; *Kova Establishment v Sasco Investments* [1998] 2 BCLC 83.
26   See *Re Quest Cae* [1985] BCLC 266, discussed in part 4 of **CHAPTER 3** (**3.140**ff).

generally entitled to bring proceedings against the guarantor without enforcing his rights against the debtor and without proceeding against any co-guarantors.[27]

11.43 The guarantor's liability is, nevertheless, secondary to that of the principal debtor. It follows that, unless there is a contrary provision in the guarantee, the creditor is unable to proceed against the guarantor until the principal debt becomes owing by the debtor. If, therefore, the principal debt only becomes payable if demand is made on the debtor, then the creditor must do so before proceeding against the guarantor. Equally, many guarantees are only payable 'on demand' against the guarantor. This is because, in the absence of such a provision, the guarantor becomes liable as soon as the principal debtor defaults, in which event the limitation period starts to run at that point. In order to avoid this potential problem, it is common for the liability under the guarantee to be dependent on a demand being made by the creditor on the guarantor. In any event, and regardless of the documentation, it is good practice first to make demand on the debtor and then to make demand on the guarantor before taking any action against the guarantor.

Revocation of a guarantee

11.44 One common issue of construction in relation to guarantees is whether the guarantee is terminable by notice from the guarantor and, if so, what is the effect of that termination. The position can be explained by reference to two contrasting examples.

11.45 In *Offord v Davies*,[28] in consideration of C discounting bills of exchange for D, G guaranteed the repayment of such bills 'for the space of twelve calendar months'. The question arose whether the guarantee could be terminated by notice by the guarantor within the 12-month period. The Court of Common Pleas held that it could. The promise to guarantee a discounted bill only became effective in respect of that bill when it was discounted. The guarantor could therefore revoke the guarantee in respect of any future bills which had not then been discounted. The 12-month period was simply a back-stop date, beyond which G's liability could not extend, but did not prevent early revocation in respect of bills which had not then been discounted.

11.46 By contrast, in *Lloyd's v Harper*,[29] D was an underwriting member of Lloyd's of London, and G had guaranteed D's obligations to Lloyd's. The Court of Appeal held that the guarantee could not be revoked by G giving notice to Lloyd's to do so. The consideration for the guarantee (which was D becoming an underwriting member of Lloyd's) was given once and for all when the guarantee was given, and the guarantee was therefore irrevocable.

---

27 *Moschi v Lep Air Services* [1973] AC 333 at 356–357, per Lord Simon. The position was different in Roman law and is still different in many civil law jurisdictions and in some US states, where the guarantor has a right of 'discussion' before the creditor is entitled to proceed against him.

28 (1862) 12 CB NS 748.

29 (1880) 16 Ch D 290.

11.47 The distinction between the two types of case was explained by Lush LJ.[30] He distinguished two types of guarantee:

- guarantees where the consideration is entire (for instance, a guarantee of a particular contract); and
- guarantees where the consideration is divisible (for instance, a guarantee of an overdraft).

11.48 In the former case, there can be no revocation. The consideration for the guarantee has been given and the guarantor is therefore bound to perform the obligation contained in the guarantee. In the latter case, however, the consideration for the guarantee is given each time a transaction is entered into between the debtor and the creditor. In such a case, the guarantor can revoke the guarantee for the future, although he will remain liable for obligations incurred before the notice is given.

11.49 Seen in this light, it is easy to establish what the effect is of a revocation. It prevents the guarantor from becoming liable for any transactions entered into between the debtor and the creditor after receipt of notice by the creditor. The guarantee is not terminated as a result of the notice. The effect of the notice is simply to prevent the guarantor from becoming liable for transactions entered into between the debtor and the creditor after the notice has been received.[31]

11.50 Notice of revocation by the guarantor is not the only way of preventing the guarantor from becoming liable for continuing obligations in the second type of guarantee. For instance, in the case of individual guarantors, it is also determined as to the future by notice to the creditor of the death of the guarantor[32] or of his becoming of unsound mind.[33]

11.51 Where a continuing guarantee is given of a running account, such as an overdraft, practical problems can arise where the guarantee is determined for the future. Assume that G has guaranteed D's overdraft with C. If D owes £100 to C when G gives notice to determine the guarantee as to the future, in the absence of any further transactions G remains liable for the £100. If, however, C continues the account and receives credits into it and pays debits from it, the effect of the rule in *Clayton's Case*[34] is that the payments into the account will, in the absence of evidence of agreement to the contrary, go to discharge the earliest debits on the account. As a result, if the account is allowed to continue, the existing liability of £100 will gradually be reduced until the guarantor is no longer liable for anything.

11.52 Because of concerns about the way the courts approach issues of construction, it is common for guarantees to contain specific provisions concerning revocation. Where the guarantee is given in relation to a particular

---

30 (1880) 16 Ch D 290 at 319–320.
31 See *Bank of Credit and Commerce International v Simjee* [1997] CLC 135.
32 *Coulthart v Clementson* (1879) 5 QBD 42.
33 *Bradford Old Bank v Sutcliffe* [1918] 2 KB 833 at 839, per Pickford LJ.
34 *Devaynes v Noble, Clayton's Case* (1815–16) 1 Mer 572. See part 7 of **CHAPTER 7** (**7.203**ff)

facility, the consideration for the guarantee is the granting of the facility by the creditor to the debtor. In such a case, the guarantee will (in the absence of any contrary indication in the guarantee) continue to secure the debtor's obligations in relation to the entire facility. It will not be revocable. In practice, however, the guarantee will normally be expressed to be irrevocable in order to put the matter beyond doubt.

11.53   Where the guarantee does not secure a particular facility, but extends to all moneys from time to time owing by the debtor to the creditor, the guarantee will be revocable by notice by the guarantor. The guarantee will normally contain two provisions intended to limit the effect of revocation by the guarantor:

- The first is a provision by which the guarantor is required to give a certain period of notice of revocation to the creditor and that the guarantor will remain liable for all obligations of the debtor to the creditor which are created before the expiry of the notice period. In order to avoid any potential problems of construction, it is normal for such a provision to make it clear that the obligations for which the guarantor continues to be liable include those which were contingent at the date the notice expired, but which subsequently mature into actual liabilities.
- It is also common (particularly in bank guarantees) specifically to contract out of the rule in *Clayton's Case*. A clause which provides for a current account to be deemed to be ruled off when notice is received of revocation is perfectly effective.[35] If this is done, subsequent payments into the account will not reduce the amount for which the guarantor is liable.

Limits on guarantees

11.54   Limits on the guarantor's liability are common. The main types of limit are:

- limits in time;
- limits as to amount; and
- limits as to particular types of transaction.

Limits in time

11.55   Limits in time are common in guarantees given by banks but much less so in guarantees given to banks. Where there is such a limit, it must be clear what is its effect. For instance, is the guarantor liable for all obligations falling within the provisions of the guarantee which existed on a particular date? If so, does that include liabilities which are then contingent but which subsequently mature? Alternatively, is it necessary for the creditor to make a demand during the period and, if so, what is the effect of failure to do so? The types of issue which arise are similar to those considered above in relation to revocation by the guarantor.

---

35   *Westminster Bank v Cond* (1940) 46 Com Cas 60.

Limits as to amount

11.56 Limitations as to amount are common in all types of guarantee. It is again important to be clear what is the effect of the limit. For instance, where the guarantee is of a loan, is the limit an absolute one (in the sense that it is the total amount recoverable by the creditor) or does the limit only extend to the principal amount of the loan (in which event interest and costs in relation to that amount will be recoverable in addition)?

11.57 There is one issue concerning limitations as to amount which can create problems in practice. The cases distinguish between two particular types of limit as to amount. The guarantor may:

- guarantee part of the debt owing by the debtor to the creditor; or
- guarantee the whole of the debt owing by the debtor to the creditor, but subject to a limit on the amount recoverable from the guarantor.

11.58 The distinction can be important because it affects the guarantor's rights on payment of the guaranteed amount. These rights are considered in more detail in part 5 of this chapter (**11.140ff**) but, in essence, a guarantor of part of the debt who has paid off that part has greater rights of subrogation against the creditor and of proof in the debtor's insolvency than if he has guaranteed the whole of the debt subject to a limit.

11.59 It is difficult to see any justification for such a rule. It is hard to believe that guarantors (or, for that matter, most creditors) turn their minds to such an artificial distinction as whether it is a guarantee of the whole debt subject to a limit or a guarantee of part of the debt. It has no practical or commercial merit, but it is now firmly ensconced. In practice, most financial guarantees are expressed to be guarantees of the whole debt, subject to a limit.

Limits as to particular types of transaction

11.60 It is again a matter of construction which types of transaction the guarantee extends to. As has been mentioned earlier, even with an 'all monies' form of guarantee, the presumption is that the guarantee is only intended to cover transactions between the debtor and the creditor and not debts owing by the debtor to a third party which are subsequently acquired by the creditor. If it is intended to cover such transactions, they need to be specifically referred to in the guarantee.[36]

Conditions precedent

11.61 If liability under a guarantee is subject to express conditions precedent, they must clearly be complied with before the guarantee becomes effective, but difficulties do arise in relation to implied conditions precedent. One example of an implied condition precedent concerns co-guarantors. If the guarantee is

---

36   *Re Quest Cae* [1985] BCLC 266; *Re Clark's Refrigerated Transport* [1982] VR 989; *Kova Establishment v Sasco Investments* [1998] 2 BCLC 83.

expressed to be entered into by a number of guarantors, one or more of whom do not sign, it is a matter of construction whether the other guarantors are still liable, but the likelihood is that the court will regard execution of the guarantee by all intended guarantors as being a condition precedent to the liability of any of them.[37] As a result, it is common for guarantees of financial transactions to contain an express provision to the effect that the guarantee is effective against those guarantors who have signed even if others, who were intending to sign, have not done so or are not effectively bound by the guarantee.

11.62 A further example of an implied condition precedent arose in *Associated Japanese Bank (International) v Credit du Nord*.[38] In that case, a guarantee was given of leases of certain machines which did not, in fact, exist. Although the guarantee contained wording which was intended to protect the creditor from the equitable defences available to guarantors, it was held that the existence of the machines was an implied condition precedent to the liability of the guarantor; and, since they did not exist, the guarantor was not liable.

Comfort letters

11.63 In a financing transaction, it is common for a parent company to guarantee the borrowings of its subsidiary. In some cases, however, the parent company will not do so but, instead, is prepared to give a 'comfort letter' to the creditor in relation to its subsidiary's borrowings. The effect of such a comfort letter was considered by the Court of Appeal in *Kleinwort Benson v Malaysia Mining*.[39] In that case, a bank made a facility available to a company. Its parent gave a comfort letter to the bank. The comfort letter explained that the parent knew of, and approved of, the facility and contained an undertaking that the parent would not reduce its shareholding in the subsidiary. It then went on to say:

> 'It is [the parent's] policy to ensure that the business of [the subsidiary] is at all times in a position to meet its liabilities to [the bank] under the above arrangements.'

11.64 The subsidiary went into liquidation, and the bank sued the parent under the comfort letter. The Court of Appeal held that the parent was not liable under the comfort letter. There was no doubt that the undertaking not to reduce its shareholding was a contractual promise, but it had not been breached. The real question was whether the sentence described above was an implied promise by the parent to procure that the subsidiary could 'at all times' meet its liabilities to the bank, or whether it was a representation of fact. If it was the former, the bank would have a claim against the parent for breach of the implied promise. If the latter, the bank would only be able to claim against the parent if the statement was untrue at the time that it was made (and there was no evidence that this was the case).

---

37   *Evans v Bremridge* (1856) 8 De GM & G 100.
38   [1989] 1 WLR 255.
39   [1989] 1 WLR 379.

11.65 The Court of Appeal held that the sentence was a representation of fact. It did not expressly promise that the factual position would continue, and no such promise could be implied. Whether an undertaking is a contractual promise or a representation of fact is a question of fact in each case, but a statement that 'it is our policy' or 'it is our intention' would not generally be expected to give rise to a promise that the policy or intention will always continue. The position is even clearer if the statement describes the parent company's 'present' intention.

11.66 Discussion of comfort letters sometimes revolves around the question whether they are intended to create legal relations. This was not the issue in the *Kleinwort Benson* case. There was no doubt in that case that the comfort letter was intended to create legal relations. It was given in a commercial context and contained one undertaking concerning maintenance of the parent company's shareholding which was clearly intended to be legally binding. The question was not, therefore, whether the letter was legally binding, but what was meant by the particular statement contained in the letter. Comfort letters are sometimes expressed not to be legally binding, in which event they will not be. But, in the absence of such a provision, a comfort letter in a commercial transaction is likely to be legally binding – the only question being one of interpretation of what it means.

Vitiating factors

11.67 As with any other contract, an apparently effective guarantee may be void or voidable as a result of a vitiating factor, such as fraud, mistake, misrepresentation, undue influence or breach of fiduciary duty. It is beyond the scope of this chapter to discuss such matters in detail, but there are two issues which do need to be considered because of their importance in practice in relation to guarantees. They both stem from the fact that a guarantor normally does not obtain any commensurate benefit for giving the guarantee.

11.68 The first relates to corporate guarantors. The issue is whether the giving of a guarantee by one member of a group of the obligations of its parent company or its sister companies is a breach of fiduciary duty of which the creditor is aware or ought to have been aware, in which event the guarantee is voidable by the guarantor.[40] This is a particular problem in relation to guarantees because of their one-sided nature. This issue is discussed in part 2 of CHAPTER 5 (**5.17ff**).

11.69 The second issue concerns individual guarantors. A contract of guarantee, like any other contract, can be set aside if it is the subject of a vitiating factor, such as misrepresentation or undue influence. The reason why the contract can be set aside is because there has been no real consent by one party to the contract because of the actions of the other. But, in the case of guarantees, a further principle has developed, as a result of which a contract of guarantee (or a similar arrangement, such as a third party charge) can be set

---

40 There is also a statutory formulation of the principle, contained in s 238 of the Insolvency Act 1986. See part 2 of CHAPTER 9 (**9.23ff**).

aside as a result of undue influence by the debtor on the guarantor. In this type of case, the creditor is unable to rely on a contract entered into by the guarantor not because of any misconduct by the creditor, but because of misconduct by the debtor. And this can be so even if the creditor was not aware of the debtor's misconduct.

11.70 Creditors who have taken a guarantee are treated more harshly than other contracting parties because, in most cases, the guarantor will obtain no commensurate benefit for the contingent liability which is incurred as a result of giving the guarantee. Uncertainty about the precise circumstances in which a guarantee will be set aside as a result of undue influence has led to a great deal of litigation. As a result, in *Barclays Bank v O'Brien*,[41] the House of Lords were at pains to establish the circumstances in which a guarantee would be set aside for undue influence. But this decision failed to stem the flow of litigation and, as a result, less than 10 years later they had to step in again. In *Royal Bank of Scotland v Etridge (No 2)*,[42] the House of Lords re-stated, with some variations, the principles which it had laid down in *O'Brien*. Some idea of the practical problems which needed to be resolved can be gleaned from the fact that, whilst *O'Brien* took up a mere 20 pages of the law reports, *Etridge* runs to some 110 pages. It remains to be seen whether this will have the desired effect of creating some certainty in the law and reducing the amount of litigation.

11.71 The judgment in *Etridge* is, in essence, concerned with three questions:

* What amounts to undue influence?
* In what circumstances is the creditor affected by the undue influence of the debtor on the guarantor?
* If the creditor is so affected, what steps must it take to enable it to be able to rely on the guarantee?

Undue influence

11.72 Undue influence can be established in two different ways. One way is for one party to a contract to prove that the other party imposed improper pressure on him, with the effect that he did not freely consent to entering into the contract. Alternatively, instead of proving such an overt act of improper pressure, one party can establish that a relationship of trust and confidence existed between the parties to the contract and that, in that circumstance, the nature of the transaction required an explanation. In the latter type of case, it is then for the other party to provide the explanation, failing which there will be sufficient evidence of undue influence for the transaction to be set aside. A guarantee, being a one-sided transaction, is precisely the type of transaction which is likely to require an explanation if it is given by one person for the benefit of another with whom he has a relationship of trust and confidence.

11.73 Certain types of relationship give rise to the presumption that they are relationships of trust and confidence. An example is the relationship between a

---

41   [1994] 1 AC 180.
42   [2002] 2 AC 773.

parent and a child. In fact, most of the cases concerning guarantees involve relationships between husbands and wives. This is not a relationship where trust and confidence is presumed, although its existence can be established by evidence.

11.74 Accordingly, in the case of a guarantee given by a wife for the obligations of her husband or his company, if the wife can prove that, at the time the guarantee was entered into, there was a relationship of trust and confidence between them, the guarantee is likely to require an explanation, in which event the debtor will have to explain how the transaction was entered into without undue influence. In some cases, the wife might also be able to establish that there was a misrepresentation by her husband, which would then give her another basis on which to have the guarantee set aside.

Is the creditor affected?

11.75 The issues which have just been discussed are all concerned with the relationship between the debtor and the guarantor – a matter about which the creditor is likely to be ignorant, and to wish to remain so. But, in this context, ignorance is no defence. The courts have had to grapple with two conflicting principles – the importance of the certainty of transactions and the wish to protect those whose will might be overborne. And they have come out firmly in favour of the latter.

11.76 If the creditor was a party to the undue influence being exerted by the debtor on the guarantor, then the guarantee can clearly be set aside. Equally, if it knew of the undue influence, then that would be sufficient to prevent it from being able to rely on the guarantee. But the principle goes much further than this. The guarantee can be set aside even if the bank was not a party to the undue influence and was not aware of it. Because a guarantee is a one-sided contract, the creditor will be affected by the debtor's undue influence whenever a wife gives a guarantee for the obligations of her husband or of his company. Indeed, this principle is not restricted to cases of husband and wife (although the bulk of the cases have concerned such relationships). Where the creditor has taken a guarantee, it will be affected by the creditor's undue influence on the debtor if the relationship between the debtor and the creditor is not a commercial relationship. In practice, this means that, regardless of the creditor's actual knowledge of the facts, the guarantee can be set aside if there was undue influence in any case where the relationship between the guarantor and the debtor was not a commercial relationship.

11.77 The House of Lords recognised that they were establishing a very broad principle, but they justified it on the basis that it was certain and that it would effectively act as a prophylactic – using creditors to police proper standards of conduct where the relationship between the guarantor and the debtor was of a non-commercial nature. In *O'Brien*, Lord Browne-Wilkinson had justified the conceptual basis for this approach by reference to concept of constructive notice. In *Etridge*, the House of Lords recognised that the doctrine of constructive notice is concerned with property law, not the law of contract, but they nevertheless upheld (and, indeed extended) the approach of Lord Browne-Wilkinson, justifying it on practical, rather than conceptual, grounds.

What must a creditor do if it is affected?

11.78 It has been seen that the creditor will be affected by undue influence if it takes a guarantee in circumstances where the relationship between the guarantor and the creditor is a non-commercial one. The third issue with which the House of Lords had to deal was how the creditor can protect itself in such a case. They decided that what the creditor must do is to take reasonable steps to satisfy itself that the guarantor understands what she is doing – that she is entering into the guarantee with her eyes open.

11.79 Their Lordships accepted that the creditor would be unlikely to do this itself, and that it would normally be done through a solicitor. And they described what has to be done both by the solicitor and by the creditor in order to ensure that the creditor is not affected by the undue influence.

11.80 As far as the creditor is concerned, it essentially has to do three things:

●   to ensure that the guarantor obtains her own legal advice on the guarantee;
●   to provide her solicitor with sufficient financial information to be able to advise the guarantor appropriately; and
●   to obtain a confirmation from the solicitor that he has advised the guarantor.

11.81 In essence, the solicitor has to do two things:

●   to describe the nature of the transaction to the guarantor, its effect on the guarantor and the seriousness of the risks which she is running in entering into it; and
●   to make it clear to the guarantor that she had a choice whether or not to proceed and to check that she does want to proceed,

the purpose being to ensure that the guarantor understands what she is doing by entering into the guarantee.

Conclusion

11.82 There is no doubt that the principles enunciated in *Etridge* are an extension of normal equitable principles. The House of Lords recognised this, but justified it on the basis of the need to protect wives from undue influence by their husbands. The purpose of the procedure is clear – it is to make it more difficult for husbands to put pressure on their wives to enter into guarantees or third party charges. And what is good for wives is also good for any other guarantor who is in a non-commercial relationship with the debtor. The role of the creditor is to act as a policeman. By threatening the creditor with having its guarantee set aside even though it was not aware of undue influence, the courts have forced creditors, for their own protection, to take steps to satisfy themselves that the guarantor understands what she is doing. The justification, as with so much else in relation to contracts of guarantee, is that a guarantee is a one-sided contract and therefore requires special rules for the protection of guarantors.

Part 4: DISCHARGE BY CONDUCT OF THE CREDITOR

11.83 The main problem with guarantees, as far as the creditor is concerned, is the ease by which his actions can release the guarantor from all or part of his liability. The problem arises from the nature of a guarantee. Because a guarantor will frequently obtain no real benefit from the guarantee, the courts have developed various protections for him.

11.84 Although, in principle, it is understandable that the courts should want to protect guarantors, they have frequently done so in ways which have very little commercial justification. There are numerous cases, both in equity and at common law, which stretch back at least as far as the early seventeenth century. Instead of establishing a general overriding principle to the effect that actions by the creditor which materially prejudice the guarantor will release the guarantor to the extent of the prejudice, the courts have developed a detailed series of conflicting rules, the application of which depends on the nature of the creditor's action. They fall into six categories:

- The release of the debtor by the creditor.
- The debtor being given time to pay by the creditor.
- Variations to the contract between the creditor and the debtor.
- The release of co-guarantors by the creditor.
- The loss of security held by the creditor.
- Breach of contract by the creditor.

11.85 This part considers each of these categories in turn, and then discusses how the problems can be overcome in practice. Although the courts have recognised that guarantors need protection, they have also accepted that a guarantee is a contract and that it is therefore possible to contract out of these protections. In practice, most modern guarantees do so, particularly those which secure financial transactions.

Release of the debtor

11.86 In *Mahant Singh v U Ba Yi*, Lord Porter said:[43]

'A surety is discharged if the creditor, without his consent, either releases the principal debtor or enters into a binding arrangement with him to give him time.'

---

43 [1939] AC 601 at 606.

11.87 An example of the effect of this rule in relation to releases of the debtor is contained in *Commercial Bank of Tasmania v Jones*.[44] G had guaranteed D's bank account with C. Without G's consent, C and D then agreed with a third party that the bank account would be novated. The effect of the novation was to release D from its liability to C and to replace it with a new liability owing by the third party to C. The Privy Council held that this released G's liability under the guarantee.

11.88 Three different reasons have been given for the rule. The first reason is straightforward. As has been seen, the liability of a guarantor is secondary to that of the debtor. If the principal debt does not exist, then there is nothing to guarantee. In *Commercial Bank of Tasmania v Jones*, Lord Morris said that, if there is an absolute release of the debtor's liability, the guarantor is no longer liable because the guaranteed debt has been extinguished.[45]

11.89 This explanation would seem to be sufficient, but two other reasons for the rule have been given in various cases, and they are both referred to by Lord Porter in *Mahant Singh v U Ba Yi*. The first is that the release of the principal debtor interferes with the guarantor's rights of subrogation and indemnity against the debtor (which are discussed in part 5 of this chapter (**11.140ff**)). The second (which is inconsistent with the first) is that, if the guarantor continued to be liable, he would retain his rights of subrogation and indemnity against the debtor, which would therefore nullify the release.

11.90 It is necessary to examine these reasons because they underlie the way in which the courts view the effect of releases and the methods by which the problem can be averted by the creditor. If the debtor were to be released, but the guarantor continued to be liable, there are two alternative outcomes, neither of which is wholly satisfactory. The first possibility is that the guarantor, because he is still liable, would continue to have his rights of subrogation and indemnity against the debtor. This would mean that the guarantor was not prejudiced by the release, but it would have the effect that the release of the debtor would effectively be rendered nugatory. Although the creditor could not sue the debtor direct, he could still sue the guarantor, who could then claim against the debtor. The alternative outcome would be to give effect to the release by preventing the guarantor from pursuing his remedies against the debtor. But this would then clearly prejudice the guarantor, who would continue to be liable under the guarantee, but would not have his rights of subrogation and indemnity against the debtor.

11.91 Either way, the result is unsatisfactory and the courts have therefore decided that the release of the debtor will also release the guarantor.

11.92 There are two principal exceptions to this rule:

● The creditor can reserve his rights against the guarantor or, instead of releasing the guarantor, covenant not to sue him.

● The creditor can obtain the consent of the guarantor either by a provision in the guarantee or at the time of the release.

---

44 [1893] AC 313.
45 [1893] AC 313 at 316.

Covenants not to sue and reservations of rights

11.93 Although the guarantor is released if the debtor is released, it would seem that the guarantor is not released if the creditor only covenants not to sue the debtor.[46] The distinction between a release and a covenant not to sue can be seen as one of those 'hair-splitting distinctions' referred to by Harman LJ in *Yeoman Credit v Latter.*[47] The cases concerning covenants not to sue can, however, be seen in a different light.

11.94 In *Green v Wynn,*[48] G had guaranteed an obligation of D to C. D entered into a composition with his creditors which involved a transfer of his assets to a trustee and the release of D. The composition contained a proviso that it did not affect any rights which a creditor might have against anyone else in respect of any debt due by D. The Lord Chancellor held that the composition did not constitute an absolute release of the debtor. The proviso was inconsistent with such an absolute release and it was therefore just a covenant not to sue; and the guarantor was therefore still liable.

11.95 This case establishes the conceptual basis by which it can be determined whether or not the guarantor is released. It is not a question of whether the arrangement with the debtor is expressed to constitute a release or a covenant not to sue. The real question is whether the creditor has reserved his rights against the guarantor.

11.96 It is suggested that the position is as follows. The issue for the court is what is the effect of the arrangement between the debtor and the creditor? Is it intended by the parties to be a complete release of the debtor from claims against all parties (ie from the guarantor as well as from the creditor)? If so, the guarantor will be released because:

- the preservation of his rights of indemnity and reimbursement against the debtor would nullify the intended effect of the document; and
- to make the guarantor liable notwithstanding the release of his rights against the debtor would be unfair.

11.97 Alternatively, the intention of the parties may have been to release the creditor's rights against the debtor, but to preserve:

- the creditor's rights against the guarantor; and
- the guarantor's rights against the debtor.

11.98 It is a matter of construction which of these two results is intended. If the latter result is intended, it should be made clear in the documentation that the creditor is preserving his rights against the guarantors; and it would be prudent to make it clear to the debtor that the effect of this preservation of rights is that the debtor has not been completely released from his obligations because of the ability of the guarantor to claim his rights of indemnity and subrogation from the debtor.

---

46 *Mallet v Thompson* (1803, 1806, 1807) 5 Esp 178.
47 [1961] 1 WLR 828 at 835, referred to in part 2 of this chapter (**11.12**ff).
48 (1869) LR 4 Ch App 204.

Consent by the guarantor

11.99   The other (and much simpler) way of preserving the creditor's rights is to obtain the consent of the guarantor. This can be done either at the time the arrangement is entered into with the debtor or in the guarantee itself.

11.100   The liability of a guarantor is ultimately a matter of construction of the particular document concerned, and it is therefore possible to contract out of the principle that the release of the debtor will release the guarantor. In *Perry v National Provincial Bank of England*,[49] G entered into a third party charge in favour of C to secure an overdraft granted by C to D. The document provided that C could, without affecting its rights against G, 'vary, exchange or release any other securities held or to be held by [C] for or on account of the [secured liabilities]' or 'compound with, give time for payment of, and accept compositions from and make any arrangements with [D]'.

11.101   D became insolvent and entered into a scheme with its creditors by which they were given debentures in a new company in consideration for the release of their claims against D. The Court of Appeal held that this arrangement did not release G. Lord Cozens-Hardy MR acknowledged that, in a simple guarantee, a release of the debtor will release the guarantor but:[50]

> 'When you find in the instrument of suretyship itself a provision that the surety shall be liable notwithstanding certain acts being done by the creditor which would otherwise release him, these doctrines have no application at all. It is not then a simple contract of suretyship. It is true that in one sense it is a contract of suretyship, but it is a contract of suretyship containing special clauses which deliberately exclude certain rights which the surety would otherwise have had.'

11.102   He went on to say:[51]

> '[I]t is perfectly possible for a surety to contract with a creditor in the suretyship instrument that notwithstanding any composition, release, or arrangement the surety shall remain liable although the principal does not.'

11.103   Notwithstanding these clear words, there is a distinction between the release of the debtor and other actions taken by the creditor which might prejudice the debtor. As has been seen, the essence of a guarantee is that it is a secondary liability. If there is no principal debt, the guarantor can no longer be liable as a guarantor. In order to continue to be liable, the guarantor must assume a primary liability to the creditor, independent of that of the debtor. That was what the Court of Appeal held had happened in the *Perry* case, but a different conclusion was reached by the Privy Council in *Commercial Bank of Tasmania v Jones*.[52] In that case, the guarantee contained a provision by which a release of the debtor was expressed not to affect the guarantor's liability. As has been seen, the Privy Council held that a novation of the principal debt

---

49   [1910] 1 Ch 464.
50   [1910] 1 Ch 464 at 471.
51   [1910] 1 Ch 464 at 473.
52   [1893] AC 313.

released the guarantor. The judgment does not clearly explain why the express provision of the guarantee did not save the guarantor's liability, but it shows that it is preferable to ensure that the guarantee makes it very clear that the guarantor is undertaking a primary obligation as indemnifier in all cases where the principal debtor is not liable, whether this is because the principal debt is ineffective from the outset or is subsequently discharged.

11.104   In order to prevent the discharge of the guarantor by the release of the debtor, it is accordingly preferable for the guarantee not only to provide that it remains effective notwithstanding the release of the debtor, but also to contain an indemnity by which the guarantor agrees to indemnify the creditor against any loss it may suffer as a result of entering into the guaranteed transaction even if the debtor is not himself liable, either at the outset of the transaction (for example, because the primary obligation is void) or subsequently (for example, because the debtor is released). In practice, it is usual for the creditor also to require an express consent by the guarantor as a condition of the release of the debtor. If the guarantee contains appropriate wording, this is not strictly necessary, but it makes it more difficult in practice for the guarantor to argue the point.

The creditor gives time to the debtor

11.105   If the creditor enters into an agreement to give time to the debtor to perform the principal agreement, the guarantor is discharged unless he assents. The principles are very similar to those relating to the release of the principal debtor, and it is common for both principles to be considered together. It is worth repeating the statement of Lord Porter in *Mahant Singh v U Ba Yi*:[53]

> 'A surety is discharged if the creditor, without his consent, either releases the principal debtor or enters into a binding arrangement with him to give him time.'

11.106   The debtor is only released if there is a binding agreement between the creditor and the debtor. He is not released if there is simply an omission by the creditor to press for payment. In the words of Lord Eldon LC in *Samuell v Howarth*:[54]

> '[I]f a creditor, without the consent of the Surety, gives time to the principal debtor, by so doing he discharges the Surety; that is, if time is given by virtue of positive contract between the creditor and the principal – not where the creditor is merely inactive.'

11.107   If there is such a binding agreement, the guarantor is released even if he is not prejudiced by the arrangement and even if it positively benefits him.[55]

11.108   It has been seen that there were three reasons why the release of the debtor also released the guarantor. The first reason related to the nature of a

---

53   [1939] AC 601 at 606.
54   (1817) 3 Mer 272 at 278.
55   *Polak v Everett* (1876) 1 QBD 669 at 673–674, per Blackburn J.

guarantee as a secondary obligation – that it cannot exist if there is no primary obligation. That is not relevant where there is an agreement to give time to the debtor, but the other two reasons for releasing the guarantor have been held to apply equally to an agreement to give time to the debtor as they do to a release of the debtor. The granting of time either deprives the guarantor of his ability to compel the debtor to perform his obligation and thereby absolve the guarantor from liability[56] or that right is retained, in which event the creditor remains liable to the guarantor and therefore the agreement to give time is effectively nullified.[57]

11.109 It has been seen that there are two ways in which the creditor can avoid releasing the guarantor as a result of releasing the debtor. He can reserve his rights against the guarantor or he can obtain the consent of the guarantor, either prospectively in the guarantee or at the time of the arrangement. These methods are equally available to the creditor in relation to giving time to the principal debtor.[58]

11.110 As in the case of the release of the debtor, the cases indicate that the guarantor is not released by giving time to the debtor if the creditor reserves his rights against the guarantor. In *Kearsley v Cole*,[59] Parke B explained why a reservation of remedies was effective when a creditor gave time to the debtor. It was because:

- it rebutted the implication that the guarantor was meant to be discharged; and
- it prevented the guarantor's rights against the debtor from being impaired.

11.111 As Lord Eldon LC made clear in *Boultbee v Stubbs*,[60] if the creditor gives time to the debtor, but reserves his rights against the guarantor, the guarantor continues to be able to recover against the debtor if he is sued by the creditor.

11.112 It is important, when drafting such arrangements, that it should be clear that:

- the creditor is reserving his rights against the guarantor; and
- notwithstanding the arrangement with the debtor, the guarantor can still bring a claim against the debtor for any amount which he has to pay to the creditor.

11.113 In practice, the simplest way of avoiding the problem is either to obtain the consent of the guarantor at the time or to contract out of it in the guarantee.

11.114 It is difficult to understand why the rule is as strict as the courts have made it. The guarantor is completely discharged from his liability if there is a

---

56 *Moschi v Lep Air Services* [1973] AC 331 at 348, per Lord Diplock.
57 *Mahant Singh v U Ba Yi* [1939] AC 601 at 606, per Lord Porter.
58 *Perry v National Provincial Bank of England* [1910] 1 Ch 464.
59 (1846) 16 M & W 128.
60 (1810, 1811) 18 Ves Jun 20 at 26.

binding agreement to give time unless one of the exceptions referred to above apply. This is the case even if the guarantor is not prejudiced and, apparently, even if it is to his advantage. The final words should be left to Justice Cardozo:[61]

> 'The law has shaped its judgments upon the fictitious assumption that a surety, who has probably lain awake at nights for fear that payment may some day be demanded, has in truth been smarting under the repressed desire to force an unwelcome payment on a reluctant or capricious creditor.'

Variations to the principal contract

11.115   If the creditor gives the debtor time to pay, that effectively varies the contractual arrangements between them, and it has been seen that this completely releases the guarantor even if the arrangement does not prejudice him. But what is the position with respect to other variations of the principal contract between the debtor and the creditor? The basic rule is that the guarantor will be released by a variation of the principal contract which is made without his consent unless the alteration is obviously unsubstantial or clearly for the guarantor's benefit. The principle is expressed very clearly by the High Court of Australia in *Ankar v National Westminster Finance (Australia)*:[62]

> '[T]he principle applies so as to discharge the surety when conduct on the part of the creditor has the effect of altering the surety's rights, unless the alteration is unsubstantial and not prejudicial to the surety. The rule does not permit the courts to inquire into the effect of the alteration. The consequence is that, to hold the surety to its bargain, the creditor must show that the nature of the alteration can be beneficial to the surety only or that by its nature it cannot in any circumstances increase the surety's risk.'

11.116   The leading case is the decision of the Court of Appeal in *Holme v Brunskill*.[63] C let a farm to D on a yearly tenancy. The farm included a flock of sheep and G guaranteed the re-delivery of the flock in good condition at the end of the tenancy. D and C agreed to a variation of the tenancy which reduced its size and provided for a lower rental. When the tenancy terminated, the flock had been reduced in number and its quality had deteriorated. It was found as a fact that the alteration to the tenancy agreement had not materially affected the guarantor.

11.117   The Court of Appeal nevertheless decided that the guarantor was not liable. He had not been asked to assent to the alteration and should be the sole judge of what was reasonable. The principal judgment was given by Cotton LJ. He said that, if there was any agreement between the debtor and the creditor about the principal contract, the guarantor ought to be consulted. If he does not consent, then he will be discharged unless it is self-evident that the variation

---

61   Cardozo *The Nature of Judicial Process* (Yale University Press, 1921) at pp 153–154.
62   (1987) 162 CLR 549 at 559.
63   (1878) 3 QBD 495.

is unsubstantial or cannot be prejudicial to the guarantor. It is for the guarantor to be the judge of whether he accepts the variation and therefore the court will not inquire into the materiality of the variation. It is only if it is self-evidently unsubstantial or cannot be prejudicial to the guarantor that the guarantee will be preserved. On the facts of the particular case, although there was a finding of fact that the variation did not materially prejudice the guarantor, the court should not inquire into such matters and, since the variation was not self-evidently immaterial, the guarantor was discharged from liability.

11.118   The principle does not apply if the guarantor consents to the variation at the time or prospectively in the guarantee.[64] Most modern guarantees contain a provision by which the creditor is entitled to vary the underlying contract without discharging the guarantor's liability. Such clauses are effective.[65] There is some authority that a clause which simply provides that the liability of the guarantor shall be that of a principal debtor is sufficient to enable the creditor to enter into arrangements with the debtor without prejudicing the guarantee.[66] There are also suggestions that the liability of an indemnifier may not be affected by variations to the underlying contract.[67] It would, however, be preferable not to rely on such cases. Where an indemnity is given to secure the liabilities of a third party, the indemnifier has the same rights against the debtor, once he has paid, as would a guarantor. Since the justification for discharging the guarantor is the prejudice which he can suffer as a result, particularly in pursuing his remedies against the debtor, the principle ought to apply to an indemnifier (and to a guarantor who is expressed to be a principal debtor) as much as to a simple guarantor. It is therefore preferable for a creditor to ensure that the document contains clear provisions authorising the creditor to agree to variations of the principal contract without affecting the liability of the guarantor.

11.119   Variations to the principal contract raise a further issue. If the guarantor guarantees the performance by the debtor of a particular contract, it has been seen that a variation of that contract will discharge the guarantor from liability, even to the extent of the contract before the variation. This problem is solved if the guarantee provides that variations to the principal contract will not discharge the guarantor. But, even if the guarantee contains such a provision, the extent of the guarantor's liability is still a matter of construction of the guarantee. Has the guarantor agreed to guarantee the contract as varied or is he only liable under the old contract? He will only be liable under the varied contract if the guarantee expressly or impliedly makes him liable for it (and any ambiguity will be construed in favour of the guarantor). Similarly, if the variations to the contract are so substantial that they amount to a rescission of the existing contract and the creation of a new one, does the guarantee extend to that new contract? Again, this will only be the case if the guarantee provides that it does.

---

64   *Woodcock v Oxford and Worcester Railway Co* (1853) 1 Drew 521.
65   *Perry v National Provincial Bank of England* [1910] 1 Ch 464.
66   *General Produce Co v United Bank* [1979] 2 Lloyd's Rep 255.
67   *Way v Hearn* (1862) 11 CB NS 774.

11.120   An example of this problem is the decision of the Court of Appeal in *Triodos Bank v Dobbs*.[68] This case is discussed in part 4 of **CHAPTER 3** (**3.140**ff), but is worth repeating here. Mr Dobbs had guaranteed to a bank the obligations of a company under two loan agreements, by which the company was lent £900,000 to complete the first stage of a particular project. Those loan agreements were replaced by two further loan agreements in 1998 and by another one in 1999. Their effect was to increase the amount of the facility from £900,000 to £2,600,000, the purpose of the increase being to finance the second stage of the project. It was held that the guarantee did not extend to the new facilities. Even though the guarantee contained protective provisions and even though it was expressed to extend to amendments or variations of the existing facility, the new facilities were for a greatly increased amount and for new purposes. In substance, they documented a different facility from that which Mr Dobbs had guaranteed.

11.121   When drafting guarantees, there are therefore two issues which need to be borne in mind in relation to variations. In the first place, it is necessary to make sure that the guarantee does contain a clause by which variations to the principal contract will not discharge the guarantor. But such a clause will not necessarily make the guarantor liable in respect of the variations to the contract or in respect of any replacement contract. It is therefore necessary to ensure that the guaranteed obligations are drafted sufficiently widely to ensure that varied contracts and new contracts are, where appropriate, included within the definition of the guaranteed obligations.

Release of co-guarantors

11.122   Where the creditor enters into arrangements with co-guarantors, the position is rather different from when he deals with the principal debtor. If the guarantees are joint or joint and several, the release of one guarantor will release the others.[69] This follows from the general rules concerning joint liabilities. Where, however, the guarantees are only several (and were not entered into on the basis that the other guarantees would remain in force), the release of one co-guarantor will not release the others unless they suffer loss as a result (ie in relation to their rights of contribution and subrogation against the co-guarantors), and then only to the extent of that loss.[70]

11.123   In either case, the creditor will not be affected if:

- the creditor reserves his rights against co-guarantors when releasing the guarantor (because the co-guarantors' rights of contribution and subrogation will remain);[71] or
- the guarantor consents to the release either at the time or prospectively in the guarantee itself.[72]

---

68   [2005] EWCA Civ 630.
69   *Mercantile Bank of Sydney v Taylor* [1893] AC 317.
70   *Ward v The National Bank of New Zealand* (1883) 8 App Cas 755.
71   *Re Wolmershausen* (1890) 62 LT 541.
72   *Perry v National Provincial Bank of England* [1910] 1 Ch 464.

Loss of security held by the creditor

11.124 A creditor will often take security from the debtor, in addition to taking a guarantee. He may also take security from co-guarantors. Once the guarantor has paid the guaranteed debt, he is entitled to the benefit of any security held by the creditor which has been granted by the debtor and, in certain circumstances, where it has been given by co-guarantors. These rights are considered in part 5 of this chapter (**11.140ff**).

11.125 Because the guarantor has rights to the creditor's security in certain circumstances, the law recognises that the creditor owes certain duties to the guarantor in relation to that security. In essence, if the creditor either deliberately or negligently allows the value of the security to be diminished, the guarantor's liability under the guarantee is reduced by the amount of the loss which has been suffered as a result of that failure. The duty was clearly expressed by Dixon J in the High Court of Australia in *Williams v Frayne*:[73]

> 'If the guarantee is given upon a condition, whether express or implied from the circumstances, that a specific security shall be obtained, completed, protected, maintained or preserved, any failure in the performance of the condition operates to discharge the surety and the discharge is complete. But otherwise the surety can complain only if the creditor sacrifices or impairs a security, or by his neglect or default allows it to be lost or diminished, and in that case the surety is entitled in equity to be credited with the deficiency in reduction of his liability.'

11.126 It will be seen that there are two principles described here. The first is a contractual one. If the guarantee is expressly or impliedly conditional on the performance of a particular duty by the creditor, the guarantor will not be bound if that condition is not fulfilled. The second principle does not impose a duty on the creditor to act in a particular way but gives the guarantor a defence to a claim by the creditor to the extent that the creditor's actions in relation to the security have reduced its value to the guarantor.

11.127 An example of this latter type of case is *Wulff v Jay*.[74] C lent money to D which was secured by a guarantee from G and a security bill of sale over chattels owned by the debtor. The creditor failed to register the bill of sale and also failed to enforce the security when he became aware that the debtor was in default. As a result of these failures, the bill of sale was worthless. It was held that the liability of the guarantor was reduced by the amount which the bill of sale would have been worth had it been properly registered and enforced. In the words of Cockburn CJ:[75] 'it is the business of the creditor, where he has security ..., to do whatever is necessary to make that security properly available.'

11.128 It was made clear in this case that the principle applies to all security to which the guarantor would be subrogated (which, as will be seen in part 5 of

---

73   (1937) 58 CLR 710 at 738.
74   (1872) LR 7 QB 756.
75   (1872) LR 7 QB 756 at 762.

this chapter (**11.140ff**), includes security acquired by the creditor after the guarantee was entered into, even if the guarantor was unaware of it).

11.129 The principle applies where the creditor releases security[76] or fails to perfect security, for instance, by failing to register the security[77] or to give notice to a debtor of an equitable assignment.[78] In *Wulff v Jay*, it was also held to apply where the creditor failed to enforce his security, although a different decision was reached on this point by the Privy Council in *China and South Sea Bank v Tan Soon Gin*.[79] In that case, C took security over shares owned by D as well as a guarantee from G. When D defaulted, the shares were worth more than the amount of the loan, but C did not enforce the security and they subsequently became worthless. C sued G and G claimed a breach of duty by C. The Privy Council held that C was entitled to exercise his power of sale when he decided and owed no duty to the guarantor when the power of sale is to be exercised.

11.130 How is it possible to reconcile this case with *Wulff v Jay*? In the first place, the guarantee contained broad exculpatory provisions which were intended to protect the creditor from the loss of the guarantee as a result of his actions. As Lord Templeman stated, the guarantor 'does not and cannot impugn the validity of the [protective] provisions of the guarantee'.[80] Secondly, although a secured creditor has a duty to obtain the best price which can reasonably be obtained at the time he decides to enforce his security, he has a discretion as to when to exercise the security.[81] Although a creditor enforcing security owes the same duty to a guarantor as he does to a subsequent encumbrancer or the debtor,[82] the scope of the duty owed to the guarantor clearly cannot exceed that owed to those persons.

Breach of contract by the creditor

11.131 The discussion in this part has involved a consideration of the various common law and equitable protections available to a guarantor. They do not depend on express or implied terms of the contract, although they are susceptible to qualification or removal by the terms of the guarantee.

11.132 Normally a guarantee is a one-way obligation, owed by the guarantor to the creditor. Sometimes, however, the creditor will enter into an agreement with the guarantor, either in the guarantee or in a separate document. Breach of that contractual obligation will result in a damages claim by the guarantor but it might also release the guarantor from his liability under the guarantee. This will be the case if the creditor's obligation to the guarantor is a condition of the contract (so that any breach of it will release the guarantor from his

---

76   *Pledge v Buss* (1860) Johns 663.
77   *Wulff v Jay* (1872) LR 7QB 756.
78   *Northern Banking Co v Newman & Calton* [1927] IR 520.
79   [1990] 1 AC 536.
80   [1990] 1 AC 536 at 543.
81   See part 8 of CHAPTER 8 (**8.173ff**).
82   *Standard Chartered Bank v Walker* [1982] 1 WLR 1410.

obligations under the guarantee) or if the effect of the breach is to deprive the guarantor of the whole or substantially the whole of the benefit of the contract. This can be illustrated by an example.

11.133 In *Ankar v National Westminster Finance (Australia)*,[83] G entered into a third party charge to secure the hiring of machinery by D from C. The third party charge document contained an undertaking by C to notify G if D proposed to assign its interest in the machinery and C also agreed to notify G if D was in default under the hire contract, whereupon the parties would confer as to the steps to be taken. D defaulted under the hire contract and, with the consent of C, assigned its interest in the machinery. C did not notify G. The High Court of Australia held that G was discharged from liability under the guarantee because the compliance by C with these provisions was conditions precedent to the guarantor's liability.

11.134 This case is a reminder of the importance of ensuring that, if the creditor does enter into undertakings with the guarantor, the contract should make it clear whether these are simply contractual promises which, if broken, will give the guarantor a right to damages or whether they are also conditions precedent to the liability of the guarantor.

Guarantee protections in practice

11.135 The guarantor protections which have been discussed in this part broadly fall into two categories. The first category consists of cases where the debtor is released from his obligations to the creditor. Since a guarantee constitutes a secondary obligation, the absence of the principal obligation means that the guarantee falls away. This result can be avoided if the creditor reserves his rights against the guarantor, but this has the effect that the release is not totally effective to protect the creditor, since he is still subject to claims by the guarantor.

11.136 The better way of dealing with the problem is for the contract of guarantee to provide that the guarantor continues to be liable notwithstanding the release of the debtor. In view of the secondary nature of a guarantee, it is also preferable to make it clear that the guarantor is thereby undertaking a primary obligation as indemnifier. Such a clause will be effective if properly drafted, but it is nevertheless good practice to obtain the consent of the guarantor to the release at the time it is given – if only to avoid subsequent argument.

11.137 The second category consists of the other four types of case:

- giving time to the debtor;
- variations of the principal contract;
- releasing co-guarantors; and
- losing the benefit of security.

---

83   (1987) 162 CLR 549.

11.138 It might have been expected that, in such cases, the guarantor would be released if he were prejudiced, and to the extent of the prejudice. Unfortunately, the authorities do not adopt such a general rule, but treat different types of action by the creditor in different ways. In some cases (such as an agreement to give time to the debtor), any action of the relevant type will release the guarantor absolutely, regardless of any prejudice. In some cases (such as variations to the principal contract), the guarantor is absolutely discharged, but not if the variation is manifestly unsubstantial or in the guarantor's interests. In other cases, such as loss of securities, the guarantor is only released to the extent that he has suffered loss as a result of the creditor's action or inaction.

11.139 The most important consideration, however, is that all of these protections can be contracted out of in the guarantee. Although such provisions will be construed against the creditor if there is any ambiguity, there is no doubt that clear exclusions of the protections are effective. Most guarantees (particularly in financial transactions) contain detailed provisions contracting out of such protections, although it is also common to obtain the guarantor's consent at the time, not least to avoid subsequent argument. It is also good practice to treat any contract by which one person is assuming responsibility for the liabilities of another in the same way as a guarantee, including indemnities and third party charges. The reason why the courts protect guarantors is that a guarantee is a one-sided contract, and these other types of contract exhibit the same characteristic.

Part 5: THE GUARANTOR'S RIGHTS

11.140 The last part of this chapter was concerned with the circumstances in which a guarantor can deny liability as a result of actions by the creditor which can prejudice his interests. This part discusses the rights of guarantors which arise as a result of the giving of the guarantee. In both cases, the reason for protecting the guarantor is the same – the fact that the guarantor will generally obtain no commensurate benefit for entering into the guarantee.

11.141 A guarantor is given various rights against the debtor, the creditor and co-guarantors. The purpose of these rights is to enable the guarantor to recover payments which he has to make under the guarantee. This is done in three different ways:

- The guarantor has rights of indemnity against the debtor in respect of amounts paid under the guarantee.
- The guarantor has a right of contribution against co-guarantors in order to ensure that he does not pay more than his fair share.
- The guarantor has the right to be subrogated to the creditor's rights (including its security) against the debtor and co-guarantors in order to give effect to those rights of indemnity and contribution.

11.142 Although these rights were generally available at common law as well as in equity, they arise as a result of broad equitable principles and not as a result of any express or implied contract between the parties. But they can be contracted out of.

Indemnity

11.143 The guarantor has a right to be indemnified by the debtor against payments made by him under the guarantee if the guarantee is entered into at the express or implied request of the debtor.

11.144 An example of the way in which this principle works is *Re a Debtor (No 627 of 1936)*.[84] In 1933, G guaranteed D's bank account with C. In 1936, D defaulted and, following a demand by C, G paid C. G tried to obtain repayment from D. D was unable to pay and G accordingly petitioned for D's bankruptcy. This would normally have been a straightforward case of a claim under an indemnity giving rise to the ability to bankrupt the debtor if the claim was not paid. In this case, however, D was a married woman and the complication was that married women were generally not susceptible to bankruptcy proceedings before 1935, when the law was changed. As a result of the change in the law, a married woman was liable to be made bankrupt, but only in respect of obligations which arose after 1935. The question was therefore whether G's right of indemnity arose in 1933, when the guarantee was given, or in 1936, when payment was made.

11.145 The Court of Appeal held that G's right of indemnity was created at the time the guarantee was given at D's request. The right to indemnity was contingent until G actually made payment, but the obligation arose when the guarantee was entered into at the express or implied request of D. As a result, D could not be made bankrupt. The principle was expressed clearly by Greene LJ:[85]

> '[W]here "A" at the request of "B" guarantees payment of "B's" debt to "C", the law implies an undertaking by "B" to indemnify "A" in respect of any sums which he properly pays to "C" under the guarantee.'

11.146 The reference to a request by the debtor indicates the one material limitation on the principle that the guarantor is entitled to an indemnity – it is only available if it is given at the express or implied request of the debtor. In *Owen v Tate*,[86] D borrowed money from C, secured by a third party charge given by T. For the benefit of T, and without consulting D, G guaranteed D's borrowings from C, and secured the guarantee by a cash deposit with C, in consideration for which C released T's security. D protested when this was discovered but, being pressed for payment by C, requested C to utilise G's deposit in discharge of D's liability. G then claimed reimbursement from D.

---

84 [1937] Ch 156.
85 [1937] Ch 156 at 163.
86 [1976] QB 402.

11.147   The Court of Appeal held that G did not have a right of indemnity against D. G had entered into the guarantee without the knowledge or consent of D and, although the courts are ready to imply a request from the circumstances of the case, in this case no such request could be implied.

11.148   Although G's claim for an indemnity was rejected by the Court of Appeal, it is arguable that G would have been subrogated to C's claims against G as a result of payment, even though the guarantee was given without the express or implied request of D, because such a requirement does not appear to be a condition of a right of subrogation. Rights of subrogation are considered below.

11.149   If the guarantor does have a right of indemnity, he is entitled to be reimbursed by the debtor for all payments made under the guarantee, even if they are only part payments and do not discharge the guarantor's liability in full. In the words of Parke B in *Davies v Humphreys*:[87] 'there is no rule of law which requires the surety to pay the whole debt before he can call for reimbursement.'

11.150   The guarantor also has certain limited rights even before he pays the guarantor. If the creditor has an immediate right to payment from the guarantor, the guarantor can require the debtor to pay the creditor, and thereby absolve the guarantor from liability. In *Thomas v Nottingham Incorporated Football Club*,[88] G had given a continuing guarantee of D's overdraft from C and then gave notice to terminate his future obligations under the guarantee. C accordingly opened a new account for future dealings with D, thereby retaining G's liability for the amount owing at the date D received notice of the revocation. G applied to the court for an order requiring D to pay off the debt. D objected, on the basis that D had not made demand on G, and therefore G had no obligation to make an immediate payment to C.

11.151   Goff J held that G was entitled to require D to pay C on the basis that:[89] 'the surety is entitled to remove the cloud which is hanging over him ... [O]nce the account is closed and there is an accrued fixed liability, the surety is entitled to this quia timet relief.' G accordingly obtained a declaration that he was entitled to be exonerated from liability under the guarantee by payment by D to C of the amount of his guarantee liability.

Contribution

11.152   The purpose of the right of indemnity is to ensure that the person who is primarily liable for the debt has the ultimate liability to pay it. From at least the early seventeenth century,[90] the courts have recognised that, where there is more than one guarantor, the fact that the creditor happens to recover from one guarantor rather than another should not affect the rights of the

---

87   (1840) 6 M & W 153 at 167.
88   [1972] Ch 596.
89   [1972] Ch 596 at 606.
90   *Morgan v Seymour* (1637–38) 1 Rep Ch 120.

guarantors between themselves. Each guarantor is therefore entitled to a contribution from the other guarantors if he has paid more than his fair share.

11.153 This principle was recognised by the common law courts as well as by the courts of equity, and the leading case is the decision of the Court of Exchequer in *Deering v Earl of Winchelsea*.[91] G1, G2 and G3 had each entered into separate bonds with C, guaranteeing the obligations owing by D to C in respect of the due performance of a particular office. C obtained judgment against G1, and G1 then claimed a contribution from G2 and G3 in respect of his liability. It was held that G1 was entitled to a contribution from his co-guarantors. Although all three guarantors had entered into separate bonds, and there was no evidence that they had intended that there should be any rights of contribution, it was held that 'contribution is a fixed principle of justice, and is not founded in contract';[92] and that the right of contribution arose because the guarantors all had 'a common interest and a common burthen'.[93]

11.154 The right of contribution arises from basic principles of equity, regardless of whether:

● the guarantors are bound by the same or different documents;
● they are jointly or severally liable;
● they were aware of the other guarantors;
● they were created at different times; or
● they have different limits of liability.

11.155 The only question is whether the various guarantors are liable for the same liability of the debtor. If so, they are entitled to a contribution. If not, they are not. This limit on the obligation to contribute is illustrated by *Craythorne v Swinburne*.[94] D and G1 issued a joint and several bond in favour of C, G1 acting as guarantor for D. G2 then issued another bond to C as security for the first bond. G1 paid the liability in full and claimed a contribution from G2. Lord Eldon LC held that G1 was not entitled to a right of contribution. G2 and G1 had not guaranteed the same debt. G1 had guaranteed D, but G2 had guaranteed D and G1. In essence, therefore, G2 was a sub-guarantor, rather than a co-guarantor with T. A right of contribution is only available if there is what is sometimes referred to as a 'common demand', ie if the two guarantors are liable for the same debt.

11.156 The guarantor's right of contribution is to recover from his co-guarantors that part of the amount which he has paid which is in excess of his fair share. What is his fair share depends on the arrangements between the parties. If the guarantors are liable to an unlimited extent for the same debt, they will each be liable to share equally. If some of their liabilities are limited, that limit is the amount of their fair share. If one of the guarantors is insolvent,

91 (1787) 2 Bos & Pul 270, also reported as *Dering v Earl of Winchelsea* (1787) 1 Cox 319.
92 (1787) 2 Bos & Pul 270 at 272.
93 (1787) 2 Bos & Pul 270 at 273.
94 (1807) 14 Ves Jun 160.

he is ignored for the purpose of the initial loss-sharing arrangements.[95] To take an example: there are three guarantors for D's debt to C. G1 has a maximum liability of £500. G2 and G3 each have a maximum liability of £250. As between the guarantors, G1 is liable for one-half and G2 and G3 for one-quarter each. If, however, G3 is insolvent then, prima facie, G1 is liable for two-thirds and G2 for one-third.

11.157 It should be stressed that these principles only apply to the liability between the guarantors. As regards the creditor, they are liable for the full amount that they have guaranteed. It is also the case that the guarantors can agree to a different liability as between themselves.

11.158 The general rule is that a guarantor can only recover from co-guarantors once he has paid more than his share, although there is no necessity for him to pay the whole debt.[96] In *Deering v Earl of Winchelsea*,[97] however, the guarantor was allowed a right of contribution when judgment had been obtained against him, even though he had not yet paid the guaranteed debt. The basis of this principle is demonstrated in the decision of Wright J in *Wolmershausen v Gullick*.[98] If a judgment or similar ruling is obtained against a guarantor to the effect that he must pay under the guarantee, he is entitled to a declaration that, once he has paid his share, the other guarantors should pay the balance. Indeed, if C is a party to the proceedings, the court could order the other guarantors to pay their shares to the creditor. It is again important to appreciate that this only affects the rights of the guarantors between themselves and assumes that they are all solvent. The arrangements for contribution between the guarantors do not affect the rights of the creditor against the individual guarantors under the terms of their guarantees.

Subrogation

11.159 The guarantor's right of indemnity is a personal claim against the debtor for the payment of the amount paid by the guarantor. Similarly, a guarantor's right of contribution is a personal claim against co-guarantors for payment of amounts paid by the guarantor in excess of his fair share. In addition to these rights, the guarantor has the right to be subrogated to the creditor's rights against the debtor and against co-guarantors. The importance of the right of subrogation is that the debtor is subrogated not only to the creditor's personal right of repayment but also to all security and preferential rights held by the creditor in relation to the guaranteed debt, whether they are available against the debtor or against co-guarantors.

11.160 There are many similarities between the right of subrogation and the right of contribution. They are both equitable in nature, being founded on

---

95 *Lowe v Dixon* (1885) 16 QBD 455 at 458, per Lopes J.
96 *Davies v Humphreys* (1840) 6 M & W 153 at 168–169, per Parke B; *Ex p Snowdon* (1881) 17 Ch D 44.
97 (1787) 2 Bos & Pul 270.
98 [1893] 2 Ch 514.

principles of justice rather than on contract. They have been given effect by the courts since the early seventeenth century.

11.161   One of the limitations of rights of subrogation was that security is generally discharged by payment of the secured debt; and the guarantor's right to be subrogated to the creditor's security was accordingly limited. This restriction was lifted by the Mercantile Law Amendment Act 1856, s 5 of which sets out the modern basis of the law of subrogation:

> 'Every person who, being surety for the debt or duty of another, ... shall pay such debt or perform such duty, shall be entitled to have assigned to him ... every ... security which shall be held by the creditor in respect of such debt or duty, whether such ... security shall or shall not be deemed at law to have been satisfied by the payment of the debt or performance of the duty, and such person shall be entitled to stand in the place of the creditor, and to use all the remedies ... in any ... proceeding ... in order to obtain from the principal debtor, or any co-surety ... indemnification for the ... loss sustained by the person who shall have so paid such debt or performed such duty ... Provided always, that no co-surety ... shall be entitled to recover from any other co-surety ... more than the just proportion to which, as between those parties themselves, such last-mentioned person shall be justly liable.'

11.162   Like rights of contribution, rights of subrogation are not dependent on the guarantor being aware of security held by the creditor or the fact that they are acquired after the guarantee was given. As an example, in *Duncan, Fox & Co v The North and South Wales Bank*,[99] D created security in favour of C, and G endorsed a bill of exchange as guarantor on behalf of D. D became insolvent and G paid the bill of exchange and then discovered the existence of the security. The House of Lords held that G was entitled to the security even though he was previously unaware of it and had not relied on it.

11.163   The right of subrogation is, in the vernacular, described as the right of the guarantor to 'step into the shoes' of the creditor once he has paid the guaranteed debt. The guarantor is not only subrogated to security held by the creditor, but also to any priority which the creditor may have in the insolvency of the debtor. Accordingly, if the debt which was paid by the guarantor was a preferential debt, the guarantor is entitled to the same priority as the creditor would have had, even though the payment discharges the debt.[100]

11.164   The guarantor is subrogated not only to the creditor's rights against the debtor, but also to those against co-guarantors. In *Steel v Dixon*,[101] C lent £800 to D on the basis of a joint and several promissory note executed by D and G1, G2, G3 and G4. D gave security to G1 and G2, but G3 and G4 were not aware of this. D went bankrupt and each guarantor paid £200 to C. G1 and G2 then realised about £500 from their security and G3 and G4 each claimed a

---

99   (1880) 6 App Cas 1.
100   *Re Lamplugh Iron Ore Co* [1927] 1 Ch 308; Mercantile Law Amendment Act 1856, s 5.
101   (1881) 17 Ch D 825.

quarter of that amount. Fry J held that G3 and G4 were entitled to share in the security. The ultimate burden of each guarantor should be shared in proportion to their liabilities.

11.165   It has been seen that the guarantor's right of indemnity against the debtor is available as soon as the guarantor makes any payment, even if he does not pay the guaranteed liability in full; and his right of contribution against co-guarantors is available as soon as he has paid more than his fair share. The right of subrogation, however, is generally only available once the guarantor has paid the guaranteed debt in full.[102] It has been seen that there is a distinction between a guarantor being liable for the whole debt, subject to a limit, as opposed to being liable for part of the debt. If the guarantor is liable for the whole debt, his right of subrogation will only arise once the entire debt has been paid, but if he is only liable for part of the debt, he is entitled to be subrogated once he has paid that part of the debt which he has guaranteed.[103]

11.166   A guarantor's right of indemnity is only available if the guarantee was given at the express or implied request of the debtor. It does not appear that this limitation applies to rights of subrogation. On the face of it, s 5 of the Mercantile Law Amendment Act 1856 gives the guarantor a right of subrogation simply as a result of him being guarantor, although it is curious that there are circumstances in which a guarantor is unable to obtain a personal right of reimbursement from the debtor but is entitled to be subrogated to the creditor's secured rights against that debtor.

Contracting out

11.167   The creditor is not concerned with rights which the guarantor may have once the creditor has been paid in full what he is owed by the debtor. The creditor will, nevertheless, want to ensure that the guarantor is not able to proceed against the debtor or any co-guarantors until the creditor has been paid in full. To allow them to do so could prejudice the creditor's own claims against the debtor and co-guarantors. It has been seen that rights of indemnity and contribution can arise before the creditor has been paid in full. Although, as a general rule, a right of subrogation is not available until the creditor has been paid in full, the guarantor is entitled to be subrogated if he has only guaranteed part of the debt, and has paid that part in full. Accordingly, it is common for guarantees to contain provisions by which the guarantor contracts out of rights of indemnity, contribution or subrogation, until such time as the full amount of the secured obligations has been paid to the creditor.

Part 6: USING GUARANTEES IN PRACTICE

11.168   Guarantees are used a great deal in practice, largely because of the proliferation of groups of companies. Although credit will frequently be

---

102   *Ex p Brett, re Howe* (1871) 6 Ch App 838 at 841, per Mellish LJ.
103   *Midland Banking Co v Chambers* (1869) LR 4 Ch App 398.

granted to one member of the group (or to a small number of its members), the creditor will require guarantees from the other members of the group, in order to obtain direct access to them. In an insolvency, the creditor will want to be able to prove for the full amount of its debt against each group member (providing, of course, that it does not in fact recover more than the total amount owing to it). In addition, the creditor may want the ability to be able to obtain security over assets, not just from the debtor but from the guarantors. As a result, one of the most common forms of security document is the composite guarantee and debenture.

11.169   A creditor needs to be aware that it is always more difficult to enforce a guarantee than a primary obligation. Because the guarantor rarely obtains any commensurate benefit for granting the guarantee, the courts are very protective of guarantors, and have developed a number of methods by which they can deny creditors recovery from guarantors. It is nevertheless possible for the creditor to avoid most (although not necessarily all) of these pitfalls. There are essentially three steps which the creditor needs to take.

11.170   The first step is to ensure that all of the terms of the guarantee are contained in a written document, which is executed by the guarantor. The creditor would be likely to want to do this anyway, but it is particularly important, in the case of a guarantee, to ensure that there are no external oral understandings which have not been set down in the guarantee.

11.171   The second step is to ensure that the guarantee is properly drafted. There are a number of issues which need to be borne in mind, the most important of which are as follows:

- The guaranteed obligations must be clearly stated. Where the guarantee only extends to a particular facility, it needs to be clear that it will cover that facility as amended from time to time. Even in the case of an 'all monies' guarantee, it will not extend to claims against the debtor which have been acquired by a creditor from a third party unless the guarantee makes it clear that it does. The problems which arise in relation to guarantees are exactly the same as those in relation to mortgages and charges, which are discussed in part 4 of **CHAPTER 3** (**3.140**ff).
- Because, even in a commercial context, the courts are likely to construe a guarantee against the creditor, it is particularly important that its provisions are clear and unambiguous, particularly in relation to such matters as revocation and limits on guarantees.
- The guarantee should contain an indemnity to cover the circumstances where the debtor is not liable (either because the principal liability was ineffective from the start, or because the debtor has subsequently been released).
- The guarantee should contain appropriate provisions by which the guarantor contracts out of any of the protections to which he would otherwise be entitled. In particular, the guarantor should agree that his liability will not be released or prejudiced as a result of any act or other matter which would otherwise do so, including the release of the debtor or any co-guarantor, the granting of time or indulgence to the debtor, variations to the principal contract, or the loss of, or failure to enforce, any security.

- Until the creditor has been paid in full, the guarantor should contract out of any right of indemnification, contribution or subrogation.

11.172   The importance of simple, clear and all-embracing wording in any commercial document cannot be overestimated. Nor that its provisions should not be so unreasonable that a court will attempt to find a way round them. In view of the one-sided nature of a guarantee, these principles are particularly important when drafting guarantees.

11.173   This leads on to the final step. Clear drafting of the guarantee can avoid many of the problems which the creditor will otherwise encounter. But it will not assist the creditor if the guarantee is capable of being set aside. It has been seen in part 3 of this chapter (**11.31ff**) that this is most likely to occur as a result of undue influence or breach of fiduciary duty.

11.174   Where the guarantor is an individual, the creditor needs to take very seriously the requirements laid down by the House of Lords in the *Etridge* case.[104] Where the guarantor is a company, the most important consideration for the creditor is to try to ensure that there is no breach of fiduciary duty by the directors of the guarantor; and the terms of the relevant board minutes are of particular importance in establishing this. The reason that this is so important is that, if there is a breach of fiduciary duty, it is quite likely that the creditor will have constructive notice of it.

11.175   In summary, there is no reason why a creditor cannot overcome most of the hurdles which the legislature and the courts have set in his way when enforcing a guarantee. But the nature of a guarantee is such that the creditor should always be aware that, in practice, it will be more difficult to enforce a guarantee than a primary obligation.

---

104 *Royal Bank of Scotland v Etridge (No 2)* [2002] 2 AC 773.

Chapter 12

SET-OFF

Part 1: INTRODUCTION

12.1   Although a right of set-off is not a security interest, it is nevertheless an important element of the security (in its broader sense) available to a creditor when his debtor gets into financial difficulties. At its simplest, a right of set-off exists where there are cross-claims for money between the creditor and the debtor. The effect of the set-off is that both claims are discharged to the extent that they are of an equal amount, and the balance becomes owing to the party who was owed the larger amount.

12.2   To take an example, if the creditor is owed £100 by the debtor and the creditor owes £40 to the debtor, the set-off of those two cross-claims will result in:

- the discharge of the £40 owed by the creditor to the debtor; and
- the discharge of £40 of the £100 owed by the debtor to the creditor,

with the result that the creditor no longer owes anything to the debtor, and the debtor owes £60 to the creditor.

12.3   Rights of set-off have always been of particular importance to banks and other creditors involved in financial transactions. The example described above explains why this is so. The availability of the set-off gives the creditor the commercial equivalent of security over £40 of the £100 debt owing by the debtor to it. A right of set-off has a number of advantages for a creditor:

- It gives the creditor effective security without the necessity to create (and, in most cases, to register) a security interest.
- It is easier to enforce than a security interest. There is no necessity, for instance, to sell the charged asset. Indeed, on insolvency, set-off happens automatically.
- The value of the right of set-off is certain because it is expressed as a monetary amount. The value of other assets held as security will fluctuate.
- There are circumstances where a right of set-off can give the creditor greater rights than a charge (for instance, where the charge is found to be a floating charge, and therefore subject to the rights of third parties to which a right of set-off is not subject).

12.4   A right of set-off exists where there are cross-claims for money between the creditor and the debtor. The effect of the set-off is to extinguish both cross-claims to the extent that they are of an equivalent amount, and to substitute for them a single claim for the balance, owing by the party who owed the greater amount. Set-off assumes that each party owes money to the other. It needs to be distinguished from other arrangements between the parties which have an equivalent economic result, but use different legal means. In practice, the most important alternative method of achieving the same commercial result is by 'netting'.

12.5 Netting is a contractual arrangement between the debtor and the creditor by which the parties agree that transactions entered into between them will not result in individual cross-claims between them but, at any time, will only result in one amount being owed by the party who has received the greater value. It is best explained by an example. If the parties to a contract each supply goods or services to the other, they might agree that, instead of each having the obligation to pay the gross value of the goods or services supplied to it, at any time there will only be one liability to make a payment – for the party who has received the greater value to pay to the other the amount by which that value exceeds the value which it has supplied to the other party.

12.6 In short, a set-off acknowledges the existence of cross-claims between the parties and effects a discharge of them to the extent that the amounts are equivalent, whereas a netting arrangement involves just one monetary claim being owed by one party to the transaction to the other. The broad scope of set-off in English law means that the distinction between them is of little practical relevance in England. It is, however, particularly important in those jurisdictions (many of which are in continental Europe) which have restrictive rights of set-off but which give effect to contractual netting arrangements.

12.7 Rights of set-off are of various types, but they broadly fall into three categories:

- those which are available outside insolvency proceedings;
- those which are available in insolvency proceedings; and
- those which are available against assignees.

12.8 In practice, the most important type of set-off is that which is available in insolvency proceedings – in bankruptcy, liquidation and administration. This is for the obvious reason that creditors are most likely to need to rely on such rights when the debtor is insolvent. Rights of set-off outside insolvency proceedings are nevertheless of importance where the debtor is in financial difficulties but is not yet the subject of formal insolvency procedures (for instance, because it is the subject of a restructuring). Both types of set-off are only available if the cross-claims concerned are mutual. The only exception to the requirement for mutuality is rights of set-off against assignees, which are discussed in part 5 of CHAPTER 3 (**3.175**ff).

12.9 The rest of this chapter considers the following matters:

- Part 2 (**12.10**ff) – conditional payment obligations and netting: in what circumstances can the creditor deny that he is liable to the debtor (in which event he does not need to rely on set-off)?
- Part 3 (**12.39**ff) – mutuality: this is a requirement of most types of set-off; what does it mean?

- Part 4 (**12.76ff**) – set-off outside insolvency: in what circumstances does the creditor have a right of set-off if the debtor is not the subject of insolvency proceedings?
- Part 5 (**12.114ff**) – set-off in insolvency: what difference does it make if the debtor is in insolvency proceedings?
- Part 6 (**12.171ff**) – improving rights of set-off: to what extent can the creditor improve his position by contract or by taking a charge?

Part 2: CONDITIONAL PAYMENT OBLIGATIONS AND NETTING

12.10   Before considering the circumstances in which A is entitled to set off a payment due from B against a payment due to B, it is first necessary to establish whether A has an obligation to make the payment to B. The existence of a set-off depends upon A and B having cross-claims against each other. If A is claiming a right of set-off, he acknowledges the existence of B's claim, but contends that he does not have to pay the amount owing by him to the extent that an equivalent amount is owing by B. This needs to be contrasted with a case where A is contending either that he does not owe any money to B because B has failed to perform an obligation owing to A, or that he is only liable to pay to B the net amount after deduction of the amount owing by B.

12.11   In some jurisdictions, the distinction is of great importance because of the limited rights of set-off which are available, particularly in an insolvency. In English law, wide rights of set-off are available in insolvency and, therefore, the distinction is of less practical importance. But the distinction can still be of relevance. If, for instance, A is liable to B, and B's liability to A would be time-barred if A were to sue to recover it, a set-off will not assist A because he has no right to recover against B in respect of his cross-claim. But, if A's liability to B is conditional on payment by B, then A will have no liability to pay B even though A could not recover against B in an action. Similarly, if A can establish that the amount which he owes to B is in fact the net amount after deduction of the sum owing by B, A's liability to B will be reduced even though he would have no right to sue B for the amount.[1]

12.12   This part is concerned with the circumstances in which A is entitled to say that he is not liable to B because of a claim he has against B. There are two types of case:

- *Conditional payment obligation*: In this case, A is not liable to make a payment to B until such time as B has performed his obligation to A. A's obligation to B is conditional on the performance of B's obligation to A.
- *Netting*: In this case, A is only liable to pay B a net amount which takes account of the amount of B's liability to A.

---

1   *Henriksens Rederi v THZ Rolimpex, 'The Brede'* [1974] QB 233.

12.13 Each of these rights can be available to A either under the general law or as a result of specific contractual arrangements between A and B. This part will consider five examples of the application of these principles which are particularly important in practice. These illustrations concern:

- contractual conditions precedent;
- abatement;
- the banker's right to combine accounts;
- flawed assets; and
- netting agreements.

12.14 The first three arise by operation of law, the remaining two by agreement. Contractual conditions precedent and flawed assets are examples of conditional payment obligations. The other three are examples of netting.

Contractual conditions precedent

12.15 When considering the extent of a contractual obligation by A to make a payment to B, the first question to ask is whether A is under an obligation to make the payment at all. This depends on general contractual principles. A's obligation to make the payment may be subject to an express or an implied condition precedent.[2] Alternatively, A's obligation to pay may initially have arisen but have been discharged, for instance, by a repudiatory breach of contract by B.[3] These underlying principles are, of course, subject to the express provisions of the particular contract, which may require complete performance by B before A is under any obligation to pay or may provide for payments in stages following particular partial performance. But, whatever the contract provides, the first question is always whether A does, in fact, have an obligation to make a payment to B. It is only if he does that any further question arises.

Abatement

12.16 If A does have an obligation to make payment to B, the next question is whether his obligation is to pay the full amount provided for in the contract, or whether the amount of the payment is reduced by the amount of any cross-claim which A may have against B as a result of a breach of contract by B.

12.17 The general position at common law is that, once A is under an obligation to make the payment to B, B is entitled to recover that payment from A and, even if A has a cross-claim against B for breach of the contract, A has no right to reduce the amount of the payment to take account of B's breach, but must pay the full amount to B and bring a separate claim against B for damages for breach of contract. In the words of Parke B in *Mondel v Steel*:[4]

---

2   *Associated Japanese Bank (International) v Credit du Nord* [1989] 1 WLR 255.
3   For instance, if it has deprived A of substantially the whole benefit of the contract: *Hong Kong Fir Shipping Co v Kawasaki Kisen Kaisha* [1962] 2 QB 26.
4   (1841) 8 M & W 858 at 870.

'Formerly, it was the practice, where an action was brought for an agreed price of a specific chattel, sold with a warranty, or of work which was to be performed according to contract, to allow the plaintiff to recover the stipulated sum, leaving the defendant to a cross action for breach of the warranty or contract.'

12.18   Although this continues to be the underlying position at common law, as Baron Parke's comment suggests, there is an exception in relation to contracts for the sale of goods or for work and labour. During the nineteenth century, it became established that, in such cases, A was entitled to reduce the contractual payment required of him by an amount equal to the claim he had against B for damages for breach of contract if he could establish that the value of what he had obtained under the contract was reduced as a result of the breach of contract. As Baron Parke said in *Mondel v Steel*:[5]

'In all these cases of goods sold and delivered with a warranty, and work and labour, as well as the case of goods agreed to be supplied according to a contract, the rule which has been found so convenient is established; and that it is competent for the defendant, in all of those, not to set off, by a proceeding in the nature of a cross action, the amount of damages which he has sustained by breach of the contract, but simply to defend himself by showing how much less the subject-matter of the action was worth, by reason of the breach of contract; and to the extent that he obtains, or is capable of obtaining, an abatement of price on that account, he must be considered as having received satisfaction for the breach of contract, and is precluded from recovering in another action to that extent; but no more.'

12.19   This principle, that A can deduct the amount of his damages claim against B from the amount of his liability to B, only applies to two types of contract:

- contracts for the sale of goods (where the position is now regulated by statute);[6] and
- contracts for work and labour.[7]

12.20   In *Aries Tanker Corporation v Total Transport*,[8] the House of Lords confirmed that this principle does not apply to any other type of contract. In particular, that case decided that it does not apply to contracts for the carriage of goods by sea and, as a result, that it is not open to the charterer to deduct from freight owing to a shipowner the amount of damage suffered by it in respect of cargo. In the words of Lord Simon of Glaisdale:[9] 'Freight, representing the original rule, stands uneroded, like an outcrop of pre-Cambrian amid the detritus of sedimentary deposits.'

12.21   This principle has also had a limiting effect on equitable set-offs (which is discussed in part 4 of this chapter (**12.76ff**)). But, for this purpose, suffice it

---

5   (1841) 8 M & W 858 at 871 and 872.
6   Sale of Goods Act 1979, s 53(1).
7   *Mondel v Steel* (1841) 8 M & W 858.
8   [1977] 1 WLR 185.
9   [1977] 1 WLR 185 at 193.

to say that the doctrine of abatement only applies to the two types of contract described above. It is not a general principle of contract law. It also only applies to a damages claim to the extent that it reduces the value of the subject matter of the contract. To the extent that A may have a further damages claim against B for consequential loss, he must bring a separate claim against B to recover it.[10]

The banker's right to combine accounts

12.22 The right of a bank to combine (or, as it is sometimes called, consolidate) its accounts is, like abatement, also an example of a default rule (ie one which arises by operation of law). It establishes the circumstances in which a bank is only liable for the net amount owing by it to its customer after debit and credit balances on the customer's accounts with the bank have been applied against each other.

12.23 Two examples illustrate its application in practice. In *Garnett v M'Kewan*,[11] a customer held accounts with two different branches of the same bank, one of which was in credit, and the other in debit, each of an approximately equal amount. The customer drew a cheque on the bank, which it refused to honour. The Court of Exchequer held that the bank was only indebted to the customer for the net amount which was established after applying the credit balance on one account against the debit balance on the other. As a result, the bank had no obligation to honour the cheque.

12.24 The conceptual basis of a bank's right to combine accounts was considered in *Re K*.[12] In that case, the customer had three accounts with the bank – two deposit accounts, which were in credit, and one overdraft account, which was in debit. The customer was arrested for drug-related offences, and a restraint order was made prohibiting the customer from dealing with the three bank accounts. The bank applied to court to vary the order to enable it to combine the accounts. The court held that it was able to do so for two reasons. In the first place, it was held that the bank had a common law right to combine the three accounts, with the effect that it was only liable to the customer for the net balance. In the words of Otton J:[13]

> 'In my judgment, the right of a bank to combine is well established and is fundamental to the bank/customer relationship. It is a means of establishing the indebtedness of the customer to the bank and the bank to the customer. In exercising this right a bank is not asserting a claim over the moneys ... It is merely carrying out an accounting procedure so as to ascertain the existence and amount of one party's liability to the other. This can only be ascertained by discovering the ultimate balance of their mutual dealing.'

---

10 *Mondel v Steel* (1841) 8 M & W 858 at 872.
11 (1872) LR 8 Exch 10.
12 [1990] 2 QB 298.
13 [1990] 2 QB 298 at 304.

12.25 The bank had also obtained a contractual right of set-off from the customer, which it was held would have enabled the bank to exercise a contractual right of set-off. In fact, it was not necessary for the bank to rely on this, because it was only liable to the customer for the net balance.

12.26 The bank's right to combine accounts does not extend to all accounts which a customer holds with it. Where the bank is aware that an account in the name of a customer is in fact held on behalf of someone else, it is not able to combine the accounts for the same reason that it is unable to set off (as to which see part 3 of this chapter (**12.39ff**)). The types of account which can be combined are also limited. It would appear that there is no right to combine a loan account with a current account.[14] Nor does the right apply where arrangements between the bank and the customer expressly or impliedly contract out of it.

12.27 Because the right to combine accounts does not extend to all accounts and it is relatively easy for the customer to allege that the bank has contracted out of it, it is rare for banks to rely on the right of combination. In practice, as was seen in *Re K*, banks require contractual rights of set-off from their customers which are expressed to extend to all accounts and negative any implication that the right of combination is being waived by the bank. Contractual rights of set-off are considered further in part 4 of this chapter (**12.76ff**).

Flawed assets

12.28 The three examples described above all arise by operation of law without the necessity for any provision in the contract, although they are all subject to contrary agreement. The last two are examples of ways in which creditors can enhance by contract their rights against the debtor.

12.29 One concerns the use of what is sometimes known as a 'flawed asset'. The purpose of a flawed asset arrangement is to establish that A has no obligation to pay B until such time as B has fully performed its obligation to A. It is, in effect, an express condition precedent – a means of extending the concept of implied conditions precedent described above.

12.30 It is best explained by means of an example. A bank may agree to issue a letter of credit for a customer in consideration of the customer depositing cash with the bank, to be held as security for the obligation of the customer to indemnify the bank if it is called upon to make payment under the letter of credit. The parties may agree that the deposit is only to be repayable to the customer once the customer has fully indemnified the bank in respect of any payments it may make under the letter of credit. Such an arrangement is frequently described as creating a 'flawed asset' – in the sense that the customer's right to recover its asset (the deposit) is flawed – ie it is subject to the complete performance by the customer of its obligation to indemnify the bank.

---

14 *Re E J Morel* [1962] Ch 21 at 31–32; *Bradford Old Bank v Sutcliffe* [1918] 2 KB 833 at 847.

12.31   Such arrangements used to be common because of certain perceived deficiencies in the law of insolvency set-off (which have now been resolved, and are discussed in part 5 of this chapter (**12.114ff**)) and because of a perceived doubt about the ability of a bank to take a charge over its own deposit (which has also now been resolved, and is discussed in part 6 of this chapter (**12.171ff**)). Such arrangements are now of less importance than they were when those uncertainties still existed, but there is no reason why they cannot continue to be used in an appropriate case. If the customer made demand on the bank for repayment of the deposit, the bank would be able to deny liability until such time as the customer had performed its obligations to the bank.

12.32   Nevertheless, although such arrangements work in theory, in practice they are likely to be more difficult to be enforced. Unless the wording of the arrangements is so clear that there can be no doubt about its effect, it might not take a great deal of evidence to persuade a court that the real intention of the parties was not that the bank should have no liability until the customer had paid in full, but that the bank's liability should be limited to the net amount of the deposit, once the customer's obligations had been taken into account. Ultimately, this will be a matter of construction of the contractual arrangements between the parties in the light of the surrounding matrix of facts at the time they were entered into.

Netting agreements

12.33   This leads on to the other way in which A can protect itself against B by contract. The arrangements between the parties can provide that neither A nor B is liable for the gross value of the consideration provided by the other under the contract, but that the only liability of either party is for the net amount of the consideration provided by both parties from time to time. Although such arrangements can be used in commercial contracts, they are also frequently used in financial arrangements, such as in swap contracts.

12.34   The effect of such a netting arrangement is that each party is only liable for the net balance of advantage from time to time. As with flawed asset arrangements, there is no conceptual reason why such a provision should not be effective, but it is important that the contractual arrangements should be clearly drafted to this effect and that the subsequent actions of the parties do not suggest that they are varying the arrangements. If, on their true construction, the arrangements involve the creation of cross-debts owing by both parties, it will not be a netting arrangement, but a set-off arrangement.

12.35   Whilst the debtor remains outside insolvency proceedings, this is unlikely to have many adverse consequences but, in the liquidation, administration or bankruptcy of the debtor, a contractual set-off arrangement will be ineffective, and the effectiveness of the netting arrangement may therefore be crucial. In principle, a netting arrangement ought to be effective in the debtor's insolvency, but the authorities (discussed in Part 5 of the chapter) indicate it will not be if it gives the creditor more than he would have been entitled to by way of insolvency set-off. Where the netting agreement is part of a financial collateral arrangement, the Financial Collateral Arrangements

(No 2) Regulations 2003[15] make it clear that it will be enforceable even in an insolvency if it contains a 'close-out netting provision'. Financial Collateral is discussed in part 5 of CHAPTER 3 (**3.175**ff).

Conclusion

12.36 Before considering whether A is able to exercise a right of set-off against B, it is first necessary to establish whether A is, in fact, indebted to B. In some cases, A may not be indebted to B as a result of the operation of general principles of law. Alternatively, A may be able to rely on express contractual provisions in order to create the same effect. Examples of such arrangements which arise by operation of law include the common law rule of abatement and the bank's right to consolidate accounts. Contractual extensions of such arrangements include flawed asset and netting arrangements.

12.37 An alternative way of analysing these arrangements is by reference to their effect, rather than by reference to the way they were created. In some cases, the effect of these arrangements is that A is not liable to B at all until certain conditions have been fulfilled. A flawed asset arrangement is an example of such a case. Alternatively, A may only be liable to B for the net amount of the consideration provided by both parties. The common law rule of abatement, the bank's right to consolidate accounts and contractual netting arrangements are examples of this type of case.

12.38 Finally, it should be emphasised that contractual extensions of these arrangements (whether by means of flawed assets or netting arrangements) require not only careful drafting but also the likelihood that the parties will carry them out as the contractual arrangements require. If the effect of the contract in the light of its surrounding matrix of facts establishes that the arrangements between the parties do not actually result in a net amount owing by one to the other but that the parties intend there to be cross-claims which are set off, the arrangements cease to be effective as flawed assets or netting arrangements and will only be effective to the extent that a set-off agreement is effective.

Part 3: MUTUALITY

12.39 With one exception, mutuality of cross-claims is a prerequisite of all types of set-off, although the cases tend to be concerned with insolvency set-off. Before considering the various types of set-off available to a creditor, this part will accordingly analyse what is meant by 'mutuality'. Cross-claims are mutual if they satisfy four criteria:

- they are money claims;

---

15   SI 2003/3226.

- they are personal, not proprietary, claims;
- they are owing between the same persons; and
- they are owing in the same right.

Money claims

12.40 It is in the very nature of rights of set-off that they can only apply to cross-claims for money. There is no requirement that the cross-claims will result in debts – a claim for damages is equally capable of being set off – but each claim must result in an obligation to pay money to the other party. This was made clear by Lord Russell of Killowen CJ in *Palmer v Day*,[16] who said that the dealings between the parties must end in money claims owing between the parties 'otherwise the claims are incommensurable' (ie are incapable of being measured by the same standard).

12.41 This may seem self-evident, and it has always been the case that set-off outside insolvency proceedings is limited to monetary cross-claims. But, in the case of insolvency set-off, the courts have flirted with the idea of extending its scope to non-monetary claims. The issue has arisen in cases where the debtor has entered into insolvency proceedings at a time when the creditor is holding goods belonging to the debtor. On the face of it, no set-off is available in such a case. The creditor may have a lien on the goods (as to which, see **CHAPTER 10**) but will generally have no right of set-off. This is because, although the creditor may have a money claim against the debtor, the debtor's claim against the creditor is for the return of his goods.[17] In practice, though, the position is more complicated. There is a lot of case-law, and the cases divide themselves into two categories – those cases where the creditor has a power of sale over the goods held by him, and those where he does not.

12.42 Where the creditor does not have a power of sale over the goods in his possession, there were some suggestions in eighteenth-century cases that the creditor would have a right of set-off in respect of the value of the goods.[18] But, in *Rose v Hart*,[19] the Court of Common Pleas declined to follow the earlier authorities and decided that set-off was only possible where the arrangements between the parties would eventually terminate in money claims.

12.43 Where the creditor does have a power of sale, the position is more complicated. The authorities distinguish between two types of case:

- those where the creditor's authority to sell the goods continues even though the debtor goes into insolvency proceedings, and the goods are then sold; and
- those where the creditor's authority to sell the goods is revoked by the debtor's insolvency proceedings, and the goods accordingly remain unsold.

---

16 [1895] 2 QB 618 at 622.
17 Under s 3 of the Torts (Interference with Goods) Act 1977, the remedy is discretionary, but it would be awarded in the debtor's insolvency if the creditor is the owner of the goods.
18 *Ex parte Deeze* (1748) 1 Atk 228; *Oliver v Smith* (1813) 5 Taunt 56.
19 (1818) 8 Taunt 499.

12.44	An example of the first type of case is *Palmer v Day*.[20] D had deposited certain pictures with C, a firm of auctioneers, for sale, but became bankrupt whilst the pictures were still unsold. C subsequently sold the pictures, acting upon the instructions of D's trustee in bankruptcy. A Divisional Court of the Queen's Bench Division held that C had the right to set off the proceeds of sale against a debt owed from D which pre-dated the bankruptcy.

12.45	In contrast, in *Eberle's Hotels Co v Jonas*,[21] D deposited cigars with C as security for a particular debt, giving C authority to sell the cigars and credit D with the proceeds. D went into liquidation at a time when C still had cigars in his possession. The secured debt had been repaid, but C claimed to set off the value of the cigars against another debt owing by D. The Court of Appeal held that C was not entitled to a set-off. In the words of Lord Esher MR:[22]

> 'Although there may be mutual dealings, and the parties are such as come within the terms of [the statutory provision concerning set-off in insolvency], it is obvious that its provisions cannot apply unless the dealings are such that in the result the account contemplated by the section can be taken in the way described. If the claim on one side in the action and the counter-claim on the other were such as would both result in a money claim, so that for the purposes of the action there would be merely a pecuniary liability on each side, the case would, I think, come within the section.'

12.46	Since, however, it was held that C no longer had a power to sell the cigars and was bound to return them, there was no monetary liability from D to C which could be the subject of a set-off.

12.47	The position can therefore be summarised as follows:

- Where the creditor's power of sale is terminated as a result of the insolvency of the debtor before the goods are sold, no set-off will be available because the debtor's insolvency officer will have the ability to recover the goods, and there will be no monetary claim owing by the creditor to the debtor which will be capable of being set off.

- If, however, the creditor's power of sale continues after the debtor's insolvency and is exercised and, as a result, money becomes owing by the creditor to the debtor, it will be capable of being set off.

12.48	Whether or not the creditor's power of sale is revoked is a matter of ordinary agency principles. Where the debtor enters into insolvency proceedings, that will generally revoke any power of sale unless it is given by way of security or is coupled with a proprietary interest.[23]

20	[1895] 2 QB 618. It is a curious case, and is considered further in part 5 of this chapter (**12.114ff**).
21	(1887) 18 QBD 459.
22	(1887) 18 QBD 459 at 465.
23	Powers of Attorney Act 1971, s 4; *Smart v Sandars* (1848) 5 CB 895.

12.49   There is one case which is contrary to these principles. In *Rolls Razor v Cox*,[24] D got into financial difficulties at a time when it owed money to C, one of its employee salesmen. D dismissed C as an employee and then went into liquidation. At that time, C owed money to D in respect of goods which he had sold, and also held certain goods belonging to D, some of which were to be sold, and some of which were items to be used for fitting goods to be sold. By a majority, the Court of Appeal held that C had a right to set off the monies owing by him at the time of the liquidation, and also the value of the goods held by him for sale, but that he could not set off the value of the property held by him for the purpose of fitting the goods to be sold. Lord Denning MR (with whom Danckwerts LJ agreed) held that the right of set-off existed even though the power of sale had been revoked by the termination of C's contract of employment. Wynn LJ (dissenting) would have decided that the right of set-off only applied where the goods had been converted into money before the authority to sell had been withdrawn.

12.50   It is suggested that this case is one example of Lord Denning's legacy which is unlikely to survive him. It is inconsistent with *Eberle's Hotels Co v Jonas* (also a Court of Appeal decision), it is wrong in principle, and it is unlikely to be followed.

12.51   In conclusion, it is suggested that, in principle as well as on the basis of the preponderance of authority, a set-off is only available, even in insolvency proceedings, where there are monetary cross-claims between the parties.

Personal, not proprietary, claims

12.52   A set-off is not available where one of the cross-claims is proprietary rather than personal. The reason why this is the case is best explained by an example. Assume that a principal appoints an agent to sell an asset on his behalf. The agent sells the asset and receives the proceeds of sale. The principal also owes the agent money. If the parties intended the agent simply to become a debtor to the principal for the sale proceeds, the agent would, if the other requirements for a set-off were established, be able to set off the amount owing by the principal to him against the amount payable by him to the principal. If, however, as is likely to be the case, the express or implied intention of the parties was that the agent would hold the sale proceeds on trust for the principal, then the principal would, if the proceeds of sale were identifiable, have an equitable proprietary interest in them, and no set-off would be available. This is because the obligation of the agent would be to deliver the principal's asset (ie the sale proceeds) to him. The principal is entitled to receive the entire asset in which he has a beneficial interest.

12.53   That is not to say that there can be no deduction from money held on trust. If, for instance, the agent was owed a commission in respect of the sale, the parties may have intended that the commission should be deducted from the sale proceeds before the net balance was paid to the principal. If this were the case, the deduction would be permitted because the amount held on trust

---

24   [1967] 1 QB 552.

by the agent for the principal would be the net sale proceeds after deduction of commission. But if the agreement between the parties was that the agent should hold the full amount of the sale proceeds on trust, then no such deduction would be available.

12.54 The principle is, therefore, that a set-off is not available where one of the cross-claims consists of a proprietary claim. In practice, this exception has manifested itself most frequently where the creditor holds surplus proceeds of security on behalf of the debtor. This has occurred in three types of case:

- In the first type of case, D deposits property with C as security for money to be advanced by C. D subsequently enters into an insolvency procedure and his insolvency officer tenders the amount of money secured by the property. C claims to set off other money due from D. No such set-off is available. The deposit of property was by way of a limited security for a particular liability, and any surplus after repayment of that liability is held on trust for D under his equity of redemption.[25]

- In the second type of case, D owes money to C (his solicitor) in respect of unpaid costs. Before C will act further, he insists that D deposits money with him as security for future costs. D makes the deposit and then becomes bankrupt. C wishes to set off earlier costs against the deposit. No such set-off is available because the deposit was by way of a limited security for a particular liability, and any surplus after repayment of the future costs is held on trust for D under his equity of redemption.[26]

- In the third case, D and C enter into a treaty of reinsurance, C being entitled to retain out of moneys due to D a sum of money as security for the performance of D's obligations under the treaty. D goes into insolvency proceedings and, after all of its obligations to C under the treaty have been satisfied, C retains the surplus which it claims to set off against other sums due to it from D under other contracts. No such set-off is available, because the surplus moneys are held on trust for D under its equity of redemption.[27]

12.55 These cases (which are frequently described as the 'special purpose' cases) were discussed in the House of Lords in *National Westminster Bank v Halesowen Presswork and Assemblies*.[28] Lord Kilbrandon, after referring to two of them, said:[29]

'In all these cases the funds may be said to have been impressed with quasi-trust purposes, and that is sufficient to destroy the mutuality which is a prerequisite of the right to set off arising, since it is necessary that the debts were between the parties in the same right, a condition which the holding of a sum as trustee would destroy.'

---

25   *Key v Flint* (1817) 8 Taunt 21; *Buchanan v Findlay* (1829) 9 B & C 738.
26   *Re Pollitt, ex parte Minor* [1893] 1 QB 455; *Re Mid-Kent Fruit Factory* [1896] 1 Ch 567.
27   *Re City Equitable Fire Insurance Company (No 2)* [1930] 2 Ch 293. Compare *Re H E Thorne & Son* [1914] 2 Ch 438, which is inconsistent with the other cases.
28   [1972] 1 AC 785.
29   [1972] 1 AC 785 at 821.

12.56	Lord Simon took a different approach. He said:[30]

'Every payment of money, every contractual provision, is for a special or specific purpose in the ordinary sense of those words: something more is required to take the transaction out of the concept of "mutual dealings". It was suggested on behalf of the [bank] that the situation only arises when the transaction gives rise to a payment on which a quasi-trust is imposed. My only quarrel with this way of putting it is that quasi-anything gives uncertain guidance in the law. I would prefer to say that money is paid for a special (or specific) purpose so as to exclude mutuality of dealing within [the statutory provisions concerning set-off in insolvency] if the money is paid in such circumstances that it would be a misappropriation to use it for any other purpose than that for which it is paid. I think that all the cases cited on this point are explicable on this basis.'

12.57	There is much to be said for Lord Simon's observation that 'quasi-anything gives uncertain guidance in the law'. It is nevertheless suggested that Lord Kilbrandon's reference to trusts is well made, except that the cases concerned a real trust rather than a quasi-trust. In all the so-called 'special purpose' cases, an amount was owing by the creditor to the insolvent debtor which represented surplus security after payment of a secured debt. It is clear[31] that a creditor holds any such surplus on trust for the debtor. It is suggested that it is for this reason that no set-off was available in those cases. The debtor had an equitable proprietary interest in the surplus money, and, as a result, no set-off was available which would deprive the debtor of the benefit of its proprietary interest.

12.58	The moral for the creditor is clear – make sure that assets held as security are held to secure all liabilities which could be owed to it by the debtor. Taking limited security can prejudice rights of set-off.

Between the same persons

12.59	It has been seen that it is in the nature of a right of set-off that it only extends to personal claims for the payment of money. It is equally in the very nature of a right of set-off that it is only available where the cross-claims are due between the same persons.[32] If A owes money to B, and B owes money to A, there can be a set-off. But if A owes money to B, and B owes money to C, it is perfectly obvious that there can be no set-off. B cannot claim to set off against A money which he owes to someone else.

Assignments or charges

12.60	The only exception to this principle concerns assignments of debts. It has been seen in part 5 of **CHAPTER 3** (**3.175**ff) that an assignee of a right to the payment of money acquires his proprietary interest 'subject to equities'; and

---

30	[1972] 1 AC 785 at 808.
31	See s 105 of the Law of Property Act 1925.
32	*Yates v Sherrington* (1843) 11 M & W 42.

that one of those equities is rights of set-off which the counterparty has against the assignor. The reason for this principle is that the assignment should not place the counterparty to the contract in a worse position than he would have been in if the assignment had not taken place. That objective is not achieved totally. There are limits on the ability of the counterparty to set up against the assignee a right of set-off which he has against the assignor. But the cases do establish that the counterparty is entitled to a set-off against the assignee if, in broad terms, he would have been entitled to a set-off against the assignor at the time he received notice of the assignment. The principle is not restricted to assignments. It applies to any proprietary interest which is created over the debt – for instance, a charge.

12.61 To take an example. The counterparty has entered into a contract with the assignor as a result of which he has an obligation to make a payment to the assignor. The assignor assigns the benefit of that contract to the assignee, who gives notice of the assignment to the counterparty. As a result, the counterparty now has an obligation to make the payment under the contract to the assignee, rather than to the assignor. On the face of it, therefore, he would be unable to set off a liability owing by the assignor to him against his obligation to pay the assignee: the liabilities would be owing to different persons. But, because of the principle that an assignee takes subject to equities, including rights of set-off, the counterparty is entitled, as against the assignee, to set off cross-claims which either arise out of the same transaction between the assignor and the counterparty or which were owing by the assignor to the counterparty at the time he received notice of the assignment. The right of set-off in such a case is considered in more detail in part 5 of **CHAPTER 3** (**3.175ff**). For this purpose, what is important is that it is the one exception to the principle that a set-off is only available where the cross-claims are due between the same persons.

The importance of the beneficial interest

12.62 When considering whether cross-claims are owing between the same persons, it is the beneficial interests in the cross-claims which are important, rather than just the legal interests. In the words of Dixon J in the High Court of Australia in *Hiley v The Peoples Prudential Assurance Co*[33] in the context of insolvency set-off:

> '[T]he equitable or beneficial interest of the parties in the mutual debts, credits or dealings must be considered and not merely the dry legal right.'

12.63 In the case of a syndicated loan, therefore, where amounts owing by the borrower are due to the agent bank on behalf of the lenders, rights of set-off are established by reference to each lender's beneficial interest in the amounts payable by the borrower. If, for example, the debtor owes £100 to the agent on behalf of the lenders, and the agent, in its capacity as a lender, has lent £20 of that amount, a credit balance of £30 owing by the agent to the borrower can only be set off against the £20 which is owed beneficially to the agent. The

---

33   (1938) 60 CLR 468 at 497.

balance of £10 cannot be set off. The fact that the agent is, at law, owed £100 is irrelevant. It is the agent's beneficial right, rather than its legal right, which is relevant for the purpose of set-off.

12.64 Conversely, if one of the lenders had a beneficial interest in £20 of the amount owing by the borrower to the agent, and had a deposit of £20 from the borrower, it would (subject to the other requirements of an effective set-off discussed in this chapter) be entitled to set them off even though the legal right to payment of the debt was vested in the agent. Because the lender has the beneficial right to payment, it is entitled to a set-off.

12.65 Although it is the beneficial interest in the cross-claims which is the main consideration in establishing whether or not a set-off is available, it does not follow that the legal interest in the cross-claims is irrelevant. An illustration of the importance of legal title is provided by *Re Gross, ex parte Kingston.*[34] D, who was county treasurer, had two accounts with C Bank – one a private account and the other described as a 'police account'. Few of the credit items in the police account could be traced as having come from the county funds, but all cheques drawn on that account appeared to have been drawn only for county purposes. For the purposes of interest, C Bank treated the accounts as being one, and credited it to the private account. The manager of C Bank knew that D was the county treasurer and that he was in the habit of paying county money into the bank. It was held that C Bank could not set off the credit balance on the police account against A's overdrawn private account because the bank had been made sufficiently aware that one was a trust account.

12.66 The reason that the bank was not entitled to a set-off in this case was not simply because one of the accounts was a trust account, the beneficial interest in which was owned by someone else, but that it was established that the bank had notice that it was a trust account. If the bank had not had actual or constructive notice of the fact that one of the accounts was a trust account, it would have been entitled to exercise a right of set-off because the legal owner of both accounts was the same person. It was only because the bank was aware of the trust, that it was not entitled to effect the set-off.

12.67 The legal entitlement to the cross-claims is also important in another circumstance. Where it is clear that one person is the beneficial owner, although not the legal owner, of a monetary claim, a set-off will be available in respect of a monetary liability owing by that beneficial owner to the person who is liable to pay the claim. But, where there is doubt about the beneficial entitlement, a set-off will not be available. In *Ex parte Morier, Re Willis, Percival & Co,*[35] A and B kept an executorship account with C Bank; and A, who was a residuary legatee under the will, had a private account with C Bank. C Bank went into liquidation and, at that time, A's private account was overdrawn but the executorship account was in credit. The executorship had yet to be completed,

---

34 (1871) LR 6 Ch App 632.
35 (1879) 12 Ch D 491.

and the Court of Appeal held that the credit balance on the executorship account could not be set off against the debit balance on A's private account. In the words of Brett LJ:[36]

> 'My view is this, that, the account standing in the names of [A] and [B], the case would not have been brought within the rules of equitable set-off or mutual credit, unless [A] was so much the person solely beneficially interested that a Court of Equity, without any terms or any further inquiry, would have obliged [B] to transfer the account into [A's] name alone.'

12.68   Had B joined with A in acknowledging that the money in the executorship account was part of the residue belonging to A, a set-off would have been allowed on the basis that the entirety of the money was held on trust for A without the necessity for taking an account but, in the absence of such an acknowledgement or of any settlement of accounts liquidating the trust fund, there could be no set-off since the court had no power to take accounts for this purpose.[37]

12.69   The position is different where the person claiming the set-off is the legal owner of the relevant cross-claim. In *Bailey v Finch*,[38] a banking firm became bankrupt at a time when A had an overdraft of £300 on his private account. Before the bankruptcy, B had died, having appointed A the sole executor of her will, and a credit balance of £500 was transferred from the account of B at the bank to the account of A as 'executor of the late B'. A was the sole residuary legatee under B's will and, although the executorship had not been completed, A had in his hands sufficient personal assets of B to provide for unpaid bequests. A was held to be entitled to set off the credit balance on the executorship account against a claim by the trustees of the banking firm on the overdrawn private account. The result was different from that in *Ex parte Morier* because A was the legal owner of both accounts, and there was no sufficient notice of any equity to countervail A's legal right of set-off.

12.70   In summary, therefore, a set-off will be available of debts due in the same right at law provided that the person claiming the set-off does not have notice of a conflicting equitable interest. Where the debts are not due in the same right at law, set-off will only be allowed if the court can ascertain, without the taking of accounts, that the whole of the debt is held on trust for the person claiming the set-off.

In the same right

12.71   In order for cross-claims to be set off, not only must they exist between the same persons but they must be owing 'in the same right'. In practice, this requirement is of little importance any more. What it means is that a joint debt

---

36   (1879) 12 Ch D 491 at 502.
37   This principle had been established by Sir George Jessel MR in *Middleton v Pollock, ex parte Nugee* (1875) LR 20 Eq 29.
38   (1871) LR 7 QB 34.

cannot be set off against a several debt. In *Ex parte Riley*,[39] A owed money to his banker B, who owed money to a partnership consisting of A and C. B became bankrupt and A contended that he could set off the debt due by B to the partnership against a claim by B's assignees for the debt due from him to B. Lord King LC held that the joint debt owed by the partnership to B and the separate debt owed by B to A were not mutual and could not be set off.

12.72   There was some attempt in cases at the end of the eighteenth century and the beginning of the nineteenth century to find a way round this rule in order to enable joint debts to be set off against several debts.[40] Most of these cases were decisions of Lord Eldon LC and, in *Middleton v Pollock, ex parte Knight & Raymond*,[41] Sir George Jessel MR distinguished them and reiterated the basic principle that joint and several debts are incapable of being set off against each other.

12.73   In practice, this limitation is of little practical importance. It is only of relevance where one of the cross-claims is a joint (as opposed to a joint and several) debt, and such debts are rare in current commercial practice, now that most commercial activity is carried out through companies rather than partnerships

Conclusion

12.74   It has occasionally been suggested that whether or not cross-claims are mutual depends on the intention of the parties to them.[42] In fact, as has been seen, the criterion of mutuality is a matter of law, and is tested objectively without reference to the actual or presumed intention of the parties.

12.75   Cross-claims are mutual if:

● they are both claims for the payment of money;
● they are personal, not proprietary claims;
● they are owing between the same parties (and, for this purpose, it is generally the beneficial entitlement to them which is of most importance); and
● they are due in the same right (by which is meant only that a joint debt cannot be set off against a several debt).

Part 4: SET-OFF OUTSIDE INSOLVENCY

12.76   The right of set-off outside insolvency proceedings is very different from that within insolvency proceedings. Outside insolvency proceedings, the

---

39   (1731–32) Kel W 24.
40   *Ex parte Quintin* (1796) 3 Ves Jun 248; *Ex parte Hanson* (1806) 12 Ves Jun 346 and (1811) 18 Ves Jun 232; *Ex parte Stephens* (1805) 11 Ves Jun 24; *Vulliamy v Noble* (1817) 3 Mer 593.
41   (1875) LR 20 Eq 515.
42   See, for instance, Winn LJ in *Rolls Razor v Cox* [1967] 1 QB 552 at 575. His comments were criticised by Lord Kilbrandon in *National Westminster Bank v Halesowen Presswork and Assemblies* [1972] AC 785, HL.

right of set-off under the general law is quite limited, but it is capable of being increased by contract. By contrast, the general right of set-off within insolvency proceedings is extensive, but it cannot be varied by contract. For these reasons (and also because rights of set-off are more likely to be required inside an insolvency than outside one), the general right of set-off outside insolvency proceedings is much less important than that within insolvency proceedings. In practice, in financial transactions, set-off rights outside insolvency are normally created by contract, and it is rarely necessary for financial institutions to rely on the underlying law of set-off.

12.77 Outside insolvency proceedings, rights of set-off fall into two categories – those which arise by operation of law and those which are created by contract. As well as arising in different circumstances, they also have a different effect. The effect of contractual rights of set-off depends on the terms of the contract, which will normally allow one or both of the parties to exercise a right of set-off in defined circumstances (such as on default) in accordance with the terms of the contract.

12.78 By contrast, rights of set-off which arise by operation of law are procedural. A has a right of set-off if, being sued by B for the payment of a monetary sum, he is able to set up a cross-claim against B as a reason for not paying to the extent of the cross-claim. If A is entitled to a procedural right of set-off, he will have a defence to B's claim to the extent of the cross-claim. In such a case, A is not denying that he owes money to B, but simply contending that judgment should not be given to B without taking account of the cross-claim. In the words of O'Bryan J in the Victorian Supreme Court in *Re K L Tractors*:[43]

> 'A set-off is not a denial of the debt – it is a plea against its enforcement ... A plea of set-off ... in effect admits the existence of the debt, but sets up a cross-claim as being a ground on which the person against whom the claim is brought is excused from payment and entitled to judgment on the plaintiff's claim. Until judgment in favour of the defendant on grounds of set-off has been given, the plaintiff's claim is not extinguished.'

12.79 This right of set-off is now contained in the Civil Procedure Rules 1998[44] (CPR), r 16.6, which provides:

> 'Where a defendant—
>
> (a)   contends he is entitled to money from the claimant; and
> (b)   relies on this as a defence to the whole or part of the claim,
>
> the contention may be included in the defence and set off against a claim, whether or not it is also a Part 20 claim [ie a counterclaim].'

12.80 This provision is very similar to the set-off provision contained in the Rules of the Supreme Court (which were the predecessor of the CPR),[45] and it does not appear to have altered the previous law.

---

43   [1954] VLR 505 at 507; and see *Re Hiram Maxim Lamp Co* [1903] 1 Ch 70.
44   SI 1998/3132.
45   RSC Ord 18, r 17.

12.81   As has been seen in part 2 of this chapter (**12.10ff**), the position at common law is that, where A is being sued by B for a monetary claim, A cannot use a cross-claim which he has against B as a defence to B's claim. B is entitled to judgment on his claim, and A must bring a separate proceeding against B for the amount of his cross-claim.[46] In the nineteenth century, the doctrine of abatement developed, which limited A's obligation to the net amount in certain cases where B had committed a breach of contract against A, but the common law has never allowed the set-off of cross-claims.

12.82   In order to ameliorate the common law position, set-off became available in two types of case – by statute and in equity. Statutory set-off became available where the cross-claims were liquidated or where their amount was otherwise capable of being ascertained easily. Equitable set-off became available where the cross-claims arose out of the same transaction and were so closely connected with each other that it would be unfair for one claim to be paid without taking account of the other. It is these two types of set-off which are now available under CPR, r 16.6.

12.83   The rest of this part discusses statutory set-off and then equitable set-off, and it then considers the limitations which are common to both. It ends by discussing how set-off rights can be increased or limited by contract. The discussion assumes that the cross-claims to be set off are mutual. The meaning of mutuality is discussed in part 3 of this chapter (**12.39ff**).

Statutory set-off

12.84   In the early eighteenth century, concern about the effect of the common law rule that a cross-claim could not be a defence to an action led to the passing of the Statutes of Set-Off.[47] Those statutes have now been repealed, but their effect has been preserved and statutory set-off is now available under CPR, r 16.6. The circumstances in which statutory set-off is available are explained by Cockburn CJ in *Stooke v Taylor*:[48]

> 'By the Statutes of Set-off this plea is available only where the claims on both sides are in respect of liquidated debts, or money demands which can be readily and without difficulty ascertained. The plea can only be used in the way of defence to the plaintiff's action, as a shield, not as a sword.'

12.85   Set-off is, therefore, available in respect of two types of money claim:

- claims in debt for a liquidated sum:[49] and
- other money claims (including claims for damages) if their amount

---

46   See *Mondel v Steel* (1841) 8 M & W 858 at 870, per Parke B.
47   2 Geo 2 c22 (1728) and 8 Geo 2 c24 (1734).
48   (1880) 5 QBD 569 at 575.
49   For a useful discussion of the meaning of 'liquidated', see *Alexander v Ajax Insurance Co* [1956] VLR 436.

can be 'readily and without difficulty ascertained'[50] or 'ascertained with certainty,'[51] or 'ascertained with precision'.[52]

12.86   If, therefore, B is sued by A for a money claim, B can set off a money claim owing to him by A if it satisfies those criteria. As has been seen, until judgment, the cross-claims are distinct and separate.[53]

Equitable set-off

12.87   Unlike the common law courts, the courts of equity were prepared to allow a defendant to set off a cross-claim owing to him by the claimant; and, where that claim was brought against the defendant in the common law courts, they would issue an injunction to prevent the claimant from proceeding until the cross-claim had been dealt with. Since the Judicature Acts, an equitable set-off is now available in any court proceedings under CPR, r 16.6.

12.88   It is clear that it is not a requirement of an equitable set-off that the cross-claims are liquidated or capable of being ascertained with certainty. A claim for damages is available for set-off in equity even if its amount is unascertained. But it is less easy to establish the precise circumstances in which an equitable set-off is available. One of the leading cases is *Rawson v Samuel*,[54] in which Lord Cottenham LC said:[55]

> 'It will be found that this equitable set-off exists in cases where the party seeking the benefit of it can shew some equitable ground for being protected against his adversary's demands. The mere existence of cross-demands is not sufficient; ... several cases were cited in support of the injunction; but in every one of them, except *Williams v Davies*, it will be found that the equity of the Bill impeached the title to the legal demand.'

12.89   This statement is often cited in the later cases but the case provides little assistance in deciding what is an 'equitable ground for being protected' and when the equity can be said to have 'impeached the title to the legal demand'.

12.90   The leading modern case is the decision of the Court of Appeal in *Hanak v Green*.[56] In that case, the claimant sued her builder for breach of contract for failing to complete the works which he had contracted for. The defendant claimed to set off a claim on a quantum meruit in respect of extra work done outside the contract and also for loss caused by the claimant's refusal to admit the defendant's workmen. The Court of Appeal held that these amounts could be set off against the claimant's claim.

---

50   *Stooke v Taylor* (1880) 5 QBD 569 at 576, per Cockburn CJ.
51   *Hanak v Green* [1958] 2 QB 9 at 17, per Morris LJ; and *The Brede* [1974] QB 233 at 246, per Lord Denning MR.
52   *Morley v Inglis* (1837) 4 Bing NC 58 at 71, per Tindal CJ.
53   *Re Hiram Maxim Lamp Company* [1903] 1 Ch 70 at 74, per Byrne J.
54   (1839, 1840, 1841) Cr & Ph 161.
55   (1839, 1840, 1841) Cr & Ph 161 at 178 and 179.
56   [1958] 2 QB 9.

12.91 The leading judgment was given by Morris LJ who, having quoted Lord Cottenham's judgment in *Rawson v Samuel*, then reviewed the subsequent authorities and said:[57]

'On the authorities to which I have referred, it seems to me that a court of equity would say that neither of these claims [ie the claims by the claimant and by the defendant] ought to be insisted upon without taking the other into account. It would not be equitable for the plaintiff to recover [the amount owing to her] while the [amount owing by her] was owing by her under the contract.'

12.92 Morris LJ did not identify, in so many words, the test as to when an equitable set-off is available, but his discussion of *Bankes v Jarvis*[58] is instructive. In explaining why a set-off was available in that case, he said:[59]

'The conclusion seems to me to be clearly correct and obviously fair. It would have been manifestly unjust if the defendant had had to pay £50 to the plaintiff (who was an agent or trustee for her son) at a time when the defendant had an unquestioned claim for £51 against the plaintiff's son, who had left the country. There was a close relationship between the dealings and transactions which gave rise to the respective claims.'

12.93 What Morris LJ therefore considered relevant was the closeness of the dealings between the parties and the manifest injustice of having to pay one without the other.

12.94 It has been seen in part 5 of **CHAPTER 3 (3.175ff)** that similar language is used when describing the circumstances in which the counterparty under a contract can set off, as against an assignee, a claim which he has against the assignor. In *Government of Newfoundland v Newfoundland Railway Co*, Lord Hobhouse said:[60]

'There is no universal rule that claims arising out of the same contract may be set against one another in all circumstances. But Their Lordships have no hesitation in saying that in this contract [the cross-claims] ought to be set one against another ... Unliquidated damages may now be set off as between the original parties, and also against an assignee if flowing out of and inseparably connected with the dealings and transactions which also give rise to the subject of the assignment.'

12.95 In *Bank of Boston Connecticut v European Grain and Shipping*,[61] Lord Brandon (with whose judgment all their lordships agreed) referred to Lord Cottenham's test in *Rawson v Samuel* and said:[62]

'The concept of a cross-claim being such as "impeached the title to the legal demand" is not a familiar one today. A different version of the

---

57   [1958] 2 QB 9 at 26.
58   [1903] 1 KB 549.
59   [1958] 2 QB 9 at 24.
60   (1888) 13 App Cas 199 at 212–213.
61   [1989] AC 1056.
62   [1989] AC 1056 at 1102.

relevant test is to be found in the decision of the judicial committee of the
Privy Council in *Government of Newfoundland v Newfoundland
Railway Co.*'

12.96 Lord Brandon went on to decide that the test for set-off against
assignees was the same as the test for set-off between parties to the original
contract, and he clearly regarded the test set out in the *Newfoundland Railway*
case as being the correct one.

12.97 One further illustration will establish the limits of equitable set-off.
British Anzani (Felixstowe) v International Marine Management (UK)[63] is only
a first instance decision, but Forbes J explains very clearly the way in which
equitable set-offs work. In that case, the landlord of premises brought a claim
against the tenant for unpaid rent. The tenant claimed to set off damages for
loss suffered by it as a result of the failure of the landlord to make good defects
in the floor of the building which it had undertaken to do in a separate
agreement. Forbes J held that the tenant was able to set off its damages claim
against the landlord's claim for rent even though the landlord's claim was made
under the lease, and the tenant's counterclaim was made under a separate
agreement.

12.98 Forbes J said:[64]

'[I]n considering questions of this kind, it is what is obviously fair or
manifestly unjust that will determine the solution. This is because today,
while it is necessary to look back before the Judicature Act to discover the
broad principles upon which equity would grant relief, it may not be
helpful to seek to find out from the cases what a court of equity would have
done in a similar case. The principle may be derived from the older cases.
The application of that principle should be reached by a consideration of
what today will be regarded as fair or just.'

12.99 Applying that test to the facts of the case, he decided that, even though
the cross-claims arose out of different agreements:[65]

'[T]here is nevertheless here that close connection between claim and
cross-claim which equity requires ... It would in my view be manifestly
unjust to allow the landlords to recover the rent without taking into
account the damages which it is alleged the tenants have suffered through
failure by the landlords to perform their part of the agreement.'

Conclusion

12.100 In conclusion, it is suggested that there are two requirements of an
equitable set-off:

• In the first place, the cross-claims must arise out of the same transaction,
  but need not arise out of the same contract.

---

63 [1980] QB 137.
64 [1980] QB 137 at 155.
65 [1980] QB 137 at 155–156.

● Secondly, the cross-claims must be so closely connected that it would clearly be unfair to allow one to be recovered without taking account of the other.

Limitations on set-off

12.101 As a general principle, both statutory set-off and equitable set-off are applicable to any type of transaction provided that their respective requirements are complied with. There are, however, two exceptions which are worthy of note.

12.102 The first is simply an application of the general principle that certain types of monetary claim are considered as 'cash' and are therefore payable without set-off. Negotiable instruments are an example of this concept. If, for instance, A is liable to B on a bill of exchange, he cannot, as a general rule, use a cross-claim against B as a reason for not paying under the bill of exchange. In this sense, the bill is regarded as cash in the hands of B.[66] There are limited circumstances, such as fraud, where this principle does not apply.

12.103 The other exception is more difficult to justify. It has been seen, in part 2 of this chapter (**12.10**ff), that the common law right of abatement only applies to certain types of contract and that, in particular, it does not apply to contracts of carriage. This was made clear by Parke B in *Mondel v Steel*.[67] What is more difficult to understand is that the courts have used this principle as a justification for refusing to allow equitable set-off in respect of freight payable under contracts of carriage by sea, even though equitable set-off is available in respect of other types of contract to which the right of abatement does not apply. In *Aries Tanker Corporation v Total Transport*,[68] the House of Lords decided that, because the common law principle of abatement did not extend to contracts of carriage by sea, then neither did the principle of equitable set-off. It was decided that the rule was well settled. In the words of Lord Wilberforce:[69]

> 'It is said to be an arbitrary rule – and so it may be, in the sense that no very clear justification for it has ever been stated and perhaps also in the sense that the law might just, or almost, as well have settled for a rule to the opposite effect. But this does not affect its status in the law. A rule is nonetheless capable of being a rule of law, though no reason can be given for it ...'

12.104 It is therefore clear that, in contracts for the carriage of goods by sea, a charterer is unable to set up cross-claims against the owner in reduction of his obligation to pay freight to the owner. The position is less clear in relation to contracts for the carriage of goods by land, but there is first instance authority

---

66   *Nova (Jersey) Knit v Kammgarn Spinnerei* [1977] 1 WLR 713 at 732–733.
67   (1841) 8 M & W 858.
68   [1977] 1 WLR 185.
69   [1977] 1 WLR 185 at 190.

for the proposition that the 'freight exception' applies to such contracts in the same way as it applies to a contract of carriage of goods by sea.[70] The principle can, of course, be contracted out of.

Contractual set-off

12.105   Outside insolvency proceedings, rights of set-off can be, and frequently are, either extended or limited by contract. In *Gilbert-Ash (Northern) v Modern Engineering*,[71] Lord Salmon said:[72]

> 'There is nothing to prevent [the parties to a contract] from extinguishing, curtailing or enlarging their ordinary rights of set-off, provided they do so expressly or by clear implication.'

Limiting rights of set-off

12.106   An example of an express provision which limits the right of set-off is provided by *Hong Kong and Shanghai Banking Corporation v Kloeckner & Co*.[73] In that case, a bank's customer had entered into a letter of undertaking to its bank by which it irrevocably undertook to make payment in full of a particular liability 'without any discount, deduction, off-set or counterclaim whatsoever on the due date'. Hirst J held that this contractual agreement excluded any right of set-off which the customer might otherwise have had against the bank.

12.107   Provisions of this type are common in financial transactions and in some commercial transactions. Their purpose is to ensure that A will perform his obligations to B under the contract without deduction. They are, in effect, a contractual extension of the common law rule that certain types of undertaking (such as negotiable instruments) must be paid in full, without set-off. As will be seen in part 5 of this chapter (**12.114ff**), they are ineffective in a liquidation, administration or bankruptcy, but they are otherwise effective.

Extending rights of set-off

12.108   Of even more importance is the ability of parties to a contract to extend rights of set-off by agreement. An example of the use of such a provision is *Re K*,[74] which was discussed in part 2 of this chapter (**12.10ff**). In that case, a customer had agreed with her bank that:[75]

> 'In addition to the rights which you have in law, you shall also have the right at any time and without prior notice to me to combine and consolidate all or any of my accounts with the bank, and/or to set off all moneys whatsoever due by the bank to me and whether on current account

---

70   *United Carriers v Heritage Food Group (UK)* [1996] 1 WLR 371.
71   [1974] AC 689.
72   [1974] AC 689723.
73   [1990] 2 QB 514.
74   [1990] 2 QB 298.
75   [1990] 2 QB 298 at 299–300.

or deposit account … which the bank may at any time hold … for my account, against any liability incurred or to be incurred by me to the bank …'

12.109   Otton J held that this provision was effective and:[76] 'entitles the bank at any time to combine or consolidate the accounts or to set off all monies whatsoever due by the bank to [its customer] against any liability incurred by her to the bank.'

12.110   It is ubiquitous, in all types of financing transactions, for financial institutions such as banks to require their counterparties to agree that the financial institution will have a broad right of set-off. Such arrangements are contained in general banking documentation (such as mandates and letters of set-off) as well as in transactional documents (such as facility agreements and security documents). It will be seen in part 5 of this chapter (**12.114ff**) that these provisions are ineffective if the counterparty enters into liquidation, administration or bankruptcy; but they are otherwise effective.

12.111   Contractual set-off arrangements are of various types but, in practice, two types of arrangement are particularly common. The more limited form, which is frequently seen in facility agreements, enables the financial institution to set off against amounts owing by it, money then payable by the counterparty to it. Such provisions do not materially extend the institution's rights beyond those available as a result of statutory set-off, but their importance is that they provide clear evidence that it has not contracted out of any right of set-off and they enable the set-off to be effected in accordance with the terms of the contract, rather than merely as a defence to a claim in court.

12.112   The more extended form of contractual set-off arrangement purports to enable the financial institution to set off against money owing by it to the counterparty any amounts then owing by the counterparty whether they are actual (ie then payable), future (ie payable at some certain time in the future) or contingent (ie payable only on the happening of some uncertain future event). The effectiveness of such arrangements is not beyond doubt. They attempt to mirror the effect of an equitable set-off which, if available, applies not only to money which is actually payable but to amounts which will, or may, become payable in the future. The effect of an equitable set-off is to prevent the claimant from recovering against the defendant until the extent of the defendant's cross-claim against the claimant has been established. These contractual provisions try to do the same thing. As a contractual matter, there is no reason why they should not be effective. But, to the extent that they purport to enable the financial institution to appropriate the counterparty's present right to payment in discharge of a future or contingent cross-claim owing by the counterparty, they may well create a charge. There used to be concerns that, if such a charge had been created, it would only be effective in the counterparty's insolvency if it was registered at Companies House, although such concerns have now to a large extent been allayed by the Financial Collateral Arrangements (No 2) Regulations 2003,[77] which

76   [1990] 2 QB 298 at 304.
77   SI 2003/3226.

establishes that no registration is required in cases to which those Regulations apply. Nevertheless, such wide-ranging set-off provisions are less common than they used to be, creditors being more likely to take an express charge in such a case.

12.113 In conclusion, there is no doubt that a simple contractual right of set-off of amounts payable by the counterparty to the financial institution is effective. To the extent that the documentation purports to allow a set-off of future or contingent amounts, it is arguable that such arrangements create a charge. Provided the charge is not registrable, this should not matter, although it would be preferable to draft it as a charge to avoid any uncertainty, and then to take an informed decision whether or not to register it.

Part 5: SET-OFF IN INSOLVENCY

12.114 The right of set-off in insolvency is very different from the right of set-off between parties which are not in insolvency proceedings. It has developed quite independently of those other types of set-off, it is of much broader application, its effect is quite different and it cannot be contracted out of.

12.115 Its importance is illustrated by an example. A owes B £100 and B owes A £40. A goes into liquidation, administration or bankruptcy. B, by setting off his £40, receives the equivalent of full payment of £40 instead of being paid the percentage dividend on that amount which is being paid to A's other creditors. In practice, therefore, the right of set-off in insolvency is the equivalent of a substantive security right. It is not simply a matter of procedure.

12.116 The distinction between set-off in insolvency and set-off between solvent parties was explained by Parke B in *Forster v Wilson*:[78]

> 'The right of set-off in bankruptcy does not appear to rest on the same principle as the right of set-off between solvent parties. The latter is given by the statutes of set-off ... to prevent cross actions. ... But, under the bankrupt statutes, the mutual credit clause has not been so construed. The object of this clause ... is not to avoid cross actions, for none would lie against assignees, and one against the bankrupt would be unavailing, but to do substantial justice between the parties ...'

12.117 The development of set-off in insolvency in England and in other common law jurisdictions is in marked contrast to the approach of many civil law jurisdictions. In those jurisdictions, the approach has been to restrict rights of set-off because they give a creditor who owes money to the insolvent person an advantage over a creditor who does not. The creditor is expected to pay the amount owing by him in full, and then receive a dividend on the amount owing

---

78   (1843) 12 M & W 191 at 203–204.

to him. In England, the approach has been exactly the opposite. It has always been considered to be unfair for a creditor who owes money to the insolvent person to have to pay him in full but only to receive a dividend on the amount owing to him.

12.118 English law has recognised the importance of allowing a creditor a right of set-off in his debtor's insolvency for over 400 years. Although it is now enshrined in statute, the commissioners in bankruptcy allowed the set-off of mutual debts under their general powers long before the first statute permitted set-off in bankruptcy.[79] The arrangements were put on a statutory footing in 1705.[80] The history of set-off in insolvency has consisted of a gradual statutory extension of the creditor's right of set-off (with the occasional backward step prompted by decisions of the courts). The statutory provisions initially applied where the debtor became bankrupt. In 1875, they were extended to companies in liquidation.[81] When administration was introduced for insolvent companies in 1986, the rules were not initially extended to companies in administration (which therefore remained subject to the rules discussed in part 4 of this chapter (**12.76ff**)) but, in 2003, they were extended to companies in administration.

12.119 Until recently, the statutory provisions did not differ to any material extent from those contained in the Bankruptcy Act 1869. Indeed, in bankruptcy, s 323 of the Insolvency Act 1986 is still recognisably a modernised version of that provision. But, in liquidation and administration, the Insolvency (Amendment) Rules 2005[82] have amended the wording of those provisions to a considerable extent, although the amendments largely follow the case-law and do not alter the substance of the preceding law. The intention of the new provisions is to restate the preceding law more clearly than the previous legislation, rather than to amend it.

12.120 There are now three statutory provisions:

- in liquidation – r 4.90 of the Insolvency Rules 1986;[83]
- in administration – r 2.85 of the Insolvency Rules 1986;
- in bankruptcy – s 323 of the Insolvency Act 1986.

12.121 There are two prerequisites of an insolvency set-off:

- There must have been mutual credits, mutual debts or other mutual dealings between the insolvent person and a creditor proving or claiming to prove in the insolvency proceedings.
- Those mutual credits, debts or dealings must have taken place before the date specified in the legislation (referred to here as the 'relevant date').

---

79 *Powel v Stuff* (1612) 2 Bulst 26; *Anon* (1676) 1 Mod 215.
80 4/5 Anne, c 17, s 11.
81 Judicature Act 1875, s 10, as interpreted in *Mersey Steel and Iron Co v Naylor Benzon and Co* (1884) 9 App Cas 434.
82 SI 2005/527.
83 SI 1986/1925.

12.122 If those two criteria are satisfied, an account is taken of the amounts of the cross-claims, they are set off against each other and the balance of the account can (if owed to the creditor) be proved in the insolvency or must (if it is owed to the insolvent person) be paid to the appropriate insolvency officer.

12.123 The remaining sections of this part consider:

- what is the relevant date in liquidations, administrations and bankruptcies;
- what is meant by mutual debts, credits and dealings;
- how the account is taken, the set-off effected and the balance paid;
- the public policy limitations on insolvency set-off;
- the restrictions on contracting out of insolvency set-off; and
- the persons to which insolvency set-off applies.

The relevant date

12.124 A set-off is only available if the debts, credits or dealings between the parties were entered into before the relevant date. There are two elements to the concept of the relevant date. In its basic sense, the relevant date is when the debtor entered into insolvency proceedings. In liquidation, this means the date on which the debtor 'goes into liquidation'[84] – which, in the case of a voluntary liquidation, is the date of the resolution to wind up and, in the case of a compulsory liquidation, is the date of the winding-up order.[85] In bankruptcy, it means the date of commencement of the bankruptcy[86] – ie the day on which the bankruptcy order is made.[87] The position is different in administration. Because, unlike a bankruptcy or liquidation, an administration does not necessarily result in a distribution to creditors, r 2.85 of the Insolvency Rules 1986[88] only comes into effect where an administrator is authorised to make a distribution and has given notice that he proposes to do so.[89]

12.125 Although this is the basic rule, it is varied in one respect. There were concerns that creditors might obtain rights of set-off when they knew that insolvency proceedings were imminent by deliberately entering into transactions with the intention of creating a right of set-off. One way of doing so would be for a person who owed money to the debtor and who had discovered his imminent insolvency to buy debts from his creditors (at a discount) and then to use the amount he owed the debtor by way of set-off against the debts he had purchased, thereby obtaining full value on them. This led to the incorporation of a provision in the legislation by which a creditor was not able to take advantage of insolvency set-off if he entered into the transaction giving rise to the set-off when he knew that insolvency proceedings were imminent.

84　Insolvency Rules 1986, r 4.90(1).
85　Insolvency Act 1986, s 247(2).
86　Insolvency Act 1986, s 323(1).
87　Insolvency Act 1986, s 278.
88　SI 1986/1925.
89　Insolvency Rules 1986, r 2.85(1).

12.126 An example of the effect of this provision is provided by *Re Eros Films*.[90] In that case, after A had sent out to its creditors notice of its resolution to wind up, B called upon A to pay under certain guarantees and then assigned the benefit of the guarantees to its subsidiary company, C, which was a debtor of A. A subsequently passed a resolution to be wound up and C claimed that it could set off the debts because they both arose before the resolution to wind up. Buckley J held that C was unable to establish a right of set-off because it was aware, at the time it received the assignment, of the fact that A was about to go into liquidation.

12.127 The circumstances in which this limitation on set-off arises differ depending on the nature of the insolvency proceedings concerned. In bankruptcy, the only limitation is where the creditor has notice that a bankruptcy petition is pending in relation to the debtor.[91] In liquidation, the relevant provisions of r 4.90 of the Insolvency Rules 1986 are more complicated. In essence, they provide that the creditor is unable to exercise a right of set-off if his claim against the debtor was created or was acquired by him after he had notice that a meeting of creditors had been summoned preparatory to putting the company into creditors voluntary liquidation or that a winding-up petition was pending in relation to a compulsory liquidation. There are also provisions to deal with a situation where the liquidation immediately follows an administration, and the dealings took place during the administration or during a time when the creditor had notice that an administration was about to occur.[92]

12.128 There are similar provisions in relation to administrations. In this case, the matters of which the creditor requires notice are an application for an administration order being pending or a person having given notice of an intention to appoint an administrator. There are also similar provisions to deal with a situation where a liquidation immediately precedes the administration.[93]

12.129 Although the provisions relating to liquidation and administration are more elaborate than those in relation to bankruptcy, it is unlikely that they have a materially different effect. In all three cases, a creditor will not be able to avail himself of a right of set-off if it arises out of a transaction which he entered into with the debtor or a right he acquired from a third party after the earlier of:
- the date of the insolvency; and
- the date on which he became aware that steps were being taken to place the debtor into insolvency proceedings.

Debts, credits and dealings

12.130 A set-off is only available if there have been mutual debts, credits or dealings between the debtor and the creditor before the relevant date. The

---

90   [1963] 1 Ch 565.
91   Insolvency Act 1986, s 323(3).
92   Insolvency Rules 1986, r 4.90
93   Insolvency Rules 1986, r 2.85(2).

concept of mutuality has been discussed in part 3 of this chapter (**12.39ff**). This part considers what is meant by debts, credits and dealings.

12.131   Mutual debts and credits have been the subject of the legislation since it first became law in 1705. Mutual debts signify cross-claims for money which are for a liquidated amount which is presently payable. Mutual credit is a wider concept, encompassing claims which are not payable at the present date but which will become payable in the future. In the words of Lord Brougham in *Young v Bank of Bengal*:[94] 'The relation contemplated by the statute has been held to be established where the debt is immediately due from the one party and only at a future day from the other.'

12.132   The concept of mutual dealings was introduced in the Bankruptcy Act 1869 and has greatly increased the scope for set-off. Although 'mutual credit' was interpreted widely, the previous statutes only applied where the amount which ultimately became payable was a debt; and, accordingly, a claim for damages could not be set off.[95] The introduction of 'mutual dealings' increased the scope of the section so that it applied to any monetary claim, whether in debt, damages or otherwise. In the words of Brett LJ in *Peat v Jones & Co*:[96]

> 'It seems to me that the expression "mutual debts and credits" was intended to comprise all ordinary transactions between the two persons in their individual capacities, and that "mutual dealings" was added to get rid of any questions which might arise whether a transaction would end in a debt or not.'

12.133   What the legislation requires is that transactions have taken place before the relevant date which result in cross-claims for money between the debtor and the creditor. There is no requirement for the monetary cross-claims to be present liabilities as at the relevant date (ie that they are then payable) or to be future liabilities at that date (ie that they must become payable in the future). A liability which is contingent at the relevant date is capable of being set off provided that it ultimately terminates in a monetary liability. But the liability which ultimately results in the monetary claim must have existed at the relevant date. If the transaction which gave rise to the liability is entered into after the relevant date, the monetary amount ultimately becoming payable will not be the subject of a set-off.

12.134   Nor is there any requirement for a connection between the claims to be set off. They can be entirely independent of each other, even if they are contingent at the relevant date. The right of set-off is not restricted because one cross-claim is enforceable at law and the other only in equity.[97] There is no reason why a monetary claim arising out of contract cannot be set-off against a claim arising under statute, in tort or in any other way.[98] The only requirement

---

94   (1836) 1 Moo PC 150 at 165.
95   *Rose v Hart* (1817) 8 Taunt 499.
96   (1881) 8 QBD 147 at 149.
97   *Mathieson's Trustee v Burrup, Mathieson & Co* [1927] 1 Ch 562.
98   *Re D H Curtis (Builders)* [1978] Ch 162.

is that the creditor's claim must be provable in the insolvency, but this is not a material limitation in practice in view of the breadth of provable claims.

12.135 In the past, there was some doubt about whether liabilities which were 'wholly' contingent at the relevant date were capable of being set off. Following the introduction of the concept of mutual dealings in 1869, a number of Court of Appeal decisions established that a liability which was contingent at the relevant date was capable of being set off if it ultimately matured into a monetary liability.[99] Doubt was cast on the extent to which this principle applied to cases of guarantee as a result of the decision of the Court of Appeal in *Re a Debtor (No 66 of 1955)*.[100] That decision was, it is suggested, inconsistent with the earlier Court of Appeal decisions and, for this reason, the High Court of Australia refused to follow it in *Day & Dent Constructions v North Australian Properties*.[101] *Re a Debtor* did, nevertheless, create uncertainty about the extent of the availability of insolvency set-off to claims which were contingent at the relevant date.

12.136 Further problems occurred in 1986 as a result of the way in which the insolvency set-off provisions relating to companies were drafted in the Insolvency Rules 1986.[102] They provided that a set-off would not be available if the creditor had notice of the potential insolvency at the time the cross-claims 'became due'. Read literally, this suggested that, if the claim was contingent at that date, it could not be set off, although it seemed clear that this was simply a drafting error and that there had been no intention to alter the substance of the previous law.

12.137 These concerns were put to rest by the decision of the House of Lords in *Stein v Blake*.[103] That case involved the bankruptcy of an individual. The question arose whether cross-claims between the creditor and the bankrupt debtor, which had arisen out of a contract entered into before the bankruptcy but which remained contingent at the time of the bankruptcy, were to be set off. The House of Lords held that they were. The principal judgment was given by Lord Hoffmann. Having considered the difference between statutory set-off and insolvency set-off he said:[104]

> 'Bankruptcy set-off ... affects the substantive rights of the parties by enabling the bankrupt's creditor to use his indebtedness to the bankrupt as a form of security. Instead of having to prove with other creditors for the whole of his debt in the bankruptcy, he can set off pound for pound what he owes the bankrupt and prove for or pay only the balance.'

---

99   *Re Asphaltic Wood Pavement Co, Lee & Chapman's Case* (1885) 30 Ch D 216; *Re Daintrey, ex parte Mant* [1900] 1 QB 546.
100   [1956] 1 WLR 1226.
101   (1982) 150 CLR 85.
102   SI 1986/1925.
103   [1996] AC 243.
104   [1996] AC 243 at 251.

12.138 Having then quoted Baron Parke's statement in *Forster v Wilson*[105] that the purpose of insolvency set-off was 'to do substantial justice between the parties', he went on to say:[106]

> 'Bankruptcy set-off therefore requires an account to be taken of liabilities which, at the time of bankruptcy, may be due but not yet payable or may be unascertained in amount or subject to contingency.'

12.139 *Re a Debtor* was not expressly referred to in *Stein v Blake* but, in *Secretary of State for Trade and Industry v Frid*,[107] the House of Lords had to consider it directly. In that case, a company went into liquidation being owed money by Customs & Excise in respect of VAT and having a contingent liability to indemnify the Secretary of State for Trade and Industry in respect of her statutory obligation to pay redundancy payments to the company's employees. The question at issue was whether the company's liability to indemnify the Secretary of State could be set off against the company's claim for VAT. The counterparty in both cases was the Crown, but the liability owing to the Crown was contingent at the relevant date, resulting from the payment under a (statutory) guarantee after the relevant date. The case therefore directly raised the question of whether set-off was precluded by *Re a Debtor*.

12.140 The House of Lords held that it was not. They disapproved *Re a Debtor* and confirmed that monetary cross-claims arising from liabilities which were contingent before the relevant date must set off. The principal judgment was again given by Lord Hoffmann. He said:[108]

> '9.   It is not however necessary for the purposes of Rule 4.90(2) that the debt should have been due and payable before the insolvency date. It is sufficient that there should have been an obligation arising out of the terms of a contract or statute by which a debt sounding in money would become payable upon the occurrence of some future event or events ...
>
> 24.   All that is necessary therefore is that there should have been 'dealings' (in an extended sense which includes the commission of a tort or the imposition of a statutory obligation) which give rise to commensurable cross-claims.'

12.141 It is now, therefore, clear that insolvency set-off is available in relation to all mutual cross-claims which become owing between the creditor and the insolvent debtor provided that they become payable as a result of liabilities incurred before the relevant date.

12.142 The statutory provisions which apply in liquidation and administration have now been clarified in order to reflect these judicial pronouncements. Rules 2.85 and 4.90 now make it clear that a sum will be regarded as being due whether:

- it is payable at present or in the future;

---

105 (1843) 12 M & W 191 at 204.
106 [1996] AC 243 at 252.
107 [2004] 2 AC 506.
108 [2004] 2 AC 506 at 511 and 514.

- the obligation by virtue of which it is payable is certain or contingent; or
- its amount is fixed or liquidated, or is capable of being ascertained by fixed rules or as a matter of opinion.[109]

12.143 As far as bankruptcy is concerned, s 323 of the Insolvency Act 1986 has not been amended because it is more difficult to amend the Insolvency Act than the Insolvency Rules. But there is no doubt that the position is the same as in liquidation and administration.

12.144 One issue which remains to be decided is the circumstances in which a court will decide that an amount payable after the relevant date is not payable as a consequence of a liability incurred before the relevant date because an event has occurred which breaks the causative link between them. It is clear that the payment under a guarantee will not break the causative link if the guarantor had a liability to make the payment before the relevant date. But it is possible to envisage circumstances in which a debt which becomes payable after the relevant date apparently as a result of a liability entered into before that date is, in fact, payable as a result of some intervening action which has had the result of breaking the causative link.

12.145 An example of such a case is *The Ince Hall Rolling Mills Co v The Douglas Forge Co.*[110] In that case, D agreed to supply goods to C and then went into compulsory liquidation, the goods being supplied to C after the liquidation. It was held that C could not set off a debt due from D before the liquidation against the debt due from it to D in respect of the goods supplied after the liquidation. Watkin Williams J said:[111]

> 'If it could be correctly stated in the present case that the debt sued for by [D] was a debt incurred and due upon the making of the contract ... before the liquidation, although not payable until after the liquidation, the two sets of debts would have been mutual and in the same interest, and could have been set off one against the other. But in reality no debt was created until the delivery of the goods after the commencement of the liquidation, and the only remaining question is whether this delivery having taken place in a certain sense in fulfilment of a contract made before the liquidation gives the debt that character in interest and mutuality that is necessary to make it a subject of set-off against the debt of the company.'

12.146 The judge decided that it did not, saying that the delivery of the goods after the liquidation gave rise to a debt due to D in a new capacity. There is much to be said for this decision. The liquidator was not bound to supply the goods. He ought to have made it clear that he would only do so against actual payment but, not having done so, to have allowed a set-off would have given a windfall to C.

12.147 The *Ince Hall* case should be contrasted with *Palmer v Day.*[112] In that case, D deposited certain pictures with C, a firm of auctioneers, for sale, but

---

109 Insolvency Rules 1986, r 4.90(4) and (9); r 2.85(4) and (9).
110 (1882) 8 QBD 179.
111 (1882) 8 QBD 179 at 183–184.
112 [1895] 2 QB 618.

became bankrupt whilst the pictures were still unsold. C subsequently sold the pictures, acting upon the instructions of D's trustee in bankruptcy. A Divisional Court of the Queen's Bench Division held that C had a right to set off the proceeds of sale against a debt owed by D which pre-dated the bankruptcy. It is a curious case for two reasons. Although C held D's pictures before the bankruptcy, the instruction to sell came from D's trustee in bankruptcy, which ought to have broken the causal link between the pre-bankruptcy bailment and the post-bankruptcy debt. In any event, C, having sold D's goods, should have held the proceeds on trust for D, in which event no set-off should have been available in respect of D's proprietary claim to the proceeds (see part 3 of this chapter (**12.39**ff)).

12.148   A problem like that which arose in these two cases is unlikely to arise in practice. These days, an insolvency practitioner is unlikely to enable such a liability to be created without requiring that it is paid in full. But, if such a case does occur, a liability which arises as a result of an action by an insolvency practitioner after he has been appointed should, it is suggested, constitute a new liability and should not be referable back to a contract made before the relevant date.

12.149   Subject to that point, all mutual cross-claims are the subject of insolvency set-off if they become payable as a result of a transaction which was entered into or a matter which happened before the relevant date.

The account, set-off and payment

12.150   If there have been mutual debts, credits or dealings between the insolvent person and the debtor before the relevant date:

- an account is taken of the amounts which are due from each party to the other;
- those amounts are then set off against each other; and
- the balance then becomes owing by the party who owes the larger sum.

12.151   The account is taken as at the date of the liquidation or bankruptcy (or, in an administration, as at the date by reference to which a distribution is to be made by the administrator). As Lord Hoffmann makes clear in *Stein v Blake*,[113] although the calculation will, in practice, be made later, it is made by reference to that date, which is the date at which the liabilities of the insolvent person are established. In most cases, even where the liability is contingent at the relevant date, it will mature shortly after that date and it will be clear what the amount is for the purpose of the account. In *Stein v Blake*, Lord Hoffmann dealt with the situation (which is unlikely to arise frequently in practice) where the amount cannot be established at the time a distribution is to be made. In such a case, he said that a liability owing by the insolvent debtor to the creditor can be estimated; but there is no corresponding mechanism for amounts owing by the creditor to the debtor. Although this is still the case in bankruptcy, the

---

113   [1996] AC 243.

new insolvency rules which are applicable to liquidations and administrations enable the valuation of a contingent liability whether it is owing by or to the debtor company.[114]

Public policy limitations

12.152   Although it has been seen that, as a general rule, set-off in insolvency is available in relation to any type of cross-claim between the insolvent debtor and a creditor provided that there were mutual dealings between the parties at the relevant date, certain cases have established an exception based on public policy.

12.153   The principle behind these cases is that, where legislation relating to insolvency requires a person to pay money to an insolvency practitioner for the purpose of swelling the assets of the insolvent debtor, it is not possible for the person whose obligation it is to make that payment to set off a cross-claim which he may have against the insolvent debtor. The purpose of the legislation is to swell the assets of the insolvent debtor in order to enable a larger amount to be paid to unsecured creditors rateably; and it would defeat this purpose if a set-off were to be allowed.

12.154   This principle is seen most clearly in relation to liability for calls. In *Re Overend, Gurney & Co, Grissell's Case*,[115] a limited liability company was being wound up under the supervision of the court, and a contributory took out a summons asking that the liquidators be ordered to pay him a dividend on the amount owing to him by the company after deducting the amount of any calls due to be made by him. The summons was dismissed, Lord Chelmsford LC stating:[116]

> 'It appears to me to be quite clear that the amount of the call not paid cannot be set-off against the debt. The [Companies Act 1862] creates a scheme for the payment of the debts of a company ... It removes the rights and liabilities of parties out of the sphere of the ordinary relation of debtor and creditor to which the law of set-off applies. Taking the Act as a whole, the call is to come into the assets of the company, to be applied with the other assets in payment of debts. To allow a set-off against the call would be contrary to the whole scope of the Act.'

12.155   This decision was subsequently extended to compulsory liquidations[117] and to creditors voluntary liquidations.[118] There is an exception where the contributory is himself bankrupt,[119] although it would seem that this exception does not apply where the contributory is a company which is in insolvent liquidation.[120]

---

114   Insolvency Rules 1986, SI 1986/1925, rr 4.90(5)–(7) and 2.85(5)–(7).
115   (1866) LR 1 Ch App 528.
116   (1866) LR 1 Ch App 528 at 535–536.
117   *Re Paraguassu Steam Tramroad Co, Black & Co's Case* (1872) LR 8 Ch App 254.
118   *Re Whitehouse & Co* (1878) 9 Ch D 595.
119   *Re Duckworth* (1867) 2 Ch App 578.
120   *Re Auriferous Properties* [1898] 1 Ch 691.

12.156   It is now very rare for companies to have uncalled share capital, but the principle of *Grissell's Case* has been applied to other situations which are likely to be more important in practice. In particular, it applies in two types of case – in relation to claw-back and misfeasance liabilities.

12.157   Various provisions of the insolvency legislation give an insolvency practitioner the power to set aside transactions entered into in the period running up to the commencement of insolvency proceedings. They are discussed in **CHAPTER 9**. If a person has an obligation to make a payment to the insolvency practitioner as a result of one of these provisions, he will not be able to set off a claim which he has against the insolvent person. It has been held that this is the case in relation to preferences,[121] on the basis that 'if a set-off were allowed in these circumstances, it would be reducing the fraudulent preference section ... to a nullity'.[122] In principle, the same result should follow in other cases where a person has to make a payment to the company as a result of a claw-back provision of the insolvency legislation.

12.158   The same principle applies in relation to misfeasance liabilities. In *Re Anglo-French Co-operative, ex parte Pelly*,[123] Hall V-C (whose decision was affirmed by the Court of Appeal) held that the liability of an officer of the company in respect of misfeasance 'is a liability of a delinquent, and until the order directing payment in respect of it has been made should not be treated (in the delinquent's favour) as a debt due from him to the company, so as to entitle him to a set off'.[124] The words are perhaps a little harsh, but the policy is clear.

The effect of agreement

12.159   It is not possible, by contract, for the debtor and the creditor to agree either that the right of set-off in insolvency should be restricted or that it should be increased. These propositions were established in two key decisions of the House of Lords in the 1970s – *National Westminster Bank v Halesowen Presswork and Assemblies*[125] and *British Eagle International Airlines v Compagnie Nationale Air France*.[126] In the *Halesowen* case, it was decided that an agreement purporting to abolish or limit the creditor's right of set-off in insolvency was ineffective. In the *British Eagle* case, it was decided that a contractual arrangement purporting to extend the creditor's right of set-off in insolvency was also ineffective.

12.160   In the *Halesowen* case, a company had an overdrawn account with a bank. It was agreed that this account would be re-named the no 1 account and be frozen at its then limit, and that a no 2 account would be opened on a strictly credit basis. The bank agreed to keep to this scheme in the absence of materially changed circumstances. The company went into liquidation at a time

---

121   *Re A Debtor (No 82 of 1926)* [1927] 1 Ch 410.
122   [1927] 1 Ch 410 at 415–416, per Astbury J.
123   (1882) 21 Ch D 492.
124   (1882) 21 Ch D 492 at 498.
125   [1972] 1 AC 785.
126   [1975] 1 WLR 758.

when there was a credit balance on the no 2 account, and the bank claimed to set off that credit balance against the debit balance on the no 1 account. The House of Lords held that the agreement was only intended to remain operative as long as the company was a going concern, and accordingly that the parties had not intended to contract out of insolvency set-off. The case is, however, important for the statements of Their Lordships that it would not have been possible for the parties to contract out of insolvency set-off because its provisions are mandatory.

12.161 Lord Cross reviewed all the authorities, concluding that the statements in them were contradictory. He would have decided that insolvency set-off was intended solely for the benefit of the creditor and that there was no reason in principle why such a person should not be entitled to agree in advance that in the event of the insolvency of the other party he would not invoke it. But the other members of the House disagreed. Lord Simon held that insolvency set-off was not solely for the benefit of any particular person. The statutory provisions are drafted in mandatory form. The insolvency legislation lays down a code of procedure for the administration of insolvent estates in a proper and orderly way, which is a matter in which the commercial community generally has an interest. As a result, contracting out was not possible.

12.162 In spite of the mandatory wording of the insolvency set-off provisions, it is difficult to see why this should be the case. The right of set-off in insolvency is clearly intended to protect the creditor. If the commercial community generally does have an interest, it is too remote to allow it to interfere in a decision taken by the creditor. There may be good commercial reasons why a creditor might wish to contract out of a right of set-off, and it is difficult to see why anyone other than the creditor should suffer as a result. Nevertheless, although the statements of the majority of the House of Lords in the *Halesowen* case are not binding, it has generally been accepted that the legislation is mandatory in its effect and this concept underpins the subsequent decision of the House of Lords in *Stein v Blake*.[127]

12.163 It is much easier to understand why an agreement purporting to increase the creditor's right of set-off in insolvency should be ineffective, although the case in which it was decided is controversial for another reason. In the *British Eagle* case, British Eagle and Air France were both members of the International Air Transport Association (IATA), which was established as a clearing house for international airlines. The object of the clearing house was to provide a facility for the settlement of debts between international airlines which carried passengers and freight on behalf of each other. Instead of each company running up debits and credits with a number of different airlines, the members of IATA agreed that all such debits and credits would be payable through the medium of the clearing house in accordance with the regulations of IATA. Claims in respect of all airlines were cleared each month. Members in overall debit to IATA were required to pay the sums due from them within 7 days, and IATA then discharged the amounts due to members in credit within the next 7 days.

---

127 [1996] AC 243.

12.164 In the month before its liquidation, British Eagle had received services from Air France exceeding the value of those rendered to it by British Eagle. The liquidator of British Eagle accordingly claimed that Air France was indebted to it for the difference. Templeman J and the Court of Appeal (Russell, Cairns and Stamp LJJ), held that the clearing house arrangements were binding on the liquidator, that all settlements had to be made through IATA and accordingly that no debt was due to British Eagle. But a majority of the House of Lords held that the IATA clearing house arrangements were an attempt to contract out of the fundamental principle of insolvency law that the assets of the debtor should be distributed pari passu amongst his creditors and were accordingly contrary to public policy and void. The judgment of the majority (Lords Cross, Diplock and Edmund-Davies) was given by Lord Cross:[128]

> 'The "clearing house" creditors are clearly not secured creditors. They are claiming nevertheless that they ought not to be treated in the liquidation as ordinary unsecured creditors but that they have achieved by the medium of the "clearing house" agreement a position analogous to that of secured creditors without the need for the creation and registration of charges on the book debts in question ... But what [Air France] are saying here is that the parties to the "clearing house" arrangements by agreeing that simple contract debts are to be satisfied in a particular way have succeeded in "contracting out" of the provisions contained in [the equivalent of s 107 of the Insolvency Act 1986] for the payment of unsecured debts "pari passu". In such a context it is to my mind irrelevant that the parties to the "clearing house" arrangements had good business reasons for entering into them and did not direct their minds to the question how the arrangements might be affected by the insolvency of one or more of the parties. Such a "contracting out" must, to my mind, be contrary to public policy.'

12.165 The minority in the House of Lords (Lords Morris and Simon) agreed with the judgments of Templeman J and the Court of Appeal. Their view was summarised by Russell LJ in the Court of Appeal:[129]

> 'We are, in short, of the opinion that, British Eagle having contracted with every other member of the clearing house and with IATA not to enforce its net claim for services against, for example, Air France otherwise than through the clearing house, it could not while a member do so. Nor, in our judgment is the liquidator of British Eagle in any better position in respect of the claim now made against Air France: for we do not consider that the contract is one that can fairly be said to contravene the principles of our insolvency laws. Those laws require that the property of an insolvent company shall be distributed pro rata among its unsecured creditors: but the question here is whether the claim asserted against Air France is property of British Eagle. In our judgment it is not: British Eagle has long since deprived itself of any such property by agreeing to the clearing house system.'

---

128 [1975] 1 WLR 758 at 780.
129 [1975] 1 WLR 758 at 765.

12.166   The point of principle decided in the *British Eagle* case is clear – in the insolvency proceedings, a contractual arrangement which would have the effect of increasing the rights of set-off of a creditor above those provided for in the legislation is void. That principle is clearly correct, and it was assented to by all the judges who were involved in the case.

12.167   What is controversial about the case is whether the IATA clearing house arrangements did, in fact, constitute such a contract. Three members of the House of Lords thought they did. The other six judges in the case thought they did not. There is much to be said for the latter view. If the arrangements had been executed by the time of the liquidation, it is difficult to see what property of British Eagle was being applied otherwise than pari passu. An arrangement which is executory at the relevant date and which would have the effect of increasing a creditor's right of set-off is clearly void. Where, however, transactions have taken place before the relevant date as a result of which the debtor company has ceased to have rights over the assets concerned, it is difficult to see how these could be a breach of the pari passu sharing rules.

12.168   In conclusion, and in spite of the unsatisfactory nature of the *Halesowen* and *British Eagle* cases, it is clear that the insolvency set-off provisions are mandatory and that a purported contractual arrangement between the creditor and the debtor to increase or reduce the creditor's right of insolvency set-off is void.

Persons to which insolvency set-off applies

12.169   The procedural set-off rules only apply where proceedings are being brought in the English courts. Where a creditor wishes to rely on contractual set-off under English law, it can do so if the contract is governed by English law. Insolvency set-off in England only applies if the debtor goes into insolvency proceedings in England. The English courts have insolvency jurisdiction not only over persons incorporated or domiciled here, but also over certain other categories of person, such as foreign companies. The scope of this jurisdiction is considered in **CHAPTER 14**.

12.170   There are certain types of association which cannot be the subject of normal insolvency proceedings and which are not, therefore, amenable to insolvency set-off. One example is building societies. In principle (although there is no clear authority on the point), rights of set-off outside insolvency proceedings should continue to be available in such cases, including contractual rights of set-off.

Part 6: IMPROVING RIGHTS OF SET-OFF

12.171   It has been seen that rights of set-off outside insolvency proceedings are fairly limited in their scope, but that it is possible to extend them by contract. Conversely, although set-off in insolvency has a very wide ambit, it cannot be extended by contract. The purpose of this part is to consider how a creditor can improve upon his rights of set-off under the general law.

12.172 The inquiry falls into two parts. The first part considers the ways in which the creditor can use contractual arrangements to improve his position before the debtor enters into insolvency proceedings. The second part considers how a taking of a charge can improve his position in the debtor's insolvency.

Contractual arrangements

12.173 The limited nature of set-off rights outside insolvency proceedings has resulted in contractual extensions of set-off rights being commonplace in financial transactions. The creditor can, in an appropriate case, use flawed assets or netting as a means of ensuring that his liability to the debtor is conditional upon the payment by the debtor to him or, alternatively, only consists of the net amount after the balance of debits and credits between the parties has been established. These arrangements are considered in part 2 of this chapter (**12.10ff**). Alternatively, and more commonly, in cases where there are cross-claims owing between the debtor and the creditor, the creditor can extend his right of set-off by contract in the manner described in part 4 of this chapter (**12.76ff**).

12.174 An example of the use of contractual arrangements to improve rights of set-off is where a debtor is required to place a deposit with a creditor to 'secure' a future or contingent liability of the debtor to the creditor. In such a case, the documentation should provide that the creditor is entitled to retain the deposit until such time as the debtor's liability matures and then to set it off against the resulting liability. Such an arrangement is common, and is effective until such time as the debtor goes into liquidation, administration or bankruptcy.

12.175 As well as protecting itself against the debtor, the creditor can also use contractual arrangements to protect itself against third parties who might claim an interest in the deposit – such as assignees or chargees of the deposit. It has been seen, in part 5 of **CHAPTER 3** (**3.175ff**), that an assignee or chargee of a receivable will take it subject to equities, such as rights of set-off. In the example described above, if the debtor assigns the deposit, the creditor will be able to set off against the assignee cross-claims which it has against the debtor either if its claim against the debtor is due at the time it receives notice of the assignment or if the cross-claims between the creditor and the debtor arise out of the same transaction and are so closely connected that it would be unfair to allow the assignee to obtain the deposit in full without giving the creditor the benefit of a set-off. Where the debtor's liability to the creditor is contingent, the creditor cannot rely on the first of these protections, but there is no reason why it cannot ensure that there is a sufficiently close connection between the deposit and the debtor's liability to the creditor that an assignee will take subject to the creditor's right of set-off. The documentation can make it clear that the deposit is being made solely for the purpose of securing the debtor's liability.

12.176 There is another way in which the creditor can improve his position against purported assignees or chargees of the deposit. It has been seen in part

5 of **CHAPTER 3** (**3.175ff**) that an asset such as a deposit, which is created by contractual arrangement between the creditor and the debtor, is incapable of assignment to the extent that it is prohibited by the documentation creating it. Where a creditor is relying on a deposit to secure a particular liability, therefore, a provision can be inserted in the documentation which establishes the deposit to the effect that it is incapable of being assigned or charged. Such an arrangement is effective to protect the creditor from the consequences of any purported assignment or similar arrangement.

12.177   There are, therefore, various ways in which a creditor can protect itself by contract both against the debtor and against third parties before the debtor enters into insolvency proceedings.

Charges

12.178   It has been seen in part 5 of this chapter (**12.114ff**) that contractual arrangements which purport to extend the right of set-off in insolvency are void. In many cases, this will not cause any concern to the creditor. It has been seen that the right of set-off in insolvency has a very broad scope. Before the decision of the House of Lords in *Stein v Blake*,[130] there was doubt about the precise extent to which a set-off was available where the liability remained contingent at the relevant date, but any doubts on this score were removed by *Stein v Blake* and *Frid*,[131] and have been confirmed by the new wording of rr 4.90 and 2.85 of the Insolvency Rules 1986,[132] all of which are discussed in part 5 of this chapter (**12.114ff**).

12.179   In most circumstances, therefore, a creditor will be able to rely on insolvency set-off, and will have no need for any extension of its provisions. But, if the creditor does wish to improve its position, it is clear that it cannot do so by contract, and therefore that it must obtain a proprietary interest in the deposit by way of security – ie take a charge over it.

12.180   There are circumstances in which a charge over the deposit will be more advantageous to the creditor than relying on insolvency set-off. The problem with insolvency set-off is that it is both mandatory and specific. The Insolvency Rules 1986 contain detailed provisions which establish how the set-off operates. Where, for instance, one of the liabilities is a long-term contingent liability, it may require to be valued under the Insolvency Rules before it matures, in which event the amount of the valuation could be significantly different from the actual value when it does mature. More importantly in practice, foreign currency debts are translated into sterling at the date of the insolvency. This may not necessarily be the most appropriate date for conversion, particularly if the obligation to make the payment has not matured at the time of the liquidation.[133]

---

130   [1996] AC 243.
131   *Secretary of State for Trade and Industry v Frid* [2004] 2 AC 506.
132   SI 1986/1925.
133   For a consideration of other circumstances where a charge may be more advantageous than a

12.181 The advantage of a charge is its flexibility. If a creditor has to rely on insolvency set-off, there is no ability to alter the rules to meet the circumstances of the particular case. If the deposit is the subject of a charge, however, it is taken outside the scope of the insolvency and can be dealt with in accordance with the terms of the charge document.

12.182 On the other hand, rights of set-off do have some advantages over charges. They are less likely to constitute a breach of a negative pledge in the debtor's facility documentation. A right of set-off is also preferable in cases where the charge might be re-characterised as a floating charge, for instance, because it is taken over fluctuating credit balances and the bank has insufficient control over the accounts. A right of set-off is not subject to the limitations to which a floating charge is subject (which are discussed in part 5 of CHAPTER 4 (**4.79ff**)).

12.183 There used to be doubt about the ability of a bank to take a charge over its own indebtedness. The doubt was created by a statement by Millett J in *Re Charge Card Services*[134] that it is 'conceptually impossible' for a person to have a charge over a debt which he owes to another. That decision caused a great deal of controversy, and doubts were expressed about its conceptual accuracy and its practical utility. It spawned a great deal of commentary, but can now be consigned to history because, in *Re Bank of Credit and Commerce International (No 8)*,[135] the House of Lords disapproved of Millett J's statement in the *Charge Card* case and decided that it is conceptually possible for a bank to take a charge over its own deposits.

12.184 There is therefore no doubt that a bank can take a charge over indebtedness owing by it to its customer; and banks frequently do take charges over their own indebtedness. In part, this is a hangover from the days in which there was some uncertainty about the scope of insolvency set-off in relation to contingent liabilities. Even though that issue has now firmly been laid to rest, old habits die hard, and there is no doubt that the flexibility of a charge is useful in some cases.

Conclusion

12.185 A creditor can, by contractual arrangements with the debtor, substantially improve his position before the debtor enters into insolvency proceedings. These arrangements are easy to document and can provide material benefits in practice. The additional benefit obtained by taking a charge is much more marginal, but there are cases where the flexibility of a charge (as opposed to the rigidity of insolvency set-off) can be an advantage in the debtor's insolvency.

---

right of set-off, see Calnan 'Security over Deposits Again: BCCI (No 8) in the House of Lords' (1998) 4 JIBFL 125.
134 [1987] Ch 150.
135 [1998] AC 214.

INTERNATIONAL SECURITY

Chapter 13

CROSS-BORDER SECURITY

Part 1: INTRODUCTION

13.1 It is common for secured transactions governed by English law to have links with jurisdictions other than England. A facility financed out of London and governed by English law may involve:

- borrowers or guarantors incorporated in jurisdictions outside England;
- parties incorporated in England which have branches, or do business, abroad;
- tangible assets (such as land or goods) forming part of the security which are located abroad;
- intangible assets (such as contracts) forming part of the security which are governed by foreign laws.

13.2 Conversely, it is also common for financings governed by foreign laws to involve security over assets which are located in England or are governed by English law.

13.3 To the extent that English law and the relevant foreign law is the same in relation to any particular issue, this is unlikely to cause a problem. But where, as is frequently the case, the laws diverge, a conflict will arise between the result if English law is applied to the issue and that which would follow from the application of the foreign law. It is these issues of conflict of laws which are considered in this chapter.

13.4 This is a book about English law, and this chapter is concerned with English conflict of laws rules. It therefore assumes that the issue of whether a conflict has arisen and, if so, how it should be resolved, will be decided by English courts in accordance with English law. In practice, of course, this will not always be the case. In a cross-border financing, it may well be the courts of a foreign country which will decide the issue in question, and they will resolve it in accordance with their own conflict of laws rules.

13.5 Frequently, when considering the conflict of laws in the context of a secured financing, the courts which will be likely to resolve the conflict will be those in the jurisdiction where the secured assets are situated or subject to whose laws they have been created. The conflict of laws rules of foreign jurisdictions may, like its domestic laws, be different from those which would apply in England. A foreign court, faced with the question of whether it should apply its law or another law to the outcome of a particular question, may apply different principles to its resolution than would an English court. When structuring cross-border security arrangements, therefore, it is necessary to consider not only the domestic and conflict of law rules which are applicable in England, but also the domestic and conflict of law rules of any other jurisdiction which may have an effect on the arrangements.

13.6 This can be a daunting task. The companies involved in the transaction may be incorporated in a number of different jurisdictions, and may carry on business in yet other jurisdictions. The secured assets may consist of land in some jurisdictions, goods in others and contracts subject to the laws of yet others. And the facts can change during the course of the financing. Companies can set up businesses in other jurisdictions. Goods can be moved from one jurisdiction to another. A company may enter into insolvency proceedings in a jurisdiction with which it has only a minimal connection.

13.7 In practice, it is impossible to obtain advice on the domestic and conflict of law rules of every jurisdiction which may become relevant in relation to a cross-border financing. The lenders must be made aware of the risks and they will then need to decide in which jurisdictions legal advice should be taken at the outset. In this respect, there are two key jurisdictions – those where the borrower and guarantors are incorporated and those where the assets which are the subject of the security are situated (if they are tangibles) or whose law governs their creation (if they are intangibles). Advice needs to be taken in each relevant jurisdiction not only on its domestic law in relation to the issue in question but also as to its conflict of laws rules.

13.8 This chapter and the following one are concerned with the English conflict of law rules – which law will an English court apply if there is a conflict between the approach of English law and that of another jurisdiction with a link to the transaction. This chapter considers which law will govern the effectiveness of the security in a cross-border case. **CHAPTER 14** discusses what happens if the borrower or a guarantor enters into insolvency proceedings in England or in a foreign jurisdiction, and considers which laws govern the issues which arise as a result. In this chapter and the next, the expression 'debtor' will be used to describe any person who is liable to pay money to a financier under a financing transaction – whether as a borrower or as a guarantor.

Classification of the issues

13.9 The purpose of the conflict of laws rules is to establish which law should be applied to decide the issue which has arisen. Which law will be applied depends on the nature of the issue. The first thing which the court has to do therefore is to classify (or characterise or categorise – in this context these words are synonymous) the issue. In the context of a secured financing, the issue might relate to a number of different matters, such as the capacity of the debtor, the existence of the contract to create the security, the effectiveness of the security over a particular asset, or the effect of insolvency proceedings on the security. Different laws may govern each of these different issues.

13.10   The first job for the court is therefore how to classify the issue before the court. Only once the issue has been classified in this way can it be decided which law will govern it. A recent example of the importance of classification is the decision of the Court of Appeal in *Macmillan v Bishopsgate Investment Trust*.[1] The case involved a claim by Macmillan in respect of shares which it owned. The shares had been wrongfully taken from Macmillan and used as security for loans made in New York by certain banks. This case is considered in more detail in part 6 of this chapter (**13.128ff**). In this context, its importance lies in the stress placed by all three members of the Court of Appeal on the importance of the correct characterisation, classification or characterisation of the issue. In the words of Aldous LJ:[2]

'... the problem of characterising which judicial concept or category is appropriate is not easy, but it is a task which is essential for the court to complete before it can go on to decide which system of law is to be used to decide the question in issue.'

13.11   Macmillan claimed that the issue related to restitution – the shares had wrongfully been taken from it and its claim for their return was a restitutionary one. The Court of Appeal accepted that Macmillan's claim was a restitutionary in nature, but concluded that the issue in question was not whether Macmillan had a restitutionary claim (which it clearly did) but whether the banks had obtained effective security over the shares, notwithstanding the claim, because they had obtained their security in good faith and without notice of it. The issue was therefore characterised as one relating to property rights – who had a better claim to the shares, Macmillan or the banks?

13.12   Categorisation requires categories, and it is therefore important to establish which categories of issue have been established by English law for the purpose of the conflict of laws. You can only decide into which box a matter falls if you know what the boxes are. The starting point here is that English law does not characterise issues solely on the basis of domestic English law concepts. The quest for categories involves a broader consideration of the issues involved in any dispute. As Auld LJ said in the *Macmillan* case: 'The proper approach is to look beyond the formulation of the claim and to identify according to the lex fori the true issue or issues thrown up by the claim and defence.'[3] In the *Macmillan* case, the classification of the issue was relatively straightforward. In other cases, it can be much more complex.

13.13   When establishing categories, the first demarcation line which has to be drawn is between personal and proprietary rights. Even that, seemingly obvious, distinction has created problems in practice, particularly in relation to intangible assets (which are discussed in part 6 of this chapter (**13.128ff**)). It is nevertheless clear that different laws can govern the personal and proprietary effects of a contractual arrangement.

---

1   [1996] 1 WLR 387.
2   [1996] 1 WLR 387 at 417.
3   [1996] 1 WLR 387 at 407.

13.14 Within each of these categories, further categorisations are required. For instance, in relation to personal issues, distinctions need to be drawn, such as:

- whether the debtor has the capacity to enter into the contract concerned;
- whether any formalities required for its enforcement have been complied with;
- whether it can be set aside as a result of a vitiating matter such as mistake; and
- what the contract means.

13.15 As far as the proprietary effects of the security are concerned, distinctions are sometimes drawn between the creation and priority of proprietary interests, although it is suggested in part 5 of this chapter (**13.82ff**) that no sensible distinction can be drawn between them in the context of the conflict of laws. In the context of proprietary interests, the important classification is between different types of asset – movables and immovables, tangibles and intangibles.

13.16 In the context of the law of security, the most important consideration is whether the security which is purported to be taken over an asset has the proprietary effect which it is intended to have. Much of the discussion in this chapter will therefore be concerned with the proprietary effect of security. But the personal effect of security documentation cannot be ignored. A security interest is only of value to the extent that the obligations which it secures are effective. The creditor may have a valid proprietary interest over an asset but, if it is held by way of security and there are no secured obligations, the proprietary interest is worthless. This chapter is also, therefore, concerned with the personal effects of security arrangements. Since the personal issues involved in security arrangements are essentially contractual in nature, they will be described as contractual issues in this chapter (although this can have its dangers, as becomes apparent in part 6 of this chapter (**13.128ff**)).

Latin tags

13.17 The conflict of laws is plagued by Latin tags. In this chapter, they will be eschewed, as far as possible, in favour of the use of the vernacular. But they cannot entirely be avoided, not least because they are frequently used in the cases. For this reason, it is necessary briefly to explain what they mean. The following is not a complete list, but it covers those most frequently encountered in relation to security issues.

- *Lex fori* (or law of the forum) – this is the law of the jurisdiction in which the court which is resolving the issue is located. If the case is being heard by the English courts, the lex fori is English law. If the case were being heard in France, it would be French law.
- *Lex causae* (or applicable law) – this is the description given to the law which will decide the issue before the court. In the *Macmillan* case,[4] for

---

4   *Macmillan v Bishopsgate Investment Trust* [1996] 1 WLR 387.

instance, it has been seen that the issue was whether Macmillan or the banks had a better proprietary right to the shares. The Court of Appeal decided that the law which governed this issue was New York law. New York law was, therefore, the lex causae. In that case, Staughton LJ described the lex causae as the 'applicable law', and that is the expression which will be used in this chapter.

- *Governing law* – this is one of the few expressions which is normally given in English, rather than in Latin. It means the law which governs a contract – the law by which it is created and will be interpreted. In the past, it was frequently described in the English cases as the 'proper law'. Since 1990, that formulation has fallen out of favour and it is now normally referred to as the 'applicable law' or as the 'governing law'. Because the expression 'applicable law' seems better suited to describing the lex causae, in this chapter the expression 'governing law' will be used.

  In the context of the law of security, the expression 'governing law' is used in two different senses. In one sense, it is used to refer to the law which governs the contract creating the security – the mortgage or charge entered into between the debtor and the creditor. Alternatively, where the asset over which the security is created is an intangible, the expression 'governing law' may be used to describe the law under which the intangible has been created. For instance, if the asset which is the subject of the security is a contract between the debtor and a counterparty, the expression 'governing law' may refer to that contract. The distinction is drawn very clearly in Art 12 of the Rome Convention. Article 12(1) is concerned with the governing law of the contract between the debtor and the creditor, which creates the security. Article 12(2) is concerned with the governing law of the contract between the debtor and the counterparty, over which the security is created.

- *Lex domicilii* (the law of the place of incorporation or law of the domicile) – this is the law of the place where a person is permanently located. There is a very great deal of jurisprudence concerning the domicile of individuals, and it is beyond the scope of this chapter to consider that authority (not least because it is an issue which rarely arises in secured transactions). As far as corporations are concerned, it is easier to establish the lex domicilii – it is the law of the place of incorporation of the company. Since most cross-border issues arising in relation to security transactions are concerned with companies, in this chapter the expression 'law of the place of incorporation' will be used unless an individual is involved, in which case it will be described as the 'law of the domicile'.

- *Lex situs* – this means the law of the place where an asset is situated at a particular time. It is of particular importance in relation to proprietary issues arising in relation to tangible assets, such as land and goods. Because of the ubiquity of the use of the expression 'lex situs' and the difficulty of producing an acceptable shorthand English translation ('the law of the place of the location of the asset' is accurate, but does not trip off the tongue), the Latin tag will often be used in this instance.

- *Lex loci actus* – this is the law of the place where the transaction concerned is effected. In relation to the taking of security, it is also likely to be the law of the place where the asset is situated (ie the lex situs), but this is not always the case. In practice, it has little part to play in deciding which law should govern security issues.

Renvoi

13.18   There is one other technical issue concerning the conflict of laws which needs to be mentioned, albeit briefly. The expression 'renvoi' is used to describe the process by which, a court in one jurisdiction having decided that a particular issue is to be decided by the law of another jurisdiction, the application of that law requires that issue to be determined by a law other than its own law.

13.19   By way of example, assume that the courts in jurisdiction A, in accordance with the conflict of laws rules in that jurisdiction, decide that a particular matter should be determined by the laws of jurisdiction B. The courts in jurisdiction B, by applying the conflict of laws rules in jurisdiction B, may decide that it should be decided in accordance with the law of jurisdiction A (or by another law other than the domestic law of jurisdiction B). The problem arises if the courts in jurisdiction B do not just apply their domestic law to the issue but also apply their conflict of law rules and thereby decide that another court should decide it.

13.20   When does renvoi apply? In relation to issues governed by the Rome Convention (which is discussed in part 2 of this chapter (**13.24ff**)), the application of the doctrine of renvoi is excluded. When the Rome Convention requires the application of the laws of a particular jurisdiction, it is referring to the domestic laws of that jurisdiction, and not its conflict of law rules.[5] Where the issue to be decided is not governed by that Convention, it is less clear whether the doctrine of renvoi will apply. Because the position is unclear, it needs to be borne in mind in cases outside the Rome Convention that, if an English court decides that a foreign law is the applicable law, that foreign law might return the issue to the English court as a result of the doctrine of renvoi.

Conclusion

13.21   Even from this brief discussion, it can be seen that the conflict of law rules relating to the law of security are by no means straightforward. In part, this is because, the issues are complex. It is also, in part, due to the relatively small number of cases in England; and it does not help that a number of the cases which we do have are contradictory. The absence of case-law has meant that textbooks have assumed a greater importance in relation to conflict of laws than they have in other areas of English law, and the cases frequently refer to the leading textbook on conflict of laws, *Dicey and Morris*.[6]

13.22   As will be seen, some EU initiatives have helped to clarify the law. In particular, the Rome Convention, although it is not free of uncertainty, has clarified the law in a number of areas. Unfortunately, the same cannot be said

---

5   Rome Convention, Art 15.
6   *Dicey and Morris The Conflict of Laws* (Sweet & Maxwell: 13th edn, 2000) (*Dicey and Morris*).

of EU initiatives in the realm of cross-border insolvency, which, in many ways, serve to muddy waters which were already unclear. These issues are discussed further in **CHAPTER 14**.

13.23 The rest of this chapter is concerned, first, with contractual issues and then with proprietary ones. It is divided into the following parts:

- Part 2 (**13.24ff**) – contractual issues.
- Part 3 (**13.67ff**) – proprietary issues – introduction.
- Part 4 (**13.78ff**) – proprietary issues – land.
- Part 5 (**13.82ff**) – proprietary issues – goods.
- Part 6 (**13.128ff**) – proprietary issues – intangibles.
- Part 7 (**13.158ff**) – conclusion.

Part 2: CONTRACTUAL ISSUES

13.24 This part is concerned with the personal obligations of the debtor under the security documentation and the underlying facility documentation. The personal obligations of the debtor will include matters such as contractual undertakings (both positive and negative), indemnities and waivers of rights but, in this context, the most important personal obligation is the undertaking to pay the secured obligations – the liabilities which are secured by the security documents. If this obligation is ineffective, the security will be worthless. The key question in this context is, therefore, whether the debtor is bound to pay the secured obligations.

13.25 This question can be broken down further:

- Has the debtor validly entered into the documentation?
- Have the requirements of the law of contract been complied with?
- Can the documents be set aside as a result of a vitiating factor?
- What do the documents mean?

13.26 Some of these sub-questions can be broken down still further:

- Whether the debtor has validly entered into the documentation depends not only on its capacity to do so, but also on the authority of those who have entered into the documentation on its behalf.
- Whether the requirements of the law of contract have been complied with are, at least for conflict of laws purposes, broken down into:
  - substantive (or material) issues (is there an agreement?; has there been consideration?); and
  - formalities (have the requirements for writing, or a seal, or notarisation been complied with?).
- Whether the documents can be set aside may depend on:
  - the absence of any real consent by the party expressed to be bound (for instance, as a result of fraud, mistake, misrepresentation or undue influence);

- in the case of a company, the failure of its officers to act in its interests (ie breach of fiduciary duty); or
- the commencement of insolvency proceedings in relation to the debtor (and, in consequence, the possibility of their constituting transactions at an undervalue or preferences).

13.27 The applicable law in relation to these matters is not always the same. In broad terms, English conflict of laws rules distinguish between:

- capacity, authority and breach of fiduciary duty;
- formal validity;
- material validity (including the absence of real consent);
- the effect of the contract; and
- the effect of insolvency.

13.28 These categories are not, however, precise, and there is some overlap between them. As a result, the classification of a particular issue is not straightforward. The categories do tend to merge into each other, and it is ultimately a matter of judgment to decide into which category a particular issue falls.

13.29 Insolvency of the debtor raises separate issues, and these are discussed in **CHAPTER 14**. This part will accordingly discuss each of the first four categories in turn. It then considers mandatory rules and public policy and how the governing law of a contract is determined. Before doing that, however, it is necessary briefly to considers the source of English conflict of laws rules in relation to contractual matters and, in particular, the Rome Convention.

The Rome Convention

13.30 Many (but not all) of the English conflict of laws rules in relation to contractual matters are contained in the Rome Convention on the law applicable to contractual obligations, which was incorporated into English law by the Contracts (Applicable Law) Act 1990.

13.31 The basic principle is that the Rome Convention applies to 'contractual obligations in any situation involving a choice between the laws of different countries'.[7] This principle is subject to a number of exceptions.[8] In the context of the law of security, the most important exceptions are that the Rome Convention does not apply to:

- questions concerning the status or legal capacity of companies or natural persons;[9]

---

7   Rome Convention, Art 1(1).
8   It does not, for instance, apply to contracts of insurance which cover risks situated in the territories of the member states of the EU (Rome Convention, Art 1(3)), although this exception does not apply to contracts of reinsurance (Art 1(4)).
9   Rome Convention, Art 1(2)(a) and (e).

- questions involving the authority of persons entering into contracts on behalf of companies or natural persons;[10] or
- other issues concerning company law, including the winding-up of companies.[11]

13.32 The main purpose of the Rome Convention is to establish:

- how the law which governs a contract is to be determined; and
- which issues concerning the contract are to be established by reference to that governing law.

Capacity, authority and breach of fiduciary duty

13.33 The capacity of a person to enter into a transaction and the authority of agents acting on his behalf fall outside the scope of the Rome Convention.[12] Issues concerning capacity and authority are therefore governed by the common law rules which existed before the Rome Convention was introduced into English law. The scarcity of case-law authority means that it is not possible to be definitive about the rules which do apply. The basic principle is, however, clear. The capacity of a company to enter into a transaction is governed by the law of its place of incorporation, and the capacity of a natural person to do so is governed by the law of his domicile.

13.34 Unlike a natural person, a company is a creature of the legal system of a particular jurisdiction, and it is accordingly that system which governs its capacity to enter into transactions. Whether or not a transaction entered into by an English company is ultra vires that company is, in principle, a matter to be determined by English law, even if the transaction is to be entered into abroad. *Dicey and Morris* consider that its capacity can be further limited (but not extended) by the law governing the transaction into which the company is entering,[13] although it is difficult to understand why it should.

13.35 The principle that capacity is governed by the law of the company's place of incorporation is an obvious and convenient one, not least because anyone dealing with a company can easily establish where it is incorporated, conduct the necessary investigations and, if appropriate, obtain a legal opinion in the jurisdiction concerned.

13.36 In the case of individuals, their capacity is governed by the law of their domicile. This is much more difficult to establish than the law of the place of incorporation of a company. Unlike a company, an individual is not created by, and dependent on, one legal system. The law accordingly has to attribute a domicile to an individual, the establishment of which is not as clear-cut as the establishment of a place of incorporation. A person's domicile is where that person has his permanent home; and a person can have only one domicile.

---

10   Rome Convention, Art 1(2)(e) and (f).
11   Rome Convention, Art 1(2)(e).
12   Rome Convention, Art (2)(a), (e) and (f).
13   *Dicey and Morris*, r 154.

There is a great deal of authority concerning how that domicile is to be determined, and it is beyond the scope of this chapter to consider this issue.[14] *Dicey and Morris* suggest that the capacity of an individual can be extended by the law of the country with which the contract is most closely connected, although it is impossible to be precise because of the paucity of authority.[15] It is rare for security to be granted by individuals in cross-border transactions and, as a result, the problem of establishing an individual's domicile is rarely encountered in practice. More important in practice is the fact that the place of incorporation of a company can be established with certainty.

13.37 The authority of a company's directors to bind the company or of agents to bind their principal also falls outside the scope of the Rome Convention and, as with capacity, there is a dearth of case-law. In principle, it would seem that the authority of a board of directors to bind its company must be governed by the law of the company's place of incorporation. The company is a creature of that legal system, and the ability of natural persons to bind it must logically be governed by the same legal system.

13.38 Establishing that the directors have the authority to bind the company is not the end of the story. Under English law, even if the board of directors does have that authority, the transaction can be set aside if the directors have entered into it in breach of their fiduciary duty to the company and the person they have dealt with has actual or constructive notice of that fact.[16] In principle, and on the basis of the decision of the Court of Appeal in *Macmillan v Bishopsgate*,[17] it would seem that:

- whether there has been a breach of fiduciary duty and whether it can have a proprietary effect is a matter for the law of the place of incorporation of the company concerned; but
- whether the person dealing with the company is affected by it is a matter for the law which governs the proprietary effect of the arrangements (which is discussed in the following parts of this chapter).

Formal validity

13.39 English law imposes few formal requirements on the creation of contracts or of security. In certain cases, the documentation needs to be in writing, sometimes accompanied by the signature of the person to be bound; and a deed is required to transfer land. Formal requirements are most apparent in relation to dispositions of land, but formalities are also required for dispositions of equitable interests in any type of asset and also for the creation of guarantees. Apart from these relatively limited formal requirements, security can, in theory, be created entirely informally.

13.40 In other jurisdictions, however, the formal requirements for the creation of security can be more cumbersome. They may involve not simply the

---

14   See *Dicey and Morris*, chapter 6.
15   *Dicey and Morris*, r 179.
16   See part 2 of chapter 5 (**5.17ff**).
17   [1996] 1 WLR 387.

requirement of writing or of a formal type of document such as a deed, but also the involvement of a third party, such as a notary. It is therefore important to establish which law governs the formal validity of contracts creating security.

13.41 Article 9 of the Rome Convention sets out the requirements for the formal validity of a contract:

'(1) A contract concluded between persons who are in the same country is formally valid if it satisfies the formal requirements of the law which governs it under this Convention or of the law of the country where it is concluded.

(2) A contract concluded between persons who are in different countries is formally valid if it satisfies the formal requirements of the law which governs it under this Convention or of the law of one of those countries.'

13.42 If, therefore, the formal requirements of the law which governs the contract are complied with, the contract cannot be set aside on the basis of lack of formal validity. Even if the contract fails to comply with those requirements, it will still be formally valid if it complies with the formal requirements of:

- the law of the country where it is concluded if the parties are in the same country; or
- if they are not, the law of any of the countries in which the parties are located.

13.43 Where a contract is concluded by an agent, it is the country in which the agent acts which is the relevant country for these purposes.[18] There is also a special rule in relation to land. Article 9(6) provides:

'[A] contract the subject matter of which is a right in immovable property or a right to use immovable property shall be subject to the mandatory requirements of form of the law of the country where the property is situated if by that law those requirements are imposed irrespective of the country where the contract is concluded and irrespective of the law governing the contract.'

Material validity

13.44 More important in practice are the requirements which relate to the material (or, as it is sometimes called, essential) validity of the contract. This is concerned with those matters, other than formalities, which are required in order to create a valid contract. It therefore encompasses:

- the requirements for the creation of a contract (such as, in English law, consideration); and
- those matters relating to contracts generally which can vitiate a contract (such as mistake or misrepresentation).

---

18   Rome Convention, Art 9(3).

13.45 The material validity of a contract is a matter for its putative governing law. Article 8(1) of the Rome Convention provides that:

'The existence and validity of a contract, or of any term of a contract, shall be determined by the law which would govern it under this Convention if the contract or term were valid.'

13.46 The dividing line between material validity and other concepts is not always easy to draw. There is no doubt that it extends not only to the requirements for the formation of a contract (such as agreement and consideration), but also to the existence of matters which can result in the contract being set aside. But not all matters which can result in a contract being set aside are encompassed by the expression 'material validity'. It has been seen that a contract which is entered into in breach of fiduciary duty can be set aside in certain circumstances, but it seems clear that the question of whether or not there is a breach of fiduciary duty is a matter for the law of the place of incorporation of the company concerned, not the governing law of the contract. Similarly, transactions can be set aside in insolvency proceedings (if, for instance, they amount to transactions at an undervalue or preferences), but there is no doubt that the application of such rules depends on the law applicable to the insolvency, not on the law governing the contract. Material validity does, however, encompass those vitiating factors which are part of the general law of contract – such as mistake, misrepresentation, duress and undue influence.

13.47 Article 8(2) of the Rome Convention enables a party to rely upon the law of the country in which he has his habitual residence to establish that he did not consent if it appears from the circumstances that it would not be reasonable to determine the effect of his conduct in accordance with the governing law of the contract. This provision is more likely to be of relevance to individuals than companies.

The effect of the contract

13.48 The effect of the contract is a matter for its governing law. Article 10 of the Rome Convention provides that, in particular, the governing law determines:[19]

'(a) interpretation;
(b) performance;
(c) within the limits of the powers conferred on the court by its procedural law, the consequences of breach, including the assessment of damages insofar as it is governed by the rules of law;
(d) the various ways of extinguishing obligations, and prescription and limitation of actions.'

13.49 This is not an exhaustive list of the matters which are subject to the governing law of the contract, but it gives an indication of the breadth of the issues which are subject to the governing law. These include:

---

19   Article 10(1)(e) is not part of English law – s 2(2) of the Contracts (Applicable Law) Act 1990.

- how the contract is to be interpreted;
- how it is to be performed (although Art 10(2) requires regard to be had to the law of the country in which performance takes place in relation to the manner of performance and the steps to be taken in the event of defective performance);
- when the contract is breached and its consequences (although, to the extent that these matters are purely procedural, they will be governed by the law of the forum); and
- discharge of the contract.

Mandatory rules and public policy

13.50 English law (like other legal systems) will not give effect to a foreign law if:

- it is manifestly contrary to public policy; or
- it runs counter to a provision of English law which it is important should be applied even to foreign contracts.

13.51 Article 16 of the Rome Convention provides:

'The application of a rule of the law of any country specified by this Convention may be refused only if such application is manifestly incompatible with the public policy ("ordre public") of the forum.'

13.52 Although drafted in a negative form, this Article gives effect to the basic concept that the court which is conducting the litigation does not have to enforce a foreign law if it is 'manifestly incompatible' with the public policy of the place of the forum. The fact that this Article is drafted in the negative, and the use of the words 'manifestly incompatible' make it clear that it is only intended to be used in exceptional circumstances, where it is absolutely clear that to enforce a foreign law would be contrary to public policy. The concept is similar to that expressed by the American jurist, Justice Cardozo, when he said that courts will not refuse to enforce a foreign law unless it would 'violate some fundamental principle of justice, some prevalent conception of good morals, some deep-rooted tradition of the common weal'.[20]

13.53 In the context of the law of security, it is difficult to conceive of many cases in which the application of a foreign law would be regarded as being manifestly incompatible with English public policy. The mere fact that there is a conflict between the position under English law and that of the foreign law is not, of course, sufficient, since the existence of rules concerning conflict of laws is premised on the assumption that such differences do exist. One possible case where public policy might be brought into question would be where a foreign law expropriated the creditor's rights under its security documentation; but, even in such a case, it would have to be established that no reasonable system of law could provide for such an expropriation.

---

20 *Loucks v Standard Oil Co* 224 NY 99.

13.54   Article 7(2) of the Rome Convention can be seen in a similar light. It provides:[21]

> 'Nothing in this Convention shall restrict the application of the rules of the law of the forum in a situation where they are mandatory irrespective of the law otherwise applicable to the contract.'

13.55   It is, again, hard to think of many examples of such mandatory rules in the context of the law of security. One example of a statutory provision which could be regarded as being mandatory for these purposes would be the financial services legislation, to the extent that it is intended to affect contracts regardless of the law by which they are governed.[22]

13.56   Articles 16 and 7(2) of the Rome Convention enable the law of the forum to override the governing law of the contract where to do otherwise would manifestly offend against public policy or would fail to give effect to a statutory provision which was clearly intended to apply regardless of the law governing the contract. The public policy rules and mandatory rules applied in such cases are those of the law of the forum – the place where the litigation is taking place.

13.57   Article 3(3) of the Rome Convention deals with a different situation. It allows mandatory rules to be taken into account which do not form part of the governing law of the contract if they do form part of the law of the country to which 'all the other elements relevant to the situation are connected'. If, for instance, the governing law is English law but all the other elements relating to the contract point to French law being relevant, mandatory rules in France can be taken into account.

What is the governing law?

13.58   It has been seen that the law governing the contract is determinative of many of the issues which arise when considering the personal effect of contracts. In particular, the governing law of the contract establishes its material validity and effect; and a contract will be formally valid if it complies with the formalities imposed by the governing law.

13.59   The determination of the governing law of the contract is therefore crucial to many of the issues concerned with the personal contractual effect of the contract. In this respect, Art 3(1) of the Rome Convention is particularly important. It provides:

> 'A contract shall be governed by the law chosen by the parties. The choice must be expressed or demonstrated with reasonable certainty by the terms of the contract or the circumstances of the case. By their choice the parties can select the law applicable to the whole or a part only of the contract.'

13.60   It is hard to overestimate the importance of this provision. It is a principle which had been given effect by the English courts long before the

---

21   Article 7(1) is not part of English law – s 2(2) of the Contracts (Applicable Law) Act 1990.
22   This is suggested in *Dicey and Morris*, r 175.

Rome Convention was incorporated into English law, but it is now clearly expressed, without any qualifications, that the parties can choose any law to govern their contract.

13.61 In financial transactions, it is rare to find a contract (whether it is a loan agreement, a security document or otherwise) which does not have an express choice of law clause.[23] In the unlikely event that the contract does not contain an express choice of law clause, Art 4 contains the rules which apply to determine the governing law. The main principles contained in Art 4 are as follows:

- The basic principle is that, in the absence of a choice of law clause, the contract is governed by 'the law of the country with which it is most closely connected'.[24]
- There are certain presumptions which help to establish the law of the country with which the contract is most closely connected, but those presumptions 'shall be disregarded if it appears from the circumstances as a whole that the contract is more closely connected with another country'.[25]
- The main presumption is that the contract is most closely connected with the country 'where the party who is to effect the performance which is characteristic of the contract' is located.[26]
- Where the contract is entered into in the course of that party's trade or profession, 'that country shall be the country in which the principal place of business is situated or, where under the terms of the contract the performance is to be effected through a place of business other than the principal place of business, the country in which that other place of business is situated'.[27]
- Where the contract is not entered into in the course of that party's trade or profession, it will be the place where, at the time of the conclusion of the contract, that party has 'its central administration' (in the case of a body corporate or unincorporated) or 'his habitual residence' (in any other case).[28]
- To the extent that the subject matter of the contract is a right in immovable property or a right to use immovable property, it is presumed that the contract is most closely connected with the country where the immovable property is situated.[29]

13.62 The presumptions require a consideration of what is meant by the expression 'the performance which is characteristic of the contract'. In the case of a loan agreement, this would be the making of the loan, and would therefore point to the location of the creditor. In the case of security documents, it would

---

23   The one exception to this principle is letters of credit, which rarely have governing law clauses, although they should do.
24   Rome Convention, art 4(1).
25   Rome Convention, art 4(5).
26   Rome Convention, art 4(2).
27   Rome Convention, art 4(2).
28   Rome Convention, art 4(2).
29   Rome Convention, art 4(3).

refer to the granting of the security, and would therefore point the location of the debtor. This would produce the rather curious result that (unless the presumptions were disregarded) the loan agreement would be governed by the law of the creditor's location, whereas the security documents would be governed by the law of the debtor's location. In practice, this is unlikely to be much of a problem because loan agreements and security documents invariably contain choice of law clauses.

Conclusion

13.63 Although the personal effects of security arrangements are less important than their proprietary effects, they are nevertheless of importance, not least because they establish the existence and extent of the secured obligations. On the whole, the rules are clear and sensible. This is particularly the case to the extent that they are now governed by the Rome Convention, although there are still some areas of uncertainty in relation to matters which are not the subject of that Convention.

13.64 The most beneficial rule is that the parties are free to choose the law which will govern their contract; and this invitation is almost invariably taken up by the parties to financial contracts. That governing law does not determine every dispute relating to the contract, but it does determine some of the most important issues, including the existence and effect of the contract and its material validity. The contract will also be formally valid if it complies with the requirements of its governing law. Although the governing law can be subject to public policy and mandatory rules (particularly in the law of the forum), these are unlikely to be of much practical importance in relation to the law of security. Where the debtor is a company, questions concerning its capacity, the authority of its directors and the duties of its directors will be governed by the law of its place of incorporation – which the creditor is easily able to establish.

13.65 In broad terms, therefore, a creditor should be able to establish, with some degree of certainty, which laws will determine the contractual effect of its documentation. It can check the due execution of the documentation by reference to the place of incorporation of the debtor, and it can ensure the effectiveness of the contractual arrangements by choosing an appropriate governing law. That is not to say that these are the only two laws which can affect the outcome, but they are by far the most important in practice.

13.66 Finally, it should be stressed that these rules only apply where England is the forum for the dispute. Where the dispute is litigated abroad, it will be the courts of the forum concerned which will determine the conflict of law rules to be applied (although, where the country concerned is a party to the Rome Convention, there should be a substantial degree of consistency of approach to those matters to which the Convention applies).

Part 3: PROPRIETARY ISSUES – INTRODUCTION

13.67 The most important consideration when taking security is to ensure that the creditor obtains an effective proprietary interest in the assets which are the subject of the security. In cross-border transactions, therefore, it is particularly important to ensure that the creditor has obtained a proprietary interest in the appropriate jurisdictions.

13.68 The issues which can arise in practice can be illustrated by an example: The debtor creates security over goods situated in France and over a contract governed by the law of New York. The security documents are expressed to be governed by English law, and are executed in Luxembourg. The goods are subsequently moved to Spain.

13.69 The various laws which might be relevant in this case include:

- English law – being the law governing the security documents;
- Luxembourg law – being the law of the place where the security was created;
- New York law – being the law governing the contract which is the subject of the security;
- French law – being the lex situs of the goods at the time the security was created; and
- Spanish law – being the lex situs of the goods at the time the matter is to be decided.

13.70 This example is, perhaps, a little fanciful, but complicated issues of this type are not uncommon in cross-border secured financings. The purpose of the rest of this chapter is to consider which law governs the proprietary effects of the security.

13.71 It will be for the law of the forum to answer this question. If that is English law, it is clear that the answer depends on the classification of the asset over which security is taken, and that different rules apply to different types of asset. What is less clear is the classification which should be used. The classic distinction in conflict of laws cases is between movables and immovables. As Cozens-Hardy MR said in *Re Hoyles*:[30]

> 'The terms "movable" and "immovable" are not technical terms in English law, though they are often used, and conveniently used, in considering questions arising between our law and foreign systems which differ from our law.'

13.72 Although, for domestic purposes, English law distinguishes between real property and personal property, that distinction is not the same as the distinction between movables and immovables in the conflict of laws. For instance, in English domestic law, although land itself is real property many rights attached to land are regarded as personal property. By contrast, the expression 'immovable' in the conflict of laws, is used to describe not just land but also interests deriving from land, such as leases and mortgages of land; and 'movables' is used to describe any other type of asset.

13.73 This classification is doubtless useful when considering issues concerning universal transfers by operation of law on succession, but a study of

---

30   [1911] 1 Ch 179 at 183.

the cases involving consensual transfers of particular assets (including the creation of security) establishes that, although the expressions 'movables' and 'immovables' are frequently used, they do not carry forward the analysis of which law governs the proprietary effects of a particular consensual transaction. The categorisation of assets as 'movable' or 'immovable' is not particularly helpful in practice in relation to commercial transactions. It bears little relationship to what the courts actually do in practice.

13.74   A more useful classification (and one which, it is suggested, bears more relationship to the law as it is actually applied by the courts in relation to commercial transactions) is the distinction between tangible and intangible assets. It will be suggested in the rest of this chapter that, even though the authorities and the commentators do not all speak with one voice, there are two basic principles which inform the court's decision as to the law which governs the proprietary effects of a transaction. These two principles are:

- The proprietary effect of a transaction in respect of a tangible asset is decided by the law of the place where the asset is located (ie the lex situs) at the time the transaction is effected.
- The proprietary effect of a transaction in respect of an intangible asset is decided by the law under which that intangible asset has been created. Where the asset concerned is created by contract, that law will be the governing law of the contract.

13.75   For the purpose of considering these principles in more detail, it is convenient to divide tangible assets into two categories – land and goods. As a result, the following three parts of this chapter will consider the principles relating to the proprietary effect of transfers of:

- land (**13.78ff**);
- goods (**13.82ff**); and
- intangibles (**13.128ff**).

13.76   Before turning to each of these categories, however, there is one further point which should be made. It is an obvious one, but can be important in practice. A court only needs to decide between two systems of law if they are in conflict – ie if they would produce different answers to the same question. In some cases, an apparent conflict will, on examination, be shown not to involve a conflict at all.

13.77   For example, the law of jurisdiction A may allow non-possessory security interests to be created without any requirement for registration, whereas jurisdiction B may invalidate such security interests unless they are registered. On the face of it, there is a conflict between the two jurisdictions. A company in jurisdiction B may have created security over assets in jurisdiction A, but no registration may have been effected in jurisdiction B. Jurisdiction A will say that registration is not necessary. On the face of it, jurisdiction B does require registration but, on a proper understanding of the law in jurisdiction B, it may not be necessary where the security is granted over an asset situated outside jurisdiction B. Whether or not it does is, of course, a matter for the domestic law of jurisdiction B. If, under that law, it requires security to be registered wherever it is created, there will be a conflict between jurisdiction A and jurisdiction B which will need to be resolved. But if, on its true construction, the law of jurisdiction B only requires the registration of security created in jurisdiction B, there will be no conflict.

Part 4: PROPRIETARY ISSUES – LAND

13.78 There is no doubt that issues relating to the creation or transfer of proprietary interests in land are governed by the law of the jurisdiction in which the land is located (the lex situs). This principle applies not just to land itself, but also to rights derived from the land, such as rights under leases and land mortgages, even if they are regarded as personal property under domestic English law principles.

13.79 There are few cases which consider the issue. This is doubtless because the rule is obvious and it is extremely unusual for a document creating or transferring an interest in land to be governed by any law other than the law of the jurisdiction in which the land is located.

13.80 An example of the approach of the English courts is *Norton v Florence Land and Public Works Co.*[31] A company incorporated in England owned property in Florence. It created certain 'Obligations' to secure loans made to it in England. It subsequently created a mortgage under Italian law over the property in Florence in favour of a bank. The holders of the Obligations claimed that they had security over the land and that it ranked in priority to that obtained by the bank. Sir George Jessel MR decided that the Obligations did not create security, but he also considered what the position would have been if they had done so. He decided that an English form of security would be ineffective to create a proprietary interest in land located in Italy if the security did not comply with the Italian rules concerning the creation of security. In response to a contention that the Obligations created security which was effective against anyone with notice of it, Sir George Jessel replied:[32]

> 'The answer is very simple. It depends on the law of the country where the immovable property is situated. If the contract according to the law of that country binds the immovable property, as it does in this country, when for value, that may be so, but if it does not bind the immovable property, then it is not so. You cannot by reason of notice to a third person of a contract which does not bind the property thereby bind the property if the law of the country in which the immovable property is situate does not so bind it.'

13.81 The moral is clear. When taking security over land, the proprietary effect of the documentation will be governed by the lex situs and, in practice, any security documentation should comply with, and be expressed to be governed by, that law.

---

31 (1877) 7 Ch D 332.
32 (1877) 7 Ch D at 336–337.

Part 5: PROPRIETARY ISSUES – GOODS

13.82 In this context, the expression 'goods' encompasses all forms of tangible property other than land. It therefore extends not just to goods in the ordinary sense of that term, but also to intangibles which are the subject of a document of title, the transfer of which (with any necessary endorsement) passes title not just to the document but also to the underlying intangible (examples of which include negotiable instruments and bearer securities).[33]

The basic principle

13.83 The basic principle is that the proprietary effect of a transaction in respect of goods is governed by the lex situs – ie the law of the place where the goods are located – at the time of the transaction. The principle applies to any transaction relating to the transfer or creation of a proprietary interest in goods, whether legal or equitable, whether outright or by way of security, and whether consensual or by operation of law. It does not, however, apply to general transfers of goods by operation of law, for instance, under the rules of succession on death or on bankruptcy. The effectiveness of such general transfers by operation of law is a matter for the law of the domicile of the person concerned. But the effectiveness of specific transfers is, as a general rule, governed by the lex situs of the goods at the relevant time.

13.84 The application of this principle in practice will be considered by reference to three cases – the first two of which concern outright transfers, and the third of which involves a transfer by way of security.

13.85 The first case is *Cammell v Sewell*.[34] The claimants had insured goods shipped to Hull. The vessel was wrecked in Norway, the claimants paid for them as a total loss and, as a result, they became the owners of the goods. The master of the vessel arranged for the goods to be sold in judicial proceedings in Norway. Their purchaser then delivered them to the defendants in London by way of security for a loan. It was established that, under English law, the master had no authority to sell the goods and, as a result, the purchaser would not have obtained title to them. It was also established that, under Norwegian law, the sale was effective to pass title to the purchaser.

13.86 The issue was whether Norwegian law or English law applied. If Norwegian law applied, the purchaser owned the goods and the defendants were therefore entitled to retain them as against the claimants. If English law applied, the goods remained in the ownership of the claimants and the defendants would therefore have no right to retain them.

13.87 The case was first heard by the Court of Exchequer, which decided in favour of the defendants on the ground that the matter in dispute between the parties had been concluded by the judgment of the Norwegian court in the

---

33 The expression 'goods' will be used in preference to 'chattels' because it is the more modern usage.

34 (1858) 3 H & N 617; (1860) 5 H & N 728.

judicial proceedings for the sale of the goods. On appeal to the Court of Exchequer Chamber, that court also found in favour of the defendants, but this time not on the ground that the Norwegian judgment was conclusive but on the broader ground that the effect of the purported sale of the goods in Norway was a matter to be decided by Norwegian law. The judgment of the majority of the court was given by Crompton J, who said:[35]

'We think that the law on this subject was correctly stated by the Lord Chief Baron [Pollock CB] in the course of the argument in the Court below, where he says "if personal property is disposed of in a manner binding according to the law of the country where it is, that disposition is binding everywhere." And we do not think that it makes any difference that the goods were wrecked, and not intended to be sent to the country where they were sold.'

13.88 The court also decided that the fact that the goods were subsequently brought to England could not alter the position of the parties.[36]

13.89 The court accepted that there was very little pre-existing authority on this point, and the case is accordingly important as laying down clearly the principle that the proprietary effect of a purported transfer of goods is governed by the law of the place where the goods were located (the lex situs) at that time.

13.90 The second case is *Winkworth v Christie Manson and Woods.*[37] The claimant was the owner of works of art which were stolen from him in England, taken to Italy and sold in Italy to the defendant. The defendant sent them to Christies in England to be auctioned. The claimant brought proceedings to recover the goods. The issue to be decided was whether English law or Italian law governed the proprietary effects of the purported sale in Italy. Under English law, the sale would be ineffective even if the defendant acquired them in good faith. Under Italian law, it appeared that the defendant would have acquired a good title to them.

13.91 Relying principally on *Cammell v Sewell*, Slade J decided that the issue was governed by Italian law, not English law. He relied on:[38]

'... the general principle of private international law that, if personal property is disposed of in a manner binding according to the law of the country where it is, that disposition is binding everywhere.'

13.92 This case is important in illustrating the breadth of the proposition that the proprietary effects of a transfer of goods are governed by the lex situs at the time of the transfer. It was Italian law which governed the proprietary effects of the transfer even though the goods had been stolen from England, were taken to Italy without the owner's consent and were subsequently returned to England.

---

35   (1860) 5 H & N at 744–745.
36   (1860) 5 H & N at 742–743.
37   [1980] Ch 496.
38   [1980] Ch 496 at 505.

13.93   The third example concerns a transfer by way of security. In *Inglis v Robertson*,[39] A, who was domiciled in England, stored goods in a warehouse in Scotland. A created security over the goods in favour of B, who was also domiciled in England. C, another creditor of A, obtained execution against the goods in Scotland. The question at issue was whether the security in favour of B was effective against C. If English law were applied to the question, it would have been; but, if Scots law were applied, it would not, because the more onerous requirements of Scots law concerning the creation of security had not been complied with.

13.94   The House of Lords decided that the issue as to whether B had obtained effective security over the goods was a matter of Scots law, because that was where the goods were located. Much of the discussion in the case involves the construction of certain statutory provisions, but the principle is clearly expressed by Lord Watson, who said:[40]

> 'The *situs* of the goods was in Scotland. The Scottish creditors who claim their proceeds did not make any English contract; and in order to attach them they made use of the execution which the law of Scotland permits for converting their personal claim against the owner into a real charge upon the goods themselves. It would, in my opinion, be contrary to the elementary principles of international law, and, so far as I know, without authority, to hold that the right of a Scottish creditor when so perfected can be defeated by a transaction between his debtor and the citizen of a foreign country which would be according to the laws of that country, but is not according to the law of Scotland, sufficient to create a real right in the goods.'

13.95   In this case, the House of Lords was sitting as the final appeal court from Scotland, but there is no doubt that the principle expounded by Lord Watson is as much a part of English law as it is of Scots law. The proprietary effect of a security interest over goods is decided by the law of the place where the goods are located at the time the interest is purported to be created.

To what type of assets does the principle apply?

13.96   The three cases which have just been discussed concern goods in the ordinary sense of that word. *Alcock v Smith*[41] establishes that the same principle applies to documents of title to intangible assets. That case involved a bill of exchange, drawn and accepted by English parties in England, which found its way to Norway, was endorsed in blank and then seized in execution and sold in Norway. Under English law, the sale would not have been effective to pass an unencumbered title to the purchaser but, under Norwegian law, it was. The bill was then sent for collection in England, and the question arose

---

39   [1898] AC 616.
40   [1898] AC 616 at 625.
41   [1892] 1 Ch 238.

whether the purchaser had good title to it. The Court of Appeal held that he did. The efficacy of the transfer of the bill of exchange in Norway was a matter of Norwegian law.

13.97   Some confusion has been caused by the statement of Kay LJ that:[42]

'As to personal chattels, it is settled that the validity of a transfer depends, not upon the law of the domicil of the owner, but upon the law of the country in which the transfer takes place.'

13.98   This suggests that the reason why Norwegian law was chosen was not because it was the law of the place where the bill was located at the time of the transfer (ie the lex situs), but because it was the law of the place where the transfer was effected (ie the lex loci actus). Kay LJ did, however, cite *Cammell v Sewell*[43] as authority for the proposition. In this case, the lex situs and the lex loci actus were the same. It is now clear from the decision of the Court of Appeal in *Macmillan v Bishopsgate*[44] that it is the lex situs, not the lex loci actus which is the applicable law.

13.99   In summary, the principle that the proprietary effects of a transfer of goods is a matter for the law of the place that the goods are located at the time of the transfer applies not just to goods in the ordinary sense of that term but also to intangibles which are the subject of a document of title which can be transferred by delivery. In *Alcock v Smith*, the asset was a negotiable instrument, but the principle applies equally to transferable instruments such as bearer securities. The key point is not that the instrument is negotiable (ie that it can be transferred free of encumbrances) but that it can be transferred by delivery (and, if necessary, endorsement) of a document. The principle applies to these types of instrument because – like goods – they are transferable by delivery.

The extent of the principle

13.100   The principle is of very broad application. The cases which have been discussed establish that the proprietary effect of a transaction is governed by the law of the jurisdiction where the goods are located at the time of transaction even if:

- the goods were removed to that jurisdiction without the knowledge or consent of their owner; and
- the goods are subsequently returned to the jurisdiction in which they were originally located.

13.101   In *Glencore International v Metro Trading International*,[45] Moore-Bick J decided that the principle also applies even where the contest is between the original parties to the transaction. In that case, sellers had sold oil to the buyer

---

42   [1892] 1 Ch 238 at 267.
43   (1858) 3 H & N 617; (1860) 5 H & N 728.
44   [1996] 1 WLR 387.
45   [2001] 1 Lloyd's Rep 284.

under contracts governed by English law, but the oil was located in Fujairah. Questions arose concerning the passing of title to the oil. The sellers contended that, since the issue in contention was one solely between the sellers and the buyer, that issue should be decided in accordance with the governing law of the contract.

13.102   Moore-Bick J rejected this contention, and decided that the proprietary effects of the transfer were governed by the lex situs, which was the law of Fujairah. He decided that the authorities support the adoption of the lex situs rule as a rule of general application and that, in the interests of certainty, consistency and practical reality, the rule applied whether or not third parties were involved. He approved the following statement of Diplock LJ in *Hardwick Game Farm v Suffolk Agricultural Poultry Producers Association*:[46]

> 'The proper law governing the transfer of corporeal movable property is the *lex situs*. A contract made in England and governed by English law for the sale of specific goods situated in Germany, although it would be effective to pass the property in the goods at the moment the contract was made if the goods were situate in England, would not have that effect if under German law (as I believe to be the case) delivery of the goods was required in order to transfer the property in them. This can only be because the property passes at the place where the goods themselves are.'

Exceptions to the principle

13.103   It is generally accepted that the principle that the proprietary effects of a transfer are governed by the lex situs is not an absolute rule. As Blackburn J said in *Castrique v Imrie*,[47] after quoting the principle: 'This, we think, as a general rule, is correct, though no doubt it may be open to exceptions and qualifications.'

13.104   One exception is clear. It will not be applied if to do so would be manifestly contrary to English public policy. Byles J gave a dissenting judgment in *Cammell v Sewell*[48] on this ground. Having considered the law of Norway on the point at issue, he decided it should not be followed, saying that 'small islands and petty states might be tempted to establish it, and thereby become public nuisances to the traffic of maritime nations'. In giving the judgment of the majority, Crompton J expressly countered this point saying that:[49] 'It does not appear to us that there is anything so barbarous or monstrous in this state of the law as that we can say that it should not be recognised by us.'

13.105   In part 2 of this chapter (**13.24ff**), when considering public policy as an exception to the application of the governing law of a contract, it was suggested that English public policy would very rarely require the governing law of the contract to be overridden in a commercial transaction involving the

---

46   [1966] 1 WLR 287 at 330.
47   (1870) LR 4 HL 414 at 429.
48   (1860) 5 H & N 728 at 747–752.
49   (1860) 5 H & N 728 at 743.

granting of security. The same holds true of public policy as an exception to the application of the lex situs to proprietary disputes. It is difficult to envisage what rule of public policy would require the English courts to depart from the principle that the lex situs determines the proprietary effect of a transaction.

13.106 In this respect, other laws may not be so accommodating. Because English law recognises a broad concept of non-possessory security, it is unlikely to find that security created in accordance with a foreign law offends against fundamental principles of the English law of security. The same may not always be the case in jurisdictions which have a more restrictive concept of non-possessory security. In Scotland, for instance, there is authority for the proposition that a security interest created in another jurisdiction in accordance with its laws is ineffective in Scotland if it does not comply with the more stringent requirements of Scots law as to the creation of security.[50]

13.107 In summary, English law is unlikely to refuse to apply the lex situs on the grounds of public policy, but jurisdictions with more restrictive laws (and there are many of those in civil law jurisdictions) may refuse to recognise security created in a more liberal jurisdiction if the asset concerned is brought into its own jurisdiction and the security does not comply with its requirements.

13.108 Four other potential exceptions were discussed by Slade J in *Winkworth v Christie*.[51] The first is not an exception at all, but simply a recognition that the lex situs principle applies to particular transfers of goods, not to general assignments of goods on bankruptcy or succession.

13.109 The second suggested exception is expressed to be[52] 'where a purchaser claiming title has not acted *bona fide*'. This (rather curious) suggested exception was doubted by Moore-Bick J in the *Metro Trading* case. He said:[53]

'For my own part, however, I would regard the absence of good faith as essentially a matter for the *lex situs*, subject only to the right of the English Court to refuse to recognise the transfer on well established public policy grounds if it regarded its effect as morally repugnant.'

13.110 The third exception was suggested to be a case where:[54] 'a statute in force in the country which is the forum in which the case is heard obliges the court to apply the law of its own country.' This is also probably best regarded as a further example of the public policy exception.

13.111 That only leaves the final proposed exception (taken from *Dicey and Morris*) that:[55] 'If a tangible movable is in transit, and its situs is casual or not known, a transfer which is valid and effective by its applicable law will (*semble*) be valid and effective in England.' In practice, such a case is likely to occur in

---

50 *Hammer and Sohne v HWT Realisations* 1985 SLT 21.
51 [1980] Ch 496.
52 [1980] Ch 496 at 501.
53 *Glencore International v Metro Trading International* [2001] 1 Lloyd's Rep 284 at 295.
54 [1980] Ch 496 at 501.
55 *Dicey and Morris*, Exception to Rule 116.

very few circumstances. Of more importance in practice is the fact that, for at least some purposes, the lex situs of a registered ship or aircraft is the jurisdiction where it is registered. It is beyond the scope of this chapter to consider this issue in any detail but, when taking security over ships or aircraft, it is usual to do so by reference to the law of the jurisdiction where the asset is registered.

13.112 Of the exceptions discussed in *Winkworth v Christie*, therefore, it is suggested that there is only one material exception – public policy; and that even this is hardly ever likely to apply in practice in England.

Priorities

13.113 It is sometimes suggested that the lex situs principle does not apply to determine the priority of two security interests created over the same asset; and that the decision of the Privy Council in *The Halcyon Isle*[56] indicates that priority disputes are governed by the law of the forum (the lex fori).

13.114 If that were the case, it would be surprising. Cases such as *Cammell v Sewell*[57] and *Winkworth v Christie*[58] establish that the lex situs governs the proprietary effect of transfers of goods; and *Inglis v Robertson*[59] shows that it also governs the creation of proprietary interests by way of security. What distinguishes a proprietary right from a personal one is the ability of the owner of the right to enforce it against persons other than those by whom it was created. If it is correct to state that the lex situs principle governs the effect of the creation of a proprietary interest in goods, it should follow that it determines not only whether the transfer is effective as between its immediate parties, but also the extent to which it is effective against third parties.

13.115 Although the creation and priority of security involve different issues, in practice a priority dispute is no different in kind from a dispute concerning the creation or transfer of a proprietary right. If there is a dispute about the effect of a transaction, the question to be determined is what rights have been obtained over the asset as a result of the transaction. Strictly, this involves two questions – first, whether a proprietary interest has been created and, secondly, whether it has priority over anyone else claiming an interest in the asset concerned. In practice though, there is just one issue – does the claimant have a proprietary interest in the asset which is effective against the defendant? It would be impracticable to apply two legal systems to the determination of what is, in essence, one question.

13.116 In principle, and on the basis of authority, therefore, the lex situs at the time of the transaction should govern all issues relating to the proprietary effect of a transaction involving goods. In fact, *The Halcyon Isle*[60] does not say

---

56 *Bankers Trust International v Todd Shipyards Corpn, The Halcyon Isle* [1981] AC 221.
57 (1858) 3 H & N 617; (1860) 5 H & N 728.
58 [1980] Ch 496.
59 [1898] AC 616.
60 [1981] AC 221.

anything to the contrary. In that case, a bank had taken a mortgage of a British ship. American ship-repairers carried out repairs on the ship in New York. The ship was arrested and sold in Singapore, and there were insufficient proceeds to pay both the bank and the repairers. Under New York law, the repairers were entitled to a maritime lien for the cost of the repairs which would take priority over the bank's mortgage. In Singapore (as in England) they would not have been entitled to such a maritime lien. By a majority, the Privy Council decided that the bank's mortgage took priority over the repairers' maritime lien, deciding that the priority and enforceability of maritime liens was a matter to be determined in accordance with the law of the forum – Singapore. None of the cases referred to earlier were discussed. The opinions given in the case were concerned entirely with the nature and effect of maritime liens, and laid down no general principle that the law of the forum governs issues of priority.

13.117 In conclusion, therefore, is suggested that there is not a separate rule for priorities. All issues concerning the proprietary effect of a transaction concerning goods should be determined by the lex situs of the goods at the time of the transaction.

Examples

13.118 In the absence of much case-law, the effect of this principle is best understood by considering a series of examples, which assume that it will be English law which decides the issue.

Example 1

13.119 A security interest is created over goods located in jurisdiction A in accordance with the law of jurisdiction A. The goods are then moved to jurisdiction B.
The validity of the security will be recognised in jurisdiction B because it was created in accordance with the lex situs at the time of the transaction. Although some jurisdictions, such as Scotland, may, as a matter of public policy, not recognise the security interest if it does not comply with its own legal requirements, this is not the case in England.

Example 2

13.120 A security interest is created over goods located in jurisdiction A in accordance with the law of jurisdiction A. The goods are then moved to jurisdiction B, where they are sold in breach of the terms of the security interest.
The effectiveness of the security interest is a matter to be decided in accordance with the laws of jurisdiction A (because that is where it was located at the time the security interest was created), but the rights of the purchaser are governed by the law of jurisdiction B (because that is the jurisdiction in which the purported transfer to him was effected).

Example 3

13.121 The facts are the same as in Example 2, but the goods are then returned to jurisdiction A.

This will not make any difference. The purchaser's rights acquired in jurisdiction B will be recognised by jurisdiction A unless and until there is a further dealing with them in jurisdiction A.

Example 4

13.122 A security interest is created over goods located in jurisdiction A in accordance with the law of jurisdiction A. The goods are then taken to jurisdiction B and, in breach of the terms of the security interest, a further security interest is created over them.

The effectiveness of the first security interest is a matter to be decided in accordance with the laws of jurisdiction A (being the lex situs of the goods at the time the first security interest was created). The effectiveness of the second security interest, and whether or not it takes priority over the first, is a matter for the law of jurisdiction B (being the lex situs of the goods at the time the second security interest was created).

Example 5

13.123 A security interest is created by a company incorporated in jurisdiction A over goods located in jurisdiction B. The requirements of jurisdiction B relating to the creation of security are complied with, but not those of jurisdiction A.

The first question is whether, under the domestic law of jurisdiction A, its requirements are intended to apply to assets located abroad. If they are not, there is no conflict. If they are, the requirements of the law of jurisdiction A need to be characterised. They may go to the capacity of the company to create the security interest. If so, the issue will be governed by the law of jurisdiction A. Alternatively (and more likely) they may relate to the effectiveness of the security as a proprietary matter, in which event the requirements of jurisdiction A will be disregarded because the lex situs of the asset at the time the security interest was created was jurisdiction B, and it is the lex situs which governs such matters.

Example 6

13.124 The facts are the same as in Example 5, except that the goods are then moved to jurisdiction A.

As in Example 3, this should not make any difference. The courts in jurisdiction A ought to recognise that, if the failure to comply with the law of jurisdiction A relates to a proprietary matter, it should be disregarded in favour of jurisdiction B, which was the lex situs at the time the transaction was entered into.

Conclusion

13.125 There is no doubt as to the identity of the basic principle: the proprietary effects of a transaction concerning goods are determined by the law of the place where the goods are located (the *lex situs*) at the time of the transaction. Although it is recognised that there may be exceptions from the principle, in practice only two are of any significance. The principle will give way to a manifest public policy objection, although it is difficult to see in practice how one would occur under English law. And, in the case of registered ships and aircraft, the law of the registry can be as important a criterion as the actual location of the asset concerned.

13.126 There is much to be said in favour of this conclusion. In the *Metro Trading* case,[61] Moore-Bick J considered the efficacy of the *lex situs* principle, and decided that it was justified because it reflects both what are likely to be the natural expectations of the parties and the practical realities of control over goods which are movable. These are both compelling reasons for the principle. Certainty and consistency are also crucial in financial transactions, and these are best served by adopting a principle to which there are few exceptions and which enables the parties to the transaction to be able to establish with certainty the law which will govern the effect of the transaction.

13.127 When taking security over goods in cross-border transactions, therefore, it is crucial to consider the law of the place where the goods are located at the time the security is created, and to ensure that that law is complied with. Where possible, the law governing the security document should also be the law of that jurisdiction, not least because it will avoid the necessity to prove foreign law in the event of a dispute over the enforcement of the security. In practice, of course, it is also preferable to ensure that the security also complies with the law of the place of the debtor's incorporation. It is obviously better to avoid a conflict if possible, particularly if all that is required to register the security.

Part 6: PROPRIETARY ISSUES – INTANGIBLES

13.128 When it comes to establishing the law which governs the proprietary effect of transactions involving intangible assets, the position is much less clear than it is in relation to tangible assets. There are two main reasons for this. In the first place, there are relatively few cases which are concerned with the proprietary aspects of transactions involving intangibles. Many of the leading cases concerning transfers of intangibles (such as *Republica de Guatemala v Nunez*[62]) are concerned with other issues. And, secondly, the leading textbook, *Dicey and Morris*, has changed its mind on the issue over the years.

---

61   *Glencore International v Metro Trading International* [2001] 1 Lloyd's Rep 284.
62   [1927] I KB 669.

13.129   There are two main contenders for the position of the law which governs the proprietary effect of transactions involving intangibles:

- the law of the place where the intangible asset is located (the lex situs) at the time of the transaction; and
- the which governs the intangible asset (ie, in the case of an intangible asset created by contract, the law which governs that contract).

13.130   *Dicey* initially favoured the first alternative (the lex situs) and, as a result, a number of cases adopt that view. Later, *Dicey and Morris* changed its mind, in favour of the law which governs the intangible asset concerned. In the case of intangible assets created by contract, these uncertainties would appear to have been resolved by Art 12(2) of the Rome Convention, which provides that the applicable law in such a case is the governing law of that contract. Although it is still not absolutely clear that the issue has been resolved by the Rome Convention, there is now Court of Appeal authority for the proposition that it has.

13.131   In the remaining sections of this part, Art 12 will be considered first in order to establish whether, and if so to what extent, it has resolved the issue. There will then be a discussion of the extent (if at all) to which the lex situs is relevant to the issue. The particular rules relating to shares and financial collateral will then be considered. Finally, the pros and cons of the competing principles will be discussed.

Article 12 of the Rome Convention

13.132   Article 12 of the Rome Convention is in the following terms:

'1   The mutual obligations of assignor and assignee under a voluntary assignment of a right against another person ("the debtor") shall be governed by the law which under this Convention applies to the contract between the assignor and the assignee.

2   The law governing the right to which the assignment relates shall determine its assignability, the relationship between the assignee and the debtor, the conditions under which the assignment can be invoked against the debtor and any question whether the debtor's obligations have been discharged.'

13.133   Article 12(1) simply expresses what is implicit in the earlier articles of the Rome Convention – that the personal rights and obligations of the assignor and assignee are governed by the law of the contract between them. Of much more importance, is Art 12(2). This establishes that the 'law governing the right to which the assignment relates' (ie the law which governs the intangible concerned) determines:

- its assignability (ie whether the right is of a kind which can be assigned as a matter of general law, and whether any contractual prohibition on assignment is effective);
- the relationship between the assignee and the debtor and the conditions under which the assignment can be invoked against the debtor (ie whether, as a result of the assignment, the assignee is entitled to recovery from the debtor); and

● any question whether the debtor's obligations have been discharged (ie the circumstances in which the debtor has to pay the assignee and will not obtain a good discharge by paying the assignor).

13.134 On the face of it, Art 12(2) directly answers the question of which law governs the proprietary effect of a transaction in relation to an intangible. Although it refers to 'assignments', it would appear to extend to any consensual transaction by which proprietary rights are transferred or created, including by means of a charge.

13.135 There are nevertheless some limits on its application. In the first place, it only applies where there has been 'a voluntary assignment of a right against another person'. It does not, therefore, have any bearing on general assignments on bankruptcy or succession, in respect of which there are separate rules (in relation to both tangibles and intangibles) which look to the law of the domicile of the person concerned. Secondly, it does not apply to transfers of all types of intangible. It does not extend to transfers of shares[63] or to certain types of insurance contract,[64] although these are relatively minor exceptions. There are also particular rules for financial collateral.

13.136 In spite of the fact that, on the face of it, Art 12(2) governs the question of the transfer or creation of proprietary rights in most types of intangible, there is a substantial body of opinion that it does not do so, and that these issues are, in fact, governed by the lex situs of the intangible asset concerned. The main reason for this view is that the Rome Convention is concerned with contractual matters, not with proprietary issues.

13.137 As a general proposition, this is a correct description of the effect of the Rome Convention, and it is reinforced by the Giuliano-Lagarde report on the Convention.[65] Article 12(1) is clearly concerned with the personal effect of the contract between the assignor and the assignee. But Art 12(2) is different. It deals not with the relationship between assignor and assignee but with their relationship with the debtor. The juxtaposition of the two paragraphs of Art 12 make it clear that a distinction is being drawn between the law which governs the relationship between the assignor and the assignee and the law which governs their relationship with the debtor. The former is concerned with the personal effects of the assignment, the latter with its proprietary effects. A proprietary right is a right which is available not just against the other contracting party (in this case, the assignor) but also against other persons (in this case, the debtor). Because Art 12(2) is dealing not with the relationship between the assignor and the assignee but with their relationship with a third party (the debtor), it necessarily has a proprietary effect. It expressly deals with the assignability of the debt, the relationship between the assignee and the debtor and the relationship between the assignor and the debtor, all of which concern the proprietary effect of the assignment.

---

63   Article 1(2)(e).
64   Article 1(3) and (4).
65   [1980] OJ C282.

13.138 In short, Art 12(2) is concerned with the question whether the assignee is owed (and therefore owns) the debt, which is necessarily a proprietary issue. It is accordingly suggested that Art 12(2) requires the proprietary effect of a transaction involving an intangible (other than those limited types of intangible which are not the subject of the Rome Convention) to be determined in accordance with the law which governs the intangible concerned.

13.139 The leading English case on this subject, *Raiffeisen Zentralbank Österreich v Five Star Trading* (the '*Mount I*'),[66] confirms that it is Art 12(2) of the Rome Convention which governs these issues. A bank had lent money to the owners of a vessel, secured by a mortgage over the vessel and an assignment by way of security of its insurances. The insurances were governed by English law, as was the assignment, but the insurers were French companies carrying on business in France. Creditors of the owners obtained attachments in France over the insurances, and the question arose as to the priority of the bank and those creditors in respect of the insurances. As a matter of English law, the bank had an effective security interest in the insurances and would take priority over the attaching creditors. But the requirements of French law as to the perfection of the security interest had not been complied with and, as a result, under French law the execution creditors would take priority.

13.140 In court, the dispute between the bank and the execution creditors resolved itself into the question of whether the bank's rights under its assignment were contractual or proprietary. The bank argued that they were contractual, that Art 12(2) of the Rome Convention applied to them and therefore that they were governed by English law, as the law governing the insurances. The execution creditors, on the other hand, argued that whether the bank had any rights under the assignment was a proprietary issue, that proprietary issues were governed by the lex situs of the asset concerned, that the residence of the insurers was in France and therefore the lex situs of the insurances was in France, and accordingly that French law applied to the question of the effectiveness of the bank's security.

13.141 In the Court of Appeal, Mance LJ declined to accept either submission in its entirety. In his judgment 'a more nuanced analysis is required'.[67] His conclusion was that English law was the applicable law because that was the effect of Art 12(2) of the Rome Convention:[68]

'In my view, there is a short answer to both characterisation and resolution of the present issue ... it is that art. 12(2) of the Rome Convention manifests the clear intention to embrace the issue and to state the appropriate law by which it must be determined. Article 12(1) regulates the position of the assignor and the assignee as between themselves. Under art. 12(2), the contract giving rise to the obligation governs not merely its assignability, but also "the relationship between the assignee and the debtor" and "the conditions under which the assignment can be invoked

66   [2001] QB 825.
67   [2001] QB 825 at [20].
68   [2001] QB 825 at [43].

against the debtor", as well as "any question whether the debtor's obligations have been discharged". On its face, art. 12(2) treats as matters within its scope, and expressly provides for, issues both as to whether the debtor owes moneys to and must pay the assignee (their "relationship") and under what "conditions", e.g. as regards the giving of notice.'

13.142 As Mance LJ pointed out, Art 12(2) clearly governs the question of the respective rights of the assignor and the assignee against the debtor. To that extent, the characterisation of the issue as contractual or proprietary is less pressing. But it is nevertheless important to establish the nature of the issues involved. Mance LJ saw the issue more as a contractual than a proprietary one[69] but this was to some extent prompted by the way in which the parties put their cases. Much of the discussion of the issue by Mance LJ is understandably aimed at considering the opposing contentions of the bank and the execution creditors; and their contentions contained a number of non-sequiturs. It is not correct to state that, if the issue is a proprietary one, the lex situs will apply, whereas, if it is a contractual one, it will be the governing law of the underlying contract. The terms 'contractual' and 'proprietary' are not opposites. Most proprietary rights are created by contract. Article 12(1) deals with the personal rights and duties of the assignor and the assignee arising under the contract of assignment. Article 12(2) deals with the proprietary rights between the assignor, the assignee and the debtor which arise out of the same contract. They are both contractual, but one is personal and the other proprietary.

13.143 For the reasons expressed earlier, it is suggested that the issue is in fact a proprietary one. But, whatever the outcome of that debate, what is clear from the *Mount I* is that the Court of Appeal has confirmed that Art 12(2) does have the effect which it appears to have – that the rights of an assignee or chargee of most types of intangible asset are determined by the law governing that asset, and not by its lex situs.

Is the lex situs relevant?

13.144 There is no doubt that, if necessary, it is possible to attribute a location to an intangible asset. In particular, this has been required for tax purposes in a number of cases. There are, therefore, rules which can be applied for attributing a location to an intangible. But there is equally no doubt that to do so involves a very artificial and imprecise exercise. By its very nature, an intangible asset does not have a location, and rules attributing a location to it have proved to be complex and lacking in certainty. As Atkin LJ said in *New York Life Assurance Company v Public Trustee*:[70]

'The question as to the locality, the situation of a debt, or a chose in action is obviously difficult, because it involves consideration of what must be considered to be legal fictions. A debt, or a chose in action, as a matter of fact, is not a matter of which you can predicate position ...'

---

69   [2001] QB 825 at [34] and [48].
70   [1924] 2 Ch 101 at 119.

13.145 The problems and uncertainties created in trying to attribute an artificial location to an intangible are illustrated by a brief consideration of r 112 of *Dicey and Morris*, which states that: 'Choses in action generally are situate in the country where they are properly recoverable or can be enforced.' This statement has been approved on a number of occasions by the courts, but many cases have been required in order to establish what it really means. In the *New York Life Assurance* case, it was decided that, as a general rule, a debt is located where the debtor is resident, but that, where a corporation has more than one residence, the debt is located where it is payable. The uncertainties involved in this type of formulation are manifest, and it deals only with debts, not with other types of intangible asset. It may be necessary to attribute an artificial location to an intangible asset for the purpose of particular statutes, but that is no reason to extend the search for a location when there is no reason to do so.

13.146 Luckily, there are very few cases which do decide that the proprietary effects of the transfer of an intangible are governed by its lex situs. An example is *Re Maudslay, Sons & Field*.[71] In that case, an English company had created a floating charge under English law over all of its assets in favour of debenture holders. The debenture holders appointed receivers. One of the assets of the company was a debt due from a French firm, over which unsecured creditors of the company obtained execution in France. Since the execution creditors were English, the debenture holders applied to court to prevent them from obtaining payment of the debt. Cozens-Hardy J held that, although the debenture holders had valid security under English law, they did not have valid security over the debt under French law and, as a result, were not entitled to prevent the execution creditors from obtaining payment of the debt. He applied by analogy cases concerning land and goods and decided that the debt was located in France and that the effectiveness of the bank's security was to be determined by the lex situs of the debt, ie French law.

13.147 The actual decision in the case is clearly correct. But its authority for the application of the lex situs principle to intangibles is undermined by three matters:

* the judge relied on *Dicey* (now *Dicey and Morris*), which has now changed its view on the issue;
* the debt was governed by French law and therefore the result would have been exactly the same if it had been decided by reference to the governing law of the debt; and
* Art 12(2) of the Rome Convention now requires the effectiveness of the assignment as between the assignee and the debtor to be determined in accordance with the governing law of the debt concerned.

13.148 It is therefore suggested that there can no longer be any basis on which issues concerning the effectiveness of security over debts can be determined by the lex situs of the debt.

---

71   [1900] 1 Ch 602.

Shares

13.149 It has been seen that the Rome Convention does not apply to the transfer of shares. It would appear from *Macmillan v Bishopsgate Investment Trust*[72] that the proprietary effect of a transfer of shares is governed by the *lex situs* of the shares. That case has been briefly discussed in part 1 of this chapter at **13.10**ff. Macmillan was the owner of shares which, in breach of fiduciary duty by its directors, were taken from it and delivered by way of security to certain banks to secure loans made to an associated company. The issue was whether the banks took their interest in the shares subject to Macmillan's equitable proprietary interest.

13.150 At first instance, Millett J decided that this question was to be determined in accordance with the law of the place where the transactions with the banks had taken place (the lex loci actus), which was New York. The Court of Appeal agreed that the issue was one of New York law, but for a different reason. All three judges agreed that the proprietary effect of the purported security interest granted to the banks was to be determined by reference to the law of the place where the shares were located (the lex situs). They did not, however, agree on what the lex situs was. Aldous LJ decided that the lex situs was the law of the place of incorporation of the company whose shares were in dispute. Staughton LJ agreed that this would normally be the case, but accepted that there might be cases where it would be the law of the place where the share register was kept. Auld LJ held that the lex situs was normally the place where the share register was kept, which was usually, but not always, the country of incorporation.

13.151 In this case, the shares in issue were shares in a company incorporated in New York whose share register was held in New York. The case is accordingly authority for the following propositions:

- The proprietary effect of a transaction concerning shares is governed by the lex situs of the shares at the time of the transfer.
- The lex situs is the place of incorporation of the company whose shares are in dispute, but it is open for argument in a subsequent case as to whether, in exceptional circumstances, it might be the law of the place where the register is kept, if that is different.

13.152 There is no doubt that the decision in *Macmillan v Bishopsgate* is correct. The issue of the bank's entitlement should have been governed by New York law, but the route by which the Court of Appeal reached that conclusion was rather a roundabout one. They decided the matter by reference to the lex situs, and said that it was (at least in most cases) the law of the place of incorporation of the company whose shares were in dispute. This two-stage process seems rather unnecessary. Although Art 12(2) does not expressly apply to transfers of shares, the logic behind Art 12(2) (which is that a transfer of an intangible should be governed by the law by which that intangible has been created) is equally relevant to shares. There is much to be said for the proposition that the creation of a proprietary interest in shares should be

---

72   [1996] 1 WLR 387.

governed by the law of the place of incorporation of the company whose shares are in dispute because that is the law which governs the shares. The company is a creature of that law, and so are its shares. The use of the law of the place of incorporation is both certain and apposite. *Macmillan v Bishopsgate* has produced the same result, but by a two-stage process.

Financial collateral

13.153 In the case of financial collateral arrangements, there are particular rules which govern conflict of laws issues where security is taken over securities the title to which is evidenced by book-entries in accounts with intermediaries. In such cases, the proprietary effect of the security is governed by the domestic law of the country in which the relevant account is maintained.[73] Financial collateral arrangements are discussed in part 5 of chapter 3 (**3.175ff**).

Conclusion

13.154 As a result of the Rome Convention, the proprietary effects of transactions concerning most intangible assets are determined by the law which governs the intangible concerned. In those circumstances where the Rome Convention does not apply, *Dicey and Morris* suggest that it should be applied by analogy,[74] and this has much to recommend it. Apart from the particular rules for financial collateral held through intermediaries, the only clear exception to this principle concerns shares, in respect of which the proprietary effects of the transfer are governed by the lex situs. In practice, however, shares are in the same position as other intangible assets because the lex situs will generally be the law of the place of incorporation of the company whose shares are in dispute, and that will be the law which governs the shares.

13.155 The problem with having the proprietary effects of transfers governed by the lex situs of an intangible is that it is:

• artificial (and therefore does not always correspond with commercial reality); and

• uncertain (as can be seen from the amount of litigation which there has been as to the *situs* of intangibles and the problems caused by establishing the situs of shares in *Macmillan v Bishopsgate*[75]).

13.156 The use of the governing law of the intangible, on the other hand:

• acknowledges the real differences between tangibles and intangibles and the fact that it is not possible simply to apply to intangibles rules which were created for tangibles;

• acknowledges that an intangible only exists because it has been created by a legal system and that it is therefore appropriate that its proprietary effects should be governed by that system; and

---

73 Financial Collateral Arrangements (No 2) Regulations 2003, SI 2003/3226, reg 19.
74 *Dicey and Morris*, r 118.
75 *Macmillan v Bishopsgate Investment Trust* [1996] 1 WLR 387.

- is consistent with the parties' reasonable expectation of what the rules should be.

13.157 There is doubtless a problem with so-called 'global' assignments, under which intangibles governed by various laws are transferred in one transaction, but the same problem would arise if it was the lex situs which governed the proprietary effects of the transaction. For a creditor taking security over intangibles, the principle that its proprietary effects are determined by the governing law enables the creditor to ascertain with certainty which laws are relevant and to decide to what extent it is appropriate to investigate their effect.

Part 7: CROSS-BORDER SECURITY IN PRACTICE

13.158 When taking security in cross-border transactions, it is nearly always the case that a practical decision has to be taken about the extent to which it is possible to investigate the laws of other jurisdictions which may be relevant. It is rarely possible to be assured that the security will be effective in every jurisdiction which may be relevant. In some cases, this results from the sheer volume of the security being taken and the number of jurisdictions involved. In most cases, it is also a function of the fact that tangible assets which start in one jurisdiction may move to another, and that companies can end up in insolvency proceedings in the most unlikely jurisdictions.

13.159 Nevertheless, it is possible for creditors to obtain a broad level of comfort that they have considered the main issues in the appropriate legal systems concerned:

- As far as the underlying facility documentation is concerned, the parties can choose which law will govern it, and most of the important personal effects of a contract will be determined by its governing law.
- Whether or not a debtor has duly executed the documentation it has entered into is, to a large extent, a matter for the law of its place of incorporation, which will resolve issues such as capacity and authority.
- Both the governing law of the contracts and the law of the place of incorporation of the debtor can be ascertained with certainty, and appropriate investigations can be made. These laws will not necessarily cover every issue which might arise in relation to the documents, but complying with them can certainly go a long way towards ensuring that the main problems concerning the personal effect of the transaction have been resolved.
- As far as the proprietary effects of the transaction are concerned, the key distinction is between tangible and intangible assets.
- As far as tangible assets are concerned, the law is reasonably clear. The proprietary effect of a transaction is determined by the lex situs of the asset concerned at the time of the transaction, and this is normally easy to identify. There are exceptions to the lex situs principle, but these are relatively unimportant.

- The position is less clear in relation to intangibles, but Art 12(2) of the Rome Convention and the decision of the Court of Appeal in the *Mount I*[76] do indicate that the law which governs the proprietary effect of a transaction in respect of most types of intangible is the law which governs the intangible concerned. Apart from financial collateral held through intermediaries, the main exception is shares, where the lex situs appears to be the determining factor but, even here, the lex situs will almost always be the law of the place of incorporation of the company whose shares are in dispute, and that will itself be the law which governs those shares. In practice, therefore, the key determinant in relation to intangibles is the law which governs the intangible, which will normally be easy to identify.
- When considering the proprietary effect of a transaction, therefore, it is necessary to consider:
  - the lex situs of the tangibles which form part of the security; and
  - the governing law of the intangibles which form part of the security.
- Since the effectiveness of the proprietary elements of security will be determined by these laws, it is preferable for the security document to be governed by the law concerned. If the same security document extends to assets in, or governed by, the laws of more than one jurisdiction, it should be governed by the law which represents the preponderance of the assets, and advice needs to be taken in the other jurisdictions that this is appropriate.
- Potential insolvency issues also need to be considered, and these are discussed in **CHAPTER 14**.

---

76   *Raiffeisen Zentralbank Österreich v Five Star Trading* [2001] QB 825.

Chapter 14

CROSS-BORDER INSOLVENCY

Part 1: INTRODUCTION

14.1 CHAPTER 9 considers the effect of insolvency procedures on the rights of a secured creditor in the context of a domestic transaction to which only English law is relevant. CHAPTER 13 contains a general discussion of the rights of secured creditors in a cross-border context. This chapter is specifically concerned with the effect which insolvency procedures can have on a secured creditor in the context of a cross-border financing.

14.2 One of the main concerns of a secured creditor faced with a cross-border transaction will be the extent to which his security can be affected by foreign insolvency laws. This chapter cannot directly assist with that question – it is primarily a matter for the foreign law concerned. What this chapter can do is to consider the converse – how an English court will approach insolvency proceedings where there is a foreign element involved, such as a foreign debtor. In doing so, it discusses the same types of issue which would need to be considered by a foreign court in a similar situation. It should also be borne in mind that much of the law governing this area is now derived from EU legislation – the Council Regulation of 29 May 2000 on Insolvency proceedings[1] (referred to in this chapter as the 'EC Regulation') – and that, at least within the EU, there should be some measure of consistency of approach.

14.3 There are two things which a secured creditor wants to know in the context of cross-border insolvency. The first is to establish in which jurisdictions the debtor (which, in this context, includes a guarantor) can enter into insolvency proceedings. The second is to understand the effect which those proceedings will have on the security.

14.4 In principle, the two main ways in which a secured creditor can be affected by insolvency proceedings concern:

- the validity of the security – can the security be set aside if it was granted in the period running up to the insolvency?; and
- the enforceability of the security – can the creditor's ability to enforce the security be suspended by a moratorium?

---

1   Regulation 1346/2000/EC, as amended by Regulation 603/2005/EC of 12 April 2005.

14.5 In addition, a further issue may be important to a creditor (whether secured or unsecured) – the extent to which his rights of set-off will continue in the event of the insolvency of the debtor.

14.6 The following parts of this chapter will accordingly discuss the following issues:

- Part 2 (**14.19ff**) – the scope of the EC Regulation.
- Part 3 (**14.17ff**) – the circumstances in which a foreign debtor can be placed into insolvency proceedings in England.
- Part 4 (**16.62ff**) – the effect which English insolvency proceedings will have on foreign security.
- Part 5 (**14.98ff**) – the effect which foreign insolvency proceedings will have on English security.
- Part 6 (**14.111ff**) – the way in which the position of a secured creditor will change if the UNCITRAL Model Law on cross-border insolvency is brought into effect.

14.7 It should be stressed that this chapter is concerned with the way in which English law deals with these issues. Foreign laws may deal with them differently. As well as obtaining advice in relevant foreign jurisdictions on the effectiveness of the security, a secured creditor should, in an appropriate case, also obtain advice on the effect of insolvency proceedings in those jurisdictions.

14.8 In an international transaction, the debtor will almost invariably be a company, and this chapter will therefore concentrate on insolvency procedures relating to companies. The main differences which arise where the debtor is an individual will, however, be described briefly.

Part 2: THE EC REGULATION

The scope of the EC Regulation

14.9 The EC Regulation[2] came into effect in 2002. Its purpose is not to harmonise the content of the insolvency laws of the members of the EU but to establish, within the EU, in which jurisdictions insolvency proceedings should be instituted and to ensure that they are recognised in the other EU member states. The EC Regulation will be discussed in detail in the following parts of this chapter, but a few points should be made clear at this stage concerning its scope:

- It extends both to corporate and to individual debtors.
- It applies if there are 'collective insolvency proceedings'.[3] In England, that expression includes bankruptcy, compulsory liquidation and

---

2   Regulation 1346/2000/EC, as amended by Regulation 603/2005/EC of 12 April 2005.
3   EC Regulation, Art 1(1).

administration, but not receivership (which, as has been seen in CHAPTER 8, is an enforcement procedure by a secured creditor rather than a collective insolvency procedure).

- It only applies to collective insolvency proceedings where the debtor's 'centre of main interests' is located in the EU. The expression 'centre of main interests' is discussed below. For this purpose, what is important is that the EC Regulation has no application where the debtor's centre of main interests is located outside the EU. Many cross-border insolvencies are concerned with debtors in such jurisdictions, and the EC Regulation has no part to play in these cases except, possibly, by analogy.
- Denmark did not participate in the introduction of the EC Regulation and is not bound by it. In this chapter, therefore, references to the 'EU' or to 'member states' are references to the members of the EU other than Denmark. Denmark is, for this purpose, in the same position as if it were not an EU member.

14.10 In those cases to which it applies, the EC Regulation limits the circumstances in which a debtor whose centre of main interests is within the EU can be placed into collective insolvency proceedings within the EU. It also provides for the recognition within the EU of collective insolvency proceedings commenced in a member state and specifically deals with the rights of secured creditors in a cross-border insolvency.

14.11 As a result of the limitations on its application, there are now two bodies of law to consider – one where the EC Regulation applies, and the other where it does not.

The centre of main interests

14.12 English law has traditionally taken the view that issues concerning the existence, status and management of a company are a matter for the law of its place of incorporation. In Continental Europe, on the other hand, there is more emphasis on the place where the company has its 'seat'. The seat of a company may be its place of incorporation but can be located elsewhere if, for instance, the company does not carry on any material business in its place of incorporation. It is this latter approach which has informed the EC Regulation. The fundamental feature of the EC Regulation is that its applicability depends on the company concerned having its centre of main interests in the EU (rather than on it being incorporated within the EU). So, for instance, a company incorporated in France which has its centre of main interests in Switzerland will fall outside the scope of the EU Regulation, whereas a company incorporated in Delaware which has its centre of main interests in England will fall within the scope of the Regulation. As has been seen, for this purpose Denmark is treated as if it is not in the EU.

14.13 Although the concept of the 'centre of main interests' is central to the approach of the EC Regulation, it is not defined. The Regulation does, however, give us two clues to its meaning. Recital (13) provides that 'the "centre of main interests" should correspond to the place where the debtor conducts the administration of his interests on a regular basis and is therefore ascertainable by third parties'. And Art 3(1) provides that 'in the case of a company or legal person, the place of the registered office shall be presumed to be the centre of its main interests in the absence of proof to the contrary'.

14.14 Although it does not say so, it is clear from the EC Regulation that a company has only one centre of main interests at any particular time. Where the company concerned only carries on business in its jurisdiction of incorporation, there will be no problem – the centre of main interests and the place of incorporation will be the same. Where, as is frequently the case, a company carries on business in more than one jurisdiction, it is often very unclear where the centre of its main interests is situated. The presumption that it is where the company's registered office is located can be rebutted by evidence to the contrary, the test contained in Recital (13) is extremely vague, and experience of the workings of the EC Regulation since it was introduced has shown that the concept of centre of main interests provides an uncertain and confusing basis on which to establish insolvency jurisdiction.

14.15 The purpose of the EC Regulation was to prevent forum shopping.[4] Experience in practice suggests that it has achieved quite the opposite. There have been a number of examples of courts in one jurisdiction deciding that the centre of main interests of a company is in their jurisdiction notwithstanding that it is incorporated elsewhere, and there have been concerns that a court in the place of incorporation might have taken a different view. The approach of the EC Regulation to conflicts of this kind appears to be based on the principle that the decision by the first court to assume jurisdiction should be accepted by other courts within the EU.[5] It is, nevertheless, unfortunate that such a key issue as the circumstances in which the Regulation applies should depend on such an uncertain concept. The certainty required in international financial transactions would have been better achieved if jurisdiction had depended on the place of incorporation, rather than the centre of main interests, of the company concerned.

The effect of the EC Regulation

14.16 The intention of the EC Regulation was to simplify cross-border insolvencies and to avoid forum shopping. As will be seen, it does helpfully clarify a number of areas, particularly in relation to the rights of secured creditors. But it suffers from two major weaknesses. The first is its emphasis on the debtor's centre of main interests, rather than on its place of incorporation. There would be far less litigation if the vague and uncertain concept of 'centre of main interests' were to be replaced by the clear and certain test of the debtor's place of incorporation. The other weakness is that it is limited to debtors whose centres of main interests are within the EU. This is understandable, but it has resulted in the fragmentation of English law (and the law of other member states) in relation to cross-border insolvencies. The following discussion will illustrate how complicated the position now is.

---

4   EC Regulation, Recital (4).
5   EC Regulation, Recital (22).

Part 3: PUTTING FOREIGN DEBTORS INTO ENGLISH INSOLVENCY PROCEDURES

14.17   Before the introduction of the EC Regulation[6] in 2002, the English courts had, for a long time, had the jurisdiction to make a foreign individual bankrupt if he had a sufficient connection with England. Under s 265 of the Insolvency Act 1986, a debtor may be adjudicated bankrupt in England if:

- he is domiciled in England;
- he is personally present in England on the day on which the bankruptcy petition is presented; or
- at any time within the 3 years before presentation of the bankruptcy petition, he was ordinarily resident or had a place of residence in England, or carried on business in England himself or as a member of a partnership.

14.18   It will be seen that this gives English courts a very broad jurisdiction to make an individual bankrupt even though he is not domiciled in England. This can be done not only if at any time during the 3-year period before the bankruptcy he lived here or carried on business here, but also if his only connection with England is that he is personally present here on the date the bankruptcy petition is presented. But its scope is limited by the EC Regulation if the debtor's centre of main interests is in the EU.

14.19   Before 2002, the jurisdiction of the English courts in relation to companies was in some respects wider, and in others narrower. The English courts had a very wide jurisdiction to wind up foreign companies, the precise scope of which varied over the years but which had for many years required only a very slight connection with England. This was in stark contrast to the jurisdiction of the English courts in relation to administration. Until recently, that jurisdiction was generally limited to English companies, although it was extended in 2005 to give the English courts the jurisdiction to put some foreign companies into administration. As a result, the extent of insolvency jurisdiction over foreign companies is not straightforward, depending as it does on the nature of the insolvency procedure concerned. Since 2002, the position has been complicated still further as a result of the introduction of the EC Regulation, which has limited the jurisdiction of the English courts in cases where the debtor's centre of main interests is in the EU.

14.20   When considering these principles in more detail, the discussion will be divided between liquidation and administration because the rules in relation to them are very different. As far as other types of insolvency proceedings are concerned, the rules relating to schemes of arrangement[7] are the same as those relating to liquidation; and the rules for company voluntary arrangements[8] are the same as those for administration. As far as bankruptcy is concerned, the

---

6   Regulation 1346/2000/EC, as amended by Regulation 603/2005/EC of 12 April 2005.
7   Under s 425 of the Companies Act 1985.
8   Under Part 1 of the Insolvency Act 1986.

general jurisdiction of the English courts has already been briefly discussed, and the effect of the EC Regulation on bankruptcy is broadly the same as it is on liquidation.

Liquidation

14.21   As an artificial legal person, a company is created by the legal system in its place of incorporation, and English law considers that it is the law of that place under which the company is created, managed and dissolved.[9] The obvious place, therefore, in which a company should be liquidated is its jurisdiction of incorporation. But English law also recognises that this is not the only place in which it can be liquidated. In appropriate circumstances, a foreign company can be liquidated in England.

14.22   The extent of the jurisdiction of an English court to wind up a foreign company depends on whether the EC Regulation applies. It has restricted the jurisdiction of the English courts to wind up foreign companies, but it only applies in certain cases. It requires a distinction to be drawn between two types of case:

●   those where the debtor's centre of main interests is in the EU; and
●   those where the debtor's centre of main interests is elsewhere.

14.23   In the latter case, the court's jurisdiction to wind up foreign companies is very broad. In the former case, that jurisdiction is restricted by the EC Regulation. Because the jurisdiction of the English court to wind up insolvent companies depends on whether the company concerned has its centre of main interests within the EU or outside it, these two possibilities need to be considered separately.

Where the debtor's centre of main interests is outside the EU

14.24   The jurisdiction of the English courts to wind up foreign companies is now contained in ss 220–228 of the Insolvency Act 1986, which deal with the winding-up of 'unregistered companies'. The expression 'unregistered company' includes any association and any company other than companies incorporated under the UK companies legislation.[10]

14.25   Section 221(1) provides:

'Subject to the provisions of this Part, any unregistered company may be wound up under this Act; and all the provisions of this Act and the Companies Act about winding up apply to an unregistered company with the exceptions and additions mentioned in the following sub-sections.'

14.26   Under s 221(5)(b), an unregistered company may be wound up 'if the company is unable to pay its debts …'. This must be done by the court (ie in a

---

9   See *Dicey and Morris The Conflict of Laws* (Sweet & Maxwell: 13th edn, 2000) chapter 30.
10   Insolvency Act 1986, s 220(1).

compulsory liquidation). A foreign company cannot go into voluntary liquidation.[11] If a foreign company has been carrying on business in Great Britain, it can be wound up even though it has been dissolved under the laws of its place of incorporation.[12]

14.27 At first sight, these provisions suggest that the courts have an unlimited jurisdiction to wind up insolvent foreign companies, but the courts have limited the circumstances in which they will do so. An insolvent foreign company will only be wound up in England if it has a connection with England and there is a reasonable possibility of benefit to creditors from the winding up. These requirements are sometimes considered to limit the jurisdiction of the court to wind up foreign companies.[13] But, in *Re Drax Holdings*,[14] Lawrence Collins J held that they were not matters which restricted the court's jurisdiction, but were reasons why the court will exercise its discretion not to make a winding-up order.[15]

14.28 Even if it has the jurisdiction to do so, there is no doubt that a court has a discretion whether or not to put a company into liquidation (or, indeed, to make an individual bankrupt). Where the company concerned is incorporated in England and is insolvent, a winding-up order will be made unless there are compelling reasons not to do so. Where, however, the insolvent company is incorporated abroad, the courts have adopted a more restrictive approach to the circumstances in which the winding-up order should be made.

14.29 The nature of the requirements which must be satisfied in relation to a foreign company has changed over the years. It was initially considered that it was a requirement that the company concerned should have had a branch office in England or a place of business of some kind.[16] This requirement was then abandoned in favour of the looser test that the company should have assets in England.[17] In *Re Compania Merabello San Nicholas*,[18] Megarry J held that, in order to make a winding-up order in respect of a foreign company, there is no need to establish that the company ever carried on business in England, but that:[19]

'... a proper connection with the jurisdiction must be established by sufficient evidence to show (a) that the company has some asset or assets within the jurisdiction, and (b) that there are one or more persons concerned in the proper distribution of the assets over whom the jurisdiction is exercisable.'

14.30 He decided that the assets need not be distributable to creditors by the liquidator in the winding up. All that is necessary is that the making of the winding-up order will be of benefit to a creditor.

---

11 Insolvency Act 1986, s 221(4).
12 Insolvency Act 1986, s 225.
13 *Re A Company (No 00359 of 1987)* [1988] 1 Ch 210 at 221.
14 [2004] 1 WLR 1049.
15 [2004] 1 WLR 1049 at [26].
16 *Re Lloyd Generale Italiano* (1885) 29 Ch D 219.
17 *Banque des Marchands de Moscou (Koupetschesky) v Kindersley* [1951] Ch 112.
18 [1973] 1 Ch 75.
19 [1973] 1 Ch 75 at 91–92.

14.31 The jurisdiction was widened again in *Re A Company (No 00359 of 1987)*,[20] in which Peter Gibson J said:[21]

'[T]he presence of assets in this country is not an essential condition for the court to have jurisdiction in relation to the winding up of a foreign company. In my judgement, provided a sufficient connection with the jurisdiction is shown, and there is a reasonable possibility of benefit for the creditors from the winding up, the court has a jurisdiction to wind up the foreign company.'

14.32 He went on to say that the court would also take into account whether there was any more appropriate jurisdiction to wind up the company.

14.33 In *Re Real Estate Development Co*,[22] Knox J accepted that, in addition to the requirements for a connection with the jurisdiction and the reasonable prospect of benefit to creditors, there was a third requirement (which had been mentioned by Megarry J in *Re Compania Merabello San Nicholas*) that there must be persons interested in the distribution of the company's assets over whom the court can exercise jurisdiction. This threefold characterisation was adopted by the Court of Appeal in *Stocznia Gdanska v Latreefers (No 2)*.[23] Morritt LJ, giving the judgment of the court, described the requirements as follows:[24]

'(1) There must be a sufficient connection with England and Wales which may, but does not necessarily have to, consist of assets within the jurisdiction.

(2) There must be a reasonable possibility, if a winding-up order is made, of benefit to those applying for the winding-up order.

(3) One or more persons interested in the distribution of assets of the company must be persons over whom the court can exercise a jurisdiction.'

14.34 The breadth of this approach can be seen from the circumstances in which the courts have been prepared to make winding-up orders against insolvent foreign companies. In the *Compania Merabello San Nicholas* case, a winding-up order was made even though the company's only asset in England would, on the making of the winding-up order, vest in the petitioning creditors under the Third Parties (Rights Against Insurers) Act 1930, with the effect that there would be no assets available to the English liquidator. In *Re A Company (No 00359 of 1987)*, a winding-up order was made even though the company had no assets in England, because of the possibility that the liquidator would be able to make recoveries from directors under the provisions of the Insolvency Act 1986 dealing with fraudulent and wrongful trading.

14.35 In summary, therefore, the English court has the jurisdiction to wind up any insolvent foreign company whose centre of main interests is outside the EU, but will only do so if the company has a connection with England and a

---

20   [1988] 1 Ch 210.
21   [1988] 1 Ch 210 at 225–226.
22   [1991] BCLC 210.
23   [2001] 2 BCLC 116.
24   [2001] 2 BCLC 116 at 120.

creditor of the company over whom the court can exercise jurisdiction will benefit. The precise formulation of the requirements has changed from time to time, and may change again, but the two key concepts of connection with the jurisdiction and benefit from the winding-up order are unlikely to change.

Where the debtor's centre of main interests is within the EU

14.36 Where a company's centre of main interests is within the EU, the effect of the EC Regulation is to limit the jurisdiction of the English courts to wind up foreign companies. The Regulation distinguishes between two types of proceedings:

- main proceedings; and
- territorial (or secondary) proceedings.

14.37 The purpose of the EC Regulation is to restrict main proceedings to the place where the company has its centre of main interests, with the effect that all other proceedings are territorial (in the sense that the proceedings are limited to assets within the jurisdiction concerned) and are also likely to be secondary (in the sense that, if main proceedings are opened, they will be ancillary to those proceedings). A discussion of the jurisdiction of the English courts to wind up foreign companies must therefore distinguish between those which are main proceedings and those which are territorial.

14.38 Main proceedings can only be opened where the debtor has its centre of main interests.[25] Main proceedings can consist of any type of collective insolvency procedure. In England, this means bankruptcy, compulsory liquidation, administration and company voluntary arrangements.[26] Receivership (whether administrative receivership or otherwise) is not included because it is not a collective insolvency procedure. Neither are voluntary liquidation or schemes of arrangement with creditors included, even though they are (in the case of voluntary liquidation) or can be (in the case of schemes of arrangement with creditors) collective insolvency procedures.

14.39 Main proceedings have all the normal characteristics of insolvency proceedings. In particular, they extend to all of the debtor's assets, wherever they are located.

14.40 Territorial proceedings are more limited in nature than main proceedings. As their name suggests, territorial proceedings are limited to assets within the jurisdiction where the insolvency proceedings are taking place.[27] The types of proceedings are also limited. A territorial proceeding must be either a bankruptcy or a compulsory liquidation.[28] This needs to be contrasted with main proceedings, which includes an administration and a company voluntary arrangement.

---

25 EC Regulation, Art 3(1).

26 EC Regulation, Art 2(a) and Annex A. Also included are winding-up subject to the supervision of the court and creditors' voluntary winding-up (with confirmation by the court) – but these procedures are not used in practice.

27 EC Regulation, Art 3(2).

28 EC Regulation, Arts 3(3), 2(c) and Annex B. It can also be an administration, but not in its primary sense of a rescue procedure – only once it has become a distribution mechanism.

14.41 Although the nature and effect of territorial proceedings is more limited than main proceedings, they are available more widely. It has been seen that main proceedings can only be instituted if the debtor has its centre of main interests in the jurisdiction concerned. Territorial proceedings, on the other hand, can be opened if the debtor has an establishment within the jurisdiction concerned.[29] Article 2(h) defines 'establishment' as 'any place of operations where the debtor carries out a non-transitory economic activity with human means and goods'. This definition is almost as unhelpful as that of a 'centre of main interests', but it clearly requires something more than the presence of assets within the jurisdiction. What is needed is some form of branch organisation in the jurisdiction concerned.

14.42 There is one further restriction on the opening of territorial proceedings. They can only be opened before main proceedings have been opened in two circumstances.[30] The first is where main proceedings are not possible under the law of the jurisdiction in which the debtor has its centre of main interests. This is unlikely to occur very frequently in practice. More important is the second circumstance. Territorial proceedings can be opened before the main proceedings if they are requested by a creditor:[31]

'... who has his domicile, habitual residence or registered office in the Member State within the territory of which the establishment is situated, or whose claim arises from the operation of that establishment.'

Summary

14.43 The jurisdiction of the English courts to wind up foreign companies differs markedly depending on whether or not the company concerned has its centre of main interests within the EU. If the company's centre of main interests is outside the EU, the English courts continue to have a very broad jurisdiction to wind up foreign companies provided they have some connection with the jurisdiction and some benefit to a creditor is likely to result. But, where the company's centre of main interests is within the EU, the jurisdiction is much narrower. Main proceedings can only be opened if the centre of main interests is in England; and territorial proceedings can only be opened if the company has an establishment here. In this respect, we have gone full circle, back to the approach of the English courts in the late nineteenth century, which would only wind up a foreign company which had a branch office within the jurisdiction.[32] It remains to be seen to what extent this limitation will alter the courts' approach to winding up companies whose centre of main interests is outside the EU.

14.44 Further complications exist where the English insolvency proceedings are not the only insolvency proceedings relating to the company concerned. This issue will be discussed later but, first, it is necessary to consider the jurisdiction of the English courts to place companies into administration.

---

29 EC Regulation, Art 3(2).
30 EC Regulation, Art 3(4).
31 EC Regulation, Art 3(4)(b).
32 *Re Lloyd Generale Italiano* (1885) 29 Ch D 219.

Administration

14.45 When administration was introduced in 1986, it was generally only available in relation to companies incorporated in England. The only recognised exception was that an administration order could be made at the request of a foreign court under s 426 of the Insolvency Act 1986, which requires the English courts to assist insolvency courts in other parts of the United Kingdom or in certain designated countries (mainly Commonwealth states and others with an historical link with the United Kingdom).[33]

14.46 Following the introduction of the EC Regulation, it was decided in *Re BRAC Rent-A-Car*[34] that it gave English courts the jurisdiction to place any company into administration if it had its centre of main interests here. This was a curious decision in view of the purpose of the Regulation, which was to impose limits on the international insolvency jurisdiction of EU members, rather than to extend it.[35] But the position has been clarified by the Insolvency Act 1986 (Amendment) Regulations 2005,[36] which now enable the following types of company to go into administration:

- a company incorporated under the Companies Acts;
- a company incorporated in an EEA state other than the UK; and
- a company not incorporated in an EEA state but having its centre of main interests in a member state of the EU other than Denmark.[37]

14.47 The general jurisdiction of the English courts to place companies into administration has, as a result, been extended, but it is still less extensive than the jurisdiction in relation to winding up. It extends to English companies,[38] to companies incorporated in other EEA states, and to any other companies whose centre of main interests is in the EU. But, as in the case of liquidation, the apparent breadth of this jurisdiction is limited by the EC Regulation.

14.48 Where the centre of main interests of the company is in the EU, it can generally only be placed in administration in England if its centre of main interests is here. The effect of the EC Regulation on administrations is different from its effect on liquidations. It has been seen that a liquidation can constitute either main proceedings or territorial proceedings, that the former are only available where the company's centre of main interests is located in England, but that the latter are available if the company has an establishment here. As far as administrations are concerned, however, the general principle is that administration proceedings are only available if they are the main proceedings, and therefore that they can only be instituted if the company's centre of main interests is in England. This is because territorial proceedings which are opened after main proceedings have been opened (and which are described in the

---

33   *Re Dallhold Estates (UK)* [1992] BCLC 621.
34   [2003] 1 WLR 1421.
35   EC Regulation, Recital (15).
36   SI 2005/879.
37   Insolvency Act 1986 (Amendment) Regulations 2005, reg 2(4). The jurisdiction is identical in relation to company voluntary arrangements – reg 2(2).
38   So long as they are incorporated under the companies legislation.

Regulation as secondary proceedings) must be what the Regulation describes as 'winding-up proceedings' – ie compulsory liquidation or bankruptcy,[39] and only includes administration in its secondary role as a distribution procedure, not in its primary role as a rescue procedure. Where, therefore, main proceedings have already commenced in another member state, it is not generally possible to institute territorial administration proceedings in England.

14.49 Territorial administration proceedings are, nevertheless, available under the EC Regulation in one circumstance – where main proceedings have not been instituted in another jurisdiction at the time the administration proceedings are commenced in England. It has been seen that the circumstances in which this can be done are, generally, restricted to a case where the creditor is based in England or his claim arises from the operation of the debtor's establishment in England.[40]

14.50 In summary, the extent of the ability of a foreign company to enter into administration depends on whether its centre of main interests is within, or outside, the EU:

- Where the company's centre of main interests is outside the EU, it can be placed into administration if it is incorporated under the English companies legislation or in another EEA State.
- Where the company's centre of main interests is within the EU, it can enter into:
  - main administration proceedings if its centre of main interests is in England; or
  - territorial administration proceedings if it has an establishment here and proceedings are instituted here before main proceedings are instituted in another jurisdiction (or if the administration is only being used as a distribution procedure).

14.51 So much for the EC Regulation simplifying international insolvencies.

Multiple insolvency proceedings

14.52 It is not unusual for debtors to enter into insolvency proceedings in more than one jurisdiction. In the case of corporate debtors, English courts have had to grapple with this problem since the second half of the nineteenth century. Indeed, it was the existence of multiple insolvency proceedings and the likelihood of their increase which led to the EC Insolvency Regulation, the purpose of which was not to eradicate them but to regulate them. But since, as has been seen, the EC Regulation only applies where the debtor's centre of main interests is located within the EU, it is necessary to consider the way in which English law approached the issue before the EC Regulation, as well as how that Regulation has changed matters. For the purpose of the following discussion, it is assumed that the company concerned is incorporated abroad,

---

39   EC Regulation, Arts 3(3) and 2(c).
40   EC Regulation, Art 3(4).

that it is in insolvency proceedings in its jurisdiction of incorporation and that it is also the subject of insolvency proceedings in England.

Where the debtor's centre of main interests is outside the EU

14.53 Where the debtor's centre of main interests is outside the EU, the law is derived from the cases which pre-dated the EC Regulation. Those cases evidenced two (potentially conflicting) approaches to the problem which arises where a company is subject to insolvency proceedings both in its country of incorporation and in England. One approach is to treat the liquidation in England in exactly the same way as any other English liquidation. The other approach is to treat the English liquidation as being ancillary to that main procedure, and to adapt English insolvency rules accordingly. The issue is how these two approaches can be reconciled.

14.54 The starting point is that, if a debtor is in insolvency proceedings in England, they must be governed by English law. It is clear that, in principle, the liquidation of a foreign company is a liquidation of that company as a whole, not simply of its English assets.[41] Similarly, the company's worldwide assets are distributable amongst its worldwide creditors[42]. As Browne-Wilkinson V-C said in *Re Bank of Credit and Commercial International*:[43]

'The attempt to put a ring fence around either the assets or the creditors to be found in any one jurisdiction is, at least under English law as I understand it, not correct, and destined to failure.'

14.55 There are nevertheless a number of cases in which the courts have expressed the view that an English liquidation of a foreign company is 'ancillary' to insolvency proceedings in its place of incorporation, although it was not always made entirely clear what effect this had in practice. The issue came to a head in *Re Bank of Credit and Commerce International (No 10)*[44] – referred to in this chapter as *BCCI (No 10)*. In that case, the company concerned was incorporated in Luxembourg but carried on much of its business in England. It was in insolvent liquidation in both Luxembourg and England, and arrangements had been put in place between both sets of liquidators to promote the orderly distribution of its assets. The question arose as to the extent to which the English liquidators could depart from English insolvency rules in order to assist in this process.

14.56 Scott V-C reviewed the authorities concerning ancillary liquidations and drew the following conclusions from them:[45]

'(1) Where a foreign company is in liquidation in its country of incorporation, a winding up order made in England will normally be regarded as giving rise to a winding up ancillary to that being conducted in the country of incorporation.

---

41 *Re Bank of Credit and Commerce International (No 2)* [1992] BCLC 579 at 581.
42 *Re Azoff-Don Commercial Bank* [1954] Ch 315.
43 [1992] BCLC 570 at 577.
44 [1997] Ch 213.
45 [1997] Ch 213 at 246.

(2) The winding up in England will be ancillary in the sense that it will not be within the power of the English liquidators to get in and realise all the assets of the company worldwide. They will necessarily have to concentrate on getting in and realising the English assets.

(3) Since in order to achieve a *pari passu* distribution between all the company's creditors it will be necessary for there to be a pooling of the company's assets worldwide and for a dividend to be declared out of the assets comprised in that pool, the winding up in England will be ancillary in the sense, also, that it will be the liquidators in the principal liquidation who will be best placed to declare the dividend and to distribute the assets in the pool accordingly.

(4) None the less, the ancillary character of an English winding up does not relieve an English court of the obligation to apply English law, including English insolvency law, to the resolution of any issue arising in the winding-up which is brought before the court. It may be, of course, that English conflicts of law rules will lead to the application of some foreign law principle in order to resolve a particular issue.'

14.57   This is an important statement and deserves a little elaboration:

• The starting point is that an English insolvency procedure must be conducted in accordance with English insolvency law.

• But, where the liquidation is ancillary, in the sense that there is another insolvency procedure being conducted in the company's place of incorporation, this principle is subject to two limitations.

• The first limitation is a practical one. Although every English liquidation extends to all of the company's assets worldwide, the court will not expect liquidators in an ancillary liquidation to collect assets abroad if it is impracticable to do so. Where there are main proceedings elsewhere, the liquidators will generally only be expected to collect assets within the jurisdiction of the English courts.

• The second limitation is that it is recognised that it is preferable to have one distribution of assets to creditors, rather than multiple distributions, and that the English liquidators are accordingly entitled to co-operate with the liquidators in the main proceedings to enable the main liquidators to make the distribution to all creditors. In practice, this requires the English liquidators to pay the net proceeds of their recoveries to the main liquidators, provided that the distribution will comply with the basic English law requirement that it is made to all unsecured creditors who could claim in the English liquidation. The English liquidators must accordingly retain sufficient funds to enable them to ensure that the requirements of English insolvency law are complied with.

• It can therefore be seen that the statement that the English liquidation is ancillary means very little. The English liquidators are not required to collect overseas assets but, in practice, they would be unlikely to be able to do so anyway. Nor are the English liquidators required to make their own distributions to creditors, but they must ensure that creditors receive what they would have done if the separate distributions had been made. In other words, although the form of the distribution mechanism will not follow English law, the legal substance must comply with English law.

Where the debtor's centre of main interests is within the EU

14.58   Where the debtor's centre of main interests is within the EU, the EC Regulation distinguishes between main proceedings and territorial (or secondary) proceedings.

14.59   If the debtor's centre of main interests is in England, it can be subject to main insolvency proceedings here even if it is incorporated abroad. If the debtor's centre of main interests is in a member state other than the United Kingdom, the only proceedings which can be brought in England are territorial proceedings, even if it is incorporated in England. It has been seen that such proceedings are subject to various restrictions. In this context, two are of particular importance. The first is that the proceedings which can be brought are limited to the assets of the company situated in England.[46] The second is that, where main proceedings have already been started, the English proceedings will be secondary proceedings.[47] The effect of the secondary proceedings is described in Art 33(1):

> 'The court, which opened the secondary proceedings, shall stay the process of liquidation in whole or in part on receipt of a request from the liquidator in the main proceedings, provided that in that event it may require the liquidator in the main proceedings to take any suitable measure to guarantee the interests of the creditors in the secondary proceedings and of individual classes of creditors.'

14.60   The proviso to Art 33(1) gives creditors in the English liquidation the comfort that they should not lose what they would otherwise be entitled to under English law. The result is therefore broadly the same as under *BCCI (No 10)*.

Summary

14.61   Although the jurisdiction of the English courts differs depending on whether the debtor's centre of main interests is within or outside the EU, the effect of an ancillary (or secondary) liquidation is very similar under both regimes. Where there are main proceedings in another jurisdiction, the ancillary (or secondary) proceedings will be governed by English law, but they will be subject to two principal limitations. The first is that the liquidation will only extend to assets in England. The second is that the main liquidator will control the distribution process, but subject to the important requirement that the English liquidator should ensure that creditors who could claim in the English liquidation will not suffer as a result.

Part 4: THE EFFECT OF ENGLISH INSOLVENCY PROCEEDINGS ON FOREIGN SECURITY

14.62   The purpose of this part is to consider how the institution of English insolvency proceedings will affect security which has a foreign element. The

---

46   EC Regulation, Art 3(2).
47   EC Regulation, Art 3(3).

converse issue is discussed in the part 5 (**14.98**ff) – the extent to which foreign insolvency proceedings will affect English security. Both issues are considered from the point of view of English law. Where the transaction involves a foreign element, the law of other jurisdictions is also likely to be relevant.

14.63 It is assumed, for the purpose of this part, that the debtor has entered into an English insolvency procedure, but that there is a foreign element to the security which has been created, such as that the debtor is incorporated abroad or carries on business abroad, or that the security is over assets located abroad or which are governed by a foreign law.

14.64 Where the transaction is entirely domestic:

- security entered into during the period running up to the insolvency is capable of being set aside in certain circumstances (for instance, as a preference or if the security is a floating charge which secures existing indebtedness);
- there is a moratorium on the enforcement of security in an administration (but not in liquidation or bankruptcy); and
- rights of set-off are protected in liquidation, administration and bankruptcy.[48]

14.65 To what extent do these provisions apply if the transaction has a foreign element? These issues are the subject of the EC Regulation[49] but, as has been seen in earlier parts of this chapter, it is only applicable where the debtor's centre of main interests is located within the EU. It is, therefore, still necessary to consider how English law dealt with this issue before the introduction of the EC Regulation because that will continue to govern the position where the debtor's centre of main interests is outside the EU.

Where the debtor's centre of main interests is outside the EU

14.66 Where the debtor's centre of main interests is outside the EU, the EC Regulation does not apply, and it is necessary to consider the pre-existing case-law. That case-law establishes that, in English insolvency procedures, English law will be applied to questions concerning claw-back, the moratorium and rights of set-off even where the security has a foreign element.

Claw-back

14.67 As a matter of domestic English law, it is now clear that the claw-back provisions of the Insolvency Act 1986 are equally applicable to foreign creditors as they are to English ones. In *Re Paramount Airways*,[50] the administrators of an English company sought to have a transaction with a foreign bank set aside on the basis that it was a transaction at an undervalue. The bank was incorporated in Jersey, carried on business there, and did not

---

48 See **CHAPTERS 9** and **12**.
49 Regulation 1346/2000/EC, as amended by Regulation 603/2005/EC of 12 April 2005.
50 [1993] Ch 223.

carry on business in England. At first instance, it was decided that the claw-back provisions of the Insolvency Act 1986 did not have extra-territorial effect and did not, therefore, apply to a foreign person resident abroad, on the basis that there was a general principle of statutory interpretation to the effect that a statute is not intended to apply to foreigners unless it is clearly expressed to do so.

14.68 The Court of Appeal overruled this decision, deciding that the legislation applied even where the defendant was foreign. It was impossible to identify any clear limitation on the general words of the statute and, as a result, the legislation must be taken to mean what it says – that, if the conditions for its exercise are satisfied, it can be exercised against anyone, whether English or foreign.

14.69 Although the claw-back legislation has extra-territorial effect, the court stressed the importance of two safeguards for foreign creditors faced with English proceedings to set aside their security. The first relates to the discretion which the court has, under the relevant provisions, concerning the type of order which it makes. In the words of Nicholls V-C:[51]

'The discretion is wide enough to enable the court, if justice so requires, to make no order against the other party to the transaction or the person to whom the preference was given. In particular, if a foreign element is involved the court will need to be satisfied that, in respect of the relief sought against him, the defendant is sufficiently connected with England for it to be just and proper to make the order against him despite the foreign element ... Thus in considering whether there is a sufficient connection with this country the court will look at all the circumstances, including the residence and place of business of the defendant, his connection with the insolvent, the nature and purpose of the transaction being impugned, the nature and locality of the property involved, the circumstances in which the defendant became involved in the transaction or received a benefit from it or acquired the property in question, whether the defendant acted in good faith, and whether under any relevant foreign law the defendant acquired an unimpeachable title free from any claims even if the insolvent had been adjudged bankrupt or wound up locally. The importance to be attached to these factors will vary from case to case. By taking into account and weighing these and any other relevant circumstances, the court will ensure that it does not seek to exercise oppressively or unreasonably the very wide jurisdiction conferred by the sections.'

14.70 The other safeguard is the practical one that, in order to commence proceedings in England, it may be necessary to obtain a court order authorising the service of the proceedings abroad. Where a foreign element is involved, in deciding whether to allow service outside the jurisdiction the court will take into account the apparent strength or weakness of the claim and whether the defendant has a sufficient connection with England.

---

51 [1993] Ch 223 at 239–240.

14.71   The *Paramount Airways* case involved the administration of an English company, but there seems little doubt that the same principle would be applied where the company concerned was incorporated abroad. As *BCCI (No 10)*[52] makes clear, even where the English insolvency procedure is ancillary to a main foreign procedure, the English courts apply English law to issues which arise in the insolvency proceedings. But the fact that the company is incorporated abroad is clearly a relevant factor to be taken into account in considering whether there is a sufficiently close connection between the defendant and England for the court to exercise its discretion to set aside the transaction.

14.72   In summary, it is clear that English claw-back rules will be applied in an English insolvency procedure (even an ancillary procedure) if the defendant has a sufficiently close connection with England that it is proper to set aside the transaction. Although the test is clear, it leaves such a degree of discretion to the court that it will be of scant comfort to a foreign creditor weighing up the risks of having security set aside in England.

Moratorium

14.73   The second main concern for a secured creditor is whether he is prevented from enforcing his security as a result of a moratorium. Under English law, there is no moratorium on action by secured creditors in a liquidation or a bankruptcy, but there is such a moratorium in administration. It has been seen that the jurisdiction to place a foreign company into administration is narrower than the corresponding rules concerning liquidation.

14.74   Although there is no clear authority on the point, there seems little doubt that the principle as regards the moratorium is the same as that which applies to claw-back procedures. The moratorium, which is expressed in very broad terms, will have extra-territorial effect, but the court will be mindful of the extent of the creditors' connection with England before deciding whether or not to enforce it. In other words, the approach of the Court of Appeal in the *Paramount Airways* case is likely to be equally applicable to the moratorium.

14.75   In view of the concern that to breach the moratorium under the Insolvency Act 1986 will constitute a contempt of court, in an appropriate case the secured creditor might wish to obtain the guidance of the English court before enforcing security in apparent breach of the moratorium. This would be particularly likely to be appropriate where the secured creditor carries on business in England, even if the actual security itself is located abroad.

Set-off

14.76   The third concern for a secured creditor is to establish whether or not it would have a right of set-off in English insolvency proceedings. The answer to that question is clear. The set-off provisions of the Insolvency Act 1986 and

---

52   *Re Bank of Credit and Commerce International (No 10)* [1997] Ch 213.

Rules[53] (which are discussed in detail in CHAPTER **12**), have no territorial limitations and, in *BCCI (No 10)*, Scott V-C decided that they are applicable even in an ancillary liquidation.

14.77 The background to that case has already been discussed. The main issue was whether English set-off rules would apply in the English ancillary liquidation. The concern arose from the fact that, although English set-off rules in insolvency are very broad and give great protection to creditors, set-off rules in Luxembourg (which is where the company was incorporated and where the main insolvency proceedings were being conducted) are much narrower. Scott V-C decided that, even though the English liquidation was ancillary to the Luxembourg one, English set-off rules must be applied in respect of creditors claiming in the English liquidation, with the effect that claims against them by the company were automatically discharged to the extent that they did not exceed amounts owing by the company to them.

Summary

14.78 Where the debtor's centre of main interests is outside the EU:

- English claw-back rules and the English moratorium in an administration will apply even where the transaction has a foreign element, but the court will only act such a case if the secured creditor and the transaction are sufficiently connected with England that it would be proper for the court to do so; and

- any creditor who claims in the English insolvency will have the benefit of English set-off provisions.

14.79 These principles apply whenever there are English insolvency proceedings – whether they are main proceedings or ancillary proceedings.

Where the debtor's centre of main interests is within the EU

14.80 Where the debtor's centre of main interests is within the EU, the EC Regulation applies. The basic principle is contained in Art 4. It provides that:

'(1) Save as otherwise provided in this Regulation, the law applicable to insolvency proceedings and their effects shall be that of the Member State within the territory of which such proceedings are open, hereafter referred to as the "State of the opening of proceedings".

(2) The law of the State of the opening of proceedings shall determine the conditions for the opening of those proceedings, their conduct and their closure ...'

---

53   Insolvency Rules 1986, SI 1986/1925.

Claw-back

14.81 The Article then lists a series of matters which, in particular, are determined by the law of the state of the opening of proceedings.[54] One of those matters (contained in Art 4(2)(m)) is 'the rules relating to the voidness, voidability or unenforceability of legal acts detrimental to all the creditors'. Article 28 makes it clear that there is no distinction, in this respect, between main proceedings and secondary proceedings.

14.82 Claw-back provisions under the Insolvency Act 1986 clearly fall within Art 4(2)(m), and are therefore subject to the law of the insolvency proceedings. The EC Regulation does, however, contain a protection for secured creditors in Art 13. It provides:

> 'Article 4(2)(m) shall not apply where the person who benefited from an act detrimental to all the creditors provides proof that:
>
> – the said act is subject to the law of a Member State other than that of the State of the opening of proceedings, and
> – that law does not allow any means of challenging that act in the relevant case.'

14.83 The result is that, in English insolvency proceedings (whether they are main proceedings or secondary proceedings), English claw-back rules will apply, but the secured creditor will have a defence if the proprietary effect of the security is governed by the law of another member state which does not allow the transaction to be set aside 'in the relevant case'. These last words indicate that whether or not the security can be set aside in that other member state is to be determined in accordance with the facts as they are at the time. If the debtor is not in insolvency proceedings in that member state and therefore there are no claw-back provisions operative, the creditor will have a good defence even if claw-back would have been available in that member state had the debtor been subject to insolvency proceedings there. But if there are other means of setting aside the transaction even outside insolvency proceedings (such as for breach of fiduciary duty), the defence may not be applicable.

14.84 The position of a secured creditor in relation to claw-back proceedings is, therefore, more advantageous if the debtor's centre of main interests is within the EU than if it is outside it. The basic principle in both cases is that English law will apply, although the court will only exercise its discretion to set the transaction aside if it has a sufficient connection with England. But, where the debtor's centre of main interests is within the EU, the creditor has the additional protection of Art 13 of the EC Regulation.

Moratorium

14.85 The distinction between cases where the EC Regulation applies, and those where it does not, is even more stark in relation to the moratorium on enforcement of security. Article 5 of the EC Regulation provides as follows:

---

54 See also Recital (23).

'(1) The opening of insolvency proceedings shall not affect the rights in rem of creditors or third parties in respect of tangible or intangible, moveable or immovable assets – both specific assets and collections of indefinite assets as a whole which change from time to time – belonging to the debtor which are situated within the territory of another Member State at the time of the opening of proceedings.'

14.86   Article 5(4) makes it clear that this does not preclude the bringing of claw-back proceedings under the law of the insolvency. But, subject to that, Art 5 establishes that rights in rem (ie proprietary rights) are not affected by the insolvency proceedings if they are 'situated within the territory of another Member State' when the insolvency proceedings commence. If, therefore, there are insolvency proceedings in England (whether main proceedings or territorial ones), nothing in English insolvency law can affect the secured creditor's proprietary rights if the assets concerned are located in another member state. This provision does not apply where the assets are situated outside the EU, but it does give substantial protection to secured creditors in cases where the secured assets are situated within the EU, but not in the member state in which the insolvency proceedings are taking place.

14.87   The expression 'the Member State in which assets are situated' is defined, in Art 2(g) to mean:

'... in the case of:

–   tangible property, the Member State within the territory of which the property is situated,

–   property and rights ownership of or entitlement to which must be entered in a public register, the Member State under the authority of which the register is kept,

–   claims, the Member State within the territory of which the third party required to meet them has the centre of his main interests, as determined in Article 3(1); ...'

14.88   The first limb of this definition is clear, and accords with the basic conflict of law principle under English law which is discussed in CHAPTER 13 – that the proprietary effect of security over tangible property is governed by the law of the place where the property is situated. The second limb deals with asset registries (such as those relating to land, ships and aircraft), and establishes that it is the law of the place where the register is kept which is the relevant law.

14.89   The third limb is more puzzling. It has been seen in CHAPTER 13 that the basic conflict of law principle of English law is that the proprietary effect of rights over intangibles is determined by the law which governs the intangible. Article 2(g) diverts from this principle and establishes that, 'claims' (which would certainly include contractual rights), are to be dealt with according to the place they are 'situated', and that they are situated within the jurisdiction in which the person required to pay them has the centre of his main interests. If, therefore, security is granted over a contract which is entered into between English parties and is governed by English law and the centre of main interests of the counterparty to the contract is in the United States, the contract will not be situated within the territory of another member state, and therefore Art 5 will not apply to it – a curious result.

14.90 In spite of this, Art 5 gives considerable protection to secured creditors. The reason for the extent of the protection is explained in Recital (25):

> 'There is a particular need for a special reference diverging from the law of the opening State in the case of rights in rem, since these are of considerable importance for the granting of credit. The basis, validity and extent of such a right in rem should therefore normally be determined according to the lex situs and not be affected by the opening of insolvency proceedings ...'

14.91 Where the insolvency proceedings are in England, but the secured asset is situated within the territory of another member state, the general effect of Art 5 is that English insolvency rules cannot affect the rights of the secured creditor. Apart from claw-back mechanisms (which continue to apply as an exception to the principle contained in Art 5), the other main way in which rights of secured creditors can be affected by English insolvency proceedings is by the application of the moratorium on the enforcement of secured creditors' rights in an administration. The effect of Art 5 is that, although the moratorium is effective in relation to assets situated in England and (at least as a matter of English law) to assets situated outside the EU, it is ineffective where the assets are situated within another member state of the EU. In order to obtain a moratorium, it will be necessary for the administrator to start secondary proceedings in that other member state. Even then, a moratorium will only be available if it is available in the insolvency proceeding concerned in that jurisdiction.

14.92 As far as the moratorium is concerned, therefore, the position of a secured creditor is substantially more advantageous if:

- the debtor's centre of main interests is within the EU; and
- the secured assets are situated in a member state other than the UK.

14.93 In such a case, the English moratorium will be ineffective, whether the English insolvency proceedings are main proceedings or secondary ones.

14.94 If, however:

- the debtor's centre of main interests is outside the EU; or
- the charged assets are situated outside the EU,

the moratorium will, as a matter of English law, be effective if the transaction has a sufficient connection with England, and subject always to the practicality of enforcing it outside England. Nevertheless, the approach of the EC Regulation may inform the attitude of the English courts even in cases to which it does not apply – by making them less willing to attempt to use the moratorium where the secured assets are abroad.

Set-off

14.95 The third issue for creditors relates to the extent of rights of set-off. Article 4(2)(d) establishes that the law of the insolvency will govern 'the conditions under which set-offs may be invoked'. If the creditor has a right of set-off under the law of the insolvency, he will be entitled to rely on it. If not, Art 6 gives the creditor an alternative right of set-off. Article 6(1) provides:[55]

> 'The opening of insolvency proceedings shall not affect the right of creditors to demand the set-off of their claims against the claims of the debtor, where such a set-off is permitted by the law applicable to the insolvent debtor's claim.'

14.96 The result of Art 6 is that, if no set-off is available under the law of the insolvency, the creditor will still be entitled to a set-off if it is available under the law which governs the claim by the debtor against the creditor. In practice, where the insolvency proceeding is taking place in England, there will be no necessity to rely on Art 6, because of the breadth of insolvency set-off under English law, which is discussed in CHAPTER 12.

Summary

14.97 Where the debtor's centre of main interests is within the EU, the EC Regulation gives secured creditors more protection than they have where the centre of main interests is outside the EU. Where the insolvency proceeding is in England, this will have little effect on rights of set-off, because of the general breadth of insolvency set-off under English law. As far as claw-back is concerned, the secured creditor is given an additional right to defend claw-back proceedings if the transaction would not be set aside under its governing law. Even more importantly, the secured creditor can avoid the administration moratorium if the charged assets are situated outside the UK but within another member state. It is quite possible that these broader protections for secured creditors will influence the English courts' discretion whether or not to enforce English claw-back and moratorium provisions where the security is located outside the EU.

Part 5: THE EFFECT OF FOREIGN INSOLVENCY PROCEEDINGS ON ENGLISH SECURITY

14.98 In this part, it will be assumed that the debtor is subject to insolvency proceedings abroad, but that the creditor has obtained security over tangible assets located in England or over intangible assets governed by English law. To what extent will the security be affected by the foreign insolvency?

---

55 See also Recital (26). This principle is subject to claw-back – Art 6(2).

14.99   It is again necessary to distinguish between cases where the debtor's centre of main interests is within the EU, and those cases where it is not. The former are governed by the EC Regulation,[56] the latter are not. But the distinction between these two types of case is less clear than in the preceding parts of this chapter. This is because there is very little case-law concerning the approach of an English court to this question and, as a result, the English courts may be even more inclined to apply the EU Regulation by analogy than in cases where the law is more settled. For this reason, this part will not divide the discussion first into cases which fall outside the EC Regulation and then into those which fall within it. Instead, it will consider each of the three types of case discussed in the previous part – claw-back, moratorium and set-off – and, in relation to each of them, will consider the position both under the EC Regulation and outside it.

14.100   First, however, the general approach of the English courts to foreign insolvency proceedings should be considered. There is very little authority concerning the way in which English courts will approach the question concerning the effect of foreign insolvency proceedings on English security. There are two relevant principles, which may conflict. The first is that the proprietary effect of security is a matter for the law which governs the security – generally, in the case of security over tangible assets, the lex situs and, in the case of intangible assets, the law governing the intangible concerned. The other relevant principle is that the law governing insolvency proceedings is the law of the place where the insolvency proceedings are conducted. These two principles will conflict where insolvency law purports to affect the rights of secured creditors.

14.101   In the context of security, there is no clear authority which establishes which principle should take priority. *Felixstowe Dock & Railway Co v United States Lines*[57] did not involve a secured creditor but did consider the extent to which an English court would give effect to a foreign insolvency procedure. In that case, Hirst J refused to give effect in England to a moratorium imposed under Chapter 11 of the US Bankruptcy Code because he was concerned that, on the facts of that particular case, the arrangements in the bankruptcy would have an adverse affect on European creditors. But Hirst J did, say:[58]

> 'I wish however to stress that the court would in principle always wish to co-operate in every proper way with an order like the present one made by a court in a friendly jurisdiction (of which the United States is a most conspicuous example). But whether this is appropriate in any given case, and if so the precise nature and extent of such co-operation, must depend on the particular sphere of activity in question and the English law applicable thereto as discussed in the ensuing section of this judgment, together with the overall circumstances.'

14.102   The approach of the courts in subsequent cases has been to stress the importance of comity,[59] but these cases did not involve conflicts between

---

56   Regulation 1346/2000/EC, as amended by Regulation 603/2005/EC of 12 April 2005.
57   [1989] 1 QB 360.
58   [1989] 1 QB 360 at 376.
59   See, for instance, *Barclays Bank v Homan* [1993] BCLC 680.

foreign insolvency laws and the rights of secured creditors who had security in England, and they are therefore only of rather tenuous authority. Outside the scope of the EC Regulation, therefore, there is little indication of the way in which English courts will approach these issues and, for that reason, there is much to be said for applying the principles contained in the EC Regulation by analogy, even in cases where it is not directly applicable.

14.103 Under s 426 of the Insolvency Act 1986, the English courts have a duty to assist insolvency courts in other parts of the United Kingdom and in other specified jurisdictions which have an historical link with this country, most of which are outside the EU[60]. The nature of the assistance is at the discretion of the court[61] but, even in relation to these jurisdictions, it is suggested that it is unlikely that the courts will go any further in the interference with security rights than is permitted by the EC Regulation.

Claw-back

14.104 Where the debtor's centre of main interests is in the EU and the debtor is in insolvency proceedings in another member state, the apparent effect of Art 4(2)(m) is that the secured creditor will be subject to the claw-back provisions of the law of the insolvency proceedings. In practice, however, the secured creditor is likely to be able to avoid this consequence as a result of Art 13, which gives him a defence to a claw-back claim if the security on which he is relying is subject to the law of another member state and that law does not allow any means of challenging the security in the relevant case. If the debtor is not the subject of insolvency proceedings in England, the claw-back provisions in insolvency will not apply and, as a result, Art 13 will provide a defence for the secured creditor. The only circumstance in which this will not be the case is where, even though the debtor is not in insolvency proceedings, there is an alternative basis on which the security can be attacked, such as breach of fiduciary duty.

14.105 Where the debtor's centre of main interests is outside the EU or the foreign insolvency is being conducted outside the EU, the EC Regulation does not apply although, in the absence of any clear pre-existing English case-law, there is much to be said for applying it by analogy, not least in order to establish consistency.

Moratorium

14.106 Where the debtor's centre of main interests is in the EU, Art 5 establishes that foreign insolvency proceedings will not affect the proprietary rights of a secured creditor where the assets are situated in another member state. If, therefore, the debtor's centre of main interests is within the EU, there are foreign insolvency proceedings in relation to the debtor and the security is

---

60 Co-operation of Insolvency Courts (Designation of Relevant Countries and Territories) Orders 1986 (SI 1986/2123), 1996 (SI 1996/253) and 1998 (SI 1998/2766).

61 *Hughes v Hannover* [1997] 1 BCLC 526.

situated in England, any moratorium contained in the foreign insolvency law will be disregarded in England. That is clearly of great benefit to the secured creditor, but a warning note should be sounded. Under Art 2(g), 'claims' (which includes contract rights and receivables) are situated in the place where the person required to make the payment has the centre of his main interests; and this may not necessarily be the same jurisdiction as that which governs the effectiveness of the security over the claim – an unnecessary complication.

14.107 Where the debtor's centre of main interests is outside the EU, the EC Regulation will not apply. But there is, again, much to be said for the idea that it should be applied by analogy in such cases. If it is, it will mean that English courts will not give effect to the worldwide stay in a US bankruptcy. In view of the apparent sentiments of English Chancery judges since the *Felixstowe Docks* case (that the English courts should be prepared to give effect to foreign insolvency laws on the basis of comity), this may seem a surprising result. But the purpose of the EC Regulation is clear – to protect the rights of secured creditors; and it would be curious if continental European moratoria were to be ignored but US moratoria complied with.

Set-off

14.108 Where the debtor's centre of main interests is within the EU, an English creditor is entitled to any set-off available under the law of the foreign insolvency under Art 4 of the EC Regulation. Alternatively, he can rely on Art 6 if the claim by the debtor against him is governed by English law and a set-off would be available under English law. If the debtor is not subject to insolvency proceedings in England, the creditor would be entitled to utilise any contractual rights of set-off it may have against the debtor under Art 6.

14.109 Where the debtor's centre of main interests is outside the EU, the absence of clear authority means that it is quite possible that the English court will apply Art 6 by analogy in such a case.

Summary

14.110 Where the security is in England and there are foreign insolvency proceedings, but no English insolvency proceedings, there is little English case-law. Where the EC Regulation applies, the secured creditor is in quite a strong position. He can ignore any moratorium under the foreign insolvency proceedings and may have a defence to foreign claw-back proceedings if he can establish that the security could not be set aside in England. He should also generally be able to rely on contractual rights of set-off in England, even if set-off is not available in the foreign proceedings.

14.111 Where the EC Regulation does not apply, the position is unclear. There is much to be said for the idea that the EC Regulation should be applied by analogy in order to fill the vacuum. That would provide a neat solution as a matter of English law but, where the insolvency proceedings are in a non-EU jurisdiction (such as the United States) and those proceedings contain a worldwide moratorium (as do Chapter 11 proceedings in the United States), it may be insufficient for the creditor to rely on English law. In many cases, the creditor will have a connection with that other jurisdiction and a breach of the moratorium might constitute a contempt of court, for which it might suffer material penalties.[62]

Part 6: THE UNCITRAL MODEL LAW

14.112   The government proposes to introduce the UNCITRAL Model Law on cross-border insolvency[63] into English law in 2006. It will do so in the Cross-Border Insolvency Regulations 2006.[64] Because the Regulations are not yet in final form, it is not possible to be definitive about the scope of the new law. But, since the government's intention is to introduce the Model Law with as few changes to its text as possible, it is possible to give a reasonable idea of the likely position once the Model Law has been introduced.

14.113   The principal purpose of the Model Law is to enable a foreign representative (ie the person who is administering a foreign insolvency procedure) to seek the assistance of the English courts. It is, therefore, less wide-ranging than the EC Regulation,[65] although it has a wider geographic coverage because it applies to all foreign debtors, not just those whose centre of main interests is in the EU. If it conflicts with the EC Regulation it is the EC Regulation which will prevail,[66] and it will therefore have most effect in cases where the debtor's centre of main interests is outside the EU.

14.114   The Model Law, if it is implemented, will make two principal changes to the issues discussed in this chapter. It will give the foreign representative various rights in England even though there is no insolvency procedure here; and it will limit the jurisdiction of the English court to wind up a debtor whose centre of main interests is outside the EU.

14.115   The principal change which will be made by the Model Law will be to alter the way in which foreign insolvency proceedings can impinge on English security – a topic which is discussed in part 5 of this chapter (**14.98ff**). It will give a foreign representative the ability to have the foreign insolvency procedure recognised in England.[67] If the foreign proceeding is taking place in the state where the debtor has the centre of its main interests, that proceeding is described as a 'foreign main proceeding'. If it is taking place in a state where the debtor has an establishment, it is described as a 'foreign non-main proceeding'.

---

62   This is one of the issues discussed in the *Felixstowe Docks* case [1989] 1 QB 360.
63   This is the Model Law on cross-border insolvency as adopted by the United Nations Commission on International Trade Law on 30 May 1997.
64   Published in draft by the DTI in August 2005.
65   Regulation 1346/2000/EC, as amended by Regulation 603/2005/EC of 12 April 2005.
66   Model Law, art 3.
67   Model Law, arts 15 and 17.

14.116 In the case of a foreign main proceeding, the effect of recognition in England is to establish an automatic moratorium as if the debtor were bankrupt or in compulsory liquidation in England.[68] Unlike an administration, the moratorium in a bankruptcy or liquidation does not prevent a secured creditor from enforcing his security and, as a result, this will not affect the position of a secured creditor.

14.117 In addition, the court has the power, in its discretion, to grant 'any appropriate relief' where it is 'necessary to protect the assets of the debtor or the interests of the creditor' if a foreign proceeding is recognised in England, whether that proceeding is a foreign main proceeding or a foreign non-main proceeding.[69] Neither power can be exercised if there is an English insolvency procedure on foot and it would be inconsistent with that procedure.[70]

14.118 Unlike the EC Regulation, the Model Law does not specifically provide that the court is not entitled to prejudice the rights of a secured creditor but, in the light of the fact that the automatic moratorium in a main proceeding will not prevent a secured creditor from enforcing his security, it is unlikely that the discretionary power would be exercised in order to prevent a secured creditor from doing so. As a result, it is unlikely that the introduction of the Model Law will prevent a secured creditor from enforcing his security.

14.119 The Model Law will also give the foreign representative the ability to apply to the court for an order under the claw-back provisions of the Insolvency Act 1986.[71] As a result, even if there are no insolvency proceedings on foot in England, it will be possible for the English claw-back provisions to be exercised. This could affect a secured creditor although, in view of the fact that secondary insolvency proceedings could generally be instituted in England (in which case the claw-back provisions would apply in any event), it is unlikely that this will have a material effect on secured creditors.

14.120 The other change relates to the jurisdiction of the English courts. It has been seen in part 3 of this chapter (**14.17**ff) that the court's jurisdiction to wind up a foreign debtor is broader where the debtor's centre of main interests is outside the EU than where it is within the EU. Once a foreign main proceeding has been recognised in England, the effect of the Model Law will be to limit the jurisdiction of the English court to a case where the debtor has assets in England.[72]

14.121 It is not yet clear when the Model Law will be incorporated into English law or the precise terms on which this will be done. On the basis of the initial draft of the proposed legislation, it is unlikely that it will have a material effect on the rights of a secured creditor.

---

68 Model Law, art 20.
69 Model Law, art 21.
70 Model Law, art 29.
71 Model Law, art 23.
72 Model Law, art 28.

INDEX